1,50

Rick Steves

PROVENCE &
THE FRENCH RIVIERA

Rick Steves & Steve Smith

CONTENTS

INTRODUCTION 1

PROVENCE 20

▸ **Arles** 40

▸ **Near Arles** 73
Les Baux 74
St-Rémy-de-Provence 83
The Camargue.............. 90

▸ **Avignon** 95

▸ **Near Avignon**............. 122
Nîmes..................... 124
Pont du Gard............... 136
Uzès 141

▸ **Orange & the Côtes du Rhône** 144
Orange 146
Near Orange:
    Châteauneuf-du-Pape...... 153
Vaison-la-Romaine 157
Best of the Côtes
    du Rhône Villages......... 166
More Côtes du Rhône
    Drives.................... 179

▸ **Hill Towns of the Luberon**... 183
Isle-sur-la-Sorgue........... 186
Heart of the Luberon........ 195
More Luberon Towns....... 203

▸ **Marseille & Nearby** 220
Marseille 220
Cassis..................... 240
Aix-en-Provence........... 252

THE FRENCH RIVIERA.. 272

▸ **Nice**..................... 284

▸ **East of Nice**.............. 339
Villefranche-sur-Mer 340
The Three Corniches........ 351
Cap Ferrat 353
Villa Kérylos 360
Eze-le-Village 361
Le Trophée des Alpes 364
Quickie Riviera Bus Tour 366

▸ **Monaco** 370
Menton 384

▸ **Antibes & Nearby**......... 386
Antibes 386
Cannes 405
St-Tropez 411

▸ **Inland Riviera**............. 416
Inland Riviera Driving Tour ... 417
St-Paul-de-Vence........... 419
Vence..................... 422
Between Vence
    and Grasse 427
Grasse 428
Grand Canyon du Verdon ... 431

▸ **Traveling with Children** ... 438

▸ **Shopping** 445

▸ **France: Past & Present** 452

▸ **Practicalities** 461
Tourist Information 461
Travel Tips 462
Money 463
Sightseeing 469
Sleeping 471
Eating 482
Staying Connected 498
Transportation............. 503
Resources from Rick Steves.. 526

▸ **Appendix**................ 529
Useful Contacts 529
Holidays and Festivals 530
Books and Films........... 531
Conversions and Climate 533
Packing Checklist........... 536
Pronunciation Guide
    for Place Names 537
French Survival Phrases..... 539

▸ **Index** 541

▸ **Map Index** 555

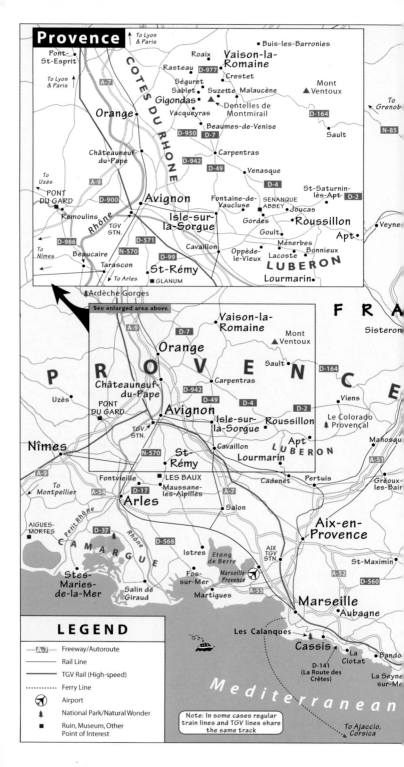

A sun-dappled café in the Luberon

Summer beach scene in Antibes

Nice's old port

Market day in Provence

Roussillon huddling atop its ochre cliffs

Rick Steves®

PROVENCE &
THE FRENCH RIVIERA

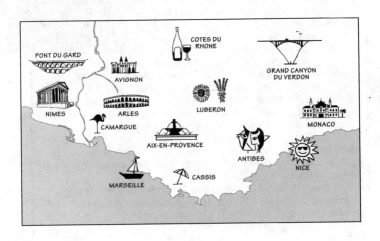

Welcome to Rick Steves' Europe

Travel is intensified living—maximum thrills per minute and one of the last great sources of legal adventure. Travel is freedom. It's recess, and we need it.

I discovered a passion for European travel as a teen and have been sharing it ever since—through my tours, public television and radio shows, and travel guidebooks. Over the years, I've taught thousands of travelers how to best enjoy Europe's blockbuster sights—and experience "Back Door" discoveries that most tourists miss.

Written with my talented co-author, Steve Smith, this book offers you a balanced mix of Provence and the Riviera's lively cities and cozy towns, from happening Nice to the romantic hill towns of the Luberon. And it's selective—rather than listing dozens of beach towns, we recommend only the best three.

Our self-guided museum tours and city walks give insight into Provence and the Riviera's vibrant history and today's living, breathing culture.

We advocate traveling simply and smartly. Take advantage of our money- and time-saving tips on sightseeing, transportation, and more. Try local, characteristic alternatives to expensive hotels and restaurants. In many ways, spending more money only builds a thicker wall between you and what you traveled so far to see.

We visit Provence and the Riviera to experience it—to become temporary locals. Thoughtful travel engages us with the world, as we learn to appreciate other cultures and new ways to measure quality of life.

Judging from the positive feedback we receive from readers, this book will help you enjoy a fun, affordable, and rewarding vacation—whether it's your first trip or your 10th.

Bon voyage! Happy travels!

Rick Steves

INTRODUCTION

Provence and the French Riviera are an intoxicating bouillabaisse of enjoyable cities, warm stone villages, Roman ruins, contemporary art, and breathtaking coastlines steaming with sunshine and stirred by the wind. There's something about the play of light in this region, where natural and man-made beauty mingle to dazzle the senses and nourish the soul. It all adds up to *une magnifique* vacation.

Provence and the Riviera stretch along France's southeast Mediterranean coast from the Camargue (south of Arles) to Monaco, and ramble north along the Rhône Valley into the Alps. The regions combined are about the same size as Massachusetts—you can take a train or drive from one end to the other in just three hours—yet they contain more sightseeing opportunities and let's-live-here villages than anywhere else in France. Marseille and Nice, the country's second- and fifth-largest cities, provide good transportation and an urban perspective to this otherwise laid-back region, where every day feels like Sunday.

In Provence, gnarled sycamores line the roads that twist their way through stone towns and between oceans of vineyards. France's Riviera is about the sea and money—it's populated by a yacht-happy crowd wondering where the next "scene" will be. Provence feels older and more *español* (with paella on menus and bullfights on Sundays), while the Riviera feels downright Italian—with fresh-Parmesan-topped pasta and red-orange, pastel-colored buildings. For every Roman ruin in Provence, there's a modern-art museum in the Riviera. Provence is famous for its wines and wind, while the bikini and ravioli were conceived on the Riviera.

This book covers the predictable biggies, from jet-setting beach resorts to famous museums, but it also mixes in a healthy dose of Back Door intimacy. Along with the Pont du Gard, Nice,

INTRODUCTION

Provence & the French Riviera

Ardèche Gorges
To Lyon & Paris
Nyons
F R A
A-7
Vaison-la-Romaine
To Lyon & Paris
D-977
TGV
Orange
Mont Ventoux ▲
Uzès
Châteauneuf-du-Pape
A-9
P R O V E N C E
PONT DU GARD
Avignon
Isle-sur-la-Sorgue
To Montpellier
Nîmes
A-9
E-80
AVIGNON TGV STN.
Cavaillon
Roussillon
Le Colorado Provençal
N-100
N-100
Apt
D-99
St-Rémy
L U B E R O N
Petit Rhône
Les Baux
TGV
Lourmarin
Aigues-Mortes
D-570
Arles
D-543
A-51
C A M A R G U E
Rhône
A-7
Gréoux-les-Bains
Stes-Maries-de-la-Mer
AIX TGV STN.
A-51
Aix-en-Provence
Marseille-Provence ✈
A-55
A-52
A-8
Marseille
A-50
Paris
FRANCE
TGV
Cassis
The Calanques
A-50
100 Miles
Mediterranean Sea
Toulon

Note: In some cases regular train lines and TGV lines share the same track

and Avignon, we'll introduce you to our favorite villages and scenic walks. You'll marvel at ancient monuments, take a canoe trip down the meandering Sorgue River, and settle into a shaded café on a made-for-movies square. Claim your favorite beach to call home, and at day's end dive headfirst into a southern France sunset. You'll enjoy tasty-yet-affordable wines while feasting on a healthy cuisine bursting with olives, tomatoes, and spices.

This book is selective, including only the most exciting sights and romantic villages. There are *beaucoup de* Provençal hill towns... but we cover only the most intriguing. And though there are scads of beach towns on the Riviera, we recommend our favorite three.

The best is, of course, only our opinion. But after spending more than half of our adult lives writing and lecturing about travel, guiding tours, and gaining an appreciation for all things French,

we've developed a sixth sense for what touches the traveler's imagination.

ABOUT THIS BOOK

Rick Steves Provence & the French Riviera is a personal tour guide in your pocket. Better yet, it's actually two tour guides in your pocket: The co-author of this book is Steve Smith. Steve, who has lived in France, now travels there annually (as he has since 1986) as a guide, a researcher, a homeowner, and a devout Francophile. He has restored an old farmhouse in Burgundy and today keeps one foot on each side of the Atlantic. Together, Steve and I keep this book up-to-date and accurate (though for simplicity, from this point "we" will shed our respective egos and become "I").

This book is organized by destinations. Each is a mini vacation on its own, filled with exciting sights, strollable neighborhoods,

INTRODUCTION

Provence & the French Riviera Almanac

Official Name: Provence and the French Riviera are part of the Provence-Alpes-Côte-d'Azur (PACA), one of 13 administrative regions of France.

Capital: Marseille is the region's capital city.

Regional Population: Over 4.9 million.

Main Cities: Marseille (855,000), Nice (344,000), Aix-en-Provence (140,000), Avignon (90,000), Antibes (75,000), Cannes (73,000), Arles (52,000), St-Tropez (5,600).

Language: French is the official language. More than 1.5 million people in the south of France speak one of two lesser-known dialects: Occitan, and specifically in the Provence region, Provençal (both dialects are closely related to Catalan, a dialect of Spanish).

Geography: Located in the southeast of France, the Provence-Alpes-Côte-d'Azur region spans over 71 miles of Mediterranean coastline, from Marseille and Toulon in the west, to Monaco and the Italian border in the east, where the Alps stretch to the north.

Climate: The Hautes-Alpes and Rhône-Alpes shield the region from severe weather and give Provence and the Riviera the highest average temperatures in France. Locals enjoy more than 300 days of sun per year, but experience more storms than other parts of France.

Economy: The Provence-Alpes-Côte-d'Azur region is the third wealthiest in France and annually contributes nearly $158 billion (7%) to France's GDP. Tourism and service industries account for 80 percent of jobs, but the region is also a leading center for agriculture, biotechnology, and microelectronics.

Agriculture: Provence is known for its herbs (such as oregano,

affordable places to stay, and memorable places to eat. The content consists of two obvious parts: Provence and the Riviera (although almost everything covered in this book is officially considered part of the "Provence-Alpes-Côte d'Azur region" by the French government). The Provence half highlights Arles, Nîmes, and Avignon, and their day-trip destinations; the photogenic hill towns of the Côtes du Rhône and Luberon; and the coastal towns of Marseille and Cassis, and nearby Aix-en-Provence. On the high-rolling French Riviera, I cover the waterfront destinations of Nice, Villefranche-sur-Mer, Cap Ferrat, Monaco, Antibes, Cannes, and St-Tropez—plus the best of the inland hill towns and the truly grand Grand Canyon du Verdon.

The introductions to **Provence** and **The French Riviera** acquaint you with the history, cuisine, and wine of the places you'll be visiting, and give practical advice on what to see, how to get

thyme, and rosemary), vegetables, and olive oil, and the region produces nearly two-thirds of France's olives. These ingredients, combined with elements of French, Spanish, and Italian cooking, make Provence's cuisine fresh, colorful, and flavorful.

Crafts: In the 17th century, Marseille began manufacturing expen-sive and colorful printed linens called "Indiennes," inspired by fabrics imported from India. Though most traditional textile factories are closed today, Provence still produces cotton fabrics (scarves, shawls) using original "Indienne" techniques and featuring the local cicada (*cigale*) in their designs.

Tourism: The Provence-Alpes-Côte-d'Azur region welcomes over 34 million tourists every year. Celebrities and wealthy Brits have vacationed on the French Riviera since the 19th century (giving the Promenade des Anglais in Nice its name). Nowadays, the Riviera attracts more than just celebrities: More than 5 million tourists visit every summer, with Nice at the center of the tourist commotion.

Famous Residents: The rich and famous have homes throughout Provence and the Riviera, including actors Brigitte Bardot, Sean Connery, Mel Gibson, Brad Pitt; musicians Bono, Elton John, Tina Turner, Bill Wyman, and Rod Stewart; and billionaire Bill Gates.

around, and lots more. Don't overlook the valuable tips in these chapters.

In the destination chapters, you'll find these sections:

Planning Your Time suggests a schedule for how to best to use your limited time.

Orientation has specifics on public transportation, helpful hints, local tour options, easy-to-read maps, and tourist information.

Sights describes the top attractions and includes their cost and hours.

Self-Guided Walks and **Tours** help you explore these fascinating towns and sights: Avignon, Nîmes, Arles, Marseille, Aix-en-Provence, Les Baux, Isle-sur-la-Sorgue, Roussillon, Nice (Promenade des Anglais, Vieux Nice, and the Chagall Museum), Monaco, Antibes, Villefranche-sur-Mer, and Cannes. **Self-guided driving tours** let you explore the Côtes du Rhône wine road, the

Grand Canyon du Verdon, and inland hill towns of the Riviera with the knowledge of a local.

Sleeping describes my favorite hotels, from good-value deals to cushy splurges.

Eating serves up a buffet of options, from inexpensive cafés to fancy restaurants.

Connections outlines your options for traveling to destinations by train and bus, plus route tips for drivers.

The book also includes detailed chapters on these key topics:

Traveling with Children offers general tips and destination-specific advice on finding kid-friendly sights, hotels, and restaurants. Kids have greatly enriched my travels, and I hope the same will be true for you.

Shopping has suggestions for this region's best souvenirs and bargains. My longtime friendships with shopkeepers, local guides, and vintners have contributed greatly to the savvy shopping advice.

France: Past & Present gives you a quick overview of the country's history and current political issues.

The **Practicalities** chapter near the end of this book is a traveler's tool kit, with my best advice about money, sightseeing, sleeping, eating, staying connected, and transportation (trains, buses, car rentals, driving, and flights).

The **appendix** has the nuts-and-bolts: useful phone numbers and websites, a holiday and festival list, recommended books and films, a climate chart, a handy packing checklist, and French survival phrases.

Throughout this book, you'll find money- and time-saving tips for sightseeing, transportation, and more. Some businesses—especially hotels and walking tour companies—offer special discounts to my readers, indicated in their listings.

Browse through this book, choose your favorite destinations, and link them up. Then have a *très bon voyage!* Traveling like a temporary local, you'll get the absolute most out of every mile, minute, and dollar. As you visit places I know and love, I'm happy that you'll be meeting some of my favorite French people.

Planning

This section will help you get started planning your trip—with advice on trip costs, when to go, and what you should know before you take off.

TRIP COSTS

Five components make up your trip costs: airfare to Europe, transportation in Europe, room and board, sightseeing and entertainment, and shopping and miscellany.

The Language Barrier and That French Attitude

You've probably heard that the French are "cold and refuse to speak English." This preconception is left over from the days of Charles de Gaulle—and is especially untrue in the laid-back south. In these lands kissed by the sun and sea, you'll find your hosts more jovial and easygoing (like their Italian neighbors) than in the more serious north. Still, be reasonable in your expectations: French waiters are paid to be efficient, not chatty.

My best advice? Slow down. Hurried, impatient travelers who skip the subtle pleasures of people-watching from a sun-dappled café often misinterpret French attitudes. With five weeks of paid vacation and 35-hour workweeks, your hosts can't fathom why anyone would rush through their time off. By slowing your pace and making an effort to understand French culture, you're likely to have a richer experience.

The French take great pride in their customs and cling to a sense of their own cultural superiority. Polite and formal, the French respect the fine points of culture and tradition. Here, strolling down the street with a big grin and saying hello to strangers is a sign of senility, not friendliness (seriously). Recognize sincerity and look for kindness.

Communication difficulties are exaggerated. To hurdle the language barrier, start with the French survival phrases in this book (see the appendix). In transactions, a small notepad and pen minimize misunderstandings; have vendors write down the price. Keep a French/English dictionary or translation app handy.

Though many French people speak English—especially those in the tourist trade, and in big cities—you'll get better treatment if you use French pleasantries. Learn these five phrases: *bonjour* (good day), *pardon* (pardon me), *s'il vous plaît* (please), *merci* (thank you), and *au revoir* (good-bye). Begin every encounter with *"Bonjour* (or *S'il vous plaît*), *madame* (or *monsieur*),"* and end every encounter with *"Au revoir, madame* (or *monsieur*)."* When spelling out your name, you'll find that most letters are pronounced very differently in French: *a* is pronounced "ah," *e* is pronounced "eh," and *i* is pronounced "ee." To avoid confusion, say *"a,* Anne," *"e,* euro," and *"i,* Isabelle."

When you do endeavor to speak French, you may be politely corrected—*c'est normal* (to be expected). The French are linguistic perfectionists—they take their language (and other languages) seriously. Often they speak more English than they let on. This isn't a tourist-baiting tactic, but timidity on their part about speaking another language less than fluently. To ask a French person to speak English, say, *"Bonjour, madame* (or *monsieur*). *Parlez-vous anglais?"* They may say *"non,"* but as you continue you'll probably find they speak more English than you speak French.

For more tips, consider the *Rick Steves French Phrase Book* (available at www.ricksteves.com).

Provence and the French Riviera at a Glance

Provence

▲▲▲**Arles** Once-important Roman outpost, now a bustling town famous for its market days, ancient amphitheater, and as a site that inspired Vincent van Gogh.

▲▲**Near Arles** Several compelling sights: the cliff-topping castle ruins at Les Baux; St-Rémy with Roman ruins and a mental hospital that treated Van Gogh; and the Camargue—a nature lover's refuge, with flamingos, bulls, and white horses.

▲**Avignon** Fourteenth-century residence of the popes, today a youthful city with atmospheric cafés, lively squares and pedestrian areas, and a famous broken bridge.

▲▲▲**Near Avignon** Three worthy destinations, including the stunning Pont du Gard aqueduct; thriving Nîmes, with world-class Roman monuments; and pedestrian-friendly Uzès, a refreshing break from power monuments and busy cities.

▲▲▲**Orange and the Côtes du Rhône** Starring Orange's remarkably intact Roman theater, plus the sunny Côtes du Rhône wine road, cozy villages, and fields of lavender, anchored by charming Vaison-la-Romaine.

▲▲**Hill Towns of the Luberon** Boasting crumbled castles, ocher canyons, and meditative abbeys; the sturdy market town of Isle-sur-la-Sorgue; and delightful rock-top villages like Roussillon, Lacoste, and Ménerbes.

Airfare to Europe: Nice is the handiest airport for Provence and the Riviera (Marseille is a good second choice). A basic round-trip flight from the US to Nice or Paris can cost, on average, about $1,000-2,000 total, depending on where you fly from and when (cheaper in winter). Smaller budget airlines may provide bargain service from Paris and other European cities to places such as Marseille, Toulouse, Avignon, and Montpellier (see "Flights" on page 525 for details). If your trip covers a wide area, consider saving time and money in Europe by flying into one city and out of another—for instance, into Nice and out of Paris. Overall, Kayak.com is the best place to start searching for flights on a combination of mainstream and budget carriers.

Transportation in Europe: Allow $30 per day per person for public transportation (trains, buses, and taxis). If you'll be renting a car, allow at least $250 per week, not including tolls, gas,

▲▲Marseille and Nearby Photogenic port of Marseille with a gritty charm; the beach town of Cassis, home of the *calanques* (Mediterranean fjords); and inland, the genteel city of Aix-en-Provence.

The French Riviera

▲▲▲Nice The Riviera's metropolis, with a sun-drenched promenade, a delightful French-Italian old city, and museums dedicated to Chagall and Matisse.

▲▲▲East of Nice Small, Italianate beach town of Villefranche-sur-Mer, ritzy but woodsy Cap Ferrat, and little cliff-topping Eze-le-Village—linked by the panoramic roads known as the Three Corniches.

▲▲Monaco Tiny independent principality, known for its Grand Prix car race and classy casino.

▲Antibes and Nearby The Riviera's west: laid-back Antibes, with a medieval old town and Picasso Museum; glamorous Cannes, with sandy beaches and movie stars; and the luxurious port town of St-Tropez.

▲▲Inland Riviera Perfectly perched hill towns of Vence and St-Paul-de-Vence (France's most-visited village), the perfume capital of Grasse, and the spectacular Grand Canyon du Verdon.

and supplemental insurance. If you need the car for three weeks or more, leasing can save you money on insurance and taxes. A short flight can be cheaper than the train (check www.skyscanner.com for intra-European flights).

Room and Board: You can thrive in Provence and the Riviera on $140 a day per person for room and board. This allows an average of $12 for breakfast, $18 for lunch, $40 for dinner with drinks, and $70 for lodging (based on two people splitting the cost of a $140 double room). Students and tightwads can enjoy Provence and the Riviera for as little as $60 a day ($30 per bed, $30 for meals and snacks).

Sightseeing and Entertainment: Figure about $10 per major sight ($9-10 for Arles' Roman Arena or Nice's Chagall Museum, $13 for Avignon's Palace of the Popes), around $6 for minor ones (e.g., climbing church towers), $30 for guided walks, and $40-70 for splurge experiences (such as bullfights or concerts). An over-all average of $25 a day works for most people. Don't skimp here. After all, this category is the driving force behind your trip—you came to sightsee, enjoy, and experience this wonderfully French region.

Shopping and Miscellany: Figure $4 per ice-cream cone, café au lait, or soft drink. Shopping can vary in cost from nearly nothing to a small fortune. Good budget travelers find that this category has little to do with assembling a trip full of lifelong memories.

SIGHTSEEING PRIORITIES

So much to see, so little time. How to choose? Depending on the length of your trip, and taking geographic proximity into account, here are my recommended priorities:

6 days:	Arles and day trips to Pont du Gard and Les Baux, a night in a Côtes du Rhône village, and Nice with a day trip to Monaco
9 days, add:	A second night in a Côtes du Rhône village with a day trip to Avignon en route, and two nights in Cassis
12 days, add:	Luberon, Grand Canyon du Verdon, and one more night in Nice with a day trip to Antibes
14 days, add:	Two nights in Aix-en-Provence and side-trips to Nîmes, Marseille, and the Camargue

This includes nearly everything on the map on page 13. If you don't have time to see it all, prioritize according to your interests. The "Provence and the Riviera at a Glance" sidebar can help you decide where to go (page 8). For a day-by-day itinerary of a two-week trip, see this chapter's two recommended routes (by car, and by train and bus).

WHEN TO GO

With more than 300 days of sunshine per year, Provence and the Riviera enjoy France's sunniest weather. Spring and fall are best, with generally comfortable weather—though crowds can be a problem, particularly during holiday weekends and major events (May is worst). April can be damp, and any month can be windy. Don't be fooled by sunny forecasts in shoulder season (April and October)—if the wind is blowing it can be chilly.

Summer means festivals, lavender (late June through July), sunflowers, steamy weather, long hours at sights, and longer lines of cars along the Riviera. Europeans vacation in July and August, jamming the Riviera, the Gorges du Verdon, and Ardèche (worst from mid-July through mid-Aug), but leaving the rest of this region relatively calm. Though many French businesses close in August, the traveler hardly notices.

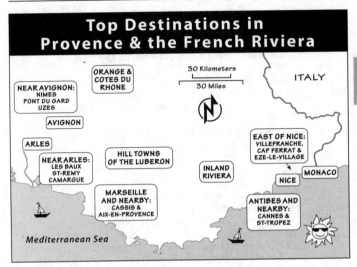

Top Destinations in Provence & the French Riviera

September brings the grape harvest, when small wineries are off-limits to taste-seeking travelers (for information on wine tasting, see page 32). Late fall delivers beautiful foliage and a return to tranquility.

Winter travel is OK in Nice, Aix-en-Provence, and Avignon, but you'll find smaller cities and villages buttoned up tight. Sights and tourist-information offices keep shorter hours, and some tourist activities (such as English-language castle tours) vanish altogether.

Thanks to Provence's temperate climate, fields of flowers greet the traveler much of the year:

May: Wild red poppies *(coquelicots)* sprout.

June: Lavender begins to bloom in the lower hills of Provence, generally during the last week of the month.

July: Lavender is in full swing in Provence, and sunflowers are awakening. If you can find adjacent fields with lavender and sunflowers, celebrate! Cities, towns, and villages everywhere overflow with carefully tended flowers.

August-September: Sunflowers flourish.

October: In the latter half of the month, the countryside glistens with fall colors (most trees are deciduous). Vineyards go for the gold.

Before You Go

You'll have a smoother trip if you tackle a few things ahead of time. For more information on these topics, see the Practicalities chapter (and www.ricksteves.com, which has helpful travel tips and talks).

Best Two-Week Trip of Provence & the French Riviera by Car

Day   Plan

1   **Fly into Nice.** Settle in at your hotel, then follow my self-guided walk along the Promenade des Anglais. Sleep in or near Nice.

2   **All Day in Nice.** Start the morning with my self-guided walk through Vieux Nice. Take time to smell the *fougasse* and sample *un café*. Spend your afternoon at one or more of Nice's fine museums. Have dinner on the beach. Sleep in or near Nice.

3   **Coastal Route to Monaco.** Take the train or bus to nearby Villefranche-sur-Mer, explore, and have lunch. Consider my recommended seaside walks in Cap Ferrat, or take the one-hour boat cruise from Nice's port. Spend the afternoon or evening in almost neighboring Monaco. Sleep in or near Nice.

4   **Inland Riviera.** Pick up your rental car as early as possible in Nice. Drive north to Vence or Grasse (you choose), then continue on to the Gorges du Verdon and sleep in tiny Aiguines or Moustiers-Ste-Marie.

5   **Drive to Provence.** Continue west into the Luberon and explore the villages of the Provençal heartland—*la Provence profonde*. Stay in or near Roussillon.

6   **Luberon Hill Towns.** Spend your day sampling hill towns in the Luberon. Taste a village market, then drive over the hills to the valley of the Côtes du Rhône. Sleep in or near Vaison-la-Romaine (Mon arrival is ideal because market day is Tue). From late June to late July, when the lavender blooms, the drive to Vaison-la-Romaine via Sault is a must.

7   **Côtes du Rhône Villages.** Explore Vaison-la-Romaine's upper medieval village and lower Roman city. Set sail along the Côtes du Rhône wine road (following my self-guided driving tour) and visit a winery or wine cooperative. Tour little Crestet and take a walk above Gigondas. Sleep in or near Vaison-la-Romaine.

8   **Orange and Châteauneuf-du-Pape.** Start your day touring the Roman theater in Orange and consider a quick stop in Châteauneuf-du-Pape. Continue south and set up in Avignon. In the afternoon, take my self-guided Avignon walks and enjoy dinner on one of the town's many atmospheric squares. Sleep in Avignon.

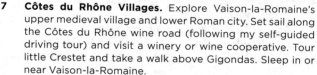

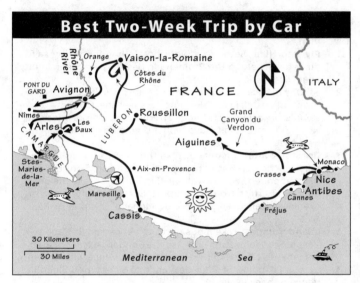

Best Two-Week Trip by Car

9 **Nîmes and Pont du Gard.** Spend the day visiting Nîmes (Roman amphitheater) and the Pont du Gard (Nîmes works better first). If the weather's good, bring your swimsuit and float on your back for views of the 2,000-year-old aqueduct. Sleep in Avignon.

10 **The Camargue.** Take a joyride through the Camargue (but if it's summer, when flamingos are scarce and mosquitoes aren't, skip it and visit Les Baux instead). Wind up in Arles (big Saturday morning market). Sleep in Arles.

11 **All Day in and near Arles.** Spend most of your day in Arles. Drive to Les Baux for late afternoon sightseeing and dinner. Sleep in Arles.

12 **Aix-en-Provence or Marseille.** Drive to Cassis, stopping for lunch and a midday visit to Aix-en-Provence or Marseille (Marseille is dicier by car). Set up in Cassis and watch the sun set from the old port while you savor a bouillabaisse dinner. Sleep in Cassis.

13 **All Day in Cassis.** Spend all day in Cassis enjoying *la vie douce*. Take a boat trip or hike to the *calanques,* watch the *pétanque* balls fly, and end your day with a drive up Cap Canaille. Sleep in Cassis.

14 **Fly Away.** Fly out of Marseille today or, if leaving from Nice, drive to Antibes and spend your final day and evening there.

15 **Trip over.**

Best Two-Week Trip of Provence & the French Riviera by Train and Bus

Note that on Sundays, fewer trains run, and buses often disappear.

Day	Plan
1	**Fly into Nice.** Settle in at your hotel, then follow my self-guided walk along the Promenade des Anglais. Sleep in or near Nice.
2	**All Day in Nice.** Start the morning with my self-guided walk through Vieux Nice. Take time to smell the *fougasse* and sample *un café*. Spend your afternoon at one or more of Nice's fine museums. Have dinner on the beach. Sleep in or near Nice.
3	**Coastal Route to Monaco.** Take the train or bus to nearby Villefranche-sur-Mer, explore, and have lunch. Consider my recommended seaside walks in Cap Ferrat, or take the one-hour boat cruise from Nice's port. Spend the afternoon or evening in (almost) neighboring Monaco. Sleep in or near Nice.
4	**Inland Villages.** Take a bus north to Vence and St-Paul-de-Vence. Stop for a stroll and visit the Fondation Maeght and/or Matisse's Chapel of the Rosary. Or link Vence with Grasse by bus (skipping St-Paul-de-Vence to save time). Sleep in Vence or back in Nice.
5	**Isle-sur-la-Sorgue.** Take a train to Isle-sur-la-Sorgue via Marseille or Nice (best to arrive on Sat or Wed and awaken the next morning for market day). Wander and explore the town. Consider a canoe ride down the crystal-clear Sorgue River. Sleep in Isle-sur-la-Sorgue.
6	**Isle-sur-la-Sorgue and Avignon.** Enjoy market day this morning, then take a train to Avignon. Take my self-guided Avignon walks this afternoon and enjoy dinner on one of Avignon's many atmospheric squares. Sleep in Avignon.
7	**Day Trip to Nîmes and Pont du Gard.** Visit Nîmes (Roman amphitheater) in the morning and Pont du Gard in the afternoon. If the weather's good, bring your swimsuit and float on your back for views of the 2,000-year-old aqueduct.

Make sure your passport is valid. If it's due to expire within six months of your ticketed date of return, you need to renew it. Allow up to six weeks to renew or get a passport (www.travel.state.gov).

Arrange your transportation. Book your international flights. Figure out your main form of transportation within Provence and the Riviera: It's worth thinking about buying train tickets online in advance, renting a car, or booking cheap European flights. (You can wing it once you're there, but it may cost more.)

Rail passes only make sense if you are traveling beyond

Have dinner and sleep back in Avignon.

8   **Vaison-la-Romaine.** Take a bus to Vaison-la-Romaine or ride a morning train to Orange (frequent departures), then connect to a less frequent bus to Vaison-la-Romaine (market day is Tue, so a Mon arrival is ideal). Set up in Vaison-la-Romaine for two nights. Explore the town's upper medieval village and lower Roman city this afternoon.

9   **Côtes du Rhône Villages.** Get to a wine village near Vaison-la-Romaine. Take a minivan tour of the wine road (see "Tours in Provence" on page 24), bike to Séguret and Gigondas, or hike to Crestet for lunch (taxi back). Sleep in Vaison-la-Romaine.

10   **Orange and Arles.** Take a morning bus back to Orange (bag check available near the train station), visit the Roman theater, then hop a train to Arles (big Sat morning market) and explore the city this afternoon. Check into Arles for the next two nights.

11   **Les Baux and Arles.** Take a minivan tour or a taxi (or, in summer, a bus) to Les Baux and have breakfast with a view. Return to Arles by taxi or bus (minivan tours will probably include other destinations), and spend your afternoon there; or take a taxi from Les Baux to St-Rémy, explore there, then catch a bus back to Arles.

12   **Marseille, then Cassis.** Hop the train to Marseille, check your bags at the station, and take my walking tour of the ancient center. End your day in Cassis and watch the sunset from the old port while you savor a bouillabaisse dinner. Sleep in Cassis.

13   **Cassis.** Spend all day in Cassis enjoying *la vie douce.* Take a boat trip or hike to the *calanques,* then watch the *pétanque* balls fly. Sleep in Cassis.

14   **Fly Away.** Fly out of nearby Marseille or, if leaving from Nice, take a train back to Nice and savor a last night on the Promenade des Anglais. Sleep in Nice.

15   **Trip over.**

Provence and the Riviera, as distances are short and point-to-point fares are reasonable. Note that all high-speed trains (TGV; also called "InOui") in France require a seat reservation; book as early as possible, as these trains fill fast. If you're using a rail pass, book even earlier—there's a tight limit on seat reservations for passholders. Most trains between Marseille and Nice are TGV, so think about reserving that trip ahead.

Book rooms well in advance, especially if your trip falls during peak season or any major holidays or festivals.

Consider travel insurance. Compare the cost of the insurance to the cost of your potential loss. Check whether your existing insurance (health, homeowners, or renters) covers you and your possessions overseas.

Call your bank. Alert your bank that you'll be using your debit and credit cards in Europe. Ask about transaction fees, and get the PIN number for your credit card. You don't need to bring euros for your trip; you can withdraw euros from cash machines in Europe.

Use your smartphone smartly. Sign up for an international service plan to reduce your costs, or rely on Wi-Fi in Europe instead. Download any apps you'll want on the road, such as maps, translation, transit schedules, and Rick Steves Audio Europe (see page 528).

Pack light. You'll walk with your luggage more than you think. I travel for weeks with a single carry-on bag and a daypack. Use the packing checklist in the appendix as a guide.

Travel Smart

If you have a positive attitude, equip yourself with good information (this book), and expect to travel smart, you will.

Read—and reread—this book. To have an "A" trip, be an "A" student. Note opening hours of sights, closed days, crowd-beating tips, and whether reservations are required or advisable. Check the latest at www.ricksteves.com/update.

Be your own tour guide. As you travel, get up-to-date info on sights, reserve tickets and tours, reconfirm hotels and travel arrangements, and check transit connections. Visit local tourist information offices (TIs). Upon arrival in a new town, lay the groundwork for a smooth departure; confirm the train, bus, or road you'll take when you leave.

Outsmart thieves. Pickpockets abound in crowded places where tourists congregate. Treat commotions as smokescreens for theft. Keep your cash, credit cards, and passport secure in a money belt tucked under your clothes; carry only a day's spending money in your front pocket. Don't set valuable items down on counters or café tabletops, where they can be quickly stolen or easily forgotten.

Minimize potential loss. Keep expensive gear to a minimum. Bring photocopies or take photos of important documents (passport and cards) to aid in replacement if they're lost or stolen.

Beat the summer heat. If you wilt easily, choose a hotel with air-conditioning, start your day early, take a midday siesta at your hotel, and resume your sightseeing later. Churches offer a cool haven (modest attire is appreciated). Take frequent breaks.

Guard your time and energy. Taking a taxi can be a good value if it saves you a long wait for a cheap bus or an exhausting walk across town. Use the tips throughout this book to organize your sightseeing efficiently.

Be flexible. Even if you have a well-planned itinerary, expect changes, strikes, closures, sore feet, bad weather, and so on. Your Plan B could turn out to be even better.

Attempt the language. Many French—especially in the tourist trade and in cities—speak English, but if you learn some French, even just a few phrases, you'll get more smiles and make more friends. Practice the survival phrases near the end of this book, and even better, bring a phrase book.

Connect with the culture. Interacting with locals carbonates your experience. Enjoy the friendliness of the French people. The

French adore enthusiastic reactions to their landscapes, sights, food, and wine. Ask questions; most locals are happy to point you in their idea of the right direction. Cheer for your favorite bowler at a *boules* match, leave no chair unturned in your quest for the best café, find that perfect hill-town view, and make friends with a waiter (it happens). When an opportunity pops up, make it a habit to say "yes."

France...here you come!

PROVENCE

PROVENCE

"There are treasures to carry away in this land, which has not found a spokesman worthy of the riches it offers."

—Paul Cézanne

The magnificent region of Provence is shaped like a giant wedge of quiche. From its sunburned crust, fanning out along the Mediterranean coast from the Camargue to Marseille, it stretches north along the Rhône Valley to Orange. The Romans were here in force and left many ruins—some of the best anywhere (the region's name comes from its status as the first Roman province). Seven popes, artists such as Vincent van Gogh and Paul Cézanne, and author Peter Mayle all enjoyed their years in Provence. This destination features a splendid recipe of arid climate, oceans of vineyards, dramatic scenery, lively cities, and adorable hill-capping villages.

Explore the ghost town that is ancient Les Baux, and see France's greatest Roman ruins—the Pont du Gard aqueduct, the theater in Orange, and the arena in Nîmes. Admire the skill of ball-tossing *boules* players in small squares in every Provençal village and city. Spend a few Van Gogh-inspired starry, starry nights in Arles. Youthful but classy Avignon bustles in the shadow of its brooding Palace of the Popes. Stylish and self-confident Aix-en-Provence lies 30 minutes from the sea and feels more Mediterranean. It's a short hop from Arles or Avignon into the splendid scenery and villages of the Côtes du Rhône and Luberon regions. To properly understand southern France, day-trip into gritty Marseille. If you prefer a perfectly Provençal beach fix, find Cassis, just to the east.

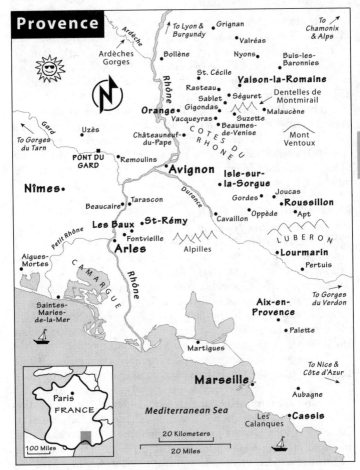

CHOOSING A HOME BASE

With limited time, make Arles or Avignon your sightseeing base—particularly without a car. Italophiles prefer smaller Arles, while poodles pick urban Avignon. Many enjoy nights in both cities. (With a car, head for St-Rémy or the hill towns.)

Arles has a blue-collar quality; the entire city feels like Van Gogh's bedroom. It also has this region's best-value hotels and is handy to Les Baux, St-Rémy, and the Camargue.

Avignon—double the size of Arles—feels sophisticated, with more nightlife and shopping. Avignon makes a good base for non-drivers thanks to its convenient public-transit options (within an hour, you can reach Pont du Gard, Uzès, Nîmes, and St-Rémy by bus, or Marseille by train; within a half-hour, you can reach Arles, Isle-sur-la-Sorgue, and Aix-en-Provence by train).

For drivers who prefer a smaller-town base, **St-Rémy-de-Provence** is manageable and central. It offers a nice range of hotels with free and easy parking, good restaurants, and a few sights of its own. The towns of **Vaison-la-Romaine** (in the Côtes du Rhône region) and **Roussillon** (in the Luberon) are two good but remote hill-town options.

Aix-en-Provence works well as a base for Provence sights east of Arles and Avignon, with easy access to Marseille, Cassis, and some Luberon villages. About halfway between Arles and Nice, Aix-en-Provence also makes a convenient stopover, and if you're flying in or out of Marseille, Aix has quick access to the airport, making it a convenient first- or last-day stop.

PLANNING YOUR TIME

The bare minimum you should spend in Provence is three days: one day for sightseeing in Arles and Les Baux (Arles is best on Wed or Sat, when it's market day); a day for Pont du Gard and Nîmes; and a full day for Orange and the Côtes du Rhône villages. Add two more days to explore Avignon, Uzès or St-Rémy, and more Provençal villages. Allow an additional two days in Cassis, using one of them for a day trip to Marseille or Aix-en-Provence (or both). Ideally, see the cities—Arles, Nîmes, Avignon, Aix-en-Provence, and Marseille—by train, then rent a car for the countryside.

To measure the pulse of rural Provence, spend at least a few nights in the smaller towns. Provençal villages come to life on market days, but can be quiet on Mondays—when shops are shuttered tight—and are terminally quiet from mid-October to Easter. I've described many towns in the Côtes du Rhône and Luberon. The Côtes du Rhône is ideal for wine connoisseurs and an easy stop for those heading to or from the north. The Luberon was made for hill-town lovers and works well for travelers heading east, toward Aix-en-Provence or the Riviera. Avoid speeding through these areas. Provençal village evenings are what books are written about—spend the night, or two, or...

The small port town of Cassis is a marvelous Mediterranean meander between Provence and the Riviera (and more appealing than most Riviera resorts). It has easy day-trip connections to Marseille and Aix-en-Provence.

Depending on the length of your trip, here are my recommended priorities for Provence:

4 days:	Arles and Les Baux; Pont du Gard and Nîmes; and Orange and Côtes du Rhône villages
5-6 days, add:	Cassis, Marseille, and Aix-en-Provence
7-8 days, add:	Luberon hill towns
9-10 days, add:	Avignon and either St-Rémy or Uzès

HELPFUL HINTS

Resources: Imagine Tours (near Avignon) offers free assistance to travelers. They can work with you to plan your itinerary, book hotels, or help you deal with problems that might arise during your trip (for contact information, see page 26).

Cruise-Ship Sightseeing: Cruise lines that visit Provence call at either Marseille or La Seyne-sur-Mer/Toulon (about 40 miles east of Marseille; see page 239). Public-transit options are limited—with a short day, only Marseille, Cassis, and Aix-en-Provence are doable. (It's possible to visit Avignon or Arles from Marseille—but only with a long day in port.) To journey beyond the immediate area and/or connect several sights in one busy day, join a cruise-line excursion, hire a driver or guide (see "Tours in Provence," later), or rent a car. For in-depth coverage, consider my guidebook, *Rick Steves Mediterranean Cruise Ports.*

GETTING AROUND PROVENCE

By Bus or Train: Public transit is good between cities and decent to some towns, but marginal at best to the smaller villages. Frequent trains link Avignon, Arles, and Nîmes (no more than an hour between each). Avignon has good train connections with Orange and adequate service to Isle-sur-la-Sorgue. Marseille is well-connected to all cities in Provence, with frequent service to Cassis (25 minutes) and Aix-en-Provence (45 minutes).

Buses connect many smaller towns, though service can be sporadic. From Arles you can catch a bus to Les Baux (high season only), Stes-Maries-de-la-Mer (in the Camargue), or St-Rémy. From Avignon, you can bus to Pont du Gard, St-Rémy, Uzès, Isle-sur-la-Sorgue (also by train), and to some Côtes du Rhône villages. St-Rémy, Isle-sur-la-Sorgue, and Uzès are the most accessible and interesting small towns. Vaison-la-Romaine—my favorite town—is a manageable bus ride from Orange (with fast and frequent train connections to Avignon). A visit here works well with a tour of Orange's Roman Theater.

While a tour of the Côtes du Rhône or Luberon is best on your own by car, a variety of minivan tours and basic bus excursions are available. (TIs in Arles and Avignon also have information on bus excursions to regional sights that are hard to reach *sans* car; see "Tours in Provence," later.)

By Car: The region is made to order for a car, though travel time between some sights will surprise you—thanks, in part, to narrow roads and endless roundabouts (for example, figure an hour from Les Baux to Pont du Gard, and two hours from Arles to Vaison-la-Romaine). Michelin map #527 (1:275,000 scale) covers this area perfectly. Michelin maps #332 (Luberon and Côtes du Rhône) and #340 (Arles area) are also worth considering. I've described key sights and a variety of full-day drives deep into the countryside. Be wary of thieves: Park only in well-monitored spaces and leave nothing valuable in your car. Drivers are smart to offload bags at hotels before sightseeing.

Avignon (pop. 90,000) is a headache for drivers. Arles (pop. 52,000) is easier but still challenging. Les Baux and St-Rémy work well from Arles or Avignon (or vice versa). Nîmes and Pont du Gard are a short hop west of Avignon. The town of Orange ties in tidily with a trip to the Côtes du Rhône villages and with destinations farther north. If you're heading north from Provence, consider a half-day detour through the spectacular Ardèche Gorges. The Luberon villages are about halfway between Arles or Avignon and Aix-en-Provence (little Lourmarin works as a base for day trips to Aix-en-Provence). And if you're continuing on to the Riviera, let yourself be lured into the Grand Canyon du Verdon detour (see the Inland Riviera chapter). Most drivers will prefer exploring congested Marseille on foot—take the train from Cassis or Aix-en-Provence (both towns have parking at their train stations with frequent trains and buses to the center of Marseille).

By Bike: Wind, heat, and hilly terrain make this region a challenge to bike. If you're determined, I list bike rental options in most cities (including electric bikes). Telecycles will deliver your bike to hotels within about 12 miles of St-Rémy (tel. 04 90 92 83 15 or 06 11 64 04 69, www.telecycles-location.com).

TOURS IN PROVENCE

Towns with a lot of tourism generally have English-speaking guides available for private hire (about €130 for a 3-hour guided walk). It's also possible to take half-day or full-day excursions to most of the sights in Provence. TIs have wads of brochures on day trips and can help you make a reservation. Excursions are best from Avignon, where most tours can pick you up at your hotel, the TI, or at either of the city's train stations. Here are several good options to consider:

Tours with a Wine Focus
Wine Safari
Dutchman Mike Rijken runs a one-man show, taking travelers through the region he adopted 25 years ago. His English is fluent, and though his focus is on wine and wine villages, Mike knows the region thoroughly and is a good teacher of its history (per person: €75/half-day, €130/day, 2-6-person groups; pickups possible in Arles, Avignon, Lyon, Marseille, or Aix-en-Provence; tel. 04 90 35 59 21, mobile 06 19 29 50 81, www.winesafari.net, mikeswinesafari@orange.fr).

Top 10 Provençal Towns and Vi...

1. **Roussillon,** a beautiful hill town sitting atop a huge ochre deposit, giving it a red-rock appeal, popular with American tourists; see page 195.
2. **Uzès,** a chic town with manicured pedestrian streets, popular with European tourists; see page 141.
3. **Joucas,** an adorable little village where flowers and stones are lovingly maintained, a magnet for artists; see page 202.
4. **Brantes,** a spectacularly situated cliff village literally at the end of the road, with few tourists; see page 181.
5. **Vaison-la-Romaine,** a bustling midsize town that spans both sides of a river and has Roman ruins, popular with tourists; see page 157.
6. **Lourmarin,** a lovely upscale village, busy during the day but quiet at night; see page 217.
7. **Crestet,** an overlooked village with a sensational hilltop location and one commercial enterprise; see page 170.
8. **Séguret,** a linear hillside village with memorable views, many day-trippers, but few overnighters; see page 169.
9. **Gigondas,** a world-famous wine village with a nice balance of commercial activity and quiet; see page 176.
10. **Nyons,** an overlooked midsize town with a few pedestrian streets, famous for its olive oil and ideal climate; see page 180.

Le Vin à la Bouche

Charming Céline Viany—a sommelier and easy-to-be-with tour guide—is an expert on her region and its chief product (from €200/half-day for 2 people, from €250/day for 2-7 people, price depends on pickup location and number of clients, tel. 04 90 46 90 80, mobile 06 76 59 56 30, www.levinalabouche.com, contact@degustation-levinalabouche.com).

Avignon Wine Tour

For a playful and distinctly French perspective on wines of the Côtes du Rhône region, contact François Marcou, who runs his tours with passion and energy (€110/person for all-day wine tours that include 4 tastings, €80/person for half-day tours, €350 for private groups, less in winter, mobile 06 28 05 33 84, www.avignon-wine-tour.com, contact@avignon-wine-tour.com).

Wine Uncovered

Passionate Englishman Olivier Hickman takes small groups on focused tours of selected wineries in Châteauneuf-du-Pape and in the villages near Vaison-la-Romaine. Olivier knows his subject matter

PROVENCE

and out. His in-depth tastings include a half-day tour of ... or three wineries (€40-75/person for half-day to full-day tours, prices subject to minimum tour fees, mobile 06 75 10 10 01, www.wine-uncovered.com, olivier.hickman@orange.fr).

Tours du Rhône

American Doug Graves, who owns a small wine *domaine* in the Côtes du Rhône, runs custom tours of Châteauneuf-du-Pape, the villages of the Côtes du Rhône, and the Luberon Valley (per person: €135/day, up to 4 people, includes lunch; mobile 06 37 16 04 56, www.toursdurhone.com, doug@masdelalionne.com).

Winery Plus Tours

This company offers small group tours centered on wine and food with a good dose of history and local culture. Experienced guide and wine connoisseur Joe McLean's tours focus on the wines of Uzès, Châteauneuf-du-Pape, and the Côtes du Rhône (per person: €90/half-day, €130-160/day, prices include pickup from Uzès hotels; custom tours possible from Arles and Avignon, no tours on Sun, tel. 06 73 08 23 97, www.wineryplustours.com, contact@wineryplustours.com).

Provence & Wine

Romain Gouvernet is a young and sincere wine guide concentrating on the Côtes du Rhône. Ask about his evening wine tours (per person: €90/half-day, €140/day; tel. 06 86 49 56 76, www.provenceandwine.com, provenceandwine@gmail.com).

Cultural/Historical Tours
Imagine Tours

This organization focuses on cultural excursions, offering personalized tours that allow visitors to discover the "true heart of Provence and Occitania." Itineraries are adapted to your interests, and your guide can meet you at your hotel or the departure point of your choice (€190/half-day, €315/day, prices for up to 4 people starting from near Avignon or Arles, mobile 06 89 22 19 87, www.imagine-tours.net, imagine.tours@gmail.com). They can also help plan your itinerary, book hotel rooms, or address other travel issues.

Local Guides

Catherine D'antuono is a smart, capable, licensed guide for Aix-en-Provence and the region. She guides tours as far west as Pont du Gard and as far east as St-Tropez (€460/day for 2 people, €15 extra for each additional person, 8-person maximum, mobile 06 17 94 69 61, www.provence-travel.com, tour.designer@provence-travel.com).

Discover Provence was founded by England-born Sarah Pernet, who has lived in Aix-en-Provence since 2001. She and her small team offer a variety of well-organized, easygoing, small-group tours to the Luberon, Cassis, Arles, and St-Rémy (from €130/person for half-day, mobile 06 16 86 40 24, www.discover-provence.net, sarah@discover-provence.net).

Basic Transportation-Only Tours
Visit Provence
This company runs day tours from Avignon, Arles, Marseille, and in Aix-en-Provence. Tours from Avignon run year-round and cover a variety of destinations; more limited tours from other cities run April through September only. Tours provide introductory commentary, but no guiding at the actual sights. They use eight-seat, air-conditioned minivans (per person: about €65-80/half-day, €100-125/day). Ask about their cheaper big-bus excursions, or consider hiring a van and driver for your private use (allow about €230/half-day, €500/day, tel. 04 90 14 70 00, www.provence-reservation.com).

THE ROMANS IN PROVENCE
Provence is littered with Roman ruins. Many scholars claim the best-preserved ancient Roman buildings are not in Italy, but in France. These ancient stones will be an important part of your sightseeing agenda in this region, so it's worth learning about how they came to be.

Classical Rome endured from about 500 B.C. through A.D. 500—spending about 500 years growing, 200 years peaking, and 300 years declining. Julius Caesar conquered Gaul—which included Provence—during the Gallic Wars (58-51 B.C.), then crossed the Rubicon River in 49 B.C. to incite civil war within the Roman Republic. He erected a temple to Jupiter on the future site of Paris' Notre-Dame Cathedral.

The concept of one-man rule lived on with his grandnephew, Octavian (whom he had also adopted as his son). Octavian killed Brutus, eliminated his rivals (Mark Antony and Cleopatra), and united Rome's warring factions. He took the title "Augustus" and became the first in a line of emperors who would control Rome for the next 500 years—ruling like a king, with the backing of the army and the rubber-stamp approval of the Senate. Rome morphed from a Republic into an Empire: a collection of many diverse territories ruled by a single man.

Augustus' reign marked the start of 200 years of peace, prosperity, and expansion known as the *Pax Romana*. At its peak (c. A.D. 117), the Roman Empire had 54 million people and stretched from Scotland in the north to Egypt in the south, as far west as Spain and as far east as modern-day Iraq. To the northeast, Rome was bounded by the Rhine and Danube Rivers. On Roman maps,

Top 10 Roman Sights in Provence

1. Pont du Gard aqueduct and its museum
2. Roman Theater in Orange
3. Maison Carrée in Nîmes
4. Ancient History Museum in Arles
5. Arena in Nîmes
6. Arena in Arles
7. Roman city of Glanum (in St-Rémy)
8. Ruined aqueduct near Fontvieille
9. Roman city of Vaison-la-Romaine
10. Julien Bridge (near Roussillon)

the Mediterranean was labeled *Mare Nostrum* ("Our Sea"). At its peak, "Rome" didn't just refer to the city, but to the entire civilized Western world.

The Romans were successful not only because they were good soldiers, but also because they were smart administrators and businessmen. People in conquered territories knew they had joined the winning team and that political stability would replace barbarian invasions. Trade thrived. Conquered peoples were welcomed into the fold of prosperity, linked by roads, education, common laws and gods, and the Latin language.

Provence, with its strategic location, benefited greatly from Rome's global economy and grew to become an important part of its worldwide empire. After Julius Caesar conquered Gaul, Emperor Augustus set out to Romanize it, building and renovating cities in the image of Rome. Most cities had a theater (some had several), baths, and aqueducts; the most important cities had sports arenas. The Romans also  erected an elaborate infrastructure of roads, post offices, schools (teaching in Latin), police stations, and water-supply systems.

With a standard language and currency, Roman merchants were able to trade wine, salt, and olive oil for foreign goods. The empire invested heavily in cities that were strategically important for trade. For example, the Roman-built city of Arles was a crucial link in the trade route from Italy to Spain, so they built a bridge across the Rhône River and fortified the town.

A typical Roman city (such as Nîmes, Arles, Orange, or Vaison-la-Romaine) was a garrison town, laid out on a grid plan with two main roads: one running north-south (the *cardus*), the other east-west (the *decumanus*). Approaching the city on your chariot, you'd pass by the cemetery, which was located outside of town for hygienic reasons. You'd enter the main gate and wheel past warehouses and apartment houses to the town square (forum). Facing the square were the most important temples, dedicated to the patron gods of the city. Nearby, you'd find bathhouses; like today's fitness clubs, these served the almost sacred dedication to personal vigor. Also close by were businesses that catered to the citizens' needs: the marketplace, bakeries, banks, and brothels.

Aqueducts brought fresh water for drinking, filling the baths, and delighting the citizens with bubbling fountains. Men flocked to the stadiums in Arles and Nîmes to bet on gladiator games; eager couples attended elaborate plays at theaters in Orange, Arles, and Vaison-la-Romaine. Marketplaces brimmed with exotic fruits,

vegetables, and animals from the far reaches of the empire. Some cities in Provence were more urban 2,000 years ago than they are today. For instance, Roman Arles had a population of 100,000—double today's size. Think about that when you visit.

You'll come across rounded arches throughout Provence. These were constructed by piling two stacks of heavy stone blocks, connecting them with an arch (supported with wooden scaffolding), then inserting an inverted keystone where the stacks met. *Voilà!* The heavy stones were able to support not only themselves, but also a great deal of weight above the arch. The Romans didn't invent the rounded arch, but they exploited it better than their predecessors, stacking arches to build arenas and theaters, stringing them side by side for aqueducts, stretching out their legs to create barrel-vaulted ceilings, and building freestanding "triumphal" arches to celebrate conquering generals.

When it came to construction, the Romans' magic building ingredient was concrete. A mixture of volcanic ash, lime, water, and small rocks, concrete—easier to work than stone, longer-lasting than wood—served as flooring, roofing, filler, glue, and support. Builders would start with a foundation of brick, then fill it in with poured concrete. They would then cover important structures, such as basilicas, in sheets of expensive marble (held on with nails), or decorate floors and walls with mosaics—proving just how talented the Romans were at turning the functional into art.

PROVENCE

PROVENCE'S CUISINE SCENE

Provence has been called France's "garden market," featuring farm-fresh food (vegetables, fruits, and meats) prepared in a simple way, and meant to be savored with family and friends. Grilled foods are common, as are dishes derived from lengthy simmering—in part a reflection of long days spent in the fields. Colorful and lively, Provençal cuisine hammers the senses with an extravagant use (by French standards) of garlic, olive oil, and herbs. Order anything *à la provençale,* and you'll be rewarded with aromatic food heightened by rich and pungent sauces. Thanks to the proximity of the Riviera, many seafood dishes show up on Provençal menus (see "The Riviera's Cuisine Scene" on page 282).

Unlike other French regional cuisines, the food of Provence is inviting for nibblers. Appetizers (hors d'oeuvres) often consist of bowls of olives (try the plump, full-flavored black *tanche* or the green, buttery *picholine*), as well as plates of fresh vegetables served with lusty sauces ready for dipping. These same sauces adorn dishes of hard-boiled eggs, fish, or meat. Look for tapenade, a paste of pureed olives, capers, anchovies, herbs, and sometimes tuna. True anchovy lovers dig into *anchoïade* (a spread of garlic, anchovy, and parsley) or *bagna cauda* (a warm sauce of anchovies and melted butter or olive oil).

Aioli—a rich, garlicky mayonnaise spread over vegetables, potatoes, fish, or whatever—is another Provençal favorite. In the summertime, entire village festivals celebrate this sauce. Watch for signs announcing *aioli monstre* ("monster aioli") and, for a few euros, dive into a deeply French eating experience.

Despite the heat, soup is a favorite in Provence. *Soupe au pistou* is a thin yet flavorful vegetable soup with a sauce (called *pistou*) of basil, garlic, and cheese—pesto minus the pine nuts. Or try *soupe à l'ail* (garlic soup, called *aigo bouido* in the Provençal dialect). For details on seafood soups, see page 282.

Provençal main courses venerate fresh vegetables and meats. (Eat seafood on the Riviera and meat in Provence.) Ratatouille is a mixture of Provençal vegetables (eggplant, zucchini, onions, and peppers are the usual suspects) in a thick, herb-flavored tomato sauce. It's readily found in charcuteries and often served at room temperature, making it the perfect picnic food. Ratatouille veggies also show up on their own, stuffed and served in spicy sauces. Look for *aubergines* (eggplants), *tomates* (tomatoes), *poivrons* (sweet peppers), and *courgettes* (zucchini—especially *fleurs de courgettes,* stuffed and batter-fried zucchini flowers). *Tians* are gratin-like vegetable dishes named for the deep terra-cotta dish in which they are cooked and served. *Artichauts à la barigoule* are stuffed artichokes flavored with garlic, ham, and herbs (*barigoule* is from the Provençal word for thyme, *farigoule*). Also look for *riz de Camargue*—the reddish, chewy, nutty-tasting rice that has taken over the Camargue area, a marshy region that is otherwise useless for agriculture.

The famous herbs of Provence influence food long before it's cooked. The locally renowned lambs of the *garrigue* (shrub-covered hills), as well as rabbits and other small edible beasts in Provence, dine on wild herbs and spicy shrubs—preseasoning their delicate meat. Regional specialties include lamb (*agneau*, most often leg of lamb, *gigot d'agneau*), grilled and served no-frills, or the delicious *lapin à la provençale*—rabbit served with garlic, mustard, tomatoes, and herbs in white wine. Locals have a curious passion for quail *(caille)*. These tiny, bony birds are often grilled and served with any variety of sauces, including those sweetened with Provençal cherries or honey and lavender. *Daube,* named for the traditional cooking vessel *daubière,* is generally beef simmered in wine with spices and herbs—and perhaps a touch of orange zest—until it is spoon-tender; it's then served with noodles or the local rice. *Taureau* (bull's meat), usually raised in the marshy Camargue, melts in your mouth.

By American standards, the French undercook meats: *bleu* (bluh) is virtually raw (just flame-kissed); *saignant* (seh-nyahn) is close to raw; *à point* (ah pwahn)—their version of "medium"—is rare; and *bien cuit* (bee-yehn kwee, "well cooked") is medium. (Because French cows are raised on grass rather than corn, the beef is leaner than in the US, so limiting the cooking time keeps the meat tender.)

You'll want to steer clear of these dishes: *Pieds et paquets* is a scary dish of sheep's feet and tripe (no amount of Provençal sauce can hide this flavor). *Tourte de blettes* is a confused "pie" made with Swiss chard; both savory and sweet, it can't decide whether it should be a first course or dessert (it shows up as both).

Eat goat cheese *(fromage de chèvre)* in Provence. Look for *banon de banon* or *banon à la feuille* (dipped in *eau-de-vie* to kill bad mold, then wrapped in a chestnut leaf), spicy *picodon* (the name means "spicy" in the old language), or the fresh, creamy *brousse du Rove* (often served mixed with cream and sugar for dessert). On Provençal cheese platters, you'll find small rounds of bite-size chèvres, each flavored with a different herb or spice—and some even rolled in chopped garlic.

Desserts tend to be light and fruit-filled, or traditionally French. Treat yourself to fresh tarts made with seasonal fruit, regional Cavaillon melons (cantaloupes, served cut in half with a trickle of the sweet Rhône wine Beaumes-de-Venise), and ice cream or sorbet sweetened with honey and flavored with various herbs such as lavender, thyme, or rosemary. Don't miss the region's delicious cherries and apricots, which are often turned into jams and candied fruits.

Provence also produces some of France's great wines at relatively reasonable prices (€5-10/bottle on average). Look for wines from Gigondas, Rasteau, Cairanne, Beaumes-de-Venise, Vacqueyras, and Châteauneuf-du-Pape. For the cheapest but still tasty wines, look for labels showing Côtes du Rhône Villages or Côtes de Provence. If you like rosé, you win. Rosés from Tavel are considered among the best in Provence. For reds, splurge for Châteauneuf-du-Pape or Gigondas, and for a fine aperitif wine or a dessert wine, try the Muscat from Beaumes-de-Venise.

Remember, restaurants serve only during lunch (12:00-14:00) and dinner (19:00-21:00, later in bigger cities), but some cafés serve food throughout the day. For details on dining in France's restaurants, cafés, and brasseries, getting takeout, and assembling a picnic—as well as a rundown of French cuisine—see the "Eating" section in the Practicalities chapter.

WINES OF PROVENCE

For many, a highlight of a visit to Provence is tasting its fine and famous wines. Enjoying a glass of Rhône wine—especially when poured by someone whose family name has been on the label for two centuries—is a memorably rich, and quintessentially Provençal, experience.

The American wine-tasting experience (I'm thinking Napa Valley) is generally informal, chatty, and entrepreneurial (logo-adorned baseball caps and golf shirts). Although Provençal vintners are welcoming and more easygoing than in other parts of France, it's still a serious, wine-focused experience. Your hosts are not there to make small talk, and they're likely to be "all business." Still, Provence's shorts-and-T-shirt climate and abundance of hearty, reasonably priced wines make for an enjoyable experience, particularly if you're patient and willing to learn. See the "French Wine-Tasting 101" sidebar (page 34) for the basics.

Provence saw the first grapes planted in France, in about 600 B.C., by the Greeks. Romans built on what the Greeks started, realizing 2,000 years ago that Provence had an ideal climate for producing wine: mild winters and long, warm summers—but not too hot, thanks to the cooling winds. This sunbaked, wine-happy region offers Americans a chance to sample wines blended from several grapes—resulting in flavors unlike anything we get at home. (Yes, we have good cabernet sauvignons, merlots, and pinot noirs, but Rhône wines are new to many of us.)

In France, wine production is strictly controlled by the government to preserve the overall quality. This ensures that vintners use specified grapes that grow best in that region and follow certain grape-growing procedures. The *Appellation d'Origine Controlée* (AOC) label found on many bottles is the government's seal of approval, indicating that a wine has met various requirements. The type and percentages of grapes used, vinification methods, and taste are all controlled and verified.

Provençal vintners can blend wines using a maximum of 13 different types of grapes (five white and eight red)—unique in France. Only in Châteauneuf-du-Pape are all 13 grapes used; most vintners blend four or five types of grapes. (In Burgundy and Alsace, only one grape variety is used for each wine—so pinot noir, chardonnay, Riesling, Tokay, and pinot gris are each 100 percent from that grape.) This blending allows Provençal winemakers great range in personalizing their wine. The most prevalent types of red grapes are grenache, mourvèdre, syrah, carignan, and cinsault. The white grapes include grenache blanc, roussanne, marsanne, bourboulenc, and clairette.

There are three primary growing areas in Provence: Côtes du Rhône, Côtes de Provence, and Côteaux d'Aix-en-Provence. A few wines are also made along the Provençal Mediterranean coast. All regions produce rich, fruity reds and dry, fresh rosés. Only about five percent of wine produced here is white (the best of which comes from Cassis and Châteauneuf-du-Pape). Most Provençal whites are light, tart, with plenty of citrus and minerals, and work best as a predinner drink or in a *kir*.

In Provence, I often drink rosé instead of white. French rosé is generally crisp and fruity, a perfect match to the hot days and Mediterranean cuisine. Rosé wines are made from red grapes. After the grapes are crushed, their clear juice is left in contact with their dark-red skins just long enough to produce the pinkish color (no more than 24 hours). Rosés from Tavel (20 minutes north and west of Avignon) are the darkest in color and best-known outside of Provence, but you'll find many good producers at affordable prices in other areas as well. If you're unaccustomed to drinking rosés, try one here.

Here's some terminology to help you decipher what you'll see on bottles:

appellation: area in which a wine's grapes are grown
bouquet: bouquet (the fragrance when first opened)
cave: cellar (or wine shop)
cépage: grape variety (syrah, chardonnay, etc.)
côte, côteaux: hillside or slope
domaine: wine estate
étiquette: label
fût, tonneau: wine barrel
grand vin: excellent wine

PROVENCE

French Wine-Tasting 101

France is peppered with wineries and wine-tasting opportunities. For some visitors, trying to make sense of the vast range of French wines can be overwhelming, particularly when faced with a no-nonsense winemaker or sommelier. Take a deep breath, do your best to follow my guidance, and don't linger where you don't feel welcome.

Visit several private wineries or stop by a *cave coopérative* or a *caveau* to taste wines from a number of local vintners in a single, less intimidating setting. (Throughout this book, I've tried to identify which vineyards are most accepting of wine novices.) At wineries, you'll have a better experience if you call ahead to let them know you're coming (even if it's open all day; ask your hotelier for help). Avoid visiting places between noon and 14:00: Many wineries close midday, and those that don't are staffed by people who would rather be at lunch.

Winemakers and sommeliers are usually happy to work with you...especially if they can figure out what you want. It helps to know what you like (drier or sweeter, lighter or full-bodied, fruity or more tannic, and so on). The people serving you may know those words in English, but you're wise to learn the key words in French (see the "French Wine Lingo" section).

French wines usually have a lower alcohol level than American or Australian wines. While Americans commonly like a big, full-bodied wine, most French prefer subtler flavors. They judge a wine by how well it pairs with a meal—and a big, oaky wine would overwhelm most French cuisine. The French enjoy sampling younger wines and divining how they will taste in a few years, allowing them to buy bottles at cheaper prices and stash them in their cellars. Americans want it now—for today's picnic.

At wine tastings, vintners and wine shops are hoping you'll buy a bottle or two. If you don't, you may be asked to pay a small fee for a tasting. They understand that North Americans can't take much wine with them, but they do hope you'll look for their wines when you're back home. Some places will ship your purchase—ask.

French Wine Lingo

Here are some phrases to get you started when wine-tasting:

Hello, madam/sir.
Bonjour, madame/monsieur.
(bohn-zhoor, mah-dahm/muhs-yur)

We would like to taste a few wines.
Nous voudrions déguster quelques vins.
(noo voo-dree-ohn day-goo-stay kehl-kuh van)

We would like a wine that is _____ and _____ .
Nous voudrions un vin _____ et _____ .
(noo voo-dree-ohn uhn van _____ ay _____)

Fill in the blanks with your favorites from this list:

English	French
wine	*vin* (van)
red	*rouge* (roozh)
white	*blanc* (blahn)
rosé	*rosé* (roh-zay)
light	*léger* (lay-zhay)
full-bodied	*robuste* (roh-bewst)
fruity	*fruité* (frwee-tay)
sweet	*doux* (doo)
tannic	*tannique* (tah-neek)
fine	*fin, avec finesse* (fan, ah-vehk fee-nehs)
ready to drink (mature)	*prêt à boire* (preh tah bwar)
not ready to drink	*fermé* (fair-may)
oaky	*goût de fût de chêne* (goo duh few duh shehn)
from old vines	*de vieilles vignes* (duh vee-yay-ee veen-yah)
sparkling	*pétillant* (pay-tee-yahn)

millésimé: wine from a given year

mis en bouteille au château/au domaine: estate-bottled (bottled where it was made)

vin de table: table wine (can be a blend of several wines)

vin de pays: wine from a given area (a step up from *vin de table*)

Côtes du Rhône Wines

The king of Provençal wines hails from the Côtes du Rhône, the area along the Rhône River from just south of Lyon to near Avignon. My focus is on the southern section, roughly from Vaison-la-Romaine to Avignon (though wine lovers should also try the big, complex reds found in the northern Rhône wines of St-Joseph, Crozes-Hermitage, and Cornas, as well as the tasty whites of Condrieu). The wines of the southern Rhône are consistently good, sometimes exceptional, and usually inexpensive. The reds are full-bodied, rosés are dry and fruity, and whites are dry and fragrant. (For more on this wine region, including a self-guided driving tour of the area's villages and vintners, see the Orange & the Côtes du Rhône chapter.)

Many subareas of the southern Côtes du Rhône are recognized for producing outstandingly good wines, and have been awarded their own *appellations* (like Châteauneuf-du-Pape, Gigondas, Beaumes-de-Venise, Côtes de Ventoux, Tavel, and Côtes du Luberon). Wines often are named for the villages that produce them. The "Côtes du Rhône Villages" *appellation* is less prestigious, covering 20 villages on the eastern side of the Côtes du Rhône, including Séguret, Sablet, Rasteau, and Cairanne. Strict guidelines govern the production of these wines (called *appellation controllée*).

Here's a summary of what you might find on a Côtes du Rhône *carte des vins* (wine list):

Châteauneuf-du-Pape: Almost all wines from this famous village are reds (often blends; the most dominant grapes are grenache, mourvèdre, and syrah). These wines have a velvety quality and can be spicy, with flavors of licorice and prunes. A few delicious whites are made here and worth sampling. Châteauneuf-du-Pape red wines merit lengthy aging. Château de Beaucastel, Le Vieux Télégraphe, Clos des Papes, and Château la Nerthe are traditionally considered among the best producers. Domaine Roger Sabon and Domaine Durieu are up-and-coming producers. You should find most of these wines in North America. It's also worth seeking out lesser-known names and smaller wineries (many of which are listed in this book).

Gigondas: These wines have many of the same qualities as Châteauneuf-du-Pape, but are lesser known and usually cheaper. Gigondas red wines are spicy, meaty, and can be pretty tannic. Again, aging is necessary to bring out the full qualities of the wine. Near Gigondas look for Domaine du Terme, Domaine Les Goubert, or Château de Montmirail. The following places also make fine Gigondas—and are more scenically set along my Côtes du Rhône wine road tour: Domaines de Coyeux and Cassan (both near La Fare), or Domaine de la Garance in Suzette.

Beaumes-de-Venise: While this village produces reds that are rich and flavorful, Beaumes-de-Venise is most famous for its Muscat—a sweet, fragrant wine usually served as an aperitif or with dessert. It often has flavors of apricots and peaches, and it should be consumed within two years of bottling. Try Domaine de Coyeux, Domaine de Durban, and Château Redortier, or visit the *cave coopérative* in Beaumes-de-Venise.

Rasteau: This village sits across the valley from Gigondas and shares many of its qualities—at lower prices. Rasteau makes fine rosés, robust (at times "rough") and fruity reds, and a naturally sweet wine (Vin Doux Naturel). Their Côtes du Rhône Villages can be excellent. The cooperative in Rasteau is good, as are the wines from Domaine des Girasols and Domaine de Beaurenard.

Sablet: This village lies down in the valley below Gigondas and makes decent, fruity, and inexpensive reds and rosés.

Tavel: The queen of French rosés comes from this area 20 minutes north and west of Avignon, close to Pont du Gard. Tavel produces a rosé that is dry, crisp, higher in alcohol, darker, and more full-bodied than other rosés from the region. Look for any rosé from Tavel.

Côtes de Provence Wines

The lesser-known vineyards of the Côtes de Provence run east from Aix-en-Provence almost to St-Tropez. Typical grapes are cinsault, mourvèdre, grenache, carignan, and a little cabernet sauvignon and syrah. The wines are commonly full-bodied and fruity, and are meant to be drunk when they're young. They cost less than Côtes du Rhônes wines and have similar characteristics. But the region is most famous for its "big" rosés that can be served with meat and garlic dishes (rosé accounts for 60 percent of production).

For one-stop shopping, make it a point to find the superb **La Maison des Vins Côtes de Provence** on RN-7 in Les Arcs-sur-Argens (a few minutes north of the A-8 autoroute, about halfway between Aix-en-Provence and Nice). This English-speaking wine shop and tasting center represents hundreds of producers, selling bottles at vineyard prices and offering good tastings (daily 10:00-

The Rules of *Boules*

The game of *boules*—also called *pétanque*—is the horseshoes of France. Invented here in the early 1900s, it's a social yet serious sport, and endlessly entertaining to watch—even more so if you understand the rules.

The game is played with heavy metal balls and a small wooden target ball called a *cochonnet* (piglet). Whoever gets his *boule* closest to the *cochonnet* is awarded points. Teams commonly have specialist players: a *pointeur* and a *tireur*. The *pointeur's* goal is to lob his balls as close to the target as he can. The *tireur's* job is to blast away opponents' *boules.*

In teams of two, each player gets three *boules.* The starting team traces a small circle in the dirt (in which players must stand when launching their *boules*), and tosses the *cochonnet* about 30 feet to establish the target. The *boule* must be thrown underhand, and can be rolled, launched sky-high, or rocketed at its target. The first *pointeur* shoots, then the opposing *pointeur* shoots until his *boule* gets closer. Once the second team lands a *boule* nearest the *cochonnet,* the first team goes again. If the other team's *boule* is very near the *cochonnet,* the *tireur* will likely attempt to knock it away.

Once all *boules* have been launched, the tally is taken. The team with a *boule* closest to the *cochonnet* wins the round, and they receive a point for each *boule* closer to the target than their opponents' nearest *boule.* The first team to get to 13 points wins. A regulation *boules* field is 10 feet by 43 feet, but the game is played everywhere—just scratch a throwing circle in the sand, toss the *cochonnet,* and you're off.

19:00, Oct-March until 18:00 and closed all day Sun, tel. 04 94 99 50 20, www.maison-des-vins.fr).

Côteaux d'Aix-en-Provence Wines

This large growing region, between Les Baux and Aix-en-Provence, produces some interesting reds, whites, and rosés. Commonly used grapes are the same as in Côtes de Provence, though several producers (mainly around Les Baux) use a higher concentration of cabernet sauvignon, which helps distinguish their wines. The vintners around Les Baux produce some exceptionally good wines, and many of their vineyards are organic. Try Domaine d'Eole or Domaine Gourgonnier. The tiny wine-producing area of Palette houses only three wineries, all of which make exceptional rosés; one (Château Simone) also makes a delicious white wine. The

Côtes de Provence-Sainte-Victoire wineries, with their beautiful views of Mont Ste-Victoire (famously painted by Cézanne), also produce some excellent rosés.

Provençal Mediterranean Wines

Barely east of Marseille, Cassis and Bandol sit side by side, over-looking the Mediterranean. Though very close together, they are designated as separate wine-growing areas because of the distinctive nature of their wines. Cassis is one of France's smallest wine regions and is known for its strong, fresh, and very dry whites (made with the Marsanne grape)—arguably the best white wine in Provence. Bandol is known for its luscious, velvety reds. This wine, aged in old oak and made primarily from the mourvèdre grape, is one of your author's favorites.

ARLES

Arles (pronounced "arl") is an amiable slice of Provence, with evocative Roman ruins, an eclectic assortment of museums, made-for-ice-cream pedestrian zones, and squares that play hide-and-seek with visitors.

Back in Roman times, the city earned the imperial nod by helping Julius Caesar defeat his archrival Gnaeus Pompeius Magnus (a.k.a. Pompey) at Marseille, and grew into an important port. Site of the first bridge over the Rhône River, Arles was a key stop on the Roman road from Italy to Spain, the Via Domitia. After reigning as the seat of an important archbishop and as a trading center for centuries, the city became a sleepy backwater of little importance in the 1700s. Vincent van Gogh settled here in the late 1800s, but left only a chunk of his ear (now long gone). American bombers destroyed much of Arles in World War II as the townsfolk hid out in its underground Roman galleries.

Today Arles thrives again. A city in search of an economy, workaday Arles feels unpolished and even a little dirty compared to nearby Avignon and Nimes. But to me, that's part of its charm. Locals display a genuine *joie de vivre* that's hard to sense in Arles' larger, more cosmopolitan neighbors.

PLANNING YOUR TIME

Start at the Ancient History Museum (at the edge of town, closed Tue; see page 59) for a helpful overview—drivers should try to do this museum on their way into Arles—then head to the city-center sights, linked by my Arles City Walk. For cost-efficient sightseeing, get the Liberty Passport, which covers the ancient monuments and the Ancient History Museum (see "Helpful Hints").

Orientation to Arles

Arles faces the Mediterranean, turning its back on Paris. And although the town is built along the Rhône, it largely ignores the river. Landmarks hide in Arles' medieval tangle of narrow, winding streets. Hotels have good, free city maps, and helpful street-corner signs point you toward sights and hotels.

TOURIST INFORMATION

The TI is on the ring road Boulevard des Lices, at Esplanade Charles de Gaulle (daily 9:00-18:45; Oct-March Mon-Sat 9:00-16:45, Sun 10:00-13:00; tel. 04 90 18 41 20, www.arlestourisme. com). While there, take advantage of free Wi-Fi, pick up the city map and bus schedules, and request English information on nearby destinations such as the Camargue. Ask about walking tours and "bullgames" in Arles and nearby towns (Provence's more humane version of bullfights—see page 63). The TI sells the worthwhile Liberty Passport (see "Helpful Hints," later).

ARRIVAL IN ARLES

By Train or Bus: The train station is on the river, a 10-minute walk from the town center. There's no baggage storage at the station, but you can walk 10 minutes to stow it at Hôtel Régence (see "Helpful Hints," later). The main bus station is on big Boulevard Georges Clémenceau, but some buses stop at the train station.

To reach the town center or Ancient History Museum from the train station, wait for the free **Navia shuttle** at the glass shelter facing away from the station (cross the street and veer left, 2/hour Mon-Sat 7:00-19:00, none Sun). The bus makes a counterclockwise loop around Arles, stopping near most of my recommended hotels (see map on page 66 for stops). **Taxis** usually wait in front of the station (if there's not a taxi waiting, call 04 90 96 52 76 or the posted telephone numbers, or ask the info desk staff to call for you). Allow about €10-15 to any of my recommended hotels.

By Car: Driving in Arles old center is difficult; it's easiest to enter on foot after stowing your car (at least temporarily) at Arles' only parking garage, **Parking des Lices,** near the TI on Boulevard des Lices (€1.50/hour, €16/24 hours), or at the lots around the big roundabout called Place Lamartine. All of my recommended hotels are within a 10-minute walk of these parking options. (There are small lots closer to most hotels than this garage, but they can be hard to get to.) Most hotels have parking deals for about €7-12/day, either at one of these lots or at Parking des Lices (ask before you arrive).

Lots and curbside parking spots in Arles center are metered 9:00-19:00 Mon-Sat (some limited to 2.5 hours, free daily 19:00-9:00 and all day Sun). You'll find easy-to-access metered lots along the city wall at Place Lamartine (except Tue night, when it is restricted). To find these, first follow signs to *Centre-Ville*, then *Gare SNCF* (train station) until you come to the roundabout with a Monoprix department store to the right. The hotels I list are no more than a 15-minute walk from here.

HELPFUL HINTS

Sightseeing Tips: Arles has a smart ticket-and-hours plan for its sightseeing. Ancient monuments, such as the Roman Arena and Classical Theater, share the **same hours** (daily 9:00-19:00, April and Oct until 18:00, Nov-March 10:00-17:00). A good-value combo-ticket called the **Liberty Passport** (€11, €12 July-Aug, Le Passeport Liberté) covers any four monuments, the Ancient History Museum, and the Réattu Museum (and offers a discount at the Fondation Van Gogh gallery). Buy the pass at the TI or any included sight.

While only the Ancient History Museum and Roman Arena are essential to enter, the pass makes the city fun to explore, as you can pop into nearly everything, even for just a couple of minutes.

Market Days: The big markets are on Wednesdays and Saturdays (see page 447 for more on French markets).

Crowds: An international photo event jams hotels the second weekend of July. The let-'er-rip, twice-yearly Féria draws crowds over Easter and in mid-September (described on page 64).

Baggage Storage and Bike Rental: The recommended **Hôtel Régence** will store your bags for €3 (daily 7:30-22:00, closed in winter, 5 Rue Marius Jouveau). They also rent bikes (€7/half-day, €15/day, electric bikes available, reserve ahead, one-way rentals within Provence possible, same hours as baggage storage). From Arles you can ride to Les Baux (25 miles round-trip). It's a darn steep climb going into Les Baux—an electric bike can help. Those in great shape can consider biking into the Camargue (level 30-40-mile round-trip, forget it on windy days).

Laundry: A launderette is at 41 Rue du 4 Septembre (daily 7:30-22:00).

Car Rental: Europcar and **Hertz** are downtown (Europcar is at 61 Avenue de Stalingrad, tel. 04 90 93 23 24; Hertz is closer

Arles at a Glance

▲▲**Roman Arena** This big amphitheater, once used by gladiators, today hosts summer "bullgames" and occasional bullfights. **Hours:** Daily 9:00-19:00, April and Oct until 18:00, Nov-March 10:00-17:00. See page 49.

▲▲**Ancient History Museum** Filled with models and sculptures, this museum takes you back to Arles' Roman days. **Hours:** Wed-Mon 10:00-18:00, closed Tue. See page 59.

▲▲**St. Trophime Church** Church with exquisite Romanesque entrance. **Hours:** Church—daily 9:00-12:00 & 14:00-18:30, until 17:00 Oct-March; cloisters—same hours as Arena. See page 53.

▲**Forum Square** Lively, café-crammed square that was once the Roman forum. **Hours:** Always open. See page 57.

▲**Réattu Museum** Decent, mostly modern art collection in a fine 15th-century mansion. **Hours:** Tue-Sun 10:00-18:00, Nov-Feb until 17:00, closed Mon year-round. See page 63.

▲**Fondation Van Gogh** Small gallery with works by major contemporary artists paying homage to Van Gogh. **Hours:** Generally daily 11:00-19:00, closed Mon off-season. See page 56.

ARLES

to Place Voltaire at 10 Boulevard Emile Combes, tel. 04 90 96 75 23).

Local Guides: Charming **Agnes Barrier,** who knows Arles and nearby sights intimately, enjoys her work. Her tours cover Van Gogh and Roman history (€130/3 hours, mobile 06 11 23 03 73, agnes.barrier@hotmail.fr). **Alice Vallat** offers a variety of scheduled visits of Arles' key sights (€25/person for 1.5-hour group tour, €130 for 3-hour private tour, mobile 06 74 01 22 54, www.guidearles.com, alice.vallat13@gmail.com).

English Book Exchange: A small exchange is available at the recommended **Soleileis** ice-cream shop.

Public Pools: Arles has three pools (indoor and outdoor). Ask at the TI or your hotel.

Boules: The local "*boul*ing alley" is by the river on Place Lamartine. After their afternoon naps, the old boys congregate here for a game of *pétanque* (see page 38 for more on this popular local pastime).

Frank Gehry Tower: The buzz in Arles is the 180-foot-tall Gehry-designed aluminum tower rising in a rundown neighborhood southeast of the center. The LUMA Foundation will provide a

Arles

ARLES

Arles City Walk

1. The Yellow House (Easel)
2. Starry Night over the Rhône (Easel)
3. Rue de la Cavalerie
4. Old Town
5. Arena (Easel)
6. Roman Arena
7. Alpilles Mountains View
8. L'Entrée du Jardin Public (Easel)
9. Classical Theater
10. Republic Square
11. Cryptoporticos
12. St. Trophime Church
13. St. Trophime Cloisters
14. Rue de la République
15. Espace Van Gogh (Easel)
16. Fondation Van Gogh
17. Rue du Docteur Fanton
18. Place du Forum & Café at Night (Easel)

Other

19. Hôtel Régence (Bag Storage & Bike Rental)
20. Launderette
21. To Europcar Car Rental
22. Hertz Car Rental

TRINQUETAILLE

RUE DES CAPUCINS

RUE DE LA VERRIERE

RUE CAMARGUE

QUAI ST. PIERRE

Rhône

TRINQUETAILLE BRIDGE

QUAI MARX DORMOY

R. DE LA TOUR DU FABRE

R. DR. FANTON

TRUCHET

16

LIBERTE

⚓ Van Gogh Easels

Ⓑ Shuttle Bus Stops

Ⓑ

QUAI A. FRANCE

R. JOUVENE

ARLATEN FOLK MUSEUM (REOPENS IN 2019)

Ⓑ

QUAI DE LA ROQUETTE

Place Paul Doumier

R. DES PORCELETS

RUE DE LA REPUBLIQUE

RUE GAMBETTA

14

Ⓑ

RUE DE LA ROQUETTE

RUE CROIX ROUGE

LA ROQUETTE

RUE DE CHARTROUSE

RUE JEAN GRANAUD

15 ⚓

ESPACE VAN GOGH

R. PRES WILSON

To Ancient History Museum

Place Genive

RUE RAILLON

RUE FLEURY PRUDHON

RUE MOLIERE

RUE MOLIERE

MAIN BUS STATION

To Nîmes via A-84

Ⓑ

To Ancient History Museum

BLVD. G CLEMENCEAU

Ⓑ

RUE PARMENTIER

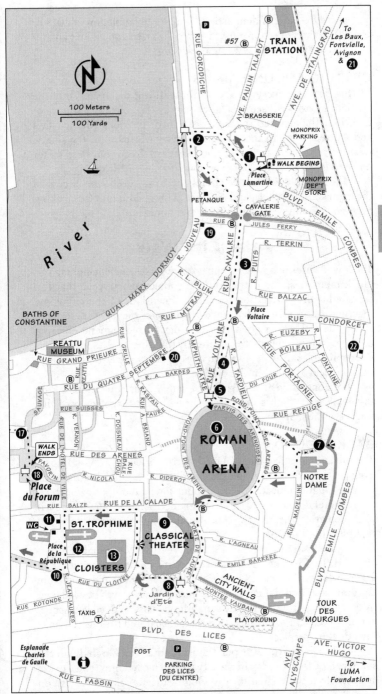

ARLES

space for independent artists. Slated for completion in 2018 or 2019, the project promises to revitalize that zone with galleries and apartments (www.luma-arles.org).

GETTING AROUND ARLES

In this flat city, everything's within **walking** distance. Only the Ancient History Museum is far enough out to consider a shuttle or taxi ride. The elevated riverside promenade provides Rhône views and a direct route to the Ancient History Museum (to the southwest) and the train station (to the northeast). Keep your head up for *Starry Night* memories, but eyes down for doggie droppings.

The free **Navia shuttle** circles the town, useful for access to the train station, hotels, and Ancient History Museum (see map on page 66, 2/hour, Mon-Sat 7:00-19:00, none Sun).

Arles City Walk

The joy of Arles is how its compact core mixes ancient sights, Van Gogh memories, and a raw and real contemporary scene that can be delightfully covered on foot. All dimensions of the city come together in this self-guided walk. If you enter the sights described, this walk will take a good part of a day. (I recommend entering them, even if briefly; all are covered by the Liberty Passport). Consider splitting this walk over two days or doing the latter half (after the Classical Theater) in the evening.

For context, visit the Ancient History Museum before taking this walk (see "Sights in Arles," later). To trace the route of this walk, see the map on page 44.

BACKGROUND

The life and artistic times of Dutch artist **Vincent van Gogh** form a big part of Arles' draw, and the city does a fine job of highlighting its Van Gogh connection: Throughout town, about a dozen steel-and-concrete panels, or "easels," provide then-and-now comparisons, depicting the artist's paintings alongside the current view of that painting's subject.

In the dead of winter in 1888, 35-year-old Van Gogh left big-city Paris for Provence, hoping to jump-start his floundering career and social life. He was as inspired as he was lonely. Coming from the gray skies and flat lands of the north, Vincent was bowled over by everything Provençal—the sun, bright colors, rugged landscape, and raw people. For the next two years he painted furiously, cranking out a masterpiece every few days.

Only a few of the 200-plus paintings that Van Gogh did in the south can be found today in the city that so moved him (you can see at least one at the Fondation Van Gogh gallery, which we'll visit on this stroll). But here you can walk the same streets he knew and see the places he painted.

• *Start at the north gate of the city, just outside the medieval wall in Place Lamartine (100 yards in front of the medieval gate, with the big Monoprix store across the street to the right, beyond the roundabout). A four-foot-tall easel shows Van Gogh's painting.*

❶ *The Yellow House* Easel

Vincent arrived in Arles on February 20, 1888, to a foot of snow. He rented a small house on the north side of Place Lamartine.

The house was destroyed in 1944 by an errant bridge-seeking bomb, but the four-story building behind it—where you see the brasserie—still stands (find it in the painting). The house had four rooms, including a small studio and the cramped trapezoid-shaped bedroom made famous in paintings. It was painted yellow inside and out, and Vincent named it…"The Yellow House." In the distance, the painting shows the same bridges you see today, as well as a steam train—which was a rather recent invention in France, allowing people like Vincent to travel greater distances and be jarred by new experiences. (Today's TGV system continues that trend.)

Freezing Arles was buttoned up tight when Vincent arrived, so he was forced to work inside, where he painted still lifes and self-portraits—anything to keep his brush moving. In late March, spring finally arrived. In those days, a short walk from Place Lamartine led to open fields. Donning his straw hat, Vincent set up his easel outdoors and painted quickly, capturing what he saw and felt—the blossoming fruit trees, gnarled olive trees, peasants sowing and reaping, jagged peaks, and windblown fields, all lit by a brilliant sun that drove him to use ever-brighter paints.

• *Walk directly to the river. You'll pass a monument in honor of two WWII American pilots killed in action during the liberation of Arles (erected in 2002 as a post-9/11 sign of solidarity with Americans), a post celebrating Arles' many sister cities (left), and a big concrete high school (right).*

At the river, find the easel in the wall where ramps lead down.

ARLES

The Roman bridge stood here (look for a few stones directly across), and just upstream are the remains of a modern bridge bombed by the Allies in World War II. This is the busier-than-ever cruise port, which brings crowds into the city throughout the season. Looking downstream, notice the new embankment constructed in recent years. Now, turn your attention to the...

❷ *Starry Night over the Rhône* Easel

One night, Vincent set up shop along the river and painted the stars boiling above the city skyline. Vincent looked to the night sky for  the divine and was the first to paint outside after dark, adapting his straw hat to hold candles (which must have blown the minds of locals back then). As his paintings progressed, the stars became larger and more animated (like Vincent himself). The lone couple in the painting pops up again and again in his work. Experts say that Vincent was desperate for a close relationship with another being...someone to stroll the riverbank with under a star-filled sky. (Note: This painting is not the *Starry Night* you're thinking of—that one was painted later, in St-Rémy.)

To his sister Wilhelmina, Vincent wrote, "At present I absolutely want to paint a starry sky. It often seems to me that night is still more richly colored than the day; having hues of the most intense violets, blues, and greens. If only you pay attention to it, you will see that certain stars are lemon-yellow, others pink or a green, blue, and forget-me-not brilliance." Vincent painted this scene on his last night in Arles. If you're taking this walk in the daytime, come back at night to match his painting with today's scene.

• *With your back to the river, angle right through the scruffy park of sycamore trees, where the old boys gather for* pétanque *(a favorite French pastime). Observe the action. If you're inclined (and charming), you may be invited to give it a try. Continue into town through the park and between the stumpy 14th-century stone towers where the city gates once stood.*

❸ Rue de la Cavalerie

Van Gogh walked into town the same way. Arles' 19th-century red light district was just east of Rue de la Cavalerie, and the far-from-home Dutchman spent many lonely nights in its bars and brothels. The street still has a certain edgy local color. Saddle up to the bar in the down-and-dirty café at Hôtel de Paris for a taste. It's a friendly watering hole with fun paintings of football and bull fighting.

• *Continuing along, you'll come to an ornately decorated fountain from*

1887: two columns with a mosaic celebrating the high culture of Provence (she's the winged woman who obviously loves music and reading).

Stay left and keep walking to Place Voltaire, a center of this working-class neighborhood (you'll see the local Communist Party headquarters across on the left). Arles is famously red; its communist mayor is in his third term and quite popular.

❹ Old Town

You've left the bombed-out part of town and entered the old town, with buildings predating World War II. The stony white arches of the ancient Roman Arena ahead mark your destination. As you hike up Rue Voltaire, notice the shutters, which contribute to Arles' character. The old town is strictly preserved: These traditional shutters come in a variety of styles but cannot be changed.

• *Keep straight up Rue Voltaire, climb to the Roman Arena, and find the* Arena *easel at the top of the stairs, to the right.*

ARLES

❺ *Arena* Easel

All summer long, fueled by sun and alcohol, Vincent painted the town. He loved the bullfights in the arena and sketched the colorful surge of the crowds, spending more time studying the people than watching the bullfights (notice how the bull is barely visible). Vincent had little interest in Arles' antiquity—it was people and nature that fascinated him.

• *Now, let's visit the actual...*

❻ Roman Arena (Amphithéâtre)

This well-preserved arena is worth ▲▲ and is still in use today. Nearly 2,000 years ago, gladiators fought wild animals here to the delight of 20,000 screaming fans. Now local daredevils still fight wild animals here—"bullgame" posters around the arena advertise upcoming spectacles (see page 63). Don't miss the tower climb for fantastic views over Arles, the arena, and the Rhône River.

Cost and Hours: €8 (€9 July-Aug) combo-ticket with Classical Theater, covered by Liberty Passport; open daily 9:00-19:00, April and Oct until 18:00, Nov-March 10:00-17:00, Rond-point des Arènes, tel. 04 90 49 36 86, www.arenes-arles.com.

Visiting the Arena: After passing the ticket kiosk, find the helpful English display under the second arch, where you can read about the arena's history and renovation. Then take a seat in the theater.

Thirty-four rows of stone bleachers extended all the way

to the top of those vacant **arches** that circle the arena. All arches were numbered to help distracted fans find their seats. The many passageways you'll see (called *vomitoires*) allowed for rapid dispersal after the games—fights would break out among frenzied fans if they couldn't leave quickly.

The arena takes its name from the central **floor** where the action took place—"arena" derives from the Latin word for sand, which was spread across the floor to absorb the blood. Wild animals were caged in passages and storage areas underneath the floor and hoisted up on an elevator to make surprise appearances. (While Rome could afford exotic beasts, places like Arles made do with snarling local fauna...bulls, wild boars, and lots of bears.) The standard fight was as real as professional wrestling is today—mostly just crowd-pleasing.

The arena is a fine example of Roman engineering...and propaganda. In the spirit of "give them bread and circuses," games were free—sponsored by city bigwigs. The idea was to create a populace that was thoroughly Roman—enjoying the same activities, entertainment, and thoughts (something like how US television contributes to the American psyche).

After Rome fell and stability was replaced by Dark Ages chaos, this huge structure was put to good use: Throughout medieval times and until the early 1800s, the stadium became a fortified town—with arches bricked up and 200 humble homes crammed within its circular defenses. Parts of three of the medieval **towers** survive.

To climb one of those towers and enjoy magnificent **views** over Arles and the arena, find the "*To the Tower*" sign after the ticket booth.

For more on Roman amphitheaters, see the description of Nîmes' Arena on page 128.

• *After climbing the tower and returning to street level, circumnavigate the stadium and savor the receding views of arches and fine stonework. A quarter of the way around, go up the cute stepped lane (Rue Renan). Take three steps and turn around to study the arena. The big stones are Roman; the little medieval stones—more like rubble—filling the two upper-level archways are a reminder of the arena's time as a fortified town in the Middle Ages. You can even see roof lines and beam holes where the Roman structure provided a solid foundation to lean on.*

Hike up the pretty lane through the parking lot, keeping to the left of the stark and stony church to the highest point in Arles. Take in the view.

❼ Alpilles Mountains View

This view pretty much matches what Vincent van Gogh, an avid walker, would have seen. Imagine him hauling his easel into those fields under intense sun, leaning against a ferocious wind, struggling to keep his hat on. He trekked into the pastoral countryside many times during his stay in Arles, just to paint the farm workers. Vincent venerated but didn't deify peasants. Wanting to accurately show their lives and their struggles, he reproached Renoir and Monet for glorifying common people in their works.

Vincent carried his easel as far as the medieval Abbey of Montmajour, that bulky structure three miles straight ahead on the hill. The St. Paul Hospital, where he was eventually treated in St-Rémy, is on the other side of the Alpilles mountains (which look more like hills to me), several miles beyond Montmajour.

• *Now might be a good time to take a break. Several good restaurant options are nearby (see map on page 66). When you're ready, continue circling the arena. At the high point, turn left and walk out Rue de Porte de Laure. (You'll pass the Classical Theater on your right, which we'll see later.) After a couple of blocks, just after the street turns left, go right, down the curved staircase into the park. At the bottom of the stairs take the second right (through the gate and into the park) and find the...*

❽ *L'Entrée du Jardin Public* Easel

Vincent spent many a sunny day painting the leafy Jardin d'Eté. In another letter to his sister, Vincent wrote, "I don't know whether you can understand that one may make a poem by arranging colors...In a similar manner, the bizarre lines, purposely selected and multiplied, meandering all through the picture may not present a literal image of the garden, but they may present it to our minds as if in a dream."

• *Hike uphill through the park toward the three-story surviving tower of the ancient Roman Theater. On the right in the grass is a monument that reads "to 1.5 million Armenian victims of the 1915 Genocide." (French law makes it a crime to deny the Ottoman Empire's genocide of Armenians, causing tension with today's Turkey.) At the ancient tower, follow the white metal fence to the left along "le jardin" of stone—a collection of ancient carved bits of a once-grand Roman theater. Go up four steps and around to the right for a fine view of the...*

❾ Classical Theater (Théâtre Antique)

This first-century B.C. Roman theater once seated 10,000...just like the theater in nearby Orange. But unlike Orange, here in Arles there was no hillside to provide structural support. Instead, this elegant, three-level structure had 27 buttress arches radiating out behind the seats. From the outside, it looked much like the adjacent arena.

Cost and Hours: €8 (€9

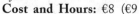

July-Aug) combo-ticket with Roman Arena, covered by Liberty Passport, same hours as Arena.

Visiting the Theater: Start with the 10-minute video outside, which provides background information that makes it easier to imagine the scattered stones back in place (crouch in front to make out the small English subtitles).

Then walk into the theater and pull up a stone seat in a center aisle. (For more context, read the description of Orange's Roman theater on page 148 while you rest.) Imagine that for 500 years, ancient Romans gathered here for entertainment. The original structure was much higher, with 33 rows of seats covering three levels to accommodate demand. During the Middle Ages, the old theater became a convenient town quarry—much of St. Trophime Church was built from theater rubble. Precious little of the original theater survives—though it still is used for events, with seating for 2,000 spectators.

Two lonely Corinthian columns are all that remain of a three-story stage wall that once featured more than 100 columns and statues painted in vibrant colors (a model in the Ancient History Museum shows the complete theater). Principal actors entered through the central arch, over which a grandiose statue of Caesar Augustus stood (it's now on display at the Ancient History Museum). Bit players entered through side arches. The orchestra section is defined by a semicircular pattern in the stone in front of you. Stepping up onto the left side of the stage, look down to the slender channel that allowed the brilliant-red curtain to disappear below, like magic. The stage, which was built of wood, was about 160 feet across and 20 feet deep. The actors' changing rooms are backstage, down the steps.

• *From the theater, walk downhill on Rue de la Calade. Take the first left into a big square.*

⑩ Republic Square (Place de la République)

This square used to be called "Place Royale"...until the French Revolution. The obelisk was the former centerpiece of Arles' Roman Circus (outside of town). The lions at its base are the symbol of the city, whose slogan is (roughly) "the gentle lion." Observe the age-old scene: tourists, peasants, shoppers, pilgrims, children, and street musicians. The City Hall (Hôtel de Ville) has a French Baroque facade, built in the same generation as Versailles. Where there's a City Hall, there's always a free WC (if you win the Revolution, you can pee for free at the mayor's home). Notice the flags: The yellow-and-red of Provence is the same as the yellow-and-red of Catalunya, its linguistic cousin in Spain.

• *Today's City Hall sits upon an ancient city center. Inside, admire the*

*engineering of the ceiling and find the entrance to an ancient cryptopor-
tico (foundation).*

⓫ Cryptoporticos (Cryptoportiques)

This dark, drippy underworld of Roman arches was constructed to
support the upper half of Forum Square. Two thousand years ago,
most of this gallery of arches was at or above street level; modern
Arles has buried about 20 feet of its history over the millennia.
Through the tiny windows high up you would have seen the sandals
of Romans on their way to the forum. Other than dark arches and
broken bits of forum littering the dirt floor, there's not much down
here beyond ancient memories (€3.50, covered by Liberty Passport,
same hours as Arena).

• *The highlight of Place de la République is...*

⓬ St. Trophime Church

Named after a third-century bishop of Arles, this church, worth
▲▲, sports the finest Romanesque main entrance I've seen anywhere. The Romanesque and Gothic interior—with tapestries, relics, and a rare painting from the French Revolution when this was
a "Temple of Reason"—is worth a visit.

Cost and Hours: Free, daily 9:00-12:00 & 14:00-18:30, until
17:00 Oct-March.

Exterior: Like a Roman triumphal arch, the church **facade**
trumpets the promise of Judgment Day. The tympanum (the semi-

circular area above the door) is filled
with Christian symbolism. Christ
sits in majesty, surrounded by symbols of the four evangelists: Matthew (the winged man), Mark (the
winged lion), Luke (the ox), and John
(the eagle). The 12 apostles are lined
up below Jesus. It's Judgment Day...
some are saved and others aren't. Notice the condemned (on the right)—a
chain gang doing a sad bunny-hop over the fires of hell. For them,
the tune trumpeted by the three angels above Christ is not a happy
one. Below the chain gang, St. Stephen is being stoned to death,
with his soul leaving through his mouth and instantly being welcomed by angels. Study the exquisite detail. In an illiterate world,
long before the vivid images of our Technicolor time, this was col-
orfully painted, like a neon billboard over the town square. It's full
of meaning, and a medieval pilgrim understood it all.

Interior: Just inside the door on the right, a yellow chart lo-
cates the interior highlights and helps explain the carvings you just
saw on the tympanum. The tall 12th-century Romanesque nave is

ARLES

decorated by a set of tapestries (typical in the Middle Ages) showing scenes from the life of Mary (17th century, from the French town of Aubusson). Circle the church counterclockwise.

Stop into the first open chapel, the **Chapel of Baptism,** to view a statue of St. John Paul II under the window. Facing the window, look to the right wall where you'll see a faded painting of a triangle with a sunburst from 1789. The French Revolution secularized the country and made churches "Temples of Reason." This painting is the only example I've seen of church decor from this age.

Amble around the ambulatory toward the **Gothic apse.** Choose which chapel you need or want: If you have the plague or cholera, visit the chapel devoted to St. Roch—notice the testimonial plaques of gratitude on the wall. Some spaces are still available...if you hurry.

Two-thirds of the way around, find the **relic chapel** behind the ornate wrought iron gate, with its fine golden boxes that hold long-venerated bones of obscure saints. These relics generated lots of money for the church from pilgrims through the ages. Pop in a coin to share some light. The next chapel houses the skull of St. Anthony of the Desert.

Nearing the exit, look for two black columns and the early-Christian **sarcophagi** from Roman Arles (dated about A.D. 300). One sarcophagus shows Moses and the Israelites crossing the Red Sea. You'll see Christians wearing togas and praying like evangelicals do today—hands raised. The heads were likely lopped off during the French Revolution.

This church is a stop on the ancient pilgrimage route to Santiago de Compostela in northwest Spain. For 800 years pilgrims on their way to Santiago have paused here...and they still do today. Notice the modern-day pilgrimages advertised on the far right near the church's entry.

• *To reach the adjacent peaceful cloister, leave the church, turn left, then left again through a courtyard.*

⓭ St. Trophime Cloisters

Worth seeing if you have the Liberty Passport (otherwise €4.50, same hours as Arena), the cloisters' many small columns were scavenged from the ancient Roman theater and used to create an oasis of peace in Arles' center. Enjoy the delicate, sculpted capitals, the rounded Romanesque arches (12th century), and the pointed Gothic ones (14th century). The pretty vaulted hall exhibits 17th-century tapestries showing scenes from the First Crusade to the Holy Land. There's an instructive video and a chance to walk outside along an angled rooftop designed to catch rainwater: Notice the slanted gutter that channeled the water into a cistern and the heavy roof slabs covering the tapestry hall below.

• *From Place de la République, exit on the far corner (opposite the church and kitty-corner from where you entered) to stroll a delightful pedestrian street.*

⑭ Rue de la République

Rue da la République is Arles' primary shopping street. Walk downhill, enjoying the scene and popping into shops that catch your interest.

Near the start is **Maison Soulier Bakery.** Inside you'll be tempted by *fougasse* (bread studded with herbs, olives, and bacon bits), *sablés Provençal* (cookies made with honey and almonds), *tarte lavande* (a sweet almond lavender tart), and big crispy meringues (the egg-white-and-sugar answer to cotton candy—a cheap favorite of local kids). A few doors down is **Restaurant L'Atelier** (with two prized Michelin stars), **L'Occitane en Provence** (local perfumes), **Puyricard Chocolate** (with enticing €1 treats and *calisson,* a sweet almond delight), as well as local design and antique shops. The fragile spiral columns on the right (just before the tourist-pleasing Lavender Boutique on the corner) show what 400 years of weather can do to decorative stonework.

• *Take the first left onto Rue Président Wilson. Just after the butcher shop (Chez Mère Grand, with local pork-and-bull sausages hanging above a counter filled with precooked dishes to take home and heat up), turn right to find the **Hôtel Dieu,** a hospital made famous by one of its patients: Vincent van Gogh.*

⑮ *Espace Van Gogh* Easel

In December 1888, shortly after his famous ear-cutting incident (see *Café at Night* easel, described later), Vincent was admitted

into the local hospital—today's Espace Van Gogh cultural center (the Espace is free, but only the courtyard is open to the public). It surrounds a flowery courtyard that the artist loved and painted, when he was being treated for blood loss, hallucinations, and severe depression that left him bedridden for a month. The citizens of Arles circulated a petition demanding that the mad Dutchman be kept under medical supervision. Félix Rey, Vincent's kind doctor, worked out a compromise: The artist could leave during the day so that he could continue painting, but he had to sleep at the hospital at night. Look through the postcards sold in the courtyard and find a painting of Vincent's ward showing nuns at-

tending to patients in a gray hall *(Ward of Arles Hospital)*.

• *Return to Rue de la République. Take a left and continue two blocks downhill. Take the second right up Rue Tour de Fabre and follow signs to* Fondation Van Gogh. *After a few steps, you'll pass* **La Main Qui Pense** *(The Hand That Thinks) pottery shop and workshop, where Cécile Cayrol is busy creating and teaching. A couple blocks farther down, turn right onto Rue du Docteur Fanton (where you see "Vincent"). On your immediate right is the...*

⑯ Fondation Van Gogh

This art foundation, worth ▲, delivers a refreshing stop for modern-art lovers and Van Gogh fans, with two temporary exhibits per year in which contemporary artists pay homage to Vincent through thought-provoking interpretations of his works. You'll also see at least one original work by Van Gogh (painted during his time in the region). The gift shop has a variety of souvenirs, prints, and postcards.

Cost and Hours: €9, discount with Liberty Passport, daily 11:00-19:00 except closed between exhibits and Mon off-season—check website for current hours, audioguide-€3, Hôtel Leautaud de Donines, 35 Rue du Docteur Fanton, tel. 04 90 49 94 04, www.fondation-vincentvangogh-arles.org.

• *Continue on Rue du Docteur Fanton.*

⑰ Rue du Docteur Fanton

A string of recommended restaurants is on the left. On the right is the **Crèche Municipale.** Open workdays, this is a free government-funded daycare where parents can drop off their infants up to two years old. The notion: No worker should face financial hardship in order to receive quality childcare. At the next corner is the recommended **Soleileis,** Arles' top ice cream shop.

At the strawberry-and-vanilla ice cream cone, turn right and step into **Bar El Paseo** at 4 Rue des Thermes. The main museum-like room is absolutely full of bull—including the mounted heads of three big ones who died in the local arena and a big black-and-white photo of Arles' arena packed to capacity. Señora Leal—whose family is famous for its bullfighters—has wallpapered the place with photos and bullfighting memorabilia, and serves good Spanish Rioja wine and sangria.

• *A few steps further is...*

⑱ Forum Square (Place du Forum) and *Café at Night* Easel

Named for the Roman forum that once stood here, **Forum Square,** worth ▲, was the political and religious center of Roman Arles. Still lively, this café-crammed square is a local watering hole and popular for a *pastis* (anise-based apéritif). The bistros on the square can put together a passable salad or *plat du jour*—and when you sprinkle on the ambience, that's €14 well spent.

At the corner of Grand Hôtel Nord-Pinus (a favorite of Pablo Picasso), a plaque shows how the Romans built a foundation of galleries to make the main square level in order to compensate for Arles' slope down to the river. The two columns are all that survive from the upper story of the entry to the forum. Steps leading to the entrance are buried—the Roman street level was about 20 feet below you.

ARLES

The statue on the square is of **Frédéric Mistral** (1830-1914). This popular poet, who wrote in the local dialect rather than in French, was a champion of Provençal culture. After receiving the Nobel Prize in Literature in 1904, Mistral used his prize money to preserve and display the folk identity of Provence. He founded a regional folk museum (the Arlaten Folk Museum, closed until 2019) at a time when France was rapidly centralizing and regions like Provence were losing their unique identities. (The local mistral wind—literally "master"—has nothing to do with his name.)

• *Facing the brightly painted yellow café, find your final Van Gogh easel—Café at Night.*

In October 1888, lonely Vincent—who dreamed of making Arles a magnet for fellow artists—persuaded his friend Paul Gauguin to come. He decorated Gauguin's room with several humble canvases of sunflowers (now some of the world's priciest paintings), knowing that Gauguin had admired a similar painting he'd done in Paris. Their plan was for Gauguin to be the "dean" of a new art school in Arles, and Vincent its instructor-in-chief. At first, the two got along well. They spent days side by side, rendering the same subjects in their two distinct styles. At night they hit the bars and brothels. Van Gogh's well-known *Café at Night* captures the glow of an absinthe buzz at Café la Nuit on Place du Forum.

After two months together, the two artists clashed over art and personality differences (Vincent was a slob around the house, whereas Gauguin was meticulous). The night of December 23, they were drinking absinthe at the café when Vincent suddenly went ballistic. He threw his glass at Gauguin. Gauguin left. Walking through Place Victor Hugo, Gauguin heard footsteps behind him and turned to see Vincent coming at him, brandishing a razor. Gauguin quickly fled town. The local paper reported what happened next: "At 11:30 p.m., Vincent van Gogh, painter from Holland, appeared at the brothel at no. 1, asked for Rachel, and gave her his cut-off earlobe, saying, 'Treasure this precious object.' Then he vanished." He woke up the next morning at home with his head wrapped in a bloody towel and his earlobe missing. Was Vincent emulating a successful matador, whose prize is cutting off the bull's ear?

The **bright-yellow café**—called Café la Nuit—was the subject of one of Vincent van Gogh's most famous works in Arles. Although his painting showed the café in a brilliant yellow from the glow of gas lamps, the facade was bare limestone, just like the other cafés on this square. The café is now a tourist trap that its current owners painted to match Van Gogh's version...and to cash in on the Vincent-crazed hordes who pay too much to eat or drink here.

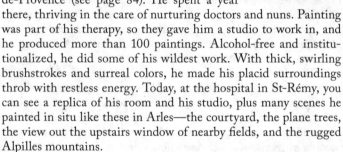

In spring 1889, the bipolar genius (a modern diagnosis) checked himself into the St. Paul Monastery and Hospital in St-Rémy-de-Provence (see page 84). He spent a year there, thriving in the care of nurturing doctors and nuns. Painting was part of his therapy, so they gave him a studio to work in, and he produced more than 100 paintings. Alcohol-free and institutionalized, he did some of his wildest work. With thick, swirling brushstrokes and surreal colors, he made his placid surroundings throb with restless energy. Today, at the hospital in St-Rémy, you can see a replica of his room and his studio, plus many scenes he painted in situ like these in Arles—the courtyard, the plane trees, the view out the upstairs window of nearby fields, and the rugged Alpilles mountains.

Eventually, Vincent's torment became unbearable. In the spring of 1890, he left Provence to be cared for by a sympathetic doctor in Auvers-sur-Oise, just north of Paris. On July 27, he wandered into a field and shot himself. He died two days later.

• *With this walk, you have seen the best of Arles. The colorful Roquette District and the charming Réattu Museum are each a short walk away (both described later). But I'd rather enjoy a drink on the Place du Forum and savor the joy of experiencing the essence of Provence.*

Sights in Arles

The Ancient History Museum provides valuable background on Arles' Roman history: Visit it first, before delving into the rest of the city's sights (drivers should stop on the way into town). For a deeper understanding, read "The Romans in Provence" on page 27. Many of Arles' city-center sights are covered on my self-guided walk, earlier.

ON THE OUTSKIRTS

▲▲Ancient History Museum
(Musée Départemental Arles Antique)

Begin your town visit here, for Roman Arles 101. Located on the site of the Roman chariot racecourse (the arc of which defines today's parking lot), this air-conditioned, all-on-one-floor museum is just west of central Arles along the river. Models and original sculptures re-create the Roman city, making workaday life and culture easier to imagine. While this excellent museum describes most of its treasures only in French, the English brochure gives general descriptions.

Cost and Hours: €8, free first Sun of the month, covered by Liberty Passport, open Wed-Mon 10:00-18:00, closed Tue, Presqu'île du Cirque Romain, tel. 04 13 31 51 03.

Getting There: Drivers will see signs for the museum as you enter the city. Without a car, to reach the museum from the city center, take the free **Navia shuttle** (stops at the train station and along Rue du 4 Septembre, then along the river—see map on page 44; 2/hour Mon-Sat, none Sun). The museum is about a 20-minute **walk** from the city center: Turn left at the river and take the scruffy riverside path under two bridges to the big, modern blue building (or better, stroll through Arles' enjoyable La Roquette neighborhood, described later). As you approach the museum, you'll pass the verdant Hortus Garden—designed to recall the Roman circus and chariot racecourse that were located here. A **taxi** ride costs €11 (museum can call a taxi for your return).

Visiting the Museum: The permanent collection is housed in a large hall flooded with natural light. Highlights include models of the ancient city and its major landmarks, a 2,000-year-old Roman boat, statues, mosaics, and sarcophagi. Here's a rundown on what you'll see.

A wall **map** of the region during the Roman era greets visitors and shows the geographic importance of Arles:

ARLES

A Day in the Life of an Arles Citizen in the Roman Era

Ancient Rome has often been compared to America...without cars or electricity, but with slaves to make up for it. Rome's wealth made a lifestyle possible that was the envy of the known world. Let's look at a typical well-to-do Arles citizen and his family in the era of Roman rule over the course of a day.

In the morning, Nebulus reviews the finances of the country farm with his caretaker/accountant/slave. He's interrupted by a "client," one of many poorer people dependent upon him for favors. The client, a shoemaker, wants permission from the government to open a new shop. He asks Nebulus to cut through the red tape. Nebulus promises to consult a lawyer friend in the basilica, or legal building.

Hungry, Nebulus stops at Burger Emp to grab a typical fast-food lunch. Most city dwellers don't cook in their cramped, wooden apartments because of the fire hazard. After a siesta, he walks to the baths for a workout and a little business networking. He discusses plans for donating money to build a new aqueduct for the city.

The children, Raucous and Ubiquitous, say good-bye to the pet dog and head off to school in the Forum. Nothing funny happens on the way. At school, it's down to business. They learn the basic three Rs. When they get older, they'll study literature, Greek, and public speaking. (The saving grace of this dreary education is that they don't have to take Latin.)

Work done, Nebulus heads for the stadium. The public is

Three important Roman trade routes—vias Domitia, Grippa, and Aurelia—all converged on or near Arles.

After a small exhibit on pre-Roman Arles you'll come to fascinating **models of the Roman city** and the impressive Roman structures in (and near) Arles. These breathe life into the buildings, showing how they looked 2,000 years ago. Start with the model of Roman Arles and ponder the city's splendor when Arles' population was double that of today. Find the forum—it's still the center of town, although only two columns survive (the smaller section of the forum is where today's Place du Forum is built). Look at the space Romans devoted to their

crazy about the chariot races. There are 12 per day, 240 days a year. Four teams dominate the competition (Reds, Whites, Blues, and Greens), and Nebulus has always been a die-hard Blue.

Back home, Nebulus' wife, Vapid, tends to the household affairs. She pauses in the bedroom to offer a prayer to her personal goddess for good weather for tonight. Meanwhile, the servants clean the house and send clothing to the laundry. A typical outfit is a simple woolen tunic: two pieces of cloth, front and back, sewn together at the sides. But tonight they'll dress up for a dinner party. She'll wear silk, with a wreath of flowers, and Nebulus will wear his best toga, a 20-foot-long white cloth. It's heavy and hard to put on, but it's all the rage. Nebulus dons his phallic-shaped necklace, which serves as an amulet against the evil eye and as a symbol of good luck in health, business, and bed.

At the dinner party, Vapid marvels over the chef's creation: ham soaked with honey, pasted in flour and baked. The guests toast each other with clay goblets bearing inscriptions like "Fill me up," and "Love me, baby!" Reclining on a couch, waited on by slaves, Nebulus orders a bowl of larks' tongues and a roast pig stuffed with live birds, then washes it down with wine. He calls for a feather, vomits, and starts all over. He catches the eye of a dark-skinned slave dancer from Egypt, and he takes her to the bedroom just down the hall...

...Or so went the stories. In fact, the legendary Roman orgy was just that—legendary. Romans advocated moderation and fidelity. Stuffiness and business sense were the rule. The family unit was considered sacred. If anything, the decadence of Roman life was confined to the upper classes in the later years of the empire.

arena and huge racecourse—a reminder that a passion for sports is not unique to modern civilizations (the museum you're in is at the far end of the racecourse). The model also illustrates how little Arles' core has changed over two millennia, with its houses still clustered around the city center, and warehouses still located on the opposite side of the river.

At the museum's center stands the original **statue of Julius Caesar,** which once graced Arles' ancient theater's magnificent stage wall. Look for a **model of the theater** and its wall, as well as models of the ancient town's other major buildings. You'll see the elaborately elegant forum; the floating wooden bridge over the widest, slowest part of the river—giving Arles a strategic advantage; the arena with its movable cover to shelter spectators from sun or rain; and the hydraulic mill of Barbegal with its 16 waterwheels cascading water down a hillside.

Don't miss the large model of the **chariot racecourse.** Part of the original racecourse was just outside the windows, and although long gone, it likely resembled Rome's Circus Maximus.

Next, step into the hall dedicated to the museum's newest and most exciting exhibit: a **Gallo-Roman vessel** and much of its cargo (English translations on panels). This almost-100-foot-long Roman barge was hauled out of the Rhône in 2010, along with some 280 amphorae and 3,000 ceramic artifacts. It was typical of flat-bottomed barges used to shuttle goods between Arles and ports along the Mediterranean (vessels were manually towed upriver). This one hauled limestone slabs and big rocks—no wonder it sunk. A worthwhile 20-minute video about the barge (with English subtitles) plays continuously in a tiny theater at the end of the hall.

Elsewhere in the museum, you'll see displays of pottery, jewelry, metal, and glass artifacts. You'll also see well-crafted mosaic floors that illustrate how Roman Arles was a city of art and culture. The many **statues** are all original, except for the greatest—the *Venus of Arles,* which Louis XIV took a liking to and had moved to Versailles. It's now in the Louvre—and, as locals say, "When it's in Paris...bye-bye."

The final section is dedicated to expertly carved pagan and early-Christian **sarcophagi** (from the second to fifth century A.D.). These would have lined the Via Aurelia outside the town wall. In the early days of the Church, Jesus was often portrayed beardless and as the good shepherd, with a lamb over his shoulder.

MORE SIGHTS IN ARLES
La Roquette District

To escape the tourist beat in Arles, take a detour into Arles' little-visited western fringe. Find Rue des Porcelets near the Trinquetaille Bridge and stroll several blocks into pleasing Place Paul Doumier, where you'll find a lively assortment of cafés, bakeries, and inexpensive bistros with nary a tourist in sight. Continue along Rue de la Roquette and turn right on charming Rue Croix Rouge to reach the river. Those walking to or from the Ancient History Museum can use this appealing stroll as a shortcut.

Baths of Constantine (Thermes de Constantin)

These partly intact Roman baths were built in the early fourth century when Emperor Constantine declared Arles an imperial residence. Roman cities such as Arles had several public baths like this, fed by aqueducts and used as much for exercising, networking, and chatting with friends as for bathing. These baths were located near the Rhône River for easy water disposal. You can get a pretty good look at the baths through the fence. If you enter you'll walk elevated metal corridors at the original floor level. Imagine the elaborate engineering: the hypocaust system for heating the floor and big tubs with various temperatures—hot, tepid, and cold—next to a sauna and steam room heated by slave-stoked, wood-burning ovens.

Cost and Hours: €3, covered by Liberty Passport, same hours as Roman Arena—daily 9:00-19:00, April and Oct until 18:00, Nov-March 10:00-17:00.

▲Réattu Museum (Musée Réattu)

Housed in the former Grand Priory of the Knights of Malta, this modern-art collection, while always changing, is a stimulating and well-lit mix of new and old. Picasso loved Arles and came here regularly for the bullfights. At the end of his life in 1973, he gave the city a series of his paintings, some of which are always on display here. The permanent collection usually includes a series of works by homegrown Neoclassical artist Jacques Réattu.

Cost and Hours: €8, covered by Liberty Passport, Tue-Sun 10:00-18:00, Nov-Feb until 17:00, closed Mon year-round, 10 Rue du Grand Prieuré, tel. 04 90 49 37 58, www.museereattu.arles.fr.

ARLES

Experiences in Arles

▲▲Markets

On Wednesday and Saturday mornings, Arles' ring road erupts into an open-air festival of fish, flowers, produce...and everything Provençal. The main event is on Saturday, with vendors jamming the ring road from Boulevard Emile Combes to the east, along Boulevard des Lices near the TI (the heart of the market), and continuing down Boulevard Georges Clemenceau to the west. Wednesday's market runs only along Boulevard Emile Combes, between Place Lamartine and Avenue Victor Hugo; the segment nearest Place Lamartine is all about food, and the upper half features clothing, tablecloths, purses, and so on. On the first Wednesday of the month, a flea market doubles the size of the usual Wednesday market along Boulevard des Lices near the main TI. Both markets are open until about 12:30. Dive in: Buy some flowers for your hotelier, try the olives, sample some wine, swat a pickpocket, and speak some Arabic.

Part of the market has a North African feel, thanks to the many Algerians and Moroccans who live in Arles. As with immigrants in any rich country, they came to do the lowly city jobs that locals didn't want, and now they mostly do the region's labor-intensive agricultural jobs (picking olives, harvesting fruit, and working in local greenhouses; see sidebar on page 223).

▲▲Bullgames (Courses Camarguaises)

Provençal "bullgames" are held in Arles and in neighboring towns. Those in Arles occupy the same seats that fans have used for nearly

2,000 years, and deliver the city's most memorable experience—the *courses camarguaises* in the ancient arena. The nonviolent bull-games are more sporting than bloody bullfights (though traditional Spanish-style bullfights still take place on occasion). The bulls of Arles (who, locals insist, "die of old age") are promoted in posters even more boldly than their human foes. In the bullgame, a ribbon *(cocarde)* is laced between the bull's horns. The *razeteur,* dressed in white and carrying a special hook, has 15 minutes to snare the ribbon. Local businessmen encourage a *razeteur* by shouting out how much money they'll pay for the *cocarde*. If the bull pulls a good stunt, the band plays the famous "Toreador" song from *Carmen*. The following day, newspapers report on the games, including how many *Carmens* the bull earned.

Three classes of bullgames—determined by the experience of the *razeteurs*—are advertised in posters: The *course de protection* is for rookies. The *trophée de l'Avenir* comes with more experience. And the *trophée des As* features top professionals. During Easter *(Féria de Pâques)* and the fall rice-harvest festival *(Féria du Riz),* the arena hosts traditional Spanish bullfights (look for *corrida*) with outfits, swords, spikes, and the whole gory shebang. (Nearby villages stage *courses camarguaises* in small wooden bullrings nearly every weekend; TIs have the latest schedule.)

Bullgame tickets usually run €11-20; bullfights are pricier (€36-100). Schedules for bullgames vary (usually July-Aug on Wed and Fri)—ask at the TI or check www.arenes-arles.com.

Easter and Fall Fairs (Féria de Pâques and Féria du Riz)

For 150 years, Arles has thrown citywide parties to celebrate the arrival of spring and fall. During the four days that each event lasts, more than 500,000 people pile into Arles for bullfights, street concerts, piles of paella, and parties *(Feria de Pâques* is Fri-Mon of Easter weekend, and *Feria du Riz* is Fri-Mon on the second weekend of Sept). The Easter event kicks off the bullfighting season, while the September event celebrates the land and traditions of Arles. Only during these fairs are bulls killed in the bullfights and only during these events does Arles feel overrun.

Sleeping in Arles

Hotels are a great value here—many are air-conditioned, though few have elevators. The Calendal, Musée, and Régence hotels offer exceptional value.

$$ Hôtel le Calendal*** is a service-with-a-smile place ideally located between the Roman Arena and Classical Theater. The hotel opens to the street with airy lounges and a lovely palm-shaded courtyard, providing an enjoyable refuge. You'll find snacks and drinks in the café/sandwich bar (daily 8:00-20:00). The modern rooms, decorated with art from local artists, come in random shapes and sizes (some with balcony, family rooms, air-con, free spa for adults, good-value parking, just above arena at 5 Rue Porte de Laure, tel. 04 90 96 11 89, www.lecalendal.com, contact@lecalendal.com). They also run the nearby budget Hostel Arles City Center, described later.

$ Hôtel du Musée** is a quiet, affordable manor-home hideaway tucked deep in Arles (if driving, call the hotel from the street—they'll open the barrier so you can drive in to drop off your bags). This delightful place comes with 29 wood-floored rooms, a flowery courtyard, and comfortable lounges. Lighthearted Claude and English-speaking Laurence are good hosts (family rooms, no elevator, pay parking garage, follow *Réattu Museum* signs to 11 Rue du Grand Prieuré, tel. 04 90 93 88 88, www.hoteldumusee.com, contact@hoteldumusee.com).

$ Hôtel de la Muette** is a small, good-value hotel located in a quiet corner of Arles, run by hard-working owners Brigitte and Alain. Its tasteful rooms and bathrooms come with tiled floors and stone walls (RS%, family rooms, no elevator, pay private garage, 15 Rue des Suisses, tel. 04 90 96 15 39, www.hotel-muette.com, hotel.muette@wanadoo.fr).

$ Hôtel Régence,** a top budget deal, has a riverfront location near the train station, comfortable Provençal rooms, and safe parking (family rooms, choose river-view or quieter courtyard rooms, good buffet breakfast extra, no elevator but only two floors, pay parking garage; from Place Lamartine, turn right after passing between towers to reach 5 Rue Marius Jouveau; tel. 04 90 96 39 85, www.hotel-regence.com, contact@hotel-regence.com). Gentle Valérie and Eric speak English.

$ Hôtel Acacias,*** just off Place Lamartine and inside the old city walls, is a modern hotel with small yet inviting and comfortable rooms (family rooms, air-con, pay parking garage, 2 Rue de la Cavalerie, tel. 04 90 96 37 88, www.hotel-acacias.com, contact@hotel-acacias.com).

¢ Hôtel Voltaire rents 12 small, spartan rooms with ceiling fans and nifty balconies overlooking a colorful, working-class square. A block below the arena, the rooms have some rough edges but are cheap. "Mr." Ferran loves the States, and hopes you'll add to his license plate or postcard collection (cheaper rooms with shared bath, no air-con, no elevator, Wi-Fi in restaurant only,

ARLES

ARLES

Arles Hotels & Restaurants

Accommodations

1 Hôtel/Rest. le Calendal & Hostel Arles City Center
2 Hôtel du Musée
3 Hôtel de la Muette
4 Hôtel Régence
5 Hôtel Acacias
6 Hôtel/Rest. Voltaire
7 To Mas du Petit Grava & Mas Petit Fourchon
8 To Domaine de Laforest

Eateries

9 Le Comptoir d'Italie
10 Cafés de la Major
11 Cuisine de Comptoir
12 Rue du Dr. Fanton Eateries
13 La Chistera
14 Le Criquet
15 Delicate et Saine Wine Bar
16 L'Atelier & A Côté
17 Soleileis Ice Cream
18 Glacier Arelatis
19 Maison Soulier Bakery

RUE DES CAPUCINS
RUE ROBESPIERRE
RUE DE LA VERRIERE
RUE CAMARGUE
TRINQUETAILLE
QUAI ST. PIERRE

Rhône

TRINQUETAILLE BRIDGE

QUAI MARX DORMOY
R DE LA TOUR DU FABRE
R. DR. FANTON
R. TRUCHET
FONDATION VAN GOGH
RUE A. FRANCE
R. JOUVENE
LIBERTE

B Shuttle Bus Stops

ARLATEN FOLK MUSEUM
(REOPENS IN 2019)

QUAI DE LA ROQUETTE

R. DES PORCELETS
Place Paul Doumier

RUE DE LA REPUBLIQUE

RUE DE LA ROQUETTE
RUE DE CHARTROUSE
RUE JEAN GRANAUD
RUE GAMBETTA

ESPACE VAN GOGH

To Ancient History Museum

LA ROQUETTE

RUE CROIX ROUGE

RUE MOLIERE
MAIN BUS STATION

RUE PRES. WILSON

Place Genive

To Nîmes via A-84

RUE RAILLON
RUE FLEURY PRUDHON

To Ancient History Museum

BLVD. G. CLEMENCEAU
RUE PARMENTIER

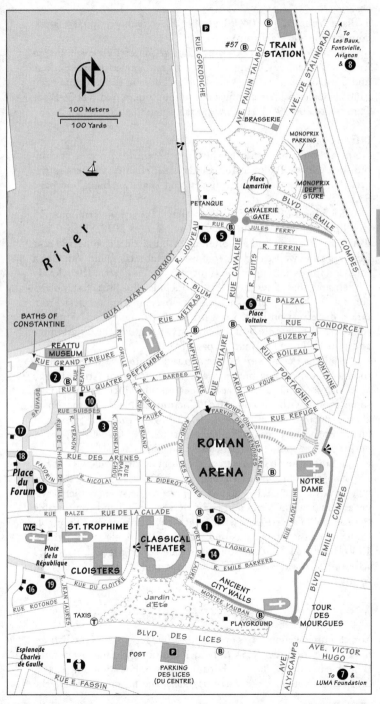

ARLES

1 Place Voltaire, tel. 04 90 96 49 18, www.hotel-voltaire-arles. com, levoltaire13@aol.com).

¢ **Hostel Arles City Center** offers good dorm rooms, a shared kitchen, and homey living area. It's a great value for backpackers and those on a shoestring. Check in next door at the recommended Hôtel le Calendal (air-con, just above the Roman Arena at 26 Place Pomme, tel. 06 99 71 11 89, www.arles-pelerins.fr).

NEAR ARLES

Many drivers, particularly those with families, prefer staying outside Arles in the peaceful countryside, with easy access to the area's sights. (See also "Sleeping in and near Les Baux," on page 81.)

$$ **Mas du Petit Grava** is a vintage Provençal farmhouse 15 tree-lined minutes east of Arles (may close in 2018). Here California refugees Jim and Ike offer an enthusiastic welcome and rent four large and well-cared-for rooms with tubs, tiles, and Van Gogh themes (Jim is an expert on Vincent's life and art). Their lovely garden surrounds a swimming pool (includes fine breakfast, no air-con, tel. 04 90 98 35 66, management@masdupetitgrava.net). From Arles, drive east on D-453 toward St-Martin de Crau (1.5 miles), then turn left on route St. Hippolyte to the right of the large white-and-blue building (see map on page 74).

$$ **Mas Petit Fourchon** is a grand farmhouse with spacious rooms on a sprawling property a few minutes from Arles. There's acres of room to roam and a big, heated pool (includes breakfast, some rooms with air-con, 1070 Chemin de Nadal in the Fourchon suburb; take exit 6 from N-113 toward *l'hôpital,* turn right just after the hospital and follow signs; tel. 04 90 96 16 35, www. petitfourchon.com, info@petitfourchon.com).

$ **Domaine de Laforest,** a few minutes' drive below Fontvieille, near the aqueduct of Barbegal, is a 320-acre spread engulfed by vineyards, rice fields, and swaying trees. The sweet owners (Sylvie and mama Mariette) rent eight well-equipped and comfortable two-bedroom apartments with great weekly rates (may be rentable for fewer days, air-con, washing machines, pool, big lawn, swings, 1000 Route de l'Aqueduc Romain—see map on page 74, tel. 06 23 73 44 59, www.domaine-laforest.com, contact@domaine-laforest. com).

Eating in Arles

You can dine well in Arles on a modest budget (most of my listings have *menus* for under €25). Sunday is a quiet night for restaurants, though eateries on Place du Forum are open. For a portable snack, try Maison Soulier Bakery (see page 55), and for groceries, use the big, Monoprix supermarket/department store on Place Lamartine (Mon-Sat 8:30-19:30, closed Sun).

PLACE DU FORUM NEIGHBORHOOD

Great atmosphere and mediocre food at fair prices await on Place du Forum. Avoid the garish yellow Café la Nuit. Other cafés on the square deliver acceptable quality and terrific ambience. For serious cuisine, wander away from the square.

Before dinner on the main square, consider one of the most local rituals you can enjoy in Arles: enjoying a *pastis*. This anise-based apéritif is served straight with ice, along with a carafe of water—dilute to taste. Wherever you dine, consider finishing with a portable dessert at Soleileis or Glacier Arelatis.

$ Le Comptoir d'Italie offers good-enough and inexpensive meals on Place du Forum, with a good selection of salads and pizzas (daily, 9 Place du Forum, tel. 09 81 80 50 22).

$ Cafés de la Major is *the* place to go to recharge with some serious coffee or tea (Tue-Sat 8:30-19:00, closed Sun-Mon, 7 bis Rue Réattu, tel. 04 90 96 14 15).

$ Cuisine de Comptoir offers light and cheap dinners of *tartine*—a cross between pizza and bruschetta, served with soup or salad for €11—and offers a fun array of pizza-style *tartine* toppings. This Provençal answer to a pizzeria—run by Vincent—has indoor seating only (closed Sun year-round, closed evenings Dec-April, just off the lower end of Place du Forum at 10 Rue de la Liberté, tel. 04 90 96 86 28).

On Rue du Docteur Fanton

This pedestrian-friendly street—with a pleasing lineup of restaurants, all with good outside and inside dining—is my favorite place to comparison-shop for dinner. Come here to peruse your options side-by-side. And, for your dessert pleasure, one of the town's best ice cream places is just across the street

$$$ Le Galoubet is a trendy local spot, blending a warm interior, traditional French cuisine, and friendly service, thanks to owner Frank. It's the most expensive of the places I list on this street and the least flexible, serving €27 and €32 *menus* only. If it's cold, a roaring fire keeps you toasty (closed Sun-Mon, great fries and desserts, 18 Rue du Docteur Fanton, tel. 04 90 93 18 11).

$$ Les Filles du 16 is a warm, affordable place to enjoy a fine Provençal two- or three-course dinner inside or out. The choices, while tasty, are limited, so check the selection before sitting down (closed Sat-Sun, 16 Rue du Docteur Fanton, tel. 04 90 93 77 36).

$$ Le Plaza la Paillotte buzzes with happy diners enjoying delicious, well-presented Provençal cuisine at good prices. Attentive owners Stéphane and Graziela (he cooks, she serves) welcome diners with a comfortable terrace and a smart interior (reservations recommended, closed Wed Oct-March, 28 Rue du Docteur Fanton, tel. 04 90 96 33 15).

Nearby: For a less-touristy-feeling dining experience, wander into the La Roquette neighborhood (described under "More Sights in Arles," earlier). Have a drink on Place Paul Doumier and consider staying for dinner. **$$ La Chistera,** an intimate, local spot, dishes up classic dishes with Basque accents at good prices and fine quality (closed Wed, 16 Rue des Porcelets, tel. 04 90 96 86 13).

NEAR THE ROMAN ARENA

Several little restaurants overlook the Roman Arena, offering a stony and ancient backdrop for your dinner.

$$ Le Criquet, possibly the best value in Arles, is a sweet little place two blocks above the arena, serving well-presented and delicious Provençal classics with joy at good prices. Sisters Lili and Charlotte serve while mama and papa run the kitchen. If you're really hungry, try the mouth-watering €25 *bourride*—a creamy fish soup thickened with aioli and garlic and stuffed with mussels, clams, calamari, and more. Book ahead for an outdoor table (closed Wed and Sun, 21 Rue Porte de Laure, tel. 04 90 96 80 51).

$ Delicate et Saine Wine Bar has no real kitchen and only a handful of outdoor tables, but the enticing €5-10 gourmet dishes, matched with a nice list of wine by the glass come with huge arena views (closed Sun evening and all day Mon, 30 Rond-Point des Arènes, tel. 06 15 80 73 14).

$ Le Comptoir du Calendal, in the recommended Hotel le Calendal around the corner from the arena, serves light seasonal food in its lovely courtyard or at the café (delicious and cheap little sandwiches, daily 8:00-20:00, guest computer available, 5 Rue Porte de Laure, tel. 04 90 96 11 89).

$ Hôtel Voltaire, on a low-key square away from most tourists, serves simple three-course lunches and dinners at honest prices, including hearty *plats* and filling salads for €11—try the *salade Latine,* or, if tapenade is your thing, the filling *assiette Provençale* (closed Sun evening, on Place Voltaire below the arena).

A GASTRONOMIC DINING EXPERIENCE

One of France's most recognized chefs, Jean-Luc Rabanel, runs two very different places 50 yards from Place de la République (at 7 Rue des Carmes). They sit side by side, both offering indoor and terrace seating.

$$$$ L'Atelier, a destination restaurant with two Michelin stars (notice the red plaque), attracts people from great distances to happily pay €125 or more for dinner with wine (about half that for lunch). There is no menu, just a parade of delicious taste sensations served in artsy dishes (called "*touches de gout*"—taste touches). Don't plan on a quick dinner, and don't come for a traditional setting: Everything is enthusiastically contemporary. You'll probably see or hear the famous chef with his long salt-and-pepper hair and deep voice (closed Mon-Tue, book ahead, friendly servers will hold your hand through this palate-widening experience, tel. 04 90 91 07 69, www.rabanel.com).

$$$ A Côté, next door, offers a smart wine bar/bistro ambience and top-quality cuisine for much less money. Here you can sample the famous chef's talents with the €32 three-course *menu* (limited selection of wines by the glass, closed Mon-Tue, tel. 04 90 47 61 13, www.bistro-acote.com).

AND FOR DESSERT...
Soleileis scoops up fine ice cream made with organic milk, fresh fruit, all-natural ingredients, and creative flavors that fit the season. There's also a shelf of English books for exchange (daily 14:00-18:30, later on weekends, closed in winter, a block off the Forum at 9 Rue du Docteur Fanton, run by Marijtje). **Glacier Arelatis** advertises "gourmet ice cream," which looks more like tasty gelato to me (9 Place du Forum, daily until late).

Arles Connections

BY TRAIN
Note that some trains in and out of Arles require a reservation. These include connections with Nice to the east and Bordeaux to the west (including intermediary stops). Ask at the station.

Compare train and bus schedules: For some nearby destinations the bus may be the better choice, and it's usually cheaper.

From Arles by Train to: Paris (11/day, 2 direct TGVs—4 hours, 9 more with transfer in Avignon—5 hours), **Avignon Centre-Ville** (roughly hourly, 20 minutes), **Nîmes** (9/day, 30 minutes), **Orange** (4/day direct, 35 minutes, more with transfer in Avignon), **Aix-en-Provence Centre-Ville** (10/day, 2 hours, transfer in Marseille, train may separate midway—be sure your section is going to Aix-en-Provence), **Marseille** (11/day, 1 hour), **Cassis** (7/day, 2 hours), **Carcassonne** (4/day direct, 2.5 hours, more with transfer in Narbonne, direct trains may require reservations), **Beaune** (10/day, 5 hours), **Nice** (11/day, 4 hours, most require transfer in Marseille), **Barcelona** (3/day, 4.5 hours, transfer in Nîmes), **Italy** (3/day, transfer in Marseille and Nice; from Arles, it's 5 hours to Ventimiglia on the border, 8 hours to Milan, 9 hours to Cinque Terre, 11 hours to Florence, and 13 hours to Venice or Rome).

BY BUS

Arles' bus company office is located on the main boulevard a few blocks from the TI. All buses to regional destinations depart from here, except bus #57 to Les Baux/St Rémy, which leaves from the train station. Most bus trips cost under €2. Get schedules at the TI or from the bus company (office open Mon-Fri 7:30-18:30, Sat 7:30-12:00 & 14:00-17:30, 24 Boulevard Georges Clémenceau, tel. 08 10 00 08 18, www.lepilote.com).

From Arles Train Station to Avignon TGV Station: The direct SNCF bus is easier than the train (€7.10, 8/day, 1 hour, included with rail pass). You can also take the train from Arles to Avignon's Centre-Ville Station, then catch the *navette* (shuttle bus) to the TGV station (2-block walk, see page 96).

From Arles by Bus to Les Baux and St-Rémy: Bus #57 connects Arles to St-Rémy-de-Provence via Les Baux (6/day daily July-Aug, Sat-Sun only in May-June and Sept, none Oct-April; departing from the train station; 35 minutes to Les Baux, 50 minutes to St-Rémy, then runs to Avignon). Bus #54 also goes to St-Rémy but not via Les Baux (5/day Mon-Fri, 3/day Sat, none on Sun, 1 hour). For other ways to reach Les Baux and St-Rémy, see page 75.

By Bus to Other Destinations: Nîmes (8/day Mon-Fri, 2/day Sat-Sun, 1 hour), **Aix-en-Provence** (faster than trains, 5/day Mon-Fri, 2/day Sat-Sun, 1.5 hours), **Fontvieille** (6/day, 10 minutes), **Camargue/Stes-Maries-de-la-Mer** (bus #20, 6/day Mon-Sat, 3/day Sun, 1 hour).

NEAR ARLES

Les Baux • St-Rémy •
The Camargue

The diverse terrain around Arles harbors many worthwhile and easy day trips. The medieval ghost town of Les Baux haunts the eerie Alpilles mountains, while chic and compact St-Rémy-de-Provence awaits just over the hills, offering Roman ruins and memories of Vincent van Gogh. For an entirely different experience, the flat Camargue wetlands region knocks on Arles' southern door with sandy beaches, saltwater lakes, rice paddies, flamingos, wild horses, and wild black bulls.

PLANNING YOUR TIME

Because public transportation in this area is sparse, these sights are most convenient by car, taxi, or minivan tour. For a memorable one-day road trip from Arles or Avignon, spend the morning in Les Baux (before the crowds), have lunch in St-Rémy and explore its sights, then finish at the Roman aqueduct of Barbegal. Nondrivers can do the same day trip (cheaper without the aqueduct) by bus and taxi. If you have more time or are a nature or bird-watching buff, head for the Camargue. A good market pops up on Friday mornings in little Eyguières (near Les Baux and St-Rémy).

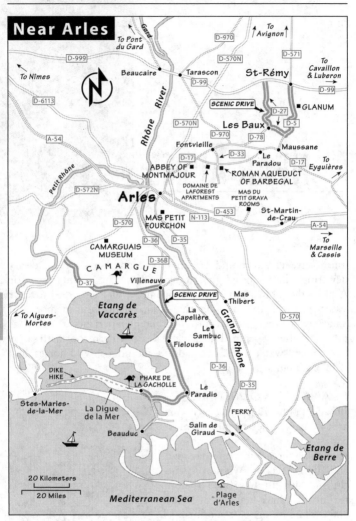

NEAR ARLES

Les Baux

The hilltop town of Les Baux crowns the rugged Alpilles (ahl-pee) mountains, evoking a tumultuous medieval history. Here, you can imagine the struggles of a strong community that lived a rough-and-tumble life—thankful more for their top-notch fortifications than for their dramatic views. It's mobbed with tourists most of the day, but Les Baux rewards those who arrive by 9:00 or after 17:30. (Although the hilltop citadel's entry closes at the end of the day, once you're inside, you're welcome to live out your medieval fantasies all night long, even with a picnic.) Sunsets are dramatic, the castle is brilliantly illuminated after dark, and nights in Les Baux are pin-drop peaceful. (If you like what you see here, but want a way more off-the-beaten-path experience, head for the Luberon and find Fort de Buoux—see page 215).

GETTING TO LES BAUX

By Car: Les Baux is a 20-minute drive from Arles: Follow signs for *Avignon*, then *Les Baux*. Drivers can combine Les Baux with St-Rémy (15 minutes away) and the ruined Roman aqueduct of Barbegal.

On arrival in Les Baux, drivers pay €6 to park near the village or several blocks below (parking is squirreled all around the site). Those parking in lots close to the site pay at the small office near the village entrance (look for the big star icon on a glass door). Those parking along the road pay at meters. Wherever you park, put your receipt on the dash of your car. You can park a 15-minute walk away for free at the quarry-cave called Carrières de Lumières (described later, under "Near Les Baux").

By Bus: From Arles, Cartreize **bus #57** runs to Les Baux (daily July-Aug, in May-June and Sept Sat-Sun only, none Oct-April, 6/ day, 35 minutes; via Abbey of Montmajour, Fontvieille, and Le Paradou; destination: St-Rémy, timetables at www.lepilote.com).

St-Rémy, about seven miles north of Les Baux, is a workable transit point for those home-basing in Avignon: Ride Cartreize bus #57 from Avignon to St-Rémy (10/day Mon-Sat, 6/day Sun, 45 minutes); you can continue to Les Baux on the same bus daily in July-August and on weekends in May-June and September (none Oct-April, timetables at www.lepilote.com). Otherwise, continue to Les Baux by taxi (next).

By Taxi: If buses aren't running to Les Baux, you can taxi there from St-Rémy, then take another taxi to return to St-Rémy or to your home base. Figure €30 for a taxi one-way to Les Baux from Arles, €55 from Avignon, and €20 from St-Rémy (mobile 06 80 27 60 92).

By Minivan Tour: The best option for many is a minivan tour, which can be both efficient and economical (easiest from Avignon; see page 24).

Orientation to Les Baux

Les Baux is actually two visits in one: castle ruins perched on an al-most lunar landscape, and a medieval town below. Savor the castle, then tour—or blitz—the lower town's polished-stone gauntlet of boutiques (a Provençal dream come true for shoppers). While the town, which lives entirely off tourism, is packed with shops, cafés, and tourist knickknacks, the castle above stays manageable because crowds are dispersed over a big area. The town's main drag leads directly to the castle—just keep going uphill (a 10-minute walk).

Tourist Information: The TI is immediately on the left as you enter the village (Mon-Fri 9:00-18:00, Sat-Sun until 17:00; Nov-March Mon-Sat 9:30-17:00, closed Sun). The TI has free Wi-Fi and can call a cab for you.

Sights in Les Baux

▲▲▲THE CASTLE RUINS (CHATEAU DES BAUX)

The sun-bleached ruins of the stone fortress of Les Baux are carved into, out of, and on top of a rock 650 feet above the valley floor.

Many of the ancient walls of this striking castle still stand as a testament to
the proud past of this once-feisty village.

Cost and Hours: €9, €11 if there's
"entertainment" (described next), €16
Pass Provence combo-ticket with Carrières de Lumières and Yves Brayer
Museum, entry fees include excellent
audioguide; daily Easter-Sept 9:00-
19:15, July-Aug until 20:15, March
and Oct 9:30-18:30, Nov-Feb 10:00-17:00, www.chateau-baux-
provence.com. If you're inside the castle when the entry closes, you can stay as long as you like.

Entertainment: Every weekend from April through early September and daily in summer, the castle presents medieval pageantry, tournaments, demonstrations of catapults and crossbows, and jousting matches. Pick up a schedule as you enter (or check online).

Picnicking: While no food or drink is sold inside the castle grounds, you're welcome to bring your own and use one of several picnic tables (the best view table is at the edge near the siege weaponry). Sunset dinner picnics are memorable.

Background: Imagine the importance of this citadel in the Middle Ages, when the Lords of Baux were notorious warriors (who could trace their lineage back to one of the "three kings" of Christmas-carol fame, Balthazar). In the 11th century, Les Baux was a powerhouse in southern France, controlling about 80 towns. The Lords of Baux fought the counts of Barcelona for control of Provence...and eventually lost. But while in power, these guys were mean. One ruler enjoyed forcing unransomed prisoners to jump off his castle walls.

In 1426, Les Baux was incorporated into Provence and France.

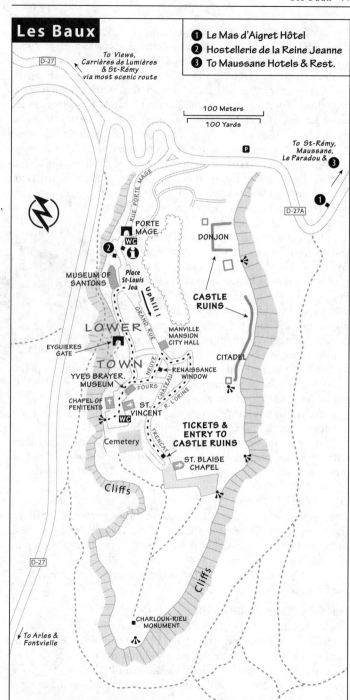

Les Baux

1 Le Mas d'Aigret Hôtel
2 Hostellerie de la Reine Jeanne
3 To Maussane Hotels & Rest.

To Views,
Carrières de Lumières
& St-Rémy via most scenic route

D-27

100 Meters
100 Yards

P

To St-Rémy,
Maussane,
Le Paradou & 3

1

D-27A

RUE PORTE MAGE

PORTE
MAGE

WC

DONJON

Place
St-Louis
Jou

Uphill !

GRAND RUE

MUSEUM OF
SANTONS

CASTLE
RUINS

LOWER

MANVILLE
MANSION
CITY HALL

EYGUIERES
GATE

CITADEL

TOWN

NEUVE

YVES BRAYER
MUSEUM

FOURS

CHATEAU

RENAISSANCE
WINDOW

R. L'ORME

CHAPEL OF
PENITENTS

ST.
VINCENT

WC

Cemetery

TRENCAT

**TICKETS &
ENTRY TO
CASTLE RUINS**

ST. BLAISE
CHAPEL

Cliffs

D-27

Cliffs

To Arles &
Fontvieille

CHARLOUN-RIEU
MONUMENT

NEAR ARLES

Not accustomed to playing second fiddle, Les Baux struggled with the French king, who responded by destroying the fortress in 1483. Later, Les Baux regained some importance and emerged as a center of Protestantism. Arguing with Rome was a high-stakes game in the 17th century, and Les Baux's association with the Huguenots brought destruction again in 1632 when Cardinal Richelieu (under King Louis XIII) demolished the castle. Louis rubbed salt in the wound by billing Les Baux's residents for his demolition expenses. The once-powerful town of 4,000 was forever crushed.

Visiting the Castle: Buy your ticket in the old olive mill and inspect the models of Les Baux before its 17th-century destruction.

Pick up your audioguide when you enter. As you wander, key in the number for any of the 30 narrated stops that interest you.

The sight is exceptionally well presented. As you walk on the windblown spur (*baux* in French), you'll pass kid-thrilling medieval siege weaponry (go ahead, try the battering ram). Good displays in English and big paintings in key locations help reconstruct the place. Imagine 4,000 people living up here. Notice the water-catchment system (a slanted field that caught rainwater and drained it into cisterns—necessary during a siege) and find the reservoir cut into the rock below the castle's highest point. Look for post holes throughout the stone walls that reveal where beams once supported floors.

For the most sensational views, climb to the blustery top of the citadel—hold tight if the mistral wind is blowing.

The St. Blaise chapel across from the entry/exit runs videos with Provençal themes (plays continuously; just images and music, no words).

▲LOWER TOWN

After your castle visit, you can shop and eat your way back through the lower town. Or, escape some of the crowds by visiting these minor but worthwhile sights as you descend. I've linked the sights with walking directions.

• *Follow the main drag about 100 yards through the town and look for the flags marking...*

Manville Mansion City Hall

The 15th-century City Hall offers art exhibits under its cool vaults. It often flies the red-and-white flag of Monaco amid several others, a reminder that the Grimaldi family (longtime rulers of the tiny principality of Monaco) owned Les Baux until the French Revolution (1789). In fact, in 1982, Princess Grace Kelly and her royal husband, Prince Rainier Grimaldi, came to Les Baux to receive the key to the city.

Exit left and walk uphill 20 steps to the empty 1571 **Renaissance window frame.** This beautiful stone frame stands as a reminder of this town's Protestant history. This was probably a place of Huguenot worship—the words carved into the lintel, *Post tenebras lux,* were a popular Calvinist slogan: "After the shadow comes the light."

• *Continue walking uphill, and turn right on Rue des Fours to find the...*

Yves Brayer Museum (Musée Yves Brayer)

This enjoyable museum lets you peruse three floors of paintings (Van Gogh-like Expressionism) by Yves Brayer (1907-1990), who spent his final years here in Les Baux. Like Van Gogh, Brayer was inspired by all that surrounded him, and by his travels through Morocco, Spain, and the rest of the Mediterranean world. Pick up the descriptive English sheet at the entry.

Cost and Hours: €8, €16 Pass Provence combo-ticket with castle and Carrières de Lumières, daily 10:00-12:30 & 14:00-18:30, shorter hours and closed Tue Oct-Dec and March, closed Jan-Feb, tel. 04 90 54 36 99, www.yvesbrayer.com.

• *Next door is...*

St. Vincent Church

This 12th-century Romanesque church was built short and wide to fit the terrain. The center chapel on the right (partially carved out of the rock) houses the town's traditional Provençal processional chariot. Each Christmas Eve, a ram pulled this cart—holding a lamb, symbolizing Jesus, and surrounded by candles—through town to the church.

• *As you leave the church, WCs are to the left (dug into the stone wall) and up the stairs. Directly in front of the church is a vast view, making clear the strategic value of this rocky bluff's natural fortifications. A few steps away is the...*

Chapel of Penitents

The elaborate Nativity scene painted by Yves Brayer covers the entire interior and illustrates the local legend that says Jesus was born in Les Baux.

• *As you leave the church, turn left and find the old town "laundry"— with a pig-snout faucet and 14th-century stone washing surface designed for short women.*

Continue past the Yves Brayer Museum again, keep left, and walk 100 yards down steep Rue de la Calade, passing a view café, the town's fortified wall, and one of its two gates. Before long, you'll run into the...

Museum of Santons

This free and fun "museum" displays a collection of *santons* ("little saints"), popular folk figurines that decorate local Christmas mangers. Notice how the Nativity scene "proves" once again that Jesus was born in Les Baux. These painted clay dolls show off local dress and traditions (with good English descriptions).

NEAR LES BAUX

▲Carrières de Lumières (Quarries of Light)

A 10-minute walk from Les Baux, this colossal quarry-cave with immense vertical walls offers a mesmerizing sound-and-slide experience. Enter a darkened world filled with floor-to-ceiling images and booming music. Wander through a complex of cathedral-like aisles, transepts, and choirs (no seating provided) as you experience the spectacle. There's no storyline to follow, but information panels by the café give some background. The show lasts 40 minutes and runs continuously. If you'd like an intermission, you can exit the "show" into a part of the quarry that opens to the sky and take a break at the café before re-entering. Dress warmly, as the cave is cool.

Cost and Hours: €11, €16 Pass Provence combo-ticket with Les Baux castle ruins and Yves Brayer Museum, daily 9:30-19:30, March and Oct-Dec 10:00-18:00, closed Jan-Feb, tel. 04 90 54 47 37, www.carrieres-lumieres.com.

Les Baux Views and St-Rémy Loop Trip

A half-mile beyond Les Baux, D-27 (toward Maillane) leads to dramatic views of the hill town. There are pullouts with great vistas, and cavernous caves in former limestone quarries dating back to the Middle Ages. (The limestone is easy to cut, but gets hard and nicely polished when exposed to the weather.) In 1821, the rocks and soil of this area were found to contain an important mineral for making aluminum. It was named after the town: bauxite.

For sensational views over Les Baux, continue up D-27 to the top, turn right on the paved road (at the red *Al.110* sign), and find a pullout among the rocks. You'll see walking trails nearby (ask at TIs for info on hikes in the Alpilles; Les Baux to St-Rémy is a 2.5-hour hike).

D-27 continues to St-Rémy, allowing for a handy loop trip (to complete the loop, return from St-Rémy to Les Baux via D-5). For details, see "Getting to St-Rémy" on page 83.

BETWEEN LES BAUX AND ARLES

The following stops are worthwhile for drivers.

Abbey of Montmajour

This brooding hulk of a ruin, just a few minutes' drive from Arles toward Les Baux, was once a thriving abbey and a convenient papal retreat (c. A.D. 950). Today, the vacant abbey church is a massive example of Romanesque architecture that comes with great views from its tower. Film buffs will appreciate this sight as the setting for *The Lion in Winter*, where Eleanor of Aquitaine (played by Katharine Hepburn) battled with her husband, Henry II (Peter O'Toole). For more on abbeys, see the sidebar on page 206.

The surrounding fields were a favorite of Van Gogh, who walked here from Arles to paint his famous wheat fields.

Cost and Hours: €6, closed Mon Nov-March, tel. 04 90 54 64 17.

▲Roman Aqueduct of Barbegal

To be all alone with evocative Roman ruins, drivers can take a quick detour to the crumbled arches of ancient Arles' principal aqueduct.

The aqueduct *(L'Aqueduc Romain)* is a few minutes south of Fontvieille on the D-82 (well signed off the D-17 to Arles). Park at the dirt pullout (just after the *Los Pozos Blancos* sign, where the ruins of the aqueduct cross the road).

From the parking area, follow the dirt path through the olive grove and along the aqueduct ruins for 200 yards. Approaching the bluff with the grand view, you'll see that the water canal is split into two troughs: One takes a 90-degree right turn and heads for Arles; the other goes straight to the bluff and over, where it once sent water cascading down to power eight grinding mills. Romans grew wheat on the vast fields you see from here, then brought it down to the mega-watermill of Barbegal. Historians figure that this mill produced enough flour each day to feed 12,000 hungry Romans. If you saw the model of this eight-tiered mill in Arles' Ancient History Museum, the milling is easy to visualize—making a visit here quite an exciting experience.

Returning to your car, find the broken bit of aqueduct—it's positioned like a children's playground slide—and take a look at the waterproofing mortar that lined all Roman aqueducts.

Sleeping in and near Les Baux

IN LES BAUX

$$ Le Mas d'Aigret*** is a 10-minute walk east of Les Baux on the road to St-Rémy (D-27). From this refuge, you can stare up at the castle walls rising beyond the heated swimming pool, or enjoy valley views from the groomed terraces. The rooms are simple and slightly worn (breakfast extra, convenient half-pension dinner and breakfast option, air-con, rooms have some daytime road noise, tel.

04 90 54 20 00, www.masdaigret. com, contact@masdaigret.com, Dutch Marieke and French Eric are wonderful hosts).

$ Hostellerie de la Reine Jeanne** is just inside the gate to Les Baux, across from the TI. The young owners rent four good-value rooms above their busy restaurant (family rooms, air-con, for view deck ask for *chambre avec terrasse*, tel. 04 90 54 32 06, www.la-reinejeanne.com, marc.braglia@wanadoo.fr).

IN MAUSSANE

The untouristed village of Maussane lies a few minutes' drive south of Les Baux (15 minutes from Arles). It has a few hotels, a handful of restaurants, and a smattering of shops that revolve around its inviting café-lined square. If St-Rémy feels too busy, sleep here. There's also a small TI (tel. 04 90 54 33 60, www.maussane.com). These two accommodations are worth considering.

$ Hôtel les Magnanarelles,** in the center of Maussane, gives solid two-star value in its 18 tastefully designed rooms above a handsome restaurant and swimming pool (ask for room off the street, no air-con, 104 Avenue de la Vallée des Baux, tel. 04 90 54 30 25, www.logishotels.com, hotel.magnanarelles@wanadoo.fr).

$ Le Mas de l'Esparou *chambres d'hôte* is welcoming and kid-friendly, with four simple-yet-spacious rooms, a big swimming pool, table tennis, swings, and distant views of Les Baux. Jacqueline loves her job, and her lack of English only makes her more animated. She dislikes email though, so you'll have to call (cash only, no air-con, between Les Baux and Maussane on D-5, look for white sign with green lettering, close to the *gendarmerie*, tel. 04 90 54 41 32).

Eating in and near Les Baux

You'll find quiet cafés with views as you follow my walking directions through Les Baux's lower town.

The recommended **$ Hostellerie de la Reine Jeanne** offers friendly service and good-value meals indoors or out (open daily).

In nearby Maussane, you'll find several worthwhile places. **Place de la Fontaine,** the town's central square, makes a good stop for café fare. **$ Pizza Brun** has tasty wood-fired pizza to take out or eat in with fun seating indoors and out (1 Rue Edouard Foscalina; with your back to Place de la Fontaine, walk to the right for about 10 minutes and look for colored tables in an alleyway; tel. 04 90 54 40 73).

NEAR ARLES

St-Rémy-de-Provence

Sophisticated and sassy, St-Rémy (sahn ray-mee) gave birth to Nostradamus and cared for a distraught artist. Today, it caters to shoppers and Van Gogh fans. A few minutes from the town center, you can visit the once-thriving Roman city called Glanum and the psychiatric ward where Vincent van Gogh was sent after lopping off his earlobe. Best of all is the chance to elbow your way through St-Rémy's raucous Wednesday market (until 12:30). A ring road hems in a fun-filled pedestrian-friendly center that's fully loaded with fine foods, beauticians, art galleries, and the latest Provençal fashions.

Popular St-Rémy offers good hotel options and makes a fine base for day trips to Arles, Avignon, Les Baux, and the Luberon.

GETTING TO ST-REMY-DE-PROVENCE

By Car: From Les Baux, St-Rémy is a spectacular 15-minute drive over the hills and through the woods. Roads D-5 and D-27 each provide scenic routes between these towns, making a loop drive between them worthwhile. The most scenic approach is on D-27; from Les Baux, take the road toward Maillane that passes the Carrière des Lumières. Take advantage of the many good pullouts and get out of your car for the view.

Parking in St-Rémy is tricky; it's easiest at the pay lot by the TI. You can park for free but less centrally in several other lots (see map page 85).

By Bus: It's one hour from Arles via **bus #54** (5/day Mon-Fri, 3/day Sat, none on Sun) or **bus #57** (6/day, daily July-Aug, Sat-Sun only in May-June and Sept, none Oct-April) and 45 minutes from Avignon via bus #57 (10/day Mon-Sat, 6/day Sun). If arriving in St-Rémy by bus, get off on the ring road at the République stop and continue uphill. The TI is a block up Avenue Durand Maillane (to the right).

By Taxi: From Les Baux, allow €20 one-way; from Avignon, count on €40 (mobile 06 14 81 34 85 or 06 25 17 00 73). St-Rémy's four taxis park on Place de la République, next to the bus stop, but it's best to have the TI call for you.

By Bike: Sun-e-Bike rents electric bikes in St-Rémy (€38/day, short walk from town center at 2 Rue Camille Pelletan—see map on page 85 for location, tel. 04 32 62 08 39, www.sun-e-bike.com).

Orientation to St-Rémy-de-Provence

From St-Rémy's circular center, it's a 15-minute walk along a busy road with no sidewalk to Glanum and the St. Paul Monastery (Van Gogh's psychiatric hospital).

St-Remy's Wednesday market swallows Place de République with clothing, fabric, and bric-a-brac, and spreads along the town's traffic-free lanes selling anything Provençal. You'll find produce on picturesque Place Pelisser (by City Hall). The market wraps up by about 12:30.

Each year during the last week of September, St-Rémy celebrates *les fêtes votives*, a tradition in the Camargue region honoring the town's patron saint. The carnival-like festivities include bull-fights, parades, and *boules* competitions.

Tourist Information: The TI is two blocks toward Les Baux from the ring road (Mon-Sat 9:00-12:30 & 14:00-18:30, Sun 10:00-12:30, free Wi-Fi, tel. 04 90 92 05 22, www.saintremy-de-provence.com). Pick up bus schedules, hiking trail maps, and a town map that includes Van Gogh's favorite painting locations (the *Starry Night* panel is just outside the TI).

NEAR ARLES

Sights in St-Rémy-de-Provence

St-Rémy's key sights—the ruins at Glanum and the hospital where Vincent van Gogh was treated—are an unappealing 15-minute walk south of the TI. If you're driving, you can park for free at the St. Paul Monastery (coming from Les Baux, it's the first right after passing Glanum) and walk a few minutes on a footpath to Glanum from there (or pay €3 to park at the Glanum site; leave nothing of value in your car).

▲St. Paul Monastery and Hospital
(Le Monastère St. Paul de Mausole)

The still-functioning psychiatric hospital (Clinique St. Paul) that treated Vincent van Gogh from 1889 to 1890 is a popular pilgrimage for Van Gogh fans. Here you'll enter Vincent's temporarily peaceful world: a small chapel, intimate cloisters, a re-creation of his room, and a small lavender field with several large displays featuring copies of his paintings. Inside, read the thoughtful English explanations about Vincent's tortured life. Amazingly, in his 53 weeks here he completed 143 paintings and more than 100 drawings. The contrast between the utter simplicity of his room (and his life) and the multimillion-dollar value of his paintings today is jarring.

"I wanted you to know that I think I've done well to come here, first, in seeing the reality of life for the diverse mad or crazy

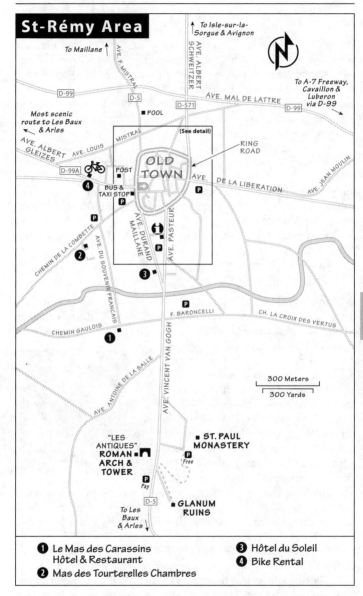

St-Rémy Area

To Maillane ↑

To Isle-sur-la-Sorgue & Avignon ↑

To A-7 Freeway, Cavaillon & Luberon via D-99

Most scenic route to Les Baux & Arles ←

■ POOL

(See detail)

RING ROAD

OLD TOWN

POST

BUS & TAXI STOP

❹ Bike Rental

AVE. MAL DE LATTRE

AVE. DE LA LIBERATION

AVE. JEAN MOULIN

AVE. ALBERT SCHWEITZER

AVE. F. MISTRAL

MISTRAL

AVE. ALBERT GLEIZES

AVE. LOUIS

CHEMIN DE LA COMBETTE

AVE. DU SOUVENIR FRANCAIS

AVE. DURAND MAILLANE

AVE. PASTEUR

❷

CHEMIN GAULOIS

❶

F. BARONCELLI

CH. LA CROIX DES VERTUS

AVE. ANTOINE DE LA SALLE

AVE. VINCENT VAN GOGH

❸

300 Meters

300 Yards

"LES ANTIQUES" ROMAN ■ ARCH & TOWER

■ ST. PAUL MONASTERY

Free

Pay

■ GLANUM RUINS

To Les Baux & Arles ↓

D-5

NEAR ARLES

❶ Le Mas des Carassins Hôtel & Restaurant
❷ Mas des Tourterelles Chambres
❸ Hôtel du Soleil
❹ Bike Rental

people in this menagerie, I'm losing the vague dread, the fear of the thing. And little by little I can consider my madness as being an illness like any other. And the change of surroundings is doing me good, I imagine. The idea of the duty to work comes back to me a lot."

—Vincent van Gogh's letter to brother Theo, May 9, 1889

In the spring of 1890, Vincent left St-Rémy and traveled to Auvers-sur-Oise near Paris to enter the care of Dr. Paul Gachet, whom he hoped could help stabilize his mental condition. Gachet advised the artist to throw himself into his work as a remedy for his illness, which he did—Vincent spent the last 70 days of his life knocking out a painting a day. On July 27, 1890, Vincent wandered into the famous Auvers wheat field and shot himself, dying of his injuries two days later.

In and around the complex, you'll see copies of Vincent's works—some located right where he painted them. The TI has a map with a list of the reproductions and where to find them. Stand among flame-like cypress trees, gaze over the distant skyline of St-Rémy, and realize you're in the midst of Van Gogh's most famous work, *The Starry Night*.

For more on Vincent van Gogh's time in this region, see the "Arles" chapter.

Cost and Hours: €5, daily 9:30-19:00, Oct-March 10:15-17:00, tel. 04 90 92 77 00.

▲Glanum Ruins

These crumbling stones are the foundations of a Roman market town, located at the crossroads of two ancient trade routes between Italy and Spain. A stubby Roman arch and tall tower stand across the road from the site as proud reminders of the town's glory days. These lonely monuments marked the entry to Glanum 2,000 years ago. The plump triumphal arch, now missing its upper level, was designed to impress visitors with scenes of Rome's power—and by association, Glanum's prestige.

The three-level tower was built as a mausoleum by one of Glanum's most distinguished families. The battle scene relief on the lowest level is dripping with intensity: The Romans were not just good builders, but skilled artists as well.

Cost and Hours: €8; daily 9:30-18:30; Oct-March Tue-Sun 10:00-17:00, closed Mon; parking-€3/day, tel. 04 90 92 23 79.

Visiting the Ruins: Start with the helpful little museum at the entrance, which offers good English explanations of key buildings and the excavation process, as well as a helpful model of Glanum in its prime. The free English handout and information panels scattered about the site provide more context to the ruins you'll see. Serious students of ancient Rome will want to spring for the well-done *Itineraries* book (€7).

While the ruins are, well...ruined, their setting at the base of the rocky Alpilles is splendid. It's also unshaded and can be very hot (making it easier to enjoy early or late).

The Roman site was founded in 27 B.C. and occupied for about 30 years. About 2,500 people lived in Glanum at its zenith (the Roman city was about seven times bigger than the ruins you see today). And though this was an important town, with grand villas, temples, a basilica, a forum, a wooden dam, and aqueducts, it was not important enough to justify an arena or a theater (such as those in Arles, Nîmes, and Orange). Locals had to charter buses to reach events in those cities.

Stroll up Glanum's main street and see remains of a market hall, a forum, thermal baths, reservoirs, and more. The view from the belvedere justifies the effort. These ruins highlight the range and prosperity of the Roman Empire. Taken together with other Roman monuments in Provence, they paint a more complete picture of Roman life. For more on Roman history, see page 27.

Sleeping in St-Rémy-de-Provence

Unless otherwise noted, the following hotels have easy parking and air-conditioning.

$$$$ Le Mas des Carassins,*** a 15-minute walk from the center, is well-run by Michel and Pierre. Luxury is affordable here, with two generously sized pools, ample outdoor lounging spaces, big gardens, and everything just so. The 22 rooms are split between the more traditional main building and the newer annex, which comes with larger rooms and more modern decor (American-style breakfast, table tennis, 1 Chemin Gaulois, tel. 04 90 92 15 48, www.masdescarassins.com, info@masdescarassins.com).

$$ Mas des Tourterelles Chambres, a Provençal farmhouse in a pleasant neighborhood, is a 10-minute walk from the town center. It has six sharp rooms and an apartment, pool, and small garden with outdoor picnic facilities including a fridge, glasses, and plates (2-night minimum, air-con in top-floor rooms—others don't need it, 21 Chemin de la Combette, tel. 09 54 64 83 30 or 06 15 87 24 55, www.masdestourterelles.com, contact@masdestourterelles.com). Turn right at the top of Place de la République onto Chemin de la Combette; after 400 yards look for the brown sign down a lane on the left (just after the second speed bump).

$$ Hôtel du Soleil,** a quick walk from St-Rémy's center, is a sharp hotel, with fresh white stone and beige decor throughout. Its spotless rooms cluster around a courtyard and pool (5 rooms have small terraces, 2-room apartment, easy parking, a block above the TI at 35 Avenue Pasteur, tel. 04 90 92 00 63, www.hotelsoleil.com, info@hotelsoleil.com).

Food Lovers' Guide to St-Rémy

Wednesday is market day in St-Rémy, but you don't have to fast until then. Foodies will appreciate these shops clustered around the ring road in St-Rémy, near the turnoff to Les Baux.

L'Epicerie Calanquet, in the same family for five generations, is where locals buy olive oil. The shop encourages you to sample olives, tapenades, and jams (daily, in the town center at 8 Rue de la Commune).

Le Petit Duc offers a remarkable introduction to traditional cookies (daily, 7 Boulevard Victor Hugo, tel. 04 90 92 08 31).

Just one whiff from **Joel Durand Chocolates** will lure chocoholics inside. Ask for a sample and learn the letter-coded system. The lavender is surprisingly good (daily, a few doors down from Le Petit Duc at 3 Boulevard Victor Hugo, tel. 04 90 92 38 25).

$ Sommeil des Fées Chambres rents five simple, fairly priced rooms in the center of St-Rémy (air con, 4 Rue du 8 Mai, tel. 04 90 92 17 66, www.angesetfees-stremy.com).

Eating in St-Rémy-de-Provence

The town is packed with restaurants, each trying to outdo the other. Join the evening strollers and compare.

$$$ Le Mas des Carassins offers a four-course food experience worth booking ahead. One *menu* is prepared each night and served in a country-classy setting inside or out. Service is friendly, kids are welcome, and the cuisine is utterly delicious. Review their website to see what's cooking before booking a table (see listing under "Sleeping in St-Rémy," earlier).

$ Crêperie Lou Planet, on pleasant Place Favier, is cheap and peaceful, with outdoor seating in summer, tasty crêpes, good salads, and inexpensive, fine house wine. Say *bonjour* to owner Jean, who has been here for decades and still hasn't changed the menu (daily April-Sept 12:00-22:00, behind Hôtel de Ville at Place Favier, next to Musée des Alpilles).

$$ Bar-Tabac des Alpilles, popular with locals, has an old-school-meets-new-world feel, with wine barrels, wood tables, and modern art on the walls. The menu offers just enough choice, in-

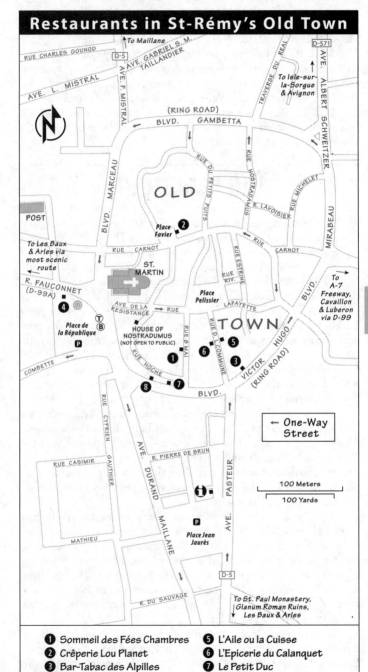

Restaurants in St-Rémy's Old Town

RUE CHARLES GOUNOD · D-5 · AVE. GABRIEL S. M. TAILLANDIER · D-571 · AVE. ALBERT SCHWEITZER

AVE. L. MISTRAL

To Maillane

AVE. F. MISTRAL

(RING ROAD)

BLVD. GAMBETTA

Traverse du Réal

To Isle-sur-la-Sorgue & Avignon

OLD

RUE DU PETIT PUITS

RUE NOSTRADAMUS

R. LAVOISIER

RUE MICHELET

MIRABEAU

BLVD. MARCEAU

POST

To Les Baux & Arles via most scenic route

Place Favier ❷

RUE CARNOT

CARNOT

ST. MARTIN

Place Pelissier

RUE RIV.

RUE ESTRINE

RUE LAFAYETTE

BLVD. HUGO VICTOR (RING ROAD)

To A-7 Freeway, Cavaillon & Luberon via D-99

R. FAUCONNET (D-99A)

❹

Place de la République

Ⓣ Ⓑ

Ⓟ

COMBETTE

AVE. DE LA RESISTANCE

RUE

HOUSE OF NOSTRADUMUS (NOT OPEN TO PUBLIC)

RUE & MAI

RUE D. COMMUNE

TOWN

❶ ❻ ❺ ❸

RUE HOCHE

❽ ❼

BLVD.

← One-Way Street

RUE CYPRIEN

RUE GAUTHIER

AVE. DURAND

R. PIERRE DE BRUN

AVE. PASTEUR

ℹ

100 Meters

100 Yards

RUE CASIMIR

Ⓟ

Place Jean Jaurès

MATHIEU

MAILLANE

D-5

R. DU SAUVAGE

To St. Paul Monastery, Glanum Roman Ruins, Les Baux & Arles

❶ Sommeil des Fées Chambres
❷ Crêperie Lou Planet
❸ Bar-Tabac des Alpilles
❹ Café de la Place
❺ L'Aile ou la Cuisse
❻ L'Epicerie du Calanquet
❼ Le Petit Duc
❽ Joel Durand Chocolates

NEAR ARLES

cluding salads and a fairly priced *menu* (daily, 21 Boulevard Victor Hugo, tel. 04 90 92 02 17).

$$ Café de la Place, on Place de la République behind the parking lot, is a hit with St-Rémy's young people (as well as aging travel writers). Come for a coffee, a drink, or a good meal of basic café fare (big *terrasse,* free Wi-Fi, open daily, tel. 04 90 92 02 13).

$$$ L'Aile ou la Cuisse is St-Rémy's vintage bistro, with a warm, classy interior and traditional cuisine (daily, 5 Rue de la Commune, tel. 04 32 62 00 25).

The Camargue

The Camargue region, occupying the vast delta of the Rhône River, is one of Europe's most important wetlands. This marshy area exists where the Rhône splits into two branches (big and little), just before it flows into the Mediterranean. Over the millennia, a steady flow of sediment has been deposited at the mouth of the rivers—thoroughly land-locking villages that once faced the sea.

Since World War II, farmers have converted large northern tracts of the Camargue to rice fields, making the delta a major producer of France's rice. Salt is the other key industry in the Camargue: You can see vast salt marshes and evaporation beds around the town of Salin de Giraud. Because the salt marshes were long considered useless, the land has remained relatively untouched, leaving it a popular nature destination today.

Today the Camargue Regional Nature Park is a protected "wild" area, where pink flamingos, wild bulls, nasty boars, nastier mosquitoes (in every season but winter—come prepared), and the famous white horses wander freely through lagoons and tall grass. The dark bulls are harder to spot than the white horses and flamingos, so go slow and make use of the viewing platforms. For more on these animals, see the sidebar.

The Camargue's subtle wetlands beauty makes it a worthwhile joyride for naturalists. The Everglades-like scenery is a birder's paradise, and occasional bulls and wild horses add to the enjoyment. But for avid city sightseers, this can feel like a big swamp—interesting to drive through, but where's the excitement? The best time to visit is in spring, when the flamingos are out in full force; the worst time to visit is in summer, when birds are fewest and the mosquitoes are most abundant.

If you have children, a picnic on the long sandy beach at Plage d'Arles may be just what the doctor ordered. Also called Plage de Piemanço, this public beach is six miles (10 kilometers) after Salin

The Wildlife of the Camargue

In this nature reserve, amusing flamingos and countless other bird species flourish—attracting birdwatchers from all over the world. Once an endangered species, the flamingos flock here because of all that salt—which is why they come to the Camargue rather than to, say, the sandy beaches of the Riviera. Ten thousand flamingos leave here each fall, heading to warmer climates, and then return in March to pink up the Camargue (a visit here in the spring reaps big, pink rewards). To see a formation of these long, clumsy-looking birds in flight is an experience you won't soon forget.

The black bulls are raised for bullfights (by local cowboys called *gardians*) and eventually end up on plates in Arles' restaurants (you may have met one already). The *gardians,* who have patrolled the Camargue on local horses for centuries, give the area a Wild West aura. The region's unique small horses—born brown or black, later turning light gray or white—are one of the oldest breeds in the world, and may have existed in the area since prehistoric times.

With the continual loss of wetlands throughout the world, it's critical that places like this remain preserved and that we understand their significance.

de Giraud (see map on page 74). Bring everything you might need, as there are no vendors.

GETTING TO THE CAMARGUE

If you don't have a car, there are several ways to experience the Camargue: horseback, mountain bikes, and jeep safaris. All three options are available in Stes-Maries-de-la-Mer, and jeep safaris are also offered from Arles (ask at TI). Hiking is not good in the Camargue, as there are few decent trails. The best biking is across the Digue (dike) to Phare de la Gacholle.

By Scenic Drive: There are two primary driving routes from Arles through the Camargue: to Stes-Maries-de-la-Mer, and toward Salin de Giraud.

My favorite route is toward **Salin de Giraud** (see map on page 74): Leave Arles driving clockwise on its ring road, then find signs to *Stes-Maries-de-la-Mer* and join D-570. Skip the D-36 turnoff to Salin de Giraud (you'll return along this route). After about 3.5 miles (6 kilometers), enthusiasts can consider a stop at the **Camargue Museum** (described later). Next, continue along D-570 past swampy rice fields, then turn left on D-37 and follow it as it skirts the Etang de Vaccarès lagoon. The lagoon is off-limits, but this area has opportunities to get out of the car for views and to smell the marshes (look for viewing stands, but any dirt turnoff works). Turn right off D-37 onto the tiny road at Villeneuve, following signs for C-134 to *La Capelière* and *La Fiélouse* (poorly marked—it's where D-36b leads back to Arles).

Make time for a stop at **La Capelière** (headquarters for Camargue sightseers), where you can pick up a good map, ask the staff questions, and enjoy a small exhibit (€3, handheld English explanations) and one-mile walking trail with some English information on the Camargue (daily 9:00-13:00 & 14:00-18:00, Oct-March until 17:00). Birders can check the register to see what birds have been spotted recently (observations in English are in red), and can buy the Camargue booklet in English.

The best part of this drive (particularly in spring) is the next stretch to and around **La Digue de la Mer,** about six scenic miles past La Capelière, where you're most likely to witness the memorable sight of platoons of flamingos in flight. At La Digue de la Mer, get out of your car and walk a few hundred yards past the pavement's end, where the dirt road curves left, to reach a good spot. This is a critical reproduction area for flamingos (about 13,000 couples produce 5,000 offspring annually). If you rented a mountain bike, now would be the right time to use it: It's about eight bumpy but engaging miles between water and sand dunes to Stes-Maries-de-la-Mer.

From here, most will want to retrace their route back to Villeneuve, then continue straight onto D-36b, which leads back to Arles.

By Bus: Buses serve the Camargue (stopping at Camarguais Museum and Stes-Maries-de-la-Mer) from Arles' bus or train station (bus #20, 6/day Mon-Sat, 3/day Sun, 1 hour, tel. 08 10 00 13 26, www.lepilote.com).

Sights and Towns in the Camargue

Camargue Museum (Musée de la Camargue)

Located in a traditional Camargue barn on the road to Stes-Maries-de-la-Mer, this well-designed folk museum does a good job of describing the natural features and cultural traditions of the Camargue. The costumes, tools, and helpful exhibits come with some English explanations (look for handouts and small screens). A two-mile nature trail, picnic tables, and a WC round out the amenities.

Cost and Hours: €5; daily 9:00-12:30 & 13:00-18:00, Oct-March Wed-Mon 10:00-12:30 & 13:00-17:00, English handout; 8 miles from Arles on D-570 toward Stes-Maries-de-la-Mer, at Mas du Pont de Rousty farmhouse; tel. 04 90 97 10 82, www.parc-camargue.fr.

Stes-Maries-de-la-Mer

At the western end of the Camargue lies this whitewashed, Spanish-feeling seafront town with acres of flamingos, bulls, and horses at its doorstep. From the bus stop, walk to the church (10 minutes) to get oriented. The place is so popular that it's best avoided on weekends and during holidays. It's a French Coney Island—a trinket-selling, perennially windy place.

The town is also famous as a mecca for the Roma (Gypsies). Every May, Roma from all over Europe pile in their caravans and migrate to Stes-Maries-de-la-Mer to venerate the town's statue of Saint Sarah. Legend has it that Mary Magdalene made landfall here in a boat with no oars after an epic journey across the Mediterranean from Egypt. Fleeing persecution for practicing the new and unpopular Christian faith, she was accompanied by two other "Stes-Maries": Mary of Clopas, the mother of the apostle James the Less, and Mary Salome, the mother of the apostles James the Great and John. Also in the boat was "Black Sarah," an Egyptian servant. Sarah collected alms for the poor; over time, her request for handouts became associated with the Roma people, who embrace her as their patron saint (the name Gypsy comes from the label Europeans gave those who came across from Egypt—*Gyptians*). Today's impressive spectacle to honor Sarah is like a sprawling flea market spilling out from the town for two weeks.

Tourist Information: Stes-Maries-de-la-Mer's TI is located along its waterfront promenade (daily 9:00-19:00, until 20:00 in summer, Oct-March until 17:00, 5 Avenue Van Gogh, tel. 04 90 97 82 55, www.saintesmaries.com).

Sights and Activities: Outside of May, the town of Stes-Maries-de-la-Mer has little to offer except its beachfront promenade, bullring, and towering five-belled fortified church. The **church** interior is worth a look for its unusual decorations and artifacts, including the statue of Saint Sarah (€3 to climb to roof for Camargue and sea views). Avoid the women with flowers and the assertive palm readers, who often cluster near the church.

Most tourists come to take a horse, a jeep, or a bike into the Camargue—and there's no lack of outfits ready to take you for a ride. The TIs in Arles and Stes-Maries-de-la-Mer have long lists. Rental **bikes** (for the ride out to La Digue de la Mer) and advice on the best routes are available at Le Vélo Saintois (€18/day, 19 Rue de la République in Stes-Maries-de-la-Mer, tel. 04 90 97 74 56, www.levelosaintois.camargue.fr). Jerry Perkins offers **Jeep excursions** at Nature et Découverte (2-hour trips from €40, pickup in Stes-Maries-de-la-Mer, tel. 06 12 44 64 74, www.visite-camargue.com). Les Cabanes de Cacharel gives **horseback tours** (€20 one-hour ride, Route de Cacharel near Stes-Maries-de-la-Mer, tel. 04 90 97 84 10, www.cabanesdecacharel.com, info@camargueacheval.com).

NEAR ARLES

Aigues-Mortes

This strange walled city, on the western edge of the Camargue (20 miles from Nîmes), was built by Louis IX as a jumping-off point for his Crusades to the Holy Land. Although Aigues-Mortes was a strategically situated royal port city, it was actually never near the sea—ships reached it via canals that were dug through an immense lagoon. Today its tall towers and thick fortifications seem oddly out of place, surrounded by nothing but salt marshes and flamingos. The name "Aigues-Mortes" means "Dead Waters," which says it all. Skip it unless you need more souvenirs and crowded streets, although drivers going between Nîmes and Arles can detour to Aigues-Mortes for a quick-and-easy taste of the Camargue. Aigues-Mortes and Nîmes are linked by buses (6/day, 50 minutes) and trains (6/day, 45 minutes).

NEAR ARLES

AVIGNON

Famous for its nursery rhyme, medieval bridge, and brooding Palace of the Popes, contemporary Avignon (ah-veen-yohn) bustles and prospers behind its mighty walls. For nearly 100 years (1309-1403) Avignon was the capital of Christendom, home to seven popes. (And, for a difficult period after that—during the Great Schism when there were two competing popes—Avignon was "the other Rome.") During this time, it grew from a quiet village into a thriving city. Today, with its large student population and fashionable shops, Avignon is an intriguing blend of medieval history, youthful energy, and urban sophistication. Street performers entertain the international throngs who fill Avignon's ubiquitous cafés and trendy boutiques. And each July the city goes crazy during its huge theater festival (with about 2,000 performances, big crowds, higher prices, and hotels booked up long in advance). Clean, lively, and popular with tourists, Avignon is more impressive for its outdoor ambience than for its museums and monuments.

Orientation to Avignon

Cours Jean Jaurès, which turns into Rue de la République, runs straight from the Centre-Ville train station to Place de l'Horloge and the Palace of the Popes, splitting Avignon in two. The larger eastern half is where the action is. Climb to the Jardin du Rochers des Doms for the town's best view, tour the pope's immense palace, lose yourself in Avignon's back streets (following my "Discovering Avignon's Back Streets" self-guided walk), and find a shady square to call home.

TOURIST INFORMATION

The TI is located on the main street linking the Centre-Ville train station to the old town (Mon-Sat 9:00-18:00 except Sat until 17:00 Nov-March, Sun 10:00-17:00 except until 12:00 Nov-March, daily until 19:00 in July, free Wi-Fi, 41 Cours Jean Jaurès, tel. 04 32 74 32 74, www.avignon-tourisme.com).

At the TI, pick up the free **Avignon Passion Pass** (for up to five family members, includes map and short guidebook). Have it stamped at the first sight you visit to receive discounts at others—for example, €2 off at the Palace of the Popes and a €3 discount at the Petit Palais. The TI also offers several good (but tricky to follow) walking tours and bike maps for good rides in the area, including the Ile de la Barthelasse.

ARRIVAL IN AVIGNON
By Train

Avignon has two train stations: Centre-Ville and TGV (linked to downtown by shuttle trains). Some TGV trains stop at Centre-Ville—verify your station in advance.

The **Centre-Ville station** *(Gare Avignon Centre-Ville)* gets all non-TGV trains (and a few TGV trains). To reach the town center, cross the busy street in front of the station and walk through the city walls onto Cours Jean Jaurès. The TI is three blocks down, at #41; baggage storage is close by (see "Helpful Hints," later).

The **TGV station** *(Gare TGV)*, on the outskirts of town, has a summer-only TI (short hours), but no baggage storage (see "Helpful Hints," later, for bag storage). Car rental, buses, and taxis are outside the north exit *(sortie nord)*. To reach the city center, take the **shuttle train** from platform A or B to the Centre-Ville station (€1.60, 2/hour, 5 minutes, buy ticket from machine on platform or at *billeterie* in main hall). A **taxi** ride between the TGV station and downtown Avignon costs about €16.

If you're connecting from the TGV station to other points, you'll find **buses** to Arles' Centre-Ville station at the second bus shelter (€7.20, 9/day, 1 hour, included with rail pass, schedule posted on shelter and available at info booths inside TGV station).

If you're **driving** a rental car directly to St-Rémy-de-Provence, Les Baux, or the Luberon, leave the station following signs to *Avignon Sud*, then *La Rocade*. You'll soon see exits to Arles (best for St-Rémy and Les Baux) and Cavaillon (for Luberon villages). Arles is well signed from the station for drivers.

AVIGNON

By Bus

The efficient bus station *(gare routière)* is 100 yards to the right as you leave the Centre-Ville train station, beyond and below Hôtel Ibis (info desk open Mon-Sat 7:00-19:30, closed Sun, tel. 04 90 82 07 35).

By Car

Drivers entering Avignon follow *Centre-Ville* and *Gare SNCF* (train station) signs. You'll find central pay lots (about €12/half-day, €20/24 hours) in the garage next to the Centre-Ville train station and at the Parking Jean Jaurès under the ramparts across from the station (enter the old city through the Porte St-Michel gate). Hotels have advice for overnight parking, and some offer parking deals.

Two free parking lots have complimentary shuttle buses to the center except on Sunday (follow *P Gratuit* signs): **Parking de l'Ile Piot** is across Daladier Bridge (Pont Daladier) on Ile de la Barthelasse, with shuttles to Place Crillon; **Parking des Italiens** is along the river east of the Palace of the Popes, with shuttles to Place Pie (allow 30 minutes to walk from either to the center). Street parking is €3 for about three hours 9:00-12:00 and 14:00-19:00 (and free 12:00-14:00 and 19:00-9:00). Hint: If you put €3 in the meter anytime between 19:00 and 9:00, you're good until 14:00.

No matter where you park, leave nothing of value in your car.

HELPFUL HINTS

Book Ahead for July: During the July theater festival, rooms are sparse—reserve very early, or stay in Arles or St-Rémy.

Local Help: David at **Imagine Tours,** a nonprofit group whose goal is to promote this region, can help with hotel emergencies and special-event tickets (mobile 06 89 22 19 87, www.imagine-tours.net, imagine.tours@gmail.com). If you don't get an answer, leave a message.

Wi-Fi: The TI has free Wi-Fi, as does the park next door (one hour/day only).

English Bookstore: Try **Camili Books & Tea,** a second-hand bookshop with a refreshing courtyard and hot drinks (Tue-Sat 12:00-19:00, closed Sun-Mon, free Wi-Fi, 155 Rue Carreterie, in Avignon's northeast corner).

Baggage Storage: La Consigne is near the TI (€10/day; June-Aug daily 8:00-21:00; Sept-May Mon-Sat 9:00-18:00, closed Sun; 1 Avenue Marechal de Lattre de Tassigny, may move to train station in the future, tel. 09 82 45 20 24, www.consigne-avignon.fr).

Laundry: At **La Blanchisseuse,** you can drop off your laundry and pick it up the same day (daily 7:00-21:00, a few blocks

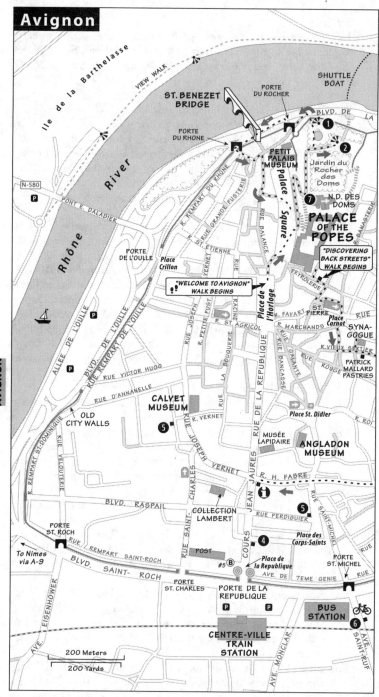

Avignon

AVIGNON

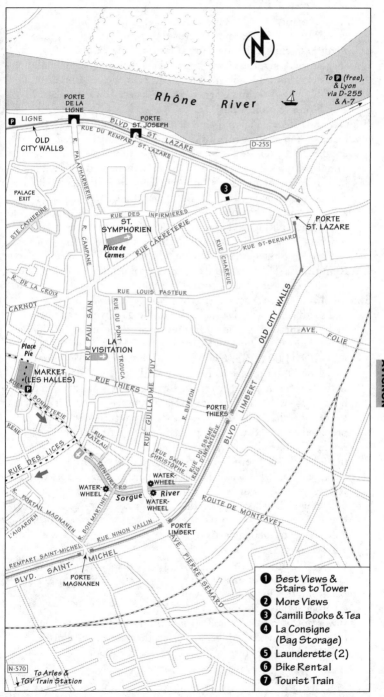

1 Best Views & Stairs to Tower
2 More Views
3 Camili Books & Tea
4 La Consigne (Bag Storage)
5 Launderette (2)
6 Bike Rental
7 Tourist Train

west of main TI at 24 Rue Lanterne, tel. 04 90 85 58 80). The launderette at 66 Place des Corps-Saints, where Rue Agricol Perdiguier ends, is handy to most hotels (daily 7:00-20:00).

Grocery Store: Carrefour City is central and has long hours daily (2 blocks from TI, toward Place de l'Horloge on Rue de la République). A second Carrefour City is near Les Halles at 19 Rue Florence (same hours).

Bike Rental: Rent pedal and electric bikes and scooters near the train station at **Provence Bike** (April-Oct 9:00-18:30, 7 Avenue St. Ruf, tel. 04 90 27 92 61, www.provence-bike.com). You'll enjoy riding on the Ile de la Barthelasse (the TI has bike maps), but biking is better in and around Isle-sur-la-Sorgue (described in the Hill Towns of the Luberon chapter) and Vaison-la-Romaine (consider taking a bike on the train to Bédarrides, biking from there to Châteauneuf-du-Pape and on to Orange, then taking it on the train back to Avignon; see the "Orange and the Côtes du Rhône" chapter).

Car Rental: The TGV station has counters for all the big companies; only Avis is at the Centre-Ville station.

Shuttle Boat: A free shuttle boat, the *Navette Fluviale,* plies back and forth across the river (as it did in the days when the town had no functioning bridge) from near St. Bénezet Bridge (3/hour, daily April-June and Sept 10:00-12:15 & 14:00-18:00, July-Aug 11:00-20:45; Oct-March weekends and Wed afternoons only). It drops you on the peaceful Ile de la Barthelasse, with its recommended riverside restaurant, grassy walks, and bike rides with terrific city views. If you stay on the island for dinner, check the schedule for the last return boat—or be prepared for a taxi ride or a pleasant 25-minute walk back to town.

Commanding City Views: For great views of Avignon and the river, walk or drive across Daladier Bridge, or ferry across the Rhône on the *Navette Fluviale*  (described above). I'd take the boat across the river, walk the view path to Daladier Bridge, and then cross back over the bridge (45-minute walk). You can enjoy other impressive vistas from the top of the Jardin du Rochers des Doms, from the tower in the Palace of the Popes, from the end of the famous, broken St. Bénezet Bridge, and from the entrance to Fort St. André, across the river in Villeneuve-lès-Avignon.

Festival d'Avignon

Avignon hosts a massive theater festival for three weeks each July with more than 1,500 official performances and countless events in the streets. Every possible venue is in action as the event creates a Mardi Gras-like atmosphere. Contemporary theater groups come from throughout Europe. While many performances book up well in advance, many more are available the same day (tickets generally €15-20). The festival is indoors, but venues overflow onto the streets. Organizers need 20 different venues to hold all the performances, from actual theater spaces to small chapels to the inner courtyard of the Palace of the Popes, which seats 800. There's also a "fringe festival," called Avignon-Off, which adds another 100 sites and countless performances, as well as a children's theater festival, with storytellers, dance, musicals, and marionettes. During the festival, the entire city is a stage, with mimes, fire-breathers, singers, and musicians filling the streets. Most performances are in French, but many are in English, and many dance performances don't require language at all (www.festival-avignon.com and www.avignonleoff.com).

Tours in Avignon

Local Guide: Isabelle Magny is a good local guide for the city and region (€160/half-day, €330/full-day, no car, tel. 06 11 82 17 92, isabellemagny@sfr.fr).

Food Tour: The Avignon Gourmet Walking Tour is a wonderful experience if you like to eat. Charming and passionate Aurélie meets small groups daily (except Sun and Mon) at the TI at 9:00 for a well-designed three-hour, eight-stop walk. Her tour is filled with information and tastes of top-quality local foods and drinks, and finishes in the market hall (€59/person, 2-8 people per group, tel. 06 35 32 08 96, www.avignongourmetours.com). Book in advance on her website.

Tourist Train: The little train leaves regularly from in front of the Palace of the Popes and offers a decent overview of the city, including the Jardin du Rochers des Doms and St. Bénezet Bridge (€8, 2/hour, 40 minutes, English commentary, mid-March-Oct daily 10:00-18:00, until 20:00 July-Aug).

Guided Excursions from Avignon: Several minivan tour companies based in Avignon offer transportation to destinations described in this book, including Pont du Gard, the Luberon, and the Camargue (see "Tours in Provence" on page 24).

AVIGNON

Avignon at a Glance

▲▲Scenic Squares Numerous hide-and-seek squares ideal for postcard-writing and people-watching—pick your favorite: Place des Corps-Saints, Place St. Pierre, Place des Châtaignes (adjacent to Place St. Pierre), Place Crillon, Place St. Didier (near the recommended Caveau du Théâtre restaurant), and the big Place Pie (see map on page 98).

▲▲Palace of the Popes Fourteenth-century Gothic palace built by the popes who made Avignon their home. **Hours:** Daily March-Oct 9:00-19:00, July-Aug until 20:00, Nov-Feb 9:30-17:45. See page 106.

▲Jardin du Rochers des Doms Park and ramparts at the hill-top where Avignon was first settled, with great views of the Rhône River Valley and the famous broken bridge. **Hours:** Daily April-May and Sept 7:30-20:00, June-Aug 7:30-21:00, Oct-March 7:30-18:00. See page 104.

▲St. Bénezet Bridge The "Pont d'Avignon" of nursery-rhyme fame, once connecting the pope's territory to France. **Hours:** Daily March-Oct 9:00-19:00, July-Aug until 20:00, Nov-Feb 9:30-17:45. See page 105.

▲Tower of Philip the Fair Massive tower across St. Bénezet Bridge, featuring the best view over Avignon and the Rhône basin. **Hours:** Tue-Sun 10:00-12:30 & 14:00-18:00, Feb-April and Nov 14:00-17:00 only, closed Dec-Jan and Mon year-round. See page 111.

Walks in Avignon

For a fine overview of the city, combine the following two self-guided walks. "Welcome to Avignon" covers the major sights, while "Discovering Avignon's Back Streets" leads you along the lanes less taken, delving beyond the surface of this historic city.

WELCOME TO AVIGNON WALK

Start this ▲▲ tour where the Romans did, on Place de l'Horloge, in front of City Hall (Hôtel de Ville).

Place de l'Horloge

In ancient Roman times this was the forum, and in medieval times it was the market square. The square is named for the clock tower (now hiding behind the more recently built City Hall) that, in its day, was a humanist statement. In medieval France, the only bells in town rang from the church tower to indicate not the hours but the calls to prayer. With the dawn of the modern age, secular clock towers like this rang out the hours as people organized their lives.

Taking humanism a step further, the City Hall (Hôtel de Ville), built after the French Revolution, obstructed the view of the old clock tower while celebrating a new era. The slogan "liberty, equality, and brotherhood" is a reminder that the people supersede the king and the church. And today, judging from the square's jammed cafés and restaurants, it is indeed the people who rule.

The square's present popularity arrived with the trains in 1854. Facing City Hall, look left down the main drag, Rue de la République. When the trains came to Avignon, proud city fathers wanted a direct, impressive way to link the new station to the heart of the city—so they plowed over homes to create Rue de la République and widened Place de l'Horloge. This main drag's Parisian feel is intentional—it was built not in the Provençal manner, but in the Haussmann style that is so dominant in Paris (characterized by broad, straight boulevards lined with stately buildings). Today, this Champs-Elysées of Avignon is lined with department stores and banks.

• *Walk slightly uphill past the neo–Renaissance facade of the theater and the carousel (public WCs behind). Look back to see the late Gothic bell tower. Then veer right at the Palace of the Popes and continue into...*

Palace Square (Place du Palais)

Pull up a concrete stump just past the café. Nicknamed *bites* (slang for penis), these effectively keep cars from double-parking in areas designed for people. Many of the metal ones slide up and down by remote control to let privileged cars come and go.

Now take in the scene. This grand square is lined with the Palace of the Popes, the Petit Palais, and the cathedral. In the 1300s the entire headquarters of the Roman Catholic Church was moved to Avignon. The Church bought Avignon and gave it a complete makeover. Along with clearing out vast spaces like this square and building a three-acre palace, the Church erected more than three miles of protective wall (with 39 towers), "appropriate" housing for cardinals (read: mansions), and residences for its entire bureaucracy. The city was Europe's largest construction zone. Avignon's population grew from 6,000 to 25,000 in short order. (Today, 13,000 people live within the walls.) The limits of pre-papal Avignon are outlined on your city map: Rues Joseph Vernet, Henri Fabre, des Lices, and Philonarde all follow the route of the city's earlier defensive wall (about half the diameter of today's wall).

The imposing facade behind you, across the square from the Palace of the Popes' main entry, was "the papal mint," which served as the finance department for the Holy See. The Petit Palais (Little

Palace) seals the uphill end of the square and was built for a cardinal; today it houses medieval paintings.

Avignon's 12th-century Romanesque cathedral, just to the left of the Palace of the Popes, has been the seat of the local bishop for more than a thousand years. Predating the Church's purchase of Avignon by 200 years, its simplicity reflects Avignon's modest, pre-papal population. The gilded Mary was added in 1854, when the Vatican established the doctrine of her Immaculate Conception.

• *You can visit the massive* **Palace of the Popes** *(described on page 106) now, but it works better to visit that palace at the end of this walk, then continue directly to the "Discovering Avignon's Back Streets" walk.*

Now is a good time to take in the...

Petit Palais Museum (Musée du Petit Palais)

This former cardinal's palace now displays the Church's collection of (mostly) art. You'll find some English information but not a lot of detail. Still, a visit here before going to the Palace of the Popes helps furnish and populate that otherwise barren building. You'll see bits of statues and tombs—an inventory of the destruction of exquisite Church art that was wrought by the French Revolution (which tackled established French society with Taliban-esque fervor). Then you'll see many rooms filled with religious Italian paintings, organized in chronological order from early Gothic to late Renaissance. Room 10 holds two paintings by Botticelli (acquired recently from the Louvre Museum in Paris).

Cost and Hours: €6, discount with Avignon Passion Pass, Wed-Mon 10:00-13:00 & 14:00-18:00, closed Tue, at north end of Palace Square, tel. 04 90 86 44 58, www.petit-palais.org.

• *From Palace Square, head up to the cathedral (enjoy the viewpoint overlooking the square), fill your water bottle just past the gate, ponder the war memorial (World War I and World War II, as well as Algeria 1954-1962), then side-trip 20 yards to the left to pause at a memorial to the 300 Jews deported from here to concentration camps by the Nazis. Now zigzag up the ramps to the top of a rocky hill where Avignon was first settled. Atop the hill is an inviting café and pond in a park—the Jardin du Rocher des Doms. At the far side is a viewpoint high above the river from where you can see Avignon's beloved broken bridge.*

▲Jardin du Rocher des Doms

Enjoy the view from this bluff. On a clear day, the tallest peak you see, with its white limestone cap, is Mont Ventoux ("Windy Mountain"). Below and just to the right, you'll spot free passenger ferries shuttling across the river, and—tucked amidst the trees on the far side of the river—a fun, recommended restaurant, Le Bercail, a local favorite. The island in the river is the Ile de la Barthelasse, a

lush nature preserve where Avignon can breathe. In the distance to the left is the TGV rail bridge.

The Rhône River marked the border of Vatican territory in medieval times. Fort St. André—across the river on the hill—was in the kingdom of France. The fort was built in 1360, shortly after the pope moved to Avignon, to counter the papal incursion into this part of Europe. Avignon's famous bridge was a key border crossing, with towers on either end—one was French, and the other was the pope's. The French one, across the river, is the Tower of Philip the Fair (described later, under "More Sights in Avignon").

Cost and Hours: Free, park gates open daily April-May and Sept 7:30-20:00, June-Aug until 21:00, Oct-March until 18:00.

• *Take the walkway down to the left and find the stairs (closed at dusk) leading down to the tower. You'll catch glimpses of the...*

Ramparts

The only bit of the rampart you can walk on is accessed from St. Bénezet Bridge (pay to enter—see next). Just after the papacy took control of Avignon, the walls were extended to take in the convents and monasteries that had been outside the city. What you see today was partially restored in the 19th century.

• *When you come out of the tower on street level, exit out of the walls, then turn left along the wall to the old bridge. Pass under the bridge to find its entrance shortly after.*

▲St. Bénezet Bridge (Pont St. Bénezet)

This bridge, whose construction and location were inspired by a shepherd's religious vision, is the "Pont d'Avignon" of nursery-

rhyme fame. The ditty (which you've probably been humming all day) dates back to the 15th century: *Sur le Pont d'Avignon, on y danse, on y danse, sur le Pont d'Avignon, on y danse tous en rond* ("On the bridge of Avignon, we will dance, we will dance, on the bridge of Avignon, we will dance all in a circle").

And the bridge was a big deal even outside its kiddie-tune fame. Built between 1171 and 1185, it was strategic—one of only three bridges crossing the mighty Rhône in the Middle Ages, important to pilgrims, merchants, and armies. It was damaged several times by floods and subsequently rebuilt. In 1668 most of it was knocked out for the last time by a disastrous icy flood. The townsfolk decided not to rebuild this time, and for more than a century, Avignon had no bridge across the Rhône. While only four arches survive today, the original bridge was huge: Imagine a 22-arch, 3,000-foot-long bridge extending from Vatican territory across the island to the lonely Tower of Philip the Fair, which marked the beginning of France (see displays of the bridge's original length).

Cost and Hours: €5, includes audioguide, €14.50 combo-ticket includes Palace of the Popes, daily March-Oct 9:00-19:00, July-Aug until 20:00, Nov-Feb 9:30-17:45, last entry one hour before closing, tel. 04 90 27 51 16.

Useful App: Download the free "Avignon 3D" app before your visit to see what the bridge looked like in the 14th and 17th centuries (the bright Provençal sun makes it difficult to use the app on the bridge, so skip the €2 tablet).

Visiting the Bridge: The ticket booth is housed in what was a medieval hospital for the poor (funded by bridge tolls). Admission includes a small room that displays a 3-D reconstruction of the bridge and your only chance to walk a bit of the ramparts (enter both from the tower). A Romanesque chapel on the bridge is dedicated to St. Bénezet. Though there's not much to see on the bridge, the audioguide included with your ticket tells a good enough story. It's also fun to be in the breezy middle of the river with a sweeping city view.

• *To get to the Palace of the Popes from here, leave via the riverfront exit, turn left, then turn left again back into the walls. Walk to the end of the short street, then turn right following signs to* Palais des Papes. *Next, look for brown signs leading left under the passageway, then stay the course up the narrow steps to Palace Square.*

▲▲Palace of the Popes (Palais des Papes)

In 1309 a French pope was elected (Pope Clément V). His Holiness decided that dangerous Italy was no place for a pope, so he moved the whole operation to Avignon for a secure rule under a supportive French king. The Catholic Church literally bought Avignon (then a two-bit town) and built the Palace of the Popes, where the popes resided until 1403. Meanwhile, Italians demanded a Roman pope, so from 1378 on, there were twin popes—one in Rome and one in Avignon—causing a schism in the Catholic Church that wasn't fully resolved until 1417.

Cost and Hours: €12, includes multimedia Histopad; €14.50 combo-ticket includes St. Bénezet Bridge, discount with Avignon Passion Pass, daily March-Oct 9:00-19:00, July-Aug until 20:00, Nov-Feb 9:30-17:45, last entry one hour before closing; tel. 04 90 27 50 00, www.palais-des-papes.com.

Visiting the Palace: Visitors follow a one-way route. A big room near the start functions as "the museum," with artifacts (such as cool 14th-century arrowheads) and a good intro video.

The palace was built stark and strong, before the popes knew how long they'd be staying (and before the affluence and fanciness of the Renaissance and Baroque ages). This was the most fortified palace of the time (remember, the pope left Rome to be more secure). With 10-foot-thick walls, it was a symbol of power. There are huge ceremonial rooms (rarely used) and more intimate living quarters. The bedroom comes with the original wall paintings, a decorated wooden ceiling, and a fine tiled floor. And there's one big "chapel" (twice the size of the adjacent cathedral), which, while simple, is majestic in its pure French Gothic lines.

This largest surviving Gothic palace in Europe was built to accommodate 500 people as the administrative center of the Holy See and home of the pope. Seven popes ruled from here, making this the center of Christianity for nearly 100 years. The last pope checked out in 1403, but the Church owned Avignon until the French Revolution in 1791. During this interim period, the palace still housed Church authorities. Avignon residents, many of whom had come from Rome, spoke Italian for a century after the pope left, making the town a cultural oddity within France.

The palace is pretty empty today—nothing portable survived both the pope's return to Rome and the French Revolution. In fact, Revolutionary leaders (who called the building "the Bastille of the South") decreed that it be demolished but lacked the money to carry out the destruction. With the Napoleonic age, the palace found a practical use, housing about 1,800 troops. It remained a barracks until 1906.

You can climb the tower (Tour de la Gâche) for grand views. The artillery room is now a gift shop channeling all visitors on a full tour of knick-knacks for sale.

• *You'll exit at the rear of the palace, where my next walk, "Discovering Avignon's Back Streets," begins. Or, to return to Palace Square, make two rights after exiting the palace.*

DISCOVERING AVIGNON'S BACK STREETS

Use the map in this chapter or the TI map to navigate this easy, level, 30-minute walk, worth ▲▲. We'll begin in the small square (Place de la Mirande) behind the Palace of the Popes. If you've toured the palace, this is where you exit. Otherwise, from the front of the palace, follow the narrow, cobbled Rue de la Peyrolerie—carved out of the rock—around the palace on the right side as you face it.

• *Our walk begins at the...*

Hôtel La Mirande: Located on the square, Avignon's finest hotel welcomes visitors. Find the atrium lounge and consider a coffee break amid the understated luxury (€11 afternoon tea served daily 15:00-18:00).

• *Turn left out of the hotel and left again on Rue de la Peyrolerie ("Coppersmiths Street"), then take your first right on Rue des Ciseaux d'Or ("Street of the Golden Scissors"). On the small square ahead you'll find the...*

Church of St. Pierre: The original walnut doors were carved in 1551, when tales of New World discoveries raced across Europe. (Notice the Indian headdress, top center of left-side door.) The fine Annunciation (eye level on right-side door) shows Gabriel giving Mary the exciting news in impressive Renaissance 3-D. The five niches are empty except for one mismatched Mary and Child filling the center niche. (The original was ransacked by the Revolution.) Now take 10 steps back from the door and look way up. The tiny statue breaking the skyline of the church is the pagan god Bacchus, with oodles of grapes. What's he doing sitting atop a Christian church? No one knows. The church's interior holds a beautiful Baroque altar.

• *Facing the church door, turn left and pass the recommended L'Epicerie restaurant, then follow the alley, which was covered and turned into a tunnel during the town's population boom. It leads into...*

Place des Châtaignes: The cloister of St. Pierre is named for the chestnut *(châtaigne)* trees that once stood here (now replaced by plane trees). The practical atheists of the French Revolution destroyed the cloister, leaving only faint traces of the arches along the church side of the square.

• *Continue around the church and cross the busy street. At the start of little Rue des Fourbisseurs find the classy...*

15th-Century Building: With its original beamed eaves showing, this is a rare vestige from the Middle Ages. Notice how this building widens the higher it gets. A medieval loophole based taxes on ground-floor square footage—everything above was tax-free. Walking down Rue des Fourbisseurs ("Street of the Animal Furriers"), notice how the top floors almost touch. Fire was a constant danger in the Middle Ages, as flames leapt easily from one home to the next. In fact, the lookout guard's primary responsibility was watching for fires, not the enemy.

• *Walk down Rue des Fourbisseurs past lots of shops and turn left onto the traffic-free Rue du Vieux Sextier ("Street of the Old Balance," for weighing items); another left under the first arch leads in 10 yards to one of France's oldest synagogues.*

Synagogue: Jews first arrived in Avignon with the Diaspora (exile after the Romans destroyed their great temple) in the first century. Avignon's Jews were nicknamed "the Pope's Jews" because of the protection that the Church offered to Jews expelled from France. Although the original synagogue dates from the 1220s, in the mid-19th century it was completely rebuilt in a Neoclassical Greek-temple style by a non-Jewish architect. This is the only synagogue under a rotunda. It's an intimate, classy place—where a community of 200 local Jews worships—dressed with white colonnades and walnut furnishings (free, Mon-Fri 9:00-11:00, email ahead or ring doorbell on gray door, closed Sat-Sun and holidays, 2 Place Jerusalem, tel. 06 18 85 67 13, abinacia@hotmail.fr).

• *Retrace your steps to Rue du Vieux Sextier and turn left. A few steps down the street (on the right) is Patrick Mallard—the most venerable pastry shop in town. It's one of two shops authorized to sell Avignon's one-of-a-kind, thistle-shaped candy called* papalines d'Avignon *(dark chocolate wrapped in pink-hued chocolate and filled with a liquor made from local plants).*

Continue down Rue du Vieux Sextier to the big square (across the busy street) and find the big, boxy market building with the hydroponic garden growing out its front wall.

Market (Les Halles): In 1970, the town's open-air market was replaced by this modern one. The market's jungle-like hydroponic

green wall reflects the changes of seasons and helps mitigate its otherwise stark exterior (Tue-Sun until 13:00, closed Mon). Step inside for a sensual experience of organic breads, olives, and festival-of-mold cheeses. Cheap cafés, bars, and good cheese shops are mostly on the right—the stinky fish stalls are on the left. This is a terrific place for lunch (doors close weekdays at 13:30, Sat-Sun at 14:00)—especially if you'd fancy a big plate of mixed seafood with a glass of white wine (see "Eating in Avignon," later).

• *Walk through the market and exit out the back door, turn left on Rue de la Bonneterie ("Street of Hosiery"), and track the street for five minutes to the plane trees, where it becomes...*

Rue des Teinturiers: This "Street of the Dyers" is a tie-dyed, tree- and stream-lined lane, home to earthy cafés and galleries. This was the cloth industry's dyeing and textile center in the 1800s. The stream is a branch of the Sorgue River. Those stylish Provençal fabrics and patterns you see for sale everywhere were first made here, after a pattern imported from India.

About three small bridges down, you'll pass the Grey Penitents chapel on the right. The upper facade shows the GPs, who dressed up in robes and pointy hoods to do their anonymous good deeds back in the 13th century. (While the American KKK dresses in hoods to hide their hateful racism, these hoods symbolized how all are equal in God's eyes.) As you stroll on, you'll see the work of amateur sculptors, who have carved whimsical car barriers out of limestone. Fun restaurants on this atmospheric street are recommended later, under "Eating in Avignon."

• *Farther down Rue des Teinturiers, you'll come to the...*

Waterwheel: Standing here, imagine the Sorgue River—which hits the mighty Rhône in Avignon—being broken into several canals in order to turn 23 such wheels.  Starting in about 1800, waterwheels powered the town's industries. The little cogwheel above the big one could be shoved into place, kicking another machine into gear behind the wall. (For more on the Sorgue River and its waterwheels, see my self-guided walk of Isle-sur-la-Sorgue on page 189.)

• *To return to the center of town, double back on Rue des Teinturiers and turn left on Rue des Lices, which traces the first medieval wall. (A* lice *is the no-man's-land along a protective wall.) After a long block you'll pass a striking four-story building that was a home for the poor in the 1600s, an army barracks in the 1800s, a fine-arts school in the 1900s, and is a deluxe condominium today (much of this neighborhood is going high-class residential). Eventually you'll return to Rue de la République, Avignon's main drag.*

More Sights in Avignon

Most of Avignon's top sights are covered earlier by my self-guided walks. With more time, consider these options.

Angladon Museum (Musée Angladon)

Visiting this museum is like being invited into the elegant home of a rich and passionate art collector. It houses a small but enjoyable collection of art from Post-Impressionists to Cubists (including Paul Cézanne, Vincent van Gogh, Edgar Degas, and Pablo Picasso), with re-created art studios and furnishings from many periods. It's a quiet place with a few superb paintings and good temporary exhibits.

Cost and Hours: €8, Tue-Sun 13:00-18:00, closed Mon, 5 Rue Laboureur, tel. 04 90 82 29 03, www.angladon.com.

Calvet Museum (Musée Calvet)

This fine-arts museum, ignored by most, impressively displays a collection highlighting French Baroque works and Northern masters such as Hieronymus Bosch and Pieter Bruegel. You'll find a few gems upstairs: a painting each by Manet, Sisley, Géricault, and David. On the ground floor is a room dedicated to more modern artists, with works by Soutine, Bonnard, and Vlamnick.

Cost and Hours: €6, includes audioguide, discount with Avignon Passion Pass, Wed-Mon 10:00-13:00 & 14:00-18:00, closed Tue, in the western half of town at 65 Rue Joseph Vernet, tel. 04 90 86 33 84, www.musee-calvet-avignon.com.

Nearby: The museum's antiquities collection, **Le Musée Lapidaire,** is hosted in a church a few blocks away at 27 Rue de la République. If you plan to visit this small museum, get your Avignon Passion Pass stamped here first for the best discount (€2 without pass, €7 combo-ticket with Calvet Museum; same hours except open Tue and closed Mon, tel. 04 90 85 75 38, www.musee-calvet-avignon.com).

Collection Lambert

This new modern art museum, situated in a grand 18th-century mansion, is the talk of Avignon. The collection, with works from the 1960s to the present, came from the famous art dealer Yvon Lambert, who was determined to make well-known contemporary art accessible outside Paris. The recommended Le Violette restaurant in the courtyard is worth the visit alone.

Cost and Hours: €10, discount with Avignon Passion Pass, Tue-Sun 11:00-18:00, closed Mon except July-Aug when it's open until 19:00, 5 Rue Violette, tel. 04 90 16 56 20, www.collectionlambert.fr.

NEAR AVIGNON

▲Tower of Philip the Fair (Tour Philippe-le-Bel)

Built to protect access to St. Bénezet Bridge in 1307, this hulking tower, located in nearby Villeneuve-lès-Avignon, offers a terrific view over Avignon and the Rhône basin. It's best late in the day.

Cost and Hours: €2.50; Tue-Sun 10:00-12:30 & 14:00-18:00, Feb-April and Nov 14:00-17:00 only, closed Dec-Jan and Mon year-round.

Getting There: To reach the tower from Avignon, drive five minutes (cross Daladier Bridge, follow signs to *Villeneuve-lès-Avignon*), or take bus #5 (2/hour, bus stops in front of post office on Cours Président Kennedy, across from train station, but because of

AVIGNON

construction, you may need to go to main bus station, next to the train station).

Sleeping in Avignon

Hotel values are better in Arles, though I've found some pretty good deals in Avignon. Avignon is crazy during its July festival, when you must book long ahead and pay inflated prices. Drivers should ask about parking discounts through hotels.

NEAR CENTRE-VILLE STATION

These listings are a 5- to 10-minute walk from the Centre-Ville train station.

$$ Hôtel Bristol*** is a big, professionally run place on the main drag, offering predictable "American" comforts at fair rates. Enjoy spacious public spaces, large rooms with neutral tones, and a generous buffet breakfast (family rooms, pay parking—reserve ahead, 44 Cours Jean Jaurès, tel. 04 90 16 48 48, www.bristol-avignon.com, contact@bristol-avignon.com).

$ Hôtel Ibis Centre Gare*** offers predictable comfort and generous public spaces near the central train and bus stations (42 Boulevard St. Roch, tel. 04 90 85 38 38, www.ibishotel.com, h0944@accor.com).

$ Hôtel Colbert** is on a quiet lane, with a dozen spacious rooms gathered on four floors around a skinny spiral staircase (no elevator). Patrice decorates each room as if it were his own, with a colorful (occasionally erotic) flair. There are warm public spaces and a sweet little patio (some tight bathrooms, rooms off the patio can be musty, closed Nov-March, 7 Rue Agricol Perdiguier, tel. 04 90 86 20 20, www.lecolbert-hotel.com, contact@avignon-hotel-colbert.com).

$ Hôtel les Corps Saints,** run by young and eager Agnes and Fabrice, rents 16 bright rooms with tight baths at fair rates (no elevator, 17 Rue Agricol Perdiguier, tel. 04 90 86 14 46, www.hotel-les-corps-saints.fr, corpssaints.avignon@gmail.com).

$ At Hôtel Boquier,** helpful owner Frédéric offers 13 quiet, good-value, and homey rooms under wood beams in a central location (family rooms, steep and narrow stairways to some rooms, no elevator, pay parking nearby, near the TI at 6 Rue du Portail Boquier, tel. 04 90 82 34 43, www.hotel-boquier.com, contact@hotel-boquier.com).

¢ Hôtel Innova/Cardabella* is a shy little place with 11 modest rooms at good rates (cheaper rooms with shared bath, no aircon, no elevator, 100 Rue Joseph Vernet, tel. 04 90 82 54 10, www.hotel-innova.fr, innova.hotel@wanadoo.fr).

IN THE CENTER, NEAR PLACE DE L'HORLOGE

$$$$ Hôtel d'Europe,***** one of Avignon's most prestigious addresses, lets peasants sleep royally without losing their shirts—but only if they land one of the 13 reasonable *"classique"* rooms. Though the staff seems a bit stiff, you'll enjoy the spacious lounges and shady courtyard. The hotel is located on the handsome Place Crillon, near the river (pay garage parking, near Daladier Bridge at 12 Place Crillon, tel. 04 90 14 76 76, www.heurope.com, reservations@heurope.com). The hotel's fine restaurant is described in "Eating in Avignon," later. Readers seeking top comfort should compare this hotel with Hôtel la Mirande, next.

$$$$ Hôtel la Mirande pampers its guests with très traditional luxury in a quiet, central location behind the Palace of the Popes. The welcoming staff delivers service with a smile, public spaces are comfy and welcoming, and the rooms are exquisitely decorated. The hotel also houses a well-respected restaurant and offers cooking classes (4 Place de l'Amirande, tel. 04 90 14 20 20, www.la-mirande.fr).

$$$ Hôtel de l'Horloge**** is as central as it gets—on Place de l'Horloge. It offers 66 unimaginative but comfortable rooms at fair rates, some with terraces and views of the city and the Palace of the Popes (elaborate €18 buffet breakfast served until 11:00, 1 Rue Félicien David, tel. 04 90 16 42 00, www.hotel-avignon-horloge.com, hotel.horloge@hotels-ocre-azur.com).

$$$ Hôtel Mercure Palais des Papes,**** about a block from the Palace of the Popes, has an ugly exterior but 86 big, smartly designed rooms, many with small balconies (about half the rooms have views over Place de l'Horloge, others are quieter with views over the Palace of the Popes, 1 Rue Jean Vilar, tel. 04 90 80 93 00, www.mercure.com, h1952@accor.com).

$$$ Hôtel Pont d'Avignon,**** just inside the walls near St. Bénezet Bridge, is part of the same chain as Hôtel Mercure Palais des Papes, with the same prices for its 87 rooms. There's an airy atrium breakfast room and small garden terrace (direct access to a garage makes parking easier than at the other Mercure hotel, parking deals, on Rue Ferruce, tel. 04 90 80 93 93, www.mercure.com, h0549@accor.com).

$$ Autour du Petit Paradis Apartments and **Aux Augustins,** run by Sabine and Patrick, offer 22 contemporary, well-furnished apartments spread over two locations. Petit Paradis, in a restored 17th-century mansion, is a bit more centrally located; Augustins has bigger rooms, all on a shaded courtyard, and lovely stone from its time as a 14th-century monastery (2-night minimum, no elevator, 5 Rue Noël Biret and 16 Rue Carreterie, tel. 04 90 81 00 42, www.autourdupetitparadis.com, contact@autourdupetitparadis.com).

AVIGNON

Avignon Hotels & Restaurants

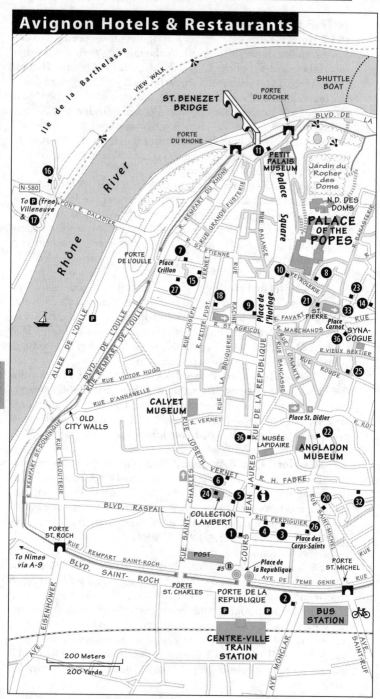

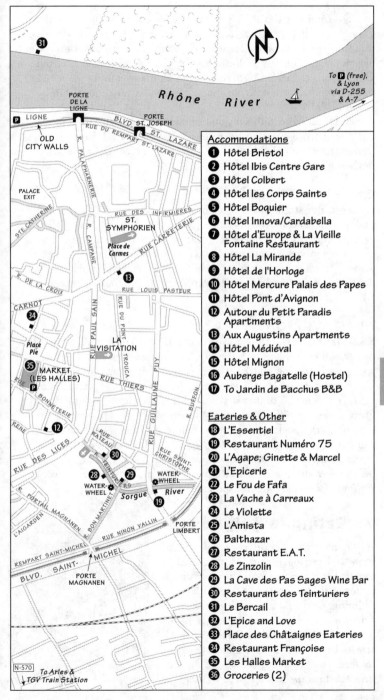

Accommodations
1 Hôtel Bristol
2 Hôtel Ibis Centre Gare
3 Hôtel Colbert
4 Hôtel les Corps Saints
5 Hôtel Boquier
6 Hôtel Innova/Cardabella
7 Hôtel d'Europe & La Vieille Fontaine Restaurant
8 Hôtel La Mirande
9 Hôtel de l'Horloge
10 Hôtel Mercure Palais des Papes
11 Hôtel Pont d'Avignon
12 Autour du Petit Paradis Apartments
13 Aux Augustins Apartments
14 Hôtel Médiéval
15 Hôtel Mignon
16 Auberge Bagatelle (Hostel)
17 To Jardin de Bacchus B&B

Eateries & Other
18 L'Essentiel
19 Restaurant Numéro 75
20 L'Agape; Ginette & Marcel
21 L'Epicerie
22 Le Fou de Fafa
23 La Vache à Carreaux
24 Le Violette
25 L'Amista
26 Balthazar
27 Restaurant E.A.T.
28 Le Zinzolin
29 La Cave des Pas Sages Wine Bar
30 Restaurant des Teinturiers
31 Le Bercail
32 L'Epice and Love
33 Place des Châtaignes Eateries
34 Restaurant Françoise
35 Les Halles Market
36 Groceries (2)

AVIGNON

$ Hôtel Médiéval,** burrowed deep a few blocks from the Church of St. Pierre, was built as a cardinal's home. This stone mansion's grand staircase leads to 35 comfortable, pastel rooms (no elevator, kitchenettes, 5 blocks east of Place de l'Horloge, behind Church of St. Pierre at 15 Rue Petite Saunerie, tel. 04 90 86 11 06, www.hotelmedieval.com, hotel.medieval@wanadoo.fr, run by helpful Régis).

$ Hôtel Mignon* is a good one-star place with fair comfort but tiny bathrooms (family rooms, no elevator, 12 Rue Joseph Vernet, tel. 09 70 35 37 67, www.hotel-mignon.com, reservation@hotel-mignon.fr).

ON THE OUTSKIRTS

Auberge Bagatelle offers dirt-cheap beds in two buildings—a **$** budget hotel and a **¢** youth hostel—and has a young and lively vibe, café, grocery store, launderette, great views of Avignon, and campers for neighbors (cheaper rooms with shared bath, family rooms, across Daladier Bridge on Ile de la Barthelasse, bus #5, tel. 04 90 86 30 39, www.hotel-bagatelle.com, auberge.bagatelle@wanadoo.fr).

NEAR AVIGNON

$$ At **Jardin de Bacchus**, a 15-minute drive northwest of Avignon by car and convenient to Pont du Gard, enthusiastic and English-speaking Christine and Erik offer two double rooms in their village home overlooking the famous rosé vineyards of Tavel (includes breakfast, fine €30 dinner if arranged in advance, swimming pool, great patio, possible bike rentals). They also offer apartments for two or four people (4-night minimum in off-season, one-week minimum in summer, tel. 04 66 90 28 62 or 06 74 41 77 94, www.jardindebacchus.fr, jardindebacchus@gmail.com). By car, it's just off the A-9 autoroute (exit 22); by bus, it's a 30-minute ride from Avignon (www.edgard-transport.fr).

Eating in Avignon

Avignon offers a good range of restaurants and settings, from lively squares to atmospheric streets. Skip the overpriced, underwhelming restaurants on Place de l'Horloge and find a more intimate location for your dinner. Avignon is brimming with delightful squares and back streets lined with little restaurants eager to feed you. If you need to dine early, find **Restaurant Françoise** on Place Pie

AVIGNON

(www.melido.fr), described later. At the finer places, reservations are generally smart (especially on weekends); your hotel can call for you.

FINE DINING WORTH THE SPLURGE

$$$$ L'Essentiel is where in-the-know locals go for a fine meal at reasonable prices. The setting is classy-contemporary inside, the back terrace is romantic, the wine list is extensive, the cuisine is classic French, and gentle owner Dominique makes timid diners feel at ease (indoor and outdoor seating, €36-48 *menus,* closed Sun-Mon, 2 Rue Petite Fusterie, reservations recommended, tel. 04 90 85 87 12, www.restaurantlessentiel.com).

$$$$ La Vieille Fontaine, just inside the gates of Hôtel d'Europe, serves gourmet traditional cuisine in an elegant dining room and on a spacious courtyard terrace. Do your best to dress up for this place, and plan to spend about €60 for the dinner *menu* (€40 for lunch, closed Sun-Mon, near Daladier Bridge at 12 Place Crillon, tel. 04 90 14 76 76, www.heurope.com).

$$$ Restaurant Numéro 75 is worth the walk. It fills the Pernod mansion (of *pastis* liquor fame) with a romantic, chandeliered, Old World dining hall that extends to a leafy, gravelly courtyard. They serve delightful lunch salads, fish is a forte, and the French cuisine is beautifully presented (Mon-Sat 12:00-14:00 & 19:30-22:00, closed Sun, 75 Rue Guillaume Puy, tel. 04 90 27 16 00, www.numero75.com).

$$$ L'Agape shares an atmospheric square with cafés and cheaper places. Here, discerning diners can eat well while enjoying great outdoor ambience (closed Sun-Mon, 21 Place des Corps-Saints, tel. 04 90 85 04 06).

DINING WELL IN THE OLD CENTER ON A MODERATE BUDGET

$$$ L'Epicerie sits alone under green awnings on the romantic Place St-Pierre square and is ideal for dinner outside (or in the small but cozy interior). The cuisine is as delicious as the setting (daily, 10 Place St-Pierre, tel. 04 90 82 74 22).

$$$ Le Fou de Fafa is a warm place with ample space between its 12 tables and a menu of delicious cuisine at good prices. Delightful Antonia serves while her husband cooks (inside dining only, book ahead or arrive early, Tue-Sat from 18:30, closed Sun-Mon, 17 Rue des Trois Faucons, tel. 04 32 76 35 13).

$$ La Vache à Carreaux venerates cheese and wine while offering a range of choices from its big chalkboard. It's a young, lively place, with colorful decor, easygoing service (thanks to owner Jean-Charles), and a reasonable wine list featuring €5 wines by the glass (daily, evenings only, just off atmospheric Place des Châtaignes at 14 Rue de la Peyrolerie, tel. 04 90 80 09 05).

$$ Le Violette, in the peaceful courtyard of the Collection Lambert modern art museum, serves fresh modern cuisine and is gorgeous when lit by the museum rooms at night (July-Aug daily, Sept-June closed Sun afternoon and all day Mon, 5 Rue Violette, tel. 04 90 85 36 42).

$$ L'Amista ("the spot to meet friends"), a cozy, welcoming place run by Delphine, offers a Provençal/Spanish-inspired menu that always includes vegetarian options. Tapas-style snacks are great for sharing, and daily specials are a tasty value. Desserts are homemade (daily 12:00-22:00, closed Sun-Mon off-season, off the main street at 23 Rue Bonneterie, tel. 09 86 19 36 86).

$$ Balthazar doubles as a bar and small restaurant serving tasty traditional French cuisine. The interior is tight, but the atmospheric outdoor seats offer ample room (Mon-Sat 8:00-24:00, closed Sun, 74 Place des Corps Saints, tel. 04 88 07 36 09).

$$ Restaurant E.A.T., just off Place du Crillon, is inviting and locally popular with mouthwatering smells coming from its open kitchen. The chef creates traditional *plats* with a creative twist (closed Wed, reservations recommended, 8 Rue Mazan, tel. 04 90 83 46 74).

BOHEMIAN CHIC, CANALSIDE ON RUE DES TEINTURIERS

Rue des Teinturiers' fun concentration of midrange, popular-with-the-locals eateries justifies the long walk. It's a trendy, youthful area, spiffed up but with little hint of tourism. You'll find wine bars, vegetarian options, and live music at rickety metal tables under shady trees along the canal. I'd walk the street's entire length to find the best ambience before making a choice. (Note that the finer Restaurant Numéro 75, listed earlier, is just around the corner.)

$$ Le Zinzolin is a bohemian bistro serving international cuisine at fair prices with a few vegetarian options. The atmosphere is good inside and out—check out the €14 meal-size salads (daily, 22 Rue des Teinturiers, tel. 04 90 82 41 55).

$ La Cave des Pas Sages, a characteristic wine bar, is a fun place to start your evening (even if you're not eating in the area). Linger with the locals over a cheap glass of regional wine or beer. Choose from the blackboard by the bar that lists all the open bottles, then join the gang outside by the canal (Mon-Sat 12:00-24:00, closed Sun, across from waterwheel at 41 Rue des Teinturiers).

$$ Restaurant des Teinturiers, run by chef Guillaume, combines a casual setting with upscale nouvelle French cuisine and presentation. Guests leave comments on the chalkboard about their "semi-gastronomic meals" (Mon-Tue and Thu-Sat 12:00-14:30 &

19:00-22:00 except no Sat lunch, closed Wed and Sun, reservations smart, near the waterwheel at 5 Rue des Teinturiers; tel. 04 90 33 43 83, http://restaurantdesteinturiers.com).

LOCAL FAVORITE ACROSS THE RHONE

$$$ Le Bercail offers a fun opportunity to get out of town (barely) and take in *le fresh air* with a terrific riverfront view of Avignon, all while enjoying big portions of Provençal cooking (daily May-Oct, Nov-April closed Mon-Tue all day plus Wed and Sun for dinner, reservations recommended, tel. 04 90 82 20 22, www.restaurant-lebercail.fr). Take the free shuttle boat (located near St. Bénezet Bridge) to the Ile de la Barthelasse, turn right, and walk five minutes. As the boat usually stops running at about 18:00 (except in July-Aug, when it runs until 20:45), you can either taxi back or walk 25 minutes along the pleasant riverside path and over Daladier Bridge.

GOOD BUDGET PLACES IN THE CENTER

$ L'Epice and Love (pronounced "lay peace and love") is a tiny, flower-child-like restaurant with a few colorfully decorated tables (inside only). Friendly, English-speaking owner Marie stokes the conviviality and changes her selections weekly: tasty meat, fish, and vegetarian/vegan dishes with a Provençal flavor, all served at good prices (evenings only, closed Sun-Mon, €16-20 *menus,* cash only, 30 Rue des Lices, tel. 04 90 82 45 96).

Place des Châtaignes: This square offers **$** cheap meals and a fun commotion of tables. The **Crêperie du Cloître** makes OK dinner crêpes and salads but has the best seating on the square (daily). **La Pause Gourmande** bakery/deli is tops on the square for lunch (great *fougasse*, quiche with salad, or *plats*; lunch only, closed Sun).

Place des Corps-Saints: This welcoming square offers the best feeling of a neighborhood dining, drinking, and simply living outdoors together. It's my choice for outdoor dining in Avignon, with several eateries in all price ranges sharing the same great setting under big plane trees. Survey the square before deciding. With tables crammed into every nook and cranny, there's standard café fare, Italian options, and finer dining choices. **$ Ginette & Marcel: Bistrot à Tartines** serves salads, big slices of toast smothered in a variety of toppings, and has tasty desserts (daily, tel. 04 90 85 58 70).

Place Pie: Avignon's youth make their home on this big square filled with cafés. Just off the square, **$ Restaurant Françoise** is a fine deli-café, where fresh-baked tarts—savory and sweet—and a variety of salads and soups make a healthful meal, and vegetarian options are plentiful. Order at the counter and eat inside or out

AVIGNON

(Wi-Fi, Mon-Sat 8:00-21:00, closed Sun, a block off Place Pie at 6 Rue Général Leclerc, tel. 04 32 76 24 77).

Farmers Market Hall: Les Halles (described in the "Discovering Avignon's Back Streets" walk) has a handful of wonderfully characteristic and cheap places serving locals the freshest of food surrounded by all that market fun. You'll need to be done by 13:30 (14:00 on weekends), as that's when they lock the place up (closed Mon). For **seafood,** the shops in either far corner can't be beat. They'll assemble the plate of your dreams at a painless price (e.g., a big assortment for two on ice for €18) and pour you a glass of local white wine...and you're set. While the prices at both these places are about the same, one spot feels like a little restaurant and the other a picnic at the marina.

Avignon Connections

BY TRAIN
Remember, there are two train stations in Avignon: the suburban TGV station and the Centre-Ville station in the city center (€1.60 shuttle trains connect the stations, buy ticket from machine on platforms or at a counter, 2/hour, 5 minutes). TGV trains usually serve the TGV station only, though a few depart from Centre-Ville station (check your ticket). The TGV station has almost all the car rental agencies; only Avis is at Centre-Ville station. Some cities are served by slower local trains from Centre-Ville station as well as by faster TGV trains from the TGV station; I've listed the most convenient stations for each trip.

From Avignon's Centre-Ville Station to: Arles (roughly hourly, 20 minutes, less frequent in the afternoon), **Orange** (15/day, 20 minutes), **Nîmes** (12/day, 30 minutes), **Isle-sur-la-Sorgue** (10/day on weekdays, 5/day on weekends, 30 minutes), **Lyon** (10/day, 2 hours; also from TGV station, 70 minutes), **Carcassonne** (8/day, 7 with transfer in Narbonne or Nîmes, 3 hours), **Barcelona** (2/day, 5.75 hours with changes).

From Avignon's TGV Station to: Nice (10/day, most by TGV, 4 hours, many require transfer in Marseille), **Marseille** (10/day, 35 minutes), **Cassis** (7/day, transfer in Marseille, 1.5 hours), **Aix-en-Provence TGV** (12/day, 25 minutes), **Lyon** (12/day, 70 minutes, also from Centre-Ville station—see above), **Paris' Gare de Lyon** (10/day direct, 2.5 hours; more connections with transfer, 3-4 hours), **Paris' Charles de Gaulle airport** (7/day, 3.25 hours), **Barcelona** (1 direct/day, 4 hours).

BY BUS
The bus station *(gare routière)* is just past and below Hôtel Ibis, to the right as you exit the train station. Nearly all buses leave from

this station (a few leave from the ring road outside the station—ask, buy tickets on bus, small bills only). Service is reduced or nonexistent on Sundays and holidays. Check your departure time beforehand, and make sure to verify your destination with the driver.

From Avignon to Pont du Gard: Take bus #A15 to this famous Roman aqueduct (5/day, 50 minutes). For a more worthwhile day trip, see my suggested train/bus excursion that combines Nîmes and Pont du Gard (see "Planning Your Time," next chapter).

By Bus to Other Regional Destinations: Arles (8/day, 1 hour, leaves from TGV station), **Nîmes** (10/day, 1 hour), **Aix-en-Provence** (6/day Mon-Sat, 3/day Sun, 75 minutes, faster and easier than train), **Uzès** (5/day, 60-80 minutes, stops at Pont du Gard); **St-Rémy-de-Provence** (Cartreize #57 bus, 10/day Mon-Sat, 6/day Sun, 45 minutes); **Orange** (Mon-Sat hourly, 5/day Sun, 1 hour—take the train instead); **Isle-sur-la-Sorgue** (bus #6, 8-10/day Mon-Sat, 2/day Sun, 45 minutes). For the **Côtes du Rhône** area, the bus runs to **Vaison-la-Romaine, Nyons, Sablet,** and **Séguret** (3-6/day; all buses pass through Orange—faster to take train to Orange, and transfer to bus there). For the **Luberon** area—including **Lourmarin, Roussillon,** and **Gordes**—take bus #13 to Cavaillon, then take bus #8 toward Pertuis and connect with #19 to Lourmarin (3/day) or bus #17 for Gordes/Roussillon (only 1/day); you must reserve a day ahead for buses from Cavaillon (tel. 04 90 74 20 21).

AVIGNON

NEAR AVIGNON

Nîmes • Pont du Gard • Uzès

Although Avignon lacks Roman monuments of its own, some of Europe's greatest Roman sights are an easy, breezy day trip away. (To get the most out of these sights, read "The Romans in Provence" on page 27 before you visit.) The Pont du Gard aqueduct is a magnificent structure to experience, as is the city it served 2,000 years ago, Nîmes, which wraps a handful of intriguing Roman monuments together in a mellow, bigger-city package. The pedestrian-friendly town of Uzès, between Nîmes and Pont du Gard, offers a refreshing break from power monuments and busy cities. Combining these three sights makes a memorable (if busy) day trip into the Languedoc-Roussillon region. Traveling by car, you'll drive scenic roads between Uzès and Nîmes that show off the rugged *garrigue* landscape that makes this area famous.

PLANNING YOUR TIME

Consider getting away from the tourists and spending the night in classy Nîmes or cozy Uzès; both beat Avignon for quick and easy access to Pont du Gard. If you're on a tight schedule, this region's sights are easy to cover as day trips from Avignon, even without a car. Avignon to Pont du Gard is a 30-minute drive; it's 45 minutes to Uzès, and 45 minutes to Nîmes. Car-less day-trippers from Avignon have these options:

Minivan Tour: An army of companies run day trips from Avignon to Pont du Gard, Uzès, and other popular destinations (see page 24). For example, **Visit Provence Tours** offers a package that includes Nimes, Uzès, and Pont du Gard for about €70 per person (www.provence-reservation.com). Avignon's **TI** can suggest other options.

Bus, Train, and/or Taxi: With as few as three buses a day connecting Avignon with Pont du Gard and Uzès, plan carefully—

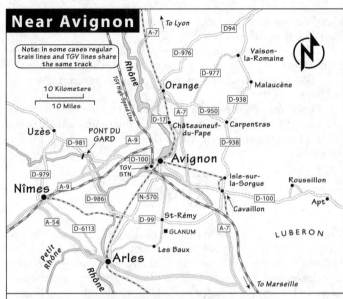

Near Avignon

Note: In some cases regular train lines and TGV lines share the same track

10 Kilometers
10 Miles

To Lyon
D94
D-976
Vaison-la-Romaine
D-977
Malaucène
Orange
D-938
D-950
D-17
Châteauneuf-du-Pape
Carpentras
Uzès
PONT DU GARD
D-981
A-9
D-938
D-100
TGV STN
Avignon
Isle-sur-la-Sorgue
Roussillon
D-979
Nîmes
A-9
D-100
Apt
D-986
N-570
Cavaillon
A-54
D-99
St-Rémy
A-7
LUBERON
D-6113
GLANUM
Petit Rhône
Les Baux
Arles
To Marseille
Rhône
Rhône

Distance By Bus/Train From Avignon

Orange: 20 minutes by train; 60 minutes by bus

Isle-sur-la-Sorgue: 30 minutes by train; 45 minutes by bus

Nîmes: 30 minutes by train; 60 minutes by bus

Uzès: 60–80 minutes by bus only

Pont du Gard: 45 minutes by bus only

Arles: 20 minutes by train; 60 minutes by bus

St-Rémy-de-Provence: 45 minutes by bus only;
   Les Baux is 20 minutes more by bus.

Vaison-la-Romaine: 60-90 minutes by bus;
   faster via train to Orange, then bus.

particularly off-season when weekend service all but vanishes. Check schedules at Avignon's bus station (see page 120), at a TI, or at Edgard-Transport.fr (tel. 08 10 33 42 73). Arrive at bus stops at least five minutes early, pay the driver (coins or small bills), and verify your stop and direction with the driver.

Buses (€2) take around 45 minutes from Avignon or Nîmes to Pont du Gard; almost hourly trains (€10) take 30 minutes to connect Avignon and Nîmes. Allow €60 and 30 minutes for a one-way taxi ride from Avignon or Nîmes to Pont du Gard.

Here are three day-trip plans to consider. The first buses usually depart Avignon for Pont du Gard at about 8:45 and 11:40. Double-check all departure times before you set out.

Day Trip to Pont du Gard Only: Take a morning bus from Avignon's bus station to Pont du Gard, tour the site, then hop on an afternoon bus back to Avignon. For more flexibility, catch a cab from Avignon, then ride the bus back.

Day Trip to Pont du Gard and Nîmes: Take a morning bus from Avignon to Pont du Gard, tour the site, then take an early-afternoon bus to Nîmes for more sightseeing. Return by train to Avignon.

Day Trip to Pont du Gard and Uzès: Take a morning bus from Avignon to Pont du Gard, tour the site, then catch a midday bus to Uzès and stroll the town. Catch the late-afternoon bus back to Avignon.

Nîmes

Most travelers make time in their schedules for Arles and Avignon, but ignore Nîmes. Arles and Avignon may have more touristic appeal, but Nîmes—which feels richer and surer of itself—is refreshingly lacking in overnight tourists. This thriving town of classy shops and serious businesses is studded with world-class Roman monuments and laced with traffic-free lanes. (And if you've visited the magnificent Pont du Gard, you gotta be curious where all that water went.)

Since the Middle Ages, Nîmes has exported a famous fabric: The word "denim" actually comes from here (*de Nîmes* = "from Nîmes"). Denim caught on in the United States in the 1800s, when a Bavarian immigrant, Levi Strauss, popularized its use in the American West.

Today, Nîmes is officially in the Languedoc-Roussillon region (for administrative purposes), yet historically the town has been a key player in the evolution of Provence. Only 30 minutes by train from Arles or Avignon, and three hours from Paris on the TGV, Nîmes is easy to reach. The city keeps its clean and tranquil old center a secret for its well-heeled residents. (Locals admit they don't need the tourism money as much as other Provençal towns.) While most visitors understandably prefer sleeping in Arles or Avignon, a night here provides a good escape from tourist crowds and a truer taste of a Provençal city.

Orientation to Nîmes

Nîmes ("neem") has no river or natural landmark to navigate by, so it's easy to become disoriented. For a quick visit, limit yourself to the manageable triangle within the ring of roads formed by boulevards Victor Hugo, Amiral Courbet, and Gambetta.

The town's landmarks are connected by 10-minute walks: It's

10 minutes from the train station to the arena, 10 minutes from the arena to the Roman temple of Maison Carrée, and 10 minutes from Maison Carrée to either the Castellum or the Fountain Garden. Apart from seeing this handful of ancient monuments, appreciate the city's traffic-free old center—a delight for browsing, strolling, sipping coffee, and people-watching.

TOURIST INFORMATION

The TI, across the street and a half-block up from Maison Carrée, is a 20-minute walk from the train station (Mon-Sat 9:00-19:00, Sun 10:00-18:00, shorter hours Oct-March, 6 Rue Auguste, tel. 04 66 58 38 00, www.nimes-tourisme.com). Pick up the English-language pamphlet, which includes a map with a description of the city's sights and museums and a worthwhile Old City walk.

ARRIVAL IN NIMES

By Train and Bus: Trains and buses use the same station (handy if you're combining Pont du Gard with Nîmes). There's baggage storage near the station at Hôtel Abalone (see "Helpful Hints," below). Confirm return schedules before leaving the station (beware of gaps in train service to Arles).

The bus station and bus information office are out the rear of the train station. Find the bright yellow *Edgard* office banners a block straight out the station's back door (Mon-Fri 8:00-18:45, Sat until 12:00, closed Sun, www.edgard-transport.fr). If departing from Nîmes by bus, arrive early to double-check schedules and ask which stall your bus leaves from (usually between 8 and 15; the shelters are to the right out the rear exit of the train station). Confirm your destination and pay the driver (about €2 one-way to Pont du Gard, use small bills or coins).

The arena is a pleasant 10-minute walk out the front of the train station (see map on page 126). Head up the pedestrian parkway, go left at the big plaza, curve right, and you'll see the arena (to find its entrance, walk counterclockwise around it). The Maison Carrée and TI are an enjoyable stroll from the arena through Nîmes' traffic-free Old City.

By Car: Follow signs for *Centre-Ville* and *TI*, then *Arènes Parking*, and pay to park underneath the arena. (It's a huge garage; make a note of where you parked.) If the garage is full, Parking des Feuchères is nearby (behind the train station), and Parking Maison Carrée is close to the TI (around €9/4 hours; not all pay machines accept bills, so bring coins).

HELPFUL HINTS

Summer Thursdays: The "Jeudi de Nîmes" (Thursdays of Nîmes) tradition turns the entire old center of town into a festival of

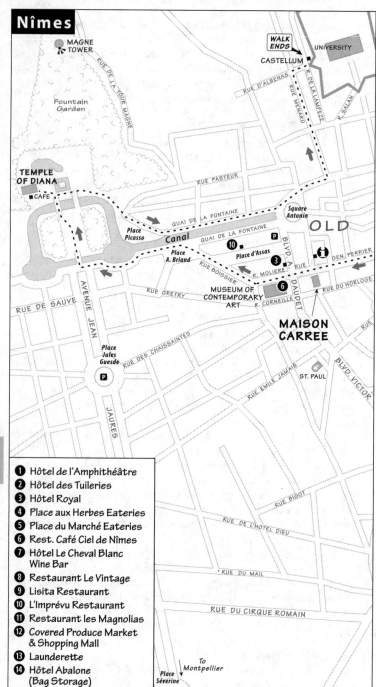

Nîmes

NEAR AVIGNON

1 Hôtel de l'Amphithéâtre
2 Hôtel des Tuileries
3 Hôtel Royal
4 Place aux Herbes Eateries
5 Place du Marché Eateries
6 Rest. Café Ciel de Nîmes
7 Hôtel Le Cheval Blanc Wine Bar
8 Restaurant Le Vintage
9 Lisita Restaurant
10 L'Imprévu Restaurant
11 Restaurant les Magnolias
12 Covered Produce Market & Shopping Mall
13 Launderette
14 Hôtel Abalone (Bag Storage)

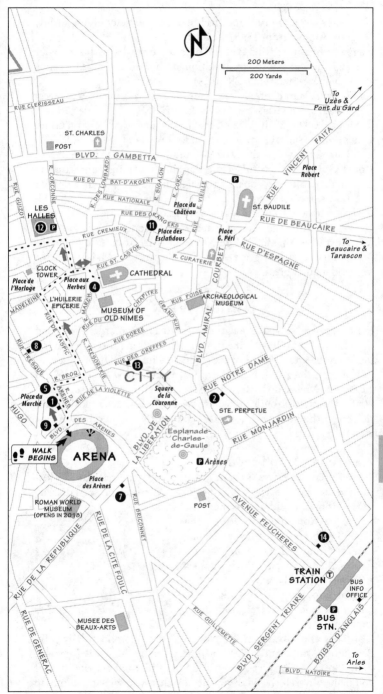

shops, street music, and liveliness on Thursday nights in July and August from 18:00 until late.

Baggage Storage: The **Hôtel Abalone** stores bags. It's to your right as you exit the train station (daily 7:00-22:00, 23 Avenue Feuchères, tel. 04 66 29 20 14).

Laundry: A launderette is near many of my recommended hotels at 1 Rue des Fourbisseurs (daily 7:00-21:00).

Taxi: Call 04 66 29 40 11 for a cab. It's about €60 to Pont du Gard.

Car Rental: Near the station, you'll find **Avis** (tel. 04 34 14 80 15), **Europcar** (tel. 04 66 29 07 94), and **Hertz** (tel. 04 66 76 25 91).

Local Guide: Delightful **Sylvie Pagnard**'s walking tours are top quality. She also does regional tours (€145/3 hours, €360/8 hours, a little extra if she drives her car, tel. 04 66 20 33 14, mobile 06 03 21 37 33, sylviepagnard@gmail.com).

View Café: Ride the glass elevator to the recommended, top-floor **Restaurant Café Ciel de Nîmes** at the Museum of Contemporary Art for a great view over the ancient Maison Carrée and a quiet break.

Nîmes Walk

I've described Nîmes' best sights below in a logical order for a good daylong visit, and have linked them with walking directions starting from the arena. Many of the sights I mention are free; the major exception is the arena. Near the arena, a brand-new **Roman World Museum** (Musée de la Romanité) is slated to open in the spring of 2018. Its futuristic building will showcase an archaeological collection from the area, with a rooftop garden that should deliver fine views over old Nîmes (ask for details at the TI).

▲▲Arena (Amphithéâtre)

Nîmes' arena dates from about A.D. 100 and is more than 425 feet in diameter and 65 feet tall. Considered the best-preserved arena

of the Roman world, it's a superb example of Roman engineering. The 24,000 seats could be filled and emptied in minutes (through 60 passageways called *vomitoires*). The games that were held here were free and designed to keep the populace entertained...and distracted from other concerns.

Cost and Hours: €10, includes great audioguide; daily July-Aug 9:00-20:00, until 19:00 in June, until 18:30 April-May and Sept; closes earlier Oct-March. Buy the €13 combo-ticket only if you plan to watch the Maison Carrée's cheesy movie and climb up to the Magne Tower (both described later, but skippable). Tel. 04 66 21 82 56, www.arenes-nimes.com.

Visiting the Arena: Pick up the included audioguide (or pay extra for the fancy tablet tour). You'll find helpful information panels in English as you tour the arena; these combine with the excellent audioguide to give a thorough and enjoyable history lesson. Don't miss the panels describing the different types of gladiators.

Climb to the very **top.** This is a rare opportunity to enjoy the view from a surviving high point—the nosebleed seats—of a Roman arena. An amphitheater is literally a double theater: two theaters facing each other, designed so that twice the people could view a *Dirty Harry* spectacle—without the acoustics provided by the back wall of a theater stage. (You may think of this as a "colosseum," but that's not a generic term. Rome's Colosseum was a one-of-a-kind arena—named for a colossal statue of Nero that stood nearby.)

As at the arena in Arles and other Roman arenas, the floor here would have been covered in sand (to absorb blood). Underground were tunnels and rooms for storage. An elevator raised angry animals (bulls, bears, and boars mostly) to the floor level to do battle with gladiators.

After Rome fell, and stability was replaced by Dark Age chaos, the huge structure was put to good use—bricked up and made into a fortress (as in Arles). In the 13th century, after the region was incorporated into France, the arena became a gated community housing about 700 people—with streets, plumbing, and even gardens on the top level. Only in 1809 did Napoleon decide to scrape away the dwellings and make this a historic monument, thus letting the ancient grandeur of Roman France shine.

Two **multimedia exhibits** on the arena's ground floor are each well covered by the audioguide (see numbers before entering). *Couleurs des Corridas* (V104) shows the thrilling Camargue bull games in action, as well as a serious Spanish-style bullfight. And the *Quartier des Gladiateurs* (gladiators' locker room, at V106) brings bullfighting and gladiating to life in a kid-friendly way. Since 1850, Nîmes' arena has been a venue for Spanish-style bullfights and rock concerts featuring musical gladiators from Sting to Santana.

• *From the arena, enter Nîmes' "protected sector"—the Old City.*

▲▲Old City

Those coming to Nîmes only for its famous Roman sights are enchanted by its carefully preserved old center. Here, you can study how elements from medieval and Renaissance times artfully survive in the buildings: Shop interiors incorporate medieval brick with stone arches, windows expose Gothic finery, and Renaissance staircases grace peaceful courtyards.

Roman Nîmes

Born a Celtic city (about 500 B.C.), Nîmes joined the Roman Empire in the first century B.C. Because it had a privileged status within the Roman Empire, Nîmes was never really considered part of the conquered barbarian world. It rated highly enough to merit one of the longest protective walls in the Roman world and to have a 30-mile-long aqueduct (Pont du Gard) built to serve its growing population.

Today, the physical remains of Roman Nîmes testify to its former importance. The city's emblem—a crocodile tied to a palm tree—is a reminder that Nîmes was a favorite retirement home for Roman officers who had conquered Egypt. (The crocodile is Egypt, and the palm tree symbolizes victory.) All over town, little bronze croc-palm medallions shine on the sidewalks. In the City Hall, 400-year-old statues of crocodiles actually swing from the top of a monumental staircase (worth a look).

• *With your back to the arena's ticket office, angle right to follow Rue des Arènes one block into...*

Place du Marché

With an inviting café ambience, including a wispy palm-tree-and-crocodile fountain (Nîmes' emblem in Roman times—see sidebar), this fine square is ideal for lunch or a coffee break. Facing the fountain, the recommended **Courtois Café/Pâtisserie** is the class act of the square—check out its old-time interior. Marie Manuelle can explain how it's been in her family since 1892. If you have a sweet tooth, let the sweet women here serve you the house specialty, a chocolate-dipped *nélusko;* it's like a cross between a cake and a cookie, and the oldest recipe of the house. Or try a Nîmes specialty, *caladon*—literally "cobble," like on the street—a hard honey-and-almond cookie.

• *Leave the square, passing the croc on your right (on Rue des Broquiers), then turn left on Rue de l'Aspic, the town's primary shopping spine. Follow Rue de l'Aspic straight past lots of shops several blocks to Place de l'Horloge (with its freestanding bell tower of the city government), the center of the Old City. From here pedestrian-friendly streets fan out in all directions, including directly to Maison Carrée. We'll take unsigned Rue de la Madeleine, the first street to the right as you enter Place de l'Horloge, to the...*

▲Place aux Herbes

This inviting square is the site of Nîmes' oldest market. At the center of the Old City, it's a good hub for a bit of sightseeing and café lounging (see "Eating in Nîmes," later). The next three sights are on or within a block of this square.

Nîmes Cathedral: While its Romanesque facade survives from the 12th century, the cathedral's interior—gutted over centuries of dynastic squabbles, Reformation, and Revolution—is unremarkable Neo-Romanesque, mostly from the 19th century.

Museum of Old Nîmes: Turning left as you leave the cathedral leads you to this humble museum, inhabiting a 17th-century bishop's palace. You'll get a sense of how the bishop lived; see a room of fine, carved hutches; and learn the story of indigo, 19th-century denimwear, and early Levi's (free, Tue-Sun 10:00-18:00, closed Mon, tel. 04 66 76 73 70). Take an English booklet at the entrance or read the touch screen in the first room.

Old-Time Spice Shop: L'Huilerie Epicerie is a charming time warp displaying spices and herbs, oils, and candy (Tue-Sun 9:00-12:30 & 14:30-19:00, closed Mon; 50 yards from the church, down the small lane by Le Petit Moka café, at 10 Rue des Marchands). To revel in more of Nîmes' medieval atmosphere, find the nearby Passage du Vieux Nîmes.

• *With your back to the church door, leave the square at the far right corner and go one block down Rue des Halles. Cross Rue Général Perrier and enter the big, modern black-and-green market hall.*

Covered Produce Market

Les Halles Centre Commercial looks black and ugly on the outside, but inside its ground floor is a thriving, colorful market, well worth exploring (Tue-Sun until 13:00, closed Mon). Within the market, **Halles Auberge** is a cheap and characteristic lunch-only spot. If it's hot, and/or you need to shop, escalate a floor up to the air-conditioned mall.

• *Leaving the market, take a right on Rue Général Perrier, and walk several blocks to the...*

▲▲▲Maison Carrée

This stunning temple rivals Rome's Pantheon as the most complete and splendid building that survives from the Roman Empire.

Admire the original columns and Corinthian capitals. The temple survived in part because it's been in constant use for the last thousand years—as a church, a City Hall, a private stable, an archive during the Revolution, a people's art gallery after the Revolution (like Paris' Louvre), and finally as the monument you visit today. It's a textbook example of a pseudoperipteral temple (surrounded by columns, half of which support the roof over a porch, and half of which merely decorate the rest of the building) and a "six-column temple" (a standard proportion—if it's six columns wide, it must be eleven columns deep).

The lettering across the front is long gone, but the tiny surviving "nail holes" presented archaeologists with a fun challenge: Assuming each letter would leave a particular series of nail holes as evidence, derive the words. Archaeologists agree: This temple was built to honor Caius and Lucius, the sons of Emperor Augustus. And from this information, they date the temple to the year A.D. 4.

Maison Carrée ("Square House"—named before they had a word for "rectangle") was the centerpiece of a fancy plaza surrounded by a U-shaped commercial, political, and religious forum. This marked the core of Roman Nîmes. As was the case in all Roman temples, only the priest went inside. Worshippers gathered for religious rituals at the foot of the steps. Climb the steps as a priest would—starting and ending with your right foot...*dexter* (from the Latin for "right") rather than *sinister* ("left"). Put your right foot forward for good karma.

Inside, the cheesy "Nemausus—The Birth of Nîmes" **movie** tells the story of Nîmes...it's like watching a 25-minute TV dramatization (€6, every 30 minutes, daily July-Aug 9:30-20:00, April-June and Sept 10:00-19:00, March and Oct until 18:00, shorter hours Nov-Feb, soundtrack in Latin and French with English subtitles).

Nearby: The modern building facing the temple is Nîmes' **Carré d'Art** ("Square of Art"), designed by British architect Lord Norman Foster. It's home to the city's Museum of Contemporary Art (Tue-Sun 10:00-18:00, closed Mon, WCs, recommended view café). Nîmes' TI is across the street and a few steps up from Maison Carrée.

• Next, walk down Rue Molière with the Museum of Contemporary Art on your left. Dogleg right until you hit the tree-lined canal, then follow the canal left until you reach the...

▲Fountain Garden (Jardin de la Fontaine)

Centuries before the Romans arrived in Nîmes, the Spring of Nemo was here (named, like the town itself, for a Celtic god). Rather than bulldoze the Nemo temple, the Romans built a shrine to Emperor Augustus around alongside it and welcomed Nemo into their own pantheon (as was their more-gods-the-merrier tradition). Today, the spring remains, though the temple is gone.

Cost and Hours: Free, daily 7:30-22:00, March and Sept until 20:00, Oct-Feb until 18:30.

Visiting the Garden: Walk into the center of the Fountain Garden and look into the canal. In the early 1700s, Nîmes needed a reliable source of water for its textile industry—to power its mills and provide water for the indigo dyes for the fabric *serge de Nîmes* (denim). About 1735, the city began a project to route a canal through the city and discovered a Roman temple. The city eventually agreed to fund a grander project that resulted in what you see today: a lavish Versailles-type park, complete with an ornate network of canals and boulevards. It was finished just 50 years after the construction of Versailles, and to the French, this place has a special significance: These were the first grand gardens not meant for a king, but for the public. The industrial canals built then still wind throughout the city.

• *Hiding behind trees in the back-left corner of Fountain Garden, find the...*

▲Temple of Diana

This first-century "temple," which modern archaeologists now believe was more likely a Roman library, has long been considered one of the best examples of ancient stonework. Its roof—a round Roman barrel vault laced together with still-visible metal pegs (find the panel with a drawing of the temple before entering)—survived until it was hit by a blast in the 1500s, during the Catholic-Protestant Wars of Religion.

Cost and Hours: Free; same hours as Fountain Garden.

Visiting the Temple: At first glance, all the graffiti seems odd. But it's actually part of the temple's story. For centuries, France had a highly esteemed guild of stone-, metal-, and woodworkers called the Compagnons, founded by Gothic-church builders in the Middle Ages. As part of their ritualistic training, these craftsmen would visit many buildings—including the great structures of antiquity (such as this one)—for inspiration. Walk through the side aisle for a close look at the razor-accurate stonework and the 17th-, 18th-, and 19th-century signatures of the Compagnon craftsmen inspired by this building. Notice how their signatures match their era—no-nonsense "Enlightened" chiseling of the 18th century gives way to ornate script in the Romantic 19th century.

Skip the hike up to the Magne Tower (at the top of the gardens), which has two remaining levels of a Roman tower; the view is worth neither the sweat nor the €3.50 entry fee. Instead, consider a coffee break or snack at the park's café, located next to the Temple of Diana.

• *The next sight is a 10-minute walk away. Angle back across the park, turning left at the canal (Quai de la Fontaine). Halfway to the end, notice that one of the trees that line the canal is actually a carving of a diving nymph (Nemausa) with her legs gracefully fluttering up in the sky. After the little waterfall at the busy road, continue straight another block. Just after the tiny park, turn left onto tiny Rue Ménard. Follow it uphill for three blocks, then head right on Rue d'Albenas, which ends at the...*

▲Castellum

This small excavation site, sitting next to the street, is free and always open. It shows a modest-looking water distribution tank that was once the grand finale of the 30-mile-long Pont du Gard aqueduct.

Discovered in the 1850s, this is one of only two known Roman distribution tanks (the other is in Pompeii). Over time, the water needs of Roman Nîmes grew beyond the capacity of its local springs. Imagine the jubilation on the day (in A.D. 50) that this system was finally operational. Suddenly, the town had an abundance of water—for basic needs as well as for cool extras like public fountains.

Notice the square hole marking the end of the aqueduct, a pool, a lower water channel, and the water-distribution holes. The lower channel, which runs under you, served top-priority needs, providing water via stone and lead pipes to the public wells that graced neighborhood squares. The higher holes—which got wet only when the supply was plentiful—routed water to the homes of the wealthy, to public baths, and to nonessential fountains. (For more on this impressive example of Roman engineering, see the "Pont du Gard" section, later.)

Sleeping in Nîmes

$ Hôtel de l'Amphithéâtre*** is ideally located on a pedestrian street a spear's toss from the arena. Run by gracious Ghislaine and Marcus, this is a top Nîmes value, with quiet, spacious, and sharp rooms at good rates (no elevator, 4 Rue des Arènes, tel. 04 66 67 28 51, www.hoteldelamphitheatre.com, contact@hoteldelamphitheatre.com).

$ Hôtel des Tuileries** is a sure value, with helpful English hosts (Andrew and Caryn) and a central location 10 minutes on foot from the train station. Rooms are carpeted, large, and modern, and most have balconies (22 Rue de Roussy, tel. 04 66 21 31 15, www.hoteldestuileries.com, les-tuileries@wanadoo.fr).

$ Hôtel Royal*** rents comfortable rooms and makes a sleepable fallback if other hotels are full. It's an artsy place well located on a main street near Maison Carrée (no elevator, back rooms are quieter but lack light, 1 Place d'Assas, tel. 04 66 58 28 27, www.royalhotel-nimes.com, contact@royalhotel-nimes.com).

Eating in Nîmes

LUNCH

Enjoy the elegance of Nîmes by eating lunch on one of its charming squares. Most of these cafés serve lunch but close for dinner.

Place aux Herbes: This square, beautifully situated in the shadow of the cathedral, boasts several popular bistros where you can lunch for €10. All close daily at 19:00 and all day on Sundays.

Place du Marché: A block from the arena, this square is home to several worthwhile eateries. **$ Courtois Café/Pâtisserie,** with a fine €12.50 *salade Nîmoise* (local pâté, tapenade, and *brandade*) and trademark desserts (described under my self-guided walk—see page 130) makes a good choice (daily July-Aug 8:00-24:00, Sept-Oct and May-June Thu-Tue until 20:00, closed Wed; Nov-April until 19:30, closed Wed; tel. 04 66 67 20 09).

Overlooking the Maison Carrée: Filling a terrace atop the city's Norman Foster-designed contemporary art gallery, **$$ Restaurant Café Ciel de Nîmes** offers great views of the Roman temple (Tue-Sun 10:00-18:00, closed Mon, Place de la Maison Carrée, tel. 04 66 36 71 70). Facing the temple, you'll see the terrace at the top of the modern building on your right. The elevator is to the right upon entering the glassy building.

DINNER

Many places close on Sunday and Monday.

At the wine bar **$$$ Hôtel Le Cheval Blanc,** diners can start, end, or spend their entire evening. It's a cozy place serving good wine, appetizers, and full meals (closed Sun, 1 Place des Arènes, tel. 04 66 76 19 59).

$$ Restaurant Le Vintage, a cool and contemporary wine bar/bistro, offers local cuisine and wines with an easygoing ambience inside or outside on a sweet little terrace (reasonable wine prices, closed Sun-Mon Oct-May, a few blocks up Rue Fresque from Place du Marché at 7 Rue de Bernis, tel. 04 66 21 04 45, www.restaurant-levintage-nimes.com).

$$$ Lisita, a dressy place a few steps from the arena, serves serious French cuisine and has a smart interior and terrific exterior seating. The chef refused a Michelin star to keep the prices affordable—that's amazing (daily July-Aug, otherwise closed Sun-Mon, 2 Boulevard des Arènes, tel. 04 66 67 29 15, www.lelisita.com).

$$ L'Imprévu is a modern bistro serving traditional cuisine on a breezy square. It's a popular place with locals and has fine terrace seating and a well-appointed interior (closed Tue-Wed, 6 Place d'Assas, tel. 04 66 38 99 59).

Place des Esclafidous: Four colorful restaurants serving a variety of cuisines ring this cute little square with outdoor tables. The

NEAR AVIGNON

square is two blocks behind the cathedral: Find the post office on Rue Crémieux and walk behind it. At **$$ Restaurant les Magnolias,** meals are tasty, with a big variety of Mediterranean specialties. Plus, it's open on weekends (€23-27 *menus,* big salads, closed Tue, tel. 04 66 21 64 01).

Nîmes Connections

Trains and buses depart from the same station in Nîmes (see "Arrival in Nîmes," earlier).

From Nîmes by Train to: Arles (9/day, 30 minutes, beware of gaps in the afternoon), **Avignon** (12/day, 30 minutes), **Aigues-Mortes** in the Camargue (6/day Mon-Fri, 2/day Sat-Sun, 45 minutes), **Carcassonne** (8/day, 2.5 hours, transfer in Narbonne), **Paris** (10/day, 3 hours).

By Bus to: Uzès (#B21 or #E52, 7/day Mon-Fri, 3/day Sat, 2/day Sun, 40 minutes), **Pont du Gard** (#B21, 6/day Mon-Fri, 4/day Sat, 2/day Sun, no buses on weekends Nov-April, 40 minutes), **Aigues-Mortes** in the Camargue (6/day, 50 minutes), **Arles** (8/day Mon-Sat, 3/day Sun, 1 hour).

Pont du Gard

Throughout the ancient world, aqueducts were like flags of stone that heralded the greatness of Rome. A visit to this impressively preserved sight still works to proclaim the wonders of that age.

In the first century A.D., the Romans built a 30-mile aqueduct that ran to Nîmes, one of ancient Europe's largest cities. While most of it ran on or below the ground, at Pont du Gard the aqueduct spans a canyon on a massive bridge over the Gardon River—one of the most remarkable surviving Roman ruins anywhere. The aqueduct supported a small canal that dropped one inch for every 350 feet, supplying the city of Nîmes with nine million gallons of water per day (about 100 gallons per second). Allow about four or five hours for visiting Pont du Gard (including transportation time from Avignon).

GETTING THERE

The famous aqueduct is between Remoulins and Vers-Pont du Gard on D-981, 17 miles from Nîmes and 13 miles from Avignon.

By Car: Pont du Gard is a 30-minute drive due west of Avignon (follow N-100 from Avignon, tracking signs to *Nîmes* and *Remoulins,* then *Pont du Gard* and *Rive Gauche*), and 45 minutes northwest of Arles (via Tarascon on D-6113). If going to Arles

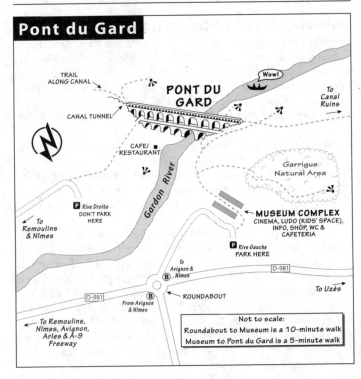

from Pont du Gard, follow signs to *Nîmes* (not *Avignon*), then D-6113, or A-54 (autoroute) to Arles.

By Bus: Buses run to Pont du Gard (on the Rive Gauche side) from Avignon (#A15, 5/day, 50 minutes), Nîmes, and Uzès. Combining Pont du Gard with Nîmes and/or Uzès makes a good day-trip excursion from Avignon.

Buses stop at the traffic roundabout 400 yards from the museum (stop name: Rond Point Pont du Gard; see Pont du Gard map). If leaving by bus, make sure you're waiting on the correct side of the traffic circle (stops have schedules posted), and wave your hand to signal the bus to stop for you—otherwise, it may drive on by. Buy your ticket when you get on and verify your destination with the driver.

By Taxi: From Avignon, it's about €60 for a taxi to Pont du Gard (tel. 04 90 82 20 20). If you're staying in Avignon and only want to see the Pont du Gard (and not Nîmes or Uzès), consider splurging on a taxi to the aqueduct in the morning, then take the early-afternoon bus back.

NEAR AVIGNON

ORIENTATION TO PONT DU GARD

There are two riversides at Pont du Gard: the Left Bank (Rive Gauche) and Right Bank (Rive Droite). Park on the Rive Gauche, where you'll find the museums, ticket booth, TI, ATM, cafeteria, WCs, and shops—all built into a modern plaza. A restaurant and ice-cream kiosk are on the Rive Droite side. You'll see the aqueduct in two parts: first the fine museum complex, then the actual river gorge spanned by the ancient bridge.

Cost: €8.50. This gives you access to the aqueduct, museum, film, and outdoor *garrigue* nature area.

Hours: Daily May-June 9:00-21:00—museum closes at 19:00; July-Aug until 23:30—museum closes at 19:30; April and Sept-Oct until 18:30, Nov-March until 17:00; possibly closed two weeks in Jan.

Information: Tel. 04 66 37 50 99, www.pontdugard.fr.

Pont du Gard After Hours: During summer months, the site is open late so that people can hike, enjoy a picnic or the riverside restaurant, and watch the light show projected on the monument. The parking lot is staffed and guarded until 24:00, and after the museum closes you'll pay only €3/person to enter. If you don't care to see the museum, seeing Pont du Gard in the evening is dramatic (and cheap). The light show is projected from the north, so those in the picnic area and at the restaurant enjoy a good view.

Hiking Tour Across Pont Du Gard: In July and August, several 30-minute tours a day go through the water channel at the top of the aqueduct (€11.50 includes tour, site, and museum; commentary in French and English, maximum 33 people, 1-2 tours/day off-season, check times at the museum entrance or online—where you can reserve). If you do this tour, notice the massive calcium buildup lining the channel from more than 400 years of flowing water.

Canoe Rental: Floating under Pont du Gard by canoe is an unforgettable experience. Collias Canoes will pick you up at Pont du Gard (or elsewhere, if prearranged) and shuttle you to the town of Collias. You'll float down the river to the nearby town of Remoulins, where they'll pick you up and take you back to Pont du Gard (€23, kids under age 12-€12, usually 2 hours—though you can take as long as you like, reserve the day before in July-Aug, tel. 04 66 22 87 20, www.canoe-collias.com).

Plan Ahead for Swimming and Hiking: Pont du Gard is perhaps best enjoyed on your back and in the water—bring along a swimsuit and flip-flops for the rocks. (Note that local guides warn that the bridge can create whirlpools and be dangerous to swim under.) The best Pont du Gard viewpoints are up steep hills with uneven footing—bring good shoes, too.

SIGHTS AT PONT DU GARD
▲Museum

In this state-of-the-art museum (well presented in English), you'll enter to the sound of water and understand the critical role fresh water played in the Roman "art of living." You'll see copies of lead pipes, faucets, and siphons; walk through a mock rock quarry; and learn how they moved those huge rocks into place and how those massive arches were made. A wooden model shows how Roman engineers determined the proper slope. While actual artifacts from the aqueduct are few, the exhibit shows the immensity of the undertaking as well as the payoff. Imagine the jubilation when this extravagant supply of water finally tumbled into Nîmes. A relaxing highlight is the scenic video of a helicopter ride along the entire 30-mile course of the structure, from its start at Uzès all the way to the Castellum in Nîmes.

Other Activities

Several additional attractions are designed to give the sight more meaning (but for most visitors, the museum is sufficient). A 15-minute film plays on a loop in the same building as the museum. The nearby kids' museum, called *Ludo*, offers a scratch-and-sniff teaching experience (in English) of various aspects of Roman life and the importance of water. The extensive outdoor *garrigue* natural area, closer to the aqueduct, features historic crops and landscapes of the Mediterranean.

▲▲▲Viewing the Aqueduct

A parklike path leads to the aqueduct. Until a few years ago, this was an actual road—adjacent to the aqueduct—that had spanned the river since 1743. Before you cross the bridge, walk to the riverside viewpoint: Pass under the bridge and aqueduct and hike about 300 feet along the riverbank to the concrete steps leading down to a grand view of the world's second-highest standing Roman structure. (Rome's Colosseum is only 6 feet taller.)

This was the biggest bridge in the whole 30-mile-long aqueduct. The arches are twice the width of standard aqueducts, and the main arch is the largest the Romans ever built—80 feet across (the width of the river). The bridge is about 160 feet high and was originally about 1,200 feet long.

Though the distance from the source (in Uzès, on the museum side of the site) to Nîmes was only 12 miles as the eagle flew, engineers chose the most economical route, winding and zigzagging 30 miles. The water made the trip in 24 hours with a drop of only 40 feet. Ninety percent of the aqueduct is on or under the ground, but a few river canyons like this required bridges. A stone lid hides a four-foot-wide, six-foot-tall chamber lined with waterproof mortar that carried the stream for more than 400 years. For 150 years, this system provided Nîmes with good drinking water. Expert as the Romans were, they miscalculated the backup caused by a downstream corner, and had to add the thin extra layer you can see just under the lid to make the channel deeper.

The bridge and the river below provide great fun for holiday-goers. While parents suntan on rocks, kids splash into the gorge from under the aqueduct. For the most refreshing view, float flat on your back underneath the structure (but beware of whirlpools, which can be dangerous).

The appearance of the entire gorge changed in 2002, when a huge flood flushed lots of greenery downstream. Those floodwaters put Roman provisions to the test. Notice the triangular-shaped buttresses at the lower level—designed to split and divert the force of any flood *around* the feet of the arches rather than *into* them. The 2002 floodwaters reached the top of those buttresses. Anxious park rangers winced at the sounds of trees crashing onto the ancient stones...but the arches stood strong.

The stones that jut out—giving the aqueduct a rough, unfinished appearance—supported the original scaffolding. The protuberances were left, rather than cut off, in anticipation of future repair needs. The lips under the arches supported wooden templates that allowed the stones in the round arches to rest on something until the all-important keystone was dropped into place. Each stone weighs from two to six tons. The structure stands with no mortar (except at the very top, where the water flowed)—taking full advantage of the innovative Roman arch, made strong by gravity.

Hike over the bridge for a closer look and the best views. Steps lead up a high trail (marked *view point/panorama*) to a superb vista (go right at the top; best views are soon after the trail starts descending). You'll also see where the aqueduct meets a rock tunnel, which was built in the 1800s to try to reuse the aqueduct and provide water to Nîmes (it failed). Notice how the aqueduct curves left before the tunnel.

Back on the museum side, steps lead up to the Rive Gauche side of the aqueduct, where you can follow the canal path along a trail (marked with red-and-white horizontal lines) to find some remains of the Roman canal. You'll soon reach another *panorama* with more great views of the aqueduct. Hikers can continue along the path, following the red-and-white markings that lead through a forest, after which you'll come across more remains of the canal (much of which are covered by vegetation). There's not much left to see because of medieval cannibalization—frugal builders couldn't resist the precut stones as they constructed area churches. The path continues for about 15 miles, but there's little reason to go farther.

Uzès

Located near the source of the spring that fed the Pont du Gard aqueduct, this intriguing, less-trampled town is officially in Languedoc-Roussillon, not Provence. Uzès (oo-zehs) feels like it must have been important once—and it was, as a bishopric from the fifth century until 1789. Today Uzès offers a refreshing small-town break from serious sightseeing. If you sleep here, try to arrive on a Tuesday or Friday night to enjoy the next morning's market.

GETTING TO UZES

Uzès is a short hop west of Pont du Gard. It can be reached easily by a €1.50 **bus** from Nîmes (Edgard buses #E52 and #B21, direction: Pont St-Esprit, 7/day Mon-Fri, 3/day Sat, 2/day Sun, 40 minutes), but less so from Avignon (Edgard bus #A15, direction: Alès, 5/day, 60-80 minutes, stops near Pont du Gard). Check Edgard-Transport.fr or call 08 10 33 42 73 for schedules. The bus stop for Uzès is labeled "Esplanade."

By **car,** Uzès is 15 minutes from Pont du Gard and 45 minutes from Nîmes and Avignon. Drivers will circle the old town on the busy ring road. The TI and one hotel that I list are on this ring road.

Orientation to Uzès

The **TI** sits at the top of the ring road on Place Albert I. Pick up the brief self-guided tour brochure in English, with a map of the town—available outside when the TI is closed (Mon-Fri 10:00-18:00, Sat-Sun 10:00-13:00 & 14:00-17:00; shorter hours and closed Sun Oct-May; tel. 04 66 22 68 88, www.pays-uzes-tourisme.com).

NEAR AVIGNON

Sights in Uzès

Strolling the Town

The traffic-free, tastefully restored town itself is the sight. It's best seen slowly on foot, with a lingering coffee break in its arcaded and mellow main square, **Place aux Herbes** (not so mellow during the colorful Wed morning market and even bigger all-day Sat market).

In spite of all those bishops, there are no important sights to visit in Uzès. You can follow the TI's self-guided walking tour, but skip their sad app tour and avoid the dull, overpriced Palace of the Duché de Uzès (the courtyard view is free). The town's trendy boutiques are as numerous as its English-speaking visitors, which give the place an upscale, international feel. The unusual circular tower called Tour Fenestrelle is all that remains of a 12th-century cathedral.

Medieval Garden

Even if you're not a plant enthusiast, pop into the Medieval Garden, a "living herbarium" with plants thought to have curative qualities. The garden is at the foot of the King's and Bishop's towers. The entrance fee includes a little shot of lemongrass tea lovingly delivered by the volunteers who care for this sight (€6, daily 14:00-18:00, plus 10:30-12:30 Sat-Sun and daily July-Aug; Oct daily until 17:00; closed Nov-March, English handout, tel. 04 66 22 38 21).

NEAR UZES

The **Musée du Bonbon** candy museum, a mile and a half below Uzès on the road to Avignon and Pont du Gard, explains the history and manufacturing process of Haribo (of Gummi Bears fame). It's interactive and makes a worthwhile detour for the kids (adults-€7, kids ages 5-15-€5, kids under 5 free, July-Aug daily 10:00-19:00, shorter hours and closed Mon Sept-June, last entry one hour before closing, tel. 04 66 22 74 39, www.museeharibo.fr).

To taste wines near Uzès, consider a stop at **La Gramière winery** or at **La Grange,** next door, both run by a delightful American couple (Amy Lillard and Matthew Kling) who are making a splash with their excellent wines just a hop, skip, and a jump from Pont du Gard (Place de la Fontaine Vers Pont du Gard, tel. 06 89 38 08 29, www.lagramiere.com and www.lagrangedevers.com).

Sleeping and Eating in Uzès

Sleeping: Hotels in Uzès mirror the upscale flavor of the town. Pale-green signs direct drivers to hotels from the ring road.

$$$$ La Maison d'Uzès,***** in the heart of the old town, is filled with modern luxury and nestled in the charm of a beautifully restored 17th-century building. In this boutique hotel, you'll find sumptuous lounges, a gastronomic restaurant, a spa complete with a waterfall Roman bath, and nine well-designed rooms (elevator serves half the rooms, 18 Rue du Docteur Blanchard, tel. 04 66 20 07 00, www.lamaisonduzes.fr, contact@lamaisonduzes.fr).

$$ L'Hostellerie Provençale,*** a charming place with nine plush rooms and four *chambres d'hôte*, is just off the ring road, a few blocks after the TI. Breakfast and dinner can be served on their splendid rooftop terrace or downstairs in the cozy restaurant (pricey breakfast on terrace, breakfast included for the four B&B rooms, kitchenette, no elevator, pay parking, restaurant closed Sun-Mon, 1 Rue de la Grande Bourgade, tel. 04 66 22 11 06, www. hostellerieprovencale.com, contact@hostellerieprovencale.com).

Eating: When the weather cooperates, it's hard to resist meals on Place aux Herbes, which is lined with appealing café options. The **$** café, restaurant, and boutique **Terroirs** has inviting seats at one corner of the square and is ideal for enjoying Provençal tapas with a glass of local wine (daily, long hours, Nov-Feb until 18:30 only, 5 Place aux Herbes, tel. 04 66 03 41 90).

$ Le Zanelli Italian, dishing up pizzas and more, is located on the most prized, tucked-away terrace in the center of Uzès. Leave Place aux Herbes through the passage between #17 and #19 (closed Tue all day and Thu and Sun for lunch, Place Nicolas Froment, tel. 04 66 03 01 93).

$$ Restaurant TEN, located one street north of Place aux Herbes, serves international cuisine in an appealing historic building. Choose between dining under the arcades outside, the cozy interior, or the peaceful interior courtyard (closed Mon-Tue, 10 Place Dampmartin, tel. 04 66 22 10 93).

To dine well indoors or high above the town on their rooftop terrace, find **$$$$ La Parenthèse** restaurant (closed Sun-Mon) in the recommended L'Hostellerie Provençale.

NEAR AVIGNON

ORANGE & THE COTES DU RHONE

Orange • Châteauneuf-du-Pape • Vaison-la-Romaine • Best of the Côtes du Rhône Villages • More Côtes du Rhône Drives

The sunny Côtes du Rhône wine road—one of France's most engaging—starts at Avignon's doorstep and winds north along a mountainous landscape carpeted with vines, studded with warm stone villages, and presided over by the Vesuvius-like Mont Ventoux. The wines of the Côtes du Rhône (grown on the *côtes,* or hillsides, of the Rhône River Valley) are easy on the palate and on your budget. But this hospitable place offers more than wine—its hill-capping villages inspire travel posters, its Roman ruins add a historical perspective, and the locals are often as excited about their region as you are.

Located 30 minutes north of Avignon, the ancient town of Orange has vineyards on its outskirts. But it's because of its well-preserved Roman Theater that Orange gets (and deserves) attention.

PLANNING YOUR TIME

Vaison-la-Romaine is the handy small-town hub of this region, offering limited bus connections with Avignon and Orange, bike rental, and a mini Pompeii in the town center. Nearby, you can visit the impressive Roman Theater in Orange, drive to the top of Mont Ventoux, follow my self-guided driving tour of Côtes du Rhône villages and wineries, or pedal along peaceful roads to nearby towns. The vineyards' centerpiece, the Dentelles de Montmirail mountains, are laced with hiking trails.

To explore this area, allow two nights for a decent dabble. Drivers should head for the hills (read this chapter's self-guided driving tour before deciding where to stay). Those without wheels find that Vaison-la-Romaine or Orange make the only practical home bases (or, maybe better, consider a minivan tour for this area).

GETTING AROUND THE COTES DU RHONE

By Car: Pick up Michelin maps #332 or #527. Landmarks like the Dentelles de Montmirail and Mont Ventoux make it easy to get your bearings. I've described my favorite driving route on page 167.

For a scenic spin, connect the Côtes du Rhône with the **Luberon** (next chapter) via Mont Ventoux between mid-April and mid-November—check with the TI beforehand to make sure the summit is open (follow signs to *Malaucène,* then to *Mont Ventoux,* allowing 2 hours to Roussillon). This route is one of the most spectacular in Provence. But if the summit is closed (in bad weather years, the reopening can be delayed through May), skip the long, underwhelming alternative route through Bédoin. Instead, zip to the Luberon by taking the autoroute via Orange and Cavaillon. A third, more direct route takes you through the traffic-snarled, difficult-to-navigate city of Carpentras, which is better avoided. Get advice from your hotelier.

By Bus: Buses run to Vaison-la-Romaine from Orange and Avignon (3-6/day, 45 minutes from Orange, 1.5 hours from Avignon—taking the train from Avignon to Orange and then the bus is best) and connect several wine villages with Vaison-la-Romaine and Nyons to the north. Limited bus service is available from Vaison-la-Romaine to Carpentras, serving Crestet, Malaucène, and Le Barroux (3/day Mon-Sat, none on Sun, tel. 04 90 36 05 22, www.cars-lieutaud.fr). All routes provide scenic rides through this area.

By Train: Trains get you as far as Orange (from Avignon: 15/day, 20 minutes).

By Minivan Tour: There's no shortage of people willing to take you for a ride through this marvelous region—so buyer beware. For my recommendations on wine-focused tours, more general tours, and private guides, see "Tours in Provence" on page 24.

COTES DU RHONE MARKET DAYS

Monday: Bédoin (intimate market, between Vaison-la-Romaine and Mont Ventoux)

Tuesday: Vaison-la-Romaine (great market with produce and antiques/flea market)

Wednesday: Malaucène (good and less-touristy market with produce and antiques/flea market, near Vaison-la-Romaine), Buis-les-Barronies (on recommended loop drive north into the Drôme Provençale), and Sault (handy if you're driving to the Luberon area)

Thursday: Orange (produce and local goods), Nyons (great market with produce and antiques/flea market), and Vacqueyras

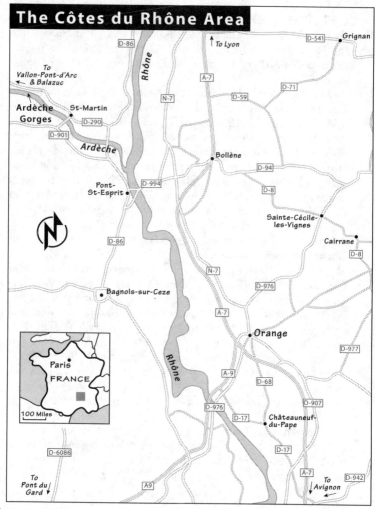

The Côtes du Rhône Area

Friday: Châteauneuf-du-Pape (small market) and Carpentras (big market)

Saturday: Sainte-Cécile-les-Vignes, near Vaison-la-Romaine

Orange

Orange, called *Arausio* in Roman times, is notable for its Roman arch and grand Roman Theater. Orange was a thriving city in ancient times—strategically situated on the Via Agrippa, connecting the important Roman cities of Lyon and Arles. It was founded as

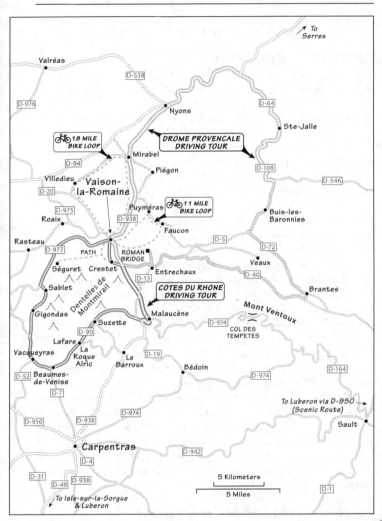

a comfortable place for Roman army officers to enjoy their retirement. Even in Roman times, professional military men retired with time for a second career. Did the emperor want thousands of well-trained, relatively young guys hanging around Rome? No way. What to do? "How about a nice place in the south of France...?"

Today's Orange (oh-rahnzh) is a busy, workaday city with a gritty charm that reminds me of Arles. Leafy café-lined squares, a handful of traffic-free streets, a gorgeous Hôtel de Ville (City Hall), and that theater all give the town some serious street appeal. For some, Orange works well as a base, with its quick access to the Côtes du Rhône wine villages by car (slower but OK by bus) and quick rail access to Avignon (which even drivers should consider).

Orientation to Orange

TOURIST INFORMATION

The unnecessary TI is located next to the fountain and parking area at 5 Cours Aristide Briand (April-Sept Mon-Sat 9:00-12:30 & 14:00-18:00— no lunch break July-Aug, Sun 9:00-12:30; shorter hours and closed Sun off-season; tel. 04 90 34 70 88, www.orange-tourisme.fr).

Market Day: Thursday is market day, and it's a big deal here, with all the town's streets and squares crammed with produce and local goods for sale until 12:30. I like this market because it focuses on locals' needs and not touristy kitsch.

ARRIVAL IN ORANGE

By Train: Orange's train station is a level 15-minute walk from the Roman Theater (or an €8 taxi ride, mobile 06 66 71 58 02). The recommended Hôtel de Provence, across from the station, will keep your bags for no charge, though it's polite to buy a drink from the café (see "Sleeping and Eating in Orange," later). To walk into town from the train station, head straight out of the station (down Avenue Frédéric Mistral), merge left onto Orange's main shopping street (Rue de la République), then turn left on Rue Caristie; you'll run into the Roman Theater's massive stage wall.

By Bus: Buses stop at the train station and Place Pourtoules, two blocks from the Roman Theater (www.pacamobilite.fr).

By Car: Follow *Centre-Ville* signs, then *Théâtre Antique* signs, and park as close to the Roman Theater's huge wall as you can. If coming from Avignon on D-907, park at *Parking Théâtre* signs; if coming from the autoroute, park near the TI. If arriving on a Thursday morning (market day), expect lots of traffic and scarce parking; look for parking on the road leading to the train station (15-minute walk to the theater).

Sights in Orange

▲▲▲Roman Theater (Théâtre Antique)

Orange's ancient theater is the best-preserved in existence, and the only one in Europe with its (awesome) acoustic wall still standing.

Cost and Hours: €9.50, drops to €8.50 one hour before closing; ticket includes good audioguide (not available if you arrive within an hour of closing), and entry to the small museum across the street; daily April-Sept 9:00-18:00, June-Aug until 19:00; Oct and March 9:30-17:30; Nov-Feb 9:30-16:30; closing times can change for evening performances or rehearsals, tel. 04 90 51 17 60, www.theatre-antique.com.

Cheap Trick: Vagabonds wanting a partial-but-free view of

COTES DU RH⟩NE

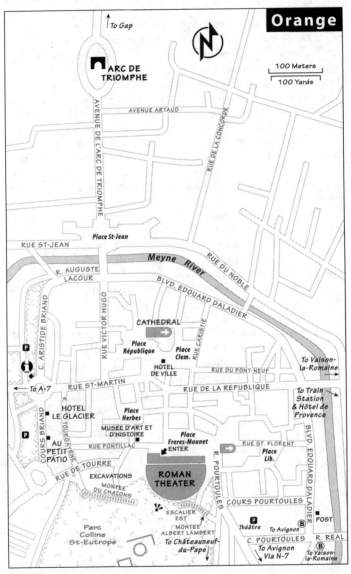

the theater (or others wanting a view from above) can find it in the Parc de la Colline St-Eutrope. Walk around to the left of the theater (see map above), and find the steps to the right, just after the *tabac*. Climb the steps, keep left at the first fork, climb for a little over 100 yards, and then take the steps to the right to the top. From here, follow the *Point de Vue* sign to the right. Benches and grassy areas make this a good picnic spot (no WCs), and you can scamper about for views of the theater from different angles.

Eating: The café in the theater, La Grotte d'Auguste, has reasonably priced snacks and lunches plus views (closed Sun-Mon, tel. 04 90 60 22 54). A shaded, café-filled square, Place de la République, is two blocks from the theater up Rue Ségond Weber.

Visiting the Theater: As you go in (to the right of the actual theater), you'll see a huge dig—the site of the Temple to the Cult of the Emperor (English explanations posted). *Arausio* is the Roman name for the town. Duck into the worthwhile 15-minute film across from the entry for a good historical account of the theater and its uses since the Romans packed up and left (English subtitles).

Now enter the theater, then climb the steep stairs to find a seat high up to appreciate the acoustics (eavesdrop on people by the stage). Contemplate the idea that 2,000 years ago, Orange residents enjoyed grand spectacles here, with high-tech sound and lighting effects—such as simulated thunder, lightning, and rain. If you've been to Arles' Ancient History Museum, conjure up the theater model there and imagine this place covered with brilliant white marble.

A grandiose **Caesar** overlooks everything, reminding attendees of who's in charge. If it seems like you've seen this statue before,

you probably have. Countless identical sculptures were mass-produced in Rome and shipped throughout the empire to grace buildings like this theater for propaganda purposes. To save money on shipping and handling, only the heads of these statues were changed with each new ruler. The permanent body wears a breastplate emblazoned with the imperial griffon (body of a lion, head and wings of an eagle) that only the emperor could wear. When a new emperor came to power, new heads were made in Rome and shipped off throughout the empire to replace the pop-off heads on all these statues. (Imagine Barack Obama's head on George W. Bush's body—on second thought...)

Archaeologists believe that a puny, vanquished Celt was included at the knee of the emperor, touching his ruler's robe respectfully—a show of humble subservience to the emperor. It's interesting to consider how an effective propaganda machine can con the masses into being impressed by their leader.

The horn has blown. It's time to find your **seat:** row 2, number 30. Sitting down, you're comforted by the "EQ GIII" carved into

CÔTES DU RHÔNE

the seat (*Equitas Gradus* #3...three rows for the Equestrian order). You're not comforted by the hard limestone bench (thinking it'll probably last 2,000 years). The theater is filled with 10,000 people. Thankfully, you mix only with your class, the nouveau riche—merchants, tradesmen, and city big shots. The people seated above you are the working class, and way up in the "chicken roost" section is the scum of the earth—slaves, beggars, prostitutes, and youth hostellers. Scanning the orchestra section (where the super-rich sit on real chairs), you notice the town dignitaries hosting some visiting VIPs.

OK, time to worship. They're parading a bust of the emperor from its sacred home in the adjacent temple around the **stage.** Next is the ritual animal sacrifice called *la pompa* (so fancy, future generations will use that word for anything full of such...pomp). Finally, you settle in for an all-day series of spectacles and dramatic entertainment. All eyes are on the big stage door in the middle—where the Angelina Jolies and Brad Pitts of the day will appear. (Lesser actors come out of the side doors.)

The play is good, but many come for the halftime shows—jugglers, acrobats, and striptease dancers. In Roman times, the theater was a festival of immorality. An ancient writer commented, "The vanquished take their revenge on us by giving us their vices through the theater."

With an audience of 10,000 and no amplification, **acoustics** were critical. A roof made of linen (called the velarium) originally covered the stage, somewhat like the glass-and-iron roof you see today (installed to protect the stage wall). The original was designed not to protect the stage from the weather, but to project the voices of the actors into the crowd. For further help, actors wore masks with leather caricature mouths that functioned as megaphones. The theater's side walls originally rose as high as the stage wall and supported a retractable roof that gave the audience some protection from the sun or rain. After leaving the theater, look up to the stage wall from the outside and notice the supports for poles that held the velarium in place, like the masts and sails of a ship.

The Roman Theater was all part of the "give them bread and circuses" approach to winning the support of the masses. The spectacle grew from 65 days of games per year when the theater was first built (and when Rome was at its height) to about 180 days each year by the time Rome finally fell.

In the fourth century (under Christian emperor Constantine), the church forced many theaters to close their doors. Later, during the barbarian invasions, the stage wall became a protective wall and the theater became a secure residence for many. Amazingly, people squatted here until the 19th century. You can still see traces of some buildings within the theater.

One floor up (to the left, with your back to the stage), you'll find the amusing *Ghosts of the Theater* **multimedia show,** which covers four periods of performance history (including rock concerts).

Nearby: Pop into the **Musée d'Art et d'Histoire** across the street (included with ticket, free audioguide) to see a few theater details and a rare marble grid, ordered by Emperor Vespasian in A.D. 79. This was to be used as the official property-ownership registry—each square represented a 120-acre plot of land.

▲Roman "Arc de Triomphe"

This 60-foot-tall arch is in the center of a big traffic circle, a level 15-minute walk north from the theater. Technically the only real Roman arches of triumph are in Rome's Forum, built to commemorate various emperors' victories. But this arch was the model for those in Rome, preceding both the famous arches of Septimius Severus and Constantine. This municipal arch was erected in about A.D. 19 to commemorate a general named Germanicus, who protected the town. The facade is covered with reliefs of military exploits, including naval battles and Romans beating up on barbarians and those rude, nasty Gauls.

Hôtel de Ville

Orange owns Provence's most beautiful City Hall, worth the short detour to appreciate it (in the heart of the old town on Place Georges Clemenceau).

Sleeping and Eating in Orange

$$ Hôtel le Glacier,*** across from the TI, is run by English-speaking and affable Philippe. It's a good value, with easy parking, a comfortable lobby with a bar, and well-designed rooms (book directly for a free upgrade when available, elevator, air-con, a few parking spaces, 46 Cours Aristide Briand, tel. 04 90 34 02 01, www.le-glacier.com, info@le-glacier.com).

Located at the train station, **$ Hôtel de Provence***** is quiet, comfortable, affordable, and air-conditioned. This traditional place is run with grace (family rooms, small rooftop pool, café, pay parking, no elevator, 60 Avenue Frédéric Mistral, tel. 04 90 34 00 23, www.hotelprovence-orange.com, hoteldeprovence84@orange.fr).

Orange has several inviting squares with ample eating choices in all price ranges. A few cafés/restaurants are across from the theater. You'll find more choices by wandering the lanes toward the Hôtel de Ville. For a more refined meal, **$$$ Au Petit Patio** delivers elegant dining and fine cuisine (closed Wed-Thu and Sun, 58 Cours Aristide Briand, tel. 04 90 29 69 27).

Orange Connections

From Orange by Train to: Avignon (15/day, 20 minutes), **Arles** (4/day direct, 35 minutes, more frequent with transfer in Avignon), **Lyon** (16/day, 2 hours).

By Bus to: Châteauneuf-du-Pape (3/day, none Sun, 30 minutes), **Vaison-la-Romaine** (6-8/day, only 1 on Sun, 1 hour), **Avignon** (Mon-Sat hourly, 3/day Sun, 1 hour—take the train instead). Buses to Vaison-la-Romaine and other wine villages depart from the train station and from Place Pourtoules (see map on page 149). Bus #4 to Vaison-la-Romaine leaves from across the street and to the right of the main shelter/stop (look for blue bus icon in front of a mansion).

Near Orange: Châteauneuf-du-Pape

This most famous of the Côtes du Rhône wine villages is busy with tourists eager to sample its famous product and stroll its climbing

lanes. While I prefer the less-famous wine villages farther north (described later, under "The Best of the Côtes du Rhône Villages"), this welcoming, wine-drenched town makes an easy day trip from Avignon and works well with a visit to nearby Orange.

Châteauneuf-du-Pape means "New Castle of the Pope," named for the pope's summer retreat—now a ruin capping the beautiful-to-see but little-to-do hill town (more interesting during the Friday market). Wine-loving popes planted the first vines

here in the 1300s. The pope's crest is embossed on all bottles of this deservedly famous wine.

Approaching from Avignon, signs announce, *"Here start the vineyards of Châteauneuf-du-Pape."* Pull over and stroll into a vineyard with a view of the hill town. Notice the rocky soil—perfect for making a good wine grape. Those stones retain the sun's heat (plentiful here) and force the vines to struggle, resulting in a lean grape—lousy for eating, but ideal for producing big wines (see "Côtes du Rhône Wines" on page 36). Eight different grapes are blended to make the local specialty, which has been strictly controlled for 80 years. Grenache dominates the blend, accounting for about 75 percent of the grapes grown. Syrah and mourvèdre are the other two most-used grapes, each contributing about 10 percent to the final blend. The most interesting white wines in Provence are also made here (a blend of up to five grapes), but the reds are what attract most visitors. Most reds show their full flavor five years after

COTES DU RHONE

bottling. For more information on the area's wines, look for the Wine Museum (described later) at the start of the village as you come from Avignon.

Orientation to Châteauneuf-du-Pape

To visit Châteauneuf-du-Pape you can take a bus from Avignon or Orange (3/day, no buses on Sun) or drive. If you're coming by car, park below the town. Follow *Château* signs up the hill to the main square, Place du Portail, with its small fountain. The helpful **TI** by Place du Portail has a long list of wineries that you can visit and good documentation on the area (Mon-Sat 9:30-18:00, closed Sun except July-Aug 9:30-12:30; off-season closed for lunch; 3 Rue de la République, tel. 04 90 83 71 08). Appealing streets fan out from here, most with cellars selling the famous wine.

Sights in Châteauneuf-du-Pape

Wine Museum (Musée du Vin)

Located at the Brotte Winery, this museum provides useful background for your Côtes du Rhône exploration. After a brief look at the basics of grape-growing, the winemaking process, and the work of a *vigneron* (audioguides are essential for the high-tech displays), enjoy a tasting. You'll need to tell them what you want; see "French Wine-Tasting 101" on page 34. The English-speaking staff is ready to help you make your choices. For a clear contrast, taste the "ready-to-drink" wine (*La Fiole du Pape*), which made the winery famous, then a wine "to keep" (*vin de garde*).

Cost and Hours: Free, daily April-Oct 9:00-13:00 & 14:00-19:00—no lunch break June-mid-Sept, Nov-March 9:00-12:00 & 14:00-18:00, on Avenue Pierre de Luxembourg, at start of village if coming from Avignon, tel. 04 90 83 59 44, www.brotte.com.

Wine Tasting

The town offers many places to taste wine, including these four cellars.

Near the TI: These two cellars are central. With your back to the TI, find (on your left) **The Best Vintage** *cave*, a top place to sample Châteauneuf-du-Pape wines. Speaking fluent English and offering wines from 35 different producers, Stéphane provides a good introduction to area wines. He can arrange shipping back to the States—expensive but you're spared the VAT tax (daily March-Oct 10:30-12:30 & 13:30-18:30, shorter hours Nov-Feb, near Place du Portail at 7 Rue de la République, tel. 04 90 83 31 75, www. thebestvintage.fr). A basic WC is next door.

Continue along this street and up the staircase. Turning left, you'll find **Vinadéa Maison des Vins,** where they sell more than

200 kinds of Châteauneuf-du-Pape appellation wines from 120 different producers and offer a free tasting selection every day. Thomas speaks English (daily June-Sept 10:00-13:00 & 14:00-18:30, shorter hours off-season, 8 Rue Maréchal Foch, tel. 04 90 83 70 69, www.vinadea.com).

Uphill from Place du Portail: These two cellars are best suited for serious tasters. **Les Caves St. Charles** offers private one-hour tastings inside a 13th-century cellar, surrounded by barrels and *beaucoup* ambience. Helpful Guy Brémond answers all your questions in superb English. Chef Jean-Claude also offers a cooking class that starts with a visit to a local market and ends with a wine tasting and a nice lunch (May-Oct Mon-Sat 10:00-19:00, closed Sun, by appointment only, reserve ahead, near the church at 10 Rue des Papes, tel. 04 90 39 13 85, www.cave-saint-charles.com).

You can huff and puff (or drive) to the fancy restaurant **Cave du Verger des Papes,** where tastings include a look at underground ruins from Roman times (free, best to call ahead, rotating selection of 3-4 wines, Mon-Sat July-Aug 10:00-19:00, Sun until 16:00; Sept-June shorter hours and closed Mon; 2 Rue Montée du Château, tel. 04 90 83 58 08, www.caveduverger.com).

NEAR CHATEAUNEUF-DU-PAPE
Mas de Lionne
Lying on the fringe of Châteauneuf-du-Pape, Mas de Lionne winery is where American Doug Graves is following his retirement dream. Doug bought this small vineyard in 2008 and has been living and working it nonstop since. He does just about everything by himself, but still has time to greet travelers and explain how his wines are made. As a *negociant*, he produces both Côtes du Rhône and Châteauneuf-du-Pape wines from grapes grown by others in the region. Doug makes light rosé and velvety red wines, including one using 100 percent grenache grapes (unusual in this area, where typically several grapes are blended). His interesting story and ability to explain winemaking to Anglophones make this a worthwhile stop for aficionados (Tue-Sat 14:00-18:00, closed Sun-Mon; find the town of Sorgues and look for *Mas de Lionne* signs off N-7, pass the first house with the small *Mas de Lionne* sign—the winery is 100 yards up the road at 948 Chemin de la Lionne, mobile 06 37 16 04 56, www.masdelalionne.com).

CÔTES DU RHÔNE

Sleeping and Eating
in Châteauneuf-du-Pape

To bed down in Châteauneuf-du-Pape, try the traditional **$ Hôtel-Restaurant La Garbure,** ideally located one door up the (mostly) pedestrian street from the TI (3 Rue Joseph Ducos, tel. 04 90 83 75 08, www.la-garbure.com).

You'll find several appealing eateries around Place du Portail on Rue Joseph Ducos. **$$ Le Pistou** serves salads and *menus* from €15 (closed Sun evening and all day Mon, #15, tel. 04 90 83 71 75). **$$ La Maisouneta,** at #7, is good for fresh pasta dishes (*menus* from €15, closed Tue evenings and all day Wed, tel. 04 90 32 55 03).

It's well worth the time and energy to follow signs up the hill to **$$$ Le Verger des Papes,** a fine restaurant where you can feast both on the terrace views and on their traditional and sophisticated cuisine (their €22 lunch *menu* is a killer deal; closed all day Mon and Sun evenings; reservations smart, 4 Rue Montée du Château—drivers can follow *Château* signs and park at the top to skip the climb, tel. 04 90 83 50 40, www.vergerdespapes.com).

For **picnic** supplies, try one of the three cafés that surround the TI, which can all make their sandwiches to go, or find the small grocery, **Le Cigalou,** halfway up Rue Joseph Ducos (Tue-Fri 8:00-12:30 & 15:30-19:30, Sat-Mon 8:00-12:30).

Côtes du Rhône

The Côtes du Rhône region features classic Provençal scenery, characteristic villages, cozy wineries, fields of fragrant lavender, and excellent good-value restaurants. If you're sleeping in this area, Vaison-la-Romaine is a handy home base. Delve into the region's highlights by following my self-guided driving tour. With more time, dig deeper into the  Côtes du Rhône with a drive up Mont Ventoux, a spin around the Drôme Provençale, or a visit to the Ardèche Gorges.

Vaison-la-Romaine

With quick access to vineyards, villages, and Mont Ventoux, this lively little town of 6,000 makes a good base for exploring the Côtes du Rhône region by car, by bike, or on foot. You get two villages for the price of one: Vaison-la-Romaine's "modern" lower city has Roman ruins, a lone pedestrian street, and a lively main square—café-lined Place Montfort. The car-free medieval hill town looms above, with meandering cobbled lanes, art galleries and cafés, and a ruined castle with a fine view from its base. (Vaison-la-Romaine is also a good place to have your hair done, since there are more than 20 hairdressers in this small town.)

Orientation to Vaison-la-Romaine

The city is split in two by the Ouvèze River. The Roman Bridge connects the lower town (Ville-Basse) with the hill-capping medieval upper town (Ville-Haute).

TOURIST INFORMATION
The TI is in the lower city, between the two Roman ruin sites, at Place du Chanoine Sautel (July-Aug Mon-Fri 9:00-18:45, Sat-Sun  9:00-12:30 & 14:00-18:45; Sept-June Mon-Sat 9:30-12:00 & 14:00-17:45, Sun 9:30-12:00—except closed Sun mid-Oct-March; tel. 04 90 36 02 11, www.vaison-ventoux-tourisme.com). Say *bonjour* to *charmante* and ever-so-patient Valerie, use the free Wi-Fi, ask about festivals and other events, and pick up information on walks and bike rides. The big wall map shows the neighboring villages.

ARRIVAL IN VAISON-LA-ROMAINE
By Bus: Bus stops are in front of the Cave la Romaine winery. Tell the driver you want the stop for the *Office de Tourisme*. When you get off the bus, walk five minutes down Avenue Général de Gaulle to reach the TI and recommended hotels.

By Car: Follow signs to *Centre-Ville*, then *Office de Tourisme*, and park in or near the big lot across from the TI. Parking is free in Vaison-la-Romaine.

HELPFUL HINTS
Market Day: Sleep in Vaison-la-Romaine on Monday night, and you'll wake to an amazing Tuesday market. If you spend a

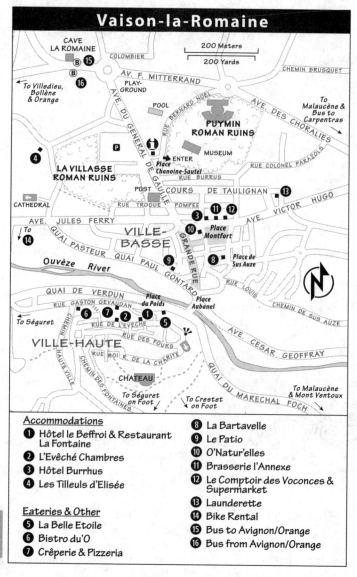

Vaison-la-Romaine

Accommodations

1. Hôtel le Beffroi & Restaurant La Fontaine
2. L'Evêché Chambres
3. Hôtel Burrhus
4. Les Tilleuls d'Elisée

Eateries & Other

5. La Belle Etoile
6. Bistro du'O
7. Crêperie & Pizzeria
8. La Bartavelle
9. Le Patio
10. O'Natur'elles
11. Brasserie l'Annexe
12. Le Comptoir des Voconces & Supermarket
13. Launderette
14. Bike Rental
15. Bus to Avignon/Orange
16. Bus from Avignon/Orange

COTES DU RHONE

Monday night, avoid parking at market sites and where signs indicate *Stationnement Interdit le Mardi*, or you won't find your car where you left it—ask your hotelier where you can park.

Wi-Fi: The **TI** and **Café Universal,** on atmospheric Place Montfort, offer free Wi-Fi.

Laundry: The self-service **Laverie la Lavandière** is on Cours Taulignan, near Avenue Victor Hugo (daily 8:00-22:00, English instructions). The friendly owners, who work next door at the dry cleaners, will do your laundry while you sightsee (dry cleaners open Mon-Fri 9:00-12:00 & 15:00-18:30, Sat 9:00-12:00, closed Sun).

Supermarket: A handy **Casino** is on Place Montfort in the thick of the cafés (Mon-Sat 7:30-13:00 & 15:30-19:30, Sun 9:00-13:00).

Bike Rental: The TI has a list. For help with bike rental and biking plans, contact John and Monique at the recommended **L'Ecole Buissonnière Chambres** (see listing later, under "Sleeping in Vaison-la-Romaine"). **Sunebike** is most central and rents electric and regular bikes (160 Avenue René Cassin, tel. 09 54 94 99 14, www.sun-e-bike.com).

Taxi: Call 04 90 36 00 04 or 04 90 46 89 42.

Car Rental: You can rent cars by the day, though they must be returned to Vaison-la-Romaine; ask at the TI for locations.

Local Guide: Scottish by birth and an attorney by profession, **Janet Henderson** offers in-depth historic walks of Vaison-la-Romaine (€30/person, minimum 3 people or €90, allow 2.5 hours, www.provencehistorytours.com, janet.henderson@wanadoo.fr).

Tourist Train: The **Petit Train** stops in front of the TI and does a loop around the town.

Cooking Classes: Charming **Barbara Schuerenberg** offers reasonably priced cooking classes from her view home in Vaison-la-Romaine, where you'll pick herbs from the garden to use in the recipes (€90, cash only, includes lunch, 4-person maximum, tel. 04 90 35 68 43, www.cuisinedeprovence.com, cuisinedeprovence@gmail.com).

Sights in Vaison-la-Romaine

Roman Ruins

Ancient Vaison-la-Romaine had a treaty that gave it a preferred "federated" relationship with Rome (rather than simply being a colony). This, along with a healthy farming economy (olives and vineyards), made it a most prosperous place...as a close look at its sprawling ruins demonstrates. About 6,000 people called Vaison-la-Romaine home 2,000 years ago. When the barbarians arrived,  the Romans were forced out, and the townspeople fled into the hills (see the sidebar on page 172). The town's population has only

CÔTES DU RHÔNE

recently recovered from those barbaric times, with the number of residents again reaching Roman-era numbers.

Cost and Hours: €9; daily June-Sept 9:30-18:30, shorter hours off-season, closed Jan-Feb; videoguide-€3 or download free app, tel. 04 90 36 50 48, www.vaison-la-romaine.com.

Visiting the Ruins: Vaison-la-Romaine's Roman ruins are split by a modern road into two sites: Puymin and La Villasse. Each is well presented, thanks to the videoguide and occasional English information panels, offering a good look at life during the Roman Empire. The Roman town extended all the way from here to the river, and its main square (forum) still lies under today's main square, Place Montfort. What  you can see is only a small fraction of the Roman town's extent— most is still buried under today's city. For helpful background about Roman civilization, read "The Romans in Provence" on page 27.

Visit **Puymin** first. Nearest the entry are the scant but impressive ruins of a sprawling mansion. Find the faint remains of a colorful frescoed wall. Climb the hill to the good little **museum** (pick up your videoguide here; exhibits also explained in English loaner booklet). Be sure to see the **film** that takes you inside the home of a wealthy Vaison resident and explores daily life some 2,000 years ago. Behind the museum is a still well-used, 6,000-seat theater, with just enough seats for the whole town (of yesterday and today).

Back across the modern road in **La Villasse,** you'll explore a "street of shops" and the foundations of more houses. You'll also see a few wells, used before Vaison's two aqueducts were built. (You can also see the sight perfectly well without entering: follow the path immediately to its left with your back to the TI.)

Lower Town (Ville-Basse)

Vaison-la-Romaine's modern town centers on café-friendly Place Montfort. Tables grab the north side of the square, conveniently sheltered from the prevailing mistral wind while enjoying the generous shade of the ubiquitous plane trees. The trees are cut way back each year to form a leafy canopy (see sidebar on page 260). Nearby, the pedestrian-only Grand Rue is a lively shopping street leading to the small river gorge and the Roman Bridge.

Roman Bridge

The Romans cut this sturdy, no-nonsense vault into the canyon rock 2,000 years ago, and it has survived ever since. Approaching from the lower town end of the bridge, find the information panel on the left. Until the 20th century, this was the only way to cross the Ouvèze River. See also the stone plaque *(Septembre 22-92...)* on the wall to the right, showing the high-water mark of the record flood that killed 30 people. The flood swept the modern top of this bridge—and several other modern bridges—downstream, but couldn't budge the 55-foot Roman arch.

Upper Town (Ville-Haute)

Although there's nothing of particular importance to see in the fortified medieval old town atop the hill, the cobbled lanes and enchanting fountains make you want to break out a sketchpad. Vaison-la-Romaine was ruled by a prince-bishop starting in the fourth century. He came under attack by the Count of Toulouse in the 12th century. Anticipating a struggle, the prince-bishop abandoned the lower town and built a castle on this rocky outcrop (about 1195). Over time, the townspeople followed, vacating the lower town and building their homes at the base of the château behind the upper town's fortified wall.

To reach the upper town, hike up from the Roman Bridge (passing memorials for both world wars) through the medieval gate, under the lone tower crowned by an 18th-century wrought-iron bell cage. Look for occasional English information plaques as you meander. The château itself is closed, but a steep, uneven trail to its base rewards hikers with a sweeping view.

▲▲Market Day

In the 16th century, the pope gave Vaison-la-Romaine market-town status. Each Tuesday morning since then, the town has hosted a farmers' market. Today merchants turn the entire place into a festival of produce and Provençal products. This market is one of France's best, but it can challenge claustrophobes. Be warned that parking is a real headache unless you arrive early (see "Helpful Hints," earlier; for tips on enjoying market day, see the Shopping chapter).

Wine Tasting

Cave la Romaine, a five-minute walk up Avenue Général de Gaulle from the TI, offers a big variety of good-value wines from nearby villages in a pleasant, well-organized tasting room (free tastes, Mon-Sat 9:00-18:30 but closes for lunch, Sun 9:00-12:00, Avenue St-Quenin, tel. 04 90 36 55 90, www.cave-la-romaine.com).

▲Hiking

The TI has information on hikes into the hills above Vaison-la-Romaine.

It's about 1.25 hours to the quiet hill town of Crestet, though views begin immediately. To find the trail, drive or walk on the road past the upper town (with the rock base and castle on your left), continue on Chemin des Fontaines (blue signs), and stay the course as far as you like (follow yellow Crestet signs). Cars are not allowed on the road after about a mile.

To find the five-mile trail to Séguret (allow 2 hours), take the same road above Vaison-la-Romaine and look for a yellow sign (*Sablet/Coste Belle*) to the right. For either route, consider hiking one way and taking a taxi back.

Biking

The TI has details on several manageable bike routes, with directions in English, as well as information on mountain-biking trails (also available at bike shops). If the air's calm, the five-mile ride to cute little Villedieu (with the recommended La Maison Bleue restaurant) is a delight. Renting an electric bike makes this an easier outing (see "Helpful Hints," earlier). The bike route is signed along small roads; from Vaison-la-Romaine, find the road to Villedieu at the roundabout by Cave La Romaine (see map on page 158). With a bit more energy, you can pedal beyond Villedieu on the lovely road to Mirabel (from Villedieu, follow signs to *Nyons*). Make a detour to Piégon (to avoid that busy section of road between Mirabel and Vaison), then rejoin the busy D-938 to reach Vaison (figure about 18 miles total). Alternatively, get a good map and connect the following villages for an enjoyable 11-mile loop ride: Vaison-la-Romaine, St-Romain-en-Viennois, Puyméras, Faucon, and St-Marcellin-lès-Vaison.

Sleeping in Vaison-la-Romaine

Hotels in Vaison-la-Romaine are a good value and are split between the upper medieval village (with all the steps) and the lower main town (with all the services). Those in the upper town (Ville-Haute) are quieter, cozier, cooler, and give you the feeling of sleeping in a hill town (some come with views), with all the services of a real town just steps away. But they require a 10-minute walk down to the town center and Roman ruins. If staying at one of the first three places, follow signs to *Cité Médiévale* and park just outside the upper village entry (driving into the Cité Médiévale itself is a challenge, with tiny lanes and nearly impossible parking).

If you have a car, consider staying in one of the Côtes du Rhône villages near Vaison-la-Romaine. I've listed a few nearby places here; for more suggestions see the "Côtes du Rhône Wine Road Driving Tour," later.

IN THE UPPER TOWN

$$ Hôtel le Beffroi*** hides deep in the upper town, just above a demonstrative bell tower (you'll hear what I mean). It offers 16th-century red-tile-and-wood-beamed-cozy lodgings with nary a level surface. The rooms—split between two buildings a few doors apart—are Old World comfy, and some have views. You'll enjoy antique-filled public spaces, a garden with view tables (meals available in good weather), a small pool with more views, and animated Nathalie at the reception (several good family rooms, closed mid-Jan-March, Rue de l'Evêché, tel. 04 90 36 04 71, www.le-beffroi. com, hotel@le-beffroi.com). The hotel's **$$$ restaurant** offers *menus* from €32 (see "Eating in Vaison-la-Romaine," later).

$$ L'Evêché Chambres, a few doors away from Hôtel le Beffroi, is a five-room melt-in-your-chair B&B. The owners (the Verdiers) have an exquisite sense of interior design and are passionate about books, making this place feel like a cross between a library and an art gallery (the *solanum* suite is worth every euro, Rue de l'Evêché, tel. 04 90 36 13 46, mobile 06 03 03 21 42, www.eveche. free.fr, eveche@aol.com).

IN THE LOWER TOWN

$ Hôtel Burrhus** is equal parts contemporary art gallery and funky-creaky hotel—but a good value. It's a central, laid-back place, with a broad, terrific terrace over Place Montfort and surprisingly good rooms (for maximum quiet, request a back room). Its floor plan will confound even the ablest navigator; the jukebox in the lobby sometimes works (air-con, 1 Place Montfort, tel. 04 90 36 00 11, www.burrhus.com, info@burrhus.com).

$ Les Tilleuls d'Elisée is a terrific *chambres d'hôte* in a stone, blue-shuttered home near the Notre-Dame de Nazareth Cathedral, a few minutes' walk below the TI. Anne and Laurent Viau run this comfortable five-room place with grace and great rates. Relax in the garden with views to the upper town and ask about wine tastings in their small cellar (includes breakfast, air-con, 1 Avenue Jules Mazen, tel. 04 90 35 63 04, www.vaisonchambres. info, anne.viau@vaisonchambres.info).

NEAR VAISON-LA-ROMAINE

$ L'Ecole Buissonnière Chambres is run by an engaging Anglo-French team, John and Monique, who share their peace and quiet 10 minutes north of Vaison-la-Romaine. This creatively restored farmhouse has three character-filled, half-timbered rooms and comfy public spaces. Getting to know John, who has lived all over the south of France, is worth the price of the room. The outdoor kitchen allows guests to picnic in high fashion in the tranquil garden (family rooms, includes breakfast, cash only; between Villedieu and Buisson on D-75—leave Vaison following signs to *Villedieu*, then follow D-51 toward Buisson and turn left onto D-75; tel. 04 90 28 95 19, www.buissonniere-provence.com, ecole. buissonniere@wanadoo.fr).

Eating in Vaison-la-Romaine

Vaison-la-Romaine offers a handful of good dining experiences—arrive by 19:30 in summer or reserve ahead, particularly on weekends. And while you can eat very well on a moderate budget in Vaison, it's well worth venturing to nearby Côtes du Rhône villages to eat. I've listed two nearby places; for recommendations farther afield see the "Côtes du Rhône Wine Road Driving Tour," later. Wherever you dine, begin with a fresh glass of Muscat from the nearby village of Beaumes-de-Venise.

IN THE UPPER TOWN

$$$ Restaurant La Fontaine, located at the recommended **Hôtel le Beffroi,** serves traditional cuisine in the lovely hotel gardens when the weather agrees, and in the pleasant dining room when it doesn't. If they're serving in the garden, you won't find a better setting in Vaison (daily, tel. 04 90 36 04 71).

$$ La Belle Etoile is a special place. Locals come here for simple, fresh, and good-value meals in a fun, eclectic setting. It's a little like eating in your hip grandma's living room. The cuisine is inspired by owner Jerome's travels, and there's no menu because the selection varies daily. Outside tables come with views over the lower town (April-Dec, closes when they run out of food or inspiration, closed Thu and Sat lunch; it's the first place you pass when coming from the lower town, tel. 04 90 37 31 45).

$$$ Bistro du'O dishes up fine, creative, and well-presented cuisine in a stone, Provençal setting in the lower part of Ville Haute (closed Sun-Mon, Rue Gaston Gevaudan, tel. 04 90 41 72 90).

$ You'll also find a simple *crêperie* with a view deck and a **pizzeria** on the main street leading up to the old town. Both have indoor and outdoor seating, some views over the river, and cheap, basic food (good for families).

IN THE LOWER TOWN

$$ La Bartavelle, run by friendly Berangère, is a good place to savor traditional French cuisine, with a tourist-friendly mix-and-match choice of local options. Her €30 *menu* gets you four courses; the €23 *menu* gives you top-end main-course selections and dessert (closed Mon and Fri lunch, also closed Sun evening off-season; outside terrace, air-con, 12 Place de Sus Auze, tel. 04 90 36 02 16).

$$$ Le Patio is the most romantic place I list, with a softly lit courtyard at night and a contemporary interior. The chef celebrates local products with a touch of Italian influence. Appetizers and a good selection of local and Italian wines are also available at the wine bar from 18:00 (*menus* from €30, closed Wed evening, Sat for lunch, and all day Sun off-season, 4 Rue du Ventoux, tel. 04 90 65 53 82).

$$ O'Natur'elles is a sweet little place. It's ideal for vegetarians, but good for all persuasions as the all-organic dishes can be served with or without meat. The cuisine is delicious, but the place is small (closed Wed, also closed Tue and Thu for dinner, reservations smart, 38 Place Montfort, tel. 04 90 65 81 67).

Cafés on Place Montfort: Come here for lighter **$$** café fare and to observe the daily flow of life in Vaison-la-Romaine. It's best to dine outside. **Brasserie l'Annexe** serves good café food and has a loyal following (open daily), while **Le Comptoir des Voconces** is the happening hangout with a pub-like ambience.

NEAR VAISON-LA-ROMAINE

$ La Maison Bleue, about four miles north of Vaison-la-Romaine on Villedieu's delightful little square, serves good pizzas and salads with great outdoor ambience. Skip it if the weather forces you inside (March-Oct Thu-Sun open for lunch and dinner, closed Mon-Wed except July-Aug closed Mon only, tel. 04 90 28 97 02).

$$ Auberge d'Anaïs, at the end of a dirt road 10 minutes from Vaison-la-Romaine, is a fun Provençal experience, ideal for a relaxing lunch. Outdoor tables gather under cheery lights with views and good cuisine. Ask for a table *sur la terrasse* (closed Sun evening and Mon, tel. 04 90 36 20 06). Heading east of Vaison-la-Romaine, follow signs to *Carpentras,* then *St. Marcellin.* Signs will guide you from there.

Vaison-la-Romaine Connections

The most central **bus stop** is a few blocks up Avenue Général de Gaulle from the TI at the main winery, Cave la Romaine. Buses to Orange and Avignon stop on the winery side. Buses to Nyons, Crestet, and Carpentras depart from the bus station farther east on that road (see map on page 158).

From Vaison-la-Romaine by Bus to: Avignon (3-6/day, all buses pass through Orange, 1.5 hours), **Orange** (3-6/day, 45 minutes), **Nyons** (3-5/day, none on Sun, 45 minutes), **Crestet** (lower village below Crestet, 3/day, none on Sun, 5 minutes), **Carpentras** (3/day, none on Sun, 45 minutes).

CÔTES DU RHÔNE

Best of the Côtes du Rhône Villages

Officially, the Côtes du Rhône vineyards follow the Rhône River from just south of Lyon to Avignon. Our focus is the southern section of the Côtes du Rhône, centering on the small area between Châteauneuf-du-Pape and Vaison-la-Romaine.

Circling the rugged Dentelles de Montmirail mountain peaks, you'll experience all that's unique about this region: its natural beauty, glowing limestone villages, inviting wineries, and rolling hills of vineyards. One hundred million years ago, the Mediterranean Sea extended this far north, leaving behind a sandy soil base for today's farmers (the wine town of Sablet's name comes from the French word *sable*, meaning sand).

PLANNING YOUR TIME

Although seeing the Côtes du Rhône is possible as a day trip by car from Arles or Avignon, you'll have a more enjoyable and intimate experience if you sleep in one of the villages (my favorite accommodations are listed under "Sleeping in Vaison-la-Romaine" on page 162).

With a car, the best one-day plan is to take the driving tour described below (allow an entire day for the 80-mile round-trip from Avignon). Try to get the first two stops done before lunch (most wineries are closed 12:00-14:00; call ahead if possible), then complete the loop in the afternoon. Some wineries are closed on Sundays, holidays, and during the harvest (mid-Sept). This area is picnic-friendly, but there are few shops along the way—stock up before you leave.

GETTING AROUND THE COTES DU RHONE VILLAGES

This area is clearly easiest if you have four wheels. Without a car, it's tougher, but a representative sampling is doable by **bike** (for ideas, see "Biking" on page 162) or by **bus** (3-6 buses/day from Avignon and Orange stop at several Côtes du Rhône villages; consider taking the bus one-way, then returning by taxi). For less effort and more expense, several of the local guides and minivan tour companies I list are happy to follow my route (see "Tours in Provence" on page 24).

Le Mistral

Provence lives with its vicious mistral winds, which blow 30-60 miles per hour, about 100 days out of the year. Locals say it blows in multiples of threes: three, six, or nine days in a row. The mistral clears people off the streets and turns lively cities into ghost towns. You'll likely spend a few hours or days taking refuge. The winds are strongest between noon and 15:00.

When the mistral blows, it's everywhere, and you can't escape. Author Peter Mayle said it could blow the ears off a donkey (I'd include the tail). According to the natives, it ruins crops, shutters, and roofs (look for stones holding tiles in place on many homes). They'll also tell you that this pernicious wind has driven many people crazy (including young Vincent van Gogh). A weak version of the wind is called a *mistralet*.

The mistral starts above the Alps and Massif Central mountains and gathers steam as it heads south, gaining momentum as it screams over the Rhône Valley (which acts like a funnel between the Alps and the Cévennes mountains) before exhausting itself when it hits the Mediterranean. And though this wind rattles shutters everywhere in the Riviera and Provence, it's strongest over the Rhône Valley...so Avignon, Arles, and the Côtes du Rhône villages bear its brunt. While wiping the dust from your eyes, remember the good news: The mistral brings clear skies.

Côtes du Rhône Wine Road Driving Tour

My self-guided driving tour (allow at least a half-day) starts in the village of Séguret, then on to Vaison-la-Romaine, and winds clockwise around the Dentelles de Montmirail, visiting the mountaintop village of Crestet, adorable little Suzette, and the renowned wine villages of Beaumes-de-Venise and Gigondas. As you drive, notice how some vineyards grow at angles—they're planted this way to compensate for the strong effect of the mistral wind.

This trip provides a crash course in Rhône Valley wine, an excuse to meet the locals who make the stuff, and breathtaking scenery—especially late in the day, when the famous Provençal sunlight causes colors to absolutely pop.

I've listed several wineries *(domaines)* along the way. Before you go, study up with "French Wine-Tasting 101" on page 34. Even if wine isn't your thing, don't miss this scenic drive. (And this region is not only about wine; you'll pass orchards of apricots, figs, cherries, and table grapes as well.) Theft is a problem in this beautiful area—leave absolutely nothing in your car.

Remember that the wineries you'll visit are serious about their

COTES DU RHONE

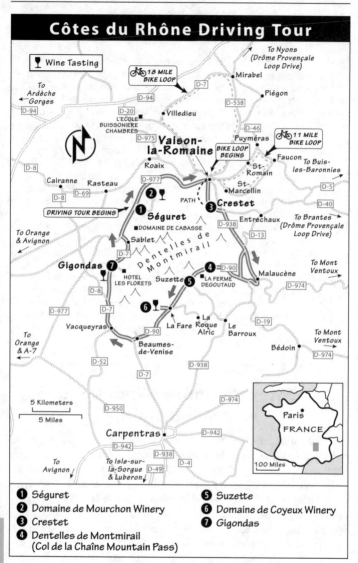

Côtes du Rhône Driving Tour

🍷 Wine Tasting

🚲 18 MILE BIKE LOOP

To Nyons
(Drôme Provençale
Loop Drive)

Mirabel

Piégon

To Ardèche Gorges

D-94

D-7

D-94

D-20

D-538

D-46

Villedieu

L'ÉCOLE
BUISSONIÈRE
CHAMBRES

D-975

Vaison-la-Romaine

BIKE LOOP BEGINS

🚲 11 MILE BIKE LOOP

Puyméras

Faucon To Buis-les-Baronnies

Roaix

St-Romain

D-8

Cairanne Rasteau

D-977

St-Marcellin

D-5

D-8 D-69

PATH

❸ Crestet

D-40

DRIVING TOUR BEGINS

❶ Séguret

Entrechaux

To Brantes
(Drôme Provençale
Loop Drive)

❷ 🍷

DOMAINE DE CABASSE

D-938

D-13

To Orange & Avignon

Sablet

D-7

Dentelles de Montmirail

To Mont Ventoux

Gigondas ❼

❹ D-90

Malaucène

HOTEL LES FLORETS

Suzette ❺

LA FERME DEGOUTAUD

D-974

D-8

D-977

D-7

❻ 🍷

La Fare

La Roque Alric

Le Barroux

D-19

To Mont Ventoux

Vacqueyras

D-90

Beaumes-de-Venise

Bédoin

D-974

To Orange & A-7

D-52

D-938

D-7

5 Kilometers

5 Miles

D-950

D-974

Carpentras

D-942

Paris
FRANCE

D-942 D-938 D-4

To Avignon

To Isle-sur-la-Sorgue & Luberon

D-49

100 Miles

❶ Séguret
❷ Domaine de Mourchon Winery
❸ Crestet
❹ Dentelles de Montmirail
   (Col de la Chaîne Mountain Pass)

❺ Suzette
❻ Domaine de Coyeux Winery
❼ Gigondas

CÔTES DU RHÔNE

wines—and they hope that you'll take them seriously, too. At private wineries, tastings are not happy-go-lucky chances to knock back a few glasses and buy a T-shirt with the property's label on it. Show genuine interest in the wines, and buy some if you enjoy your tastes.

Drivers can enjoy a wealth of country-Provençal hotel and dining opportunities in rustic settings within 15 minutes of Vaison-la-Romaine. They offer a great opportunity for drivers who want to experience rural France and get better values. All restaurants listed have some outdoor seating and should be considered for lunch or dinner.

You can start anywhere along this circular route. See below for a description of each stop, along with good restaurant and hotel options.

SEGURET TO CRESTET, SUZETTE, GIGONDAS, AND BACK

Our tour starts a bit south of Vaison-la-Romaine in little Séguret. By bike, or for a more scenic drive from Vaison-la-Romaine, cross to the Cité Médiévale side of the river, then follow D-977 signs downriver to Séguret. A hiking trail from above Vaison-la-Romaine's castle leads to Séguret in 8.5 miles (see page 162).

❶ Séguret

Blending into the hillside with a smattering of shops, two cafés, made-to-stroll lanes, and a natural spring, this hamlet is understandably popular. Séguret makes for a good coffee or ice cream stop.

Séguret's name comes from the Latin word *securitas* (meaning "security"). The bulky entry arch came with a massive gate, which drilled in the message of the village's name. In the Middle Ages, Séguret was patrolled 24/7—they never took their *securitas* for granted. Walk through the arch. To appreciate how the homes' outer walls provided security in those days, drop down the first passage on your right (near the fountain). These tunnel-like exit passages, or *poternes*, were needed in periods of peace to allow the town to expand below.

Find Séguret's open washbasin *(lavoir)*, a hotbed of social activity and gossip over the ages. The basins behind the fountain (now planted) were reserved for washing animals (which outnumbered residents in the Middle Ages); the larger ones (on the left) were for laundry only. Public washbasins like this were used right up until World War II. Farther on, take a left at the fork. The community bread oven *(four banal)* was used for festivals and celebrations. Rue Calade leads up to the unusual 12th-century St. Denis church for views (the circular village you see below is Sablet). This rock-sculpted church is usually closed, but it's worth a look from the outside. High above, a castle once protected Séguret, but all that's left today is a tower that you can barely make out (trails provide access).

At Christmas, this entire village transforms itself into one big crèche scene—a Provençal tradition that has long since died out in other villages.

Sleeping and Eating: Sure, it's a hotel and restaurant, but winemaking is also part of the business at **$$ Domaine de**

Cabasse,*** a lovely spread flanked by vineyards at the foot of Séguret (with a walking path to the village). Free tastings are offered every evening at 18:30 from April through September. Each of the 23 rooms has tasteful decor, air-conditioning, and views over vines; all the first-floor rooms have balconies or decks (elevator, big heated pool, discount for 2-3 night stay if reserved directly with hotel; on D-23 between Sablet and Séguret, entry gate opens automatically...and slowly, tel. 04 90 46 91 12, www.cabasse.fr, hotel@cabasse.fr). The **$$$** classy country **restaurant** offers fine cuisine and is worth booking ahead.

With a terrific setting in the center of the village, **$$ Restaurant/Café Côté Terrasse** delivers big portions, good prices, top quality, and cheerful service (daily from 10:00, Rue des Poternes, tel. 04 90 28 03 48).

• *Signs near Séguret's parking will lead you up, up, and away to our next stop, Domaine de Mourchon.*

❷ Domaine de Mourchon Winery

This high-flying winery blends state-of-the-art technology with traditional winemaking methods (a shiny ring of stainless-steel vats holds grapes grown on land plowed by horses). The wines are winning the respect of international critics, yet the (Scottish) owners seem eager to help anyone understand Rhône Valley wines. Language is not an issue here, nor is a lack of stunning views. Free and informative English tours of the vineyards are usually offered (wines-€9-33/bottle; winery open Mon-Sat 9:00-18:00, Sun by appointment only; from Easter-Oct, call to verify; tel. 04 90 46 70 30, info@domainedemourchon.com).

• *Next, return to Vaison-la-Romaine and follow signs toward Carpentras/Malaucène. After passing through "lower" Crestet, look for signs leading up to Le Village. Drivers should pass by the first parking lot and keep climbing to park at Place du Château at the top of town.*

❸ Crestet

This quiet village—founded after the fall of the Roman Empire, when people banded together in high places like this for protection from marauding barbarians—followed the usual hill-town evolution (see sidebar on page 172). The outer walls of the village did double duty as ramparts and house walls. The castle above (from about A.D. 850) provided a final safe haven when the village was attacked.

The Bishop of Vaison-la-Romaine was the first occupant, lending little Crestet a certain prestige. With about 500 residents in 1200, Crestet was a big deal in this region, reaching its zenith in the mid-1500s, when 660 people called it home. Crestet's gradual decline started when the bishop moved to Vaison-la-Romaine in the 1600s, though the population remained fairly stable until World War II. Today, about 35 people live within the walls year-round (about 55 during the summer boom).

Wander the peaceful lanes and appreciate the amount of work it took to put these stones in place. Notice the elaborate water channels. Crestet was served by 18 cisterns in the Middle Ages. Imagine hundreds of people living here with animals roaming everywhere. The bulky Romanesque church (unpredictable hours) is built into the hillside and has an unusual stained-glass window behind the altar.

Eating: The village's only business, the café-restaurant **$$ Le Panoramic,** is well signed at the top of town and has an upstairs terrace with a view that justifies the name...even if the food is mediocre. It serves good-enough omelets, salads, crêpes, and *plats* for too much—until you consider the vista, from what must be Provence's greatest view tables. Stop for a coffee or drink and enjoy the panorama (April-Nov daily 10:30-22:00, closed in bad weather and Dec-March, tel. 04 90 28 76 42).

Nearby: A fine lunch stop is **$$ La Fleur Bleue,** which serves fresh and local cuisine in an atmospheric setting (€15 lunch *menu*, closed Wed and Sun, no lunch on Sat, reservations smart, Chemin du Sublon, a mile from Crestet on the right towards Malaucène, tel. 04 90 36 23 45, www.lafleurbleue.fr).

• *Signs from the top of the village lead to the footpath to Vaison-La-Romaine. The trail leaves from Chemin de la Verrière at the very top of the village (by the intersection with the road from below). Look for the brown sign, which indicates that it's 8.8 kilometers (about 5 miles) to Vaison-la-Romaine, and—in a few steps—turn right, following the yellow sign that shows it's 5.1 kilometers (3 miles) to Vaison-la-Romaine (via Chemin des Fontaines).*

Drivers should carry on and reconnect with the road below, following signs to Malaucène. Entering Malaucène, turn right on D-90 (direction: Suzette) just before the gas station. After a few minutes you'll approach a pass. Look for signs on the left to Col de la Chaîne (Chain Pass). From this point on, the scenery gets better fast.

❹ Dentelles de Montmirail (Col de la Chaîne Mountain Pass)

Get out of your car at the pass (elevation: about 1,500 feet) and enjoy the breezy views. The peaks in the distance—thrusting up like the back of a stegosaurus or a bad haircut (you decide)—are

The Life of a Hill Town in Provence

Heat-seeking northerners have made Provence's hill towns prosperous and worldly. But before the 1960s, few wanted to live in these sun-drenched, rock-top settings. Like lost ships in search of safe harbor, the people of long ago took refuge here only out of necessity.

When the Romans settled Provence (125 B.C.), they brought stability to the warring locals, and hill-towners descended en masse to the Roman cities (such as Arles, Orange, Nîmes, and Vaison-la-Romaine). There they enjoyed theaters, fresh water from aqueducts, and commercial goods brought via the Roman road that stretched from Spain to Italy.

When Rome fell (A.D. 476), barbarians swept in, forcing locals back into the hills, where they'd stay for almost 1,000 years. These "Dark Ages" were when many of the villages we see today were established. Most grew up around castles, since peasants depended on their lord for security. The hill-towners gathered stones from nearby fields and built their homes side by side to form a defensive wall, terracing the hillsides to maximize the scarce arable land. But medieval life was not easy behind those walls—there were barbarians, plagues, crop failures, droughts, thieves, wars, and the everyday battle with gravity.

As the Renaissance approached, and Provence came under the protection of an increasingly centralized French nation, barbarian invasions dwindled. Just when the hill-towners thought the coast was clear to relocate below, France's religious wars (1500s) chased them back up. As Protestants and Catholics duked it out, hilltop villages prospered, welcoming refugees. Little Séguret (pop. 100 today) had almost 1,000 residents; the village of Mérindol (near Avignon) sprouted from nowhere; and Fort de Buoux (near Apt, nothing but ruins today—see page 215) was an im-

COTES DU RHONE

the Dentelles de Montmirail, a small range running just nine miles basically north to south and reaching 2,400 feet in elevation. This region's land is constantly shifting. Those rocky tops were the result of a gradual uplifting of the land, which was then blown bald by the angry mistral wind. Below, pine and oak trees mix with the shrub Scotch broom, which blooms brilliant yellow in May and June. You may see rich yellow-to-reddish patches of land—the result of deposits of ochre located deep below. The village below the peaks is Suzette (you'll be there soon). The yellow-signed hiking-only trail leads to the castle-topped village of Le Barroux (3.5 miles, mostly downhill).

The scene is gorgeous and surprisingly undeveloped. You can thank the lack of water for the absence of more homes or farms in this area. Water is everything in this parched region, and if you don't have ready access to it, you can't build or cultivate the land.

pregnable fortress. The turmoil of the Revolution (1789) continued to make the above-the-fray hill towns desirable.

Over the next century, hill towns slept peacefully as the rest of France modernized. Most of the hill towns you'll visit housed between 200 and 600 people and were self-sufficient. But 20th-century life down below required fewer stairs—and was closer to the convenience of trains, planes, and automobiles. So after World War I, down the hill-towners moved. To build in the flatlands, they pillaged the hill towns' stones, roof tiles—you name it, they took it—leaving those villages in ruin and virtual ghost towns.

In recent years, hill towns have bounced back. Real estate boomed as Parisians, northern Europeans, and (to a lesser extent) North Americans discovered the rustic charm of hill-town life. They invested huge sums—far more than most locals could afford. Today's hill towns survive in part thanks to these outsiders' deep pockets.

Today, many villages have organizations to preserve their traditions and buildings. Made up of older residents, groups like these raise money, sponsor festivals and dances, and even write collective histories of their villages. Many fear that younger folks won't have the motivation to carry on this tradition.

But hope springs eternal, as there may be a movement of locals back to these villages. Some northerners are finding hill-town life less romantic as they age, the popularity of organic produce is making it financially viable for hill-town farmers with smaller plots to make a living, and the Internet age allows some hill-towners to telecommute. Could the cycle be restarting? Armed with laptops, smartphones, and tablets, will hill-towners once again prosper when the next wave of barbarians comes?

(Some farmers have drilled as far as 1,300 feet down to try to find water.) With no water at hand, farmers here lie awake at night worrying about fire. Hot summers, dry pines, and windy days make a scary recipe for fast-traveling fires.

Now turn around and face Mont Ventoux. Are there clouds on the horizon? You're looking into the eyes of the Alps (behind Ventoux), and those "foothills" help keep Provence sunny.

• *Time to push on. You'll pass yellow trail signs along this drive. (The Dentelles provide fertile ground for walking trails.) With the medieval castle of Le Barroux topping the horizon in the distance (off to the left), drive on to little...*

COTES DU RHONE

❺ Suzette

Tiny Suzette floats on its hilltop, with a small 12th-century chapel, one café, wine tastings, a handful of residents, and the gaggle

Cicadas (*Cigales*)

In the countryside, listen for *les cigales*. They sing in the heat and are famous for announcing the arrival of summer. (Locals say their song also marks the coming of the tourists...and more money.) People here love these ugly, long-winged bugs, an integral part of Provençal life. You'll see souvenir cicadas made out of every material possible. If you look closely—they are well camouflaged—you can find live specimens on tree trunks and branches. Cicadas live for about two years, all but the last two weeks of which are spent quietly underground as larvae. But when they go public, their chirping begins with each sunrise and goes nonstop until sunset.

of houses where they live. Park in Suzette's lot, then find the big orientation board above the lot (Rome is 620 kilometers—385 miles—away). Look out to the broad shoulders of Mont Ventoux. At 6,000 feet, it always seems to have some clouds hanging around. If it's clear, the top looks like it's snow-covered; if you drive up there, you'll see it's actually white stone (see the Mont Ventoux drive on page 179). If it's very cloudy, the mountain takes on a dark, foreboding appearance.

Look to the village. A sign asks you to *Respectez son Calme* (respect its peace). Suzette's homes once lived in the shadow of an imposing castle, destroyed during the religious wars of the mid-1500s. Good picnic tables lie just past Suzette on our route. Back across the road from the orientation table is a tasting room for **Château Redortier** wines (unreliable hours, English brochure and well-explained wine list provided).

Sleeping and Eating: $ La Ferme Dégoutaud is a splendidly situated, roomy, and utterly isolated *chambres d'hôte* about halfway between Malaucène and Suzette (well signed, a mile down a dirt road). Animated Véronique (speaks minimal English, her son Thibault more) rents three country-cozy rooms with many thoughtful touches, a view pool, table tennis, picnic-perfect tables, and a barbecue at your disposal (includes breakfast, apartments available by the week, a 20-minute drive from Vaison-la-Romaine, tel. 04 90 62 99 29, www.degoutaud.fr, le.degoutaud@wanadoo.fr).

$$ Côté Vignes, off a short dirt road between Suzette and Beaumes-de-Venise, is a lighthearted wood-fired-everything place with outdoor tables flanked by fun interior dining. Young, English-speaking sister and brother Corinne and Max run the restaurant with enthusiasm; try the Camembert cheese flambé with lettuce, potatoes, and ham (salads and good pizza, *menus* from €20-36, daily May-Aug, closed Mon and also Tue-Wed evenings off-season, tel. 04 90 65 07 16).

The Phoenicians' Wine-Growing Almanac

Phoenicians brought about five grape varieties with them to southern Europe approximately 3,000 years ago. Today there

are more than 2,000 different grape varieties in the world, of which 150 are in France and 14 are in the Côtes du Rhône.

But some things have changed very little over the past three millennia: Today's Provençal farmers tend their grapes following much the same rhythm as did their Phoenician forerunners.

After a quiet winter, the plants begin waking up in March, pushing out new growth. By about mid-May, the plants are growing at a very fast pace, requiring farmers to do their first pruning of the year. Often working by hand, they pull off sucker plants and prune back new shoots, focusing the plant's energy on four to five main stalks.

Over the next three months, the farmers plow the soil, encouraging moisture to reach the plants. Every few weeks they spray for mildew (not a big problem in this dry area).

Next comes the harvest. Its precise date is dictated by how much sun and warmth the vines absorbed through the spring and summer: The hotter and drier the weather, the earlier the harvest.

In France, the grape harvest starts in the south and rolls north, ending about six weeks later in the country's northernmost vineyards, in Champagne. During the harvest, grapes are picked from the vines—either by hand or by machine—then separated from their stems. Pressing comes 2-3 weeks later, and the winemaking process is under way.

In the fall, farmers are busy watching and tweaking their wines. By December it's time for heavy pruning, when the plants are cut way back for the winter hibernation. Farmers spend the winter months catching up on maintenance, reading...and sleeping.

• *Continue from Suzette in the direction of Beaumes-de-Venise. You'll drop down into the lush little village of La Fare. Here, joyriders can take a 20-minute detour into the mountains by taking a sharp right on entering the village, following Dentelles de Montmirail signs. The* **Domaine de Cassan winery** *(tastings possible, Mon-Sat 10:00-12:00 & 14:00-18:00, closed Sun, tel. 04 90 62 96 12) lies near the end of the road that also leads to the Col du Cayron hiking trail (to the village of Gigondas). Your partner could drop you off and meet you in Gigondas (it's a 1.5-hour walk over the pass).*

But La Fare's best wine-tasting opportunity is back on our route just after leaving the village, at...

❻ Domaine de Coyeux Winery

A private road winds up and up to this impossibly beautiful setting, with the best views of the Dentelles I've found. Olive trees

frame the final approach, and *Le Caveau* signs lead to a modern tasting room (you may need to ring the buzzer). The owners and staff are sincere and take your interest in their wines seriously—skip it if you only want a quick taste or are not interested in buying. These wines have earned their excellent reputation, and are now available in the US (wines—€5-29/bottle; winery generally open daily 10:00-12:00 & 14:00-18:00, except closed Sun off-season and no midday closure July-Aug; tel. 04 90 12 42 42, www.domainedecoyeux.com/en, contact@domainedecoyeux.com, some English spoken).

• *Drive on toward Beaumes-de-Venise. You'll soon pass the recommended* **Côté Vignes** *(see page 174), a good stopping place for lunch or dinner.*

Next, navigate through Beaumes-de-Venise, following signs for Vacqueyras. At a big roundabout, you'll pass Beaumes-de-Venise's massive cave coopérative, which represents many growers in this area (big selection, but too slick for my taste). Continue following signs for Vacqueyras (a famous wine village with a Thursday market and another cave coopérative), and then signs for Gigondas and Vaison par la route touristique. As you enter Gigondas, follow signs to the TI and park on or near the tree-shaded square.

❼ Gigondas

This upscale village produces some of the region's best reds and is ideally situated for hiking, mountain-biking, and driving into the mountains. The **TI** has Wi-Fi, lists of wineries and *chambres d'hôtes*, and tips for good hikes or drives (Mon-Sat 10:00-12:30 & 14:30-18:00, closed Sun, 5 Rue du Portail, tel. 04 90 65 85 46, www.gigondas-dm.fr). The €2 *Chemins et Sentiers du Massif des Dentelles* hiking map is helpful, though not critical, because routes have good signs. Take a short walk through the village lanes, leaving from

the recommended Du Verre à l'Assiette restaurant, and find a good viewing area over the heart of the Côtes du Rhône vineyards; you'll find even better views a little higher at the church.

Several good tasting opportunities lie on the main square. **Le Caveau de Gigondas** is the best, where Sandra and Barbara await your visit in a handsome tasting room with a large and free selection of tiny bottles for sampling, filled directly from the barrel (daily 10:00-12:00 & 14:00-18:30, close to the TI on the main town square, tel. 04 90 65 82 29, www. caveaudugigondas.com). Here

you can compare wines from 75 private producers in an intimate, low-key surrounding. The provided list of wines is helpful. A self-imposed gag rule (intended to keep staff from favoring the production of a single winery in this co-op showcase) makes it hard to get a strong recommendation here, so it's best to know what you want (see "French Wine-Tasting 101" on page 34).

Sleeping and Eating: The shaded red tables of **$$ Du Verre à l'Assiette** ("From Glass to Plate") entice lunchtime eaters (also good interior ambience, €16-26 *menus,* open for lunch daily except Wed, open for dinner Fri-Sat nights and every night but Wed mid-June-mid-Sept, located diagonally across from TI, Place du Village, tel. 04 90 12 36 64).

$$ Hôtel les Florets,*** with tastefully designed rooms, is a half-mile above Gigondas, buried in the foothills of the Dentelles de Montmirail. It comes with an excellent restaurant, a vast terrace with views, and hiking trails into the mountains (annex rooms by pool have front patios, tel. 04 90 65 85 01, www.hotel-lesflorets. com, accueil@hotel-lesflorets.com).

The **$$$$ restaurant** at Hôtel les Florets is a traditional, family-run place that's well worth the price—particularly if you dine on the magnificent terrace. Dinners blend classic French cuisine with Provençal accents, served with class by English-speaking Thierry. The weighty wine list is literally encyclopedic (closed Wed, also closed Thu for lunch, service can be slow).

• *From Gigondas, follow signs to the circular wine village of Sablet—with generally inexpensive yet tasty wines (the TI and wine coopérative share a space in the town center)—then past Séguret and back to Vaison-la-Romaine, where our tour ends.*

If you haven't had your fill, consider adding on some...

Lavender

Whether or not you travel to Provence during the late-June and July lavender blossom, you'll see and smell examples of this particularly local product every-where—in shops, on tables in restau-rants, and in your hotel room. And if you come during lavender season, you'll experience one of Europe's great color events, where rich fields of purple lavender meet equally rich yellow fields of sunflowers. While lav-ender season is hot, you'll find the best fields in the cooler hills, because the flowers thrive at higher altitudes. The flowers are harvested in full

bloom (beginning in mid-July), then distilled to extract the oils for making soaps and perfume.

And though lavender seems like an indigenous part of the Provence scene, it wasn't cultivated here until about 1920, when it was imported by the local perfume-makers. Because lavender is not native to Provence, growing it successfully requires great care. Three kinds of lavender are grown in Provence: true lavender (traditionally used by perfume-mak-ers), spike lavender, and lavandin (a cloned hybrid of the first two). Today, a majority of Provence lavender fields are lavan-din—which is also mass-produced at factories, a trend that is threatening to put true lavender growers out of business.

Some of the best lavender fields bloom near Vaison-la-Romaine. Lavender blooms later the higher you go; the ones described here are listed from lowest to highest elevations. For an impressive display, drive north of Vaison-la-Romaine and ramble the tiny road between Valréas and Vinsobres (D-190 and D-46). You'll see more beautiful fields along D-538 between Nyons and Dieulefit, and still more if you climb Mont Ventoux to Sault (described on page 179).

COTES DU RHONE

VILLAGES NORTH OF THE COTES DU RHONE

Cairanne, toward Orange from Vaison-la-Romaine, is a pleasant village producing fine wines with one of the largest and most re-spected wine *coopératives* in this region. The **Cave de Cairanne,** officially known as the **Maison Camille Cayran,** has been making wine for more than 80 years with grapes from more than 60 dif-ferent farmers. Start with the free, museum-esque "sensory trail," which explores the five senses through interactive displays in Eng-lish and French and prepares you to taste their large range of wines (free, daily wine tasting 9:00-18:00 but closes at lunchtime, mu-seum closes at 17:00, lots of English spoken, on Route de Bollene on the outskirts of town on D-8—you can't miss the signs, tel. 04 90 65 98 15, www.maisoncamillecayran.com).

Eating: Consider a meal afterward at the nearby wine-bar/restaurant **$$ Le Tourne au Verre** (good value €18 lunch *menu*, closed Mon and Sun evenings, Route de Sainte-Cécile, tel. 04 90 30 72 18, www.letourneauverre.com).

More Côtes du Rhône Drives

For further explorations of the Côtes du Rhône region, consider these suggestions: a scenic mountaintop, an off-the-beaten-path countryside ramble, and an impressive gorge.

▲MONT VENTOUX AND LAVENDER

The drive to Mont Ventoux is worth ▲▲▲ if the summit is open (see later) and skies are crystal-clear, or in any weather between late June and the end of July, when the lavender blooms. It also provides a scenic connection between the Côtes du Rhône villages and the Luberon. Allow an hour to drive to the top of this 6,000-foot mountain, where you'll be greeted by cool temperatures, crowds of visitors, and acres of white stones. Most days you'll see any number of cyclists braving the long, grueling ascent, made famous by its annual inclusion in the Tour de France.

Mont Ventoux is Provence's rooftop, referred to as the "Giant of Provence" or "the Bald Mountain," with astonishing Pyrenees-to-Alps views when it's really clear (it usually isn't). But even under hazy skies, it's an interesting place. The top combines a barren and surreal lunar landscape with souvenirs, bikers, and hikers. All that chalky mess you see was once the bottom of a sea. Miles of poles stuck in the rock identify the route (the top is usually snowbound mid-Nov to April, sometimes May). **Le Vendran** restaurant (near the old observatory and Air Force control tower) offers snacks and meals with commanding views. An orientation board is available on the opposite side of the mountaintop.

Between Mont Ventoux and the Luberon, you'll duck into and out of several climate zones and remarkably diverse landscapes. The scene alternates between limestone canyons, lush meadows, and wildflowers. Forty-five minutes east of Mont Ventoux (about 16 miles), lavender fields forever surround the rock-top village of **Sault** (pronounced "soh"), which produces 40 percent of France's lavender essence.

Sault, a welcoming town in any season, goes unnoticed by most hurried travelers. It's a slow-down-and-smell-the-lavender kind of place, with a sociable "mountain market" on Wednesdays. There's no reason to sleep in Sault, but it's a fine place for lunch

CÔTES DU RHÔNE

or *un café*. **La Promenade** café has simple salads and grilled meats with territorial valley views (daily mid-April-mid-Sept, closed Tue off-season, tel. 04 90 64 14 34). Or enjoy the same views with a picnic in the adjacent, tree-lined area, the "promenade."

Getting to Mont Ventoux: Two roads lead to the peak of Mont Ventoux, both of which have small ski stations at 4,600 feet (about 4 miles from the top); Mont Serein station is on the north and Chalet Reynard station is on the south. The mountain pass between these stations (Col de Mont Ventoux), including the summit, is closed annually due to snow and ice from mid-November to mid-April (sometimes later for the north road). Confirm that the pass is open before you leave.

To reach Mont Ventoux from Vaison-la-Romaine, drive to Malaucène (15 minutes), then wind up D-974 for 45 minutes to the top. Another option is to drive around the base of the Mont, over the Col de la Madeleine (follow signs from Maulaucène) and through the quaint village of Bédoin (good Monday market); from there D-974 leads to the south road and offers a much longer, but perhaps prettier route to the top. If continuing to Sault (a worthwhile detour when the lavender blooms) or on to the Luberon (worthwhile anytime—see next chapter), follow signs to *Sault,* then *Gordes.* The *Les Routes de la Lavande* brochure suggests driving and walking routes in the area (available online at www.routes-lavande.com).

DROME PROVENCALE LOOP DRIVE

This meander north into the Drôme Provençale is overkill for many, as the scenery is only subtly different than what you'll see closer to your hotel. But if you haven't had your fill of pretty vistas, this drive is away from popular tourist areas and combines rugged scenery with overlooked towns and villages (see map on page 146). I'd only do it on Thursdays, when it's market day in Nyons, or on Wednesdays, when it's market day in Buis-les-Barronies. Allow most of a day for this up-and-down, curve-filled drive, particularly if the market in Nyons is on. Or you can just do Nyons and call it a day.

From Vaison-la-Romaine, drive to **Nyons,** an attractive mid-size town set along a river and against the hills. Here you'll find a Roman bridge with views, an olive mill, a lavender distillery, a handful of walking streets, and an arcaded square—all with few tourists. Nyons is famous for its rollicking Thursday market (until 12:30) and for producing France's best olives, which you can taste at its well-organized *coopérative* (daily 9:00-12:30 & 14:00-19:00, closes at 18:00 on Sun, slightly shorter hours off-season, interesting museum about olives, on Place Olivier de Serres, tel. 04 75 26 95 00).

From Nyons, head for the hills following signs to *Gap* on D-94, then follow signs to *Ste-Jalles* on D-64. Little Ste-Jalles hovers above the road, with a pretty Romanesque church (usually closed), two cafés (Café de Lavande overhangs the river, providing a fine backdrop for a drink, lunch, or a snack), and a small winery making crisp whites and easy reds (Domaine de Rieu Frais, daily 9:00-12:00 & 14:00-18:00, closed Sun in winter, tel. 04 75 27 31 54, www.domaine-du-rieu-frais.com, jean-yves.liotaud@wanadoo.fr, best to call ahead and let them know you're coming).

From Ste-Jalles, cross the bridge following D-108 and *Buis-les-Barronnies* signs, and start your ascent over the rocky mountains. Prepare for miles of curves, territorial views, and no guardrails. Drop down (er, drive down) and meet the Ouvèze river, then follow it into bustling **Buis-les-Barronnies** (with all the services, including a slew of cafés and an attractive old town to stroll). Buis-les-Barronnies is the linden tree capital of France and hosts an earthy outdoor market on Wednesdays with produce and crafts.

From Buis-les-Barronnies, continue south on D-5, then turn left toward Eygaliers on D-72. Follow this slow, serpentine road along the back side of Mont Ventoux and go all the way to the jewel of this trip: **Brantes**, one of Provence's most spectacularly located villages. Stop here for some fresh air, a look at the local pottery, and lunch with a Ventoux-view at **La Poterne** (daily, closed Nov-March, tel. 04 75 28 29 13).

Finally, follow signs back to Vaison-la-Romaine along the faster, less curvy D-40. A few minutes before Vaison-la-Romaine, you'll pass through pleasing little Entrechaux.

▲ARDECHE GORGES (GORGES DE L'ARDECHE)

These gorges, which wow visitors with abrupt chalky-white cliffs, follow the Ardèche River through immense canyons and thick forests. To reach the gorges from Vaison-la-Romaine, drive west 1.5 hours, passing through Bollène and Pont Saint-Esprit to **Vallon-Pont-d'Arc** (the tourist hub of the Ardèche Gorges). From Vallon-Pont-d'Arc, you can canoe along the river through some of the canyon's most spectacular scenery and under the rock arch of Pont d'Arc (half-day, all-day, and 2-day trips possible; less appealing in summer, when the river is crowded and water levels are low), and learn about hiking trails that get you above it all (**TI** tel. 04 28 91 24 10, www.pontdarc-ardeche.fr).

The Ardèche region is a hot destination, thanks to the 2015 opening of a replica of one of France's largest and most impressive prehistoric caves, the **Chauvet Pont-d'Arc,** just outside the village of Vallon-Pont-d'Arc. Not discovered until 1994, the cave holds the oldest and best preserved man-made images anywhere

CÔTES DU RHONE

(some date back over 36,000 years). The original cave is closed to the public, but the full-scale replica reproduces its art and artifacts, using cutting-edge techniques to create the same feeling that seeing the original cave inspires (€13, reservation on line at http://en.cavernedupontdarc.fr or call 04 75 94 39 40).

If continuing north toward Lyon, connect Privas and Aubenas, then head back on the autoroute. Endearing little **Balazuc**—a village north of the gorges, with narrow lanes, flowers, views, and a smattering of cafés and shops—makes a great stop.

HILL TOWNS OF THE LUBERON

France's Answer to Italy's Tuscany

Just 30 miles east of Avignon, the Luberon region hides some of France's most captivating hill towns and sensuous landscapes. Those intrigued by Peter Mayle's best-selling *A Year in Provence* love joyriding through the region, connecting I-could-live-here villages, crumbled castles, and meditative abbeys. Mayle's book describes the ruddy local culture from an Englishman's perspective as he buys a stone farmhouse, fixes it up, and adopts the region as his new home. *A Year in Provence* is a great read while you're here—or, better, get it as an audiobook and listen while you drive.

The Luberon terrain in general (much of which is a French regional natural park) is as enticing as its villages. Gnarled vineyards and wind-sculpted trees separate tidy stone structures from abandoned buildings—little more than rock piles—that challenge city slickers to fix them up. Mountains of limestone bend along vast ridges, while colorful hot-air balloons survey the scene from above. The wind is an integral part of life here. The infamous mistral wind, finishing its long ride in from Siberia, hits like a hammer (see the sidebar on page 167).

PLANNING YOUR TIME

There are no obligatory museums, monuments, or vineyards in the Luberon. Treat this area like a vacation from your vacation. Downshift your engine. Brake for views, and lose your car to take a walk. Get on a first-name basis with a village.

To enjoy the ambience of the Luberon, you'll want at least one night and a car (only Isle-sur-la-Sorgue is easily accessible by train and bus). Allow a half-day for Isle-sur-la-Sorgue if it's market day (less time if not). Add more time if you want to paddle the Sorgue River or pedal between villages. You'll also want at least a full day for the Luberon villages.

Luberon

1 Sous l'Olivier Chambres
2 Le Mas d'Estonge Chambres
3 Hôtel les Sables d'Ocre
4 Le Clos des Cigales Chambres
5 Hostellerie des Commandeurs
6 Hotel le Clos du Buis
7 Mas del Sol Chambres
8 Petit Café & Chambres

For the ultimate Luberon experience, drivers should base themselves in or near Roussillon. To lose the tourists, set up in Oppède-le Vieux, St-Saturnin-lès-Apt, or Buoux.

If you lack wheels or prefer streams to hills and like a little more action, stay in Isle-sur-la-Sorgue, located within striking distance of Avignon and on the edge of the Luberon. Adequate train service from Avignon and Marseille, and some bus service, connects Isle-sur-la-Sorgue with the real world. Level terrain, quiet, tree-lined roads, and nearby villages make Isle-sur-la-Sorgue good for biking.

The village of Lourmarin works as a southern base for visiting Luberon sights, as well as Aix-en-Provence, Cassis, and Marseille. Patient travelers can take a bus from Aix-en-Provence to reach Lourmarin.

GETTING AROUND THE LUBERON

By Car: Luberon roads are scenic and narrow. With no major landmarks, it's easy to get lost—and you will get lost—but getting lost is the point. Consider buying the Michelin map #332 or #527 to navigate, and look for free maps available at local TIs. Popular towns charge a small fee to park. Expect headaches parking in Isle-sur-la-Sorgue during its market days.

If connecting this region with the **Côtes du Rhône,** avoid

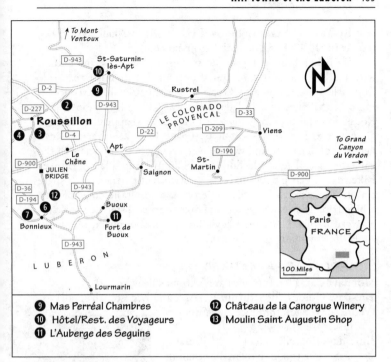

9 Mas Perréal Chambres
10 Hôtel/Rest. des Voyageurs
11 L'Auberge des Seguins
12 Château de la Canorgue Winery
13 Moulin Saint Augustin Shop

driving through Carpentras (bad traffic, confusing signage). If you're in a hurry, use the autoroute between Cavaillon and Orange. If time is not an issue, drive via Mont Ventoux—one of Provence's most spectacular routes (see end of previous chapter).

By Bus: Isle-sur-la-Sorgue is connected with Avignon's town center by the Trans Vaucluse bus line #6 (8-10/day Mon-Sat, 2/day Sun, 45 minutes, central stop—called Robert Vasse—is near post office in Isle-sur-la-Sorgue, ask for schedule at TI or download French-only schedule from www.voyages-raoux.fr/lignes/index.php). Buses also connect Isle-sur-la-Sorgue with the Marseille airport (4/day direct, 2 hours, www.info-ler.fr). Buses link Lourmarin with Aix-en-Provence (3/day, 1.5 hours, www.pacamobilite.fr). Without a car or minivan tour, skip the more famous hill towns of the Luberon.

By Train: Trains get you to Isle-sur-la-Sorgue (station called "L'Isle-Fontaine de Vaucluse") from Avignon (8/day on weekdays, 5/day on weekends, 30 minutes) or from Marseille (6/day, 1.5 hours). If you're day-tripping by train, check return times before leaving the station.

By Minivan Tour: I list several minivan tour companies and private guides who can guide you through this marvelous region (see "Tours in Provence" on page 24).

By Taxi: Contact **Luberon Taxi** (based in Maubec off D-3, mobile 06 08 49 40 57, www.luberontaxi.com).

By Bike: Isle-sur-la-Sorgue makes a good base for biking, with level terrain and good rental options. Hardy bikers can ride from Isle-sur-la-Sorgue to Gordes, then to Roussillon, connecting other villages in a full-day loop ride (30 miles round-trip to Roussillon and back, with lots of hills). Several appealing villages are closer to Isle-sur-la-Sorgue (see page 193). **Vélo Services** can help you plan a route and will deliver a rental bike anywhere in the Luberon (see "Isle-sur-la-Sorgue—Helpful Hints," later). **Sun-e-Bike** rents electric bikes and has a network of partners with spare batteries scattered across the Luberon, extending the range of your e-bike trip. They can also arrange bike tours and shuttle your bags between hotels (1 Avenue Clovis Hugues in Bonnieux, tel. 04 90 74 09 96, www.sun-e-bike.com).

LUBERON AREA MARKET DAYS

Monday: Cavaillon (produce and antiques/flea market)

Tuesday: Gordes, St-Saturnin-lès-Apt, and Lacoste (all small)

Wednesday: Sault (produce and antiques/ flea market)

Thursday: Roussillon (cute) and Isle-sur-la-Sorgue (good, but smaller than its Sunday market)

Friday: Lourmarin (very good) and Bonnieux (pretty good)

Saturday: Apt (huge produce and antiques/flea market)

Sunday: Isle-sur-la-Sorgue (granddaddy of them all, produce and antiques/ flea market) and Coustellet (very good and less touristy)

Isle-sur-la-Sorgue

This sturdy market town—literally, "Island on the Sorgue River"—sits within a split in its crisp, happy little river at the foot of the Luberon. It's a workaday town that feels refreshingly real after so many adorable villages. It also makes a good base for exploring the Luberon (15 minutes by car, doable by hardy bikers) and Avignon (30 minutes by car or train)

and can work for exploring the Côtes du Rhône by car (allow an hour to Vaison-la-Romaine).

After the arid cities and villages elsewhere in Provence, the presence of water at every turn is a welcome change. In Isle-sur-la-Sorgue—called the "Venice of Provence"—the Sorgue River's extraordinarily clear and shallow flow divides like cells, producing water, water everywhere. The river has long nourished the region's economy. The fresh spring water of the Sorgue's many branches has provided ample fish, irrigation for crops, and power for local industries for centuries. Today, antique shops power the town's economy—every other shop seems to sell some kind of antique.

Orientation to Isle-sur-la-Sorgue

Although Isle-sur-la-Sorgue is renowned for its market days (Sun and Thu), it's an otherwise pleasantly average town with no important sights and a steady trickle of tourism. It's lively on weekends but calm most weeknights. The town revolves around its river, the church square, and two pedestrian-only streets, Rue de la République and Rue Carnot.

TOURIST INFORMATION

The TI has an essential town map, Wi-Fi, hiking information, biking itineraries, and a line on rooms in private homes, all of which are outside town (April-Sept Mon-Sat 9:00-12:30 & 14:30-18:00, until 17:30 Oct-March, Sun 9:00-12:30; in town center next to church, tel. 04 90 38 04 78, www.oti-delasorgue.fr).

ARRIVAL IN ISLE-SUR-LA-SORGUE

By Car: Traffic is a mess and parking is a headache on market days (all day Sun and Thu mornings). Circle the ring road and look for parking signs. There are several lots just west of the roundabout at Le Bassin (see map on next page). **Parking les Névons** is central. You'll also pass freestyle parking on roads leaving the city. Don't leave anything visible in your car.

By Train: Remember that the train station is called "L'Isle-Fontaine de Vaucluse." To reach my recommended hotels, walk straight out of the station and turn right on the ring road.

By Bus: The bus from Avignon drops you near the post office (ask driver for "La Poste"), a block from the recommended Hôtel les Névons.

HELPFUL HINTS

Shop Hours: The antique shops this town is famous for are open Friday afternoon to Monday only.

Laundry: A *laverie automatique* is in the town center, just off

Isle-sur-la-Sorgue

Accommodations
1. La Prévôté Hôtel/Restaurant
2. To Sous l'Olivier & Le Pont des Aubes Chambres
3. Hôtel les Névons
4. Hôtel/Restaurant les Terrasses by David et Louisa

Eateries & Other
5. La Passerelle
6. Chez Stéphane & Bike Rental
7. La Balade des Saveurs
8. Café de France
9. Launderettes (2)
10. Utile Market
11. Delices de Luberon Shop

Rue de la République on Impasse de l'Hôtel de Palerme (open 24/7). Another, perhaps easier for drivers, is at the **Centre Commercial Super U** supermarket (daily 9:00-19:00, on the ring road at the roundabout, Cours Fernande Peyre).

Supermarket: A well-stocked **Utile** market is on the main ring road, near the Peugeot dealer and the train station (Mon-Sat 8:30-20:00, Sun 8:30-13:00).

Bike Rental: The TI has a good list. **Kvelo** is in the center of town (4 Rue de la République, tel. 04 90 38 59 30, www.kvelo-rent. com). **Luberon Biking,** in the nearby village of Velleron, can also deliver electric or standard bikes (daily, tel. 04 90 90 14 62, www.luberon-biking.fr).

Taxi: Try **Luberon Taxi** (tel. 04 90 76 70 08, mobile 06 08 49 40 57, www.luberontaxi.com).

Public WC: A WC is in the parking lot between the post office and the Hôtel les Névons.

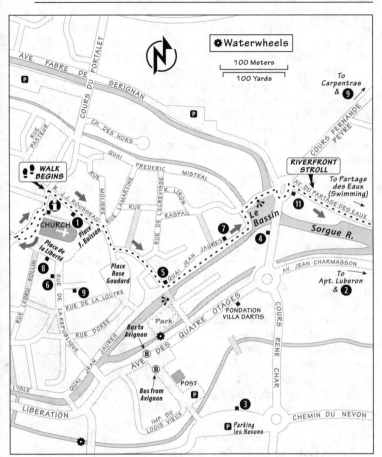

Hiking: The TI has good information on area hikes; most trails are accessible by short drives, and you can use a taxi to get there.

Isle-sur-la-Sorgue Walk

The town has crystal-clear water babbling under pedestrian bridges stuffed with flower boxes, and its old-time carousel is always spinning. For this self-guided wander (shown on map above), navigate by the town's splintered streams and nine mossy waterwheels, which, while still turning, power only memories of the town's wool and silk industries.

• *Start your tour at the church next to the TI—where all streets seem to converge—and make forays into the town from there. Go first to the church.*

   Notre-Dame des Anges: This 12th-century church has a colorful Baroque interior and feels too big for today's town. Walk in.

LUBERON

The curls and swirls and gilded statues date from an era that was all about Louis XIV, the Sun King. This is propagandist architecture, designed to wow the faithful into compliance. (It was made possible thanks to profits generated from the town's river-powered industries.) When you enter a church like this, the heavens should open up and assure you that whoever built it had celestial connections (daily 10:00-12:00 & 15:15-17:00, Mass on Sun at 10:30).

Turn right outside the church and notice the buildings' faded facades around you, recalling their previous lives (*fabrique de chaussures* was a shoemaker; *meubles* means furniture; *3 étages d'exposition* means 3 showroom floors). Admire Fauque Beyret's antique storefront. Those big porches allowed goods to be sold outside, rain or shine. Isle-sur-la-Sorgue retains a connection to its past uncommon in this renovation-happy region.

• *Wander down Rue Danton, the narrow street to the right of the* meubles *sign, to lose the crowds. Keep going until you find...*

Three Waterwheels: These big, forgotten waterwheels have been in business here since the 1200s, when they were first used for grinding flour. Paper, textile, silk, and woolen mills would later find their power from this river. At its peak, Isle-sur-la-Sorgue had 70 waterwheels; in the 1800s, the town competed with Avignon as Provence's cloth-dyeing and textile center. Those stylish Provençal fabrics and patterns you see for sale everywhere were made possible by this river.

• *Double back to the church, turn left under the arcade, then find the small stream just past the TI. Breakaway streams like this run under the town like subways run under Paris. Take a right on the first street after the stream; it leads under a long arch (along Rue J. J. Rousseau). Look up for more faded facades (bains, douches, and chambres meublées means baths, showers, and furnished rooms). Follow this straight, and veer slightly right at Place F. Buisson onto Place Rose Goudard (likely crowded with parked cars), and walk to the main river. Then turn left and walk along the many café terraces until you come to...*

Le Bassin: Literally translated as a "pond," this is where the Sorgue River crashes into the town and separates into many branches. Track as many branches as you can see (Frank Provost hides a big one), and then find the round lookout point for the best perspective (carefully placed lights make this a beautiful sight after dark). Fishing was the town's main industry until the waterwheels took over. In the 1300s, local fishermen provided the pope with his fresh-fish quota. They trapped them in nets and speared them while standing on skinny, flat-bottomed boats. Several streets are named after the fish they caught—including Rue de l'Aiguille ("Eel Street") and Rue des Écrevisses ("Crayfish Street").

The sound of the rushing water reminds us of the power that rivers can generate. With its source (a spring) a mere five miles away, the Sorgue River never floods and has a constant flow and temperature in all seasons. Despite its exposed (flat) location, Isle-sur-la-Sorgue prospered in the Middle Ages, thanks to the natural protection this river provided. Walls with big moats once ran along the river, but they were destroyed during the French Revolution.

• *Cross the busy roundabout, and walk to the orange* **Delices de Luberon** *store. Find the small tasting table with 12 scrumptious tapenades. Walk behind the store to find the river and take a refreshing…*

Riverfront Stroll: Follow the main river upstream, along the bike/pedestrian lane, as far as you like. The little road meanders about a mile, following the serene course of the river, past waterfront homes and beneath swaying trees. It ends at the Hôtel le Pescador and a riverfront café. The wide and shallow Partage des Eaux, where the water divides before entering Isle-sur-la-Sorgue, is perfect for a cool swim on a hot day.

Activities and Sights in Isle-sur-la-Sorgue

▲▲Market Days
The town erupts into a carnival-like market frenzy each Sunday and Thursday, with hardy crafts and local produce. The Sunday market is astounding and famous for its antiques; the Thursday market is more intimate and focused more on produce than antiques (see market tips in the Shopping chapter). Find a table across from the church at the Café de France and enjoy the scene.

Fondation Villa Dartis
Drop into this modern sculpture gallery to see what's on exhibit (free, May-Oct Thu-Mon 11:00-13:00 & 14:00-18:00, closed Tue-Wed and Nov-April, on the river at 7 Avenue des Quatre Otages, tel. 04 90 95 23 70, www.villadatris.com).

Antique Toy and Doll Museum
(Musée du Jouet et de la Poupée Ancienne)
The town's other main sight is a fun and funky toy museum with more than 300 dolls displayed in three small rooms. Most dolls date from 1880 to 1930.

Cost and Hours: €3.50, kids-€1.50; July-Sept daily 11:00-18:00; May-June daily 10:30-13:00 & 14:00-18:00; shorter hours and closed Mon off-season; call ahead to confirm opening times, at 26 Rue Carnot down a short alley, tel. 04 90 20 97 31, www. poupeesdelisle.com.

LUBERON

NEAR ISLE-SUR-LA-SORGUE
Fontaine-de-Vaucluse

You'll read and hear a lot about this overrun village, impressively located at the source of the Sorgue River, where the medieval Italian poet Petrarch mourned for his love, Laura. The river seems to magically appear from nowhere (the actual source is a murky, green waterhole) and flows through the town past a lineup of cafés, souvenir shops, and wall-to-river tourists. The setting is beautiful—with cliffs jutting to the sky and a ruined castle above—but the trip is worth it only if the spring is flowing (usually only after several days of hard rain or during early spring snow melt). *Sans* flowing spring, this is the most overrated sight in France. Ask your hotelier if the spring is active (*Est-ce que la source diverse?*), and arrive early or late to avoid crowds. It's a good bike ride here from Isle-sur-la-Sorgue (about five miles).

Arriving by car, you'll pay to park (€4), and then walk about 20 minutes along the sparkling river to *la source* (the spring), located in a cave at the base of the cliff. (It's an uphill hike for the last part.) The spring itself is the very definition of anticlimactic, unless it's surging. At those times, it's among the most prolific water producers in the world, with a depth no one has yet been able to determine.

The path to the spring is lined with distractions. The only stops worth your time are the riverfront cafés and restaurants—**Philip's** and **Moulin à Papier** are two to consider. Philip's (located after Moulin à Papier) offers the best seats. At the Moulin à Papier, a reproduction of a 17th-century paper mill, you'll see the value of harnessing the river's power. In the mill, a 22-foot-diameter paddle wheel turns five times a minute, driving hammers that pound paper for up to 36 hours (free, daily 9:00-19:00). As you watch the hammers pound away, imagine Isle-sur-la-Sorgue's waterwheels and the industries they once powered. The shop inside sells paper in every size.

Canoe Trips on the Sorgue

A better way to travel to Fontaine-de-Vaucluse is to canoe down the river. If you're *really* on vacation, take this five-mile, two-hour trip. The guide escorts small groups in canoes (or you can go it alone), starting in Fontaine-de-Vaucluse and ending in Isle-sur-la-Sorgue; you'll return to Fontaine-de-Vaucluse by shuttle bus (call for departure times; ask about shuttle service from Isle-sur-la-Sorgue). The company, **Kayaks Verts**, is a family operation (late April-mid-Oct, €19/person, tel. 04 90 20 35 44, www.canoe-france.com/en/sorgue). To combine bike and boat, ask about shuttling your rental bikes back to Isle-sur-la-Sorgue while you float from Fontaine-de-Vaucluse (see suggested bike route below).

Biking

Isle-sur-la-Sorgue is ideally situated for short biking forays into the mostly level terrain. Pick up a biking itinerary at the TI, or ask your bike-rental shop for suggestions. These towns make easy biking destinations from Isle-sur-la-Sorgue: **Velleron** (5 flat miles north, a tiny version of Isle-sur-la-Sorgue with waterwheels, fountains, and an evening farmers' market Mon-Sat 18:00-20:00); **Lagnes** (3 miles east, a pretty and well-restored hill town with views from its ruined château); and **Fontaine-de-Vaucluse** (5 gentle, uphill miles northeast, described above). Allow 30 miles and many hills for the round-trip ride to Roussillon.

Sleeping in and near Isle-sur-la-Sorgue

Pickings are slim for good sleeps in Isle-sur-la-Sorgue, though the few I've listed provide reliable values.

$$$ La Prévôté*** has the town's highest-priced digs. Its five meticulously decorated rooms—located above a classy restaurant—are adorned in earth tones, with high ceilings, a few exposed beams, and carefully selected furnishings. Séverine manages the hotel while chef-hubby Jean-Marie controls the kitchen (includes breakfast, limited check-in/check-out times, no elevator, rooftop deck with hot tub, no parking, one block from the church at 4 Rue J. J. Rousseau, tel. 04 90 38 57 29, www.la-prevote.fr, contact@la-prevote.fr).

$$ Sous l'Olivier is 10 minutes from Isle-sur-la-Sorgue, off D-900 near Petit Palais. Here big Julien, quiet Carole, and sons Hugo and Clovis adopt you into their sprawling old stone farmhouse, with grass to burn, a big pool, yards of chairs and lounges, and views to the Luberon range. The six rooms are big but lack air-conditioning. A good breakfast is included, and the €34 dinner is a family affair, worth every euro (three apartments available, cash only, tel. 04 90 20 33 90, www.chambresdhotesprovence.com, souslolivier@orange.fr). Heading east on D-900, it's near the *Petit Palais* sign on the road (don't go into the village). See the map on page 189.

$ Le Pont des Aubes Chambres has two huggable rooms in an old green-shuttered farmhouse right on the river a mile from town. Borrow a bike or a canoe. From here you can cross a tiny bridge and walk 15 minutes along the river into Isle-sur-la-Sorgue. Charming Martine speaks English, while husband Patrice speaks smiles (1-room apartments, cash only, a mile from town toward Apt, next to Pain d'Antan Boulangerie at 189 Route d'Apt, tel. 04 90 38 13 75, www.lepontdesaubes.com).

$ Hôtel les Névons,*** two blocks from the center (behind the post office), is concrete motel-modern outside, with well-priced and comfortable-enough rooms within, a roof deck with a small pool, and quick access to the town center (family rooms, air-con, elevator, free and safe parking, 205 Chemin des Névons, tel. 04 90 20 72 00, www.hotel-les-nevons.com, hotel-les-nevons@orange.fr).

$ Hôtel les Terrasses by David et Louisa** rents eight good-value rooms over a pleasant restaurant right on Le Bassin. Several rooms look out over the river, most have some traffic noise and queen-size beds (air-con, 2 Avenue du Général de Gaulle, tel. 04 90 38 03 16, www.lesterrassesbydavidetlouisa.com, louisaetdavid@orange.fr).

Eating in Isle-sur-la-Sorgue

Cheap and mediocre restaurants are a dime a dozen in Isle-sur-la-Sorgue. You'll see several brasseries on the river, good for views and basic café fare. The restaurants I list offer good values, but none of them is really "cheap." Dining on the river is a unique experience in this arid land, and shopping for the perfect table is half the fun. To assemble a riverside picnic, head to Rue de la République, which has bakeries, butchers, a *traiteur* (deli), cheesemongers, a wine shop, and a supermarket.

For a dirt-cheap breakfast or a good riverside lunch find **$ La Passerelle,** where charming Jennifer and Vincent serve light meals, craft beers, and more (daily until 19:30, 18 Quai Jean Jaurès, mobile 06 62 18 23 57).

Begin your dinner with a glass of wine at the cozy wine and cheese cellar **$$ Chez Stéphane.** Or for a light meal, order a selection of cheeses (great to share) with your wine and call it good (a few tables outside or find the bar hiding in the rear behind the cheese counter and wine shop; daily 9:30-19:30, 12 Rue de la République, tel. 04 90 20 70 25).

$$$ Les Terrasses by David et Louisa is a sure riverside option with fair prices, an exhaustive wine list, and tasty choices (closed Wed, 2 Avenue du Général de Gaulle, tel. 04 90 38 03 16).

$$$ La Balade des Saveurs is a refreshing change from the many run-of-the-mill riverfront places. Here, Sophie and Benjamin deliver fresh Provençal cuisine at riverside tables or in their elegantly sky-lit interior at fair prices. The asparagus soup with egg is a winning twist on a French classic (daily, 3 Quai Jean Jaurès, tel. 04 90 95 27 85, www.balade-des-saveurs.com).

$$$$ La Prévôté is the place in town to do it up. Its lovely dining room is country-classy but not stuffy. A stream runs under the restaurant, visible through glass windows (closed Tue, on narrow street that runs along left side of church as you face it, 4 Rue J. J. Rousseau, tel. 04 90 38 57 29, www.la-prevote.fr).

The Heart of the Luberon

A 15-minute drive east of Isle-sur-la-Sorgue brings you to this protected area, where canyons and ridgelines rule, and land developers take a back seat. Still-proud hill towns guard access to winsome valleys, while carefully managed vineyards (producing inexpensive wines) play hopscotch with cherry groves, lavender fields, and cypress trees.

About 30 years ago, Peter Mayle's *A Year in Provence* nudged tourism in this area into overdrive. A visit to Mayle's quintessential Provence includes many of the popular villages and sights described in this chapter. While the hill towns can be seen as subtly different variations on the same theme, each has a distinct character. Look for differences: the color of shutters, the pattern of stones, the way flowers are planted, or the number of tourist boutiques. Every village has something to offer—it's up to you to discover and celebrate it.

Stay in or near Roussillon. By village standards, Roussillon is lively and struggles to manage its popularity. When restaurant hunting, read descriptions of the villages in this chapter—many good finds are embedded in the countryside. For aerial views high above this charmed land, consider a hot-air balloon trip.

PLANNING YOUR TIME

With a car and one full day, I'd linger in Roussillon in the morning, visit the Julien Bridge, then have lunch nearby in Lacoste or Bonnieux. After lunch, continue the joyride via Ménerbes to Oppède-le-Vieux, then return through Coustellet and Gordes. With a second full day, I'd start by climbing the Fort de Buoux, then lunch nearby. After lunch, continue to Saignon and Viens, then loop back via Le Colorado Provençal and St-Saturnin-lès-Apt.

I've described sights at each stop, but you'll need to be selective—you can't (and don't need to) see them all. Read through your options and choose the ones that appeal most. Slow down and get to know a few places well, rather than dashing between every stop you can cram in. The best sight is the dreamy landscape between the villages.

Roussillon

With all the trendy charm of Santa Fe on a hilltop, photogenic Roussillon requires serious camera and café time. Roussillon has been a protected village since 1943 and has benefited from a complete absence of modern development. An enormous deposit of ochre, which gives the earth and its buildings that distinctive reddish color, provided this village with its economic base until shortly after World War II. This place is popular; it's best to visit early or late in the day.

Orientation to Roussillon

Roussillon sits atop Mont Rouge ("Red Mountain") at about 1,000 feet above sea level, and requires some uphill walking to reach. Exposed ochre cliffs form the village's southern limit.

Tourist Information: The little TI is in the center (no Wi-Fi), across from the Chez David restaurant. Hotel hunters can leaf through their binders describing area hotels and *chambres d'hôtes*. Walkers should get info on trails from Roussillon to nearby villages (TI hours are unreliable, usually Mon-Sat April-Oct 9:30-12:30 & 14:00-18:00, Nov-March 14:00-17:30, closed Sun year-round, Place de la Poste, tel. 04 90 05 60 25, http://otroussillon.pagesperso-orange.fr).

Parking: Parking lots are available at every entry to the village (free if you're staying overnight and have arranged it with your hotel). **Parking des Ocres** (also called "P2") is the large lot on the hill toward the ochre cliffs. Day-trippers should head straight here, as spots are more available and the view of Roussillon is striking. Leave nothing of value visible in your car.

Parking Sablons is next to the recommended Maison des Ocres. **Parking St-Michel** is below the town on the way to Joucas and Gordes.

Roussillon Walk

This quick self-guided walk will take you through Roussillon's village to its ochre cliffs.

• *To begin the walk, climb from any parking lot to the village center, cross the cute square, and then climb under the bell tower and the church). Continue past the church to the summit of...*

▲The Village

Find the orientation table and the **viewpoint**, often complete with a howling mistral wind. During the Middle Ages, a castle occupied this space on the top of the appropriately named Red Mountain (Mont Rouge), and watched over the village below. Although nothing remains of the castle today, the strategic advantage of this site is clear. Count how many villages you can identify, and then

Roussillon

Accommodations
1. Le Clos de la Glycine & Restaurant Chez David
2. Maison des Ocres
3. To Le Mas d'Estonge
4. To Hôtel les Sables d'Ocre & Le Clos des Cigales

Eateries & Other
5. La Treille
6. Chez Nino
7. Croqu'la Vie Bookshop

Ochre Cliffs

P

(Ochres / P-2)

WC

AVE. DE LA BURLIÈRE

To Ochre Conservatory, D-900 to Bonnieux & D-104 to Goult, Apt & 4

R. DE LA POSTE

1

POST

WC

6

R. CASTEAU

To St-Saturnin-Les-Apt & Rustrel via D-227 & 3

RUE DE LA FONTAINE

7

Place Mairie

RUE DE L'ARCADE

D-227

P (Fontaine)

ST. MICHEL

Place Mathieu

BELL TOWER

R. DU JEU

5

R. D. LAURIERS

VIEWPOINT & ORIENTATION TABLE

WALK BEGINS

CHEMIN DE RONDE

Mont Rouge

P

P (St. Michel)

WC

RUE DE LA PORTE HEUREUSE

To Murs, Joucas & Gordes via D-2

RUE DES BOURGADES

WC

P (Sablons)

D-169

2

To Gordes, Joucas & Domaine de Tara

100 Meters

100 Yards

notice how little sprawl there is in the valley below. Because the Luberon has been declared a natural reserve (Parc Naturel Régional du Luberon), development is strictly controlled.

Stroll back to the **church.** Duck into the pretty 11th-century Church of St. Michel, and appreciate the natural air-conditioning and the well-worn center aisle. The white interior tells you that the stone came from elsewhere, and the WWI memorial plaque over the side door suggests a village devastated by the war (more than 40 people from little Roussillon died).

On leaving the church, look across the way to the derelict building, a reminder of Roussillon's humble roots. After World War II, when the demand for ochre faded, this was a dusty, desolate village with zero tourist appeal. Adding to the town's economic woes, many residents fled for an easier life below, with fewer steps and modern conveniences. Abandoned buildings like this presented a serious problem (common throughout France)...until tourists discovered Roussillon, and folks began reinvesting in the village. This building is still looking for a buyer. Detour behind the building to the left down a small lane to find the Chemin de Ronde, with terrific views of the Luberon and Gordes from atop the medieval walls.

• *Return to the church and continue down to the village.*

Notice the clamped-iron beams that shore up old walls. Examine the different hues of yellow and orange. These lime-finished exteriors, called *chaux* (literally, "limes"), need to be redone about every 10 years. Locals choose their exact color...but in this town of ochre, it's never white. The church tower that you walk under once marked the entrance to the fortified town. Just before dropping down to the square, turn right and find the gigantic 150-year-old grapevine that decorates Restaurant la Treille. This is what you get when you don't prune.

Linger over *un café*, or—if it's later in the day—*un pastis*, in the picturesque village square (Place de la Mairie). Watch the

stream of shoppers. Is anyone playing *boules* at the opposite end? You could paint the entire town without ever leaving the red-and-orange corner of your palette. Many do. While Roussillon receives scads of day-trippers, mornings and evenings are romantically peaceful on this square. The **Croqu'la Vie** bookshop on the square's corner deserves a visit; a modest selection of English books are available (daily 10:00-18:00, later July-Sept).

• *With the cafés on your right, drop downhill past the lineup of shops and turn right past the TI to find the parking lot just beyond. Animals grazed here for centuries. It was later turned into a school playground. When tourists outnumbered students, it became a parking lot. Walk past the parking lot and head left uphill, hugging the cliffs to find the...*

▲▲Ochre Cliffs Trail (Le Sentier des Ocres)

Roussillon was Europe's capital for ochre production until World War II. A stroll to the south end of town, beyond the upper park-

ing lot, shows you why: Roussillon sits on the world's largest known ochre deposit. A radiant orange path leads around the richly colored, Bryce Canyon-like cliffs. Allow a minimum of 30 easy minutes of walking for a quick loop through the cliffs; a longer loop takes an hour.

Ochre is made of iron oxide and clay. When combined with sand, it creates the yellowish-red pigments you see in these buildings. Although ochre is also pro-duced in the US and Italy, the quality of France's ochre is considered *le best*.

The value of Roussillon's ochre cliffs was known even in Roman times. Once excavated, the clay ochre was rinsed with water to separate it from sand, then bricks of the stuff were dried and baked for deeper hues. The procedure for extracting the ochre did not change much over 2,000 years, until ochre mining became industrialized in the late 1700s. Used primarily for wallpaper and linoleum, ochre use reached its zenith just before World War II. (After that, cheaper substitutes took over.)

Cost and Hours: €2.50, €7.50 combo-ticket with Ochre Conservatory—described next; May-June and Sept 9:30-18:30, July-Aug 9:00-19:30, shorter hours off-season, closed Jan. Beware: Light-colored clothing (especially shoes) and orange powder don't mix.

Sights near Roussillon

▲Ochre Conservatory
(Conservatoire des Ocres et de la Couleur)

For a good introduction to the history and uses of ochre, visit this intriguing reconstructed ochre factory. Grab a pamphlet to follow the well-done self-guided tour, which shows how ochre is convert-ed from an ore to a pigment (allow 45 minutes). Your visit ends with a great bookshop and a chance to try your hand at ochre painting.

Cost and Hours: €6.50, €7.50 combo-ticket with ochre cliffs, daily 9:00-18:00 but closed for lunch, July-Aug until 19:00, about a half-mile below Roussillon toward Apt on D-104, tel. 04 90 05 66 69, www.okhra.com.

LUBERON

Domaine de Tara

Just below Roussillon, on the road to Joucas, this welcoming winery has been making excellent wines for about 15 years. Pascale runs the tasting room, and her husband makes wines to please every palate: red, white, rosé, sparkling, and sweet. Pop into the barrel room where they occasionally exhibit local artists' work. They don't mind if you picnic on the property afterward.

Cost and Hours: Prices vary by wine, daily April-Oct 10:00-19:30, Nov-March and Wed until 18:00, tel. 04 90 05 74 87, www. domainedetara.com.

Hot-Air Balloon Flight

Ply the calm morning air above the Luberon in a hot-air balloon. The **Vol-Terre** outfit offers a flight that includes a picnic and champagne (€230, around 1 hour in balloon, allow 3 hours total, maximum 4 passengers, reserve a few days ahead, mobile 06 03 54 10 92, www.montgolfiere-luberon.com).

Goult

Bigger than its sister hill towns, this surprisingly quiet village seems content to be away from the tourist path. Climb the small lanes up the hill to the panoramic view and windmill. From there, drop back down through the arch and glide down, passing the old château. Notice how many of the historic buildings are built right on top of thick rock strata. Consider having a nice meal in one of Goult's several good restaurants—where you'll have to compete with locals rather than tourists for a table. **$$ Café de la Poste** is ideal for an outdoor lunch (no dinner served). Trendier **$$$$ La Bartavelle** is *the* place in town to dine, but is darn popular (book a table a week in advance, 29 Rue du Cheval Blanc, tel. 04 90 72 33 72).

Sleeping in Roussillon

The TI posts a list of hotels and *chambres d'hôtes*. Parking is free if you sleep in Roussillon; pre-arrange with your hotelier. The village offers a couple of acceptable-value accommodations.

$$$ Le Clos de la Glycine*** delivers Roussillon's plushest accommodations with nine lovely rooms located dead-center in the village (some view rooms, off-season deals, air-con, ask about parking, located at the recommended refined restaurant Chez David—they prefer you pay for half-pension, across from the TI on Place de la Poste, tel. 04 90 05 60 13, www.luberon-hotel.com, contact@luberon-hotel.fr).

$$ Maison des Ocres,*** well-located on the edge of the village center at the Sablons parking area, is a stylish place with a spacious lounge decorated with paintings from the Maeght Foundation, handsome rooms (many with decks or balconies), a few good family rooms, and a lovely pool (private parking, Route de Gordes, tel. 04 90 05 60 50, www.lamaisondesocres-hotel.com, contact@ lamaisondesocres-hotel.com). Coming from Gordes and Joucas, it's the first building you pass in Roussillon.

NEAR ROUSSILLON

These listings are for drivers only. The last two are most easily found by turning north off D-900 at the *Roussillon/Les Huguets* sign (the second turnoff to Roussillon coming from Avignon). Joucas and St-Saturnin-lès-Apt (both described later) also have good beds near Roussillon.

$$ At Le Mas d'Estonge, Stéphane and Dominique welcome you into their little Provençal retreat located in a small neighborhood 10 minutes from Roussillon. Their four well-furnished and comfy rooms share a sweet patio, a common kitchen, and a pool (on D-227 in Hameau Des Riperts, tel. 04 90 05 63 13, www.destonge. com, destonge@gmail.com).

$$ Hôtel les Sables d'Ocre** offers 22 meticulously maintained, motel-esque rooms, a big pool, the greenest grass around, air-conditioning, and fair rates (a half-mile from Roussillon toward Apt at intersection of D-108 and D-104, tel. 04 90 05 55 55, www. sablesdocre.com, sablesdocre@orange.fr).

$ Le Clos des Cigales is a good refuge run by friendly Philippe and his wife, Brigitte. Of their five blue-shuttered, stylish bungalows, two are doubles and three are two-room suites with tiny kitchenettes; all have private patios facing a big pool. When you arrive, you'll understand the name—the cacophony from the *cigales* (cicadas) can be deafening (family rooms, includes breakfast, table tennis, hammock, 5 minutes from Roussillon toward Goult on D-104, tel. 04 90 05 73 72, www.leclosdescigales.com, philippe. lherbeil@wanadoo.fr).

Eating in Roussillon

Restaurants change with the mistral here—what's good one year disappoints the next. But I have found a few reliable places that offer a good range of prices and cuisine. Consider my suggestions (or look over my recommendations in other Luberon villages, like Goult, just a few minutes away by car).

On Place de la Poste: A good place to splurge is at **$$$$ Chez David,** at the recommended hotel Le Clos de la Glycine. You can enjoy a fine meal on the terrace or from an interior window table with point-blank views over the ochre cliffs (daily, Place de la Poste, tel. 04 90 05 60 13).

$$ La Treille hangs just above the village square and serves good value meals on a small terrace or under soft arches in an up-

Luberon Restaurants Worth the Trip

Many of the restaurants in the countryside near Roussillon are worth a detour. Use the list below as a quick reference, then flip to the full descriptions of those that sound most appealing. All are within a 20-minute drive from Roussillon. Remember that Isle-sur-la-Sorgue is a manageable 30-minute drive from Roussillon.

Dinner

Chez David, in Roussillon, offers fine cuisine and views in a formal setting (daily; see page 201).

Hôtel des Voyageurs, in St-Saturnin-lès-Apt, is a local favorite, with authentic decor and lovely hosts (page 213).

La Treille, in Roussillon, has a great setting, fair prices, and reliable cuisine (see page 201).

La Bartavalle, in overlooked Goult, offers fine cuisine and draws a foodie crowd (see page 200).

Lunch

Café de la Poste, in Goult, has a pleasant outdoor terrace and a traditional menu (see page 200).

Le Terrail, in Bonnieux, serves good-enough cuisine on an outside terrace with stunning vistas. This place works for dinner, too (see page 209).

Bar/Restaurant de France, in Lacoste, is an easygoing eatery with sensational view tables (page 209).

Petit Café, in Oppède-le-Vieux, has a charming setting facing Luberon cliffs and castle ruins (see page 212).

Le Petit Jardin Café, in remote Viens, offers an unpretentious lunch or dinner stop, with cozy interior tables and a garden terrace (see page 214).

stairs room (*souris d'agneau*—lamb shank—is the chef's specialty, closed Wed, Rue du Four, tel. 04 90 05 64 47).

$ Chez Nino cascades down the hillside with three view terraces. The chef is Sicilian and his wife is Moroccan, and the simple fare combines elements of both with regional cuisine (daily, a block behind the TI on Rue des Bourgades, tel. 04 90 74 29 17).

Joucas

This understated, quiet, and largely overlooked village offers stone lanes with carefully arranged flowers, beautiful vistas, and well-restored homes. There's not much to do or see here, except eat, sleep, and just be. Joucas has a view café, one pharmacy, a good kids' play area, and one good-value accommodation option. Sleep here for a central location and utter silence. For views, walk past the little fountain in the center and up the steep lanes as high as you want.

LUBERON

Several **hiking** trails leave from Joucas. Gordes and Roussillon are each three miles away, uphill. The three-mile hike up to the attractive village of Murs (which has several cafés/restaurants) is more scenic, though it's easier in the other direction (yellow signs point the way from the top of

the village). You don't have to go far to enjoy the natural beauty on this trail.

Sleeping and Eating: Located in the center of lovely little Joucas, **$ Hostellerie des Commandeurs**** has quite comfortable, good-value rooms and is kid-friendly, with a big pool and a sports field/play area next door. Ask for a south-facing room *(coté sud)* for the best views. All rooms have showers, air-conditioning, and mini fridges (above park at village entrance, hotel open March-Oct, tel. 04 90 05 78 01, www.lescommandeurs.com, hostellerie@ lescommandeurs.com). The traditional **$$ restaurant** offers Provençal cuisine at fair prices (succulent lamb, memorable crème brûlée with lavender, restaurant closed Wed). Village kids like to hang out around the bar's pool table.

More Luberon Towns

Le Luberon is packed with appealing villages and beautiful scenery, but it has only a handful of must-see sights. I've grouped them by area to make your sightseeing planning easier (see the Luberon map at the beginning of this chapter). The D-900 highway cuts the Luberon in half like an arrow. The more popular and visited section lies above D-900 (with Roussillon and Gordes), while the villages to the south seem a bit less trampled.

The busiest sights are in and near Gordes; I've listed those first, to encourage you to avoid afternoon crowds. Beyond that, you're free to connect the stops however you please. Rambling the Luberon's spaghetti network of small roads is a joy, and getting lost comes with the territory—go with it. None of the sights listed below is a must-see, but all are close to each other. Pick up a good map (Michelin maps #332 and #527 work for me).

I'd make a loop through these villages and sights, doing them in the order described below. If you're sleeping in or near Roussillon, start there (mornings are peaceful). Each town is about a 10-minute drive from the last, and the route is well-signed. Bonnieux looks better from a distance, and its center has no pedestrian focus—unless you're here for lunch or need a place to stay, skip it.

Gordes

The Luberon's most impressively situated hill town is worth a quick stop to admire its setting. As you approach Gordes, veer right when you see the viewpoint icon. Get out, stroll along the road, and admire the sensational view. Now consider this: In the 1960s Gordes was a ghost town of derelict buildings with no economy, where locals led simple lives and had few ambitions. Then came the theater festival in Avignon, bringing directors who wanted to re-create perfect Provençal villages on film. Parisians, Swiss, Brits, and a few Americans followed, willing to pay any price for their place in the Provençal sun.

Today Gordes is renovated top to bottom (notice how every stone seems perfectly placed), and filled with people who live in a world without calluses. Many Parisian big-shots and moneyed foreigners invested heavily, restoring dream homes and putting property values and café prices out of sight for locals. Beyond its stunning views, the village has little of interest. Move along.

SIGHTS NEAR GORDES

The first two sights—the Abbey Notre-Dame de Sénanque and the Village des Bories—are both well marked from Gordes.

Abbey Notre-Dame de Sénanque

This still-functioning and beautifully situated Cistercian abbey was built in 1148 as a back-to-basics reaction to the excesses of Benedictine abbeys. The Cistercians strove to be separate from the world and to recapture the simplicity, solitude, and poverty of the early Church. To succeed required industrious self-sufficiency—a skill these monks excelled at. Their movement spread and colonized Europe with a new form of Christianity. By 1200 there were more than 500 such monasteries and abbeys in Europe.

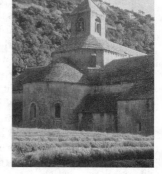

Cost and Hours: €7.50, with or without the French-only tour; tour mandatory Feb-Oct daily 11:00-17:00; individual visits Mon-Sat 9:45-11:00, no individual visits on Sun or holidays, and no visits at all 12:45-14:30, reservations strongly recommended, call or check website for tour times (tel. 04 90 72 05 72, www.senanque.fr). You can also attend Mass at various times in the abbey's church (check website or call to confirm).

Dress Code: Modest dress is required for entry—shoulders and knees must be covered.

Tours: Those arriving as the abbey opens find a peaceful place they can tour on their own (good English handout). Those arriving after 11:00 must visit the abbey on a 50-minute, French-only tour (see website for times, English booklet with translations available).

Visiting the Abbey: The abbey is best appreciated from the outside, and is worth the trip for its splendid and remote setting alone. Come first thing, or linger later and stop at a pullout for a bird's-eye view as you descend, then wander the abbey's perimeter. The abbey church is always open (except during Mass, but you're welcome to attend) and highlights the utter simplicity sought by these monks. In late June through much of July, the five hectares of lavender fields that surround the abbey make for breathtaking pictures and draw loads of visitors.

The tour covers Sénanque's church, the small cloisters, the refectory, and a *chauffoir,* a small heated room where monks could copy books year-round. The interior, which doesn't measure up to the abbey's spectacular setting, is a let-down—skip the tour and just wander the grounds.

A small monastic community still resides here. For more on monasteries, see the sidebar.

Leaving the Abbey: Leave the abbey opposite the way you arrived, following signs to *Gordes,* then *Roussillon,* then follow *Murs* and *Joucas*...and enjoy the ride.

Village des Bories

A twisting, mile-long, stone-bordered dirt road sets the mood for this mildly entertaining open-air museum of stone huts *(bories).* The vertical stones you see on the walls as you approach the site were used as counterweights to keep these mortar-free walls intact. The "village" you tour is made up of dry-laid stone structures, proving that there has always been more stone than wood in this rugged region. Stone villages like this predated the Romans—some say by 2,000 years. This one was inhabited for 200 years (from about 1600 to 1800). *Bories* can still be seen in fields throughout the Luberon; most are now used to store tools or hay.

The Village des Bories is composed of five "hamlets." Start with the short film (English subtitles), then duck into several homes and see animal pens, a community oven, and more (identified in English). Study the "beehive" stone-laying method and

Medieval Monasteries

France is littered with medieval monasteries, and Provence is no exception. Most have virtually no furnishings (they never had many), which leaves the visitor with little to reconstruct what life must have been like in these cold stone buildings a thousand years ago. A little history can help breathe life into these important yet underappreciated monuments.

After the fall of the Roman Empire, monasteries arose as refuges of peace and order in a chaotic world. While the pope got rich and famous playing power politics, monasteries worked to keep the focus on simplicity and poverty. Throughout the Middle Ages, monasteries were mediators between Man and God. In these peacefully remote abbeys, Europe's best minds struggled with the interpretation of God's words. Every sentence needed to be understood and applied. Answers later debated in universities were once contemplated in monasteries.

St. Benedict established the Middle Ages' most influential monastic order (Benedictine) in Monte Cassino, Italy, in A.D. 529. He scheduled a rigorous program of monastic duties that combined manual labor with intellectual tasks. His movement spread north and took firm root in France, where the abbey of Cluny (Burgundy) eventually controlled more than 2,000 dependent abbeys and vied with the pope for control of the Church.

Benedictine abbeys grew dot-com rich, and with wealth came excess (king-size beds and Wi-Fi). Monks lost sight of their purpose and became soft and corrupt. In the late 1100s, the determined and charismatic St. Bernard rallied the Cistercian order by

imagine the time it took to construct. The villagers had no scaffolds or support arches—just hammers and patience.

Cost and Hours: €6, buy €4 booklet of English translations to learn more, daily June-Sept 9:00-20:00, Oct-May 9:00-17:30, tel. 04 90 72 03 48, www.levillagedesbories.com.

St. Pantaléon

This postage-stamp-sized village feels lost in the valley below Gordes. It comes with an adorable 12th-century Romanesque church that has a remarkable necropolis around back, with tombs—many in the distinct shape of a human body, even one of a baby—carved right out of the rock on which the church was built. It's a peaceful, moving site.

going back to the original rule of St. Benedict. Cistercian abbeys thrived as centers of religious thought and exploration from the 13th through the 15th centuries.

Cistercian abbots ran their abbeys like little kingdoms, doling out punishment and food to the monks, and tools to peasant farmers. Abbeys were occupied by two groups: the favored monks from aristocratic families (such as St. Bernard) and a larger group of lay brothers from peasant stock, who were given the heaviest labor and could join only the Sunday services.

Monks' days were broken into three activities: prayer, reading holy texts, and labor. Monks lived in silence and poverty, with few amenities—meat was forbidden, as was cable TV. In summer, they ate two daily meals—in winter, just one. Monks slept together in a single room on threadbare mats covering solid-rock floors.

With their focus on work and discipline, Cistercian abbeys became leaders of the medieval industrial revolution. Among the few literate people in Europe, monks were keepers of technological knowledge—about clocks, waterwheels, accounting, foundries, gristmills, textiles, and agricultural techniques. Abbeys became economic engines that helped drive France out of its Middle Aged funk.

As France (and Europe) slowly got its act together in the late Middle Ages, cities reemerged as places to trade and thrive. Abbeys gradually lost their relevance in a brave new humanist world. Universities became the new center of intellectual development. Kings took over abbot selection, further degrading the abbeys' power, and Gutenberg's movable type made monks obsolete. The French Revolution closed the book on abbatial life, with troops occupying and destroying many abbeys. The still-functioning Abbey Notre-Dame de Sénanque, near Gordes, is a rare survivor.

Moulin Saint Augustin

Originally a 16th-century flour mill, this olive oil boutique is on the busy D-900 just east of Coustellet. Moulin Saint Augustin is a property with centuries of history, but you can only enter the shop. English-speaking Laure explains the qualities of the native olive varieties—yes, just like grapes, there are specific olive varieties that fare better locally (July-Aug Mon-Sat 10:00-19:00, Sept-June Mon-Sat 9:00-12:00 & 14:00-18:00, closed Sun year-round, 2800 Route d'Apt, tel. 04 90 72 43 66, www.moulin-saintaugustin.fr).

Villages and Sights South of Roussillon

These villages and sights below Roussillon and D-900 feel less visited than places north of this busy road. You'll need a good half-day to visit them all (see the map on page 184 to get oriented). They work well in the order described below, with lunch in Bonnieux or Lacoste (for recommendations, see sidebar on page 202). The first sight is situated south of Roussillon, where D-108 crosses D-900.

Julien Bridge (Pont Julien)

This delicate, three-arched bridge, named for Julius Caesar, survives as a testimony to Roman engineers—and to the importance of this rural area 2,000 years ago. It's the only surviving bridge on what was the main road from northern Italy to Provence—the primary route used by Roman armies. The 215-foot-long Roman bridge was under construction from 27 B.C. to A.D. 14. Mortar had not yet been invented, so (as with Pont du Gard) the stones were carefully set in place. Amazingly, the bridge survives

today, having outlived Roman marches, hundreds of floods, and decades of automobile traffic. A new bridge finally rerouted traffic from this beautiful structure in 2005.

Walk below the bridge. Notice how thin the layer of stone seems between the arch tops and the road. Those open niches weren't for statues, but instead allowed water to pass through when the river ran high. (At its current trickle, that's hard to fathom.) Walk under an arch and examine the pockmarks in the side—medieval thieves in search of free bronze stole the clamps.

Château de la Canorgue Winery

Well-signed halfway between the Julien Bridge and Bonnieux, this is a pretty winery; the film *A Good Year*, with Russell Crowe and French actress Marion Cotillard, was filmed here in 2006. A welcoming tasting room offers the full range of wines—from viognier and chardonnay whites to rosés and rich reds—with owner-in-waiting and winemaker Nathalie greeting guests on weekdays. For a good contrast in reds, compare the *Vendanges de Nathalie* with the *vin du pays*. Château de la Canorgue was one of the first wineries in the area to make organic wines, and they have reasonable prices.

Cost and Hours: Average bottle costs €10, Mon-Sat 9:00-19:00 except closed for lunch Sat, closed Sun, tel. 04 90 75 81 01, www.chateaulacanorgue.com.

LUBERON

Bonnieux

Spectacular from a distance, this town disappoints me up close. It lacks a pedestrian center, though the Friday-morning market briefly creates one. The main reason to visit here is to enjoy the views from a well-positioned restaurant.

Sleeping: Located in Bonnieux's center, **$$ Hôtel le Clos du Buis***** is an eight-room delight, run by eager-to-please Lydia and Pierre. Their veranda allows fine views over the Luberon (includes breakfast, pool, free parking, guest kitchen, in the middle of town on Rue Victor Hugo, tel. 04 90 75 88 48, www.leclosdubuis.fr, le-clos-du-buis@wanadoo.fr).

The country-elegant *chambres d'hôte* **$$ Mas del Sol,** between Bonnieux and Lacoste, is perfect for connoisseurs of the Luberon. Young Lucine and Richard Massol rent five bright, spacious rooms that come with views, vines, olives, and a big breakfast. The setting is unbeatable, and the stylish pool and gardens will calm your nerves (guest fridge for family picnics, loaner bikes, tel. 04 90 75 94 80, www.mas-del-sol.com, contact@mas-del-sol.com). From D-900, take the D-36 turnoff to Bonnieux and look for *Mas del Sol* signs after about three kilometers (two miles).

Eating: A local hangout is **$ Le Terrail,** serving up enjoyable cuisine with a sensational view terrace (cheap lunch *plats* and salads, good *menu* options, open daily, Place Gambetta, tel. 04 90 75 93 73).

Lacoste

Little Lacoste slumbers across the valley from Bonnieux in the shadow of its looming castle. Climb through this photogenic village of arches and stone paths, passing American art students (from the Savannah College of Art and Design) showing their work. Support an American artist, learn about the art, and then keep climbing and climbing to the ruined castle base. The view of Bonnieux from the base of Lacoste's castle is as good as it gets.

The Marquis de Sade (1740-1814) lived in this **castle** for more than 30 years. Author of pornographic novels, he was notorious for hosting orgies behind these walls, and for kidnapping peasants for scandalous purposes. He was eventually arrested and imprisoned for 30 years, and thanks to him, we have a word to describe his favorite hobby—sadism. Today, fashion designer Pierre Cardin lives in the lower part of the castle, having spent a fortune shoring up the protective walls and sponsoring a high-priced summer opera series. Some locals are critical of Cardin, claiming that he is buying up the town to create his own "faux-Provence." Could "Cardism" be next?

Eating: If it's time for lunch, find the **$$ Bar/Restaurant de France**'s outdoor tables overlooking Bonnieux and savor the view

LUBERON

(reasonably priced omelets and *plats*, daily, lunch only off-season, tel. 04 90 75 82 25). A small *épicerie* near the church has just enough fixings to make a picnic.

Abbey St. Hilaire

A dirt road off D-103 between Lacoste and Ménerbes leads down to this long-forgotten and pint-size abbey. There's not much to see here—it's more about the experience. The tranquility and isolation sought by monks 800 years ago are still palpable in the simple church and modest cloisters. Once a Cistercian outpost for the bigger abbey at Sénanque, Abbey St. Hilaire is now owned by Carmelite Friars. The lone stone bench in front is picnic-ready, and a rugged WC is cut into the rock (across the courtyard). For a pleasing loop walk, start at the abbey and cross over the D-3 road to a path running along the base of the Luberon range (details available at the abbey). Leave nothing valuable in your car at this remote site.

Ménerbes

Ménerbes, (in)famous as the village that drew author Peter Mayle's attention to this region, has an upscale but welcoming feel in its small center (€3 parking). Wine bars, cafés, and a smattering of galleries gather where key lanes intersect. To explore the linear rock-top village, follow *Eglise* signs.

At the east end of Rue Corneille you'll pass the **citadel,** built in 1584 (after the Protestants of Ménerbes were defeated in the religious wars of 1577)—and never tested. The citadel is privately owned today, but from the outside you can still enjoy the impressive facade, which spans the width of the rock. Nearby, the ancient stone prison tower is also worth a peek.

At the village's very western end, find the heavy Romanesque church (closed and under renovation) and **graveyard** (good views in all directions). You're face-to-face with the Grand Luberon ridge. Notice the quarry carved into its side, where the stone for this village came from.

On the way back, foodies can duck into the snazzy **$$$$ Maison de la Truffe et du Vin,** which offers "truffle discovery workshops," fine meals, and wine tastings (Place de l'Horloge, tel. 04 90 72 38 37, www.vin-truffe-luberon.com).

The **Corkscrew Museum** (Musée du Tire-Bouchon) is actually part of the **Domaine de la Citadelle** winery, a half-mile below Ménerbes. It is worth a stop if you're a corkscrew enthusiast or want to taste their very good wines. They have 1,200 corkscrews on display in glass cases and a well-stocked gift shop (€4 for the "museum," includes tasting, daily 10:00-12:00 & 14:00-19:00, shorter hours and closed Sun off-season, tel. 04 90 72 41 58, www.domaine-citadelle.com).

Eating: A fine lunch or snack awaits at the **$ Auzet Salon de Thé,** with a cozy interior or view tables from the small terrace. You'll find cheap quiche and savory pies with salad, delicious baked goods, and more (52 Rue du Portail Neuf, tel. 04 90 72 37 53).

▲Oppède-le-Vieux

This windy barnacle of a town clings with all its might to its hillside. There are a handful of businesses and a dusty little square at

the base of a short, ankle-twisting climb to a pretty little church and ruined castle. This off-the-beaten-path fixer-upper of a village was completely abandoned in 1910, and today has a ghost town-like feel (it once housed 200 people). The inhabited village below has a rugged character and shows little inclination for boutiques and smart hotels. It's ideal for those looking to perish in Provence.

Getting There: To find Oppède-le-Vieux from D-900, follow signs to *Oppède* and *Oppède le Village,* then *Oppède-le-Vieux,* and drive toward le Petit Luberon massif. You'll follow a long, one-way loop and be forced to park a few hundred yards from the village (unless you're sleeping there), for which you'll get to pay €3. From the lot, follow signs to *Vieux Village* up a confusing set of switchbacks—the long walk is worth it.

Sights: Plan your ascent to the **castle.** It's 20 minutes straight up—the Luberon views justify the effort. (After making this walk, you'll understand why locals abandoned it for more level terrain.) Small information panels provide a worthwhile background in English as you climb, and the upgraded paving and floodlighting will enhance your appreciation of the lovely setting. Walk under the central arch of the building across from Le Petit Café and climb. After walking under the arch, look back to notice the handsome building it supports. At the fork, you can go either way (though the path to the right is easier). Find the little church terrace. From here, tiled rooftops paint a delightful picture with the grand panorama; the flat plain of the Rhône delta is visible off to the left.

The colorful **Notre-Dame d'Alidon church** (1588) is generally open 9:30-18:30 (depending on availability of village volunteers, who are eager to answer questions). There's been a church on this site for 1,000 years. Pick up the English text and imagine having to climb this distance at least every Sunday—for your entire life. Notice the pride locals have for their church: You'll see new

LUBERON

gold-leaf accents and other efforts to spruce up the long-abandoned building. The steps to chapels on the right were necessary, thanks to the church's hillside setting.

Unfortunately, what remains of the castle is now off-limits—it's too dangerous. But the views are worth the climb.

Sleeping and Eating: Back down in the village center, consider a meal with views of the castle ruins at **$$ Petit Café,** where all-business Laurent is in charge (closed Wed and mid-Dec-Feb). Petit Café also offers simple but comfy **$** rooms, all with nice views (usually closed for check-in Tue-Wed, includes breakfast, air-con, rooftop terrace, tel. 04 90 76 74 01, www.lepetitcafe.fr).

Villages and Sights East of Roussillon

Provence can be busy with tourists, but there are still plenty of less-discovered places to explore. The area east of Roussillon, deep in the heart of Provence *(la Provence profonde)*, feels overlooked. Come here to get a sense of how most villages were before they became "destinations." Here are the key sights in the order that you'll pass them coming from the west. Allow a full day to complete this loop.

St-Saturnin-lès-Apt

This pleasant town (with a lively Tuesday market) has a ruined castle with grand views and a nifty budget hotel with a terrific restaurant. Ditch your car below the main entry to the town (just below the old city) and walk up the main drag past the Hôtel Saint Hubert (Rue de la République). You'll come to a striking church that's a fine example of Provençal Romanesque, with a tall, octagonal spire (the interior is often closed) and a perfectly situated plane tree.

From here, find the ramp with *Le Château* signs and climb. The first castle was started here a thousand years ago. Today's ruins are mostly from the 1300s and grow right out of the rock, making it difficult to tell the man-made from the natural. Go left when you see the opening and hike as high as the sun allows with no shade—faded green dots sort of guide you along. It's a scamperer's paradise, with views that rank among the best village-top vistas I've found in Provence. Find your way through the small opening to the little dam. On the opposite side of the reservoir, you'll discover fine views of the castle reflected in the water and appreciate its original scale. The small chapel at the very top is open only on Sunday mornings in summer, but at any time you can take the path to the right of the chapel back down the hill to the village, where you'll see a lovely medieval gate.

Sleeping and Eating: For a warm welcome, stay at **$$ Mas Perréal** just outside St-Saturnin-lès-Apt. American Kevin and his Parisian wife, Elisabeth, left no stone unturned as they restored their lovely farmhouse. This place features traditional rooms (a few with kitchens, each with its own terrace), a pool, 360-degree views (they own the vineyards and orchards around you), elaborate American-size breakfasts, and no language barrier (rooms without kitchens include big breakfast; tel. 04 90 75 46 31, www.masperreal.com, elisabeth-kevin@masperreal.com, closed mid-Oct-March). Mas Perréal is off D-943, between St-Saturnin-lès-Apt and D-900. Coming from D-900, turn left at Moulin à Huile Jullien, continue three-quarters of a mile, cross one "major" road, and have faith until you see the signs—it will be on your right.

$ Hôtel/Restaurant des Voyageurs,* with amiable owners Nadine and Alain (who speak no English), is a time warp that has

survived many Provençal trends without changing its look or product. The basic accommodations gather around uneven floors and a frumpy upstairs terrace that only an artist could love (rooms are just comfortable enough, 2 Place Gambetta, tel. 04 90 75 42 08, www.voyageursenprovence.fr, must reserve by phone or fax 04 90 75 50 58—what's that?). The sweet Old World **$$** restaurant, with vintage floor tiles and beams, serves traditional cuisine that locals adore (well-priced *menus* from €25, best to book a day ahead, nice outdoor terrace). Both the hotel and the restaurant are closed all day Wednesday and Thursday until 18:00. It's at the base of the old village, below the Spar store.

Le Colorado Provençal

This park has ochre cliffs similar to Roussillon's, but they're spread over a larger area, with well-signed trails. If hiking through soft, orange sand and Bryce Canyon-like rocks strikes your fancy—and you didn't get enough in Roussillon—make time for Le Colorado Provençal.

You'll be directed to a big dirt parking lot (WCs and a café) and be given a map of the two

trails. Parking attendants are available from about 9:00 until 17:00 or 18:00. Before or after those times, you can park for free (but get no map).

For the best walk, cross the little footbridge, turn right, and follow arrows leading to the Sahara trail. Do the loop counter-clockwise. The two trails (Sahara and Belvédères) are color-coded. The shorter Sahara trail (signed in blue) offers a wide spectrum of colors and provides views of the chimney formations (allow 90 minutes round-trip from your car). You can extend your walk by 40 minutes and combine both trails. Forgo light-colored clothing.

Cost and Hours: Park is free, parking—€5, always open; located a half-mile below Rustrel off D-22, between Apt and Gignac—follow signs toward the village of *Rustrel*, the gateway to Le Colorado Provençal.

Viens

Located about 15 minutes uphill and east of Le Colorado Provençal, this village is where Luberon locals go to get away. With a setting like this, it's surprising that modest Viens is not more developed.  The panoramas are higher and vaster than around Roussillon and Gordes (with some lavender fields), and the vegetation is more raw. Walk the streets of the old town (bigger than it first appears) and visit the few shops scattered about. Uphill, find the courtyard of the old château, then walk to the end of the village and relax at a picnic table to enjoy the grand view.

Eating: Just below the town's only phone booth, **$$ Le Petit Jardin Café** fits perfectly in this unpretentious town where tourists are viewed as curiosities. Come for a drink and rub shoulders with locals or, better, have a meal. Dine in the small traditional interior or outside on a garden terrace (good-value weekday *menu du jour*, more elaborate weekend *menu*, closed Sun evening and Mon, tel. 04 90 75 20 05). A small **grocery store** (closed Sun afternoon and Mon) and a **bakery** (closed Mon) are a few blocks past the café, toward St. Martin de Castillon.

To reach the next village (Saignon), follow signs to *St. Martin de Castillon*, then turn right on D-900 toward Apt.

Saignon

Sitting high atop a rock spur, this village looks down onto Apt, a city of only 11,500—which from here looks like a megalopolis after all these tiny villages. You can peek into the too-big-for-this-village Romanesque church (Notre-Dame de la Pitié) and admire its wood doors and tympanum, then follow *Le Rocher* signs through the village up to the "ship's prow." If you need to see it all, climb to the Le Rocher Bellevue for grand views over lavender fields (about three stories of stairs to the top). There are a handful of cafés and a grocery store in the linear village's center. Parking is best just above the town (hike or drive farther above town for sensational views over Saignon).

Buoux

Buoux (pronounced "by-oox"), a way-off-the-beaten-path village, is home to a remote hotel/restaurant and one of Provence's best ruined castles. A trip to this far-flung corner rewards with rocky canyons, acres of lavender, and few tourists. Start early and climb to the castle before the heat rises, then have a long, well-earned lunch at the recommended L'Auberge des Seguins (see below). If you liked Les Baux but weren't so fond of the crowds and don't need an audioguide, you'll love it here. But you'll need good shoes, stamina, and balance because much of the footing is tricky.

Buoux is south of Apt on D-113 between Saignon and Lourmarin. Ambitious travelers can combine a visit to Buoux with Lourmarin and Bonnieux.

Sights in Buoux

▲▲Fort de Buoux

The remains of this remote ridgetop castle are a playground for energetic lovers of crumbled ruins and grand views. Allow an hour for this hike.

Cost and Hours: €5, daily 10:00-17:00, closed in bad weather (wind or rain) when it's slippery and dangerous, tel. 04 90 74 25 75, www. lefortdebuoux.e-monsite.com.

Getting There: The fort is 10 minutes by car from the village of Buoux. To reach the fort from Apt and the north, drive through Buoux on D-113, drop down, and be on the lookout for small signs to *Fort de Buoux* (and *L'Auberge des Seguins*). Slow down and expect sharp turns. If coming from the south, follow signs to *Bonnieux,* then *L'Auberge des Seguins* and *Fort de Buoux.* You can use one of several dirt parking areas; you'll find the closest lot after passing two others. Once parked, walk through the gate and then about 15 easy minutes up a dirt road to the foot of the fort. From here the footing gets challenging.

LUBERON

Visiting the Fort: Floating like a cloud above the valleys below, the fort is easy to miss—it disappears beside the limestone rock cliffs that dominate the landscape. The long, rocky outcrop has been inhabited since prehistoric times. In the Middle Ages, it was home to hundreds of residents and a powerful castle that controlled a vast area. Like Les Baux, the fort was destroyed in the 1500s during the wars of religion (it was a Protestant base) and again in the 1600s by a paranoid King Louis XIII (see sidebar on page 172).

Monsieur le Gardien (the caretaker) greets you with tickets and a simple map of the sight with brief English explanations (picnic tables available and drinks sold at the entry). The map suggests a one-way route through the rocky ruins. You'll enter by the round tower and walk past what's left of the village, then scramble up and around rock piles along a stony spine to the castle remains, once home to hundreds of residents. You'll also climb around the remains of homes, a church, cisterns, and medieval storage silos. The castle keep stands at the highest point.

An unforgettable highlight of this castle is a three-story stone spiral staircase, which would never in a million years be open to the public in the US. Dating from the Bronze Age (experts think) and cut into the cliffs, it leads back down to the base. I'd skip this part (returning as you came) unless you are sure-footed and adventurous. At #36, near the grain silos (the many holes in the ground), walk under the archway and follow the faded white arrows as you leave the ruins (you'll walk uphill for 10 minutes at first). The staircase is steep with no handrails and some really big steps.

Sleeping and Eating in Buoux

$ L'Auberge des Seguins is a few stone's throws from the parking area for the fort and draws a hiking crowd. It's a modest, Shangri-la kind of place at the end of the valley, with confident young Amélie in charge. The rambling old farm is completely isolated and purposefully unmanicured—guests are encouraged to disconnect, enjoying the natural beauty and views of the fort. Come here for a light lunch (€8-10 salads and *plats*), dinner, or a drink (good local beer), or consider spending the night. The 27 rooms are simple though comfortable, clean, and squirreled about the place: Some require a dirt path to reach, and some are built into the rocky cliffs. Kids love it (there's also a big pool, but it's not heated). This place is a fine value for unpicky types—or for those on the lamb (good half-pension with dinner-€68/person, €42/person if you sleep in the cool 20-bed dorm room; coming from Fort de Buoux, take your first possible right, which turns into a dirt road; tel. 04 90 74 16 37, www.aubergedesseguins.com, aubergedesseguins@gmail.com).

Lourmarin

The southernmost Luberon village of Lourmarin has a good Friday market (and a smaller one Tue evenings), a beautiful Renais-

sance château on its fringe, and an enchanting town center. Lourmarin sits on a level plane and feels peaceful and happy, away from the more-visited villages in the heart of the Luberon. This self-assured and lovely town accommodates a healthy tourist demand without feeling too overrun (though there is no lack of boutiques). It's among the best Luberon villages to enjoy in the winter when other, better-known towns rattle about with few residents and little commercial activity.

Existentialist writer Albert Camus *(The Stranger)* lived in Lourmarin in the 1950s and is buried here, lending it a certain fame that persists today. Author Peter Mayle moved here not so long ago, adding to the village's cachet...and now you're here, too. Lourmarin makes a good base for touring the southern Luberon, Aix-en-Provence, and even Marseille and maybe Cassis. From here you can tour big cities, beaches, and castles, returning every night to the comfort of your village.

Getting There: Trans Vaucluse bus #9 links Lourmarin to Aix-en-Provence (3/day, 1.5 hours, www.pacamobilite.fr).

Tourist Information: The TI is located on Place Henri Barthélémy (Mon-Sat 10:00-12:30 & 15:00-18:00, closed Sun, tel. 04 90 68 10 77, www.lourmarin.com). Free public WCs are located to the right as you exit the TI, down the stairs. Park centrally, and leave nothing of value visible in your car.

Sights in Lourmarin

Château de Lourmarin

This Renaissance château looks across a grassy meadow at the village. It's more impressive from outside than within; you'll visit a few well-furnished rooms, an intriguing kitchen and exterior galleries, and a slick double spiral staircase in stone.

LUBERON

Cost and Hours: €7, daily June-Aug 10:00-18:00, shorter hours off-season, weekends only in Jan, decent English handout and posted explanations, tel. 04 90 68 15 23, www.chateau-de-lourmarin.com.

Market Day

Little Lourmarin hosts a lively market every Friday until 13:00. Sleep here Thursday night and awake to the commotion, arrive early, or prepare for a good walk from your car.

Sleeping in Lourmarin

Try to sleep here on a Thursday, so you can be here for Friday's market. The good-value Villa St. Louis and Les Chambres de la Cordière are near each other at the very eastern end of the town center.

$$ At Les Olivettes, Americans Joseph and Elizabeth DeLiso rent five apartments only a five-minute walk from the village center. The apartments are well-furnished and very comfortable, with kitchens, living rooms, DVD players, and guest computers. Some units have stunning views of the village. They are rentable by the week or half-week in the off-season (RS%, guest washer and dryer, Avenue Henri Bosco, tel. 04 90 68 03 52, www.olivettes.com, lourmarin@olivettes.com). As it's tricky to find this place even with a GPS, ask for directions when you make a reservation.

$ Villa St. Louis is a splendid place. It's a cross between a museum, a grand old manor home, and a garage sale. The dreamy backyard is ideal for a siesta (hammock provided) and picnics. The rooms are like Grandma's, and there's a common room with a fridge (includes breakfast, cash only, secure parking, loaner bikes, 35 Rue de Henri Savournin, tel. 04 90 68 39 18, www.villasaintlouis.com, villasaintlouis@wanadoo.fr).

$ Les Chambres de la Cordière is a cool getaway. Charming owner Françoise's goal is to make you feel at home. Six cozy rooms are tucked into one of the village's oldest buildings (c. 1582), with a tiny courtyard and welcoming cats (family rooms, 4 rooms come with mini kitchens—the 3 *gîtes* with full kitchens are usually rented only by the week, cash only, some rooms have air-con, one room with a whirlpool bath, Rue Albert Camus, tel. 04 90 68 03 32, mobile 06 81 02 8 04, www.cordiere.com, cordiereluberon@aol.com).

Eating in Lourmarin

All roads seem to converge on the postcard-perfect Place de l'Ormeau. Several appealing places line the square, making comparison shopping easy. **$ Café Gaby** offers good-value café fare (salads, omelets, *steak-frites*) with authentic decor inside and a good outside terrace (daily, tel. 04 90 68 38 42). **$$ Café l'Ormeau** serves a larger selection and has tablecloths and an interior courtyard, making it a calm retreat in the middle of the village bustle (daily, tel. 04 90 68 02 11).

$ La Maison Café draws a younger crowd and is best before or after dinner (till late) with a cool upstairs terrace and cozy bar inside (closed Mon-Tue, Rue du Galinier, tel. 04 90 09 54 01).

At **$$ La Récré** owner Jean-Louis and his bright smile have been welcoming guests for more than 30 years. You'll find an inviting terrace and regional cuisine with vegetarian options (closed Wed, below the TI on Avenue Philippe de Girard, tel. 04 90 68 23 73, www.la-recre-lourmarin.com).

MARSEILLE & NEARBY

*Marseille • Cassis •
Aix-en-Provence*

In the rush to get between Avignon and the Riviera, most travelers zip through the eastern fringe of Provence. That's a shame, as this is a land of compelling cities with a strikingly beautiful coastline, all in a tight package. I cover three different-as-night-and-day places, each worth a visit. Marseille is an untouristy, semi-seedy-but-vibrant port city. The nearby coastal village of Cassis offers the perfect antidote to the big city. And just inland, polished Aix-en-Provence is the fancy yin to Marseille's working-class yang, with beautiful people to match its lovely architecture. Aix-en-Provence makes a good and easy first- or last-day stop for those using Marseille's airport.

For good regional guides who specialize in this area, see page 24.

Marseille

Marseille (mar-say) is both the Naples and the Barcelona of France. Big and gritty, it has all the color and pitfalls that come with being a seaport. It's a place with a distinct culture, a proud spirit, and a populace determined to clean up its act. Historic buildings have been renovated, cultural centers opened, daringly modern buildings erected, a sleek new tram rolled out,  and the once rough-and-tumble harbor has blossomed into an inviting and fun-loving pedestrian zone. Much of this urban renewal

Marseille & Nearby

was done in preparation for the city's year-long stint as the European Capital of Culture in 2013, which attracted more than 10 million visitors and cost over €3 billion. Marseille is on the move.

France's oldest (600 B.C.) and second biggest city (and Europe's third largest port) owns a history that goes back to ancient Greek times. Marseille is a world apart from France's other leading cities. Rather than offering blockbuster sights, it's a bustling, well-lived-in city with happy-go-lucky residents providing its ambience.

Marseille is Europe's gateway to Africa, with nearly two million people a year riding its ferries—most shuttling between it and Tunisia and Algeria. More than 25 percent of the city's population consists of immigrants from North Africa. In certain quarters you'll hear more Arabic than French. (This infuriates anti-immigrant French people who are certain that the rest of "their" country is destined to follow suit).

Most tourists leave Marseille off their itinerary, as it doesn't fit their idea of the French Riviera or of Provence. But it would be a shame to come to the south of France and not experience the region's leading city and namesake of the French national anthem. By train, it's made-to-order for a convenient day-trip from Aix-en-

Provence (30 minutes away by train), or even from Paris—just a three-hour trip by TGV.

PLANNING YOUR TIME

For a stimulating four-hour tour of Marseille, take my self-guided "Marseille City Walk." You'll head from the train station down La Canebière, dip into the North African market, wander around the hilly old town (Le Panier) as you climb to the La Charité Museum, find the cathedral, and survey the Euroméditerranée (Euromed) development, then return to the port and take the shuttle ferry across to the new town. Finally, take a bus, tourist train, or taxi up to Notre-Dame de la Garde before returning to the station.

Orientation to Marseille

Marseille is big, with 860,000 people. Keep your visit simple and focus on the area immediately around the Old Port (Vieux Port). A main boulevard (La Canebière) meets the colorful Old Port. The Panier district is the old town, blanketing a hill that tumbles down to the port. The harborside is a lively, broad promenade lined with inviting eateries, amusements, and a morning fish market. Everything described here (except Notre-Dame de la Garde) is within a 30-minute walk of the train station.

TOURIST INFORMATION

The main TI is two blocks up from the Old Port on La Canebière (Mon-Sat 9:00-19:00 except Jan-March until 18:00, Sun 10:00-17:00, free Wi-Fi, 11 La Canebière, toll tel. 08 26 50 05 00—€0.15/minute, www.marseille-tourisme.com). In summer, satellite offices open at the St. Charles train station (see next) and in a kiosk at the cruise port. Pick up the good city map, the flier with a self-guided walk through the old town, and information on museums and the weekly walking tours—but pass on their city pass.

ARRIVAL IN MARSEILLE
By Train

St. Charles Station (Gare St. Charles) is busy, modern, and user-friendly. Many services are along track A, including WCs, a grocery store, and baggage storage (daily). In summer you should find a TI sharing space

MARSEILLE

Vive la Différence

Marseille is one of Europe's greatest cultural melting pots. An important trading center since ancient times, Marseille has long been defined by the waves of immigrant peoples who have called this beautiful setting home. Accessible by land and sea to North Africa, Spain, Italy, and Greece, Marseille once attracted Phoenicians, Greeks, and Romans. Today, Marseille houses France's largest concentration of immigrants: 200,000 of its 855,000 residents are Muslim; 80,000 are Jewish (Marseille has had a large Jewish population since the Jews were expelled from Spain in 1492); 80,000 are Armenian Orthodox (escaping Ottoman injustices); and there are 70,000 Comorans (from a group of islands in the Indian Ocean).

There's a spirit of cooperation among Marseille's immigrants, who understand that what benefits one group helps them all. Unlike in Paris, immigrants in Marseille live in the city center, not the suburbs, so they are more visible and harder to ignore. And though unemployment is high among immigrants, it is not as high as in Parisian suburbs. The commercial port, a thriving high-tech industry, and tourism (mostly from cruise ships) fuel Marseille's economy. The city also has invested mightily in jobs programs and city-center renovation projects that have benefited its lower-income residents.

Marseille engenders a strong sense of identity apart from France (and the French language) that unites this city's diverse population. Locals see themselves as *Marseillais* (mar-say-ay) first and as French second (or third, after their native country). Locals' fierce pride is manifested in their passion for Olympique de Marseille, the city's soccer team. Since 1899 *Marseillais* have lived and died with the fate of their team. (A few years ago, I was here the day that 30,000 *Marseillais* fans were boarding trains to Paris for the France finals.) Olympique de Marseille has made a point of creating a team that looks like the city by recruiting players from North African countries (Zinédine Zidane is the most famous example). The strategy seems to have worked—Marseille has won the French Cup more than any other team in France.

Immigrant populations are booming in cities throughout Europe, challenging local governments to accommodate them. Many would do well to study Marseille.

with the train information office opposite track F (open Mon-Fri only). If you exit the station at track A to Square Narvik, you'll see Hôtel Ibis on your left (with car rental behind it); access to the old city by foot is to the right. With your back to the tracks, you'll find shops, lots of food options, and the bus station and its ticket office (with airport buses and more) to the far right, past track N.

Getting from the Train Station to the Old Port: To reach the Old Port, you can walk, take the Métro, or catch a taxi. On **foot** it's

MARSEILLE

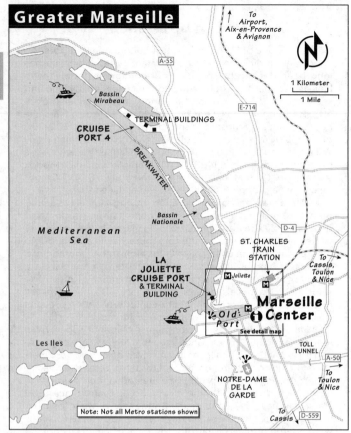

Greater Marseille

To Airport, Aix-en-Provence & Avignon

A-55

1 Kilometer

1 Mile

Bassin Mirabeau

TERMINAL BUILDINGS

CRUISE PORT 4

BREAKWATER

E-714

D-4

Bassin Nationale

Mediterranean Sea

ST. CHARLES TRAIN STATION

To Cassis, Toulon & Nice

LA JOLIETTE CRUISE PORT & TERMINAL BUILDING

Joliette

Marseille Center

See detail map

Old Port

Les Iles

TOLL TUNNEL

A-50

NOTRE-DAME DE LA GARDE

To Toulon & Nice

Note: Not all Metro stations shown

To Cassis

D-559

a 15-minute downhill gauntlet along grimy streets. Leave the station through the exit at track A (past the big departure board), veer right, and admire the view from atop the stairs (Toto, we're not in Cassis anymore). That's Notre-Dame de la Garde overlooking the city. Walk down the stairs and straight on Boulevard d'Athènes, which becomes Boulevard Dugommier. When you come to the trams, turn right onto the grand boulevard, La Canebière. This leads to the main TI and the Old Port.

By **Métro** it's an easy subterranean trip from the train station to the Old Port: Go down the escalator opposite track E and then take a longer escalator to your left. Buy a ticket from the machines or ticket window (closed 12:40-13:40). Your €1.70 ticket is good for one hour of travel on Métro or buses; an all-day pass costs €5.20 (www.rtm.fr). Take blue line M1 (direction: La Fourragère) two stops to Vieux Port (Old Port). Following *Sortie* signs, then *la Canebière* exit signs, you'll pop out within sight of the TI. To return to the station from here, take blue line M1 (direction: La Rose) two stops and get off at Gare St. Charles.

Taxis are out the front doors opposite track E. Allow €15-17 to the port and €20 to Notre-Dame de la Garde—though train station cabbies may refuse these short trips (tel. 04 91 02 20 20). Taxis elsewhere will take you on shorter rides.

By Car

Even drivers who are comfortable in big, crazy cities will be frustrated in Marseille. Traffic is always bad here. If coming from the east (Cassis and other Riviera destinations), opt for autoroute A-50, which leads to Marseille's 1.5-mile-long tunnel (toll about €4)—avoiding much of the city's traffic-ridden center streets—and pops you out under Fort St. Nicolas at the Old Port. After you leave the autoroute from any direction, signs to *Vieux Port, Centre-Ville,* and *Office du Tourisme* take you to the Old Port. At the port, follow the blue *P* signs to the underground *Parking Charles de Gaulle-Canebière* lot. Locals claim pay lots are patrolled and safe, but I wouldn't leave anything visible in the car.

By Plane

Marseille's airport (Aéroport Marseille-Provence), about 16 miles north of the city center, is small and easy to navigate (toll tel. 08 20 81 14 14, www.marseille.aeroport.fr). Frequent buses run to Marseille's St. Charles train station (€9, 3/hour, 25 minutes) and to Aix-en-Provence (stops at Aix-en-Provence's TGV station or bus station, 2/hour, 35 minutes). A taxi to downtown Marseille takes 30 minutes and costs €60 (€75 if it's really early, late, or Sun). A five-minute shuttle bus trip connects the airport to the nearby Vitrolles Aéroport train station, which is handy for its direct service to cities west of Marseille, including Arles, Avignon, and Nîmes. (You can also take a train from this station into Marseille, but the bus described above is easier and more frequent.) For destinations east of Marseille (such as Cassis, Nice, or Italy), take the bus to Marseille's St. Charles Station and connect by train from there. If you need to sleep near the airport, consider the recommended Golden Tulip hotel.

By Cruise Ship

For information on arriving in Marseille by cruise ship, see page 239.

HELPFUL HINTS

Pickpockets: As in any big city, thieves thrive in crowds and target tourists. Wear your money belt, and assume any commotion is a smokescreen for theft. Marseille (while nowhere near as dangerous as many American cities) is the most dangerous city in France. Use a little extra caution and don't venture into sketchy areas after dark.

Save on Bus Tickets: The same tickets work on buses and the Métro, but cost €1.70 at a Métro station and €2 on the bus.

Bike Cabs: In summer, look for bicycle cabs that will zip you up and down the Old Port for €5/per ride.

Taxi to Cassis or Aix-en-Provence: A taxi from Marseille to Cassis or Aix-en-Provence runs about €65.

Car Rental: All the major companies are represented at St. Charles Station (see "Arrival in Marseille," earlier).

Local Guide: Pascale Benguigui is a smart and colorful guide for Marseille, Aix-en-Provence, St-Tropez, and anything in between (€170/half-day, €270/day, mobile 06 20 80 07 51, macpas@club-internet.fr).

Soccer Matches: *Le football* is to Marseille what American football is to Green Bay: Frenzied fans go crazy, and star worship is fickle. One of France's best-ever soccer players was raised here: Zinédine Zidane (notorious for his head-butt of an Italian opponent during the 2006 World Cup Final). If you're here during soccer season (end of July to mid-May), consider getting tickets to a match (every other Sat, from €30, sold at the TI). To get to the soccer stadium (Orange Vélodrome), take the Métro's red line M2 (direction: Ste. Marguerite-Dromel) to Rond-Point du Prado.

Tours in Marseille

Le Petit Train

These little tourist trains take two routes through town. Unfortunately, the trains depart only from the far northwest corner of the Old Port (a 15-minute walk from the TI) and have skimpy recorded information. The better Notre-Dame de la Garde route (#1) saves you the 30-minute climb to the basilica's fantastic view and runs along a nice section of Marseille's coastline (€8; allow 75 minutes for round-trip, including 20 minutes to visit the church; runs daily, about every 20 minutes 10:00-18:00, less frequent Nov-March; tel. 04 91 25 24 69, www.petit-train-marseille.com). The Vieux Marseille

Marseille at a Glance

▲▲**Notre-Dame de la Garde** Marseille's landmark sight: a huge Neo-Romanesque/Neo-Byzantine basilica, towering above everything, with panoramic views. **Hours:** Daily April-Sept 7:00-20:00, until 19:00 Oct-March. See page 235.

▲▲**Panier District** Marseille's answer to Paris' Montmartre, this charming tangle of lanes in the oldest part of town draws photographers and poets. See page 232.

▲**North African Market** Taste of North Africa in downtown Marseille. **Hours:** Open long hours except Sun. See page 230.

▲**Old Port (Vieux Port)** Economic heart of town, featuring lots of boats and a fish market, protected by two impressive fortresses. **Hours:** Port—always open; fish market—nearly daily until 13:00. See page 231.

▲**La Charité Museum** Housed in a beautiful building with Celtic, Greek, Roman, and Egyptian artifacts. **Hours:** Tue-Sun 10:00-18:00, closed Mon. See page 233.

route (#2) toots you through the Panier district—best done on foot (€8, 65 minutes including one 30-minute stop, less frequent Nov-Dec, closed Jan-March).

Bus Tours

Two companies run pricey big-bus tours. The **Color Bus** double-decker buses, with open seating up top, offer a 14-stop hop-on, hop-off route that is very similar to Le Petit Train's routes. Buses depart from near the Petit Train stop and run every 30 minutes (45 minutes in off-season), leaving you too long at most stops (€19, 75 minutes round-trip). Alternatively, red **City Tour** buses take a longer route in a two-hour round-trip, with a 40-minute stop at Notre-Dame de la Garde (€18, 4/day April-Oct, 2/day Nov-March, departs from near the TI).

Marseille City Walk

This self-guided walk strings together the main sights in the areas surrounding the Old Port (Vieux Port). I've listed the sights in roughly the order you'll come to them as you amble along La Canebière to the Old Port, from where you'll loop through the Panier district and ultimately wind up across the harbor in the new town (see the map on page 230). This route takes about four hours and is ideal for day-trippers arriving by train. (See directions for

MARSEILLE

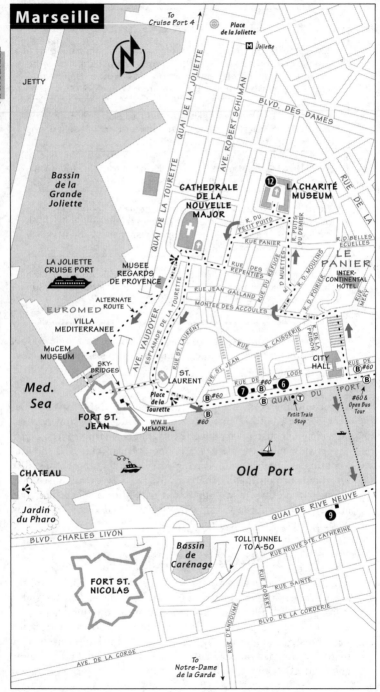

MARSEILLE

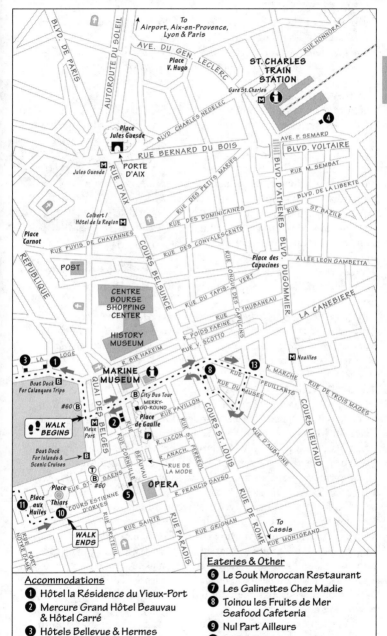

Accommodations
1. Hôtel la Résidence du Vieux-Port
2. Mercure Grand Hôtel Beauvau & Hôtel Carré
3. Hôtels Bellevue & Hermes
4. Hôtel Ibis Marseille Gare St. Charles
5. Hôtel Relax

Eateries & Other
6. Le Souk Moroccan Restaurant
7. Les Galinettes Chez Madie
8. Toinou les Fruits de Mer Seafood Cafeteria
9. Nul Part Ailleurs
10. La Cantine
11. "Restaurant Strip"
12. La Charité Museum Café
13. North African Markets

walking from the train station to the Old Port under "Arrival in Marseille, By Train" on page 222.)

• *Start at the corner of La Canebière and Boulevard Dugommier (at the Noailles Métro stop), a five-minute walk from the train station.*

Boulevard La Canebière

The Boulevard La Canebière (pronounced "can-ah' bee-air")—with its classy tramway—is the celebrated main drag of Marseille.

While strolling this stubby thoroughfare, you feel surrounded by a teeming, diverse city. Two blocks before the harbor, you'll find two museums, the TI, and a stylish shopping district. The boulevard dead-ends at the Old Port. La Canebière's name comes from the same root as cannabis—not the smoking kind but the ropemaking kind. Marseille was long the French kingdom's main naval base, and hemp was a vital ingredient in the rope used by the fleet.

• *For a taste of Africa, walk from the Noailles Métro stop a block down La Canebière to Rue Papère, and side-trip left another block to the old tram station (with another entrance to the Noailles Métro stop) and the colorful North African market filling the Place du Marché.*

▲North African Market

Marseille's huge Moroccan, Algerian, and Tunisian populations give the city a special spice. Wander downhill the length of the Place du Marché. Suddenly you're immersed in an exotic and fragrant little medina filled with commotion—and no one's speaking French. The market thrives daily except Sunday with fresh and very cheap produce. Labels show the price as well as the origin: *Maroc, Provence, Côte d'Ivoire,* and so on.

Explore a bit. Linger over a coffee at an outside table at **Café Prinder** (cheap coffee/drinks)—listen to and watch the kaleidoscope of cultures. Next, venture left on Rue Longue des Capucins. Stop by **Soleil d'Egypte** (unsigned, ask) and try a *bourek* wrap (potato and ground round), a *pastilla* wrap (chicken, almonds, onions, and egg), or the crêpe-like *mahjouba* (so nice when hot out of the oven). You'll see the kitchen behind the counter. There's €3 paella to-go next door.

At the next corner, Rue d'Aubagne, take a right and stop in for tea or a dessert (Tunisian pastries) at **La Carthage** bakery. In this inviting four-table spot you can crank up the music and be in Tunisia. A "Tunisian Plate" is lunch for €5. You could assemble an assortment of baklava-like sweets and have it with mint tea for a sticky memory.

• *Continue downhill to the big street, Cours St. Louis. The grand triumphal arch you see far to the right celebrates the Revolution and French Republic. Head toward the arch and cross to the north side of La Canebière, then turn left and continue downhill toward the Old Port. Two blocks before you hit the water, on the right side (just after the TI), you can't miss the grandiose building.*

Chamber of Commerce (Le Palais de la Bourse) and Marine Museum

Step inside and take in the grand 1860s interior (free, daily 10:00-18:00). A relief on the ceiling shows great moments in Marseille's history. The grand hall is circled by a United Nations of plaques, reminding locals that their economy is based on trade from around the world.

The small ground-floor exhibit on the city's maritime history (€2, to the right as you enter) starts with a portrait of Emperor Napoleon III, who called for the building's construction, and his wife. It then traces the growth of the city through charts of its harbor, and other rooms display models of big ships over the centuries.

Behind the Chamber of Commerce is a fancy Galeries Lafayette shopping center with a handy food court just inside the entrance; and just beyond the shopping center is the **Marseille History Museum,** with artifacts from Caesar to Louis XIV (€5, Tue-Sun 10:00-18:00, closed Mon).

• *Continue down the main boulevard, cross the busy street to the Old Port, and stop at the copper plaque in the pavement about 30 feet from the water.*

▲Old Port (Vieux Port)

This plaque marks a very central point. In fact, the monument at your feet reads: "On this spot in 600 B.C. Greek sailors landed and founded Marseille from where Western civilization rose."

Protected by two impressive fortresses at its mouth, Marseille's Old Port has long been the economic heart of town. The citadels were built in the 17th century under Louis XIV, supposedly to pro-

tect the city. But locals figured the forts were actually designed to keep an eye on Marseille (a city that was essentially autonomous until 1660) and challenge Marseille to thoroughly incorporate into the growing and ever more centralized kingdom of France.

Today, the serious shipping

is away from the center, and the Old Port is the happy domain of pleasure craft. The fish market along Quai des Belges—where you're standing—splashes and wiggles nearly every morning. The stalls are gone by 13:00.

Looking out to sea from here, the Panier district (the old town) rises to your right. The harborfront below Le Panier was destroyed in 1943 by the Nazis, who didn't want a tangled refuge for resistance fighters so close to the harbor. It's now filled with modern condos and trendy restaurants. City Hall (see the flags) is in the middle on the harborfront.

Take a spin tour to the right. Farther along is the Jesuit church San Ferreol, a Gothic building with a Neo-Baroque facade slapped on in the 19th century. Spinning past the grand boulevard, La Canebière, you come to le Ombrière ("the shade-giver"), a modern mirror-ceilinged roof on the waterfront that provides both shade and lots of photo fun (it was designed by Norman Foster for the 2013 European Capital of Culture festivities). Behind that to the left is a neighborhood of prostitutes and strip clubs and an area considered unsafe late at night. Capping the hill beyond the mirror is the Notre-Dame de la Garde basilica. And farther to the right is the new town and the Arsenal Quarter, with lots of fun restaurants and bars—the liveliest place in town after dark.

• *Walk around the port with the water on your left. Pass the departure point for tour boats. After a couple of hundred yards you'll reach the small dock (labeled* La Ligne du Ferry Boat*) for the ferry that crosses the port (€0.50, exact change, included in Métro day pass, every 10 minutes, generally 8:00-20:00). You'll be back here soon. But for now, turn around and find City Hall.*

▲▲Panier District (Old Town)

The ornate **City Hall** (Hôtel de Ville) stands across from the ferry dock. Its bust of Louis XIV overlooks the harbor. Behind that rises the Panier district. Until the mid-19th century, Marseille was just this hill-capping old town and its fortified port. Today, that historic and tangled hilltop is the best place to find the town's soul. It's a 15-minute or so hike to our next stop, La Charité Museum. But take your time. The city keeps the rent cheap here, so you'll find lots of artists and artisans working and lots of creative little commercial ventures.

• *From City Hall, walk up the broad stairway toward the 18th-century Hôtel Dieu (formerly a hospital, now an intercontinental luxury hotel). Below the hotel, turn left on the main road (Place du Mazeau); after about a hundred yards, bear right onto Montée des Accoules, and weave your way up to la Vielle Charité (head right on Rue des Moulins, then jog left on Rue des Muettes, which leads to the museum).*

▲La Charité Museum (Centre de la Vieille Charité)

Now a museum, this was once a poorhouse. In 1674 the French king decided that all the poor people on the streets were bad news. He built a huge triple-arcaded home to take in a thousand needy subjects. In 1940 the famous architect Le Corbusier declared it a shame that such a fine building was so underappreciated. Today, the striking building—renovated and beautiful in its arcaded simplicity—is used as a collection of art galleries surrounding a

Pantheon-esque church. You can stroll around the courtyard for free. (Good WCs are in the far-left corner.)

The pediment of the church features the figure of Charity taking care of orphans (as the state did with this building). She's flanked by pelicans (symbolic of charity, for the way they were said to pick flesh from their own bosom to feed their hungry chicks, according to medieval legend). The ground floor outside the church houses temporary exhibits. On the upper levels of the complex you'll find rooms with interesting collections of Celtic (c. 300 B.C.), Greek, and Roman artifacts from this region. There's also a good Egyptian collection, along with masks from Africa and the South Pacific.

Cost and Hours: €5-10 depending on exhibits, Tue-Sun 10:00-18:00, closed Mon, idyllic café/bar, tel. 04 91 14 58 80.

• *With your back to La Charité, head into the small cobbled square (with several inviting places for a bite to eat or drink), and turn right onto the small diagonal street called Rue du Petit Puits. At its end you'll run into a charming square with Le Bar des 13 Coins. Have a drink at this eclectic little bar—the inspiration for the main setting of France's most famous soap opera,* Plus Belle La Vie. *(Pétanque players enjoy the little shop opposite, with the best balls for sale and a small court for testing them.) Then descend the stairs behind the bar, go left, and take your first right to find...*

Cathédrale de la Nouvelle Major

Bam. This huge, striped cathedral seems lost out here, away from the action and above the nondescript port. The Neo-Byzantine cathedral was built in the late 1800s to replace the old cathedral that the city had outgrown. It's more impressive from

the outside, but worth a quick peek inside for its mosaics (free, Wed-Mon 10:00-18:30, Oct-March until 17:30, closed Tue).

• *Outside the cathedral, enjoy the view from the terrace. Marseille's modern port sprawls off to the right.*

Great Maritime Port of Marseille (GPMM)

The economy of Marseille is driven by its modern commercial ports, which extend 30 miles west from here (a nearby canal links Marseille inland via the Rhône River, adding to the port's importance). Over 100 million tons of freight pass through this port each year (60 percent of which is petroleum), making this one of Europe's top three ports. Container traffic is significant but is hampered by crippling strikes, for which the left-leaning city is famous. Meanwhile, cruise-ship tourism brings more than a million passengers to Marseille each year. And each year two million ferry passengers shuttle between here and Corsica, Sardinia, Algeria, and Tunisia. You're looking at Europe's gateway to Africa.

• *You now have a choice of two ways to return to the Old Port: Either hike down from the cathedral and through the vast new Euromed harbor development (described next) or view it from above as you walk up the tree-lined Esplanade de la Tourette. The Euromed complex contains three of Marseille's newest sights.*

Euroméditerranée Culture District

As Europe's Capital of Culture in 2013, Marseille gained several important cultural centers, including these impressive buildings standing side-by-side on the harbor. Euromed was a grand scheme with a big, politically correct vision to revitalize the old immigration port while tying together the great (and contentious) cultures of the Mediterranean. While the architecture is visually striking, the venues themselves host temporary exhibits that are generally of little interest to tourists.

The **Musée Regards de Provence** is in the building where immigrants were inspected and their clothing was disinfected (www.museeregardsdeprovence.com). The **Villa Méditerranée** hosts events focused on inspiring peace, brotherhood, and understanding between Mediterranean cultures. Its building, with a cantilevered top floor, was designed by Milanese architect Stefano Boeri (www.villa-mediterranee.org). And the **Musée des Civilisations de l'Europe et de la Méditerranée** (MUCEM) has a tiny permanent collection about Mediterranean cultures and hosts more special exhibits. From its rooftop (free access), which has a fine café/restaurant, you can cross the skybridge to Fortress St. Jean (www.mucem.org), which contains more exhibition space.

• *If you've explored Euromed and are coming from Fortress St. Jean, take the skybridge leading to Place de la Tourette. Otherwise, if you're coming from the cathedral, continue walking up Esplanade de la Tourette. From either direction, a fabulous view awaits you at the...*

Place de la Tourette View Terrace

Voilà! This is one of the best views of Marseille, with Notre-Dame de la Garde presiding above, and twin forts below protecting the

entrance to the Old Port. The ugly, boxy building marked "Memorial" at the base of the fort (below and to your right) is a memorial to those lost during the Nazi occupation of the city in World War II. The small church to your left is the Church of St. Laurent, which once served as a parish church for sailors and fishermen—notice the lighthouse-like tower.

• *Continue down the steps back to the Old Port. From the bottom of the steps you have a couple of options for getting to the new town: Hop on* **bus #60** *(stop is across the street and a few steps left, €2, direction: Notre-Dame de la Garde) and in 20 minutes you'll circle around the harbor to the new town (you can also ride this bus up to the Notre-Dame de la Garde basilica). Or, take a 10-minute walk halfway along the promenade (Quai du Port) to City Hall, where you'll see the fun little* **ferry boat** *that shuttles locals across the harbor to the new town (€0.50, exact change, included in Métro day pass, every 10 minutes, generally 8:00-20:00).*

New Town

Arriving in the new town aboard the ferry, you'll find popular bars and brasseries in front of the ferry dock and to the left toward the top of the harbor. These are good for a quick meal or a memorable drink. Wander in along Place aux Huiles, make your way left, and find a smart pedestrian zone crammed with cafés and restaurants.

• *You could end your walk here, but be sure to take a trip up to Notre-Dame de la Garde (30-minute walk, bus options available), described next, or consider the boat excursions described later.*

▲▲Notre-Dame de la Garde

Crowning Marseille's highest point, 500 feet above the harbor, is the city's landmark sight. This massive Neo-Romanesque/Neo-Byzantine basilica, built in the 1850s during the reign of Napoleon III, is a radiant collection of domes, gold, and mosaics. The monumental statue of Mary and the Baby Jesus towers above everything (Jesus' wrist alone is 42 inches around, and the statue weighs 9 tons). And although people come here mostly for the commanding city view, the interior (with its countless ex-voto messages of

thanks to Mary) is unforgettable. This hilltop has served as a lookout, as well as a place of worship, since ancient times. Climb to the highest lookout for an orientation table and the best views. The islands straight ahead are the Iles du Frioul, including the island of If—where the Count of Monte Cristo spent time (reachable by a boat excursion).

Cost and Hours: Free, daily April-Sept 7:00-20:00, until 19:00 Oct-March, last entry 45 minutes before closing, cafeteria and WCs are just below the view terrace.

Getting There: To reach the church, you can hike 30 minutes straight up from the harbor, catch a taxi (about €10), hop bus #60, or ride the tourist train—all stop on the harborfront near City Hall (see map on page 228).

Boat Excursions from Marseille

Boats depart from either corner (northeast and southeast) of the top of the Old Port to these destinations—look for the ticket kiosks. Get the latest schedules and info on route options at the TI.

Château d'If and Islands of Frioul (Iles du Frioul)

When King François I visited Marseille in the 16th century, he realized the potential strategic importance of a fort on the uninhabited island of If (one of the Islands of Frioul), just outside the harbor. His château was finished in 1531. The impregnable fortress, which never saw battle, became a prison—handy for locking up Protestants during the Counter-Reformation. Among its illustrious inmates was José Faria, a spiritualist priest who was the idol of Paris and whom Alexandre Dumas immortalized in *The Count of Monte Cristo*. Since 1890 the château has been open to the public, but the required two-hour stay at this French Alcatraz will leave you sensitive to the count's predicament (€6 entry). I'd bypass this prison.

The Island of Frioul (Iles du Frioul), which offers a nature break from the big city with a few hiking paths and cafés, is another 15 minutes away (the next stop after Château d'If). For most people, this is a better place to get off and stretch your legs.

Cost and Hours: €11 round-trip for one island, €16 for both, boats usually depart daily and at least hourly 9:00-17:00, last departure to visit château is 16:05, except 15:10 Nov-March, 20-minute trip to château, one-hour round-trip if you don't get off the boat, tel. 04 96 11 03 50, www.frioul-if-express.com. Boats depart from the southeast corner of the Old Port.

Calanques Cruises
For those who won't get to Cassis, **Croisières Marseille Calanques** offers day trips to the dramatic fjord-like inlets known as *calanques,* east of Marseille (€23/2.5 hours, €29/3.5 hours, tel. 04 91 58 50 58, www.croisieres-marseille-calanques.com). Boats depart from the northeast corner of the Old Port. To read up on *calanques,* see page 246.

Short and Scenic Cruise to Pointe Rouge
To appreciate Marseille's remarkable setting, take a round-trip cruise on the *navette* boat south to the Pointe Rouge neighborhood (€5 each way, departs on the hour from the southeast corner of the Old Port, about 25 minutes each way).

Sleeping in Marseille

Stay in Marseille only if you want a true urban experience. The scene is more mellow 20 minutes away in Cassis (see page 248).

$$$$ Hôtel la Résidence du Vieux-Port,**** pricey, slightly faded, but superbly located on the Old Port, offers retro-modern rooms done in primary colors. All rooms face the port. Many have balconies and are worth the extra euros (18 Quai du Port, tel. 04 91 91 91 22, www.hotel-residence-marseille.com, info@hrvpm.com).

$$$$ Mercure Grand Hôtel Beauvau**** overlooks the harbor and lets you buy away the gritty reality outside your door with business-class comfort (rates frequently reduced, pay parking, 4 Rue Beauvau, tel. 04 91 54 91 00, www.accorhotels.com, h1293@accor.com).

$$$ Hôtel Bellevue sits right on the port and comes with tasteful rooms but slightly worn-out furniture and carpets; it's above a small (view) restaurant/café. All rooms have port views and loaner iPads (no elevator, 34 Quai du Port, tel. 04 96 17 05 40, www.hotelbellevuemarseille.com, info@hotelbellevuemarseille.com).

$$ Hôtel Carré,*** a block off the port, has a mod lobby and offers modern comfort at fair rates (6 Rue Beauvau, tel. 04 91 33 02 33, www.hvpm.fr, carre@hvpm.fr).

$$ Hôtel Ibis Marseille Gare St. Charles,*** with 170 rooms, is a worthwhile value because it's right at the train station—left as you exit—and has all the services, including a restaurant, café, and bar (pay parking, look for deals on website, Square Narvik, tel. 04 91 95 62 09, www.ibishotel.com, h1390@accor.com).

$$ Hôtel Hermes,** barely off the port, houses 29 smallish, basic- but-bright rooms. The rooftop terrace delivers smashing views over the port (behind Hôtel Bellevue at 2 Rue Bonneterie, tel. 04 96 11 63 63, www.hotelmarseille.com, hotel.hermes@orange.fr).

$ Hôtel Relax* is run by sweet Houria (pronounced "oo-ree-ah," which means "Liberty" in Arabic—she's Algerian) and her husband, Ali. Despite its location in a neighborhood of bars and prostitutes, it's quiet and homey. Half of the simple rooms overlook a square—worth requesting, as the back-side rooms can be gloomy (rooms have tight bathrooms with showers, air-con, no elevator, just 2 blocks off harbor on Place de l'Opéra at 4 Rue Corneille, tel. 04 91 33 15 87, www.hotelrelax.fr, hotelrelax@free.fr).

Near the Airport: For travelers needing to catch an early flight, **$ Golden Tulip** is handy and has easy train connections to Marseille (Impasse Pythagore, Z.I. de Couperigne, 13127 Vitrolles; tel. 04 42 15 09 30, www.goldentulipmarseilleairport.com, reception@goldentulipmarseilleairport.com).

Eating in Marseille

For lunch I'd be adventurous, eating in the North African market area or up in the Panier district (around La Charité). Note the eating options mentioned in my "Marseille City Walk," earlier, for either zone. Much more forgettable and certainly stress-free is the food court in Galeries Lafayette shopping center behind the TI and Chamber of Commerce Building (also mentioned in the walk).

For dinner, I've listed five choices: Moroccan, fancy fish, cafeteria fish, fun and basic on the harbor, and elegant in the touristy restaurant zone.

$$ Le Souk Moroccan Restaurant is a quality and authentic-feeling place facing the harbor under the old town (vegetarian options, closed Mon, 100 Quai du Port, tel. 04 91 91 29 29).

$$$ Les Galinettes Chez Madie is good for bouillabaisse (the local fish stew specialty) and is also on the harbor under the old town (closed Sun evening, 138 Quai du Port, tel. 04 91 90 40 87).

$$ Toinou les Fruits de Mer Seafood Cafeteria is a fun and easy way to enjoy fresh seafood without going broke. You join the cafeteria line to pick up side dishes, sauces, dessert, and drinks—and fill out a checklist to "compose" the seafood plate of your dreams from their menu. You can survey the catch in the icy bins outside before choosing (daily 10:00-22:00, a block uphill from TI on corner with La Canebière at 3 Cours St. Louis, tel. 04 91 33 14 94).

$$ Nul Part Ailleurs, overlooking the harbor on the new-town side (near the little ferry dock), is a Corsican-run eatery with a fun and accessible menu offering pizza, salads, daily plates, and a passion for steak tartare. Their *tarte tatin* (apple pie) is big enough to split and understandably popular. It's located just beyond the tourist zone, with great seating inside and out (daily, 18 Quai de Rive Neuve, tel. 04 91 33 58 95).

$$$ La Cantine, on the Cours Honoré d'Estiene d'Orves square at #27, is surrounded by tourist joints and the Hard Rock Café, yet maintains its dignity. It's an intimate place—cozy inside and pleasant outside—that serves nicely presented Mediterranean dishes (daily, tel. 04 91 33 37 08).

The Restaurant Strip: Rue Saint-Saëns and Place aux Huiles are lined with restaurants and littered with sandwich boards listing mostly similar menus. While these places are extremely touristy, their prices are reasonable, and they offer an enticing variety of cuisines. It's a melting pot of international eateries, with choices ranging from giant salads and fresh seafood to crêpes, Vietnamese dishes, Belgian waffles, and Buffalo wings. You may enjoy surveying this scene before sitting down to eat.

Marseille Connections

BY TRAIN AND BUS

Marseille is well served by TGV and local trains and is the hub for many smaller stations in eastern Provence.

From Marseille by Train to: Cassis (2/hour, 25 minutes, bus is better—see below), **Aix-en-Provence Centre-Ville** (2/hour, 45 minutes), **Antibes** (16/day, 2.5 hours), **Nice** (18/day, 2.5 hours), **Arles** (11/day, 1.5 hours), **Avignon TGV** (10/day, 35 minutes), **Paris** (hourly, 3.25 hours), **Isle-sur-la-Sorgue** (8/day, 1.5 hours), and **London** (just 6 hours by TGV and Eurostar).

From Marseille's Train Station by Bus to: Marseille Airport (3/hour, 25 minutes), **Aix-en-Provence** (4/hour, 30-50 minutes).

From Marseille's Castellane Métro Stop by Bus to: Cassis (better than train, 6/day Mon-Sat, 4/day Sun, 40 minutes, TI has schedule—beware of afternoon gaps in service). The stop in Cassis is labeled *Gendarmerie* (on Avenue du 11 Novembre), from which it's a five-minute walk to the port.

BY CRUISE SHIP

If your cruise visits Provence, you'll arrive either at Marseille or at Toulon, about 40 miles east of Marseille.

Arrival at Marseille: The Marseille Provence Cruise Terminal (MPCT) sprawls beneath a bluff west of downtown. Cruise ships tuck themselves in between cargo vessels at the main port (Porte 4), which has several *postes* (piers).

Most cruise lines offer a convenient **shuttle bus** that takes you to downtown Marseille's Old Port in 15-20 minutes (skip the complicated public-transportation trip—it's worth springing for the shuttle). From the Old Port, you can walk to many of the sights in town or head up to the **train station** (20-minute walk or take Métro to St. Charles stop) to connect to outlying destinations, such as Aix-en-Provence or Cassis (see train connections, earlier).

Taxis meet arriving cruise ships, but rates are high (€25-29 to Old Port, Notre-Dame de la Garde, or train station; one-way to Aix-en-Provence-€65; all-day round-trip to Arles/Avignon area, including several stops-€350). Try to agree on a fixed rate up front, or make sure the meter is set to the correct rate.

Arrival at Toulon: Though the city of Toulon has a cruise terminal, most of the big cruise lines actually dock at La Seyne-sur-Mer, across the harbor from Toulon. From there you can take the cruise-line shuttle bus or a public ferry into Toulon, then connect to a train for Marseille (1 hour) or Cassis (30 minutes).

Cassis

Hunkered below impossibly high cliffs, Cassis (kah-see) is an unpretentious port town that gives travelers a sunny break from their busy vacation. Two hours away from the fray of the Côte d'Azur, Cassis is a prettier, poor man's St-Tropez. Outdoor cafés line the small port on three sides, where boaters polish their teak as they chat up café clients. Cassis is popular with the French and close enough to Marseille to be busy on weekends, April school holidays, and all summer. Come to Cassis to dine portside, swim in the glimmering-clear water, and explore its rocky *calanques* (inlets).

Orientation to Cassis

The Massif du Puget mountain hovers over little Cassis, with hills spilling down to the port. Cap Canaille cliff rises from the southeast, and the famous *calanques* inlets hide along the coast northwest of town. Hotels, restaurants, and boats line the attractive little port.

TOURIST INFORMATION

The TI is in the modern building in the middle of the port among the boats. They have free Wi-Fi, good maps for sale, and the latest on *calanques* conditions (May-Sept Mon-Sat 9:00-18:30, until 19:00 July-Aug, Sun 9:30-12:30 & 15:00-18:00; Oct-April Mon-

Sat 9:30-12:30 & 14:00-18:00, Sun 10:00-12:30, Quai des Moulins, toll tel. 08 92 39 01 03-€0.40/minute, www.ot-cassis.com, info@ot-cassis.com). If you're going to Marseille, pick up a map here.

ARRIVAL IN CASSIS

By Train: Cassis' hills forced the train station to be built two miles away, and those last two miles can be a challenge. It's a small station with no baggage storage and limited hours (Mon-Sun 8:45-12:15 & 13:45-17:25). If you need to buy tickets when the station is closed, use the machines.

A **taxi** into town costs €14 with baggage and is well worth the expense unless a Marcouline bus is soon to arrive (see below). If there's no taxi waiting, call 04 42 01 78 96. Otherwise, it's a 50-minute walk into town (turn left out of the station and follow signs).

Marcouline **buses** link the station with the town center (€1, about hourly, schedule posted at all stops) but allow extra time—bus schedules in southern France are approximate. Call the TI in advance to get the schedule and plan your arrival accordingly—and be ready to take a taxi. The bus drops you at the Casino stop in Cassis: From here, turn right on Rue de l'Arène and walk downhill five minutes to reach the port.

By Bus: Regional buses (including those from Marseille) run limited hours (check with the TI before taking one). The bus stop is a five-minute walk from the port on Avenue du 11 Novembre (stop is labeled *Gendarmerie*).

By Car: There are two exits from the autoroute for Cassis; the second (coming from Aix-en-Provence, exit #8) saves you 10 minutes, provides easy access to La Route des Crêtes (described later, under "Experiences Near Cassis"), and offers memorable views. The hills above Cassis can make it difficult to navigate. Hotels are signed, although the blue signs can be tricky to follow. Hotel parking is minimal (carefully read each hotel's listing in this book as some have more parking than others).

No matter where you park, leave nothing of value in your car. Outside of summer, drivers arriving by 10:00 usually can find curbside parking (about €1/hour, free 18:00-9:00); latecomers will likely need to park in one of the well-marked pay lots above the port (Parking de la Viguerie is closest but often full, and their *Abonnés* entrance is for locals only). Check the electronic sign-boards as you enter town to find available spaces. Parking Daudet, up the road from Parking de la Viguerie, usually has better availability, as does Parking La Madie up the road from the Casino bus stop. Another option nearby is Parking des Mimosas, which has a 400-car capacity.

MARSEILLE

Cassis

Accommodations

1. Best Western Hôtel la Rade
2. Hôtel le Golfe
3. Hôtel/Restaurant le Clos des Arômes
4. Hôtel de France Maguy
5. Hôtel Cassitel
6. Hôtel Laurence
7. Mahogany Hôtel de la Plage & Le Jardin d'Emile Hôtel
8. Le Château de Cassis

Eateries & Other

9. El Sol, L'Oustau de la Mar, Le Canaille & Chez César
10. Le 8 et Demi & Grand Marnier Crêpes
11. Le Calendal
12. Le Grand Large
13. Bada
14. La Girandole
15. Le Chai Cassidain Wine Bar
16. Grocery (2)
17. Open-Air Market
18. To Clos Ste. Magdeleine Wine Tasting
19. To La Ferme Blanche Wine Tasting
20. Launderette (2)
21. Pedal Boat Rental
22. Kayak Rental
23. Motorboat Rental & WC
24. To Bus Stop for Marseille

AVE. DE VERDUN

AVE. JEAN JAURES

AVE. DES DARDANELLES

AVE. DE

RUE ST. CLAIR

RUE DU JEUNE ANA-

QUAI

BARTH.

QUAI

AVE. DE L'AMIRAL GANTEAUME

AVE. DE L'AMIRAL GANTEAUME

P

Plage du Bestouan

AVE. DES CALANQUES

To Calanque de Port-Miou

PROMENADE ARISTIDE

Mediterranean

To Calanques

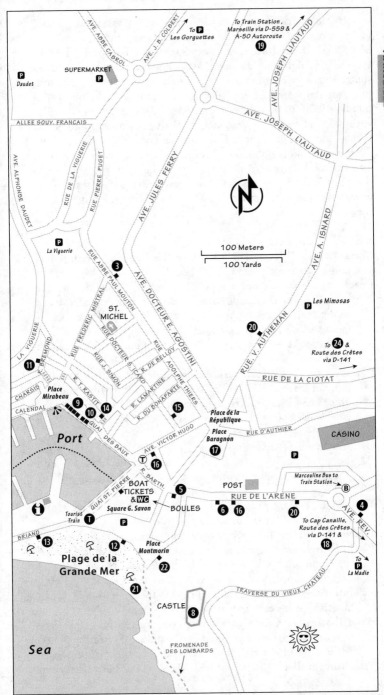

To **P** Les Gorguettes

To Train Station,
Marseille via D-559 &
A-50 Autoroute **19**

AVE. ABBÉ CABROL

AVE. J. B. COLBERT

AVE. JOSEPH LIAUTAUD

P
Daudet

SUPERMARKET **P**

ALLÉE SOUV. FRANCAIS

AVE. JOSEPH LIAUTAUD

AVE. ALPHONSE DAUDET

RUE DE LA VIGUERIE

RUE PIERRE PUGET

AVE. JULES FERRY

AVE. A. ISNARD

P
La Viguerie

RUE ABBÉ PAUL MOUTON

AVE. DOCTEUR E. AGOSTINI

3

100 Meters

100 Yards

ST.
MICHEL

P
Les Mimosas

RUE FRÉDÉRIC MISTRAL

RUE DOCTEUR S. ICARD

RUE J. SIMON

RUE R. DE BELLOY

RUE LAMARTINE

ADOLPHE THIERS

RUE V. AUTHEMAN

20

To **24** &
Route des Crêtes
via D-141

LA VIGUERIE

R. PETIT

R. BRÉMOND

R. T. KASTIL

R. DU BONAPARTE THIERS

RUE DE LA CIOTAT

11

CHARSIS

CALENDAL

Place
Mirabeau

9

10

14

QUAI DES BAUX

AVE. VICTOR HUGO

15

Place de la
République

Place
Baragnon

RUE D'AUTHIER

CASINO

Port

16

R. BARTH

17

P

5

POST

Marcouline Bus to
Train Station **B**

i

QUAI ST. PIERRE

**BOAT
TICKETS
& WC**
Square G. Savon

BOULES

6 **16**

RUE DE L'ARÈNE

20

4

AVE. REV.

Tourist
Train **T**

P

To Cap Canaille,
Route des Crêtes
via D-141 &
18

BRIAND

13

12

Place
Montmorin

22

To **P**
La Madie

**Plage de la
Grande Mer**

21

CASTLE

8

TRAVERSE DU VIEUX CHÂTEAU

Sea

PROMENADE
DES LOMBARDS

If you're driving here on weekends, holidays, during school vacation periods (April), or any day in July and August, Cassis can be packed. If need be, take advantage of the free parking at les Gorguettes, high above the town (well signed), and use the *navettes* shuttle-bus service into town (€1.60 round-trip, every 30 minutes, July-Aug daily until 24:00; April-June, Sept weekends, and school holidays 9:00-20:00). A second *navette* bypasses the town center with stops at Plage du Bestouan (with two of my recommended hotels) and goes straight to Calanque de Port-Miou, saving you a 30-minute walk (stop marked Presqu'ile, same schedule as above). To find the hiking trail from the Presqu'ile stop, exit the bus to the right and when you see the *calanque* water, swing right again to walk around to the other side where you'll find the beginning of the path.

HELPFUL HINTS

Market Days: The market fills Place Baragnon on Wednesdays and Fridays until 12:30.

Beaches: Cassis' beaches are pebbly. The big beach behind the TI—Plage de la Grande Mer—is sandier than others. You can rent a mattress with a towel (about €16/day) and pedal boats (about €15/30 minutes). Underwater springs just off the Cassis shore make the water clean, clear, and a bit cooler than at other beaches.

Laundry: A self-service *laverie automatique* is at 9 Rue Victor Autheman (daily 6:30-21:30). **K6 Pressing,** just up from the post office at 34 Rue de l'Arène, has computers to use while you get your wash done (Mon-Sat 8:30-13:00 & 14:30-19:00, closed Sun, tel. 04 42 01 10 36).

Grocery Store: The **Casino** market is next door to Hôtel le Liautaud (Thu-Tue 8:00-12:30 & 15:30-19:30, closed Wed). There's also a **Spar** market just past Hôtel Laurence on Rue de l'Arène.

Taxi: Call 04 42 01 78 96 or find the main taxi stand across from Hôtel Cassitel by the *boules* court.

Tourist Train: The little white *train touristique*, with commentary in French and English, will take you on a worthwhile 45-minute circuit out to the peninsula on the Port-Miou *calanque* and back (€8, April-Nov, usually at :15 after the hour 11:00-17:00, July-Aug until 18:00). Catch it next to the TI—where you can buy tickets; it's cash only on the train.

Wine Tasting: Le Chai Cassidain is a wine bar with a good selection of regional wines offered by the glass (€5, healthy pours) or by the bottle, with nibbles. Cassis *blanc* and rosé wines are always available (daily 10:00-13:00 & 15:00-22:00, often later,

MARSEILLE

closed Mon in winter, 4 blocks from port at 6 Rue Séverin Icard, tel. 04 42 01 99 80).

Cassis Visual Tour from the Port

Find a friendly bench in front of Hôtel le Golfe—or enjoy a drink at their café—and read this quick town intro.

Cassis was born more than 2,500 years ago (on the hill with the castle ruins, across the harbor). Ligurians, Phoenicians, maybe Greeks, certainly Romans, and plenty of barbarians all found this spot to their liking. Parts of the castle date from the eighth century, and the **fortress walls** were constructed in the 13th century to defend against seaborne barbarian raids. The Michelin family sold the fortress to investors who turned it into a luxury five-suite *chambres d'hôte*, where celebrities often hole up looking for peace and quiet (see "Sleeping in Cassis," later).

In the 18th century, life became more secure, and people moved their homes back to the waterfront. Since then, Cassis has made its living through fishing, quarrying its famous white stone, and producing well-respected white wines—which, conveniently, pair well with the local seafood dishes, and *bien sûr*, with tourists like us.

With improvements in transportation following the end of World War II, tourism rose gradually in Cassis, although crowds are still sparse by Riviera standards. While foreigners overwhelm nearby resorts, Cassis is popular mostly with the French and still feels unspoiled. The town's protected status limits the height of the buildings along the waterfront. Cassis' port is home to some nice boats...but they're dinghies compared with those in the glitzier harbors farther east.

The big cliff towering above the castle hill is **Cap Canaille.** Europe's highest maritime cliff, it was sculpted by receding glaciers (wrap your brain around that concept), and today drops 1,200 feet straight down. You can—and should—drive or taxi along the top for staggering views (see "Above Cassis: La Route des Crêtes," later). Return to this bench at sunset, when the Cap glows a deep red.

The rocky shore off to the right looks as if it were cut away just for sunbathers. But Cassis was once an important **quarry,** and stones were sliced right out of this beach for easy transport to ships. Locals say that the Statue of Liberty's base sits on this rock. Cassis stone remains highly valued throughout the world...but yesterday's quarrymen have been replaced by today's sunbathers.

Experiences near Cassis

▲▲▲The *Calanques*

Until you see these exotic Mediterranean fjords—with their translucent blue water, tiny intimate beaches, and stark cliffs plunging

into the sea or forming rocky promontories—it's hard to understand what all the excitement is about.

Calanques (kah-lahnks) are narrow, steep-sided valleys partially flooded by the sea, surrounded by rugged white cliffs usually made of limestone (quarries along the *calanques* have provided building stone for centuries). The word comes from the Corsican word *calanca*, meaning "inlet"—the island of Corsica also has *calanques*. These inlets began as underwater valleys carved by the seaward flow of water at river mouths, and were later gouged deeper by glaciers. About 12,000 years ago, when the climate warmed and glaciers retreated at the end of the last Ice Age, the sea level rose partway up the steep rocky sides of the *calanques*. Today the cliffs harbor a unique habitat that includes rare plants and nesting sites for unusual raptors.

The most famous inlets are in the Massif des Calanques, which runs along a 13-mile stretch of the coast from Marseille to Cassis. This area and part of the surrounding region became a national park in 2012.

You can hike, or cruise by boat or kayak, to many *calanques*. Bring water, sunscreen, and anything else you need for the day, as there's nary a baguette for sale. Don't dawdle—to limit crowds and because of fire hazards, the most popular *calanques* can be closed to visitors in high season (June-Sept). When they are "closed," the only way to see the *calanques* is by boat or kayak. The TI can give you plenty of advice.

Cruising the *Calanques*: Several boats offer trips of various lengths (3 *calanques*-€16, 2/hour, 45 minutes; 5 *calanques*-€20, 6/day, 1 hour; 8-9 *calanques*-€23-28, 2-6/day, 1.5 hours, www. calanquesdecassis.com). The three-*calanques* tour is the most popular. Tickets are sold (and boats depart) from a small booth on the port opposite the Hôtel Liautaud. *Prochain départ* means "next departure." Boats vary in size (some seat up to 100).

Hiking to the *Calanques*: Plan ahead. From June to September, many of the *calanques* are closed in certain weather conditions due to the high risk of brush fires. For information, check with the TI or online at www.myprovence.fr/en. Conditions and closures are announced starting at 18:00 the day before. Start your hike first thing in the morning to minimize crowds.

Drivers can save 30 minutes of hiking by driving to Calanque de Port-Miou and paying €8 to park (described below). Anyone can take the *navette* shuttle bus directly from the Les Gorguettes parking lot to Port-Miou; it runs on weekends (April-June and Sept), school holidays, and during July and August (see "Arrival by Car," earlier, for hours).

The trail lacing together *calanques* Port-Miou, Port-Pin, and d'En-Vau will warm a hiker's heart. Views are glorious, and the trail is manageable if you have decent shoes (though shade is minimal).

For most, the best *calanque* by foot is **Calanque Port-Pin,** about an hour from Cassis (30 minutes after the linear, boat-lined Calanque Port-Miou, which also works as a destination if time is short). Calanque Port-Pin is well forested, with a small beach, and is relatively peaceful until early afternoon.

The most spectacular *calanque* is **Calanque d'En-Vau,** but it's a two-hour hike one-way from Cassis with a steep descent to the beach at the end. In summer (June-Sept), access is strictly controlled depending on weather conditions.

The TI's free map of Cassis gives a general idea of the *calanques* trail, and they sell a more detailed IGN *calanques* map for €9.50. Most people don't need a map for a basic hike. Start along the road behind Hôtel le Golfe and walk past Plage du Bestouan, then look for hiker signs to *Port-Miou* or *Presqu'ile* (pay attention to your route for an easier return). You'll climb up, then drop down residential streets, eventually landing at the foot of Calanque de Port-Miou, where the dirt trail begins. Follow signs to *Calanques Port-Pin* and *d'En-Vau,* walking 500 yards along a wide trail and passing through an old quarry.

You're now on the *GR (Grande Randonnée)* trail, indicated by red, white, and green markers painted on rocks, trees, and other landmarks. Follow those markers as they lead uphill (great views at top), then connect to a rough stone trail leading down to Calanque Port-Pin (nice beach, good scampering). The trail continues from here back up and on to Calanque d'En-Vau. *Bonne route!*

Other Ways to Reach the *Calanques:* From about mid-April to mid-October, you can rent a **kayak** in Cassis—or in nearby Port-Miou, which is closer to the *calanques.* In Cassis, try Club Sports Loisirs Nautiques on Place Montmorin, behind the merry-go-round (one-seater-€30/4 hours, two-seater-€45/4 hours, tel. 04 42 01 80 01, www.cassis-kayak.com, csln.cassis@gmail.com). In Port-Miou, call mobile 06 75 70 00 73. The TI has brochures for more kayak companies. You can also take a **kayak tour** (€35/half-day, €55/day, €35/sunset tour, reservations smart, mobile 06 12 95 20 12, www.provencekayakmer.fr). If the hiking trails are closed, this is the only way you'll be able to get to those *calanque* beaches.

You can rent a small **motorboat** without a special boating license at JCF Boat Services, located behind the TI toward the lighthouse (about €100/morning, €200/day, mobile 06 75 74 25 81, www.jcfboat.com, contact@jcf-boat.com).

You can also join a guided **electric mountain bike tour** to reach the *calanques* via the national park trails (€29-45, 2-3-hour tours, book with the TI).

▲▲Above Cassis: La Route des Crêtes

If you have a car, or spring for a taxi (€30 for a 30-minute trip, 4 people per taxi), consider this remarkable drive. Ride straight up to the top of Cap Canaille and toward the next town, La Ciotat. It's a twisty road, providing access to numbingly high views over Cassis and the Mediterranean. From Cassis, follow signs to *La Ciotat/Toulon*, then *La Route des Crêtes*. The towns just east of Cassis (La Ciotat, Bandol, etc.) do not merit a detour. This road is occasionally closed (because of strong winds or the high risk of brush fires June-Sept), though you can usually get partway up—before investing time and money in this trip, check at the TI.

Wine Tasting in the Hills Behind Cassis

The following places give you the chance to taste the famous (mostly white) cassis wine with the folks who make it (remember, if it's a *free* tasting, it's polite to buy a bottle).

The most reputable winery, and easiest to reach without a car, is the **Clos Ste. Magdeleine.** English tours of the vineyard and cellar are offered Monday-Saturday usually at 11:00 and 16:00, finishing with a tasting (€12, 45 minutes, Avenue du Revestel, tel. 04 42 01 70 28; confirm times in advance and book with the TI or through website, www.clossaintemagdeleine.fr, clos.sainte.magdeleine@gmail.com).

La Ferme Blanche offers tastings (but no tours) in a small shop on a busy road, right on D-559 above town. English-speaking Jeromine likes to explain what makes cassis wine so special (daily 9:00-12:00 & 14:00-19:00, tel. 04 42 01 00 74).

Sleeping in Cassis

Cassis hotels are laid-back places with less polish but lower rates than those on the Riviera (rooms average about €95). Some close from November to March, but those that stay open offer good discounts. All are busy on weekends and in summer, when many can come with late-night noise (though most hotels have effective double-paned windows). Book early for sea views. A few offer parking spots that you can reserve when booking your room. None of the places I list has an elevator. Consider skipping your hotel breakfast and head to the port for café au lait with a view.

NEAR THE PORT OR IN TOWN

$$$ Best Western Hôtel la Rade,*** a 10-minute walk uphill from the port, has good views from its lovely poolside deck and welcoming lounge. Skip the "comfort" rooms, which promise balconies and views of the pines but actually look onto a street (pay parking, Route des Calanques, 1 Avenue de Dardanelles, tel. 04 42 01 02 97, www.hotel-cassis.com, larade@hotel-cassis.com).

$$ Hôtel le Golfe,** over an easygoing (but not late-night) café, has good rates, small bathrooms with showers, and the best views of the port. Half its basic rooms come with views and small balconies—ask for a first-floor room for a bigger balcony—and are worth booking ahead. Sleep elsewhere if you can't get a view (family rooms, dim lighting, 3 pay parking spaces, nearby pay garage, 3 Place Grand Carnot, tel. 04 42 01 00 21, www.legolfe-cassis.fr, contact@legolfe-cassis.fr).

$ Hôtel le Clos des Arômes** is a basic, quiet retreat. *Très provençal,* it has a big courtyard terrace and a good restaurant. The rooms have old furnishings, poor lighting, church-bell noise (rooms on the front are quieter), thin walls, and no air-con (some have ceiling fans), but the place works in spite of these drawbacks (pay parking nearby at la Viguerie lot, 10 Rue Abbé Paul Mouton, tel. 04 42 01 71 84, www.le-clos-des-aromes.fr, closdesaromes@ orange.fr). It's best to book by email.

$ Hôtel de France Maguy** is a good eight-room place for drivers on a budget (plenty of parking) or those without wheels (friendly owner Franck will pick you up at the station if you book ahead). It's a few blocks up from the port, so it's fairly quiet. Rooms are mostly small but are well maintained. Pricier modern rooms are larger and come with tiny balconies. Four very modern, well-furnished (in black and white) apartments face the heated swimming pool and come with private terraces and a two-night minimum (breakfast and parking are included if you book directly with hotel—March-Oct only, above the Casino on Avenue du Revestel, tel. 04 42 01 72 21, www.hoteldefrancemaguy.com, hoteldefrancemaguy@gmail.com).

$ Hôtel Cassitel,** located on the harbor over a lively café (noisy on weekends), has comfortable rooms and double-paned windows that block out most portside noise. In the more expensive rooms with balconies and sea views, the shower and sink are open to the room (family rooms, pay parking garage, Place Clemenceau, tel. 04 42 01 83 44, www.hotel-cassis.com, cassitel@hotel-cassis. com).

$ Hôtel Laurence** offers good budget beds in small, simple, but clean rooms. Back rooms are quieter, and some have views of the château (closed in winter, 2 blocks off the port beyond Hôtel Cassitel at 8 Rue de l'Arène, no parking—drop bags in load zone and head to Les Mimosas lot, tel. 04 42 01 88 78, www.cassis-hotel-laurence.com, contact@cassis-hotel-laurence.com, friendly staff).

ON PLAGE DU BESTOUAN

The next two hotels are a 10-minute walk from the port on the next beach west, Plage du Bestouan. Easy parking makes them good for drivers.

$$$ Mahogany Hôtel de la Plage*** faces the beach, with a concrete exterior and mod interior, generous public spaces, a bar/restaurant facing the sea, a spa, and 30 well-conceived, quite comfortable, and mostly spacious rooms at acceptable rates. The more modern rooms offer deck and sea views, while rooms with warmer decor have no view (family rooms, air-con, pay parking—reserve ahead, closed mid-Nov-mid-Feb, tel. 04 42 01 05 70, www. hotelmahogany.com, info@hotelmahogany.com).

$$ Le Jardin d'Emile** is a villa-hotel located below the Mahogany Hôtel de la Plage. It's a charming little refuge with rich colors inside and out, plush rooms, and a green garden. Five of the seven rooms have decks, and three have sea views (air-con, free and secure parking, tel. 04 42 01 80 55, www.lejardindemile.fr, info@ lejardindemile.fr).

HIGH ABOVE THE PORT

$$$$ Le Château de Cassis, privately owned and closed to the public for many years, recently opened its doors to visitors, renting five luxurious suites as *chambres d'hôte*. Celebrities are often in residence, so access is strictly forbidden unless you have a reservation (spacious pool, gardens, views galore, all the amenities you can imagine, book well in advance, tel. 04 42 01 63 20, www. chateaudecassis.com, contact@chateaudecassis.com).

Eating in Cassis

Peruse the lineup of tempting restaurants along the port, window shop the recommended places below, and then decide for yourself (all have good interior and exterior seating). You can have a ham-and-cheese crêpe or go all-out for bouillabaisse with the same great view. Arrive by 19:30 for the view tables. Picnickers can enjoy a beggars' banquet at the benches at Hôtel le Golfe or on the beach, or discover your own quiet places along the lanes away from the port (small grocery stores open until 19:30). Local wines are terrific: red from Bandol and whites/rosés from Cassis.

DINING PORTSIDE

The first four places are ideally situated side by side, allowing diners to comparison shop.

$$$ El Sol is sharp and popular with discerning diners (closed for dinner weekdays off-season, 20 Quai des Baux, tel. 04 42 01 76 10).

$$$ L'Oustau de la Mar has a loyal following and fair prices (daily, 20 Quai des Baux, tel. 04 42 01 78 22).

$$$ Le Canaille specializes in fresh seafood platters, oysters, and other shellfish (closed Wed, 22 Quai des Baux, tel. 04 42 01 72 36).

$$$ Chez César was most popular with locals on my last visit, with good prices and selection (€27 *marmite de pêcheur*—a poor man's bouillabaisse, closed Mon, 21 Quai des Baux, tel. 04 42 01 75 47).

$ Le 8 et Demi serves crêpes, pizza, salads, and ice cream on plastic tables with front-and-center portside views (closed Thu off-season, 8 Quai des Baux, tel. 04 42 01 94 63).

The **$ Grand Marnier crêpe stand** cooks delicious dessert crêpes to go for €3—the Grand Marnier crêpe rules. This is ideal for strollers (next to Le 8 et Demi, daily April-Sept 15:00-23:30).

DINING AWAY FROM THE PORT

$$ Le Clos des Arômes, listed earlier under "Sleeping in Cassis," is the place to come for a refined candlelit dinner. Dine on a lovely enclosed terrace (daily, tel. 04 42 01 71 84).

$$$ Le Calendal serves up *menus* that feature local dishes in a warm, charming, and cozy setting. Don't be surprised if the chef visits your table (indoor or terrace seating available). If you want bouillabaisse, you must order it a day ahead of time (closed Mon, 3 Rue Brémond, tel. 04 42 01 17 70).

$$$ Le Grand Large is indeed large and owns the scenic beachfront next to the TI. Come here for a quiet drink before dinner, or to dine seaside rather than portside (open daily, Plage de Cassis, tel. 04 42 01 81 00).

$$ Bada is a trendy beachfront place behind the TI, serving breakfast, salads, and fresh *plats* with the sounds of crashing waves (daily, dinner June-Sept only, Promenade Aristide Briand, tel. 04 42 83 70 09).

$ La Girandole is an easy place for families, with cheap pizza, pasta, and salads. It's a block off the port (closed Tue year-round, 1 Rue Thérèse Rastit, tel. 04 42 01 13 39).

Cassis Connections

Cassis' train station is two miles from the port. Shuttle buses meet some trains on weekdays, and taxis are reasonable (for details, see "Arrival in Cassis," earlier). All destinations below require a transfer in Marseille.

From Cassis by Train to: Marseille (2/hour, 25 minutes), **Aix-en-Provence Centre-Ville** (hourly, 1.5 hours), **Arles** (7/day, 2 hours), **Avignon TGV** (7/day, 1.5 hours), **Nice** (hourly, 3 hours, transfer in Toulon), **Paris** (7/day, 4 hours).

From Cassis by Bus to: Marseille (6/day Mon-Sat, 4/day Sun, 40 minutes, easier than train, TI has schedule—beware of afternoon gaps in service). Buses run from the stop labeled *Gendarmerie* on Avenue du 11 Novembre (a 5-minute walk from the port) to Marseille's Castellane Métro stop.

Aix-en-Provence

Aix-en-Provence is famous for its outdoor markets and handsome pedestrian lanes, as well as its cultivated residents and their ability to embrace the good life. Nowhere else in France is *l'art de vivre* (the art of living) so stylishly displayed. It was that way when the French king made the town his administrative capital of Provence, and it's that way today. For a tourist, Aix-en-Provence (the "Aix" is pronounced "X") is happily free of any obligatory turnstiles. And there's not a single ancient site to see. It's just a wealthy town filled with 140,000 people—most of whom, it seems, know how to live well and look good. Aix-en-Provence's 40,000 well-dressed students (many from other countries) give the city a year-round youthful energy,  and its numerous squares, lined with cafés and fine shops, allow everyone a comfortable place to pose.

Orientation to Aix-en-Provence

With no "must-see" sights, Aix works well as a day trip, and is best on days when the most markets thrive (Tue, Thu, and Sat). The city can be seen in a 1.5-hour stroll from the TI or train station, though connoisseurs of southern French culture will want more time to savor it. Aix makes a handy base for day-tripping to Marseille, Cassis, and southern villages of the Luberon (such as Lourmarin).

Cours Mirabeau (the grand central boulevard) divides the stately, quiet Mazarin Quarter from the lively old town (where the action is). In the old town, picturesque squares are connected by fine pedestrian shopping lanes, many of which lead to the cathedral. Right-angle intersections define the Mazarin Quarter but are rare in the old town—expect to get turned around regularly.

TOURIST INFORMATION

The TI, France's grandest, is located at La Rotonde traffic circle. Use the free Wi-Fi and get the walking-tour brochure *In the Footsteps of Cézanne,* with the best city-center map and a good overview of excursions in the area. The TI also has maps covering areas beyond old Aix (Mon-Sat 8:30-19:00, Sun 10:00-13:00 & 14:00-18:00, shorter hours and closed Sun in winter, 300 Avenue Giuseppe Verdi, tel. 04 42 16 11 61, www.aixenprovencetourism.com).

English-language **walking tours** (shown on monitors in the TI) of the old town are offered at 10:00 on Tuesdays and Saturdays; Cézanne walking tours leave at 10:00 on Thursdays (€9, two hours, depart from the TI).

Daily **excursions** into the countryside—Luberon villages, Pont du Gard, Les Baux, wineries, Mt. Ste. Victoire, and more—are also available from the TI (figure per-person costs of €60-80/half-day and €120-140/day).

ARRIVAL IN AIX-EN-PROVENCE

By Train: Aix-en-Provence has two train stations: Centre-Ville, near the city center, and the faraway TGV station. Neither has baggage storage.

Centre-Ville Station: It's a breezy 10-minute stroll to the TI and pedestrian area. Cross the boulevard in front of the station and walk up Avenue Victor Hugo; turn left at the first intersection (you're still on Victor Hugo). At the large fountain (La Rotonde), turn left and go about a quarter of the way around the fountain to find the TI.

Aix-en-Provence TGV Station: Shuttle buses *(navettes)* connect the distant TGV station with Aix-en-Provence's city-center bus station, described next (€4.30, 4/hour, 15 minutes). From the tracks, follow signs for *Bus/Cars* to the end of the hall and downstairs (buses leave from an underpass below the tracks).

MARSEILLE

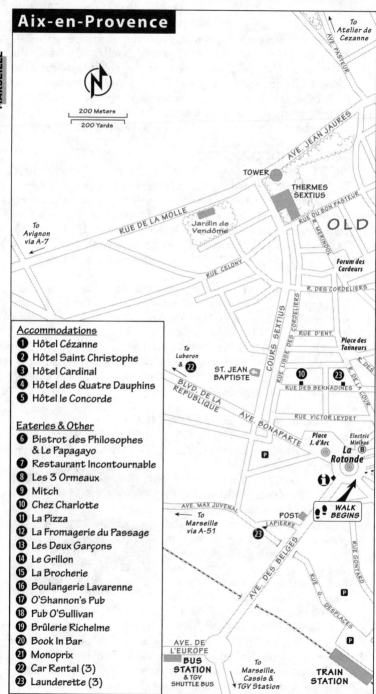

Aix-en-Provence

Accommodations
1. Hôtel Cézanne
2. Hôtel Saint Christophe
3. Hôtel Cardinal
4. Hôtel des Quatre Dauphins
5. Hôtel le Concorde

Eateries & Other
6. Bistrot des Philosophes & Le Papagayo
7. Restaurant Incontournable
8. Les 3 Ormeaux
9. Mitch
10. Chez Charlotte
11. La Pizza
12. La Fromagerie du Passage
13. Les Deux Garçons
14. Le Grillon
15. La Brocherie
16. Boulangerie Lavarenne
17. O'Shannon's Pub
18. Pub O'Sullivan
19. Brûlerie Richelme
20. Book In Bar
21. Monoprix
22. Car Rental (3)
23. Launderette (3)

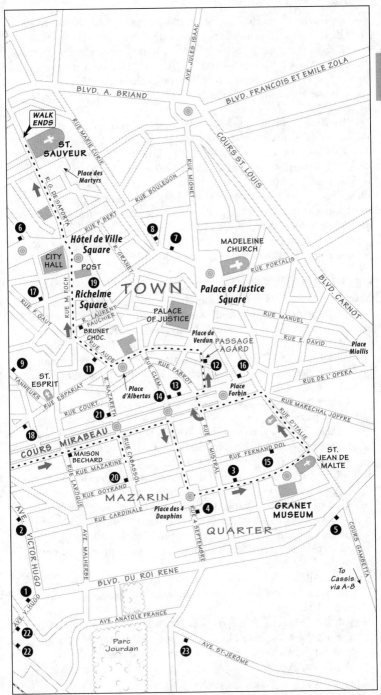

By Bus: Aix-en-Provence's bus station *(gare routière)* is on Avenue de l'Europe near its intersection with Avenue des Belges (tel. 09 69 32 82 07, some English spoken). From the bus station, it's a 10-minute walk to the town center and the TI. Head slightly uphill to the flowery roundabout, turn left on Avenue des Belges, and walk to the splashing fountain (La Rotonde, the big traffic circle by the TI).

By Plane: Buses link Marseille's airport with the bus station in Aix-en-Provence (2/hour, 30 minutes, *navette* #91).

By Car: The city is well signed (yellow for hotels, green for parking). First, follow signs to *Centre-Ville*, then the yellow signs to find your hotel (GPS is handy). If your hotel has parking, use it. Otherwise, once you've spotted your hotel sign, follow green signs to park in the first pay lot you see (I've noted the closest parking to each hotel under "Sleeping in Aix-en-Provence," later). Day-trippers should look for the La Rotonde parking area (near the TI) or park in any pay lot near the old city—allow €16/day.

HELPFUL HINTS

Markets: Aix-en-Provence bubbles over with photogenic open-air morning markets in several of its squares and streets: **Richelme** (produce daily, my favorite), **Cours Sextius/Rotonde/Cours Mirabeau** (produce and flea market Tue, Thu, and Sat—moving to the **Palace of Justice** after the square's renovation is completed in 2019), **L'Hôtel de Ville** (flower market Tue, Thu, and Sat; book market first Sun of each month), and along **Cours Mirabeau** (textiles and crafts, Tue and Thu morning). Most pack up at 13:00, except the book market, which runs all day. Saturday market days are the biggest. It's well worth planning your visit for a market day, as these markets are the sightseeing highlights of the town.

Shopping: Signs at fancy bakeries advertise *calissons d'Aix*, the city's famous homemade candy. It's made with almond paste—kind of like a marzipan cake—and makes a pleasing souvenir. You may want to pick up a pair of especially **dark sunglasses** (to be more discreet when appreciating the beautiful people of Aix-en-Provence). There's an upscale, glassy **Apple Store** next to the TI at La Rotonde.

Services: Public WCs, as they're not stylish, are rare in Aix. Take advantage of WCs in restaurants, museums, or at other stops you make.

English Bookstore: Located on the quiet side of Aix-en-Provence, the atmospheric **Book in Bar** has a good collection of adult and children's books, a good selection of tourist guides (Cassis, Arles, Avignon, and so on), and an inviting café (Mon-

Sat 9:00-19:00, closed Sun, 4 Rue Joseph Cabassol, where it crosses Rue Goyrand, tel. 04 42 26 60 07).

Laundry: Launderettes are scattered throughout the city. **Ecolav'**, with free Wi-Fi, is just behind the TI on Square Narvik at 3 Rue Lapierre (daily 7:00-21:00). Others are at 11 Rue des Bernardines (daily 8:00-19:00) and at 8 Avenue St-Jérôme (daily 8:00-19:30—opens at 9:00 on Sun).

Supermarket: Monoprix, on Cours Mirabeau, two long blocks up from La Rotonde, has a grocery store in the basement (Mon-Sat 8:30-21:30, closed Sun), but you'll find small ones all over the city.

Taxi: Call 04 42 27 71 11. A taxi from your Aix-en-Provence hotel to Marseille costs about €65 and to Cassis about €90.

Car Rental: Avis and **Hertz** are at the Centre-Ville train station (43 Avenue Victor Hugo, tel. 04 42 27 91 32), and **Europcar** is near La Rotonde (55 Boulevard de la République, toll tel. 08 25 89 69 76). All major companies have offices at the TGV station.

Tours in Aix-en-Provence

Local Guides

Pascale Benguigui is a good choice for this area (also recommended earlier for Marseille; see listing on page 226). Also consider **Catherine D'antuono** and Sarah Pernet, who runs **Discover Provence** tours (both listed on page 26).

Electric Minibus Joyride

For a mere €0.60, take a joyride through the winding lanes of the old town center on a *Diabline*—a six-seater electric-powered minibus. It leaves every 10 minutes from the La Rotonde fountain, opposite the TI (Mon-Sat 8:30-19:30, none on Sun, 40 minutes round-trip). You can also wave one down anywhere and hop on. There are three routes (A, B, and C); ask the driver for a map when you board. Line A gives you the best overview of the city and runs a route similar to the self-guided walk described later. It also gets you near Cézanne's studio. Designed with local seniors in mind, the minibus provides a fun (and less glamorous) slice-of-life experience in Aix-en-Provence.

Petit Train

Rest your feet and discover Aix-en-Provence's historic center on a 50-minute tour on the little train, while listening to English commentary (€8, departs from La Rotonde fountain).

Aix-en-Provence History

Aix-en-Provence was founded in about 120 B.C. as a Roman military camp on the site of a thermal hot spring (in France, "Aix" refers to a city built over a hot spring). The Romans' mission: to defend the Greek merchants of Marseille against the local Celts.

Strategically situated Aix-en-Provence was the first Roman base outside the Italian Peninsula—the first foreign holding of what would become a vast empire. (The region's name—Provence—comes from its status as the first Roman province.) But Rome eventually fell, and the barbarians destroyed Aix-en-Provence in the fourth century. Through the Dark Ages, Aix-en-Provence's Roman buildings were nibbled to nothing by people needing their pre-cut stones. No buildings from Roman Aix-en-Provence survive.

Aix-en-Provence was of no importance through the Middle Ages. Because the area was once owned by Barcelona, Provence has the same colors as Catalunya: gold and red. In 1481 the Count of Provence died. He was hairless (according to my guide). Without a hair, Provence was gobbled up by France. When Aix-en-Provence was made the district's administrative center, noble French families moved in, kicking off the city's beautiful age *(belle époque)*. They built about 200 *hôtels particuliers* (private mansions)—many of which survive today—giving Aix-en-Provence its classy look. As you wander, look up, peek in, and notice the stately architecture with its grandiose extra touches.

Aix-en-Provence thrived thanks to its aristocratic population. But when the Revolution made being rich dicey, Aix-en-Provence's aristocracy and clergy fled. Aix-en-Provence entered the next stage of its history as the "Sleeping Beauty city." Later in the 19th century, the town woke up and resumed its pretentious ways. In Aix-en-Provence, the custom of rich people being bobbed along in sedan chairs survived longer than anywhere else in France. After the Revolution, you couldn't have servants do it—but you could hire pallbearers in their off-hours to give you a lift. If being ostentatious ever became the norm...it happened in Aix-en-Provence.

Aix-en-Provence Walk

I've listed these streets, squares, and sights in the order of a handy, lazy orientation stroll. This self-guided walk is highlighted on the map on page 254.
• *Start on Cours Mirabeau at La Rotonde, near the statues on either side of the street, and face...*

La Rotonde

In the 1600s, the roads from Paris and Marseille met just outside the Aix-en-Provence town wall at a huge roundabout called La

Rotonde. From here locals enjoyed a sweeping view of open countryside before entering the town. As time passed, growing Aix-en-Provence needed space more than fortifications. The wall was destroyed and replaced by a grand boulevard (Cours Mirabeau). A modern grid-plan town, the Mazarin Quarter (to the right as you look up Cours Mirabeau), arose across the boulevard from the medieval town (on the left). In 1860, to give residents water and shade, the town graced La Rotonde with a fountain and a grand boulevard lined with trees. The three figures on top of the fountain represent Justice, Agriculture, and Fine Arts. *Voilà:* The modern core of Aix-en-Provence was created. The Apple store facing La Rotonde is another feather in Aix's style cap.
• *Saunter slowly up the right side of Cours Mirabeau.*

Cours Mirabeau

This "Champs-Elysées of Provence" divides the higgledy-piggledy old town (left) and the stately Mazarin Quarter (right). Designed

for the rich and famous to strut their fancy stuff, Cours Mirabeau survives much as it was: a single lane for traffic and an extravagant pedestrian promenade, shaded by plane trees (see sidebar), cafés on the sunny side, and lined by 17th- and 18th-century mansions for the aristocracy. Rich folks lived on

the right side (in the Mazarin Quarter); common folk lived on the left side (in the old town). Cross-streets were gated to keep everyone in their place. Which side are you sleeping on?

The street follows a plan based on fours: 440 meters long, 44

Plane Trees

Stately old plane trees line boulevards such as Cours Mirabeau in Aix-en-Provence and provide canopies of shade for roads and town squares all over southern France. These trees are a part of the local scene.

The plane tree is a hybrid of the Asian and American sycamores—created accidentally in a 16th-century Oxford botanical garden. The result was the perfect city tree: fast-growing, resistant to Industrial Age pollution, and hearty (it can survive with little water and lousy soil). The plane tree was imported to southern France in the 19th century to replace traditional elm trees. Napoleon planted them along roads to give his soldiers shade for their long marches. Plane trees were used to leaf up grand boulevards as towns throughout France—including Aix-en-Provence—built their Champs-Elysées wannabes. Sadly, a modern disease is taking its toll and many trees are dying.

meters wide, plane trees (originally elms) 4 meters apart, and decorated by 4 fountains. The "mossy fountains," overgrown by 200 years of neglect, trickle with water from the thermal spa that gave Aix its first name (and make steamy sights on cold winter days).

Cours Mirabeau was designed for showing off. Today, it remains a place for *tendance* (trendiness)—or even *hyper-tendance*. If French culture has a pretentious quality, it seems that such pretense was born right here. Show your stuff and strut the broad sidewalk. As you stroll up the boulevard, stop in front of Aix's oldest and most venerated *pâtisserie,* **Maison Béchard** (on the right side at 12 Cours Mirabeau) and get a whiff coming from the vent under the entry. They are famous for the candy called *calisson*. Like many local treats, these come with a history. The venerable delicacy of almond, melon, and orange rind draped in icing, whose name means "hug" in French, was concocted for a royal wedding here in the 14th century.

For a glimpse of the finest surviving mansion in the Mazarin Quarter (described below), take a side-trip from the next fountain one block right down Rue Joseph Cabassol to #3 (peek through the gate). The 17th-century Hôtel Caumont hosts the **Caumont Centre d'Art.** While it has two permanent rooms offering a feel for aristocratic luxury in the age of Louis XIV, its main attractions are its fine special exhibits, elegant café, and formal garden. Cézanne fans will enjoy the 30-minute movie about the artist in the center's theater—check show times as you enter (overpriced for most at €14, May-Sept daily 10:00-19:00, off-season until 18:00).

• *Keep strutting up Cours Mirabeau. From the mossy fountain at Rue du 4 Septembre, turn right onto Aix-en-Provence's quiet side, the pleasing little Place des Quatre Dauphins. This marks the center of the...*

Mazarin Quarter (Quartier Mazarin)

Built in a grid plan during the reign of King Louis XIV, the Mazarin Quarter remains a peaceful, elegant residential neighborhood—although each of its mansions now houses several families rather than just one. Study the quarter's Baroque and Neoclassical architecture (from the 17th and 18th centuries). The square's Fountain of the Four Dolphins, inspired by Bernini's fountains in Rome, dates from an age when Italian culture set the Baroque standard across Europe. Appreciate how calm this half of the city feels.

Wander left up Rue Cardinale to a 12th-century church facing a handsome square. St. Jean-de-Malte was built when this area was outside the town wall—500 years before the advent of the Mazarin Quarter. The adjacent **Musée Granet** features Aix's homegrown artists (including several "lesser" paintings by Cézanne). The museum is most popular for its selection of post-Impressionist works, including some by Picasso, Van Gogh, and Braque. Check its website to learn about current exhibits, or ask at the TI (€6-9, open June-Sept Tue-Sun 10:00-19:00, Oct-May Tue-Sun 12:00-18:00, closed Mon year-round, www.museegranet-aixenprovence.fr).

Walk behind the church (on the left) to the next street, and look above the window of the candy shop, on the left-hand corner, where a sweet mosaic of the Fountain of the Four Dolphins Square gives a fun glimpse of the sedan-chair elegance of this quarter back in its heyday.

• *Turn left on Rue d'Italie, lined by edible temptations. Pause and appreciate the stately architecture mixed with the patina of age. Walk along Rue d'Italie to Place Forbin, go left to the top of Cours Mirabeau, and find the statue. This is René d'Anjou, the last count of Provence, during whose rule this region joined France (c. 1450). He was nicknamed "Bon Vivant" for his cultured lifestyle and taste for the good life. Stroll down the right side of the street to #53, and spot the venerable...*

Les Deux Garçons

This café, once frequented by Paul Cézanne, remains *the* hangout on the boulevard. Peek inside at its classic old interior. The Cézanne family hat shop was next door (#55). Cézanne's dad parlayed that successful business into a bank, then into greater wealth, setting up his son to be free to enjoy his artistic pursuits.

• *From here we'll enter the lively old town, where pedestrian streets are filled with fine food stores and boutiques, and romantic street musicians. This is the place in Aix-en-Provence for shopping.*

Leave Cours Mirabeau at #55, through the tiny Passage Agard (notice the gate that was locked at night to keep the rich safe from the poor). It leads to a square dominated by the **Palace of Justice**. *When the renovation is finished in 2019, you'll find a bustling flea market here (Tue, Thu, and Sat mornings, with bric-a-brac at the near end and produce at the far end). If the market is on, explore it. Otherwise, head left along the first street you crossed as you came into the square, Rue Marius Reinaud, which hosts the top designer shops in town. Pause several blocks down when you hear the gurgling of water at the peaceful courtyard called...*

Place d'Albertas

This sweet little square was created by the guy who lived across the street. He hated the medieval mess of buildings facing his man-

sion, so he drew up a harmonious facade with a fountain, and had his ideal vision built to mask the ugly neighborhood. The long-overdue restoration of this once run-down square hit a snag. Since only two-thirds of the property owners agreed to help fund the work, one-third remains undone.

With your back to the fountain, find the large wooden door on the building across the street. Take a look at the names on the door buzzers—the Albertas family still lives here.

• *Turn right on Rue Aude, the main street of medieval Aix-en-Provence (which turns into Rue du Maréchal Foch). Notice the side streets, with their traffic-barrier stumps that lower during delivery hours. Turn right at Rue Laurent Fauchier, and detour down a few steps for what the French call a little "window licking"...*

Brunet Chocolatier and *Macarons*

In this shop (closed Sun-Mon) you'll find *macarons*, those wonderful confections made of luscious buttercreams sandwiched between two cloud-like almond meringue cookies. While popular throughout France, they are the rage in Aix. You'll find them in every flavor imaginable. Try the caramel with salted butter, pistachio, or blackcurrant violet.

• *Return to the big street and continue uphill to...*

Richelme Square (Place Richelme)

This inviting square hosts a lively market, as it has since the 1300s (daily 8:00-13:00). It's the perfect Provençal scene—lovely buildings, plane trees, and farmers selling local produce. The goat-cheese merchants here add life to the market. The cafés at the end of the square are ideal for savoring the market ambience: Pause for a drink at one or get a fresh-baked snack at Boulangerie Lavarenne. To experience the best coffee in Aix (or, perhaps a chocolate frappe), go local at La Brûlerie.

• *One block uphill is the stately...*

L'Hôtel de Ville Square (Place de l'Hôtel de Ville)

This square is anchored by a Roman column. Stand with your back to the column and face the Hôtel de Ville. The center niche of

this 17th-century City Hall once featured a bust of Louis XIV. But since the Revolution, Marianne (the Lady of the Republic) has taken his place. As throughout Europe, the three flags represent the region (Provence), country (France), and the European Union. Provence's flag carries the red and yellow of Catalunya (the proud and semiautonomous region around Barcelona in Spain) because the counts of Provence originated there. Aix-en-Provence's coat of arms over the doorway combines the Catalan flag and the French fleur-de-lis.

The 18th-century building on your left was once the town's grain exchange (today it's a post office). Its exuberant pediment features figures representing the two rivers of Provence: old man Rhône and madame Durance. While the Durance River floods frequently (here depicted overflowing its frame), it also brings fertility to the fields (hence the cornucopia).

Back toward Hôtel de Ville, the 16th-century bell tower was built in part with stones scavenged from ancient Roman buildings—notice the lighter stones at the tower's base. The niche above the arch also once displayed the bust of the king. Since the Revolution, it has housed a funerary urn that symbolically honors all who gave their lives for French liberty. Walk under the arch to see a small plaque honoring the American 3rd Division that liberated the town in 1944 (with the participation of French troops; Aix-en-Provence got through World War II relatively unscathed).

History aside, the square is a delight for its vintage French storefronts and colorful morning markets, such as the flower market (Tue, Thu, and Sat). On non-market days and each afternoon, café tables replace the market stalls.

• *Stroll under the bell tower and up Rue Gaston de Saporta, passing*

Paul Cézanne in Aix-en-Provence

Post-Impressionist artist Paul Cézanne (1839-1906) loved Aix-en-Provence. He studied law at the university (opposite the cathedral), and produced most of his paintings in and around Aix-en-Provence—even though at the time this conservative town was disinclined to understand him or his art. Today the city fathers milk anything remotely related to his years here. While there's almost no actual art by Cezanne in Aix, fans of the artist will want to pick up the *In the Footsteps of Cézanne* self-guided-tour flier at the TI, and follow the bronze pavement markers around town.

Atelier de Cézanne, the artist's last studio, has been preserved as it was when he died and is open to the public. It's a 30-minute walk from the TI, or you can get closer by riding electric minibus A or bus #5 from La Rotonde (see "Tours in Provence," earlier). Although there is no art here, his tools and personal belongings make it worthwhile for enthusiasts.

Cost and Hours: €6, daily June-Sept 10:00-18:00, April-May and Oct 10:00-12:30 & 14:00-18:00, Nov-March until 17:00, free English-language tours usually at 17:00—must book through TI, the 25-minute audioguide (€3) helps if you miss the tour, 2 miles from TI at 9 Avenue Cézanne, tel. 04 42 16 10 91, www.atelier-cezanne.com.

three stately hôtels particuliers—*now home to politics, management, and government schools*—*until you reach the...*

Cathedral of the Holy Savior (Saint-Sauveur)

This church was built atop the Roman forum—likely on the site of a pagan temple. As the cathedral grew with the city, its interior became a parade of architectural styles. The many-faceted interior is at once confusing and fascinating, with three distinct sections: Standing at the entrance, you face the Romanesque section; to the left are the Gothic and then the Baroque sections (daily 8:00-12:00 & 14:00-18:00).

Visiting the Cathedral: In the **Romanesque section** (to the right as you enter) step down and into a different age. Find the baptistery, surrounded by ancient columns with original fourth-century capitals below a Renaissance cupola. Its early Christian (fourth-century) Roman font seems dug into the floor. But 1,600 years ago, the floor was lower. The baptistery was located outside the church until the 14th century, when the church was expanded to encompass the baptistery. The font is big enough for immersion, which was the baptismal style in Roman times.

Farther down is the door to the 12th-century cloister, with its delicate carved capitals (French-only tours on the half-hour except 12:00-14:00). After passing a side chapel, find the closet-sized architectural footprint of the original Christian chapel from the Roman era (like the baptistery, it's several feet below today's floor level). This too would have been outside the current church walls until the 14th century.

In the **Gothic section,** two organs flank the nave: One works, but the other is a prop, added for looks...an appropriately symmetrical Neoclassical touch, as was the style in the 18th century (notice the lack of depth in one of them).

• *Your tour is over. Walking back through town, marvel at a place filled with people who seem to be living life very, very well.*

Sleeping in Aix-en-Provence

Hotel rooms, starting at about €75, are surprisingly reasonable in this highbrow city. Reserve ahead, particularly on weekends. Hotel stars have less meaning here. The best values are on the quiet side of Cours Mirabeau in the Mazarin Quarter.

$$$$ Hôtel Cézanne,**** a block up from the Centre-Ville train station, delivers top comfort and professional service with a smile. The lobby and 55 spacious rooms are modern and surround a generous patio (pay parking—must book ahead, 40 Avenue Victor Hugo, tel. 04 42 91 11 11, www.hotelaix.com, hotelcezanne@hotelaix.com). Charming chef Christiane serves a daily gourmet brunch for €20 (try the truffle omelet and the French toast).

$$ Hôtel Saint Christophe,*** a business-class hotel just off La Rotonde, offers acceptable rates, though the accommodations play second fiddle to a bustling brasserie. It has 67 well-equipped rooms, some with small terraces, most with double beds only (family rooms, pay parking garage, 2 Avenue Victor Hugo, tel. 04 42 26 01 24, www.hotel-saintchristophe.com, contact@hotel-saintchristophe.com).

$ Hôtel Cardinal** is a top value in Aix-en-Provence's quiet and classy Mazarin Quarter. It's a creaky old mansion that literally shakes when people walk, with tilting floors, old-time bathrooms, and spacious, 19th-century elegance under chandeliers in each room. The paintings hanging in public spaces were done by the owner Nathalie's papa (RS%, closest parking is Mignet, 24 Rue Cardinale, tel. 04 42 38 32 30, www.hotel-cardinal-aix.com, hotel. cardinal@wanadoo.fr).

$ Hôtel des Quatre Dauphins** is a cozy place in the quiet quarter with small rooms—and even smaller bathrooms—but comfortable beds and good rates (no elevator, three floors, closest parking is Mignet, 54 Rue Roux Alphéran, tel. 04 42 38 16 39, www.lesquatredauphins.fr, lesquatredauphins@wanadoo.fr).

$ Hôtel le Concorde** sits on the busy ring road, but most of its rooms gather around a quiet, convivial courtyard. Choose between rooms in the main building or the motel-esque rooms on the courtyard (thin walls, pay parking, 68 Boulevard du Roi René, tel. 04 42 26 03 95, www.hotel-aixenprovence-concorde.com, contact@hotel-leconcorde.fr).

Eating in Aix-en-Provence

In Aix-en-Provence, you can dine on bustling squares, along a grand boulevard, or on atmospheric side streets. Cours Mirabeau is good for desserts and drinks, as are many of the outdoor places lining leafy squares. While I like to sleep in a quiet neighborhood, I love the commotion of table-lined squares and the romance of a tangled old town. These recommendations offer plenty of variety. *Bon appétit!*

IN THE OLD TOWN

On Forum des Cardeurs: This traffic-free esplanade is Aix's grandiose living room—a festival of restaurants in all sizes and shapes. It is the high-energy place to be if you want to party with dinner under the sky—and dining is available on Sunday, too, when most other places are closed. Come early or reserve ahead on good-weather week-

ends. Otherwise, window shop the selection from top to bottom, then decide. Here are my two favorite places on the square:

$$$ Bistrot des Philosophes, at the top of the square at #20, is a fun place serving good quality Mediterranean dishes to happy locals. It has a cool terrace ambience and the best inside seating on the square (open daily, tel. 04 42 21 64 35).

$$ Le Papagayo, a couple of doors down from Philosophes, feels like a beach resort at chow time. It's an energetic scene with booths and tables anchored around a center island. They offer a good selection of salads, daily specials, and trendy burgers (open daily, tel. 04 42 23 98 35).

On Romantic Place des Trois Ormeaux: Two good restaurants occupy this intimate square, with tables crowding a soothing fountain. This is the candle-lit, romantic-square alternative to the more boisterous Forum des Cardeurs. The outdoor seating for both of these places is more charming than the indoor seating.

$$$ Restaurant Incontournable, serving carefully prepared, classic French cuisine with modern twists, is worth booking ahead (closed Sun-Mon, 14 Rue Montigny, tel. 09 80 32 86 32).

$$$ Les 3 Ormeaux seems less popular but delivers tasty and original *plats* in a more contemporary interior. It's a good fallback if Restaurant Incontournable is full (closed Sun-Mon, Place des Trois Ormeaux, tel. 04 42 21 59 95).

Other Favorites Buried in the Old Town: A dressier choice for a classic French dinner is **$$$ Mitch.** Enjoy the seasonal, well-presented dishes, excellent wine list, modern flair, and top-notch service that Mitch assures. Book ahead (closed Sun, no lunch, 26 Rue des Tanneurs, tel. 04 42 26 63 08, www.mitchrestaurant.com).

$ Chez Charlotte is Aix's low-key diner, where locals go for solid food at a good price served by Laurent and Nathalie in a fun back garden. While they have indoor seating, I'd dine only in the garden (open from 20:00, closed Sun-Mon, 32 Rue des Bernardines, tel. 04 42 26 77 56).

$ La Pizza has been baking pizzas for the neighborhood since 1952. It's a family-friendly place with fine outdoor seating on a pedestrian lane and a jovial interior (pizzas and hearty salads, closed Mon, 3 Rue Aude).

$$ La Fromagerie du Passage is a creative delight for anyone who's hungry and likes French cheese. Study their menu and ask for help—there's a world of fun options. I like the €20 five-cheeses-bread-and-salad deal—go right up to the cheese counter and pick what looks good (Mon-Sat 12:00-15:00 & 18:00-23:00, Sun 10:00-13:00 & 16:00-20:00, lots of wine served in small tasting portions, big charcuterie plates, off 55 Cours Mirabeau in the Passage Agard, tel. 04 42 22 90 00). They have great seating on three floors. The top-floor terrace is a find.

ALONG COURS MIRABEAU

If you're interested in a delicious view more than delicious food, eat with style on Cours Mirabeau.

$$$ Les Deux Garçons has long been the place to see and be seen: a vintage brasserie with door-to-door waiters in aprons, a lovely interior, and well-positioned outdoor tables with properly placed silverware on white tablecloths. It's busy at lunch but quiet for dinner (open daily, 53 Cours Mirabeau, tel. 04 42 26 00 51).

$$$ **Le Grillon** is a younger, more boisterous choice for a white-tablecloth dinner on Cours Mirabeau. Its bar is a hit with locals for the prime seating—front and center on the boulevard's strolling fashion show (open daily for lunch and dinner, corner of Rue Clemenceau and Cours Mirabeau, tel. 04 42 27 58 81).

IN THE MAZARIN QUARTER

$$ **La Brocherie** dishes up French rather than Provençal cuisine. Its stone-rustic, indoors-only ambience is best for cooler days. This family-owned bistro highlights food from the farm (it's about beef). Dig into the hearty self-service salad buffet (all you can eat for €12) and meats grilled over a wood fire. The €22 *menu* includes the salad bar (closed Sun, indoor seating only, 5 Rue Fernand Dol, tel. 04 42 38 33 21).

LE LATE-NIGHT

Aix is the only French city I know of with a 24/7 bakery, **Boulangerie Lavarenne.** They have two branches: on Place Richelme and at the top of Cours Mirabeau (across from 6 Rue la Tournefort). Their chocolate-chip cookies are a rare treat.

Bar Hopping: For the young—and young at heart—the best action centers on Rue de la Verrerie. **O'Shannon's Pub** (#30) makes a great starting point for your evening out, as does **Pub O'Sullivan,** near La Rotonde, next to Hôtel de France on Place des Augustins.

Aix-en-Provence Connections

Aix-en-Provence has both a TGV station and a Centre-Ville train station (see "Arrival in Aix-en-Provence," earlier). In some cases, destinations are served from both stations; I've listed the station with the best connection. And for some destinations, the bus is a faster option than the train (these are noted below).

From Aix-en-Provence's Center to the TGV Station by Bus or Car: Buses from Aix-en-Provence to the TGV station depart from the bus station (on Avenue de l'Europe, near intersection with Avenue des Belges, tel. 09 69 32 82 07, some English spoken). To find the TGV station by car from Aix-en-Provence, get on the A-51 autoroute toward *Marseille,* get off at the first exit (Les Milles), and follow signs for another 10 minutes. There's a kiosk café inside the TGV station with sandwiches, drinks, and such.

From Aix-en-Provence's Centre-Ville Station by Train to: Marseille (2/hour, 45 minutes), **Cassis** (hourly, 1.5 hours, transfer in Marseille), **Arles** (10/day, 2 hours, transfer in Marseille; train may separate midway—be sure you're in the section going to Arles).

From Aix-en-Provence's TGV Station by Train to: Avignon

TGV (12/day, 25 minutes), **Nice** (10/day, 2-3 hours, usually change in Marseille), **Paris** (14/day, 3 hours, may require transfer in Lyon).

From Aix-en-Provence by Bus to: Marseille (4/hour, 35 minutes), **Marseille's airport** (2/hour, 35 minutes), **Avignon** (6/day Mon-Sat, 1/day Sun, 75 minutes, faster and easier than train), **Arles** (faster than trains, 4-5/day, 1.5 hours), **Lourmarin** (3/day Mon-Sat, 1/day Sun, 1.5 hours), **Nice** (3/day, direct takes 2 hours, cheaper and quicker option than taking the train). All regional buses depart from the bus station on Avenue de l'Europe. Several companies operate buses from this station (www.info-ler.fr).

THE
FRENCH
RIVIERA

FRENCH RIVIERA

La Côte d'Azur

A hundred years ago, celebrities from London to Moscow flocked to the French Riviera to socialize, gamble, and escape the dreary weather at home. Today, budget vacationers and heat-seeking Europeans fill belle époque resorts at France's most sought-after fun-in-the-sun destination.

The region got its nickname from turn-of-the-20th-century vacationing Brits, who simply extended the Italian Riviera west to France to include Nice. Today, the Riviera label stretches even farther westward, running from the Italian border to St-Tropez. To the French, this summer fun zone is known for the dazzling azure color of the sea along this coast: La Côte d'Azur. All of my French Riviera destinations are on the sea, except for a few hill towns and the Gorges du Verdon.

This sunny sliver of land has been inhabited for more than 3,000 years. Ligurians were first, then Greeks, then Romans—who, as usual, had the greatest impact. After the fall of Rome, Nice became an important city in the Kingdom of Provence (along with Marseille and Arles). In the 14th century Nice's leaders voted to join the duke of Savoy's mountainous kingdom (also including several regions of northern Italy), which would later evolve into the Kingdom of Sardinia. It was not until 1860 that Nice (and Savoy) became a part of France—the result of a plebiscite. (The "vote" was made possible because the King of Sardinia had to trade the region to France as a quid pro quo for Napoleon III's support of the Italian states that wanted to break away from Austria to create modern Italy).

Nice has world-class museums, a splendid beachfront promenade, a seductive old town, and all the drawbacks of a major city (traffic, crime, pollution, and so on). The day-trip possibilities are easy and exciting: Monaco offers a royal welcome and a

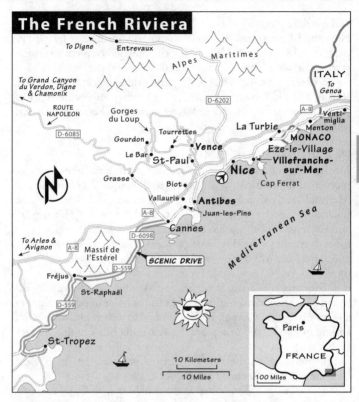

The French Riviera

fairy-tale past; Antibes has a thriving port and silky sand beaches; and image-conscious Cannes is the Riviera's self-appointed queen, with an elegant veneer hiding...very little. Yacht-happy St-Tropez swims alone an hour west. The Riviera's overlooked interior transports travelers to a world apart, with cliff-hanging villages, steep canyons, and alpine scenery—a refreshing alternative to the beach scene.

CHOOSING A HOME BASE

My favorite home bases are Nice, Antibes, and Villefranche-sur-Mer.

Nice is the region's capital and France's fifth-largest city. With convenient train and bus connections to most regional sights, this is the most practical base for train travelers. Urban Nice also has museums, a beach scene that rocks, the best selection of hotels in all price ranges, and good nightlife options. A car is a headache in Nice.

Nearby **Antibes** is smaller, with a bustling center, a lively night scene, great sandy beaches, grand vistas, good walking trails,

FRENCH RIVIERA

and a stellar Picasso museum. Antibes has frequent train service to Nice and Monaco, and quick connections by train (may not run for part of 2018) or car to Grasse. It's the most convenient overnight stop for drivers, with light traffic and easy hotel parking.

Villefranche-sur-Mer is the romantic's choice, with a serene setting and small-town warmth. It has sand-pebble beaches; quick public transportation to Nice, Monaco, and Cap Ferrat; and a small selection of hotels in most price ranges.

PLANNING YOUR TIME

Ideally, allow a day and a half for Nice itself, an afternoon to explore inland hill towns, a full day for Italianesque Villefranche-sur-Mer and lovely Cap Ferrat, a day for Monaco and the Corniches (including Eze-le-Village), and—if time allows—a day for Antibes and Cannes. If you must do St-Tropez, visit it while traveling to or from destinations farther west (such as Cassis, Aix-en-Provence, and Arles) and avoid it on weekend afternoons, as well as all summer.

Monaco is radiant at night, and Antibes works well by day (good beaches and hiking) and night (fine choice of restaurants and a lively after-hours scene). Hill-town-loving naturalists should add a night or two inland to explore the charming hill-capping hamlets near Vence.

Depending on the amount of time you have in the Riviera, here are my recommended priorities:

3 days:	Nice, Villefranche-sur-Mer with Cap Ferrat, and Monaco
5 days, add:	Antibes and hill towns near Vence
7 days, add:	Grand Canyon du Verdon and/or just slow down

HELPFUL HINTS

Medical Help: Riviera Medical Services has a list of English-speaking physicians all along the Riviera. They can help you make an appointment or call an ambulance (tel. 04 93 26 12 70, www.rivieramedical.com).

Sightseeing Tips: Mondays and Tuesdays can frustrate market lovers and museumgoers. Closed on Monday: Nice's Modern and Contemporary Art Museum, Fine Arts Museum, and Cours Saleya produce and flower market; Antibes' Picasso Museum and market hall (Sept-May). Closed on Tuesday: Chagall, Matisse, Masséna, and Archaeological museums in Nice; Renoir Museum in Cagnes-sur-Mer. Matisse's Chapel of the Rosary in Vence is closed on Friday (and has limited hours on other days).

The **French Riviera Pass** includes entry to many Riviera

museums and sights, including Nice's Chagall Museum, Monaco's Oceanography Museum, and Villa Ephrussi de Rothschild on Cap Ferrat. This pass is worthwhile only if you plan to do the included Trans Côte d'Azur cruise (see page 291) or have an aggressive sightseeing plan (€26/24 hours, €38/28 hours, €56/72 hours, tel. 04 92 14 46 14, http://en.frenchrivierapass. com). A €10 **combo-ticket for Nice** covers all of the city's museums, except the Chagall Museum.

Events: The Riviera is famous for staging major events. Unless you're actually taking part in the festivities, these occasions give you only room shortages and traffic jams. Here are the three biggies: **Nice Carnival** (two weeks in Feb, www. nicecarnaval.com), **Cannes Film Festival** (12 days in May, www.festival-cannes.com), and the **Grand Prix of Monaco** (4 days in late May, www.acm.mc). To accommodate the busy schedules of the rich and famous (and really mess up a lot of normal people), the film festival and car race often overlap.

Cruise-Ship Sightseeing: The French Riviera is a popular cruise destination. Arriving ships are divided about evenly between Nice, Villefranche-sur-Mer, and Monaco (for arrival help, see the "Connections" section at the end of each of those chapters). Because these three ports line up conveniently along a 10-mile stretch of coast—easily connected by train or bus—from any of them, those arriving by cruise have the Riviera by the tail. Hiring a local guide helps make the most of cruisers limited time in port (see "Tours in the Riviera," later). For in-depth coverage, consider my guidebook, *Rick Steves Mediterranean Cruise Ports.*

Longer-Stay Rentals: Renting an apartment, house, villa, or *gîte* can be a cost-effective way to explore the Côte d'Azur. Rentals are typically by the week, giving you time to take advantage of day-trip possibilities. **Riviera Pebbles** offers a wide range of rental apartments throughout the Riviera and gets good reviews from happy clients (www.rivierapebbles.com). See page 480 for more on longer-stay rentals.

GETTING AROUND THE RIVIERA

Trains and buses do a good job of connecting places along the coast, with bonus views along many routes. Buses also provide reasonable service to some inland hill towns. Nice makes the most convenient base for day trips, though public transport also works well from Riviera towns such as Antibes and Villefranche-sur-Mer. Driving can be challenging in this congested region (traffic, parking, etc.).

By Public Transportation

In the Riviera, buses are typically less expensive and more convenient while trains are generally faster and more expensive. For an overview of the most useful train and bus connections, see the "Public Transportation in the French Riviera" chart on page 278 (confirm all connections and last train/bus times locally). You'll also find details under each destination's "Connections" section. For a scenic inland train ride, take the narrow-gauge train into the Alps (see page 321).

If taking the train or bus, have coins handy. Ticket machines don't take US credit cards or euro bills, smaller train stations may be unstaffed, and bus drivers can't make change for large bills.

Buses: Most of the area's top destinations are connected by bus, and tickets are cheap. This is an amazing deal in the Riviera. Any one-way bus or tram **ticket** costs €1.50 (€10 for 10 tickets) whether you're riding just within Nice or to Villefranche-sur-Mer, Monaco, Antibes, or even Grasse. This ticket is good for 74 minutes of travel in one direction anywhere within the bus

system (but does not cover airport buses). Buy your bus ticket from the driver or from machines at stops, and validate it in the machine on board. Your ticket allows transfers between the buses of the Lignes d'Azur (the region's main bus company, www.lignesdazur. com) and the TAM (Transports Alpes-Maritimes); if you board a TAM bus and need a transfer, ask for *un ticket correspondance.* A €5 all-day ticket is good on Nice's city buses, tramway, and selected buses serving nearby destinations (such as Villefranche, Cap Ferrat, and Eze-le-Village). The general rule of thumb: If the bus number has one or two digits, it's covered with the all-day ticket; with three digits it's not.

You'll be able to get around most of the Riviera on the following major bus routes:

- **Bus #100** runs eastbound from **Nice** along the Low Corniche (3-4/hour) stopping in **Villefranche-sur-Mer** (20 minutes), **Beaulieu-sur-Mer** (**Villa Kérylos**; 30 minutes), **Eze-Bord-de-Mer** (40 minutes, transfer to #83 to Eze-le-Village), **Monaco** (1 hour), and **Menton** (1.5 hours).
- **Bus #81** runs eastbound from **Nice** (2-3/hour) to **Villefranche-sur-Mer** (15 minutes), **Beaulieu-sur-Mer** (**Villa Kérylos**; 20 minutes), and all **Cap Ferrat** stops, ending at **St-Jean-Cap-Ferrat** (30 minutes).
- **Buses #82 and #112** run from **Nice** and upper **Villefranche-sur-Mer** to **Eze-le-Village** (together they depart about hourly; only #82 runs on Sunday; 30 minutes to reach Eze from Nice). **Bus #112,** which runs along the scenic Middle Corniche, con-

FRENCH RIVIERA

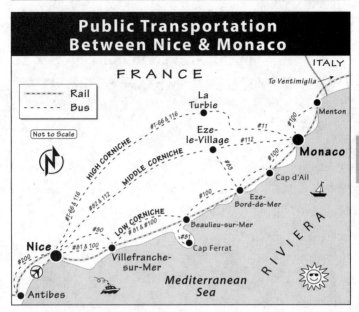

Public Transportation Between Nice & Monaco

FRANCE

ITALY

To Ventimiglia

Rail
Bus

Not to Scale

HIGH CORNICHE #1-66 & 116

La Turbie

Menton

#T-66 & 116

#11

#100

Eze-le-Village

#112

MIDDLE CORNICHE

#100

Monaco

#93

Cap d'Ail

#1-66 & 116

#82 & 112

#100

Eze-Bord-de-Mer

LOW CORNICHE #81 & #100

#80

Beaulieu-sur-Mer

R I V I E R A

Nice

#81 & 100

#81

Villefranche-sur-Mer

Cap Ferrat

#200

Mediterranean Sea

Antibes

tinues from Eze-le-Village to **Monte Carlo** in Monaco (6/day, none on Sun, 20 minutes).

- **Bus #200** goes from **Nice** westbound (4/hour Mon-Sat, 2/hour Sun) to **Cagnes-sur-Mer** (1 hour), **Biot** (1.25 hours), **Antibes** (1.5 hours), and **Cannes** (2 hours).
- For the inland towns, **bus #400** runs from **Nice** (2/hour) to **St-Paul-de-Vence** (45 minutes) and **Vence** (50 minutes); **bus #510/511** goes from Vence to **Grasse** (6/day, 50 minutes).

Trains: These are more expensive but much faster than the bus (Nice to Monaco by train is about €4), and there's no quicker way to move about the Riviera (http://en.voyages-sncf.com). Speedy trains link the Riviera's beachfront destinations—Cannes, Antibes, Nice, Villefranche-sur-Mer, Monaco, Menton, and the inland perfume town of Grasse. (Note: Grasse service may be interrupted by station construction in 2018). Never board a train without a ticket or valid pass—fare inspectors accept no excuses. The minimum fine: €70.

By Car

This is France's most challenging region to drive in. Beautifully distracting vistas (natural and human), loads of Sunday-driver tourists, and every hour being lush-hour in the summer make for a dangerous combination. Parking can be exasperating. Bring lots of coins and patience.

The Riviera is awash with scenic roads. To sample some of the

FRENCH RIVIERA

Public Transportation in the French Riviera

From ↓ / To →	Cannes	Antibes	Nice
Cannes	N/A	**Train:** 2/hr, 15 min **Bus:** #200, 2-4/hr, 35 min	**Train:** 2/hr, 30 min **Bus:** #200, 2-4/hr, 2 hrs
Antibes	**Train:** 2/hr, 15 min **Bus:** #200, 2-4/hr, 35 min	N/A	**Train:** 2/hr, 20 min **Bus:** #200, 2-4/hr, 1.5 hrs
Nice	**Train:** 2/hr, 30 min **Bus:** #200, 2-4/hr, 2 hrs	**Train:** 2/hr, 20 min **Bus:** #200, 2-4/hr, 1.5 hrs	N/A
Villefranche-sur-Mer	**Train:** 2/hr, 50 min	**Train:** 2/hr, 40 min	**Train:** 2/hr, 10 min **Bus:** #100, 3-4/hr, 20 min; also #81, 2-3/hr, 15 min
Cap Ferrat	**Bus/Train:** #81 to Beaulieu-sur-Mer (2-3/hr, 10 min), then train to Cannes (2/hr, 1 hr)	**Bus/Train:** #81 to Beaulieu-sur-Mer (2-3/hr, 10 min), then train (2/hr, 40 min) **Bus:** #81 to Nice (2-3/hr, 30 min), then #200 (2-4/hr, 1.5 hrs)	**Bus:** #81, 2-3/hr, 30 min
Eze-le-Village	**Bus/Train:** #83 to Eze-Bord-de-Mer (8/day, 15 min), then train (2/hr, 1 hour)	**Bus/Train:** #83 to Eze-Bord-de-Mer (8/day, 15 min), then train (2/hr, 45 min)	**Bus/Train:** #83 to Eze-Bord-de-Mer (8/day, 15 min), then train (2/hr, 15 min) **Bus:** #82/#112, hourly 30 min
Monaco	**Train:** 2/hr, 70 min	**Train:** 2/hr, 50 min	**Train:** 2/hr, 20 min **Bus:** #100, 3-4/hr, 1 hour

Note: Bus frequencies are given for Monday-Saturday (Sunday often has limited or no bus service).

Villefranche-sur-Mer	Cap Ferrat	Eze-le-Village	Monaco
Train: 2/hr, 50 min	**Train/Bus:** 2/hr, 1 hr to Beaulieu-sur-Mer, then bus #81 (2-3/hr, 10 min)	**Train/Bus:** 2/hr, 1 hr to Eze-Bord-de-Mer, then bus #83 (8/day, 15 min)	**Train:** 2/hr, 70 min
Train: 2/hr, 40 min	**Train/Bus:** 2/hr, 40 min to Beaulieu-sur-Mer, then bus #81 (2-3/hr, 10 min) **Bus:** #200 to Nice (2-4/hr, 1.5 hrs), then #81 (2-3/hr, 30 min)	**Train/Bus:** 2/hr, 45 min to Eze-Bord-de-Mer, then bus #83 (8/day, 15 min)	**Train:** 2/hr, 50 min
Train: 2/hr, 10 min **Bus:** #100, 3-4/hr, 20 min; also #81, 2-3/hr, 15 min	**Bus:** #81, 2-3/hr, 30 min	**Train/Bus:** 2/hr, 15 min to Eze-Bord-de-Mer, then bus #83 (8/day, 15 min) **Bus:** #82/#112, hourly, 30 min	**Train:** 2/hr, 20 min **Bus:** #100, 3-4/hr, 1 hour
N/A	**Bus:** #81, 2-3/hr, 15 min	**Train/Bus:** 2/hr, 5 min to Eze-Bord-de-Mer, then bus #83 (8/day, 15 min) **Bus:** #100 to Eze-Bord-de-Mer, then transfer to #83; also #82/#112 from upper Villefranche	**Train:** 2/hr, 10 min **Bus:** #100, 3-4/hr, 40 min
Bus: #81, 2-3/hr, 15 min	N/A	**Bus:** 20-min walk or bus #81 to #100 to Eze-Bord-de-Mer (3-4/hr, 30 min), then bus #83 (8/day, 15 min)	**Bus:** 20-min walk or bus #81 to #100 (3-4/hr, 20 min)
Bus/Train: #83 to Eze-Bord-de-Mer (8/day, 15 min), then train (2/hr, 5 min) **Bus:** #83 to Eze-Bord-de-Mer, then transfer to #100; also #82/#112 to upper Villefranche	**Bus:** #83 to Eze-Bord-de-Mer (8/day, 15 min), then #100 (3-4/hr, 30 min plus 20-min walk or transfer to #81)	N/A	**Bus:** #112, 6/day, 20 min
Train: 2/hr, 10 min **Bus:** #100, 3-4/hr, 40 min	**Bus:** #100, 3-4/hr, 20 min (plus 20-min walk or transfer to #81)	**Bus:** #112, 6/day, 20 min	N/A

Riviera's best scenery, connect Provence and the Riviera by driving the splendid coastal road between Cannes and Fréjus (D-6098 from Cannes/D-559 from Fréjus). Once in the Riviera, the most scenic and thrilling road trip is along the three coastal roads—called "corniches"—between Nice and Monaco (see page 351). Farther inland, take my recommended inland hill-towns drive (on page 417). Farther yet, explore the Grand Canyon du Verdon, with breathtaking gorges and alpine scenery. But for basic sightseeing between Monaco and Cannes, I'd ditch the car and use trains and buses.

By Boat

Trans Côte d'Azur offers seasonal boat service from Nice to Monaco or to St-Tropez, as well as between Cannes and St-Tropez (tel. 04 92 98 71 30, www.trans-cote-azur.com). For details, see the "By Boat" section under Nice Connections (page 335).

TOURS IN THE RIVIERA

Local Guides with Cars

These two energetic and delightful women have comfortable minibuses and enjoy taking couples and small groups anywhere in the region: **Sylvie Di Cristo** (€600/day, €350/half-day for up to 8 people, mobile 06 09 88 83 83, www.frenchrivieraguides. net, dicristosylvie@gmail.com) and **Ingrid Schmucker** (€490/day for 2-4 people, €550/day for 5-6 people, €200/half-day to explore old Nice on foot, tel. 06 14 83 03 33, www.kultours.fr, kultours06@ gmail.com). Their websites explain their programs well.

Charming Fouad Zarrou runs **France Azur Excursions** and offers a fun experience with less emphasis on history and more on enjoying the region's natural beauty. He can provide basic transportation in his minivan and small boat excursions as well (figure €300/half-day, tel. 06 20 68 10 70, www.franceazurexcursions. com, contact@franceazurexcursions.com).

Most hotels and TIs have information on economical shared minivan excursions from Nice (per person: roughly €50-70/half-day, €80-120/day).

Local Guides Without Cars

For a guided tour of Nice or the region using public transit or with a guide joining you in your rental car, consider **Pascale Rucker,** an art-loving guide with 25 years of experience who teaches with the joy and wonder of a flower child (€160/half-day, €260/day, tel. 06 16 24 29 52, pascalerucker@gmail.com). **Boba Vukadinovic-Millet** is an effective teacher, ideal for those wanting to dive more deeply into the region's history and art (from €250/half-day, from

FRENCH RIVIERA

Top Art Sights of the Riviera

These are listed in order of importance.

Chagall Museum (Nice)
Fondation Maeght (St-Paul-de-Vence)
Picasso Museum (Antibes)
Matisse Museum (Nice)
Museum of the Annonciade (St-Tropez)
Chapel of the Rosary (Vence)
Modern and Contemporary Art Museum (Nice)
Renoir Museum (Cagnes-sur-Mer)
Fine Arts Museum (Nice)

€350/day, tel. 06 27 45 68 39, www.yourguideboba.com, boba@ yourguideboba.com).

Foodie Tours
For food and wine walking tours and cooking classes offered in Nice, see page 292.

THE RIVIERA'S ART SCENE

The list of artists who have painted the Riviera reads like a Who's Who of 20th-century art. Pierre-Auguste Renoir, Henri Matisse, Marc Chagall, Georges Braque, Raoul Dufy, Fernand Léger, and

Pablo Picasso all lived and worked here—and raved about the region's wonderful light. Their simple, semi-abstract, and—most important-ly—colorful works reflect the pleasurable atmosphere of the Riviera. You'll experience the same landscapes they painted in this bright, sun-drenched region, punctuated with views of the "azure sea." Try to imagine the Riviera with a fraction of the people and development you see today.

But the artists were mostly drawn to the uncomplicated lifestyle of fishermen and farmers that has reigned here since time began. As the artists grew older, they retired in the sun, turned their backs on modern art's "isms," and painted with the wide-eyed wonder of children, using bright primary colors, basic outlines, and simple subjects.

A collection of modern- and contemporary-art museums (many described in this book) dot the Riviera, allowing art lovers to appreciate these masters' works while immersed in the same sun and culture that inspired them. Many of the museums were designed to blend pieces with the surrounding views, gardens, and fountains, thus highlighting that modern art is not only stimulating, but sometimes simply beautiful.

Entire books have been written about the modern-art galleries of the Riviera. If you're a fan, do some studying before your visit to be sure you know about that far-out museum of your dreams. If you've never enjoyed modern art, the two best places to give it a try here are the Fondation Maeght in St-Paul-de-Vence and the Chagall Museum in Nice.

THE RIVIERA'S CUISINE SCENE

The Riviera adds an Italian-Mediterranean flair to the food of Provence. While many of the same dishes served in Provence are available in the Riviera (see "Provence's Cuisine Scene" on page 30), there are differences, especially if you look for anything Italian or from the sea. Proximity to the water and historic ties to Italy are clear in this region's dishes.

That said, memorable restaurants that showcase the Riviera's cuisine can be difficult to find. Because most visitors come more for the sun than the food, and because the clientele is predominantly international, many restaurants aim for the middle and are hard to distinguish from one another. Trust my recommendations.

A fresh and colorful *salade niçoise* makes the perfect introduction to the Riviera's cuisine. Surprisingly, the authentic version contains no potatoes or green beans but consists of ripe tomatoes, plenty of raw vegetables (such as radishes, green peppers, celery, and perhaps artichoke or fava beans), as well as tuna (usually canned), anchovy, hard-boiled egg, and olives. This is my go-to salad for a tasty, healthy, cheap (€13), and fast lunch. I like to spend a couple of extra euros and eat it in a place with a nice ambience and view.

For lunch on the go, look for a *pan bagnat* (like a *salade niçoise* stuffed into a crusty roll drizzled with olive oil and wine vinegar). Other tasty bread treats include *pissaladière* (bread dough topped with caramelized onions, olives, and anchovies), *fougasse* (a spindly, lace-like bread sometimes flavored with nuts, herbs, olives, or ham), and *socca* (a thin chickpea-and-olive-oil crêpe, seasoned with pepper and often served in a paper cone by street vendors).

Said to have been invented in Nice, ravioli and potato gnocchi can be found on menus everywhere (ravioli can be stuffed with a variety of fillings, but the classic local version is made with beef and Swiss chard).

Bouillabaisse is the Riviera's most famous dish; you'll find it in seafront villages and cities. It's a spicy fish stew based on recipes handed down from sailors in Marseille. It must contain at least four types of fresh fish, though most have five to twelve kinds. A true bouillabaisse never has shellfish. The fish—cooked in a tomato-

and-onion-based stock and flavored with saffron (and sometimes anise and orange)—is separated from the stock, and the two are served as separate courses. Diners then heighten the soup's flavor by adding toasted croutons slathered with *rouille* sauce (a thickened reddish mayonnaise heady with garlic and spicy peppers) and topped with grated parmesan or Emmental cheese. This dish often requires a minimum order of two and can cost up to €40-60 per person.

Far less pricey than bouillabaisse and worth trying is the local *soupe de poissons* (fish soup). It's a creamy soup flavored like bouillabaisse, with anise and orange, and served with croutons and *rouille* sauce (but has no chunks of fish). For a less colorful but still tasty soup, look for *bourride*, a creamy fish concoction thickened with an aioli sauce instead of the red *rouille*.

The Riviera specializes in all sorts of fish and shellfish. Options include *fruits de mer* (platters of seafood—including tiny shellfish, from which you get the edible part only by sucking really hard), herb-infused mussels, stuffed sardines, squid (slowly simmered with tomatoes and herbs), and tuna *(thon)*. The popular *loup flambé au fenouil* is grilled sea bass, flavored with fennel and torched with *pastis* prior to serving.

For a truly local dessert, try the *Niçoise* specialty *tourte de blettes*, a sugar-dusted pie with a sweet filling of Swiss chard, rum-soaked raisins, pine nuts, and apple. In St-Tropez, the *tropézienne* is a brioche topped with sugar crystals and sandwiching with an airy vanilla cream. Desserts on the Riviera make use of the abundant local fruits, especially citrus in winter, and regional flavors such as orange flower water.

For details on dining in France's restaurants, cafés, and brasseries, getting takeout, and assembling a picnic—as well as a rundown of French cuisine—see the "Eating" section in the Practicalities chapter (page 482).

WINES OF THE RIVIERA

Do as everyone else does: Drink wines from Provence. Bandol (red) and cassis (white) are popular and from a region nearly on the Riviera. The only wines made in the Riviera are Bellet rosé and white, the latter often found in fish-shaped bottles. For more on Provençal wines, see page 34.

NICE

Nice (sounds like "niece"), with its spectacular Alps-meets-Mediterranean surroundings, is the big-city highlight of the Riviera. Its traffic-free Vieux Nice—the old town—blends Italian and French flavors to create a spicy Mediterranean dressing, while its big squares, broad seaside walkways, and long beaches invite lounging and people-watching. Nice may be nice, but it's hot and jammed in July and August—reserve ahead and get a room with air-conditioning. Everything you'll want to see in Nice is either within walking distance, or a short bike, bus, or tram ride away.

Orientation to Nice

Focus your time on the area between the beach and the train tracks (about 15 blocks apart). The city revolves around its grand Place Masséna, where pedestrian-friendly Avenue Jean Médecin meets Vieux Nice and the Promenade du Paillon parkway (with quick access to the beaches). It's a 20-minute walk (or about €14 by taxi) from the train station to the beach, and a 20-minute stroll along the promenade from the fancy Hôtel Negresco to the heart of Vieux Nice.

A 10-minute ride on the smooth-as-silk tram through the center of the city connects the train station, Place Masséna, Vieux Nice, and the port (from nearby Place Garibaldi). Work is under way on a new tram line (much of it underground) that will parallel the Promenade des Anglais and run to the airport (scheduled for completion in 2019).

TOURIST INFORMATION

Nice has three helpful TIs (tel. 08 92 70 74 07, www.nicetourisme. com), including the main branches at the **train station** and at #5 **Promenade des Anglais** (both daily 9:00-18:00, July-Aug until 19:00), and by the fountains near **Place Masséna**, called "Pavillon" (June-mid-Sept only, daily 10:00-20:00). Ask for day-trip information (including maps of Monaco, Antibes, and Cannes) and details on boat excursions, bus stop locations, and schedules.

ARRIVAL IN NICE

By Train: All trains stop at Nice's main station, called Nice-Ville. With your back to the tracks, car rentals are to the right. Bag storage is to the left inside the station; you can also stash your bags a short block away at the recommended Hôtel Belle Meunière. The TI and bus stops (including #99 to the airport) are straight out the main doors.

Nice's single tram line zips you to the center in a few minutes (several blocks to the left as you leave the station, departs every few minutes, direction: Hôpital Pasteur; see "Getting Around Nice" on page 289). To walk to the beach, Promenade des Anglais, or many of my recommended hotels, cross Avenue Thiers in front of the station, go down the steps by Hôtel Interlaken, and continue down Avenue Durante.

By Bus: For arrival by bus, see "Nice Connections," at the end of this chapter. The region's primary bus company, Lignes d'Azur, has an information office across from the train station (see "Helpful Hints," below).

By Car: To reach the city center on the autoroute from the west, take the first Nice exit (for the airport—called *Côte d'Azur, Central*) and follow signs for *Nice Centre*. Ask you hoteliers where to park (allow €18-30/day; many hotels offer deals but space is limited—arrange ahead). The parking garage at the Nice Etoile shopping center on Avenue Jean Médecin is near many recommended hotels (ticket booth on third floor, about €28/day, 18:00-8:00). Other centrally located garages have similar rates. On-street parking is metered (usually a 2-hour limit) every day but Sunday, when it is typically free.

You can avoid driving in the center—and park for free during the day (no overnight parking)—by stashing your car at a parking lot at a remote tram or bus stop. Look for blue-on-white *Parcazur* signs (find locations at www.lignesdazur.com), and ride the bus or tram into town (10/hour, 15 minutes, buy round-trip tram or bus ticket and keep it with you—you'll need it later to exit the parking lot; for tram details, see "Getting Around Nice," later). The easiest lot to use is Parcazur Henri Sappia, right off the *Nice Nord* autoroute exit. It always has room and saves you from navigating city

NICE

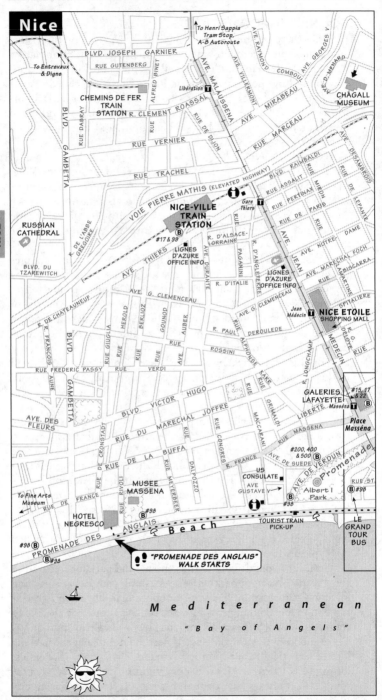

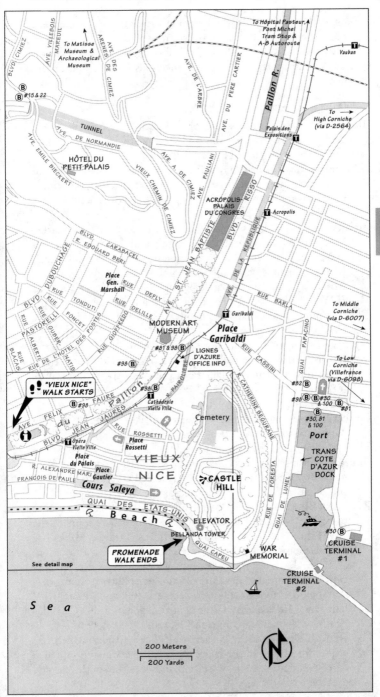

NICE

streets (daily until 2:30 in the morning). As lots are not guarded, don't leave anything of value in your car.

By Plane or Cruise Ship: For information on Nice's airport and cruise-ship port, see "Nice Connections," at the end of this chapter.

HELPFUL HINTS

Theft Alert: Nice has its share of pickpockets (especially at the train station, on the tram, and trolling the beach). Stick to main streets in Vieux Nice after dark.

Medical Help: Riviera Medical Services has a list of English-speaking physicians. They can help you make an appointment or call an ambulance (tel. 04 93 26 12 70, www.rivieramedical. com).

Sightseeing Tips: The Cours Saleya produce and flower market is closed Monday, and the Chagall and Matisse museums are closed Tuesday. All Nice museums—except the Chagall Museum—share the same €10 combo-ticket (valid 24 hours, €20/7 days, buy at any participating museum).

Wi-Fi: You'll find free Wi-Fi at TIs, at many cafés, and at large shopping centers (like Nice Etoile). All of the hotels I list have free Wi-Fi.

Baggage Storage: You can store your bags inside the train station (€5-10/bag per day), at the recommended **Hôtel Belle Meunière** (€5/bag per day), or at the **Bagguys** in Vieux Nice (€8/bag per day, daily 10:00-19:00, 22 Rue Centrale, info@ bagguys.fr).

Grocery Store: Small grocery shops are easy to find. The big **Monoprix** on Avenue Jean Médecin and Rue Biscarra has it all (open daily, see map on page 333).

Boutique Shopping: The chic streets where Rue Alphonse Karr meets Rue de la Liberté and then Rue de Paradis are known as the "Golden Square." If you need pricey stuff, shop here.

Renting a Bike (and Other Wheels): Bike-rental shops are a breeze to find in Nice, and several companies offer bike tours of the city. Bikes *(vélos)* can be taken on trains. **Holiday Bikes** has multiple locations, including one across from the train station, and they have electric bikes (www.loca-bike.fr). **Roller Station** is well-situated near the sea and rents bikes, rollerblades, skateboards, and Razor-style scooters (bikes-€5/hour, €10/ half-day, €15/day, leave ID as deposit, open daily, 49 Quai des Etats-Unis—see map on page 328, tel. 04 93 62 99 05).

Car Rental: Renting a car is easiest at Nice's airport, which has offices for all the major companies. Most companies·are also represented at Nice's train station and near the southwest side of Albert I Park.

Lignes d'Azur Bus Tickets: Very helpful information offices are at these locations in central Nice: kitty-corner from the train station at 17 Rue Thiers, at 1 Rue d'Italie, and at 4 Boulevard Jean Juarès. Office hours vary (generally Mon-Fri 9:00-18:00 or 19:00, Sat until 15:00, closed Sun). Pick up schedules, buy day passes, and get information for buses to all Riviera destinations. Ask for their helpful "Passenger Guide" brochure in English.

English Radio: Tune in to Riviera-Radio at FM 106.5.

Views: For panoramic views, climb Castle Hill (see page 320), or take a one-hour boat trip (page 291).

Beach Tips: To make life tolerable on the rocks, swimmers should buy a pair of the cheap plastic beach shoes sold at many shops. **Go Sport** at #13 on Place Masséna is a good bet (open daily, see map on page 328). Locals don't swim in July and August, as the warming sea brings swarms of stinging jellyfish. Ask before you dip.

GETTING AROUND NICE
By Public Transportation

Although you can walk to most attractions, smart travelers make good use of the buses and tram within Nice. For information on getting around the Riviera from Nice, see "Nice Connections," at the end of this chapter.

Tickets: Both buses and trams are covered by the same €1.50 single-ride ticket, or you can pay €10 for a 10-ride ticket that can be shared (each use good for 74 minutes in one direction, including transfers between bus and tram). The €5 all-day pass is valid on city buses and trams, as well as buses to some nearby destinations (but not airport buses). You must validate your ticket on every trip. Buy single tickets from the bus driver or from the ticket machines on tram platforms (coins only—press the green button once to validate choice and twice at the end to get your ticket). Passes and 10-ride tickets are also available from machines at tram stops and from the Lignes d'Azur office (see "Helpful Hints," above). Info: www.lignesdazur.com.

Buses: The bus is handy for reaching the Chagall and Matisse museums and the Russian Cathedral (for specifics, see museum listings under "Sights in Nice"). Validate your ticket in the machine—watch locals to learn how. Route diagrams in the buses identify each stop. Warning: Construction of a new tram line (see below) will likely cause changes to bus routes; ask locally.

Trams: Nice has a single modern and efficient L-shaped tram line. Trams run every few minutes along Avenue Jean Médecin and Boulevard Jean Jaurès, and connect the main train station with Place Masséna and Vieux Nice (Opéra stop), the port

(Place Garibaldi stop), and buses east along the coast (Vauban stop). Trams also stop near the Chemins de Fer de Provence train station (Libération stop)—the departure point for the scenic narrow-gauge rail journey (see page 321).

Boarding the tram in the direction of Hôpital Pasteur takes you toward the beach and Vieux Nice (direction: Henri Sappia goes the other way). Validate your ticket on the tram (http://tramway. nice.fr). Note that construction for a new tram line is under way, linking Nice with its airport (running parallel to the Promenade des Anglais a few blocks inland). The tram should begin service in around 2019.

By Taxi or Uber

While pricey, **cabs** can be useful for getting to Nice's less-central sights (figure €8 for shortest ride, €15 from Promenade des Anglais to the Chagall Museum). Cabbies normally pick up only at taxi stands *(tête de station),* or you can call 04 93 13 78 78. **Uber** works here like it does at home (including your US app and account) though there are fewer cars here. Still it's generally a better bet than a taxi. Drivers are nicer and more flexible, it's cheaper, and you usually get a car without much delay.

Tours in Nice

ON WHEELS
Hop-On, Hop-Off Bus

Le Grand Tour Bus provides a useful 14-stop, hop-on, hop-off service on an open-deck bus with good headphone commentary. The route includes the Promenade des Anglais, the old port, Cap de Nice, and the Chagall and Matisse museums (1-day pass-€23, 2-day pass-€26, night tour-€15, buy tickets on bus, 2/hour, daily 10:00-19:00, 1.5-hour loop, main stop near where Promenade des Anglais and Quai des Etats-Unis meet—across from the Plage Beau Rivage lounge, tel. 04 92 29 17 00, www.nice.opentour.com). While neither an economical nor efficient way to get to the Chagall and Matisse museums, it works well if you're looking for a city overview and want to visit these museums (best seats are up top on the left as you face forward).

Tourist Train

For €10, you can spend 45 minutes on the tourist train tooting along the promenade, through the old city, and up to Castle Hill

Nice at a Glance

▲▲▲Promenade des Anglais Nice's four-mile sun-struck seafront promenade. See page 292.

▲▲▲Chagall Museum The world's largest collection of Marc Chagall's work, popular even with people who don't like modern art. **Hours:** Wed-Mon 10:00-18:00, Nov-April until 17:00, closed Tue year-round. See page 307.

▲▲Vieux Nice Charming old city offering enjoyable atmosphere and a look at Nice's French-Italian cultural blend. See page 299.

▲Matisse Museum Modest collection of Henri Matisse's paintings, sketches, and paper cutouts. **Hours:** Wed-Mon 10:00-18:00, mid-Oct-mid-June from 11:00, closed Tue year-round. See page 314.

▲Russian Cathedral Finest Orthodox church outside Russia. **Hours:** Tue-Sat 9:00-12:00 & 14:00-19:00, Sun 9:00-12:00, closed Mon. See page 319.

▲Castle Hill Site of an ancient fort boasting great views. **Hours:** Park closes at 20:00 in summer, earlier off-season. See page 320.

Modern and Contemporary Art Museum Enjoyable collection from the 1960s and '70s, including Warhol and Lichtenstein. **Hours:** Tue-Sun 10:00-18:00, closed Mon. See page 318.

NICE

(2/hour, daily 10:00-18:00 or 19:00, recorded English commentary, meet train near Le Grand Tour Bus stop on Quai des Etats-Unis, tel. 02 99 88 47 07).

BY BOAT
▲Trans Côte d'Azur Cruise

To see Nice from the water, hop this one-hour tour run by Trans Côte d'Azur. You'll cruise in a comfortable yacht-size vessel to Cap Ferrat and past Villefranche-sur-Mer, then return to Nice with a final lap along Promenade des Anglais.

Guides enjoy pointing out mansions owned by famous people, including Elton John, Sean Connery, and Microsoft co-founder Paul Allen (€18; covered by French Riviera Pass—see page 274; April-Oct Tue-Sun 2/day, usually at 11:00 and 15:00, no boats Mon or in off-season; verify schedule, arrive 30 minutes early to get best seats). The boats leave from Nice's port, Bassin des Amiraux, just below Castle Hill—look for the ticket booth *(billeterie)* on Quai de Lunel (see map on page 286). The same company also runs boats to Monaco and St-Tropez (see "Nice Connections," at the end of this chapter).

ON FOOT
Local Guides and Walking Tours
If interested in hiring a local guide for Nice and other regional destinations, see page 280 for suggestions.

The TI on Promenade des Anglais organizes weekly walking tours of Vieux Nice in French and English (€12, May-Oct only, usually Sat morning at 9:30, 2.5 hours, reservations necessary, departs from TI, tel. 08 92 70 74 07).

Food Tours and Cooking Classes
Charming Canadian Francophile Rosa Jackson, a food journalist, Cordon Bleu-trained cook, and longtime resident of France, runs a cooking school—**Les Petits Farcis**—and offers a good food-market tour in Vieux Nice (€75/person). She also teaches cooking classes that include a morning shopping trip to the market on Cours Saleya and an afternoon cooking session (€195/person, 12 Rue Saint Joseph, tel. 06 81 67 41 22, www.petitsfarcis.com).

Walks in Nice

These two self-guided walks take you down an iconic seaside promenade ("Promenade des Anglais Walk") and through the colorful old town blending French and Italian cultures ("Vieux Nice Walk").

PROMENADE DES ANGLAIS WALK
Welcome to the Riviera. There's something for everyone along this four-mile-long promenade, worth ▲▲▲. Stroll like the belle-époque English aristocrats for whom the promenade was paved. Watch Europeans at play, admire the azure Mediterranean, anchor yourself on a blue seat, and prop your feet up on the made-to-order guardrail. Later, you can come back to join the evening parade of tans along the promenade.

The broad sidewalks of the Promenade des Anglais ("Walkway of the English") were financed by upper-crust English tourists who wanted a secure and comfortable place to stroll and admire the view. The Brits originally came to Nice seeking relief from tuberculosis; both the dry climate and the salt air helped ease their

suffering. It was an era when tanned bodies were frowned upon (aristocrats didn't want to resemble lower-class laborers who had to work outside). The walk was paved in marble in 1822 so those of gentle birth wouldn't have to dirty their shoes or smell the fishy gravel. Visitors wouldn't dare swim in the Mediterranean for another hundred years.

Length of This Walk: Allow one hour at a promenade pace for this leisurely, level walk. It's a straight one-mile line along this much-strolled beachfront, beginning near the landmark Hôtel Negresco and ending at the elevator to Castle Hill.

When to Go: While this walk is enjoyable at any time, the first half makes a great stroll before or after breakfast or dinner (meals served at some beach cafés). If you're doing the entire walk to Castle Hill, try to time it so you wind up on top of the hill at sunset.

NICE

Biking the Promenade: See page 306 for tips on cycling along the seafront.

❍ Self-Guided Walk

• *Start at the pink-domed...*

❶ Hôtel Negresco

Nice's finest hotel is also a historic monument, offering up the city's most expensive beds and a museum-like interior.

If you wonder why such a grand hotel has such an understated entry, it's because today's front door was originally the back door. In the 19th century, elegant people stayed out of the sun, and any posh hotel that cared about its clientele would design its entry on the shady north side. If you walk around to today's "back" you'll see a grand but unused front door.

The hotel is technically off-limits to non-guests, but if you explain to the doorman that you'd like to get a drink at Negresco's classy-cozy Le Relais bar (see below), you'll be allowed past the registration desk. You can also explain that you want to shop at their store, which also might get you in—*bonne chance*.

If you get in, walk straight until you reach a huge ballroom, the **Salon Royal**. The chandelier hanging from its Eiffel-built dome is made of 16,000 pieces of crystal. It was built in France for the Russian czar's Moscow palace...but thanks to the Bolshevik Revolution in 1917, he couldn't take delivery. Bronze portrait busts of Czar

Promenade des Anglais Walk

- ❶ Hôtel Negresco
- ❷ Villa Masséna
- ❸ Bay of Angels
- ❹ Palais de la Méditerranée
- ❺ Albert I Park
- ❻ Steel Girders Sculpture
- ❼ Metal Winch

Alexander III and his wife, Maria Feodorovna—who returned to her native Denmark after the revolution—are to the right, facing the shops. Circle the interior and then the perimeter to enjoy both historic and modern art. Fine portraits include Emperor Napoleon III and wife Empress Eugénie (who acquired Nice for France from Italy in 1860), and Jeanne Augier (who owns the hotel). She's quite elderly now, lives up in the cupola, and has willed the Negresco to organizations that care for orphans and stray animals.

If the **Le Relais bar** door is open, wander up the marble steps for a look into the wood-paneled interior (glass of wine-€16, mixed drinks-€30, from 11:30 in high season, from 14:30 off-season). Farther along, in the little shopping lane, nip into the toilets for either an early 20th-century powder room or a Battle of Waterloo experience. The chairs with the high, scooped backs were typical of the age (cones of silence for an afternoon nap sitting up). The hotel's **Chantecler restaurant** is one of the Riviera's best (allow €100 per person before drinks).

On your way out, pop into the **Salon Versailles** (right of entry lobby as you leave), with a grand fireplace and France's Sun King, Louis XIV, on the wall (English descriptions explain the room).

• *Across the street from the Hôtel Negresco (to the east) is...*

❷ Villa Masséna

When Nice became part of France, France invested heavily in

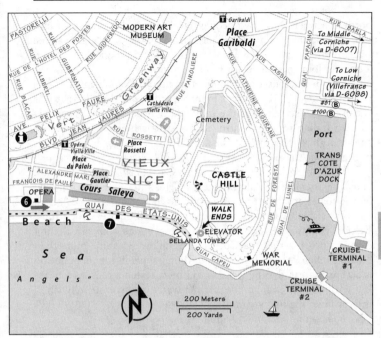

NICE

what it expected to be the country's new high society retreat—an elite resort akin to Russia's Sochi. The government built this fine palace for the military hero of the Napoleonic age, Jean-Andre Masséna and his family. Take a moment to stroll around the lovely garden (free, open daily 10:00-18:00). The Masséna Museum inside (described on page 319) offers an interesting look at belle-époque Nice.

• *From Villa Masséna, head for the beach and begin your Promenade des Anglais stroll. But first, grab a blue chair and gaze out to the...*

❸ Bay of Angels (Baie des Anges)

Face the water. The body of Nice's patron saint, Réparate, was supposedly escorted into this bay by angels in the fourth century. To

your right is where you might have been escorted into France—Nice's airport, built on a massive landfill. The tip of land beyond the runway is Cap d'Antibes. Until 1860, Antibes and Nice were in different countries—Antibes was French, but Nice was a protectorate of the Italian kingdom of Savoy-Piedmont, a.k.a. the Kingdom of Sardinia. During that period, the Var River—just west of Nice—was the geographic border between these two peoples (and to this day the river functions as a kind of cultural border). In 1850, the people here spoke Italian and ate pasta. As Italy was uniting, the region was given a choice: Join the new country of Italy or join France (which was enjoying prosperous times under the rule of Napoleon III). The majority voted in 1860 to go French...and *voilà!* (While that was the official story, in reality the Italian king needed France's support to help Italian regions controlled by Austria break away and join the emerging union of Italian states. Italy's price for France's support against Austria: the city and region of Nice.)

The lower green hill to your left is Castle Hill (where this walk ends). Farther left lie Villefranche-sur-Mer and Cap Ferrat (marked by the tower at land's end, and home to lots of millionaires), then Monaco (which you can't see, with more millionaires), then Italy. Behind you are the foothills of the Alps, which trap threatening clouds, ensuring that the Côte d'Azur enjoys sunshine more than 300 days each year. While half a million people live here, pollution is carefully treated—the water is routinely tested and is very clean. But with climate change, the warmer water is attracting jellyfish in the summer, making swimming a stinging memory.

• *With the sea on your right, begin strolling.*

The Promenade

Nearby sit two fine belle-époque establishments: the West End and Westminster hotels, both boasting English names to help those

original guests feel at home. (The West End is now part of the Best Western group...to help American guests feel at home.) These hotels symbolize Nice's arrival as a tourist mecca in the 19th century, when the combination of leisure time and a stable economy allowed visitors to find the sun even in winter.

As you walk, be careful to avoid the bike lane. The promenade you're walking on was originally only about six feet across. It's been widened and lengthened over the years to keep up with tourist

demand, including increased bicycle use.

You'll pass several rocky beaches. Despite the lack of sand, they're still a popular draw. France has a strong ethic of public access when it comes to its beaches. In response to a greedy development project in the 1970s designed to privatize a stretch of coastline, a law was passed in 1980 guaranteeing the public free access to beaches like these. All along the Riviera you'll find public beaches (and public showers).

You can go local and rent gear—about €15 for a *chaise longue* (long chair) and a *transat* (mattress), €5 for an umbrella, and €5 for a towel. You'll also pass several beach restaurants. Some of these eateries serve breakfast, all serve lunch, some do dinner, and a few have beachy bars...tailor-made for a break from this walk.

Find the easel showing a painting of La Jetée Promenade—Nice's elegant pier and first casino, built in 1883. Even a hundred years ago, there was sufficient tourism in Nice to justify constructing a palatial building to house this leisure activity imported from Venice. La Jetée Promenade stood on those white-covered pilings (with flags flapping) just offshore, until the Germans destroyed it during World War II. When La Jetée was thriving, it took gamblers two full days to get to the Riviera by train from Paris. The painting shows what an event strolling the Promenade was—like going to the Opera, it was all about dressing up, being seen, and looking good.

Although La Jetée Promenade is gone, you can still see the striking 1927 Art Nouveau facade of the ❹ **Palais de la Méditerranée,** a grand if overbearing casino, hotel, and theater. It became one of the grandest casinos in Europe, and today it is one of France's most exclusive hotels, though the casino feels cheap and cheesy.

The unappealing modern Casino Ruhl (with the most detested facade on the strip) disfigures the next block. Anyone can drop in for some one-armed-bandit fun, but to play the tables at night you'll need to dress up and bring your passport.

❺ **Albert I Park** is named for the Belgian king who enjoyed wintering here—these were his private gardens. While the English came first, the Belgians and Russians were also big fans of 19th-century Nice. That tall statue at the edge of the park commemorates the 100-year anniversary of Nice's union with France. The happy statue features two beloved women embracing the idea of union (Marianne—Ms. Liberty, Equality, and Brotherhood, and the symbol of the Republic of France—and Catherine Ségurane, a 16th-century heroine who helped Nice against the Saracen pirates).

The park is part of a long, winding greenbelt called the Promenade du Paillon. The Paillon River flows under the park on its way to the sea. This is the historical divide between Vieux Nice and the new town.

Continuing along the promenade you'll soon enter the **Quai des Etats-Unis** ("Quay of the United States"). This name was given as a tip-of-the-cap to the Americans for finally entering World War I in 1917. The big, blue chair statue celebrates the inviting symbol of this venerable walk and kicks off the best stretch of beach—

quieter and with less traffic. Check out the laid-back couches at the Plage Beau Rivage lounge and consider a beachfront drink.

Those tall, rusted ❻ **steel girders** reaching for the sky were erected in 2010 to celebrate the 150th anniversary of Nice's union with France. (The seven beams represent the seven valleys of the Nice region.) Done by the same artist who created the popular Arc of the Riviera sculpture in the parkway near Place Masséna, this "art" justifiably infuriates many locals as an ugly waste of money. But I know how to make it easier to appreciate the erection every local loves to hate: Stand directly under it, look straight up, and spin 720 degrees. Then look across the way to marvel at the 18th-century facades that line the Esplanade Georges Pompidou. Find the one that is entirely fake-painted on a flat stucco surface. Then, look down and notice the buried uplighting—a French forte. And then, give it another 720 degrees of spin and try to walk on.

At the first palm tree, some will enjoy looking left (at the delightful back side of Apollo, a couple of blocks away), while others head to the right for a view of the beach action. Topless bathing is now out of fashion. Locals say that the awareness of skin cancer and the proliferation of North African and tourist looky-loos have made it less appealing. Some say the only people still bathing topless are older ladies who remember fondly the liberation of 1968... and tourists.

A block ahead on the left, the elegant back side of Nice's opera house faces the sea. The tiny bronze Statue of Liberty (right in front of you as you face the opera) reminds all that this stretch of seafront promenade is named for the USA.

The long, low building lining the walk on the left once served the city's fishermen. Behind its gates bustles the **Cours Saleya Market**—long the heart and soul of Vieux Nice, with handy WCs under its arches.

Farther along, on the far-right side of the Quai des Etats-Unis (opposite Le Cambodia restaurant), find the three-foot-tall white ❼ **metal winch.** Long before tourism—and long before Nice dredged its harbor—hard-working fishing boats rather than vacationing tourists lined the beach. The boats were hauled in through the surf by winches like this and tied to the iron rings on either side.

• *You could end your walk here, but the view from the point just past the Hôtel la Pérouse is wonderful. Either way, you have several great options: Continue 10 minutes along the coast to the* **port,** *around the foot of Castle Hill (fine views of the entire promenade and a monumental war memorial carved into the hillside); hike or ride the elevator up to* **Castle Hill** *(catch the elevator next to Hôtel Suisse; see listing for Castle Hill on page 320); head into* **Vieux Nice** *(you can follow my "Vieux Nice Walk"); or grab a blue chair or piece of* **beach** *and just be on vacation—Riviera style.*

VIEUX NICE WALK

This self-guided walk through Nice's old town, known as Vieux Nice and worth ▲▲, gives you a helpful introduction to the city's bicultural heritage and its most interesting neighborhoods.

Length of This Walk: Allow about one hour at a leisurely pace for this level walk from Place Masséna to Place Rossetti.

When to Go: It's best done in the morning (while the outdoor market thrives—consider coffee or breakfast at a café along the Cours Saleya), and preferably not on a Sunday, when things are quiet. This ramble is also a joy at night, when fountains glow and pedestrians control the streets.

⊘ Self-Guided Walk

• *Start where Avenue Jean Médecin hits the people-friendly Place Masséna—the successful result of a long, expensive city upgrade and the new center of Nice.*

❶ Place Masséna

The grand Place Masséna is Nice's drawing room, where old meets new, and where the tramway bends between Vieux Nice and the train station. The square's black-and-white pavement feels like an elegant outdoor ballroom, with the sleek tram waltzing across its dance floor. While once congested with cars, the square today is frequented only by these trams, which swoosh silently by every couple of minutes. The men on pedestals sitting high above are modern-art additions that ar-rived with the tram. For a mood-altering experience, return after dark and watch the illuminated figures float yoga-like above. Place Masséna is at its sophisticated best after the sun goes down.

This vast square dates from 1848 and pays tribute to Jean-André Masséna, a French military leader during the Revolutionary and Napoleonic wars. Not just another pretty face in a long lineup of French military heroes, he's considered among the greatest commanders in history—anywhere, anytime. Napoleon called him "the greatest name of my military Empire." No wonder this city is proud of him.

Under the pavement, Nice's historic river, the Paillon, is flowing to the sea. For centuries this river was Nice's natural defense to the north and west (the sea protected the south, and Castle Hill defended the east). A fortified wall once ran along the river's length to the sea. It's been covered since the late 1800s.

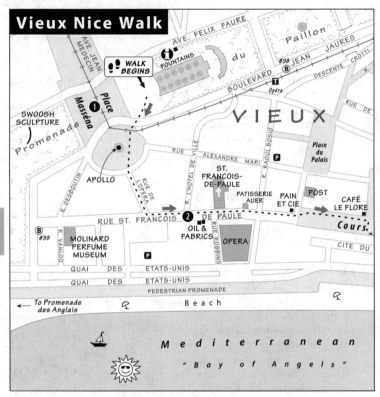

Vieux Nice Walk

NICE

Standing on the square with your back to the fountains, start a clockwise spin tour: The towering **modern swoosh sculpture** in the park is meant to represent the "curve of the French Riviera"— the arc of the bay. To the right stretches modern Nice, born with the arrival of tourism in the 1800s. **Avenue Jean Médecin,** Nice's Champs-Elysées, cuts from here through the new town to the train station. In the distance are the tracks, the freeway, and the Alps beyond. Once crammed with cars, buses, and delivery vehicles tangling with pedestrians, Avenue Jean Médecin was turned into a walking and cycling nirvana in 2007. I used to avoid this street. Now I can't get enough of it. Businesses along it flourish in the welcoming environment of generous sidewalks and no traffic.

Appreciate the city's Italian heritage—it feels more like Venice than Paris. The portico flanking Avenue Jean Médecin is Italian, not French. The rich colors of the buildings reflect the taste of previous Italian rulers.

Turn to the fountains and look east to see Nice's ongoing effort to "put the human element into the heart of the town." An ugly concrete bus station and parking structures were demolished

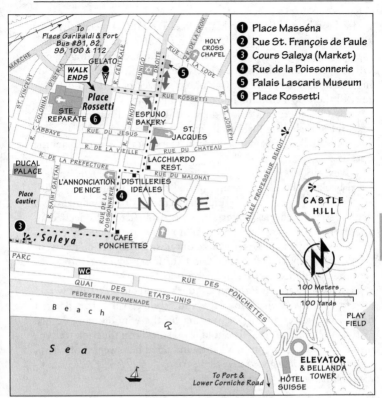

1. Place Masséna
2. Rue St. François de Paule
3. Cours Saleya (Market)
4. Rue de la Poissonnerie
5. Palais Lascaris Museum
6. Place Rossetti

NICE

not long ago, and the **Promenade du Paillon** was created to fill the space. Today, this pedestrian-friendly parkway extends from the sea to the Museum of Modern Art—a modern-day Promenade des Anglais. Forming a key spine for biking, walking, and kids at play, the Promenade du Paillon is a delight any time of day. Notice the fountain—its surprise geysers delight children by day and its fine lighting enhances romance at night. Past the fountain stands a bronze statue of the square's namesake, Masséna. The hills beyond separate Nice from Villefranche-sur-Mer.

Turn farther to the right to see **Vieux Nice,** with its jumbled and colorful facades below Castle Hill. The **statue of Apollo** has horsy hair and holds a beach towel (in the fountain) as if to say, "It's beer o'clock, let's go."

• *Walk past Apollo into Vieux Nice. A block down Rue de l'Opéra you'll see a grouping of rusted beams (described on page 298). Turn left onto Rue St. François de Paule.*

❷ Rue St. François de Paule

This colorful street leads into the heart of Vieux Nice. On the left is the Hôtel de Ville (City Hall). Peer into the **Alziari olive oil shop** (at #14 on the right). Dating from 1868, the shop produces top-quality stone-ground olive oil. The proud and charming owner, Gilles Piot, claims that stone wheels create less acidity, since grinding with metal creates heat (see photo in back over the door). Locals fill their own containers from the huge vats.

La Couqueto is a colorful shop filled with Provençal fabrics and crafts, including lovely folk characters *(santons)*. Walk in for a lavender smell sensation—is madame working the sewing machine upstairs?

Next door is Nice's grand **opera house.** Imagine this opulent jewel back in the 19th century, buried deep in Vieux Nice. With all the fancy big-city folks wintering here, this rough-edged town needed some high-class entertainment. And Victorians needed an alternative to those "devilish" gambling houses. (Queen Victoria, so disgusted by casinos, would actually close the drapes on her train window when passing Monte Carlo.) The four statues on top represent theater, dance, music, and party poopers.

Across the street, **Pâtisserie Auer**'s grand old storefront would love to tempt you with chocolates and candied fruits. It's changed little over the centuries. The writing on the window says, "Since 1820 from father to son." The gold royal shields on the back wall remind shoppers that Queen Victoria indulged her sweet tooth here.
• *Continue on, sifting your way through a cluttered block of tacky souvenir shops to the big market square.*

❸ Cours Saleya

Named for its broad exposure to the sun *(soleil),* Cours Saleya (koor sah-lay-yuh)—a commotion of color, sights, smells, and people—has been Nice's main market square since the Middle Ages (flower market all day Tue-Sun, produce market Tue-Sun until 13:00, antiques on Mon). While you're greeted by the ugly mouth of an underground parking lot, much of this square itself was a parking lot until 1980, when the mayor of Nice had this solution dug.

If you're early enough for coffee or breakfast, these places make good choices: **Pain et Cie** (at the market's entry) has a warm interior, good outdoor seating, and welcoming owners, but it's hard to beat **Café le Flore**'s outdoor tables in the heart of the market (a block up on the left).

The first section is devoted to the Riviera's largest **flower market.** In operation since the 19th century, this market offers plants and flowers that grow effortlessly and ubiquitously in this climate, including the local favorites: carnations, roses, and jasmine. Locals know the season by what's on sale (mimosas in February, violets in March, and so on). Until the recent rise in imported flowers, this region supplied all of France with flowers. Still, fresh flowers are cheap here, the best value in this notoriously expensive city. The Riviera's three big industries are tourism, flowers, and perfume (made from these flowers...take a whiff).

The boisterous **produce section** trumpets the season with mushrooms, strawberries, white asparagus, zucchini flowers, and more—whatever's fresh gets top billing. What's in season today?

The market opens up at Place Pierre Gautier. It's also called Plassa dou Gouvernou—you'll see bilingual street signs here that include the old Niçois language, an Italian dialect. This is where farmers set up stalls to sell their produce and herbs directly. For a **rooftop view** over the market, climb the steps by Le Grand Bleu restaurant (you may have to step over the trash sacks, but it's allowed).

From the steps, look up to the **hill** that dominates to the east. The city of Nice was first settled there by Greeks (circa 400 B.C.). In the Middle Ages, a massive castle stood there with soldiers at the ready. Over time, the city sprawled down to where you are now. With the river guarding one side (running under today's Promenade du Paillon parkway) and the sea the other, this mountain fortress seemed strong—until Louis XIV leveled it in 1706. Nice's medieval seawall ran along the line of two-story buildings where you're standing.

Now, look across Place Pierre Gautier to the large "palace." The **Ducal Palace** was where the kings of Sardinia, the city's Italian rulers until 1860, resided when in Nice. (For centuries, Nice was under the rule of the Italian capital of Torino.) Today, the palace is the local police headquarters. The land upon which the Cours Saleya sits was once the duke's gardens and didn't become a market until Nice's union with France.

• *Continue down Cours Saleya. The faded golden building that seals the end of the square is where Henri Matisse spent 17 years. I imagine he was inspired by his view. The **Café les Ponchettes** is perfectly positioned for you to enjoy the view too if you want a coffee break. At the café, turn onto...*

❹ Rue de la Poissonnerie

Look up at the first floor of the first building on your right. **Adam and Eve** are squaring off, each holding a zucchini-like gourd. This scene represents the annual rapprochement in Nice to make up for the sins of a too-much-fun Carnival (Mardi Gras, the pre-Lenten festival). Residents of Nice have partied hard during Carnival for more than 700 years. The **spice shop** below offers a fine selection of regional herbs.

As you continue down the street, look above the doors. The iron grills (like the one above #6) allow air to enter the buildings but keep out uninvited guests. You'll see lots of these open grills in Vieux Nice. They were part of a clever system that sucked in cool air from the sea, circulating it through homes and blowing it out through vents in the roof.

A few steps ahead, check out the small **Baroque church** (Notre-Dame de l'Annonciation) dedicated to Ste. Rita, the patron saint of desperate causes and desperate people (see display in window). She holds a special place in locals' hearts, making this the most popular church in Nice. Drop in for a peek at the dazzling Baroque decor. The first chapel on the right is dedicated to St. Erasmus, protector of mariners.

• *Turn right on the next street, where you'll pass Vieux Nice's most happening bar (the recommended* **Distilleries Ideales***), with a pirate-ship cozy interior that buzzes until the wee hours. Pause at the next corner and study the classic Vieux Nice scene in all directions. Now turn left on Rue Droite and enter an area that feels like Little Naples.*

Rue Droite

In the Middle Ages, this straight, skinny street provided the most direct route from river to sea within the old walled town. Pass the recommended restaurant Lacchiardo. Notice stepped lanes leading uphill to the castle. Stop at **Espuno bakery** (at Place du Jésus) and say *"Bonjour,* what's cooking?" to Natalie from England and her husband Fabrice, who's from here. Notice the firewood stacked behind the oven. Ask about their 2017 *Gault & Millau* award and try the house specialty, *tourte aux blettes*—a tart stuffed with Swiss chard, apples, pine nuts, and raisins. Or ask if Fabrice is making scones.

Pop into the Jesuit **Eglise St-Jacques** church (also called Eglise du Gésu) for an explosion of Baroque exuberance hidden behind that plain facade. At the wooden pulpit, notice the crucifix held by a sculpted arm. This clever support allowed the priest to focus on his sermon while reminding the congregation that Christ died for their sins.

We're turning left onto Rue Rossetti...but if you continued another block along Rue Droite you'd find the ❺ **Palais Lascaris** (c. 1647), home of one of Nice's most prestigious families. Today it's a museum and worth a quick look (covered by Nice museum combo-ticket, Wed-Mon 10:00-18:00, from 11:00 off-season, closed Tue year-round). Inside you'll find a collection of antique musical instruments—harps, guitars, violins, and violas (good English explanations)—along with elaborate tapestries and a few well-furnished rooms. The palace has four levels: The ground floor was used for storage, the first floor was devoted to reception rooms (and musical events), the owners lived a floor above that, and the servants lived at the top. Look up and make faces back at the guys under the balconies.

• *Shortly after making a left on Rue Rossetti, you'll cross Rue Benoît Bunico.*

In the 18th century, this street served as a **ghetto** for Nice's Jews. At sunset, gates would seal the street at either end, locking people in until daylight. To identify Jews as non-Christians, the men were required to wear yellow stars and the women to wear yellow scarves. Wander up the street to find the white columns across from #19 that mark what was the synagogue until 1848, when revolution ended the notion of ghettos in France.

• *Continue down Rue Rossetti to...*

NICE

❻ Place Rossetti

The most Italian of Nice's piazzas, Place Rossetti comes alive after dark—in part because of the **Fenocchio gelato shop,** popular for its many innovative flavors.

Check out the **Cathedral of St. Réparate**—an unassuming building for a big-city cathedral. It was relocated here in the 1500s, when Castle Hill was temporarily converted to military use. The name comes from Nice's patron saint, a teenage virgin named Réparate, whose martyred body floated to Nice in the fourth century accompanied by angels (remember the Bay of Angels?). The interior of the cathedral gushes Baroque, a response to the challenge of the Protestant Reformation in the 16th century. With the Catholic Church's Counter-Reformation, the theatrical energy of churches was cranked up with re-energized, high-powered saints and eye-popping decor.

• *This is the end of our walk. From here you can hike up **Castle Hill** (from Place Rossetti, take Rue Rossetti uphill; see Castle Hill listing on page 320). Or you can have an ice cream and browse the colorful lanes of Vieux Nice...or grab Apollo and hit the beach.*

Sights in Nice

▲▲▲PROMENADE DES ANGLAIS
Walking or Biking the Promenade

Enjoying Nice's four-mile seafront promenade on foot or by bike is an essential Riviera experience. Since the days when wealthy Eng-

lish tourists filled the grand seaside hotels, this stretch has been *the* place to be in Nice. (For a self-guided **walk,** see my "Promenade des Anglais Walk" under "Walks in Nice," earlier.)

To rev up the pace of your promenade saunter, rent a **bike** and glide along the coast in either or both directions (about 30 minutes each way; for rental info see page 288). Both of the following paths start along Promenade des Anglais.

To the West: The path stops just before the airport at perhaps the most scenic *boules* courts in France. Pause here to watch the old-timers while away the afternoon tossing shiny metal balls (for more on this game, see page 38).

To the East: The path rounds the hill—passing a scenic promontory and the town's memorial to both world wars—to the harbor of Nice, and gives you a chance to survey some fancy yachts. Walk or pedal around the harbor and follow the coast past the Corsica ferry terminal (you'll need to carry your bike up a flight of steps). From there the path leads to an appealing tree-lined residential district.

Beach

Beaches are free to the public (by law). Settle in on the smooth rocks, or get more comfortable by renting a lounge chair or mattress (*chaise longue* or *transat*-about €15,

umbrella-€5, towel-€5). Have lunch in your bathing suit (€14 salads and pizzas in bars and restaurants all along the beach). I enjoy stopping here first thing in the morning (before the crowds hit) for a peaceful breakfast or café au lait on the Mediterranean. *Plage Publique* signs (with English translations) explain the 10 beach no-nos.

MUSEUMS

A combo-ticket covers all of Nice's museums (except the Chagall Museum); see details under "Helpful Hints" on page 288. The Chagall Museum requires a separate admission (and is well worth it).

The first two museums (Chagall and Matisse) are a long walk northeast of Nice's city center. Because they're in the same direction and served by the same bus line (see "Getting There," below), try to visit them on the same trip. From Place Masséna, the Chagall Museum is a 10-minute bus ride, and the Matisse Museum is a few stops beyond that.

▲▲▲Chagall Museum (Musée National Marc Chagall)

Even if you don't get modern art, this museum—with the world's largest collection of Marc Chagall's work in captivity—is a delight. For fans of Chagall, it's a can't-

miss treat.

After World War II, Chagall returned from the United States to settle first in Vence and later in St-Paul-de-Vence, both not far from Nice. Between 1954 and 1967, he painted a cycle of 17 large murals designed for, and donated to, this museum. These paintings, inspired by the biblical books of Genesis, Exodus, and the Song of Songs, make up the "nave," or core, of what Chagall called the "House of Brotherhood." Combining his Russian and Jewish heritage with the Christian message, he hoped this would be a place where people of all faiths could come together and celebrate love.

Cost and Hours: €8, €2 more during frequent special exhibits; Wed-Mon 10:00-18:00, Nov-April until 17:00, closed Tue year-round; ticket includes helpful audioguide (though Chagall would suggest that you explore his art without guidance); must check daypacks, idyllic **$** café in corner of garden (salads and *plats*), tel. 04 93 53 87 20, http://en.musees-nationaux-alpesmaritimes.fr.

Getting There: The museum is located on Avenue Docteur Ménard. **Taxis** to and from the city center cost about €15. **Buses** connect the museum with downtown Nice and the train station. From downtown, catch bus #15 (Mon-Sat 6/hour, 10 minutes); on Sunday take bus #22. Catch either bus from the east end of the Galeries Lafayette department store, near the Masséna tram stop, on Rue Sacha Guitry (see map on page 308). Watch for a *Musée Chagall* sign on the bus shelter where you'll get off (on Boulevard de Cimiez).

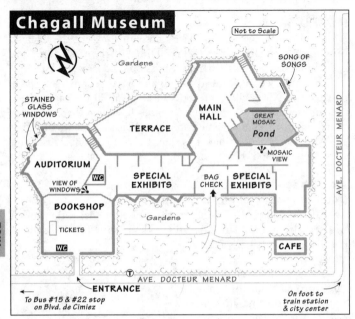

Chagall Museum

Not to Scale

Gardens

SONG OF SONGS

STAINED GLASS WINDOWS

MAIN HALL

GREAT MOSAIC
Pond

TERRACE

MOSAIC VIEW

AUDITORIUM

WC

VIEW OF WINDOWS

SPECIAL EXHIBITS

BAG CHECK

SPECIAL EXHIBITS

BOOKSHOP

TICKETS

Gardens

WC

CAFE

AVE. DOCTEUR MENARD

ENTRANCE

AVE. DOCTEUR MENARD

← To Bus #15 & #22 stop on Blvd. de Cimiez

On foot to train station & city center

NICE

Overview

This small museum consists of six rooms: two rooms (the main hall and Song of Songs room) with the 17 murals, two rooms for special exhibits, an auditorium with stained-glass windows, and a mosaic-lined pond (viewed from inside). It takes about one hour to see the whole thing. In the main hall you'll find the core of the collection (Genesis and Exodus scenes). The adjacent octagonal Song of Songs room houses five more paintings.

At the end of this tour, in the auditorium, you can see a wonderful film about Chagall (52 minutes), which plays at the top of each hour (alternately in French and English—ask about showtimes when you arrive—you may want to see the movie first, then tour the museum; no showings during special exhibits). Even the French version offers a fascinating look at old clips of the master and a chance to see the creative energy and charisma in his eyes.

❂ Self-Guided Tour

• *Buy your ticket, pass through the garden, and enter the museum at the baggage-check counter. Pick up your included audioguide and step into the main hall.*

Main Hall: Old Testament Scenes

Each painting is a lighter-than-air collage of images that draws from Chagall's Russian folk-village youth, his Jewish heritage, the Bible, and his feeling that he existed somewhere between heaven and earth. He believed that the Bible was a synonym for nature, and that both color and biblical themes were key for understanding God's love for his creation. Chagall's brilliant blues and reds celebrate nature, as do his spiritual and folk themes. Notice the focus on couples. To Chagall, humans loving each other mirrored God's love of creation.

The paintings are described below in the order you should see them, going counterclockwise around the room.

Abraham and the Three Angels: In the heat of the day, Abraham looked up and saw three men. He said, "Let a little food and water be brought, so you can be refreshed..." (Genesis 18:1-5)

Abraham refreshes God's angels on this red-hot day and, in return, they promise Abraham a son (in the bubble, at right), thus making him the father of the future Israelite nation.

The Sacrifice of Isaac: Abraham bound his son Isaac and laid him on the altar. Then he took the knife to slay his son. But the angel of the Lord called out to him from heaven, "Abraham!" (Genesis 22:9-11)

Tested by God, Abraham prepares to kill his only son, but the angel stops him in time. Notice that Isaac is posed exactly as Adam is in *The Creation* (described next). Abraham's sacrifice echoes three others: the sacrifice all men must make (Adam, the everyman), the sacrifice of atonement (the goat tied to a tree at left), and even God's sacrifice of his own son (Christ carrying the cross, upper right).

The Creation: God said, "Let us make man in our image, in our likeness..." (Genesis 1:26)

A pure-white angel descends through the blue sky and carries a still-sleeping Adam from radiant red-yellow heaven to earth. Heaven is a whirling dervish of activity, spinning out all the events of future history, from the tablets of the Ten Commandments to the Crucifixion—an overture of many images that we'll see in later paintings. (Though not a Christian, Chagall saw the Crucifixion as a universal symbol of man's suffering.)

Moses Receives the Ten Commandments: The Lord gave him the two tablets of the Law, the tablets of stone inscribed by the finger of God... (Exodus 31:18)

An astonished Moses stretches toward heaven, where God

Chagall's Style

Chagall uses a deceptively simple, almost childlike style to paint a world that's hidden to the eye—the magical, mystical world below the surface. Here are some of the characteristics of his paintings:

Deep, radiant colors, inspired by Expressionism and Fauvism (an art movement pioneered by Matisse and other French painters).

Personal imagery, particularly from his childhood in Russia—smiling barnyard animals, fiddlers on the roof, flower bouquets, huts, and blissful sweethearts.

A Hasidic Jewish perspective, the idea that God is everywhere, appearing in everyday things like nature, animals, and humdrum activities.

A fragmented Cubist style, multifaceted and multidimensional, a perfect style to mirror the complexity of God's creation.

Overlapping images, like double-exposure photography, with faint imagery that bleeds through, suggesting there's more to life under the surface.

Stained-glass-esque technique of dark, deep, earthy, "potent" colors, and simplified, iconic, symbolic figures.

Gravity-defying compositions, with lovers, animals, and angels twirling blissfully in midair.

Happy (not tragic) mood depicting a world of personal joy, despite the violence and turmoil of world wars and revolution.

Childlike simplicity, drawn with simple, heavy outlines, filled in with Crayola colors that often spill over the lines. Major characters in a scene are bigger than the lesser characters. The grinning barnyard animals, the bright colors, the magical events presented as literal truth...Was Chagall a lightweight? Or a lighter-than-air-weight?

reaches out from a cloud to hand him the Ten Commandments. While Moses tilts one way, Mount Sinai slants the other, leading our eye up to the left, where a golden calf is being worshipped by the wayward Children of Israel. But down to the right, Aaron and the menorah assure us that Moses will set things right. In this radiant final panel, the Jewish tradition—after a long struggle—is finally established.

• *Skip around the corner to...*

Driven from Paradise: So God banished him from the Garden of Eden...and placed cherubim and a flaming sword to guard the way... (Genesis 3:23-24)

An angel drives them out with a fire hose of blue (there's Adam still cradling his flaming-red *coq*), while a sparkling yellow, flower-filled tree stands like a wall preventing them from ever returning. Deep in the green colors, the painting offers us glimpses of the future—Eve giving birth (lower-right corner) and the yellow sacrificial goat of atonement (top right).

Paradise: God put him in the Garden of Eden...and said, "You must not eat from the tree of the knowledge of good and evil..." (Genesis 2:15-17)

Paradise is a rich, earth-as-seen-from-space pool of blue, green, and white. On the left, amoebic, still-evolving animals float around Adam (celibately practicing yoga) and Eve (with lusty-red hair). On the right, an angel guards the tempting tree, but Eve offers an apple and Adam reaches around to sample the forbidden fruit while the snake gawks knowingly.

The Rainbow: God said, "I have set my rainbow in the clouds as a sign of the covenant between me and the earth." (Genesis 9:13)

A flaming angel sets the rainbow in the sky, while Noah rests beneath it and his family offers a sacrifice of thanks. The pure-white rainbow's missing colors are found radiating from the features of the survivors.

Jacob's Ladder: He had a dream in which he saw a ladder resting on the earth with its top reaching to heaven, and the angels of God were ascending and descending on it... (Genesis 28:12)

In the left half, Jacob (Abraham's grandson, in red) slumps asleep and dreams of a ladder between heaven and earth. On the right, a lofty angel with a menorah represents how heaven and earth are bridged by the rituals of the Jewish tradition.

Jacob Wrestles with an Angel: So Jacob wrestled with him till daybreak. Jacob said, "I will not let you go unless you bless me..." (Genesis 32: 24, 26)

Jacob holds on while the angel blesses him with descendants (the Children of Israel) and sends out rays from his hands. On the right are scenes from Jacob's life, including his son Joseph being stripped of his bright-red coat and sold into slavery by his brothers.

Noah's Ark: Then he sent out a dove to see if the water had receded... (Genesis 8:8)

Adam and Eve's descendants have become so wicked that God destroys the earth with a flood, engulfing the sad crowd on the right. Only righteous Noah (center), his family (lower right), and the animals (including our yellow goat) are spared inside an ark. Here Noah opens the ark's window and sends out a dove to test the waters.

Moses Brings Water from the Rock: The Lord said, "Strike the rock, and water will come out of it for the people to drink..." (Exodus 17:5-6)

Marc Chagall (1887-1985)

1887-1910: Russia

Chagall is born in the small town of Vitebsk, Belarus. He's the oldest of nine children in a traditional Russian Hasidic Jewish family.

He studies realistic art in his hometown. In St. Petersburg, he is first exposed to the Modernist work of Paul Cézanne and the Fauves.

1910-1914: Paris

A patron finances a four-year stay in Paris. Chagall hobnobs with the avant-garde and learns technique from the Cubists, but he never abandons painting recognizable figures or his own personal fantasies. (Some say his relative poverty forced him to paint over used canvases, which gave him the idea of overlapping images that bleed through. Hmm.)

1914-1922: Russia

Returning to his hometown, Chagall marries Bella Rosenfeld (1915), whose love will inspire him for decades. He paints happy scenes despite the turmoil of wars and the Communist Revolution. Moving to Moscow (1920), he paints his first large-scale works, sets for the New Jewish Theater. These would inspire many of his later large-scale works.

In the brown desert, Moses nourishes his thirsty people with water miraculously spouting from a rock. From the (red-yellow) divine source, it rains down actual (blue) water, but also a gush of spiritual yellow light.

Moses and the Burning Bush: The angel of the Lord appeared to him in flames of fire from within a bush... (Exodus 3:2)

Horned Moses—Chagall depicts him according to a medieval tradition—kneels awestruck before the burning bush, the event that calls him to God's service. On the left, we see Moses after the call, his face radiant, leading the Israelites out of captivity across the Red Sea, while Pharaoh's men drown (lower half of Moses' robe). The Ten Commandments loom ahead.

• *Return to Moses Receives the Ten Commandments, then walk past a window into a room with five red paintings.*

Song of Songs

Chagall wrote, "I've been fascinated by the Bible ever since my earliest childhood. I have always thought of it as the most extraordinary source of poetic inspiration imaginable. As far as I am concerned, perfection in art and in life has its source in the Bible, and

1923-1941: France and Palestine

Chagall returns to France. In 1931 he travels to Palestine, where the bright sun and his Jewish roots inspire a series of gouaches (opaque watercolor paintings). These gouaches would later inspire 105 etchings to illustrate the Bible (1931-1952), which would eventually influence the 17 large canvases of biblical scenes in the Chagall Museum (1954-1967).

1941-1947: United States/World War II

Fearing persecution for his Jewish faith, Chagall emigrates to New York, where he spends the war years. The Crucifixion starts to appear in his paintings—not as a Christian symbol, but as a representation of the violence mankind perpetrates on itself. In 1944 his beloved Bella dies, and he stops painting for months.

1947-1985: South of France

After the war, Chagall returns to France, eventually settling in St-Paul-de-Vence. In 1952 he remarries. His new love, Valentina Brodsky, plus the southern sunshine, brings Chagall a revived creativity—he is extremely prolific for the rest of his life. He experiments with new techniques and media—ceramics, sculpture, book illustrations, tapestry, and mosaic. In 1956 he's commissioned for his first stained-glass project. Eventually he does windows for cathedrals in Metz and Reims, and a synagogue in Jerusalem (1960). The Chagall Museum opens in 1973.

NICE

exercises in the mechanics of the merely rational are fruitless. In art as well as in life, anything is possible, provided there is love."

The paintings in this room were inspired by the Old Testament Song of Songs. Chagall cherished verses such as: I sleep, but

my heart is awake (5:2). Until the day breaks and the shadows flee, turn, my lover, and be like a gazelle or like a young stag on the rugged hills (2:17). Your stature is like that of the palm, and your breasts like clusters of fruit (7:7). Chagall, who dedicated this room to his wife Valentina (Vava), saw divine love and physical love as a natural mix.

Chagall enjoyed the love of two women in his long life—his first wife, Bella, then Valentina, who gave him a second wind as he was painting these late works. Chagall was one of the few "serious" 20th-century artists to portray unabashed love. Where the Bible uses the metaphor of earthly, physical, sexual love to describe God's love for humans, Chagall uses unearthly colors and a mystical ambience to celebrate human love. These red-toned canvases are hard to interpret literally, but they capture the rosy spirit of a man in love with life.

• *Head back toward the entry and turn left at The Sacrifice of Isaac to find...*

The Pond

The great mosaic (which no longer reflects in the filthy reflecting pond) evokes the prophet Elijah in his chariot of fire (from the Second Book of Kings)—with Chagall's addition of the 12 signs of the zodiac, which he used to symbolize Time.

• *Return to the main hall, veer left, and exit the hall to the right. Pass through the exhibition room with temporary displays. At the end, you'll find...*

The Auditorium

This room, where the Chagall documentary film shows (see "Overview," earlier), is worth a peaceful moment to enjoy three Chagall stained-glass windows depicting the seven days of creation (right to left): the creation of light, elements, and planets (a visual big bang that's four "days" wide); the creation of animals, plants, man and woman, and the ordering of the solar system (two "days" wide, complete with fish and birds still figuring out where they belong); and the day of rest (the narrowest—only one "day" wide, imagine angels singing to the glory of God).

• *Our tour is over. From here, you can return to downtown Nice or the train station area, or head to the Matisse Museum. **Taxis** usually wait in front of the museum. For the **bus** back to downtown Nice, turn right out of the museum, then make another right down Boulevard de Cimiez, and ride bus #15 or #22 heading downhill. To continue to the Matisse Museum, catch #15 or #22 using the uphill stop located across the street, or enjoy a 20-minute walk uphill passing belle-époque villas at every turn.*

*To **walk** to the train station area from the museum (20 minutes), turn left out of the museum grounds on Avenue Docteur Ménard, and follow the street to the left at the first intersection, continuing to hug the museum grounds. Where the street curves right (by #32), take the ramps and staircases down on your left, turn left at the bottom, cross under the freeway and the train tracks, then turn right on Boulevard Raimbaldi.*

Nice's Other Museums

▲Matisse Museum (Musée Matisse)

This small, underachieving museum fills an old mansion in a park surrounded by scant Roman ruins, and houses a limited sampling of works from the various periods of Henri Matisse's artistic career. The museum offers an introduction to the artist's many styles and materials, both shaped by Mediterranean light and by fellow Côte d'Azur artists Picasso and Renoir.

Cost and Hours: Covered by €10 Nice museum combo-ticket; Wed-Mon 10:00-18:00, mid-Oct-mid-June from 11:00, closed Tue year-round, 164 Avenue des Arènes de Cimiez, tel. 04 93 81 08 08, www.musee-matisse-nice.org.

Getting There: Take a cab (€20 from Promenade des Anglais). Alternatively, hop bus #15 Mon-Sat or #22 on Sun; both leave from the east end of Galeries Lafayette (from train station catch #17). Get off at the Arènes-Matisse bus stop (look for the crumbling Roman arena that once held 10,000 spectators), then walk 50 yards into the park to find the pink villa.

Background: Henri Matisse, the master of leaving things out, could suggest a woman's body with a single curvy line—letting the viewer's mind fill in the rest. Ignoring traditional 3-D perspective, he expressed his passion for life through simplified but recognizable scenes in which dark outlines and saturated, bright blocks of color create an overall decorative pattern.

Matisse understood how colors and shapes affect us emotionally. He could create either shocking, clashing works (early Fauvism) or geometrical, balanced, harmonious ones (later cutouts). Whereas other modern artists reveled in purely abstract design, Matisse (almost) always kept the subject matter at least vaguely recognizable. He used unreal colors and distorted lines not just to portray what an object looks like, but to express its inner nature (even inanimate objects). Meditating on his paintings helps you connect with life—or so Matisse hoped.

As you tour the museum, look for Matisse's favorite motifs—including fruit, flowers, wallpaper, and sunny rooms—often with a window opening onto a sunny landscape. Another favorite subject is the *odalisque* (harem concubine), usually shown sprawled in a seductive pose and with a simplified, masklike face. You'll also see a few souvenirs from his travels, which influenced much of his work.

Visiting the Museum: The museum is in a constant state of flux, so expect changes from this description. The entrance should be moved to the basement floor by the time you arrive. The wall-hanging—Matisse's colorful paper cutout *Flowers and Fruits*—makes a fine introduction to his decorative art and shouts, "Riviera!" The basement also has a room devoted to two 25-foot-long watery cutouts for an uncompleted pool project *(La Piscine)* for the city of Nice, which shows his abiding love of deep blue.

On the mezzanine above, leaf through discarded cutouts from various papier-mâché works and find black-and-white photos of the artist at work and play.

Rooms on the street level usually contain paintings from Matisse's formative years as a student (1890s) and are the high-

Henri Matisse (1869-1954)

Here's an outline of Henri Matisse's busy life:

1880s and 1890s: At age 20, Matisse, a budding lawyer, is struck down with appendicitis. Bedridden for a year, he turns to painting as a healing escape from pain and boredom. After recovering, he studies art in Paris and produces dark-colored, realistic still lifes and landscapes. His work is exhibited at the Salons of 1896 and 1897.

1897-1905: Influenced by the Impressionists, he experiments with sunnier scenes and brighter colors. He travels to southern France, including Collioure (on the coast near Spain), and seeks still more light-filled scenes to paint. His experiments are influenced by Vincent van Gogh's bright, surrealistic colors and thick outlines, and by Paul Gauguin's primitive visions of a Tahitian paradise. From Paul Cézanne, he learns how to simplify objects into their basic geometric shapes. He also experiments (like Cézanne) with creating the illusion of 3-D not by traditional means, but by using contrasting colors for the foreground and background.

1905: Back in Paris, Matisse and his colleagues (André Derain and Maurice de Vlaminck) shock the art world with an exhibition of their experimental paintings. The thick outlines, simple forms, flattened perspective, and—most of all—bright, clashing, unrealistic colors seem to be the work of "wild animals" (fauves). Fauvism is hot, and Matisse is instantly famous. (Though notorious as a "wild animal," Matisse himself was a gentle, introspective man.)

1906-1910: After just a year, Fauvism is out, and African masks are in. This "primitive" art form inspires Matisse to simplify and distort his figures further, making them less realistic but more expressive.

1910-1917: Matisse creates his masterpiece paintings. Cubism is the rage, pioneered by Matisse's friend and rival for the World's Best Painter award, Pablo Picasso. Matisse dabbles in Cubism, simplifying forms, emphasizing outline, and muting his colors. But

light of the museum for me. Notice how quickly his work evolves: from dark still lifes (nature mortes), to colorful Impressionist scenes, to more abstract works, all in the matter of a few years. Find the translation of his "Découverte de la Lumière" (discovery of light), which the Riviera (and his various travels to sun-soaked places like Corsica, Collioure, and Tahiti) brought to his art. To appreciate the speed of change in his painting, notice the dramatic differences in his portraits of Madame Matisse, painted just five years apart.

Other rooms on this floor (or nearby) highlight Matisse's fasci-

ultimately it proves to be too austere and analytical for his deeply sensory nature. The Cubist style is most evident in his sculpture.

1920s: Burned out from years of intense experimentation, Matisse moves to Nice (spending winters there from 1917, settling permanently in 1921). Luxuriating under the bright sun, he's reborn, and he paints colorful, sensual, highly decorative works. Harem concubines lounging in their sunny, flowery apartments epitomize the lush life.

1930s: A visit to Tahiti inspires more scenes of life as a sunny paradise. Matisse experiments with bolder lines, swirling arabesques, and decorative patterns.

1940s: Duodenal cancer (in 1941) requires Matisse to undergo two operations and confines him to a wheelchair for the rest of his life. Working at an easel becomes a struggle for him, and he largely stops painting in 1941. But as World War II ends, Matisse emerges with renewed energy. Now in his 70s, he explores a new medium: paper cutouts pasted onto a watercolored surface (découpage on gouache-prepared surface). The technique plays to his strengths—the cutouts are essentially blocks of bright color (mostly blue) with a strong outline. Scissors in hand, Matisse says, "I draw straight into the color." (His doctor advises him to wear dark glasses to protect his weak eyes against the bright colors he chooses.) In 1947, Matisse's book *Jazz* is published, featuring the artist's joyful cutouts of simple figures. Like jazz music, the book is a celebration of artistic spontaneity. And like music in general, Matisse's works balance different tones and colors to create a mood.

1947-1951: Matisse's nurse becomes a Dominican nun in Vence. To thank her for her care, he spends his later years designing a chapel there. He oversees every aspect of the Chapel of the Rosary (Chapelle du Rosaire) at Vence, from the stained glass to the altar to the colors of the priest's robe (see page 423). Though Matisse is not a strong Christian, the church exudes his spirit of celebrating life and sums up his work.

1954: Matisse dies.

NICE

nation with dance and the female body. You'll see pencil and charcoal drawings, and a handful of bronze busts; he was fascinated by sculpture. *The Acrobat*—painted only two years before Matisse's death—shows the artist at his minimalist best.

The floor above features sketches and models of Matisse's famous Chapel of the Rosary in nearby Vence (see page 423) and related religious works. On the same floor, you may find paper cutouts from his *Jazz* or *Dance* series, more bronze sculptures, various personal objects, and linen embroideries inspired by his travels to Polynesia.

Leaving the Museum: Turn left from the museum into the park, exiting at the Archaeological Museum, and turn right at the street. The bus stop across the street is for bus #17, which goes to the train station, and #20, which heads to the port. For buses #15 and #22 (frequent service to downtown and the Chagall Museum), continue walking—with the Roman ruins on your right—to the small roundabout, and find the shelter (facing downhill).

Modern and Contemporary Art Museum
(Musée d'Art Moderne et d'Art Contemporain)

This ultramodern museum features an explosively colorful, far-out, yet manageable collection focused on American and European-American artists from the 1960s and 1970s (Pop Art and New Realism are highlighted; see page 281 for an overview of modern art on the Riviera). The exhibits cover three floors and include a few works by Andy Warhol, Roy Lichtenstein, and Jean Tinguely, and images of Christo's famous wrappings. You'll find rooms dedicated to Robert Indiana, Yves Klein, and Niki de Saint Phalle. The temporary exhibits can be as appealing to modern-art lovers as the permanent collection: Check the museum website for what's playing. Don't leave without exploring the views from the rooftop terrace.

Cost and Hours: Covered by €10 Nice museum combo-ticket, Tue-Sun 10:00-18:00, mid-Oct-mid-June from 11:00, closed Mon year-round, near Vieux Nice on Promenade des Arts, tel. 04 93 62 61 62, www.mamac-nice.org.

Fine Arts Museum (Musée des Beaux-Arts)

Housed in a sumptuous Riviera villa with lovely gardens, this museum lacks a compelling collection but holds 6,000 artworks from the 17th to 20th centuries. Start on the first floor and work your way up to enjoy paintings by Monet, Sisley, Bonnard, and Raoul Dufy, as well as a few sculptures by Rodin and Carpeaux.

Cost and Hours: Covered by €10 Nice museum combo-ticket, Tue-Sun 10:00-18:00, mid-Oct-mid-June from 11:00, closed Mon year-round, inconveniently located at the western end of Nice, take bus #12 from train station to Rosa Bonheur stop and walk to 3 Avenue des Baumettes; tel. 04 92 15 28 28, www.musee-beaux-arts-nice.org.

Archaeological Museum (Musée Archéologique)

This museum displays various objects from the Romans' occupation of this region. It's convenient—just below the Matisse Museum—but is of little interest except to ancient Rome aficionados (scant information in English). Entry includes access to the poorly maintained Roman bath ruins (ask for the English handout).

Cost and Hours: Covered by €10 Nice museum combo-ticket, Wed-Mon 11:00-18:00, closed Tue, near Matisse Museum at 160 Avenue des Arènes de Cimiez, tel. 04 93 81 59 57.

Masséna Museum (Musée Masséna)

Like Nice's main square, this museum was named in honor of Jean-André Masséna (born in Antibes), a highly regarded commander during France's Revolutionary and Napoleonic wars. The beach-front mansion is worth a look for its lavish decor and lovely gardens alone (no English labels in museum, but a €3 booklet in English is available).

Cost and Hours: Covered by €10 Nice museum combo-ticket, always free to enter gardens, Wed-Mon 10:00-18:00, mid-Oct–mid-June from 11:00, closed Tue year-round, 35 Promenade des Anglais, tel. 04 93 91 19 10.

Visiting the Museum: There are three levels. The elaborate reception rooms on the ground floor host occasional exhibits and give the best feeling for aristocratic Nice from 1860, when it joined France, until World War I (find Masséna's portrait to the right).

The first floor up, offering a folk-museum-like look at Nice through the years, deserves most of your time. Moving counter-clockwise around the floor, you'll find Napoleonic paraphernalia, Josephine's impressive cape and tiara, and Napoleon's vest. Next, you'll find bric-a-brac of the aristocracy and antique posters promoting vacations in Nice—look for the model and photos of the long-gone La Jetée Promenade and its casino, Nice's first. You'll see paintings of some of the Russian and British nobility who appreciated Nice's climate, and images of the city before the Promenade des Anglais was built and the town's river was covered over by Place Masséna. You'll also find paintings honoring Italian patriot and Nice favorite Giuseppe Garibaldi. The top floor is a painting gallery with temporary exhibits.

OTHER SIGHTS IN NICE
▲Russian Cathedral (Cathédrale Russe)

Nice's Russian Orthodox church—claimed by some to be the finest outside Russia—is worth a visit. Five hundred rich Russian families wintered in Nice in the late 19th century, and they needed a worthy Orthodox house of worship. Czar Nicholas I's widow provided the land and Czar Nicholas

II gave this church to the Russian community in 1912. (A few years later, Russian comrades who *didn't* winter on the Riviera assassinated him.) Here in the land of olives and anchovies, these proud onion domes seem odd. But, I imagine, so did those old Russians.

Cost and Hours: Free; daily 9:00-18:00 except during services, chanted services Sat at 18:00, Sun at 10:00; no tourist visits during services, no shorts, Avenue Nicolas II, tel. 04 93 96 88 02, www.sobor.fr.

Getting There: It's a 10-minute walk from the train station. Head west on Avenue Thiers, turn right on Avenue Gambetta, then look for signs. Or take any bus heading west from the station on Avenue Thiers and get off at Avenue Gambetta.

Visiting the Cathedral: Pick up an English info sheet on your way in. The one-room interior is filled with icons and candles, and traditional Russian music adds to the ambience. The wall of icons (iconostasis) divides the spiritual realm from the temporal world of the worshippers. Only the priest can walk between the two worlds, by using the "Royal Door."

Take a close look at items lining the front (starting in the left corner). The angel with red boots and wings—the protector of the Romanov family—stands over a symbolic tomb of Christ. The tall black hammered-copper cross commemorates the massacre of Nicholas II and his family in 1918. Notice the Jesus icon to the right of the Royal Door. According to a priest here, as worshippers meditate, staring deep into the eyes of Jesus, they enter a lake where they find their souls. Surrounded by incense, chanting, and your entire community...it could happen. Farther to the right, the icon of the Virgin and Child is decorated with semiprecious stones from the Ural Mountains. Artists worked a triangle into each iconic face—symbolic of the Trinity.

Nearby: The park around the church stays open at lunch and makes a fine setting for picnics.

▲Castle Hill (Colline du Château)

This hill—in an otherwise flat city center—offers sensational views over Nice, the port (to the east, created for trade and military use in the 15th century), the foothills of the Alps, and the Mediterranean. The views are best early, at sunset, or whenever the weather's clear.

Nice was founded on this hill. Its residents were crammed onto the hilltop until the 12th century, as it was too risky to live in the flatlands below. Today you'll find a playground, a café, and a cemetery—but no castle—on Castle Hill.

Cost and Hours: Park is free and closes at 20:00 in summer, earlier off-season.

Getting There: You can get to the top by foot, by elevator (free, daily April-Sept 9:00-19:00, until 20:00 in summer, Oct-March 10:00-18:00, next to beachfront Hôtel Suisse), or by pricey tourist train (see page 290).

See the "Promenade des Anglais Walk" on page 292 for a pleasant stroll that ends near Castle Hill.

Leaving Castle Hill: After enjoying the views and hilltop fun, you can walk via the cemetery directly down into Vieux Nice (just follow the signs), descend to the beach (via the elevator or a stepped lane next to it), or hike down the back side to Nice's port (departure point for boat trips and buses to Monaco and Ville-franche-sur-Mer).

EXCURSION FROM NICE
Narrow-Gauge Train into the Alps
(Chemins de Fer de Provence)

Leave the tourists behind and take the scenic train-bus-train combination that runs between Nice and Digne through canyons, along whitewater rivers, and through

tempting villages (4/day, departs Nice from Chemins de Fer de Provence Station, two blocks from the Libération tram stop, 4 Rue Alfred Binet, tel. 04 97 03 80 80, www. trainprovence.com).

An appealing stop on the scenic railway is little **Entrevaux,** a good destination that feels forgotten and still stuck in its medieval shell (about €25 round-trip, 1.5 scenic hours from Nice). Cross the bridge, meet someone friendly, and consider the steep hike up to the citadel (€3, TI tel. 04 93 05 45 73). Sisteron's Romanesque church and the view from the citadel above make this town worth a visit.

Nightlife in Nice

The city is a walker's delight after dark. Promenade des Anglais, Cours Saleya, Vieux Nice, Promenade du Paillon, and Place Mas-séna are all worth an evening wander. I can't get enough of the night scene on Place Masséna and around the adjacent fountains.

Nice's bars play host to a happening late-night scene, filled with jazz, rock, and trolling singles. Most activity focuses on Vieux Nice. Rue de la Préfecture and Place du Palais are ground zero for bar life, though Place Rossetti and Rue Droite are also good targets. **Distilleries Ideales** is a good place to start or end your evening, with a lively international crowd, a *Pirates of the Caribbean* interior, and a *Cheers* vibe (15 beers on tap, where Rue de la Poissonnerie and Rue Barillerie meet, happy hour 18:00-21:00). **Wayne's Bar** and others nearby are happening spots for the younger, Franco-Anglo backpacker crowd (15 Rue Préfecture; see map on page 328 for both bar locations). Along the Promenade des Anglais, the classy Le Relais bar at **Hôtel Negresco** is fancy-cigar old English with frequent live jazz.

Sleeping in Nice

Don't look for charm in Nice. Seek out a good location and modern, reliable amenities (like air-conditioning). The price rankings given here are for April through October. Prices generally drop considerably November through March, but go sky-high during the Nice Carnival (in February), the Cannes Film Festival (May), and Monaco's Grand Prix (late May). Between the film festival and the Grand Prix, the second half of May is slammed. Nice is also one of Europe's top convention cities, and June is convention month here.

I've divided my sleeping recommendations into three areas: city center, Vieux Nice, and near the Promenade des Anglais. Those in the city center are between the train station and Place Masséna (easy access to the train station and Vieux Nice via the tram, 15-minute walk to Promenade des Anglais). Those in Vieux Nice are between Place Masséna and the sea (east of the parkway, good access to the sea at Quai des Etats-Unis). And those near the Promenade des Anglais are between Boulevard Victor Hugo and the sea (a classier and quieter area, offering better access to the sea but longer walks to the train station and Vieux Nice).

For parking, ask your hotelier, or see "Arrival in Nice—By Car" on page 285.

IN THE CITY CENTER

The train station area offers Nice's cheapest sleeps, but the neighborhood feels sketchy after dark. The cheapest places are older, well-worn, and come with some street noise. Places closer to Avenue Jean Médecin are more expensive and in a more comfortable area.

$$$$ Hôtel du Petit Palais is a little belle-époque jewel with 25 handsome rooms tucked neatly into a residential area on the hill several blocks from the Chagall Museum. It's bird-chirping peaceful and plush, with tastefully designed rooms, a garden terrace, and small pool. You'll walk 15 minutes down to Vieux Nice (or use bus #15), free street parking is usually easy to find (17 Avenue Emile Bieckert, tel. 04 93 62 19 11, www.petitpalaisnice.com, reservation@petitpalaisnice.com).

$$$ Hôtel Vendôme*** gives you a whiff of the belle époque, with pink pastels, high ceilings, and grand staircases in a mansion set off the street. The modern rooms come in all sizes; many have balconies (limited pay parking—first-come, first-served, 26 Rue Pastorelli at the corner of Rue Alberti, tel. 04 93 62 00 77, www.hotel-vendome-nice.com, contact@vendome-hotel-nice.com).

$$ Hôtel Durante*** rents quiet rooms in a happy, orange building with rooms wrapped around a flowery courtyard. All but two of rooms overlook the well-maintained patio. The rooms have adequate comfort (mostly modern decor), the price is right, and the parking is free on a first-come, first-served basis (family rooms, 16 Avenue Durante, tel. 04 93 88 84 40, www.hotel-durante.com, info@hotel-durante.com).

$$ Hôtel St. Georges, ** five blocks from the station toward the sea, offers a good location, a pleasant backyard patio, and friendly Houssein at the reception. Rooms are dark and basic but adequate and fairly priced (family rooms, limited parking—book ahead, 7 Avenue Georges Clemenceau, tel. 04 93 88 79 21, www.hotelsaintgeorges.fr, contact@hotelsaintgeorges.fr).

$$ Hôtel Ibis Nice Centre Gare, *** 100 yards to the right as you leave the station, provides a secure refuge in this seedy area. It's big (200 rooms), modern, and a decent value with well-configured rooms, a refreshing pool, and cheap overnight parking (bar, café, 14 Avenue Thiers, tel. 04 93 88 85 85, www.ibishotel.com, h1396@accor.com).

$ Hôtel Belle Meunière, * in an old mansion built for Napoleon III's mistress, attracts budget-minded travelers with cheap rates a block below the train station. Simple but well-kept, the place has adequate rooms and charismatic Mademoiselle Marie-Pierre presiding with her perfect English (family rooms, air-con, no elevator, laundry service, limited pay parking, 21 Avenue Durante, tel. 04 93 88 66 15, www.bellemeuniere.com, hotel.belle.meuniere@cegetel.net).

$ B&B Nice Home Sweet Home is a good budget value. Laid-back Genevieve (a.k.a. Jennifer) Levert rents out four large rooms and one small single in her home. Her rooms (only one has a private bath) are simply decorated, with high ceilings, big windows, and space to spread out (cheaper rooms with shared bath, includes breakfast, elevator, one floor up, pay washer/dryer, kitchen access, 35 Rue Rossini at intersection with Rue Auber, mobile 06 50 83 25 85, www.nicehomesweethome.com, glevert@free.fr).

Hostel: The fun, good-value ¢ **Auberge de Jeunesse les Camélias** has a handy location, modern facilities, and lively evening

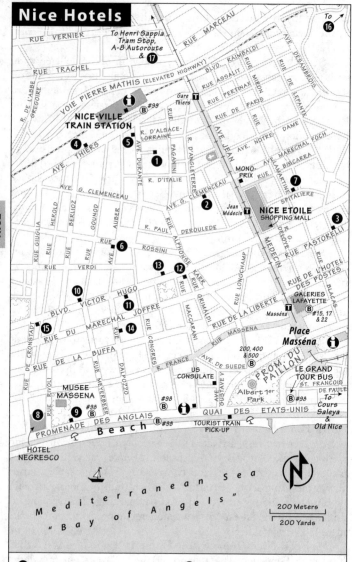

Nice Hotels

NICE

1 Hôtel Vendôme
2 Hôtel Durante
3 Hôtel St. Georges
4 Hôtel Ibis Nice Centre Gare
5 Hôtel Belle Meunière
6 B&B Nice Home Sweet Home
7 Auberge de Jeunesse les Camélias Hostel
8 Hôtel Negresco
9 Hôtel West End
10 Hôtels Splendid & Gounod
11 Hôtel Villa Victoria
12 Hôtel Le Grimaldi
13 Hôtel Carlton
14 Hôtel les Cigales
15 Hôtel Victor Hugo
16 To Hôtel du Petit Palais
17 To Chemins de Fer Station

atmosphere. Rooms accommodate four to eight people and come with showers and sinks—WCs are down the hall (includes breakfast, rooms closed 11:00-15:00 but can leave bags, laundry, kitchen, safes, bar, 3 Rue Spitalieri, tel. 04 93 62 15 54, www.hihostels.com, accueil.nice@hifrance.org).

NEAR THE PROMENADE DES ANGLAIS
These hotels are close to the beach. The Negresco and West End are big, vintage Nice hotels that open onto the sea from the heart of the Promenade des Anglais.

$$$$ Hôtel Negresco***** owns Nice's most prestigious address on the Promenade des Anglais and knows it. Still, it's the kind of place that if you were to splurge just once in your life... Rooms are opulent (see page 293 for more description), tips are expected, and it seems the women staying here have cosmetically augmented lips (some view rooms, Old World bar, 37 Promenade des Anglais, tel. 04 93 16 64 00, www.hotel-negresco-nice.com, reservations@hotel-negresco.com).

$$$$ Hôtel West End**** opens onto the Promenade des Anglais with formal service and decor, classy public spaces, and high prices (some view rooms, 31 Promenade des Anglais, tel. 04 92 14 44 00, www.hotel-westend.com, reservation@westsendnice. com).

$$$$ Hôtel Splendid**** is a worthwhile splurge if you miss your Marriott. The panoramic rooftop pool, bar/restaurant, and breakfast room almost justify the cost...but throw in plush rooms, a free gym, and spa services, and you're as good as at home (pricey pay parking, 50 Boulevard Victor Hugo, tel. 04 93 16 41 00, www. splendid-nice.com, info@splendid-nice.com).

$$$$ Hôtel Villa Victoria**** is a fine place managed by cheery and efficient Marlena and her staff, who welcome travelers into a spotless, classy old building with a spacious, attractive lobby overlooking a sprawling garden-courtyard. Rooms are plush and well-kept (pay parking, 33 Boulevard Victor Hugo, tel. 04 93 88 39 60, www.villa-victoria.com, contact@villa-victoria.com).

$$$$ Le Grimaldi**** is a traditional place with an appealing lobby, renting 48 spacious rooms with high ceilings and tasteful decor (big breakfast extra, a few suites and connecting rooms ideal for families, 15 Rue Grimaldi, tel. 04 93 16 00 24, www. le-grimaldi.com, info@le-grimaldi.com).

$$$ Hôtel Gounod*** is behind Hôtel Splendid. Because the two share the same owners, Gounod's guests are allowed free access to Splendid's pool, hot tub, and other amenities. Most rooms are quiet, with high ceilings but tired bathrooms (family rooms, pay parking, 3 Rue Gounod, tel. 04 93 16 42 00, www.gounod-nice.com, info@gounod-nice.com).

$$ Hôtel Carlton*** is well-run, unpretentious, and comfortable (26 Boulevard Victor Hugo, tel. 04 93 88 87 83, www.hotel-carlton-nice.com, info@hotel-carlton-nice.com).

$$ Hôtel les Cigales,*** a few blocks from the Promenade des Anglais, is a sweet little pastel place with 19 sharp rooms and a nifty upstairs terrace, all well-managed by friendly Veronique and Elaine (RS%, 16 Rue Dalpozzo, tel. 04 97 03 10 70, www.hotel-lescigales.com, info@hotel-lescigales.com).

$ Hôtel Victor Hugo, a traditional and spotless seven-room hotel, is an adorable time-warp place where Gilles warmly welcomes guests. It's a short walk from the Promenade des Anglais, but a hefty walk from Vieux Nice. All rooms come with mini kitchenettes (RS%, includes breakfast, 59 Boulevard Victor Hugo, tel. 04 93 88 12 39, www.hotel-victor-hugo-nice.com).

IN OR NEAR VIEUX NICE

Most of these hotels are either on the sea or within an easy walk of it. (Hôtel Lafayette and the Villa Saint Exupéry Beach hostel are more central).

$$$$ Hôtel la Perouse,*** built into the rock of Castle Hill at the east end of the bay, is a fine splurge. This refuge-hotel is top-to-bottom flawless in every detail—from its elegant rooms (satin curtains, velour headboards) and attentive staff to its rooftop terrace with hot tub, sleek pool, and lovely **$$$$** garden restaurant. Sleep here to be spoiled and escape the big city (good family options, 11 Quai Rauba Capeu, tel. 04 93 62 34 63, www.hotel-la-perouse.com, lp@hotel-la-perouse.com).

$$$$ Hôtel Suisse,*** below Castle Hill, has Nice's best sea and city views for the money, and is surprisingly quiet given the busy street below. Rooms are comfortable and the decor is tasteful. Sleep elsewhere if you don't land a view (most view rooms have balconies, 15 Quai Rauba Capeu, tel. 04 92 17 39 00, www.hotels-ocre-azur.com, hotel.suisse@hotels-ocre-azur.com).

$$$ Hôtel Albert 1er*** is a fair deal in a great location on Albert I Park, two blocks from the beach and Place Masséna. The staff is formal and the rooms are well-appointed, with heavy brown tones. Some have views of the bay, others overlook the park, and some have small decks (4 Avenue des Phocéens, tel. 04 93 85 74 01, www.hotel-albert-1er.com, info@hotel-albert1er.com).

$$$ Hôtel Mercure Marché aux Fleurs**** is ideally situated near the sea and Cours Saleya. Rooms are sharp, standard doubles are tight, and prices can be either reasonable or exorbitant (superior rooms worth the extra euros—especially those with views, 91 Quai des Etats-Unis, tel. 04 93 85 74 19, www.hotelmercure.com, h0962@accor.com).

$$ Hôtel de la Mer**** is an intimate, 12-room place with an enviable position overlooking Place Masséna, just steps from Vieux Nice. Rooms are modern, comfortable, and well-priced (4 Place Masséna, tel. 04 93 92 09 10, www.hoteldelamernice.com, hotel.mer@wanadoo.fr). They also run the **$$$$ Suites Masséna** in the same building, with huge, modern, high-ceilinged rooms—designed for two but with room for three (tel. 04 93 13 48 11, www.lessuitesmassena.com).

$$ Room With a Vue rents four, well-designed rooms (several with small balconies) right on Cours Saleya above the Pain et Cie bakery/café (3 Louis Gassin, tel. 04 93 62 94 32, roomwithavue@gmail.com, enthusiastic owner Frank).

$$ Hôtel Lafayette,* located a block behind the Galeries Lafayette department store, is a modest, homey place with 17 mostly spacious and good-value rooms—some with thin walls, some traffic noise, and all one floor up from the street (RS%, 32 Rue de l'Hôtel des Postes—see map on page 328, tel. 04 93 85 17 84, www.hotellafayettenice.com, info@hotellafayettenice.com).

Hostel: ¢ Villa Saint Exupéry Beach is a hostel-hotel in the center of Nice with a young and friendly vibe, fun bar, cheap restaurant, community kitchen, and *beaucoup* services including laundry, yoga classes, and scuba diving (no curfew, 6 Rue Sacha Guitry, tel. 04 93 16 13 45, www.villahostels.com, beach@villahostels.com).

NEAR THE AIRPORT

Several airport hotels offer a handy and cheap port-in-the-storm for those with early flights or who are just stopping in for a single night: **$$$ Hôtels Campanile** (www.campanile.fr) and **$$$ Nouvel** (www.novotel.com) are closest; **$$ Hôtel Ibis Budget Nice Aéroport** (www.ibis.com) is a few minutes away. Free shuttles connect these hotels with both airport terminals.

Eating in Nice

You'll find plenty of regional dishes and lots of Italian influence blended with classic French cuisine in this Franco-Italian city. Just because you're in a resort, don't lower your standards. Locals expect to eat well and so should you. Sundays are tricky as many places are closed, check the hours before you get your heart set on a place.

My favorite dining spots are in Vieux Nice. It's well worth booking ahead for these places. If Vieux Nice is too far, I've listed some great places handier to your hotel. Promenade des Anglais is ideal for picnic dinners on warm, languid evenings or a meal at a beachside restaurant. For a more romantic (and expensive) meal, head for nearby Villefranche-sur-Mer (see page 349). Avoid the fun-to-peruse but terribly touristy eateries lining Rue Masséna.

Vieux Nice Hotels & Restaurants

NICE

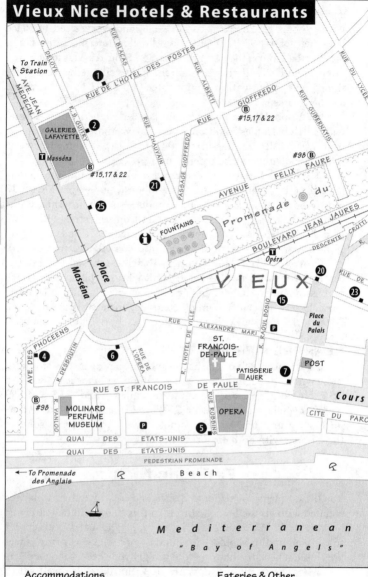

Accommodations

1 Hôtel Lafayette
2 Villa Saint Exupéry Beach Hostel
3 Hôtel la Perouse & Hôtel Suisse
4 Hôtel Albert 1er
5 Hôtel Mercure Marché aux Fleurs
6 Hôtel de la Mer & Suites Masséna
7 Room With a Vue & Pain et Cie Bakery

Eateries & Other

8 Le Safari
9 Lacchiardo
10 Chez Palmyre &
　　Petit Lascarais
11 Olive et Artichaut
12 Koko Green
13 Bistrot du Fromager

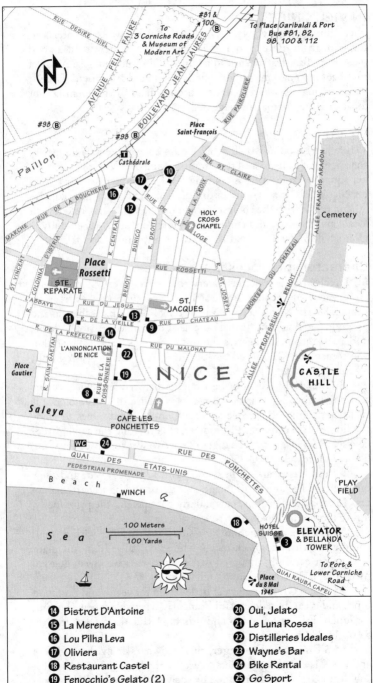

NICE

14 Bistrot D'Antoine
15 La Merenda
16 Lou Pilha Leva
17 Oliviera
18 Restaurant Castel
19 Fenocchio's Gelato (2)

20 Oui, Jelato
21 Le Luna Rossa
22 Distilleries Ideales
23 Wayne's Bar
24 Bike Rental
25 Go Sport

IN VIEUX NICE

Nice's dinner scene converges on Cours Saleya, which is entertaining enough in itself to make the generally mediocre food a good deal. It's a fun, festive spot to compare tans and mussels. Most of my recommendations are on side lanes inland from here. Even if you're eating elsewhere, wander through here in the evening. For locations, see the map on page 328.

On Cours Saleya

While local foodies would avoid Cours Saleya like a McDonalds, the energy of wall-to-wall restaurants taking over Vieux Nice's market square each evening is enticing. **$$$ Le Safari** is a fair option for Niçois cuisine and outdoor dining. This venerable place, convivial and rustic with the coolest interior on the Cours, is packed with locals and tourists, and staffed with hurried waiters (open daily, 1 Cours Saleya, tel. 04 93 80 18 44, www.restaurantsafari.fr).

Characteristic Places in Vieux Nice

$$ Lacchiardo is a homey eatery that mixes loyal clientele with hungry tourists. As soon as you sit down you know this is a treat. Its simple, hearty Niçois cuisine is served by Monsieur Acchiardo and his good-looking sons, Jean-François and Raphael. A small plaque under the menu outside says the restaurant has been run by father and son since 1927 (closed Sat-Sun and Aug, indoor seating only, 38 Rue Droite, tel. 04 93 85 51 16).

$ Chez Palmyre, your best budget bet in Vieux Nice, is tiny and popular, so book ahead (2 weeks is advised). The ambience is rustic and fun, with people squeezed onto shared tables to enjoy the home-style cooking. Philippe serves everyone the same three-course, €17 *menu*, which changes every two weeks (closed Sat-Sun, 5 Rue Droite, tel. 04 93 85 72 32).

$ Petit Lascarais sits next door with 12 tables inside and a few outside, and has a fun, rummage-sale décor and lighthearted servers. The food is delicious, particularly considering the price (daily, 5 Rue Droite, tel. 06 38 16 81 78).

$$$ Olive et Artichaut is a sharp bistro-diner with a small counter, booths, and black-meets-white floor tiles. It's a fine place to dine on carefully prepared dishes with creative twists (closed Mon-Tue, 6 Rue St. Reparate, tel. 04 89 14 97 51).

$$ Koko Green is a sweet little haven for vegan and raw-food types and is run by a delightful Franco-Kiwi couple (open Thu-Sun for lunch, Fri-Sat for lunch and dinner, 1 Rue de la Loge, tel. 07 81 63 14 88).

$$$ Bistrot du Fromager, run by owners crazy about cheese and wine, is a find. Come here to escape the heat and dine in cozy, cool, vaulted cellars surrounded by shelves of wine. You'll be treated to delicious dishes featuring fresh fish, pasta, and ham—most with cheese as a key ingredient. This is a good choice for vegetarians, and for singles who enjoy eating at the counter and watching the chef work. Book ahead (closed Sun for dinner, just off Place du Jésus at 29 Rue Benoît Bunico, tel. 04 93 13 07 83).

$$ Bistrot D'Antoine has street appeal. It's a warm, popular, vine-draped option whose menu emphasizes Niçois cuisine and good grilled selections. The food is delicious and the prices are reasonable. Call several days ahead to reserve a table—the upstairs room is quieter (closed Sun-Mon, 27 Rue de la Préfecture, tel. 04 93 85 29 57).

$$ La Merenda is a shoebox where you'll sit on small stools and dine on simple, home-style dishes in a communal environment. The menu changes with the season, but the hardworking owner, Dominique, does not. This place fills fast, so arrive early, or better yet, drop by during lunch to reserve for dinner—seatings are at 19:00 and 21:00 (closed Sat-Sun, cash only, 4 Rue Raoul Bosio, no telephone).

$ Lou Pilha Leva delivers fun and cheap lunch or dinner options with Niçois specialties and always-busy, outdoor-only, picnictable dining (daily, located where Rue de la Loge and Rue Centrale meet).

$$ Oliviera venerates the French olive. This fun shop/restaurant offers olive oil tastings and a menu of Mediterranean dishes paired with specific oils (like a wine pairing). Adorable owner Nadim speaks excellent English, knows all of his producers, and provides animated "Olive Oil 101" explanations with your dinner. It's a good place for vegetarians—try his guacamole-and-apple dish; the pesto is also excellent (closed Sun-Mon, cash only, 8 bis Rue du Collet, tel. 04 93 13 06 45).

Dining on the Beach

$$$ Restaurant Castel is a fine eat-on-the-beach option, thanks to its location at the very east end of Nice, under Castle Hill. The city vanishes as you step down to the beach. The food is nicely presented, and the tables feel elegant, even at the edge of the sand. Arrive for the sunset and you'll have an unforgettable meal (open for dinner mid-May-Aug, lunch April-Sept, 8 Quai des Etats-Unis, tel. 04 93 85 22 66, www.castelplage.com). Sunbathers can rent beach chairs and have drinks and meals served literally on the beach (lounge chairs-€16/half-day, €19/day).

And for Dessert...

Gelato lovers should save room for the tempting ice-cream stands in Vieux Nice (open daily until late). **Fenocchio** is the city's favorite, with mouthwatering displays of dozens of flavors ranging from

NICE

lavender to avocado (two locations: 2 Place Rossetti and 6 Rue de la Poissonnerie). Gelato connoisseurs should head for **Oui, Jelato,** where the quality is the priority rather than the selection (5 Rue de la Préfecture, on the Place du Palais).

IN THE CITY CENTER
Near Nice Etoile, on Rue Biscarra

An appealing lineup of bistros overflowing with outdoor tables stretches along the broad sidewalk on Rue Biscarra (just east of Avenue Jean Médecin behind Nice Etoile, all closed Sun). Come here to dine with area residents away from the tourists. **$$ Le 20 sur Vin** is a neighborhood favorite with a cozy, wine-bar-meets-café ambience (tel. 04 93 92 93 20).

Near Place Masséna

$$ Le Luna Rossa is a small neighborhood place serving delicious French-Italian dishes. Owner Christine welcomes diners with enthusiastic service and reasonable prices. Pasta dishes are copious and served in cast-iron pans, and the *assortiment* main course is a great sampler dish. Dine inside or outside on a sidewalk terrace (closed Sun-Mon, just north of parkway at 3 Rue Chauvain, tel. 04 93 85 55 66).

$ L'Ovale takes its name from the shape of a rugby ball. Come here for an unpretentious and local café-bistro experience. Young Matthieu serves while David cooks traditional dishes from southwestern France (rich and meaty). Dining is inside only. Consider the *cassoulet*, the hearty *salade de manchons* with duck and walnuts, or the €18-23 three-course *menus* (daily, 29 Rue Pastorelli, tel. 04 93 80 31 65).

$$$ Les 5 Sens ("The Five Senses") is a lively, smart, and welcoming bistro serving classic French fare at reasonable prices (daily, 37 Rue Pastorelli, tel. 09 81 06 57 00⊠).

$$ La Maison de Marie is a surprisingly high-quality refuge off Nice's touristy restaurant row. The interior tables are candlelit, white-tablecloth classy, while the tables in the courtyard enjoy a relaxed bistro feel. Expect some smokers outside. The *menu* is a good value (daily, 5 Rue Masséna, tel. 04 93 82 15 93).

Near the Train Station

$ Voyageur Nissart has blended good-value cuisine with friendly service since 1908. Kind owner Max and his able assistant Cédric are great hosts, and the quality of their food makes this place both very popular and a good choice for travelers on a budget (book ahead, leave a message in English). Try anything *à la niçoise*, including the fine *salade niçoise* (good €18 three-course *menus*, inexpensive wines, indoor and outdoor seating, closed Mon, a block

NICE

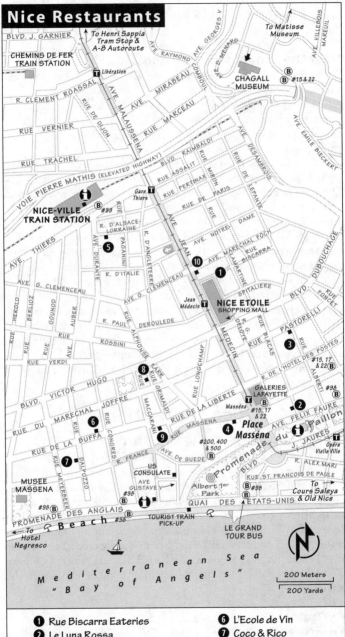

Nice Restaurants

To Henri Sappia
Tram Stop &
A-8 Autoroute

To Matisse
Museum

BLVD. J. GARNIER

CHEMINS DE FER
TRAIN STATION

Libération

CHAGALL
MUSEUM

#15 & 22

R. CLEMENT ROASSAL

AVE. RAYMOND COMBOUL

AVE. GEORGES V

AVE. D'MENARD

AVE. VILLEBOIS MAREUIL

AVE. MIRABEAU

RUE VERNIER

RUE DE DIJON

AVE. MALAUSSENA

RUE MARCEAU

AVE. EMILE BIECKERT

RUE TRACHEL

VOIE PIERRE MATHIS (ELEVATED HIGHWAY)

BLVD. RAIMBALDI

RUE ASSALIT

RUE MIRON

RUE DE LEPANTE

RUE DE DESAMBROIS

Gare
Thiers

RUE PERTINAX

RUE DE PARIS

NICE-VILLE
TRAIN STATION

#99

R. D'ALSACE-
LORRAINE

AVE. PAGANINI

AVE. DURANTE

R. D'ITALIE

AVE. THIERS

AVE. G. CLEMENCEAU

R. D'ANGLETERRE

AVE. JEAN

AVE. NOTRE-
DAME

AVE. MARECHAL FOCH

RUE LAMARTINE

RUE BISCARRA

SPITALIERE

DUBOUCHAGE

AVE. G. CLEMENCEAU

Jean
Médecin

NICE ETOILE
SHOPPING MALL

BLVD. DUBOUCHAGE

RUE FONCET

R. HEROLD

R. BERLIOZ

R. GOUNOD

R. AUBER

R. PAUL DEROULEDE

ROSSINI

MEDECIN

G. DEOYE

RUE BLACAS

PASTORELLI

RUE DE L'HOTEL DES POSTES

#15, 17
& 22

RUE VERDI

RUE VICTOR HUGO

RUE DE LA LIBERTE

KARR

RUE GRIMALDI

RUE MACCARANI

RUE LONGCHAMP

GALERIES
LAFAYETTE

Masséna

#15, 17
& 22

AVE. FELIX FAURE

RUE DE L'ALBERTI

#98

Le Paillon

BLVD. VICTOR HUGO

RUE MARECHAL JOFFRE

RUE DU

RUE DE LA BUFFA

RUE DE LA

RUE CONGRES

RUE MEYERBEER

DALPOZZO

RUE FRANCE

AVE. DE SUEDE

RUE MASSENA

Place
Masséna

#200, 400
& 500

AVE. GUSTAVE V

US
CONSULATE

Albert 1er
Park

Promenade

RUE ST. FRANCOIS DE PAULE

J. JAURES

Opéra
Vieille Ville

R. ALEX. MARI

To
Cours Saleya
& Old Nice

#98

MUSEE
MASSENA

#98

PROMENADE DES ANGLAIS

#98

QUAI DES ETATS-UNIS

To
Hotel
Negresco

Beach

TOURIST TRAIN
PICK-UP

LE GRAND
TOUR BUS

Mediterranean Sea
"Bay of Angels"

200 Meters

200 Yards

---

❶ Rue Biscarra Eateries		❻ L'Ecole de Vin
❷ Le Luna Rossa		❼ Coco & Rico
❸ L'Ovale & Les 5 Sens		❽ Mon Petit Café
❹ La Maison de Marie		❾ Crêperie Bretonne
❺ Voyageur Nissart		❿ Monoprix (Grocery)

below the train station at 19 Rue d'Alsace-Lorraine, tel. 04 93 82 19 60).

Near the Promenade des Anglais

These restaurants are handy for those sleeping in hotels near the Promenade des Anglais.

$$ L'Ecole de Vin combines a wine-bar feel with a cozy but modern restaurant, and serves a limited selection of tasty dishes complimented by a vast selection of wines (closed Sun, 16 Rue de la Buffa, tel. 04 93 81 39 30).

$$$ Coco & Rico is a find away from the tourist fray. Kind Isabelle welcomes you to her cozy bistro with homemade dishes. The cuisine and wine list represent many regions of France, with a focus on fish and fresh ingredients (closed Sun-Mon, indoor and outdoor seating, 3 Rue Dalpozzo, tel. 04 83 50 09 60).

$$$ Mon Petit Café delivers fine cuisine to appreciative diners in a warm, candlelit setting with rich colors and fine glassware, or on a pleasant front terrace. Book ahead for this upscale place and expect top service and wonderful cuisine (closed Sun-Mon, 11 bis Rue Grimaldi, tel. 04 97 20 55 36).

$ Crêperie Bretonne is the only *crêperie* I list in Nice. Dine on the broad terrace or inside, with relaxed service and jukebox-meets-gramophone ambience. Their top-end, house-special crêpes are creative and enticing. Split a salad to start—try the goat cheese salad with honey (closed Sun, on Place Grimaldi, tel. 04 93 82 28 47).

Nice Connections

GETTING AROUND THE RIVIERA

Nice is perfectly situated for exploring the Riviera by public transport. Monaco, Eze-le-Village, Villefranche-sur-Mer, Antibes, Vence, and St-Paul-de-Vence are all within about a one-hour bus or train ride. With a little planning, you can link key destinations in an all-day circuit (for example: Nice, Monaco, and Eze-le-Village or La Turbie, then loop back to Nice). For a comparison of train and bus connections from Nice to nearby coastal towns, see the "Public Transportation in the French Riviera" sidebar on page 278. It's also possible to take a boat to several destinations in the Riviera.

By Train

From Nice-Ville Station to: Cannes (2/hour, 30 minutes), **Antibes** (2/hour, 20 minutes), **Villefranche-sur-Mer** (2/hour, 10 minutes), **Eze-le-Village** (2/hour, 15 minutes to Eze-Bord-de-Mer, then bus #83 to Eze, 8/day, 15 minutes), **Monaco** (2/hour, 20 minutes),

Menton (2/hour, 25 minutes), **Grasse** (better by bus; trains not running until sometime in 2018, when they resume about 15/day, 1 hour).

By Bus

Regardless of length, most one-way rides on regional buses (except express airport buses) cost €1.50. Tickets are good for up to 74 minutes of travel in one direction, including transfers. For more info on buses in the Riviera, see page 275. To connect to regional destinations, use the following bus lines and stops (see maps on pages 324 and 328 for stop locations; www.lignesdazur.com).

Eastbound Buses: Bus #100 runs through **Villefranche-sur-Mer** (3-4/hour, 20 minutes), **Monaco** (1 hour), and **Menton** (1.5 hours). Bus #81 stops in **Villefranche-sur-Mer** (2-3/hour, 15 minutes) and around **Cap Ferrat** (30 minutes to **St-Jean-Cap-Ferrat**). Due to tram-line construction, expect some changes to stops (ask locally). For now, the closest stop for eastbound buses is near the Garibaldi tram stop, close to Place Garibaldi (see map on page 329). Bus #81 stops only at the Promenade des Arts stop at the Modern Art Museum and near the port. Bus #100 stops only at the port. Buses #82 and #112 to **Eze-le-Village** leave from the Vauban tram stop (about hourly; only #82 runs on Sundays; 30 minutes). For **La Turbie,** buses run 6/day and take 45 minutes (Mon-Sat take #116 from Vauban tram stop; on Sun catch #T-66 from Pont St. Michel tram stop). Use the tram to reach any of these eastbound buses (free transfer to all of these destinations, except Monaco).

Westbound Buses: Bus #200 goes to **Antibes** (4/hour Mon-Sat, 2/hour Sun, 1.5 hours) and **Cannes** (2 hours). Bus #400 heads to **St-Paul-de-Vence** (2/hour, 45 minutes) and **Vence** (50 minutes). Bus #500 goes to **Grasse** (2/hour, 1 hour). All three use the Albert I/Verdun stop on Avenue de Verdun, a 10-minute walk along the parkway west of Place Masséna.

By Boat

In summer, Trans Côte d'Azur offers scenic trips several days a week from Nice to Monaco and Nice to St-Tropez. Boats leave in the morning and return in the evening, giving you all day to explore your destination. Drinks and WCs are available on board.

Boats to **Monaco** depart at 9:30 and 16:00, and return at 11:00 and 17:00. The morning departure can be combined with the late-afternoon return from Monaco, allowing you a full day with Prince Albert II (€39 round-trip, €32 if you don't get off in Monaco, 45 minutes each way, June-Sept Tue, Thu, and Sat only).

Boats to **St-Tropez** depart at 9:00 and return from St-Tropez at 16:30 (€65 round-trip, 2.5 hours each way; early-July-Aug daily; late May-early-July and Sept Tue, Thu, and Sat-Sun only).

Reservations are required for both boats, and tickets for St-Tropez should be booked in advance (tel. 04 92 00 42 30, www.trans-cote-azur.com). The same company also runs one-hour round-trip cruises along the coast to Cap Ferrat (see listing under "Tours in Nice," earlier).

GETTING TO DESTINATIONS BEYOND THE RIVIERA
By Long-Distance Train

Most long-distance train connections from Nice to other French cities require a change in Marseille. The Grande Ligne train to Bordeaux (serving Antibes, Cannes, Toulon, and Marseille—and connecting from there to Arles, Nîmes, and Carcassonne) requires a reservation.

From Nice by Train to: Marseille (18/day, 2.5 hours), **Cassis** (hourly, 3 hours, transfer in Toulon or Marseille), **Arles** (11/day, 4 hours, most require transfer in Marseille or Avignon), **Avignon** (10/day, most by TGV, 4 hours, many require transfer in Marseille), **Lyon** (hourly, 4.5 hours, may require change), **Paris'** Gare de Lyon (hourly, 6 hours, may require change), **Aix-en-Provence** TGV Station (10/day, 2-3 hours, usually changes in Marseille), **Chamonix** (4/day, 10 hours, may change in St-Gervais and Lyon), **Beaune** (7/day, 7 hours, 1-2 transfers), **Florence** (6/day, 8 hours, 1-3 transfers), **Milan** (3 Thello trains/day, 4 hours, www.thello.com; or 4/day, 5 hours, most with transfers), **Venice** (5/day, 9 hours, 1-3 transfers), **Barcelona** (2/day via Montpellier or Valence, 9 hours, more with multiple changes).

By Plane

Nice's easy-to-navigate airport (Aéroport de Nice Côte d'Azur, airport code: NCE) is literally on the Mediterranean—with landfill runways, a 30-minute drive west of the city center. The two terminals are connected by shuttle buses *(navettes)*. Both terminals have TIs, banks, ATMs, and buses to Nice (tel. 04 89 88 98 28, www.nice.aeroport.fr). Planes leave roughly hourly for Paris (one-hour flight, about the same price as a train ticket, check www.easyjet.com for the cheapest flights to Paris' Orly airport).

Linking the Airport and City Center

By Taxi: A taxi into the center is expensive considering the short distance (figure €35 to Nice hotels, €60 to Villefranche-sur-Mer, €70 to Antibes, about €5 more at night and on weekends, small fee for bags). Nice's airport taxis are notorious for overcharging. Before riding, confirm your fare. It's always a good idea to ask for a receipt *(reçu)*.

By Airport Shuttle: These services vary in reliability but can be cost-effective for families or small groups. Airport shuttles are better for trips from your hotel to the airport, since they require you to book a precise pickup time in advance. Shuttle vans offer a fixed price (about €30 for one person, a little more for additional people or to Villefranche-sur-Mer). Your hotel can arrange this and I would trust their choice of company.

By Bus: Two bus lines connect the airport with the city center, offering good alternatives to high-priced taxis. **Bus #99** (airport express) runs to Nice's main train station (€6, 2/hour, 8:00-21:00, 30 minutes, drops you within a 10-minute walk of many recommended hotels). To take this bus *to* the airport, catch it right in front of the train station (departs on the half-hour). If your hotel is within walking distance of the station, #99 is your best budget bet.

Bus #98 runs along Promenade des Anglais and along the edge of Vieux Nice (€6, 3-4/hour, from the airport 6:00-23:00, to the airport until 21:00, 30 minutes, see map on page 286 for stops).

For all buses, buy tickets from the driver. To reach the bus information office and stops at Terminal 1, turn left after passing customs and exit the doors at the far end. Buses serving Terminal 2 stop across the street from the airport exit (information kiosk and ticket sales to the right as you exit).

Linking the Airport and Nearby Destinations

To get to **Villefranche-sur-Mer** from the airport, take bus #98 (described above) to Place Garibaldi. From there, use the same ticket to transfer to bus #81 or #100 (see "Getting Around the Riviera," earlier, for bus frequencies and the map on page 286 for stop locations; note that in 2017 you'll likely need to walk to the Promenade des Arts stop by the Modern Art Museum or to the port to catch eastbound buses due to work on the tram system). Consider an airport shuttle van.

To reach **Antibes**, take bus #250 from either terminal (about 2/hour, 40 minutes, €11). For **Cannes**, take bus #210 from either terminal (1-2/hour, 50 minutes on freeway, €22). Express bus #110 runs from the airport directly to **Monaco** (2/hour, 50 minutes, €22).

By Cruise Ship

Nice's port is at the eastern edge of the town center, below Castle Hill; the main promenade and Vieux Nice are on the other side of the hill. Cruise ships dock at either side of the mouth of this port: Terminal 1 to the east or Terminal 2 to the west.

Getting into the City Center: To reach Vieux Nice or the tram, head to Place Garibaldi by walking or riding the shuttle bus to the top of the port, then angling up Rue Cassini to the square (20-minute walk from either cruise terminal). From here it's a short **walk** to Vieux Nice or to the tram stop. You can ride the **tram** to Place Masséna for the start of my "Vieux Nice Walk" or to catch a bus to the Chagall or Matisse museums (#15 or #22).

If arriving at Terminal 2 and heading to Vieux Nice, you can skip the walk to Place Garibaldi and stroll directly there by heading around the base of the castle-topped hill, with the sea on your left (10-15 minutes).

Other options to get into town include a **taxi** from the terminals (about €20 to points within Nice) or the **hop-on, hop-off bus,** which has a stop at the top of the port (see page 290).

Getting to Nearby Destinations: To visit Villefranche-sur-Mer or Monaco, it's best to take **bus #100** (the train is faster, but the bus stop is much closer to Nice's port). The bus stops along the top of the port, near the right end of Place de l'Ile de Beauté (see map on page 286).

To take the **train** to Villefranche-sur-Mer, Monaco, Antibes, Cannes, or elsewhere, hop on the tram (stop near Place Garibaldi, described earlier), then ride to the Gare Thiers stop and walk one long block to the main train station. For bus and train connections to nearby destinations, see page 334.

Taxis at the terminals charge about €40 one-way to Villefranche-sur-Mer, or €95 one-way to Monaco.

EAST OF NICE

Villefranche-sur-Mer •
The Three Corniches • Cap Ferrat
• Eze-le-Village

Between Nice and Monaco lies the Riviera's richest stretch of real estate, paved with famously scenic roads (called the Three Corniches) and dotted with cliff-hanging villages, million-dollar vistas, and sea-splashed walking trails connecting beach towns. Fifteen minutes east of Nice, little Villefranche-sur-Mer stares across the bay to woodsy and exclusive Cap Ferrat. The eagle's-nest Eze-le-Village and the Corniche-topping Le Trophée des Alpes survey the scene from high above.

PLANNING YOUR TIME

Ideally, spend one day in Villefranche-sur-Mer and Cap Ferrat, and a second day in Monaco and either Eze-le-Village or La Turbie (or both if you're efficient).

If you only have one day, spend it in Villefranche-sur-Mer and Monaco: Those using Nice or Villefranche-sur-Mer as a home base can take the bus and follow my self-guided bus tour to Monaco (see the end of this chapter), arriving in Monaco in time for the changing of the guard at 11:55, then visit the casino after it opens at 14:00. If you're returning to Nice, take the train or bus back to Villefranche-sur-Mer and consider having dinner there on your way back. If you're sleeping in Villefranche-sur-Mer, return from Monaco by bus via Eze-le-Village, spend the late afternoon/early evening there, then take a taxi back to Villefranche.

Drivers can connect these destinations with some scenic driving along the Corniche roads.

Villefranche-sur-Mer

In the glitzy world of the Riviera, Villefranche-sur-Mer offers travelers an easygoing slice of small-town Mediterranean life. From here, convenient day trips let you gamble in Monaco, saunter the Promenade des Anglais in Nice, and enjoy views from Eze-le-Village and the Grande Corniche.

Villefranche-sur-Mer feels more Italian than French, with pastel-orange buildings; steep, narrow lanes spilling into the sea; and pasta on menus. Luxury yachts glisten in the bay. Cruise ships make regular calls to Villefranche-sur-Mer's deep harbor, creating periodic rush hours of frenetic shoppers and bucketlisters. Sand-pebble beaches, a handful of interesting sights, and quick access to Cap Ferrat keep other visitors just busy enough.

Originally a Roman port, Villefranche-sur-Mer was overtaken by fifth-century barbarians. Villagers fled into the hills, where they stayed and farmed their olives. In 1295 the Duke of Provence—like many in coastal Europe—needed to stand up to the Saracen Turks. He asked the olive farmers to move from the hills down to the water and establish a front line against the invaders, thus denying the enemy a base from which to attack Nice. In return for tax-free status, they stopped farming, took up fishing, and established a *Ville-* (town) *franche* (without taxes). Since there were many such towns, this one was specifically "Tax-free town on the sea" *(sur Mer)*. In about 1560, the Duke of Savoy built an immense, sprawling citadel in the town. And today, while the town has an international following, two-thirds of its 8,000 people call it their primary residence. That makes Villefranche-sur-Mer feel more like a real community than neighboring Riviera towns.

Orientation to Villefranche-sur-Mer

TOURIST INFORMATION
The TI is just off the road that runs between Nice and Monaco, located in a park (Jardin François Binon) below the Nice/Monaco bus stop, labeled *Octroi* (daily 9:00-18:00; mid-Sept-mid-June Mon-Sat 9:00-12:00 & 14:00-17:00, closed Sun; tel. 04 93 01 73 68, www.villefranche-sur-mer.com). Pick up regional bus schedules and information on seasonal sightseeing boat rides. The TI has an excellent brochure-map showing seaside walks around neigh-

Between Nice & Monaco

2 Kilometers
2 Miles

To Italy

To Antibes
A-8

MATISSE
MUSEUM
• Cimiez

RUSSIAN
CATH.

Nice

Bay of
Angels

To Antibes

Nice
Airport

LOW
CORNICHE

See Nice
Detail Maps

Ville-
franche-
sur-Mer

HIGH CORNICHE
MIDDLE CORNICHE
LOW CORNICHE

LE TROPHEE
DES ALPES

Eze-le-
Village

A-8

Roquebrune •

❸

Menton

La Turbie

❸
❶
❷
• MONACO

LOW
CORNICHE

TRAIL
Cap d'Ail
Eze-Bord-de-Mer

❶

❷
• Beaulieu-sur-Mer

■ VILLA EPHRUSSI
St-Jean-Cap Ferrat

❶

Cap Ferrat
(See Cap Ferrat
detail map)

Mediterranean Sea

❶ Low Corniche Road
(Basse Corniche or
Corniche Inférieure) &
Bus #100 Route

❷ Middle Corniche Road
(Moyenne Corniche)

❸ High Corniche Road
(Grande Corniche)

EAST OF NICE

boring Cap Ferrat and information on the Villa Ephrussi de Roth-schild's gardens.

ARRIVAL IN VILLEFRANCHE-SUR-MER

By Bus: Get off at the Octroi stop. To reach the old town, walk downhill past the TI along Avenue Général de Gaulle, take the first stairway on the left, then make a right at the street's end.

By Train: Not all trains stop in Villefranche-sur-Mer (you may need to transfer to a local train in Nice or Monaco). Ville-franche-sur-Mer's train station is just above the beach, a short stroll from the old town and most of my recommended hotels (taxis won't take such a short trip).

By Car: From Nice's port, follow signs for *Menton, Monaco,* and *Basse Corniche*. In Villefranche-sur-Mer, turn right at the TI (first signal after Hôtel la Flore) for parking and hotels. For a quick visit to the TI, park at the pay lot just below the TI (first 20 minutes free; enter license plate number). You'll pay to park in all public parking areas except from 19:00 to 9:00 (meters, €15 weekly pass). The waterfront just below the Citadel is central but expensive (Parking Wilson, €2/hour, €22/day). Some hotels have their own parking.

By Plane: Allow an hour to connect from Nice's airport to Villefranche-sur-Mer (for details, see page 337).

By Cruise Ship: For arrival by cruise ship, see page 351.

HELPFUL HINTS

Market Day: A fun bric-a-brac market enlivens Villefranche-sur-Mer on Sundays (on Place Amélie Pollonnais by Hôtel Welcome, and in Jardin François Binon by the TI). On Saturday and Wednesday mornings, a small food market sets up in Jardin François Binon. A small trinket market springs to action on Place Amélie Pollonnais whenever cruise ships grace the harbor.

Wi-Fi: There's free city Wi-Fi at the port and in cafés on Place Amélie Pollonnais.

Electric Bike Rental: The adventurous can try **Eco-Loc** electric bikes as an alternative to taking the bus to Cap Ferrat, Eze-le-Village, or even Nice. You get about 25 miles on a fully charged battery (after that you're pedaling; €20/half-day, €30/day, mid-April-Sept daily 9:00-17:00, deposit and ID required, best to reserve 24 hours in advance; helmets, locks, and baskets available; pick up bike by the cruise terminal entrance at the port, mobile 06 66 92 72 41, www.ecoloc06.fr).

Tourist Train: Skip the useless white *petit train*, which goes nowhere interesting.

Spectator Sports: Lively *boules* action takes place each evening just below the TI and the huge soccer field (see page 38).

GETTING AROUND VILLEFRANCHE-SUR-MER

By Bus: Little **minibus #80** saves you the sweat of walking uphill (and gets you within a 15-minute walk of Mont-Alban Fort, described later), but runs only about once per hour from the old port to the top of the hill, stopping at Place Amélie Pollonnais, Hôtel la Fiancée du Pirate, and the Col de Villefranche stop (for buses to Eze-le-Village), before continuing to the outlying suburban Nice Riquier train station (€1.50, runs daily 7:00-19:00, see map on page 344 for stop locations, schedule posted at stops and available at TI).

By Taxi: Beware of taxi drivers who overcharge. Normal weekday, daytime rates to outside destinations should be about €25 to Cap Ferrat, €40 to central Nice or Eze-le-Village, and €70 to the airport or Monaco. For a reliable taxi, call **Didier** (mobile 06 15 15 39 15). General taxi tel. 04 93 55 55 55.

Villefranche-sur-Mer Town Walk

For tourists, Villefranche is a tiny, easy-to-cover town that snuggles around its harbor under its citadel. This quick self-guided walk laces together everything of importance, starting at the waterfront near where cruise-ship tenders land and finishing at the citadel.

• *If arriving by bus or train, you'll walk five minutes to the starting point. Go to the end of the little pier directly in front of Hôtel Welcome, where we'll start with a spin tour (spin to the right) to get oriented.*

The Harbor: Look out to sea. Cap Ferrat, across the bay, is a landscaped paradise where the 1 percent of the 1 percent com-

pete for the best view. The Rothschild's pink mansion, Villa Ephrussi (slightly left of center, hugging the top) is the most worthwhile sight to visit in the area. To its right, in the saddle of the hill, the next home, with the big red-tiled roof, belongs to Paul Allen. Geologically, Cap Ferrat is the southern tip of the Alps. The range emerges from the sea here and arcs all across Europe, over 700 miles, to Vienna.

Today, ships bring not pirates but tourists. The bay here is generally filled with beautiful yachts. (In the evenings, you might see well-coiffed captains being ferried in by dutiful mates to pick up statuesque call girls.) Local guides keep a list of the world's 100 biggest yachts and talk about some of them as if they're part of the neighborhood.

At 2,000 feet, this is the deepest natural harbor on the Riviera and was the region's most important port until Nice built its own in the 18th century. Greek, Roman, and American naval ships appreciated the setting, as do cruise ships today. The biggest cruise ships drop their hooks here rather than in Nice or Monaco. The tiny jetty is the landing point for the cruise-ship tenders that come ashore each morning in season.

Up on the hill, the 16th-century citadel (where this walk ends) is marked by flags. The yellow fisherman's chapel (with the little-toe bell tower) has an interior painted by Jean Cocteau. Hôtel Welcome offers the balconies of dreams. Up the lane is the baroque facade of St. Michael's Church. The promenade, lined by fancy fish restaurants, leads to the town beach. Fifty yards above the beach stands the train station and above that, supported by arches, is the Low Corniche road, which leads to Monaco. Until that road was built in the 1860s, those hills were free of any development all the way to Monaco. The big yellow building beyond that is rentable for €300,000 a month (as Madonna did once for a birthday).

• *Leave the pier and walk left 30 yards past the last couple of fishing boats surviving from the town's once-prominent fishing community to find a small bronze bust of Jean Cocteau, the artist who said, "When I look at Villefranche, I see my youth." Step up to the little chapel he painted.*

Chapel of St. Pierre (Chapelle Cocteau): This chapel is the town's cultural highlight. Cocteau, who decorated the place, was a Parisian transplant who adored little Villefranche-sur-Mer and

EAST OF NICE

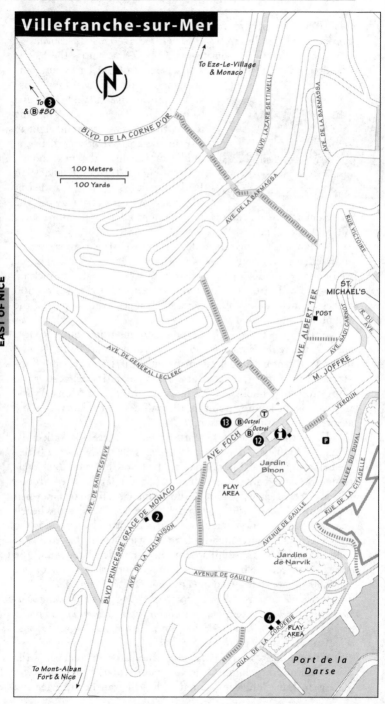

Villefranche-sur-Mer

BLVD. NAPOLEON III

TRAIN STATION

To Eze-Bord-de-Mer & Monaco via Low Corniche Road

PROMENADE DES MARINIERES

Ⓑ #80   Beach

To Cap Ferrat on foot

AVE. FERNAND MARUR

AVE. ALBERT 1ER

GALLIENI

AVE. GEORGES-CLEMENCEAU

CHEMIN DE LA FOUAN

QUAI COURBET

Place du Conseil

RUE VOLTI

RUE BARON DE BRES

OLD   R. MAY   RUE DE L'EGLISE   RUE OBSCURE   RUE DU POILU

❼

❻   ❽

Place de l'Eglise   ❺   ❶

T O W N

VALLON

SADI CARNOT

M. JOFFRE

AVE SADI CARNOT

❾   Place Amélie Pollonnais   ⓫

CHAPEL OF ST. PIERRE

👣 WALK BEGINS

Mediterranean Sea

❿

Ⓣ   Ⓑ #80   ATM

Ⓟ

GARE MARITIME (CRUISE TENDER DOCK)

WALK ENDS

CITADEL

SCENIC WALKWAY

❶ Hôtel Welcome
❷ Hôtel La Flore
❸ To Hôtel la Fiancée du Pirate
❹ Hôtel de la Darse & La Trinquette Restaurant
❺ La Grignotière Restaurant
❻ L'Aparté & Casino Grocery
❼ Le Serre Restaurant
❽ La Mère Germaine Restaurant
❾ Les Palmiers & Le Cosmo Brasseries
❿ Boat Rides & Electric Bike Rental
⓫ Dark Pelican Motor Boat Rental
⓬ Octroi Bus Stop (from Nice; to Monaco & Cap Ferrat)
⓭ Octroi Bus Stop (to Nice; from Monaco & Cap Ferrat)

whose career was distinguished by his work as an artist, poet, novelist, playwright, and filmmaker. Influenced by his pals Marcel Proust, André Gide, Edith Piaf, and Pablo Picasso, Cocteau was a leader among 20th-century avant-garde intellectuals. At the door, Marie-France—who is passionate about Cocteau's art—collects a €3 donation for a fishermen's charity. She then sets you free to enjoy the chapel's small but intriguing interior. She's happy to give explanations if you ask (open Wed-Mon 10:00-12:00 & 15:00-19:00, usually closed Tue, hours vary with cruise-ship traffic and season).

In 1955 Cocteau tattooed the barrel-vaulted chapel with heavy black lines and pastels. Each of Cocteau's Surrealist works—the Roma (Gypsies) of Stes-Maries-de-la-Mer who dance and sing to honor the Virgin, girls wearing traditional outfits, and three scenes from the life of St. Peter—is explained in English. Is that Villefranche-sur-Mer's citadel in the scene above the altar?

• *From the chapel, stroll the harbor promenade 100 yards past romantic harborside tables.* **Restaurant La Mère Germaine** *is named for Mother Germaine, who famously took care of US Navy troops in World War II (step inside to see sketches and old photos on the wall). Immediately after the restaurant, a lane leads up into the old town. Walk up a few steps until you reach a long tunnel-like street.*

Rue Obscure, the Old Town, and St. Michael's Church: Here, under these 13th-century vaults, you're in another age. Before the long stepped lane (which we'll climb later), turn right and walk to the end of Rue Obscure (which means "dark street"). At the end, wind up to the sunlight past a tiny fountain at Place du Conseil, and a few steps beyond that to a viewpoint overlooking the beach.

Turn around and stroll back past the fountain and gently downhill. At Place des Deux Garçons (the square with a namesake restaurant), turn right on Rue May and climb the stepped lane. Take your first left at the restaurant to find St. Michael's Church, facing a delightful square with a single magnolia tree (Place de l'Eglise). The deceptively large church features an 18th-century organ, a particularly engaging crucifix at the high altar, and (to the left) a fine statue of a recumbent Christ—carved, they say, from a fig tree by a galley slave in the 1600s.

• *Leaving St. Michael's, go downhill halfway to the water, where you hit the main commercial street. Go right on Rue du Poilu (browsing realestate windows if you'd like to move here), then head through the square, and angle left and up to the...*

Citadel: The town's mammoth castle was built in the 1500s by the Duke of Savoy to defend against the French. When the region joined France in 1860, the castle became just a barracks. Since the 20th century, it's housed the police station, City Hall, a summer outdoor theater, and art galleries. The single fortified entry—originally a drawbridge over a dry moat (a.k.a. kill zone)—still leads into this huge complex.

The exterior walls slope thickly at the base, indicating that they were built in the "Age of Black Powder"—the 16th century—when the advent of gunpowder made thicker, cannonball-deflecting walls a necessity for any effective fortification. The bastions are designed for smarter crossfire during an attack. The inside feels vast and empty. If you wander around, you'll find a memorial garden for victims of World War II, five free and empty museums and galleries, a garden in the bastion, and the City Hall (which offers a free WC, as all City Halls in France are required to by law).

• *And that concludes our introductory walk.*

Activities in Villefranche-sur-Mer

Boat Rides (Promenades en Mer)

To view this beautiful coastline from the sea, consider taking a quick **sightseeing cruise** with AMV (€11-21, some go as far as Monaco, select days June-Sept, departs across from Hôtel Welcome, tel. 04 93 76 65 65, www.amv-sirenes.com). You can also rent your own **motor boat** through Dark Pelican (€100/half-day, €170/day, deposit required, on the harbor at the Gare Maritime, tel. 04 93 01 76 54, www.darkpelican.com).

Seafront Walks

A seaside walkway originally used by customs agents to patrol the harbor leads under the citadel and connects the old town with the workaday harbor (Port de la Darse). At the port you'll find a few cafés, France's Institute of Oceanography (an outpost for the University of Paris oceanographic studies), and an 18th-century dry dock. This scenic walk turns downright romantic after dark. You can also wander the other direction along Villefranche-sur-Mer's waterfront and continue beyond the train station for postcard-perfect views back to Villefranche-sur-Mer (ideal in the morning—go before breakfast). You can even extend your walk to Cap Ferrat (see "Getting to Cap Ferrat" on page 355).

Hike to Mont-Alban Fort

This fort, with a remarkable setting on the high ridge that separates Nice and Villefranche-sur-Mer, is a good destination for hikers (also accessible by car and bus; info at TI). From the TI, walk on the main road toward Nice about 500 yards past Hôtel La Flore. Look for wooden trail signs labeled *Escalier de Verre* and climb about 45 minutes as the trail makes long switchbacks through the woods up to the ridge. Find your way to Mont-Alban Fort (interior closed to tourists) and its sensational view terrace over Villefranche-sur-Mer and Cap Ferrat. To visit with a much shorter hike, minibus

#80 drops you a 15-minute walk away (by the recommended Hôtel Fiancée du Pirate), and bus #14 from Nice drops you five minutes away.

Sleeping in Villefranche-sur-Mer

You have a handful of good hotels in all price ranges to choose from in Villefranche-sur-Mer. The ones I list have sea views from at least half of their rooms—well worth paying extra for.

$$$$ Hôtel Welcome**** has the best location in Villefranche-sur-Mer, and charges for it. Anchored seaside in the old town, with all of its 35 comfortable, balconied rooms overlooking the harbor and a lounge/wine bar that opens to the water, this place lowers my pulse and empties my wallet (pricey parking garage—must reserve, 3 Quai Amiral Courbet, tel. 04 93 76 27 62, www.welcomehotel.com, resa@welcomehotel.com).

$$$ Hôtel La Flore*** is a fine value—particularly if your idea of sightseeing is to enjoy a panoramic view from your spacious bedroom balcony (even street-facing rooms have nice decks). Several rooms in the annex sleep four and come with kitchenettes, views, and private hot tubs. It's a 15-minute uphill hike from the old town, but the parking is free, the bus stops for Nice and Monaco are close by, and the staff is eager to help (on main road at 5 Boulevard Princesse Grace de Monaco; tel. 04 93 76 30 30, www.hotel-la-flore.fr, infos@hotel-la-flore.fr).

$$$ Hôtel la Fiancée du Pirate*** is a family-friendly view refuge high above Villefranche-sur-Mer on the Middle Corniche with no street appeal (best for drivers, although it is on bus lines #80, #82, and #112 to Eze-le-Village and Nice). Eric and Laurence offer 15 tasteful and comfortable rooms, a large pool, a nice garden, and a terrific view lounge area. The big breakfast features homemade crêpes (RS%, laundry service, free parking, 8 Boulevard de la Corne d'Or, Moyenne Corniche/N-7, tel. 04 93 76 67 40, www.fianceedupirate.com, info@fianceedupirate.com).

$ Hôtel de la Darse** is a shy little hotel burrowed in the shadow of its highbrow neighbors and the only budget option in Villefranche. It's less central—figure 10 scenic minutes of level walking to the harbor and a steep 15-minute walk up to the main road (hourly minibus #80 stops in front; handy for drivers, free parking usually available close by). Seaview rooms are easily worth the extra euros (no elevator, tel. 04 93 01 72 54, www.hoteldeladarse.com, info@hoteldeladarse.com). From the TI, walk or drive down Avenue Général de Gaulle (walkers should turn left on Allée du Colonel Duval into the Jardins de Narvik and follow steps to the bottom).

Eating in Villefranche-sur-Mer

Locals don't come here in search of refined cuisine and nor should you. For me, dining in Villefranche-sur-Mer is about comfort food,

attitude, and ambience. Comparison-shopping is half the fun—make an event out of a predinner stroll through the old city. Check what looks good on the lively Place Amélie Pollonnais (next to Hôtel Welcome), where the whole village seems to converge at night; saunter past the string of pricey candlelit places lining the waterfront; and consider the smaller, less expensive eateries embedded in the old town. For dessert, pop into a *gelateria*, and then enjoy a floodlit, postdinner stroll along the sea.

$$$ La Grignotière, hiding in the back lanes, serves generous and tasty *plats*. Spaghetti and *gambas* (prawns) is a smart order, as is the chef's personal-recipe bouillabaisse, all served by gregarious Brigitte. Dining is mostly inside, making this a good choice for cooler days (daily except closed Wed Nov-April, 3 Rue du Poilu, tel. 04 93 76 79 83).

$$$ L'Aparté is where locals go for fresh cuisine with a focus on seafood. Outdoor tables gather under an arcade, the interior is warm with modern touches, servings are generous, and the presentation is tops (closed Mon, a few steps up from the port at 1 Rue Obscure, tel. 04 93 01 84 88).

$ Le Serre, nestled in the old town near St. Michael's Church, is a simple, cozy place that opens at 18:00 for early diners. Hard-working owner Sylvie serves well-priced dinners to a loyal local clientele and greets all clients with equal enthusiasm. Choose from the many thin crust pizzas (named after US states), salads, and meats. Try the *daube niçoise* meat stew or the three-course *menu* (open evenings only, cheap house wine, 16 Rue de May, tel. 04 93 76 79 91).

$$$$ La Mère Germaine, right on the harbor, is the only place in town classy enough to lure a yachter ashore. It's dressy, with formal service and high prices. The name commemorates the current owner's grandmother, who fed hungry GIs during World War II. Try the bouillabaisse, served with panache (daily, reserve for harborfront table, 9 Quai de l'Amiral Courbet, tel. 04 93 01 71 39, www.meregermaine.com).

$$ La Trinquette is a relaxed, low-key place away from the fray on the "other port," next to the recommended Hôtel de la Darse (a lovely 10-minute walk from the other recommended restaurants). Jean-Charles runs the place with charm, delivering reliable cuisine at good prices and a cool live-music scene on weekends (daily in summer, closed Wed off-season, 30 Avenue Général de Gaulle, tel. 04 93 16 92 48).

On Place Amélie Pollonnais: $$ Les Palmiers and **$$ Le Cosmo** each serve average brasserie fare on the town's appealing main square (daily).

Grocery Store: A handy **Casino** is a few blocks above Hôtel Welcome at 12 Rue du Poilu (Thu-Tue 8:00-12:30 & 15:30-19:30 except closed Sun afternoon and all day Wed).

Dinner Options for Drivers: If you have a car and are staying a few nights, take the short drive up to Eze-le-Village or, better still, La Turbie (dining suggestions for each later in this chapter). If it's summer (June-Sept), the best option of all is to go across to a restaurant on one of Cap Ferrat's beaches, such as Restaurant de Plage de Passable, for a before-dinner drink or a dinner you won't soon forget (see page 357).

Villefranche-sur-Mer Connections

For a comparison of connections by train and bus, see the "Public Transportation in the French Riviera" sidebar on page 278. If you're going to Nice's airport, take a cab or an airport shuttle van (see "Nice Connections," on page 337).

BY TRAIN

Trains are faster and run later than buses (until 24:00). It's a level, 10-minute walk from the port to the train station.

From Villefranche-sur-Mer by Train to: Monaco (2/hour, 10 minutes), **Nice** (2/hour, 10 minutes), **Antibes** (2/hour, 40 minutes), **Eze-Bord-de-Mer** (2/hour, 5 minutes)—transfer to bus #83 for Eze-le-Village (see page 361).

BY BUS

In Villefranche-sur-Mer, the most convenient stop is Octroi, just above the TI.

Bus #81 runs from Villefranche-sur-Mer in one direction to **Nice** (15 minutes) and in the other direction to **Beaulieu-sur-Mer** (5 minutes), around **Cap Ferrat,** and ending at the port in the village of **St-Jean** (15 minutes; for other transportation options, see "Getting to Cap Ferrat," later). The last bus departs from Nice around 20:15, and from St-Jean around 20:50.

Bus #100 runs along the coastal road from Villefranche-sur-Mer westbound to **Nice** (20 minutes) and eastbound to **Beaulieu-sur-Mer** (10 minutes), **Monaco** (40 minutes), and **Menton** (1.25 hours). The last bus from Nice to Villefranche leaves at about 19:45 and from Villefranche to Nice at about 20:30.

For more on these buses, including ticket info, routes, and frequencies, see page 275. For connections to **Eze-le-Village,** see "Getting to Eze-le-Village" on page 361.

BY CRUISE SHIP

Tenders deposit passengers at a slick terminal building (Gare Maritime) at the Port de la Santé, right in front of Villefranche-sur-Mer's old town.

Getting into Town: It's easy to **walk** to various points in Villefranche-sur-Mer. The town's charming, restaurant-lined square is a straight walk ahead from the terminal, the main road (with the TI and bus stop) is a steep hike above, and the train station is a short stroll along the beach. **Minibus #80,** which departs from in front of the cruise terminal, saves you some hiking up to the main road and bus stop (see page 342).

Getting to Nearby Towns: To connect to other towns, choose between the **bus** or **train.** Leaving the terminal, you'll see directional sights pointing left, to *Town center/bus* (a 10- to 15-minute, steeply uphill walk to the Octroi bus stop with connections west to Nice or east to Monaco); and right, to *Gare SNCF/train station* (a 10-minute, level stroll with some stairs at the end). See train and bus connections above.

Taxis wait in front of the cruise terminal and charge exorbitant rates (minimum €15 charge to train station, though most will refuse such a short ride). For farther-flung trips, see the price estimates on page 342. For an all-day trip, you can try negotiating a flat fee (e.g., €300 for a 4-hour tour).

The Three Corniches

Nice, Villefranche-sur-Mer, and Monaco are linked by three coastal routes: the Low, Middle, and High Corniches. The roads are nicknamed after the decorative frieze that runs along the top of a building (cornice). Each Corniche (kor-neesh) offers sensational views and a different perspective. You can find the three routes from Nice by driving up Boulevard Jean Jaurès past Vieux Nice. For the Low Corniche, follow signs to N-98 *(Monaco par la Basse Corniche),* which leads past Nice's port. Shortly after the turnoff to the Low Corniche, you'll see signs for N-7 *(Moyenne Corniche)* leading to the Middle Corniche. Signs for the High *(Grande)* Corniche appear a bit after that; follow D-2564 to *Col des 4 Chemins* and the *Grande Corniche.* For an overview of these three roads, see the map on page 341.

Low Corniche: The Basse Corniche (also called "Corniche

Inférieure") strings ports, beaches, and seaside villages together for a traffic-filled ground-floor view. It was built in the 1860s (along with the train line) to bring people to the casino in Monte Carlo. When this Low Corniche was finished, many hill-town villagers descended to the shore and started the communities that now line the sea. Before 1860, the population of the coast between Ville-franche-sur-Mer and Monte Carlo was zero. Think about that as you make the congested trip today.

Middle Corniche: The Moyenne Corniche is higher, quieter, and far more impressive. It runs through Eze-le-Village and provides breathtaking views over the Mediterranean, with several scenic pullouts.

High Corniche: Napoleon's crowning road-construction achievement, the Grande Corniche caps the cliffs with staggering views from almost 1,600 feet above the sea. Two thousand years ago, this was called the Via Aurelia, used by the Romans to conquer the West.

Villas: Driving from Villefranche-sur-Mer to Monaco, you'll come upon impressive villas. A particularly grand entry leads to "La Leopolda," the sprawling estate named for a previous owner, King Leopold II of Belgium in the 1930s (who owned the entire peninsula of Cap Ferrat in addition to this estate). Those driving up to the Middle Corniche from Villefranche-sur-Mer can look down on this yellow mansion and its lush garden, which fill an entire hilltop. The property was later owned by the Agnelli family (of Fiat fame and fortune), and then by the Safra family (Brazilian bankers). Its current value is a half-billion dollars.

The Best Route: For a ▲▲▲ route, **drivers** should take the Middle Corniche from Nice or Villefranche-sur-Mer to Eze-le-Village; from there, follow signs to the *Grande Corniche* and *La Turbie*, keeping an eye out for brilliant views back over Eze-le-Village, then finish by dropping down into Monaco. **Buses** travel each route; the higher the Corniche, the less frequent the buses. There are no buses between Eze-le-Village and La Turbie (45-minute walk), though buses do connect Nice and Monaco with La Turbie.

If traveling by bus, follow my self-guided bus tour to Monaco (at the end of this chapter), then consider returning to Nice or Villefranche-sur-Mer by bus via Eze-le-Village, or to Nice via La Turbie (see "Monaco Connections" on page 383).

The following villages and sights are listed from west to east, in the order you'll reach them, traveling from Villefranche-sur-Mer to Monaco.

Cap Ferrat

This exclusive peninsula, rated ▲▲, decorates Villefranche-sur-Mer's views. Cap Ferrat is a peaceful eddy off the busy Nice-Monaco route (Low Corniche). You could spend a leisurely day on this peninsula, wandering the sleepy port village of St-Jean-Cap-Ferrat (usually called "St-Jean"), touring the Villa Ephrussi de Rothschild mansion and gardens and the nearby Villa Kérylos, and walking on sections of the beautiful trails that follow the coast. If you owned a house here, some of the richest people on the planet would be your neighbors.

Tourist Information: The main TI is near the harbor in St-Jean (Mon-Sat 9:30-18:30, Sun 10:00-17:30; Oct-April Mon-Sat 9:00-17:00, closed Sun; 5 Avenue Denis Séméria, bus #81 stops here at the *office du tourisme*). A smaller TI is near the Villa Ephrussi (closed Sat off-season, closed Sun year-round, 59 Avenue Denis Séméria, tel. 04 93 76 08 90, office-tourisme@saintjeancapferrat.fr).

PLANNING YOUR TIME

Here's how I'd spend a day on the Cap: From Nice or Villefranche-sur-Mer, take bus #81 to the Villa Ephrussi de Rothschild stop (called Passable), then visit the villa. Walk 30 minutes, mostly downhill, to St-Jean for lunch (many options, including grocery shops for picnic supplies) and poke around the village. Consider the 45-minute walk on the Plage de la Paloma trail (ideal for picnics). After lunch, follow a beautiful 30-minute trail to the Villa Kérylos in Beaulieu-sur-Mer and tour that villa. Return to Villefranche-sur-Mer, Nice, or points beyond by train or bus. (If you have a car, skip the loop drive around the peninsula; there's nothing to see from the road except the walls in front of homes owned by people whose challenge in life is keeping the public out.)

You can add Eze-le-Village to this day if you skip the small town of St-Jean and walk via the seafront path directly from the Villa Ephrussi de Rothschild to the Villa Kérylos. To get to Eze-le-Village, take bus #100 (direction: *Monaco*) from the stop near the Villa Kérylos and get off at the Gare d'Eze stop, where you meet bus #83, which shuttles up and up to the village (one ticket covers both buses, get the #83 schedule at a TI or check www.lignedazur.com).

Here's an **alternative plan** for the star-gazing, nature-loving beach bum: Visit Villa Ephrussi first thing, walk to St-Jean for lunch, hike six miles around the entirety of Cap Ferrat (2-3 hours), and enjoy the late afternoon on the beach at Plage de Passable. At

EAST OF NICE

Cap Ferrat

To Villefranche-sur-Mer
& Nice

To Monaco &
Eze-le-Village

TRAIN
STATION

Beaulieu-
sur-Mer

l'Ange
Gardien
Stop

Bus #100
(Nice-to-Monaco)
Stops

VILLA
KERYLOS

Hôtel
Royal
Riviera

Golfe de St-Hospice

VILLA
EPHRUSSI
DE ROTHSCHILD

Plage de
Passable

#81
(Passable stop)

#81

#81

St-Jean-Cap-Ferrat

Plage de la
Paloma

Plage de
Passable

CHEMIN
DU ROY

ALBERTO 1

BLVD. GENERAL DE GAULLE

BLVD. GENERAL DE GAULLE

AVE. BELLEVUE

AVE. D. SEMERIA

AVE. DE GRASSEUIL

AVE. D. DURANDY

LOW CORNICHE

LOW CORNICHE

CORNICHE

LIGHTHOUSE

Mediterranean Sea

400 Meters

400 Yards

Hotels & Eateries

1 Hôtel Brise Marine

2 Hôtel Oursin & Le St. Jean
Pizzeria/Restaurant

3 Hôtel Patricia

4 Restaurant de la Plage
de Passable

5 Plage de la Paloma Restaurant

6 Restaurant La Cabane de l'Ecailler

7 Capitaine Cook Restaurant

Trails

A St-Jean to Beaulieu-sur-Mer
(30 minutes)

B Plage de la Paloma Loop
(45 minutes)

C Plage de Passable to St-Jean
(2-3 hours)

D Walk to Villefranche-sur-Mer
(1 hour)

sunset, have dinner at the recommended Restaurant de la Plage de Passable, then walk or catch a taxi back.

Warning: Late-afternoon buses back to Villefranche-sur-Mer or Nice along the Low Corniche can be jammed (worse on weekends), potentially leaving passengers stranded at stops for long periods. To avoid this, either take the train or board bus #81 on the Cap itself (before it gets crowded).

GETTING TO CAP FERRAT

From Nice or Villefranche-sur-Mer: Bus #81 (direction: *Port de St-Jean*) runs to all Cap Ferrat stops (for info on tickets, route, and frequency, see page 275). For the Villa Ephrussi de Rothschild, get off at the Passable stop (allow 30 minutes from Nice and 10 minutes from Villefranche-sur-Mer's Octroi stop). Find schedules posted at stops, or get one from a TI. The times listed for *Direction Le Port/ Cap Ferrat* are when buses depart from Nice—allow 15 minutes after that for Villefranche-sur-Mer. The return bus (direction: *Nice*) begins in St-Jean.

Cap Ferrat is quick by **car** (take the Low Corniche) or **taxi** (allow €28 one-way from Villefranche-sur-Mer, €60 from Nice).

You can also **walk** an hour from Villefranche-sur-Mer to Cap Ferrat: Go past the train station along the small beach lane, then climb the steps at the far end of the beach and walk parallel to the tracks on Avenue Louise Bordes. Continue straight past the mansions, and take the first right on Avenue de Grasseuil. You'll see signs to *Villa Ephrussi de Rothschild*, then to Cap Ferrat's port.

Sights on Cap Ferrat

▲VILLA EPHRUSSI DE ROTHSCHILD

In what seems like the ultimate in Riviera extravagance, Venice, Versailles, and the Côte d'Azur come together in the pastel-pink Villa Ephrussi. Rising above Cap Ferrat, this 1905 mansion has views west to Villefranche-sur-Mer and east to Beaulieu-sur-Mer. From this perch you'll look down on other oligarchs, but not on Microsoft cofounder Paul Allen. As you enter the grounds, look back and see the villa's neighbor—Paul Allen's mansion—on an equally prominent high point surrounded by a private forest.

Cost and Hours: Palace and gardens-€14, includes audioguide; mid-Feb-Oct daily 10:00-18:00, July-Aug until 19:00; Nov-mid-Feb Mon-Fri 14:00-18:00, Sat-Sun 10:00-18:00; tel. 04 93 01 33 09, www.villa-ephrussi.com. Kids enjoy the free treasure-hunt booklet.

Getting There: With luck, drivers can find a free spot to park along the entry road just inside the gate. There's a small turnaround at the top. The nearest bus stop is Passable, just a few minutes after the bus turns onto Cap Ferrat (bus #81, 10-minute walk uphill to the villa). If returning to Nice or Villefranche-sur-Mer by bus, check the posted schedule, and keep in mind that you're only a minute from the time-point listed for Port de St-Jean.

Visiting the Villa: Buy your ticket at the side of the building with the gift shop, then walk to the main entrance and pick up an audioguide. Start with the well-furnished belle époque interior (well-described by the audioguide). Upstairs, an 18-minute film (with English subtitles) explains the gardens and villa and gives you good background on the life of rich and eccentric Béatrice, Baroness de Rothschild, the French banking heiress who built and furnished the place. Don't miss the view over the gardens from the terrace.

As you stroll through the rooms, you'll pass royal furnishings and personal possessions, including the baroness's porcelain collection and her bathroom case for cruises. Her bedroom, sensibly, has views to the sea on both the port and starboard sides, and toward the bow, stretching like the prow of a vast cruise ship, is her garden. An appropriately classy **$$ garden-tearoom** serves drinks and lunches with a view (12:00-17:30).

The gorgeous **gardens** are why most come here (pick up the garden map when you get your audioguide). The shipshaped gardens were inspired by Béatrice's many ocean-liner trips. She even dressed her small army of gardeners like sailors. Behind the mansion, stroll through the seven lush gardens re-created from locations all over the world—and with maximum sea views. Don't miss the Jardin Exotique's wild cactus, the rose garden at the far end, and the view back to the house from the "Temple of Love" gazebo.

Walks from the Villa Ephrussi: It's a lovely 30-minute stroll, mostly downhill and east, from the Villa Ephrussi to the Villa Kérylos in Beaulieu-sur-Mer (described later) or to the port of St-Jean. To get to either, make a hard left at the stop sign below the Villa Ephrussi and follow signs along a small road toward the Hôtel Royal Riviera on Avenue Henri Honoré Sauvan (see Cap Ferrat map). When the road comes to a T, keep going straight, passing a green gate down a pedestrian path, which ends at the seafront trail—go left to reach the Villa Kérylos, or head right to get to St-Jean (be careful to follow the path left at the Villa Sonja Rello). It's about 15 minutes to either destination once you join this path.

To get to Plage de Passable from the Villa Ephrussi, turn left along the main road just below the villa; after 50 yards you'll find signs leading down to the beach.

BEACHES
Plage de Passable
This pebbly little beach, located below the Villa Ephrussi, comes with great views of Villefranche-sur-Mer. It's a peaceful place,

popular with families. One half is public (free, with snack bar, shower, and WC), and the other is run by a small restaurant (€30 includes changing locker, lounge chair, and shower; they have 260 "beds," but still reserve ahead in summer or on weekends as this is a prime spot, tel. 04 93 76 06 17). If you were ever to do the French Riviera rent-a-beach ritual, this would be the place.

To park near the beach (curbside or in a nearby lot), figure about €10/day. Bus #81 stops a 10-minute walk uphill from the beach, near Villa Euphrussi.

For me, the best reason to come here is for dinner. Arrive before sunset, then watch as darkness descends and lights flicker over Villefranche-sur-Mer's heavenly setting. **$$$ Restaurant de la Plage de Passable** is your chance to dine on the beach with romance and class (but average food) while enjoying terrific views and the sounds of children still at play (daily late May-early Sept, always make a reservation, tel. 04 93 76 06 17, www.plage-de-passable.com).

Plage de la Paloma

This half-private, half-public beach is a 10-minute walk from St-Jean-Cap-Ferrat (described below). For €25 you get a lounge chair and the freedom to relax on the elegant side. Or enjoy the pebbly free beach (with shower and WC).

$$$ Plage de la Paloma Restaurant is inviting for dining on the beach, with salads for lunch and elegant dinners (daily from 12:00 and from 20:00, closed late Sept-mid-April, tel. 04 93 01 64 71, www.paloma-beach.com).

ST-JEAN-CAP-FERRAT

This quiet harbor town lies in Cap Ferrat's center, yet is off most tourist itineraries and feels overlooked. St-Jean houses yachts,

boardwalks, views, and boutiques packaged in a "take your time, darling" atmosphere. It's a few miles off the busy Nice-to-Monaco road—convenient for drivers. A string of restaurants line the port, with just enough visitors to keep them in business. St-Jean is especially peaceful at night. Sit on a whale-tail bench, enjoy the giant clamshell flowerboxes, and work on your Cyrillic (as many signs come in Russian to cater to the needs of the town's wealthiest guests).

There's a small TI in the village center with limited hours (described earlier). The stop for the bus back to Villefranche-sur-Mer is a block above the port near Hôtel la Frégate (if you need a taxi,

EAST OF NICE

call 04 93 76 86 00). The hiking trail to Beaulieu-sur-Mer (with access to the Villa Ephrussi and Villefranche-sur-Mer for hard-core walkers) begins past the beach, to the left of the port as you look out to the water (details follow). If it's lunchtime, you'll find plenty of good options.

Eating in St-Jean: For picnics, the short pedestrian street in St-Jean has all you need (grocery store, bakery, charcuterie, and pizza to go), and you'll have no trouble finding portside or seaside seating. Plage de la Paloma, described earlier, is a 10-minute walk away.

$ Le St. Jean Pizzeria/Restaurant is central, easygoing, and cheap—on the square with a view and salads (closed Wed, Avenue Denis Séméria, tel. 04 93 76 04 75).

$$$ Restaurant La Cabane de l'Ecailler, right on the harbor, with fancy yachts for a view, is elegant and expensive but offers a reasonable two-course lunch on weekdays (Nouveau Port de Plaisance, tel. 04 93 87 39 31).

$$ Capitaine Cook is a sweet little mom-and-pop place that takes its fish seriously yet seems to turn its back on the harbor (no views). There's a patio out back and a cozy interior (good three-course *menu*, tasty *soupe de poisons* and bouillabaisse, closed Wed, a block uphill from the port toward Plage de la Paloma at 11 Avenue Jean Mermoz, tel. 04 93 76 02 66).

▲▲WALKS AROUND CAP FERRAT

The Cap is perfect for a walk; you'll find well-maintained foot trails covering most of its length. You have three easy, mostly level options of varying lengths. The TIs in Villefranche-sur-Mer and St-Jean have maps of Cap Ferrat with walking paths marked, or you can use the following itineraries with this book's map.

Between St-Jean and Beaulieu-sur-Mer (30 minutes)

A level walk takes you past sumptuous villas, great views, and fun swimming opportunities. From St-Jean's port, walk along the harbor and past the beach with the water on your right. Head up the steps to Promenade Maurice Rouvier and continue; before long you'll see smashing views of the whitewashed Villa Kérylos.

To get from Beaulieu-sur-Mer to St-Jean or the Villa Ephrussi, start at the Villa Kérylos (with the sea on your left), walk toward the Hôtel Royal Riviera, and find the trail. If going to St-Jean, stay left at the Villa Sonja Rello (about halfway down); if going to the Villa

Ephrussi, look for signs leading uphill before Villa Aurora (walk up the path to Avenue Henri Honoré Sauvan, then keep going). If you're walking from St-Jean to the Villa Ephrussi, turn left off the trail about 50 yards after passing Villa Aurora.

Plage de la Paloma Loop Trail (45 minutes)

A few blocks east of St-Jean's port, a scenic trail offers an easy sampling of Cap Ferrat's beauty. From the port, walk or drive about a quarter-mile east (with the port on your left, passing Hôtel La Voile d'Or); parking is available at the port or on streets near Plage de la Paloma. You'll find the trailhead where the road comes to a T—look for a *Plage Paloma* sign pointing left, but don't walk left. Cross the small gravel park *(Jardin de la Paix)* to start the trail, and do the walk counterclockwise. The trail is level and paved, yet uneven enough that good shoes are helpful. Plunk your picnic on one of the benches along the trail, or eat at the restaurant on Plage de la Paloma at the end of the walk (described earlier).

Plage de Passable Around the Cape to St-Jean (2-3 hours)

For a longer hike that circles the cape, follow the signs below the Villa Ephrussi marked *Plage Passable* (10 minutes downhill on foot from the villa, parking available near the trailhead). Walk down to the beach (you'll pass the recommended Restaurant de la Plage de Passable—ideal for lunch), turn left, and cross the beach. Go along a paved road behind the apartment building, and after about 60 yards, take the steps down to the trail *(Sentier Littoral)*. Walk as far as you want and double back, or do the whole enchilada—it's about six miles (10 kilometers) around the cape. Near the end of the trail, you'll pass by the port of St-Jean, where you have three options: Take bus #81 back to Villefranche-sur-Mer, walk back to the Villa Ephrussi or Plage de Passable via the shorter inland route (by reversing the directions under "Walks from the Villa Ephrussi," earlier), or continue on to Beaulieu-sur-Mer and take a bus to Monaco or Nice.

Sleeping on Cap Ferrat

In St-Jean: While St-Jean is the main town serving the notoriously wealthy community of Cap Ferrat, it does have some affordable hotels.

$$$ **Hôtel Brise Marine,** *** graced with gardens and a seaview terrace, is a peaceful retreat. Warmly run by Monsieur Maître-Henri, this aged mansion—with Old World character—feels lost in time. Most of its 16 comfortable rooms come with simple furnishings but fine views, and some have balconies—worth requesting (secure pay parking with reservation, between the port

and Plage de la Paloma at 58 Avenue Jean Mermoz, tel. 04 93 76 04 36, www.hotel-brisemarine.com, info@hotel-brisemarine.com).

$ Hôtel Oursin** is central to the port, with 13 well-priced and well-appointed rooms all on one floor. Run by mother-and-son team Chantal and Aubrey, it's a humble place with white walls that feels more like a B&B than a hotel (1 Avenue Denis Séméria, tel. 04 93 76 04 65, www.hoteloursin.com, reception@hoteloursin.com).

Between St-Jean and Villefranche-sur-Mer: Sitting across from Villefranche, at the start of Cap Ferrat, **$ Hôtel Patricia*** is a 20-minute walk to Villefranche or the Villa Ephrussi, and 10 minutes to Beaulieu-sur-Mer. Helpful owners Joelle and Franck provide 11 simple and homey rooms with eclectic decor (no elevator, no air-con, pay parking, near bus #100's l'Ange Gardien stop at 310 Avenue de l'Ange Gardien, tel. 04 93 01 06 70, www.hotelpatricia.riviera.fr, hotelpatricia@free.fr).

Villa Kérylos

The village of Beaulieu-sur-Mer, right on the Low Corniche road (just after Cap Ferrat), is busy with traffic. It's a good place to pick up the hiking trail to St-Jean and to visit the unusual Villa Kérylos. In 1902, an eccentric millionaire modeled his mansion after a Greek villa from the island of  Delos from about 200 B.C. No expense was spared in re-creating this Greek fantasy, from the floor mosaics to Carrara marble columns to exquisite wood furnishings. The rain-powered shower is fun, and the included audioguide will increase your Greek IQ. The ceramics workshop—open only high season and weekend afternoons—offers a chance to test your talents.

Cost and Hours: €12, includes audioguide; daily 10:00-19:00, Oct-May until 17:00; tel. 04 93 01 47 29, www.villakerylos.fr.

Getting There: Drivers should park near the casino in Beaulieu-sur-Mer, not on the villa's access road. Monaco-Nice bus #100 drops you at the Eglise stop in Beaulieu (5-minute walk to the Villa Kérylos), while bus #81 from Villefranche-sur-Mer and Nice stops at the villa's access road (for details on these buses, see page 350). Trains (2/hour, 10 minutes from Nice or Monaco) leave you a 10-minute walk away: Turn left out of the train station and left again down the main drag, then follow signs. The walking trail from Villa Kérylos to Cap Ferrat and the Villa Ephrussi de Rothschild begins on the other side of the bay, beneath Hôtel Royal Riviera.

Eze-le-Village

Capping a peak high above the sea, flowery and flawless Eze-le-Village (pronounced "ehz"; don't confuse it with the seafront town

of Eze-Bord-de-Mer) is entirely consumed by tourism. This *village d'art et de gastronomie* (as it calls itself) is home to perfume outlets, stylish boutiques, steep cobbled lanes, and magnificent views. Touristy as it Eze, its stony state of preservation and magnificent hilltop setting over the Mediterranean affords a fine memory. Day-tripping by bus to Eze-le-Village from Nice, Monaco, or Villefranche-sur-Mer works well. While Eze-le-Village can be tranquil early and late, during the day it is mobbed by cruise-ship and tour-bus groups.

GETTING TO EZE-LE-VILLAGE

There are two Ezes: Eze-le-Village (the spectacular hill town on the Middle Corniche) and Eze-Bord-de-Mer (a modern beach resort far below the "village" of Eze).

From Nice and upper Villefranche-sur-Mer, buses #82 and #112 together provide about hourly service to Eze-le-Village (only #82 runs on Sun, 30 minutes from Nice). To reach upper Villefranche-sur-Mer from the town's old port, you can walk or take a bus (see page 342).

From Nice, Villefranche-sur-Mer, or Monaco, you can also take the train or the Nice-Monaco bus (#100) to Eze-Bord-de-Mer, getting off at the Gare d'Eze stop. From there, take the infrequent #83 shuttle bus straight up to Eze-le-Village (8/day, daily about 9:00-18:00, schedule posted at stop, 15 minutes).

To connect Eze-le-Village directly with Monte Carlo in Monaco, take bus #112 (6/day Mon-Sat, none on Sun, 20 minutes).

There are no buses between La Turbie (Le Trophée d'Auguste) and Eze-le-Village (45-minute walk along the road's shoulder).

A taxi between the two Ezes or from Eze-le-Village to La Turbie will run you about €28 (tel. 06 09 84 17 84, or 06 14 89 34 48).

EAST OF NICE

Orientation to Eze-le-Village

Tourist Information: The helpful TI is adjacent to Eze-le-Village's main parking lot, just below the town's entry. Ask here for bus schedules. Call a week in advance to arrange a €10, one-hour English-language tour of the village that includes its gardens (garden entry extra, TI open daily 9:00-18:00, July-Aug until 19:00, Nov-March until 17:00 and closed Sun, Place de Gaulle, tel. 04 93 41 26 00, www.eze-tourisme.com).

Helpful Hints: The stop for **buses** to Nice is across the road by the Avia gas station, and the stops for buses to Eze-Bord-de-Mer and Monaco are on the village side of the main road, near the Casino grocery. Public **WCs** are just behind the TI and in the village behind the church.

Eze-le-Village Walk

This self-guided walk gives you a quick orientation to the village.

• *From the TI and parking lot, hike uphill into the town. You'll come to an exclusive hotel gate and the start of a steep trail down to the beach, marked* Eze/Mer. *For a panoramic view and an ideal picnic perch, side-trip 80 steps down this path (for details, see "Hike to Eze-Bord-de-Mer," later). Continuing up into the village, find the steps immediately after the ritzy hotel gate and climb to...*

Place du Centenaire: In this square, a stone plaque in the flower bed (behind the candy stand) celebrates the 100th anniversary of the 1860 plebiscite, the time when all 133 Eze residents voted to leave the Italian Duchy of Savoy and join France. A town map here helps you get oriented.

• *Now pass through the once-formidable town gate and climb into the 14th-century village.*

As you walk, stop to read the information plaques (in English) and contemplate the change this village has witnessed in the last 90 years. Eze-le-Village was off any traveler's radar until well after World War II (running water was made available only in the 1930s), yet today hotel rooms outnumber local residents two to one (66 to 33).

• *Wandering the narrow lanes, follow signs to the...*

Château Eza: This was the winter getaway of the Swedish royal family from 1923 until 1953; today it's a 15-room hotel. The château's tearoom (Salon de Thé), on a cliff overlooking the jagged

Riviera and sea, offers you the most scenic coffee or beer break you'll ever enjoy—for a price. The sensational view terrace is also home to an expensive-but-excellent **$$$$** restaurant (open daily, tel. 04 93 41 12 24).

• *Backtrack a bit and continue uphill (follow signs to* Jardin Exotique). *The lane ends at the hilltop castle ruins—now blanketed by the...*

Jardin d'Eze: You'll find this prickly festival of cactus and exotic plants suspended between the sea and sky at the top of Eze-le-Village. Since 1949, the ruins of an old château have been home to 400 different plants 1,400 feet above the sea (€6, usually daily 9:00-19:00, Oct-May until dusk, well-described in English, tel. 04 93 41 10 30). At the top, you'll be treated to a commanding 360-degree view, with a helpful *table d'orientation.* On a clear day (they say...) you can see Corsica. The castle was demolished by Louis XIV in 1706. Louis destroyed castles like this all over Europe (most notably along the Rhine), because he didn't want to risk having to do battle with their owners at some future date.

• *As you descend, drop by the...*

Eze Church: Though built during Napoleonic times, this church has an uncharacteristic Baroque fanciness—a reminder that 300 years of Savoy rule left the townsfolk with an Italian savoir faire and a sensibility for decor. Notice the pulpit with the arm holding a crucifix, reminding the faithful that Christ died for their sins.

Sights in Eze-le-Village

Fragonard Perfume Factory

This factory, with its huge tour-bus parking lot, lies on the Middle Corniche, 100 yards below Eze-le-Village. Designed for tour groups, it cranks them through all day long. If you've never seen mass tourism in action, this place will open your eyes. (The gravel is littered with the color-coded stickers each tourist wears so that salespeople know which guide gets the kickback.) Drop in for an informative and free tour (2/hour, 15 minutes). You'll see how the perfume and scented soaps are made before being herded into the gift shop.

Cost and Hours: Daily 8:30-18:30; best Mon-Fri 9:00-11:00 & 14:00-15:30, when people are actually working in the "factory," tel. 04 93 41 05 05.

Nearby: For a more intimate (but unguided) look at perfume, cross the main road in Eze-le-Village to visit the **Gallimard** shop. Explore the small museum (no English) and let the lovely ladies show you their scents (daily 9:00-18:00, across from Eze parking lot). They can give you a short tour if you ask.

EAST OF NICE

Hike to Eze-Bord-de-Mer

A steep trail leaves Eze-le-Village from the foot of the hill-town entry, near the fancy hotel gate (60 yards up from the main road), and descends 1,300 feet to the sea along a no-shade, all-view trail. The trail is easy to follow but uneven—allow 45 minutes (good walking shoes are essential; expect to be on all fours in certain sections). Once in Eze-Bord-de-Mer, you can catch a bus or train to all destinations between Nice and Monaco. While walking this trail in the late 1800s, Friedrich Nietzsche was moved to write his unconventionally spiritual novel, *Thus Spoke Zarathustra*.

Eating in Eze-le-Village

To enjoy Eze-le-Village in relative peace, visit at sunset and stay for dinner. There's a handy **Casino** grocery at the foot of the village by the bus stop (daily 8:00-19:30) and a sensational picnic spot at the beginning of the trail to Eze-Bord-de-Mer. **$ Le Cactus** serves crêpes, salads, and sandwiches at outdoor tables near the entry to the old town and inside their cozy, vaulted dining room (daily, tel. 04 93 41 19 02). For a real splurge, dine at **$$$$ Château Eza** (described earlier, on my "Eze-le-Village Walk").

Le Trophée des Alpes

High above Monaco, on the Grande Corniche in the overlooked village of La Turbie, lies the ancient Roman "Trophy of the Alps," one of this region's most evocative historical sights (with dramatic views over the entire country of Monaco as a bonus). Rising well above all other buildings, this massive monument, worth ▲, commemorates Augustus Caesar's conquest of the Alps and its 44 hostile tribes. It's exciting to think that, in a way, Le Trophée des Alpes (also called "Le Trophée d'Auguste" for the emperor who built it) celebrates a victory that kicked off the Pax Romana—joining Gaul and Germania, freeing up the main artery of the Roman Empire, and linking Spain and Italy.

GETTING THERE

By Car: Take the High Corniche to La Turbie, ideally from Eze-le-Village (La Turbie is 10 minutes east of, and above, Eze-le-Village), then look for signs to *Le Trophée d'Auguste.* Once in La Turbie, park in the lot in the center of town (Place Neuve, follow *Monaco* signs for a short block) and walk from there (go five minutes around the old village, with the village on your right); or drive to the site by turning right in front of La Régence Café. Those coming from farther afield can take the efficient A-8 to the La Turbie exit. To reach Eze-le-Village from La Turbie, follow signs to *Nice,* and then look for signs to *Eze-le-Village.*

By Bus: From Nice, you can get here Monday through Saturday on **buses** #116 or #T-66 (6/day each from the Vauban tram stop); on Sunday take bus #T-66 (from the Pont St. Michel tram stop). From Monaco, bus #11 connects to La Turbie (8/day Mon-Sat, 5/day Sun, 30 minutes). La Turbie's bus stop is near the post office (La Poste) on Place Neuve.

On Foot: Eze-le-Village is a 45-minute roadside walk downhill from La Turbie (no buses). There's a bike lane for half of the trip, but the rest is along a fairly quiet road with no shoulder. Follow D-2564 from La Turbie to Eze-le-Village, and don't miss the turnoff for D-45. The views of Eze-le-Village are magnificent as you get close.

ORIENTATION TO LE TROPHEE DES ALPES

Cost and Hours: €6, Tue-Sun 9:30-13:00 & 14:30-18:30, off-season 10:00-13:30 & 14:30-17:00, closed Mon year-round.

Tours and Information: The audioguide is €3. Tel. 04 93 41 20 84, www.la-turbie.monuments-nationaux.fr.

VISITING THE MONUMENT

You'll enter through a small park that offers grand views over Monaco and allows you to appreciate the remarkable setting selected by the Romans for this monument. Walk around and notice how the Romans built a fine stone exterior, filled in with rubble and coarse concrete. Flanked by the vanquished in chains, the towering inscription (one of the longest such inscriptions surviving from ancient times) tells the story: It was erected "by the senate and the people to honor the emperor."

The structure served no military purpose when built, though it was fortified in the Middle Ages (like the Roman Arena in Arles) as a safe haven for villagers. When Louis XIV ordered the destruction of the area's fortresses in the early 18th century, he sadly included this one. The monument later became a quarry before being restored in the 1930s and 1940s with money from the Tuck family of New Hampshire.

The good little one-room **museum** shows a reconstruction and translation of the dramatic inscription, which lists all the feisty alpine tribes that put up such a fight.

NEAR THE MONUMENT: LA TURBIE

The sweet old village of La Turbie sees almost no tourists, but it has plenty of cafés and restaurants. To stroll the old village, walk behind the post office and find brick footpaths that lead through the peaceful back lanes of the village.

Eating in La Turbie: Your best bet is **$$ Restaurant La Terrasse,** with tables under umbrellas and big views (daily for lunch and dinner, near the post office at the main parking lot, 17 Place Neuve, tel. 04 93 41 21 84).

Quickie Riviera Bus Tour

The Riviera from Nice to Monaco and on to Menton is so easy to tour by bus and train that those with a car should consider leaving it at their hotel. While the train laces together the charms of this dramatic stretch of Mediterranean coast as if on a scenic bracelet, the public bus affords a far better view of the crags, dreamy villas, and much-loved beaches that make it Europe's coast with the most.

PLANNING YOUR TIME

This tour works best if you ride the bus from Nice the entire route to Menton (1.5 hours), enjoy Menton, and then see Monaco and Villefranche-sur-Mer on the way back to Nice. Get an early start (and remember that Monte Carlo's casino is closed to visitors from 12:00-14:00 and the game rooms don't open until 14:00). Keep in mind that afternoon buses back to Nice are often crammed and agonizingly slow after Villefranche-sur-Mer—at these times, you can always take the train.

BUS TIPS

Bus #100 runs frequently along the Low Corniche (3-4/hour; because of construction in Nice, you must board at the city's port— see map on page 286). One simple €1.50 ticket is good for 74 minutes, no matter how far you go (one-way only). Pay the driver as you get on.

Riding from Nice toward Monaco, grab a seat on the right. To beat the beach-goers, start before 9:00. If there's a long line, you could wait for the next bus to be assured of a view seat. Stops are announced on most buses. The last bus leaves Monaco for Nice at about 20:00.

Since bus fares are cheap, consider hopping on and off at great viewpoints (the next bus is always 15-20 minutes away). All stops have names shown on overhead monitors on the bus; also usually posted on the shelter or bus stop sign)—I'll use the bus stop names to orient you as we go.

Some bus drivers on this line are in training for the Grand Prix of Monaco—hold on tight.

FROM NICE TO MONACO

This route along the Low Corniche was inaugurated with the opening of the Monte Carlo Casino in 1863. It was designed to provide easy and safe access from Nice (and the rest of France) to the gambling fun in Monaco. Here's what you'll see along the way:

Nice Harbor: This harbor—dredged by 400 convicts—was finished in the mid-1800s. Before then, boats littered Nice's beaches. You'll see some yachts, an occasional cruise ship, and the daily ferry to Corsica. The one-hour boat tour along Cap Ferrat and Villefranche-sur-Mer leaves from the right side, about halfway down (see page 291). If you return by bus #100, it's a pleasant 30-minute walk around the distant point to or from the Promenade des Anglais and Nice's old town.

From Nice to Villefranche-sur-Mer: As you glide away from Nice, look back for views of the harbor, Castle Hill, and the sweeping Bay of Angels. Imagine the views from the homes below, and imagine 007 on his deck admiring a sunset (the soft, yellow, rounded tower straight ahead near the top of the hill was part of Sean Connery's property). Elton John's home is higher up the hill (and out of view). Imagine his neighbor, Tina Turner, dropping by.

You'll soon pass the Palais Maerterlinck, one of several luxury hotels to go belly-up in recent years and be converted to luxury condos. Next, you'll come to the yacht-studded bay of Villefranche-sur-Mer and the peninsula called Cap Ferrat—playground of the rich and famous, marked by its lighthouse on the point just across the bay. This bay is a rare natural harbor along the Riviera. Since it's deeper than Nice's, it hosts huge cruise ships, which drop anchor and tender passengers in.

Villefranche-sur-Mer: To see charming Villefranche-sur-Mer, get off at the stop labeled *Octroi*.

After passing through Villefranche-sur-Mer, look for sensational views back over the town (best from the Madonne-Noire stop). Looking ahead, the Baroness Rothschild's pink Villa Ephrussi, with its red-tiled roof, breaks the horizon on Cap Ferrat's peninsula. Keep an eye out below for the small point of land with umbrella pine trees as the road arcs to the right—the Rolling Stones recorded 1972's *Exile on Main Street* in the basement of the Villa Nellcôte, the mansion below the l'Ange Gardien stop.

Cap Ferrat: This peninsula is home to the Villa Ephrussi de Rothschild, the port town of St-Jean, and some lovely seaside paths. To visit Cap Ferrat, get off at l'Ange Gardien stop. As you leave Cap Ferrat, remember that this road was built in the 1860s to bring customers to Monaco. Before then, there was nothing along this route—no one even lived here—all the way to Monaco.

Beaulieu-sur-Mer: To visit the Villa Kérylos or to take the seaside walk to St-Jean on Cap Ferrat, get off at the Eglise stop.

Just after the town of Beaulieu-sur-Mer, the cliffs create a microclimate and a zone nicknamed "Little Africa." (The bus stop is labeled *Petite Afrique*.) Exotic vegetation (including the only bananas on the Riviera) grows among private, elegant villas that made Beaulieu-sur-Mer *the* place to be in the 19th century.

Eze-Bord-de-Mer: A few minutes after leaving Beaulieu-sur-Mer, be ready for quickie views way up to the fortified town of Eze-le-Village. After passing through a rock arch, you'll swing around a big bend going left: Eze-le-Village crowns the ridge in front of you. To reach Eze-le-Village by bus, the #83 shuttle bus makes the climb from the Gare d'Eze stop in Eze-Bord-de-Mer—see page 361. To reach the village on foot (see description on page 365), find the ramp at the east end of Eze-Bord-de-Mer, to the left just before the tunnel. U-2's Bono owns a villa on the beach below.

Cap d'Ail: After passing through several tunnels, you emerge at Cap d'Ail. Near the Deux Tunnels stop, you can't miss the huge, yellowish, hospital-like building below that once thrived as a luxury hotel popular with the Russian aristocracy. Now it's luxury condos. At the first stop in the village of Cap d'Ail (stop: Cap d'Ail-Edmonds), look above at the switchbacks halfway up the barren hillside. It was at the bend connecting these two switchbacks that Princess Grace Kelly (the American movie star who married into the royal family of Monaco) was killed in a car crash in 1982. You can get off here and walk a lovely beach trail that will take you to Monaco in roughly 30 minutes.

Monaco (three bus stops): Cap d'Ail borders Monaco—you're about to leave France. You'll pass by some junky development along this no-man's-land stretch. Eventually, to the right, just before the castle-topped hill (Monaco-Ville), is Monaco's Fontvieille district, featuring tall, modern apartments all built on land reclaimed from the Mediterranean. The first Monaco stop (Place d'Armes) is best for visiting the palace and other old-town sights in Monaco-Ville.

If you stay on the bus, you'll pass through the tunnel, then emerge to follow the road that Grand Prix racers speed along. In late May you'll see blue bleachers and barriers set up for the big race.

You'll pass the second Monaco stop (on the port, named Princesse Antoinette), then enjoy the harbor and city views as you climb to the last Monaco stop (Casino), near the TI. Get off here for the casino. For information on Monaco, see the next chapter. If you stay on the bus for a few more minutes, you'll be back in France, and in 15 more minutes you'll reach the end of the line, **Menton** (described in the following chapter).

Bonne route!

MONACO

Despite high prices, wall-to-wall daytime tourists, and a Disney-esque atmosphere, Monaco is a Riviera must. Monaco is on the go. Since 1929, cars have raced around the port and in front of the casino in one of the world's most famous auto races, the Grand Prix de Monaco. The modern breakwater—constructed elsewhere and towed in by sea—enables big cruise ships to dock here, and the district of Fontvieille, reclaimed from the sea, bristles with luxury high-rise condos. But don't look for anything too deep in this glittering tax haven. Many of its 36,000 residents live here because there's no income tax—there are only about 6,000 true Monegasques.

This minuscule principality (0.75 square mile) borders only France and the Mediterranean. The country has always been tiny, but it used to be...less tiny. In an 1860 plebiscite, Monaco lost two-thirds of its territory when the region of Menton voted to join France. To compensate, France suggested that Monaco build a fancy casino and promised to connect it to the world with a road (the Low Corniche) and a train line. This started a high-class tourist boom that has yet to let up.

Although "independent," Monaco is run as a part of France. A French civil servant appointed by the French president—with the blessing of Monaco's prince—serves as state minister and manages the place. Monaco's phone system, electricity, water, and so on, are all French.

The glamorous romance and marriage of the American actress Grace Kelly to Prince Rainier added to Monaco's fairy-tale mystique. Princess Grace first came to Monaco to star in the 1955 Alfred Hitchcock movie *To Catch a Thief,* in which she was filmed racing along the Corniches. She married the prince in 1956 and adopted the country, but tragically, the much-loved princess died in 1982 after suffering a stroke while driving on one of those same scenic roads. She was just 52 years old.

The death of Prince Rainier in 2005 ended his 56-year-long enlightened reign. Today, Monaco is ruled by Prince Albert Alexandre Louis Pierre, Marquis of Baux—son of Prince Rainier and Princess Grace. Prince Albert was long considered Europe's most eligible bachelor—until he finally married on July 2, 2011, at age 53. His bride, known as Princess Charlene, is a South African commoner 20 years his junior.

A graduate of Amherst College, Albert is a bobsled enthusiast who raced in several Olympics, and an avid environmentalist who seems determined to clean up Monaco's tarnished tax-haven, money-laundering image. (Monaco is infamously known as a "sunny place for shady people.") Monaco is big business, and Prince Albert is its CEO. Its famous casino contributes only 5 percent of the state's revenue, whereas its 43 banks—which offer a hard-to-resist way to hide your money—are hugely profitable. The prince also makes money for Monaco with a value-added tax (20 percent, same as in France), plus real estate and corporate taxes.

Monaco is a special place: There are more people in Monaco's philharmonic orchestra (about 100) than in its army (about 80). Yet the princedom is well-guarded, with police and cameras on every corner. (They say you could win a million dollars at the casino and walk to the train station in the wee hours without a worry.) Stamps are printed in small quantities and increase in value almost as soon as they're available. And collectors snapped up the rare Monaco versions of euro coins (with Prince Rainier's portrait) so quickly that many Monegasques have never even seen one.

Orientation to Monaco

The principality of Monaco has three tourist areas: Monaco-Ville, Monte Carlo, and La Condamine. **Monaco-Ville** fills the rock high above everything else and is referred to by locals as Le Rocher ("The Rock"). This is the oldest part of Monaco, home to the Prince's Palace and all the key sights except the casino. **Monte Carlo** is the area around the casino. **La Condamine** is the port, which lies between Monaco-Ville and Monte Carlo. From here it's a

25-minute walk up to the Prince's Palace or to the casino, or three minutes by frequent bus to either (see "Getting Around Monaco," later).

The surgical-strike plan for most travelers is to start at Monaco-Ville (where you'll spend the most time), wander down along the port area, and finish by gambling away whatever you have left in Monte Carlo (the casino's game rooms don't open until 14:00). You can walk the entire route in about 1.5 hours, or take three bus trips and do it in 15 minutes.

TOURIST INFORMATION

The main TI is at the top of the park above the casino (Mon-Sat 9:00-19:00, Sun 11:00-13:00, 2 Boulevard des Moulins, tel. 00-377/92 16 61 16 or 00-377/92 16 61 66, www.visitmonaco.com). Note that the TI may move to another location by the time you visit, though it should remain near the casino. Another TI is at the train station (Tue-Sat 9:00-18:00, also open Sun-Mon in July-Aug, closed 12:00-14:00 off-season).

ARRIVAL IN MONACO

By Bus from Nice and Villefranche-sur-Mer: See my "Quickie Riviera Bus Tour" on page 366 to plan your route. Bus riders need to pay attention, as stops are not always announced. Cap d'Ail is the town before Monaco, so be on the lookout after that (the last stop before Monaco is called "Cimetière"). You'll enter Monaco through the modern cityscape of high-rises in the Fontvieille district. When you see the rocky outcrop of old Monaco, be ready to get off.

There are three stops in Monaco. In order from Nice, they are Place d'Armes (at the base of Monaco-Ville), Princesse Antoinette (on the port), and Monte Carlo-Casino (near the casino and the TI on Boulevard des Moulins).

Most riders will get off at **Place d'Armes** to visit Monaco-Ville first. Use the crosswalk in front of the tunnel, then, with the rock on your right, walk until you see bus stops #1 and #2 and the ramp to the palace. Casino-first types wait for the *Monte Carlo-Casino* stop. There's no reason to exit at the port stop.

By Train from Nice: The long, entirely underground train station is in the center of Monaco. From here, it's a 15-minute walk to the casino or the port, and about 25 minutes to the palace (or a few minutes by frequent local bus). The station has no baggage storage.

The TI, train-ticket windows, and WCs are up the escalator at the Italy end of the station. There are three exits from the train platform level (one at each end and one in the middle).

To reach Monaco-Ville and the palace, take the exit at the Nice end of the tracks (signed *Sortie Fontvieille/Le Rocher*), which leads through a long tunnel to the base of Monaco-Ville at Place d'Armes. From here, it's about a 15-minute hike up to the palace, or take the bus (#1 or #2).

To reach Monaco's port and the casino, take the middle exit, following *Sortie Port* signs down the steps and escalators, and then *Accès Port* signs until you pop out at the port, where you'll see the stop for buses #1 and #2 across the busy street. From here, it's a 20-minute walk to the casino (up Avenue d'Ostende to your left), or a short trip via bus #1 or #2.

To return to Nice by train after 20:30, when ticket windows close, buy your return tickets on arrival or be sure to have about €4 in coins for the ticket machines.

By Car: Follow *Centre-Ville* signs into Monaco (warning: traffic can be heavy), then watch for the signs to parking garages at *Le Casino* (for Monte Carlo) or *Le Palais* (for Monaco-Ville). You'll pay about €12 for four hours.

By Cruise Ship: See "Monaco Connections," near the end of this chapter.

HELPFUL HINTS

Grand Prix Prep: If you come anytime in May, you'll encounter construction detours as the country prepares for its largest event of the year, the Grand Prix de Monaco.

Combo-Tickets: If you plan to see both of Monaco's big sights (Prince's Palace and Oceanography Museum), buy the €20.50 combo-ticket. Another combo-ticket includes the Prince's private car collection in Fontvieille (not covered in this book).

Changing of the Guard: This popular event takes place daily (in good weather) at 11:55 at the Prince's Palace. Arrive by 11:30 to get a good viewing spot.

Loop Trip by Bus or Train: From Nice, you can get to Monaco by bus or train, then take a bus from Monaco to Eze-le-Village or La Turbie, and return to Nice from there by bus. For bus numbers, frequencies, and stop locations, see "Monaco Connections," near the end of this chapter.

Evening Events: Monaco's **Philharmonic Orchestra** (tel. 00-377/98 06 28 28, www.opmc.mc) and **Monte Carlo Ballet** (tel. 00-377/99 99 30 00, www.balletsdemontecarlo.com) offer performances at reasonable prices.

Passport Stamp: For an official memento of your visit, get your passport stamped at the TI.

Post Office: The handiest post office for local stamps is in Monaco-Ville (described on my self-guided walk; Mon-Fri 8:00-19:00, Sat until 13:00, closed Sun).

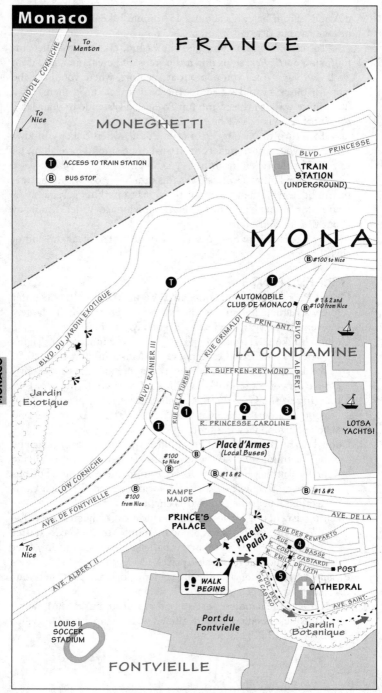

Monaco

MONACO

FRANCE

To Menton

Middle Corniche

To Nice

MONEGHETTI

T ACCESS TO TRAIN STATION

B BUS STOP

BLVD. PRINCESSE

TRAIN STATION (UNDERGROUND)

MONA

B #100 to Nice

T

T

AUTOMOBILE CLUB DE MONACO

B # 1 & 2 and #100 from Nice

BLVD. DU JARDIN EXOTIQUE

RUE GRIMALDI

R. PRIN. ANT.

BLVD. ALBERT I

LA CONDAMINE

R. SUFFREN-REYMOND

Jardin Exotique

BLVD. RAINIER III

RUE DE LA TURBIE

1

2

3

R. PRINCESSE CAROLINE

T

LOTSA YACHTS!

Place d'Armes
(Local Buses)

B

#100 to Nice

B #1 & #2

Low Corniche

RAMPE MAJOR

B #1 & #2

AVE. DE LA

AVE. DE FONTVIEILLE

B #100 from Nice

To Nice

PRINCE'S PALACE

Place du Palais

RUE DES REMPARTS

4

RUE BASSE

R. COMTE GASTARDI

R. EMILE DE LOTH

POST

AVE. ALBERT II

WALK BEGINS

R. COL. BELL DE CASTRO

5

CATHEDRAL

AVE. SAINT-

LOUIS II SOCCER STADIUM

Port du Fontvieille

Jardin Botanique

FONTVIEILLE

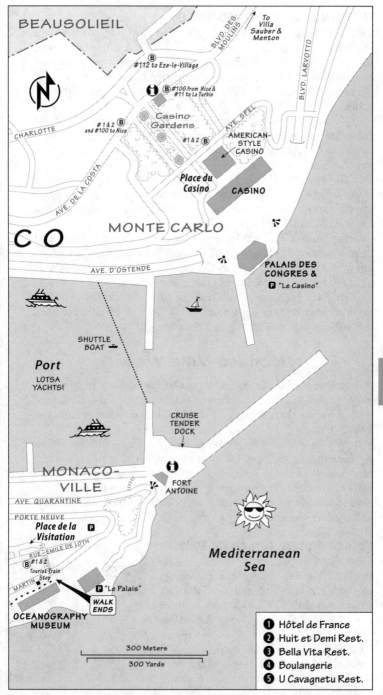

BEAUSOLEIL

To Villa Sauber & Menton

BLVD. DES MOULINS

BLVD. LARVOTTO

B #112 to Eze-le-Village

ℹ B #100 from Nice & #11 to La Turbie

AVE. SPEL

Casino Gardens

CHARLOTTE

#1 & 2 B and #100 to Nice

#1 & 2 B

AMERICAN-STYLE CASINO

AVE. DE LA COSTA

Place du Casino

CASINO

C O

MONTE CARLO

AVE. D'OSTENDE

PALAIS DES CONGRES & P "Le Casino"

SHUTTLE BOAT

Port

LOTSA YACHTS!

CRUISE TENDER DOCK

MONACO-VILLE

ℹ FORT ANTOINE

Mediterranean Sea

AVE. QUARANTINE

PORTE NEUVE

Place de la Visitation P

RUE EMILE DE LOTH

B #1 & 2 Tourist Train Stop

MARTIN

P "Le Palais"

WALK ENDS

OCEANOGRAPHY MUSEUM

300 Meters

300 Yards

❶ Hôtel de France
❷ Huit et Demi Rest.
❸ Bella Vita Rest.
❹ Boulangerie
❺ U Cavagnetu Rest.

MONACO

GETTING AROUND MONACO

By Local Bus: Buses #1 and #2 link all areas with frequent service (10/hour, fewer on Sun, buses run until 21:00). A single ticket is €2 (6 tickets-€11, day pass-€5.50, pay driver or save 50 percent at red curbside machines). You can split a six-ride ticket with your travel partners. Bus tickets are good for a free transfer if used within 30 minutes.

For a **cheap and scenic loop ride** through Monaco, ride bus #2 from one end to the other and back (25 minutes each way). You'll need two tickets and must get off the bus at the last stop and then get on again.

By Open Bus Tour: You could pay €22 for a hop-on, hop-off open-deck bus tour that makes 12 stops in Monaco, but I wouldn't. If you want a scenic tour of the principality that includes its best views, take local bus #2 (see above).

By Tourist Train: Monaco Tours tourist trains are an efficient way to enjoy a blitz tour of Monaco. They begin at the Oceanography Museum and pass by the port, casino, and palace (€9, 2/hour, 40 minutes, recorded English commentary).

By Taxi: If you've lost all track of time at the casino, you can call the 24-hour taxi service (tel. 00-377/93 15 01 01)...provided you still have enough money to pay for the cab home.

Monaco-Ville Walk

All of Monaco's major sights (except the casino) are in Monaco-Ville, packed within a few cheerfully tidy blocks. This self-guided walk connects these sights in a tight little loop, starting from the palace square.

• *To get from anywhere in Monaco to the palace square (Monaco-Ville's sightseeing center and home of the palace), take bus #1 or #2 to the end of the line at Place de la Visitation. Turn right as you step off the bus and walk five minutes down Rue Emile de Loth. You'll pass the post office, a worthwhile stop for its collection of valuable Monegasque stamps (we'll go there later—to visit it now, see page 379).*

Palace Square (Place du Palais)

This square is the best place to get oriented to Monaco. Facing the palace, go to the right and look out over the city (er...principality). This rock gave birth to the little pastel Hong Kong look-alike in 1215, and it's managed to remain an independent country for most of its 800 years. Looking beyond the glitzy port, notice the faded green roof above and to

the right: It belongs to the casino that put Monaco on the map in the 1800s. The casino was located away from Monaco-Ville because Prince Charles III (r. 1856-1889) wanted to shield his people from low-life gamblers.

The modern buildings just past the casino mark the eastern limit of Monaco. The famous Grand Prix runs along the port and then up the ramp to the casino (at top speeds of 180 mph). Italy is so close, you can almost smell the pesto. Just beyond the casino is France again (it flanks Monaco on both sides)—you could walk one-way from France to France, passing through Monaco, in about 60 minutes.

The odd statue of a woman with a fishing net is dedicated to the glorious reign of **Prince Albert I** (1889-1922). The son of Charles III (who built the casino), Albert I was a true Renaissance Man. He had a Jacques Cousteau-like fascination with the sea (and built Monaco's famous aquarium, the Oceanography Museum) and was a determined pacifist who made many attempts to dissuade Germany's Kaiser Wilhelm II from becoming involved in World War I.

Escape the crowds for a moment with a short detour up the street, keeping the view on your left. Gawk at the houses lining the street and imagine waking up to that view every day.

• *Head toward the palace, passing electric car chargers (Prince Albert is an environmentalist), and find a statue of a monk grasping a sword.*

Meet **François Grimaldi,** a renegade sword-carrying Italian dressed as a monk, who captured Monaco in 1297 and began the dynasty that still rules the principality. Prince Albert is his great-great-great...grandson, which gives Monaco's royal family the distinction of being the longest-lasting dynasty in Europe.

• *Now walk to the...*

Prince's Palace (Palais Princier)

A medieval castle once sat where the palace is today. Its strategic setting has had a lot to do with Monaco's ability to resist attackers.

Today, Prince Albert and his wife live in the palace, while poor Princesses Stephanie and Caroline live down the street. The palace guards protect the prince 24/7 and still stage a **Changing of the Guard** ceremony with all the pageantry of an important nation (daily  at 11:55 in good weather, fun to watch but jam-packed, arrive by 11:30). An audioguide takes you through part of the prince's lavish palace in 30 minutes. The rooms are well-furnished and impressive, but interesting only if you haven't seen a château lately.

Cost and Hours: €8, includes audioguide, €20.50 combo-ticket includes Oceanography Museum; hours vary but generally daily 10:00-18:00, July-Aug until 19:00, closed Nov-March; buy ticket at the *Billeterie* at the souvenir stand 75 yards opposite the palace entrance; tel. 00-377/93 25 18 31, www.palais.mc.

• *Head to the west end of the palace square. Below the cannonballs is the district known as...*

Fontvieille

Monaco's newest, reclaimed-from-the-sea area has seen much of Monaco's post-WWII growth (residential and commercial—notice the lushly planted building tops). Prince Rainier continued—some say, was obsessed with—Monaco's economic growth, creating landfills (topped with apartments, such as in Fontvieille), flashy ports, more beaches, a big sports stadium marked by tall arches, and a rail station. (An ambitious new landfill project is in the works and would add still more prime real estate to Monaco's portfolio.) Today, thanks to Prince Rainier's past efforts, tiny Monaco is a member of the United Nations. (If you have kids with you, check out the nifty play area just below.)

• *With your back to the palace, leave the square through the arch at the far right (onto Rue Colonel Bellando de Castro) and find the...*

Cathedral of Monaco (Cathédrale de Monaco)

The somber but beautifully lit cathedral, rebuilt in 1878, shows that Monaco cared for more than just its new casino. It's where centuries of Grimaldis are buried, and where Princess Grace and Prince Rainier were married. Inside, circle slowly behind the altar (counterclockwise). The second tomb is that of Albert I, who did much to put Monaco on the world stage. The second-to-last tomb—inscribed *"Gratia Patricia, MCMLXXXII"* and displaying the 1956 wedding photo of Princess Grace and Prince Rainier—is where the princess was buried in 1982. Prince Rainier's tomb lies next to hers (cathedral open daily 8:30-19:15).

• *Leave the cathedral and dip into the immaculately maintained **Jardin Botanique**, with more fine views. In the gardens, turn left. Eventually you'll find the impressive building housing the...*

Oceanography Museum
(Musée Océanographique)

Prince Albert I had this cliff-hanging museum built in 1910 as a monument to his enthusiasm for things from the sea. The museum's aquarium, which Jacques Cousteau captained for 32 years, has 2,000 different specimens, representing 250 species. You'll find Mediterranean fish and colorful tropical species (all well-described in English). Rotating exhibits occupy the entry floor. Upstairs, the fancy Albert I Hall is filled with ship models, whale skeletons, oceanographic instruments and tools, and scenes of Albert and his beachcombers hard at work—but sadly, only scant English information. Don't miss the elevator to the rooftop terrace view café.

Cost and Hours: €11-16, kids-€7-12 (price depends on season), €20.50 combo-ticket includes Prince's Palace; daily 10:00-19:00, longer hours July-Aug, Oct-March until 18:00; down the steps from Monaco-Ville bus stop, at the opposite end of Monaco-Ville from the palace; tel. 00-377/93 15 36 00, www.oceano.mc.

• *The red-brick steps across from the Oceanography Museum lead up to stops for buses #1 and #2, both of which run to the port, the casino, and the train station. To walk back to the palace and through the old city, turn left at the top of the brick steps. If you're into stamps, walk down Rue Emile de Loth to find the post office, where philatelists and postcard writers with panache can buy—or just gaze in awe at—the impressive collection of Monegasque stamps.*

Sights in Monaco

Jardin Exotique

This cliffside municipal garden, located above Monaco-Ville, has eye-popping views from France to Italy. It's home to more than a thousand species of cacti (some giant) and other succulent plants, but worth the entry only for view-loving botanists (some posted English explanations provided). Your ticket includes entry to a skippable natural cave, an anthropological museum, and a view snack bar/café. You can get similar views over Monaco for free from behind the souvenir stand at the Jardin's bus stop; or, for even grander vistas, cross the street and hike toward La Turbie.

Cost and Hours: €7.20, daily 9:00-19:00, Oct-April until about dusk, take bus #2 from any stop in Monaco, tel. 00-377/93 15 29 80, www.jardin-exotique.com.

▲Monte Carlo Casino (Casino de Monte-Carlo)

Monte Carlo, which means "Charles' Hill" in Spanish, is named for the prince who presided over Monaco's 19th-century makeover. In the mid-1800s, olive groves stood here. Then, with the construction of casino and spas, and easy road and train access, one of Europe's poorest countries was on the Grand Tour map—*the* place

for the vacationing aristocracy to play. Today, Monaco has the world's highest per-capita income.

The Monte Carlo casino is intended to make you feel comfortable while losing your retirement nest egg. Charles Garnier designed the place (with an opera house inside) in 1878, in part to thank the prince for his financial help in completing Paris' Opéra Garnier (which the architect also designed). The central doors provide access to slot machines, gaming rooms, and the opera house. The gaming rooms occupy the left wing of the building. Cruise ship visitors can jam the entry from 14:00 to 16:30.

The odd bubble-like structures that line the parkway above the casino are temporary, and house high-end boutiques relocated from nearby for a long-term construction project.

Cost and Hours: Entry fees and hours are shuffled regularly. Plan on €10 to enter at any hour, whether you gamble or not, and expect lines at the entrance. Public areas are open daily 9:00-12:00 (no gambling). Take an English brochure and tour on your own. From 14:00 to very late, the gaming rooms are open to appropriately attired humans over 18 (bring your passport as proof). Tel. 00-377/92 16 20 00, www.montecarlocasinos.com.

Dress Code: Before 19:00, walking shorts are allowed in the atrium area (but no short shorts, torn jeans, etc.). You'll need decent attire to go any farther. After 19:00, shorts and tennis shoes are off-limits everywhere. Men should wear a jacket and slacks, and women should dress appropriately.

Eating: The casino has two dining options. The **$$$$ Train Bleu** restaurant is for deep pockets for whom price is no object and elegance is everything. **$$$ Le Salon Rose** offers brasserie food—big salads and pasta dishes in a classy setting. Show your casino ticket to be reimbursed for the entrance fee before asking for the bill.

Visiting the Casino: Count the counts and Rolls-Royces in front of **Hôtel de Paris.** The hotel was built at the same time as the casino to house gamblers—transportation back to Nice was not so fast (visitors allowed in the hotel, no shorts, www.montecarloresort.com).

Enter the casino to the sumptuous **atrium.** This is the lobby for the 520-seat opera house (open Nov-April only for performanc-

MONACO

Le Grand Prix Automobile de Monaco

The Grand Prix de Monaco focuses the world's attention on this little country. The race started as an enthusiasts' car rally

by the Automobile Club de Monaco (and is still run by the same group, more than 80 years later). The first race, held in 1929, was won by a Bugatti at a screaming average speed of...48 mph (today's cars triple that speed). To this day, drivers consider this one of the most important races on their circuits. The race takes place every year toward the end of May (www.acm.mc).

By Grand Prix standards, it's an unusual course, running through the streets of this tiny principality, sardined between mountains and sea. The hilly landscape means that the streets are narrow, with tight curves, steep climbs, and extremely short straightaways. Each lap is about two miles, beginning and ending at the port. Cars climb along the sea from the port, pass in front of the casino, race through the commercial district, and do a few dandy turns back to the port. The race lasts 78 laps, and whoever is still rolling at the end wins (most don't finish).

The Formula 1 cars look like overgrown toys that kids might pedal up and down their neighborhood street (if you're here a week or so before the race, feel free to browse the parking structure below Monaco-Ville, where many race cars are kept). Time trials to establish pole position begin three days before the race, which is always on a Sunday. More than 150,000 people attend the gala event; like the nearby film festival in Cannes, it's an excuse for yacht parties, restaurant splurges, and four-digit bar tabs at luxury hotels. During this event, hotel rates in Nice and beyond rocket up (even for budget places).

Fans wanting to touch the storied past of this race can window-shop the Automobile Club de Monaco's headquarters and patronize its boutique next door (on the port at 23 Boulevard Albert 1er).

es). A model of the opera house is at the far-right side of the room, near the marble WCs.

The **first gambling rooms** (Salle Renaissance, Salon de l'Europe, and Salle des Amériques) offer European and English roulette, plus Trente et Quarante, Punto Banco—a version of baccarat—and slot machines. The more glamorous **game rooms** (Salons Touzet, Salle Medecin, and Terrasse Salle Blanche) have those same games and Ultimate Texas Hold 'em poker, but you play against the cashier with higher stakes.

The scene, flooded with camera-toting tourists during the day, is great at night—and downright James Bond-like in the private rooms. This is your chance to rub elbows with some high rollers.

The **park** behind the casino offers a peaceful place with a good view of the building's rear facade and of Monaco-Ville.

Take the Money and Run: The stop for buses returning to Nice and Villefranche-sur-Mer, and for local buses #1 and #2, is on Avenue de la Costa, at the top of the park above the casino (at the small shopping mall; for location, see map on page 374). To reach the train station from the casino, take bus #1 or #2 from this stop, or find Boulevard Princesse Charlotte (parallels Avenue de la Costa one block above) and walk 15 minutes.

Sleeping and Eating in Monaco

Sleeping: Centrally located in Monaco-Ville, **$$ Hôtel de France**** is comfortable, well run by friendly Sylvie, and reasonably priced—for Monaco (includes breakfast, air-con, no elevator; exit west from train station, 15-minute walk to 6 Rue de la Turbie, tel. 00-377/93 30 24 64, www.hoteldefrance.mc, hoteldefrance@monaco.mc).

Eating on the Port: Several cafés serve basic, inexpensive fare (day and night) on the port. Troll the places that line the flowery and traffic-free Rue Princesse Caroline between Rue Grimaldi and the port. **$$$ Huit et Demi** is a reliable choice, with a white-tablecloth-meets-director's-chair ambience and good outdoor seating (closed Sun, 7 Rue Princesse Caroline, tel. 00-377/93 50 97 02). A few blocks below, **$$ Bella Vita**—an easygoing place for salads, Italian fare, and classic French dishes—has a large terrace and modern interior (daily, serves nonstop from morning to late, 21 Rue Princesse Caroline, tel. 00-377/93 50 42 02).

Eating in Monaco-Ville: You'll find sandwiches—including the massive *pan bagnat*, basically *salade niçoise* on country bread—and quiche at the yellow-bannered **$ Boulangerie** (daily until 19:00, near Place du Palais at 8 Rue Basse). At **$$ U Cavagnetu,** just a block from Albert's palace, you'll dine cheaply on specialties from Monaco (daily, serves nonstop 11:00-23:00, 14 Rue Comte Félix Gastaldi, tel. 00-377/97 98 20 40). Monaco-Ville has other pizzerias, *crêperies,* and sandwich stands, but the neighborhood is dead at night.

MONACO

Monaco Connections

BY TRAIN

For a comparison of train and bus connections, see the "Public Transportation in the French Riviera" sidebar on pages 278. Most trains heading west will stop in Villefranche-sur-Mer and Nice (ask). Note that the last train leaves Monaco for Villefranche-sur-Mer and Nice at about 23:30. If you plan to leave Monaco on a late train (after 20:30, when ticket windows close), buy tickets in advance or bring enough coins (about €4) for the machines.

From Monaco by Train to: Villefranche-sur-Mer, Nice, Antibes, or **Cannes** (2/hour).

BY BUS

Frequent **bus #100,** which runs along the Low Corniche back to **Nice** (1 hour), is often crowded. For a better chance of securing a seat, board at the stop near the TI on Avenue de la Costa (see map on page 374) rather than the stop near Place d'Armes. Bus #100 also stops near **Cap Ferrat** (20 minutes plus 20-minute walk or transfer to bus #81) and in **Villefranche-sur-Mer** (40 minutes). The last bus leaves Monaco for Nice at about 20:00. In the other direction bus #100 goes to **Menton** (30 minutes). For bus details, including tickets, routes, frequencies, and travel times, see page 275.

Bus #112, which goes along the scenic Middle Corniche to **Eze-le-Village** (6/day Mon-Sat, none on Sun, 20 minutes), departs Monaco from Place de la Crémaillère, one block above the main TI and casino park. Walk up Rue Iris with Barclays Bank to your left, curve right, and find the bus shelter across the street at the green La Crémaillère café (bus number not posted).

Bus #11 to **La Turbie** (8/day Mon-Sat, 5/day Sun, 30 minutes) stops in front of the TI (same side of street).

Bus #110 express takes the freeway to **Nice Airport** (2/hour, 50 minutes, €22).

BY CRUISE SHIP

Cruise ships tender passengers to the end of Monaco's yacht harbor, a short walk from downtown. It's a long walk or a short bus ride to most sights in town. To reach other towns, such as Villefranche-sur-Mer or Nice, you can take public transportation. To summon a taxi (assuming none are waiting when you disembark), look for the gray taxi call box near the tender dock—just press the button and wait for your cab to arrive.

Getting into Town: To reach **Monaco-Ville,** which towers high over the cruise terminal, you can either hike steeply and scenically up to the top of the hill, or walk to Place d'Armes and hop on bus #1 or #2, which will take you up sweat-free. It's a 15-minute,

MONACO

level walk to the bus stop from the port: Cross Boulevard Albert I, follow green *Gare S.N.C.F./Ferroviare* signs, and take the public elevator to Place d'Armes.

The ritzy skyscraper zone of **Monte Carlo** is across the harbor from the tender dock, about a 25-minute walk. You can also ride the little electric "bateau bus" shuttle boat across the mouth of the harbor (works with a bus ticket). To reach the upper part of Monte Carlo—with the TI and handy bus stops (including for Eze-le-Village and La Turbie)—catch bus #1 or #2 at the top of the yacht harbor, along Boulevard Albert I.

Getting to Sights Beyond Monaco: Monaco is connected to most nearby sights by both train and bus. **Trains** run about twice hourly to Villefranche-sur-Mer (10 minutes), then on to Nice (20 minutes). The train station is about a 20-minute walk from the tender harbor—first walk to Place d'Armes (directions above), then follow Rue Grimaldi to find stairs and an elevator to the station.

Buses run regularly to nearby towns (see "By Bus," earlier, for bus stop locations and frequencies). If taking bus #112 to Eze-le-Village or bus #11 to La Turbie, first ride bus #1 or #2 to the TI and casino, then follow the directions above.

Menton

If you wish the Riviera were less glitzy and more like a place where humble locals take their families to lick ice cream and make sand castles, visit Menton (east of Monaco). Menton feels like a poor man's Nice. It's unrefined and unpretentious, with lower prices, fewer rentable umbrellas, and lots of Italians day-tripping in from just over the border (five miles away). There's not an American in sight.

Getting There: While trains serve Menton regularly, the station is a 15-minute walk from the action. Buses are more convenient, as they run frequently and drop visitors right on the beach promenade (bus #100; see page 276 for details). To return to Monaco or Nice, catch bus #100 on Avenue Thiers, just off Avenue de Verdun.

Visiting Menton: Though a bit rough, the Menton beach is a joy. An inviting promenade lines the beach, and seaside cafés serve light meals and salads (much cheaper than in Nice). A snooze or stroll here is a fine Riviera experience. From the promenade, a pedestrian street leads through town. Small squares are alive with jazz bands playing crowd-pleasers under palm trees.

Stepping into the old town—which blankets a hill capped by a fascinating cemetery—you're immersed in a pastel-painted, yet dark-and-tangled Old World scene with (strangely) almost no commerce. A few elegant restaurants dig in at the base of the towering centuries-old apartment flats. The richly decorated Baroque St. Michael's Church (midway up the hill, Mon-Fri 10:00-12:00 & 15:00-17:15, closed to visitors Sat-Sun) is a reminder that, until 1860, Menton was a thriving part of the larger state of Monaco. Climbing past sun-grabbing flower boxes and people who don't get out much anymore, the steep stepped lanes finally deposit you at the ornate gate of a grand cemetery that fills the old castle walls. Explore the cemetery, which is the final resting place of many aristocratic Russians (buried here in the early 1900s) and offers breathtaking Mediterranean views.

ANTIBES & NEARBY

Antibes • Cannes • St-Tropez

The Riviera opens up west of Nice with bigger, sandier beaches and an overabundance of tasteless beachfront development. Ancient Antibes and superficial Cannes buck the slap-it-up high-rise trend, both with thriving centers busy with pedestrians and yachts. Glamorous St-Tropez, a scenic 1.5-hour drive from Antibes, marks the western edge of the French Riviera.

PLANNING YOUR TIME

Antibes works well by car, bus, or train. You can day-trip in from Nice or, better, sleep here (hotels have easier parking than in Nice or Villefranche-sur-Mer, and train/bus service to nearby destinations is efficient). Allow a full day for Antibes sights (two nights is good). Antibes also works as a base for day trips: Cannes is a short hop away by bus, train, or car (train is best); and Grasse (covered in the next chapter) is also easy by car, bus, or train (note that trains to Grasse may not run while its station is renovated). St-Tropez—a 1.5-hour drive from Antibes—is best visited on your way in or out of the Riviera.

Antibes

Antibes has a down-to-earth, easygoing ambience. Its old town is a warren of narrow streets and red-tile roofs rising above the blue Med, protected by twin medieval towers and wrapped in extensive ramparts. Visitors making the short trip from Nice can browse Europe's biggest yacht harbor, snooze on a sandy beach, loiter through an enjoyable old town, and hike along a sea-swept trail. The town's

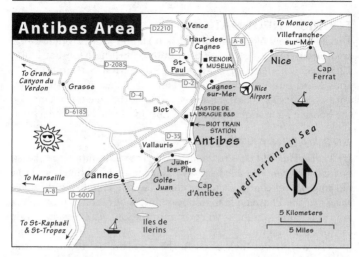

Antibes Area

To Monaco
Vence
Villefranche-
sur-Mer
D2210
Haut-des-
Cagnes
A-8
D-7
RENOIR
MUSEUM
Nice
St-
Paul
Cap
Ferrat
D-2085
To Grand
Canyon du
Verdon
Grasse
D-2
Cagnes-
sur-Mer
Nice
Airport
D-4
D-6185
Biot
BASTIDE DE
LA BRAGUE B&B
BIOT TRAIN
STATION
Mediterranean Sea
D-35
Antibes
Vallauris
Juan-
les-Pins
To Marseille
Cannes
Golfe-
Juan
Cap
d'Antibes
A-8
D-6007
N
To St-Raphaël
& St-Tropez
Iles de
lerins
5 Kilometers
5 Miles

cultural claim to fame, the Picasso Museum (closed on Mondays), shows off its appealing collection in a fine old building.

Though much smaller than Nice, Antibes has a history that dates back just as far. Both towns were founded by Greek traders in the fifth century B.C. To the Greeks, Antibes was "Antipolis"—the town *(polis)* opposite *(anti)* Nice. For the next several centuries, Antibes remained in the shadow of its neighbor. By the turn of the 20th century, the town was a military base—so the rich and famous partied elsewhere. But when the army checked out after World War I, Antibes was "discovered" and enjoyed a particularly roaring '20s—with the help of party animals like Rudolph Valentino and the rowdy (yet silent) Charlie Chaplin. Fun seekers even invented water-skiing right here in the 1920s.

Orientation to Antibes

Antibes' old town lies between the port and Boulevard Albert I and

Avenue Robert Soleau. Place Nationale is the old town's hub of activity. Stroll above the sea between the old port and Place Albert I (where Boulevard Albert I meets the water). The best beaches lie just beyond Place Albert I, and the easy walk there is beautiful. Good play areas for children are along this path and on Place des Martyrs de la Résistance (close to recommended Hôtel Relais du Postillon).

ANTIBES & NEARBY

TOURIST INFORMATION

The TI is a few blocks from the train station at 42 Avenue Robert Soleau (July-Aug daily 9:00-19:00; Sept-June Mon-Sat 9:00-12:30 & 13:30-18:00, Sun 9:00-13:00; Mon-Sat until 17:00 and closed Sun in winter; free Wi-Fi, tel. 04 22 10 60 10, www.antibesjuanlespins.com). Hikers should get the free tourist map of the Sentier Touristique de Tirepoil hike (described on page 399).

ARRIVAL IN ANTIBES

By Train: Bus #14 runs frequently from the train station to the city bus station (*gare routière*; near several recommended hotels and the old town), and continues to the fine Plage de la Salis, with quick access to the Phare de la Garoupe trail (2/hour, none on Sun, bus stop 100 yards to right as you exit train station). **Taxis** usually wait in front of the station.

To **walk** from the station to the port, the old town, and the Picasso Museum (15 minutes), cross the street in front of the station, skirting left of the café, and follow Avenue de la Libération downhill as it bends left. At the end of the street, head to the right along the port. If you walk on the water's edge, you'll see the yachts get bigger as you go.

To walk directly to the TI and recommended hotels in the old town, turn right out of the station and walk down Avenue Robert Soleau.

There's no baggage check in Antibes. The last train back to Nice leaves at about midnight.

By Bus: Antibes has two bus stations—one for regional buses and one for city buses. **Regional buses** (including bus #200 from Nice and airport bus #250) don't enter the city center, stopping instead at the bus station behind the train station (called the *Pôle d'Echange*; take the pedestrian overpass from behind the train station to reach it). Buses to and from Nice stop at the far right (east) end (info office open Mon-Fri 7:00-19:00, Sat 9:00-12:30 & 14:00-17:00, closed Sun).

City buses use the bus station at the edge of the old town on Place Guynemer, a block below Place Général de Gaulle (info desk open Mon-Fri 7:30-19:00, Sat 8:30-12:00 & 14:30-17:30, closed Sun, www.envibus.fr).

By Car: Day-trippers follow signs to *Centre-Ville*, then *Port Vauban*. The easiest place to park is a convenient but pricey underground parking lot located outside the ramparts near the archway leading into the old town (€9/4 hours, €20/12 hours, just south of Port Vauban—see map on page 392). A free lot is available opposite Fort Carré (north of the port). It's a 15-minute walk to the old town from here; you can also catch bus #14. Street parking is free

Monday through Friday (12:00-14:00 & 19:00-8:00), and all day Saturday and Sunday.

If you're sleeping in Antibes, follow *Centre-Ville* signs, then signs to your hotel. The most appealing hotels in Antibes are best by car, and Antibes works well for drivers—compared with Nice, parking is easy, traffic is minimal, and it's a convenient springboard for the Inland Riviera. Pay parking is available at Antibes' train station, so drivers can ditch their cars here and day-trip from Antibes by train.

HELPFUL HINTS

Markets: Antibes' old-time market hall (Marché Provençal) hosts a vibrant produce market (daily until 13:00, closed Mon Sept-May), and a lively antiques/flea market fills Place Nationale and Place Audiberti, next to the port (Thu and Sat 7:00-18:00). A clothing market winds through the streets around the post office on Rue Lacan (Thu 9:00-18:00).

English Bookstore: Antibes Books has a welcoming vibe and a good selection of new and used books, with many guidebooks—including mine (Tue-Sat 10:00-19:00, Sun-Mon 11:00-18:00, 13 Rue Georges Clemenceau, tel. 04 93 61 96 47, www.antibesbooks.com).

Laundry: There's a launderette at 19 Avenue du Grand Cavalier (daily 8:00-20:45).

Bike Rental: The TI has a list of places where you can rent bikes (including electric bikes). A bike path leads along the sea toward Nice, and bikes are a good way for nondrivers to reach the hikes described later in this chapter.

Taxi: For a taxi, call tel. 04 93 67 67 67.

Car Rental: The big-name agencies have offices in Antibes (all close Mon-Sat 12:00-14:00 and all day Sun). The most central are **Avis** (at the train station, tel. 04 93 34 65 15) and **Hertz** (across from the train station at 52 Avenue Robert Soleau, tel. 04 92 91 28 00).

Boat Rental: You can motor your own seven-person yacht thanks to **Antibes Bateaux Services** (€100/half-day, at the small fish market on the port, mobile 06 15 75 44 36, www.antibes-bateaux.com).

GETTING AROUND ANTIBES

Antibes' buses (Envibus) cost €1 and are handiest for carless travelers wanting access to Cap d'Antibes. **Bus #14** links the train station, city bus station, old town, and Plage de la Salis. It also takes you to Fort Carré, where free parking is available. **Bus #2** provides access to the best beaches, the path to La Phare de la Garoupe, and the Cap d'Antibes trail. It runs from the city bus station down

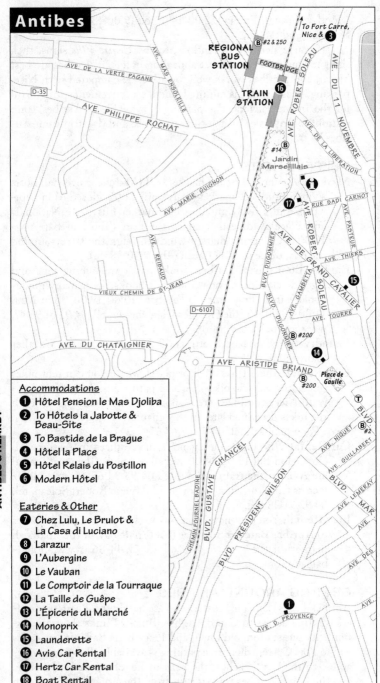

Antibes

ANTIBES & NEARBY

To Fort Carré, Nice & ③

B #2 & 250

REGIONAL BUS STATION

FOOTBRIDGE

TRAIN STATION

⑯

AVE. DE LA VERTE PAGANE

AVE. MAS ENSOLEILLE

D-35

AVE. PHILIPPE ROCHAT

AVE. ROBERT SOLEAU

AVE. DU 11 NOVEMBRE

AVE. DE LA LIBERATION

#14 B
Jardin Marseillais

RUE SADI CARNOT

⑰

AVE. MARIE GUIGNON

AVE. REIBAUD

AVE. ROBERT SOLEAU

AVE. PASTEUR

AVE. THIERS

AVE. DE GRAND CAVALIER

AVE. GAMBETTA

BLVD. DUGOMMIER

BLVD. DUGONNIER

⑮

AVE. TOURRE

VIEUX CHEMIN DE ST-JEAN

D-6107

B #200

⑭

AVE. DU CHATAIGNIER

AVE. ARISTIDE BRIAND

Place de Gaulle

B #200

Ⓣ

BLVD.

B #2

AVE. NIQUET

AVE. GUILLABERT

BLVD. LEMERAY

BLVD. MAR.

CHEMIN FOURNEL BADINE

BLVD. GUSTAVE CHANCEL

BLVD. PRÉSIDENT WILSON

AVE. DES

①

AVE. D. PROVENCE

Accommodations

① Hôtel Pension le Mas Djoliba
② To Hôtels la Jabotte & Beau-Site
③ To Bastide de la Brague
④ Hôtel la Place
⑤ Hôtel Relais du Postillon
⑥ Modern Hôtel

Eateries & Other

⑦ Chez Lulu, Le Brulot & La Casa di Luciano
⑧ Larazur
⑨ L'Aubergine
⑩ Le Vauban
⑪ Le Comptoir de la Tourraque
⑫ La Taille de Guêpe
⑬ L'Épicerie du Marché
⑭ Monoprix
⑮ Launderette
⑯ Avis Car Rental
⑰ Hertz Car Rental
⑱ Boat Rental

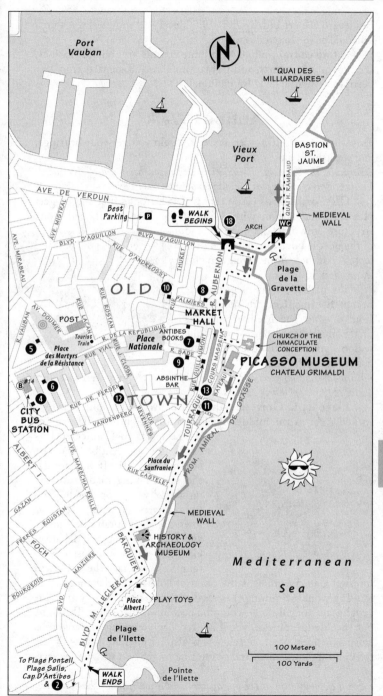

Port Vauban

"QUAI DES MILLIARDAIRES"

Vieux Port

BASTION ST. JAUME

AVE. DE VERDUN

Best Parking

WALK BEGINS

18

ARCH

WC

MEDIEVAL WALL

AVE. MISTRAL

AVE. MIRABEAU

BLVD. D'AGUILLON

BLVD. D'AGUILLON

RUE D'ANDREOSSY

RUE THURET

R. AUBERNON

Plage de la Gravette

OLD

RUE ROSTAN

RUE LACAN

AVE. DOUMER

R. VAUBAN

POST

Tourist Train

Place Nationale

RUE DE LA RÉPUBLIQUE

RUE PALMIERS

10

8

MARKET HALL

RUE SADE

Antibes Books

7

RUE GUILLAUMONT

CHURCH OF THE IMMACULATE CONCEPTION

Place des Martyrs de la Résistance

5

RUE VIAL

RUE CLOSE

9

ABSINTHE BAR

COURS MASSENA

PICASSO MUSEUM

CHATEAU GRIMALDI

B #14

6

4

CITY BUS STATION

RUE DE FERSEL

12

TOWN

13

11

RUE TOURRAQUE

RUE DU BATEAU

RUE DE GRASSE

R. G. VANDENBERG

RUE REVENNES

Place du Sanfranier

RUE CASTELET

ROM. AMIRAL DE GRASSE

ALBERT I

AVE. MARECHAL REILLE

GAZAN

FRERES ROUSTAN

FOCH

MEDIEVAL WALL

BOURGEOIS

BLVD. G. RAIMBAUD

BARQUIER

HISTORY & ARCHAEOLOGY MUSEUM

Mediterranean

Sea

BLVD. M. LECLERC

Place Albert I

PLAY TOYS

Plage de l'Ilette

To Plage Pontell, Plage Salis, Cap D'Antibes & **2**

WALK ENDS

Pointe de l'Ilette

100 Meters

100 Yards

ANTIBES & NEARBY

Boulevard Albert I (daily 7:00-19:00, every 40 minutes). Pick up a schedule at the bus station.

A **tourist train** offers 40-minute circuits around old Antibes, the port, the ramparts, and to Juan-les-Pins (€8, departs from pedestrian-only Rue de la République).

Antibes Walk

This 40-minute self-guided walk will help you get your bearings, and works well day or night.

• *Begin at the old port (Vieux Port) at the southern end of Avenue de Verdun. Stand at the port, across from the archway with the clock.*

Old Port: Locals claim that this is Europe's first and biggest pleasure-boat harbor, with 1,600 stalls. That star-shaped stone structure crowning the opposite end of the port is **Fort Carré,** which protected Antibes from foreigners for more than 500 years.

The pathetic remains of a oncehearty **fishing fleet** are moored in front of you. The Mediterranean is pretty much fished out. Most of the seafood you'll eat here comes from fish farms or the Atlantic.

• *With the port on your left, walk a block past the sorry fleet and duck under the first open arch to the shell-shaped...*

Plage de la Gravette: This normally quiet public beach is tucked right in the middle of old Antibes. Consider the scale of

the ramparts that protected this town. Because Antibes was the last fort before the Italian border, the French king made sure the ramparts were top-notch. The twin towers crowning the old town are the church's bell tower and the tower topping Château Grimaldi (today's Picasso Museum). As you face the old town, forested Cap d'Antibes is the point of land in the distance to the left. Is anyone swimming? Locals don't swim much in July and August because of jellyfish—common now in warmer water. Throughout the Mediterranean, you'll see red flags warning of dangerous storms or tides. Many beaches now also have white flags with jellyfish symbols warning that swimming might be a stinging experience.

• *For a close-up look at the megayachts and a walk along the ramparts, follow this fun detour. Otherwise, skip ahead to the "Old Antibes" directions.*

Antibes' Megayacht Harbor: Take a three-block detour to the north as you leave Plage de la Gravette for a glimpse at the epitome of conspicuous consumption. You'll walk along the harbor under the ramparts; enjoy the historic drawings and photos of the port along the wall.

You'll eventually reach a restricted area harboring massive yachts. Walk in and browse the line of huge pleasure craft stern-tied to the pier (which was built in the 1970s with financial aid from mostly Saudi Arabian yacht owners, who wanted a decent place to tie up). Locals call this the *Quai des Milliardaires* ("billionaire's dock"). The Union Jacks fluttering above most of the boats show that they're registered in the Cayman Islands (can you say tax dodge?). The crews you see keep these toys shipshape all year long—even though many of them are used for just a few days a year. Today, Antibes is the haunt of a large community of English, Irish, and Aussie boaters who help crew these giant yachts. (That explains the Irish pubs and English bookstores.)

Just outside the restricted area, climb up the rampart and make your way to the **modern white sculpture.** *Nomade*—a man of letters looking pensively out to sea—was created in 2010 by the Spaniard Jaume Plensa. You can sit in it and ponder how communication forms who we are and links all people.

Old Antibes: Now let's backtrack to where we started and enter Antibes' old town through the arch under the clock.

• *You can walk directly up the main street to get to our next stop, but here's a more scenic option: Passing through the gate, turn immediately left, walk along the wall and then up the stairs. At the terrace corner is another fine viewpoint. Turn right and walk straight through the arch at #14 and into Place du Revely, the most picturesque corner of the old town. On Place du Revely, turn right, and go down the ramp under several arches, then turn left uphill straight into the old town and Antibes' market hall, Le Marché Provençal.*

Market Hall: Antibes' market hall bustles under a 19th-century canopy, with flowers, produce, Provençal products, and beach accessories. The market wears many hats: produce until 13:30 (daily except closed Mon Sept-May), handicrafts most afternoons (Thu-Sun), and fun outdoor dining in the evenings, on Cours Masséna.

On the right (at the corner of Rue Sade), a pretty shop hides an atmospheric **absinthe bar** in its ninth-century vaulted cellar. You're welcome to

ANTIBES & NEARBY

go through the shop (or enter via Rue Sade) and descend to find an amazing collection of absinthe fountains, the oldest dating from the 1860s. Frédéric will gladly show you his memorabilia. You can even taste the now-legal drink to better understand Picasso's paintings. On Friday and Saturday nights, the basement is transformed into an absinthe-infused jazz bar lounge with 1920s ambience.

• *Facing the front of the market, go left uphill on Rue Christian Chessel and find the pretty pastel...*

Church of the Immaculate Conception: Built on the site of a Greek temple, this is worth a peek inside. A church has stood on this site since the 12th century. This one served as the area's cathedral until the mid-1200s. The stone bell tower standing in front of the church predates it by 600 years, when it was part of the city's defenses. Many of those heavy stones were pillaged from Antibes' Roman monuments.

• *Looming above the church on prime real estate is the white-stone...*

Château Grimaldi: This site was home to the acropolis of the Greek city of Antipolis and later a Roman fort. Later still, the château was the residence of the Grimaldi family (a branch of which still rules Monaco). Today it houses Antibes' Picasso Museum. Its proximity to the cathedral symbolized the sometimes too-cozy relationship between society's two dominant landowning classes: the Church and the nobility. (In 1789, the French Revolution changed all that.)

• *After visiting the **Picasso Museum** (see page 395), exit it to the left. Work your way through the warren of pretty lanes, then head out to the water, turn right along the ramparts, and find a sweeping sea view. As you walk, you'll pass a charming neighborhood (La Commune Libre du Safranier) on your right. The rampart walk leads to a viewpoint atop the History and Archaeology Museum.*

Viewpoint: From this perch you can enjoy a clear view of **Cap d'Antibes** (to the south), crowned by its lighthouse and studded with mansions (a proposed hike here is described later). The Cap was long the refuge of Antibes' rich and famous, and a favorite haunt of F. Scott Fitzgerald and Ernest Hemingway.

• *After taking a quick spin through the **History and Archaeology Museum** (see page 398), continue hugging the shore past Place Albert I until you see the views back to old Antibes. Benches and soft sand await (a few copies of famous artists' paintings of Antibes are placed on bronze displays along the beach walkway). You're on your own from here—energetic walkers can continue on the trail, which leads all the way to Cap d'Antibes (see page 399); others can return to old Antibes and wander around in its peaceful back lanes.*

Sights in Antibes

▲▲Picasso Museum (Musée Picasso)

Sitting serenely where the old town meets the sea, this compact three-floor museum offers a manageable collection of Picasso's

paintings, sketches, and ceramics. Picasso lived in this castle for part of 1946, when he cranked out an amazing amount of art (most of the paintings you'll see are from this short but prolific stretch of his long and varied career). He was elated by the end of World War II, and his works show a celebration of color and a rediscovery of light after France's long nightmare of war. Picasso was also reenergized by his young and lovely companion, Françoise Gilot (with whom he would father two children). The resulting collection (donated by Picasso) put Antibes on the tourist map. For more on Picasso's life, see the sidebar on page 396.

Cost and Hours: €6; Tue-Sun 10:00-18:00, mid-Sept-mid-June closes 12:00-14:00, closed Mon year-round; tel. 04 92 90 54 26, www.antibes-juanlespins.com.

Visiting the Museum: After buying your ticket, go through the glass door. Before heading inside, pause in the **sculpture garden** to appreciate Picasso's working environment (and wonder why he spent only a few months here).

The museum's interior is a calm place of white walls, soft arches, and ample natural light—a great space for exhibiting art. Tour the museum clockwise, noticing the focus on sea creatures, tridents, and other marine themes (*oursin* is a sea urchin, *poulpe* is an octopus, and *poisson* is, well, fishy). *Nature morte* means still life, and you'll see many of these in the collection. Each room has helpful English explanations posted.

The **ground floor** houses a cool collection of paintings by Norwegian artist Ann-Eva Bergmen and her husband, Hans Hartung, who spent their last years in Antibes. The **first floor** up holds temporary exhibitions (usually related to Picasso) and a small collection of intriguing paintings by Nicholas de Stael, whose style was greatly influenced by southern France and artists such as Henri Matisse (the painting of Antibes' Fort Carré is mood altering).

The museum's highlight is on the **top floor,** where you'll find the permanent collection of Picasso's works. Visitors are greeted by a large image of Picasso and a display of photographs of the artist at work and play during his time in Antibes. Times were tough in

ANTIBES & NEARBY

Pablo Picasso (1881-1973)

Pablo Picasso was the most famous and, for me, the greatest artist of the 20th century. Always exploring, he became the master of many styles (Cubism, Surrealism, Expressionism) and of many media (painting, sculpture, prints, ceramics, assemblages). Still, he could make anything he touched look unmistakably like "a Picasso."

Born in Málaga, Spain, Picasso was the son of an art teacher. At a very young age, he quickly advanced beyond his teachers. Picasso's teenage works are stunningly realistic and capture the inner complexities of the people he painted. As a youth in Barcelona, he fell in with a bohemian crowd that mixed wine, women, and art.

In 1900, at age 19, Picasso started making trips to Paris. Four years later, he moved to the City of Light and absorbed the styles of many painters (especially Henri de Toulouse-Lautrec) while searching for his own artist's voice. His paintings of beggars and other social outcasts show the empathy of a man who was himself a poor, homesick foreigner. When his best friend, Spanish artist Carlos Casagemas, committed suicide, Picasso plunged into a **Blue Period** (1901-1904)—so called because the dominant color in these paintings matches their melancholy mood and subject matter (emaciated beggars, hard-eyed pimps).

In 1904, Picasso got a steady girlfriend (Fernande Olivier) and suddenly saw the world through rose-colored glasses—the **Rose Period.** He was further jolted out of his Blue Period by the "flat" look of the Fauve paintings being made around him. Not satisfied with their take on 3-D, Picasso played with the "building blocks" of line and color to find new ways to reconstruct the real world on canvas.

At his studio in Montmartre, Picasso and his neighbor Georges Braque worked together in poverty so dire they often didn't know where their next bottle of wine was coming from. And then, at age 25, Picasso reinvented painting. Fascinated by the primitive power of African tribal masks, he sketched human faces with simple outlines and almond eyes. Intrigued by his girlfriend's body, he sketched Fernande from every angle, then experimented with showing several different views on the same canvas. A hundred paintings and nine months later, Picasso gave birth to a monstrous canvas of five nude, fragmented prostitutes with mask-like faces—*Les Demoiselles d'Avignon* (1907).

This bold new style was called **Cubism.** With Cubism, Picasso shattered the Old World and put it back together in a new way. The subjects are somewhat recognizable (with the help of the titles), but they're built with geometric shards (let's call them "cubes")—it's like viewing the world through a kaleidoscope of brown and gray. Cubism presents several different angles of the subject at once—say, a woman seen from the front and side simultaneously, resulting in two eyes on the same side of the nose. Cubism showed the traditional three dimensions, plus Einstein's new fourth dimension—the time it takes to walk around the subject to see other angles.

In 1918, Picasso married his first wife, Olga Kokhlova. He then traveled to Rome and entered a **Classical Period** (1920s) of more realistic, full-bodied women and children, inspired by the three-dimensional sturdiness of ancient statues. While he flirted with abstraction, throughout his life Picasso always kept a grip on "reality." His favorite subject was people. The anatomy might be jumbled, but it's all there.

Though he lived in France and Italy, Picasso remained a Spaniard at heart, incorporating Spanish motifs into his work. Unrepentantly macho, he loved bullfights, seeing them as a metaphor for the timeless human interaction between the genders. The horse—clad with blinders and pummeled by the bull—is just a pawn in the battle between bull and matador. To Picasso, the horse symbolizes the feminine, and the bull, the masculine. Spanish imagery—bulls, screaming horses, a Madonna—appears in Picasso's most famous work, *Guernica* (1937). The monumental canvas of a bombed village summed up the pain of Spain's brutal civil war (1936-1939) and foreshadowed the onslaught of World War II.

At war's end, Picasso left Paris, his wife, and his emotional baggage behind, finding fun in the **south of France.** Sun! Color! Water! Freedom! Senior citizen Pablo Picasso was reborn, enjoying worldwide fame. He lived at first with the beautiful young painter Françoise Gilot, mother of two of his children, but it was another young beauty, Jacqueline Roque, who became his second wife. Dressed in rolled-up white pants and a striped sailor's shirt, bursting with pent-up creativity, Picasso often cranked out a painting a day. Picasso's Riviera works set the tone for the rest of his life. They're sunny, lighthearted, and childlike; filled with motifs of the sea, Greek mythology (fauns, centaurs), and animals; and freely experimental in their use of new media. The simple drawing of doves Picasso made at this time became emblematic of the artist and an international symbol of peace.

Picasso made collages, built "statues" out of wood, wire, ceramics, papier-mâché, or whatever, and even turned everyday household objects into statues (like his famous bull's head made of a bicycle seat with handlebar horns). **Multimedia** works like these have become so standard today that we forget how revolutionary they once were. His last works have the playfulness of someone much younger. As it is often said of Picasso, "When he was a child, he painted like a man. When he was old, he painted like a child."

1946. Artists had to improvise. Picasso experimented with materials and surfaces like industrial paint on recycled canvases, random pieces of plywood, and even concrete. Try not to analyze too much. He's happy and in the French Riviera. Remember: The war's over and he's in love—this is pure happiness.

The first gallery room (up the small staircase to your left) houses several famous works, including the lively, frolicking, and big-breasted *La Joie de Vivre* painting (from 1946). This Greek bacchanal sums up the newfound freedom in a just-liberated France and sets the tone for the rest of the collection. You'll also see the colorless, three-paneled *Satyr, Faun and Centaur with Trident* and several ceramic creations. As you leave this room don't miss the adorable (pregnant?) goat.

Throughout, you'll see both black-and-white and colorful ink sketches that challenge the imagination—these show off Picasso's skill as a cartoonist and caricaturist. Look also for the cute Basque fishermen (*Pecheur attablé*) and several Cubist-style nudes *(nus couchés)*, one painted on plywood.

Near the end, don't miss the wall devoted to Picasso's ceramic plates. In 1947, inspired by a visit to a ceramics factory in nearby Vallauris, Picasso discovered the joy of this medium. He was smitten by the texture of soft clay and devoted a great deal of time to exploring how to work with it—producing over 2,000 pieces in one year. In the same room, the wall-sized painting *Ulysses and the Sirens* screams action and anxiety. Lashed to the ship mast, Ulysses survives the temptation of the sirens.

History and Archaeology Museum
(Musée d'Histoire et d'Archéologie)

More than 2,000 years ago, Antibes was the center of a thriving maritime culture. It was an important Roman city with aqueducts, theaters, baths, and so on. This museum—the only place to get a sense of the city's ancient roots—displays Greek, Roman, and Etruscan odds and ends in two simple halls (no English descriptions). Your visit starts at an 1894 model of Antibes and continues past displays of Roman coins, cups, plates, and scads of amphorae. The lanky lead pipe connected to a center box was used as a bilge pump; nearby is a good display of Roman anchors made of lead.

Cost and Hours: €3; Tue-Sun 10:00-12:00 & 14:00-18:00, mid-Sept-mid-June 10:00-13:00 & 14:00-17:00, closed Mon year-round, on the water between Picasso Museum and Place Albert I, tel. 04 92 95 85 98, www.antibes-juanlespins.com.

Fort Carré

This impressively situated, mid-16th-century citadel, on the headland overlooking the harbor, protected Antibes from Nice (which until 1860 wasn't part of France). You can tour this unusual star-shaped fort (€3) for the fantastic views over Antibes, but there's little to see inside.

▲Beaches *(Plages)*

Good beaches stretch from the south end of Antibes toward Cap d'Antibes. They're busy but manageable in summer and on weekends, with cheap snack stands and good views of the old town. The closest beach to the old town is at the port (Plage de la Gravette), which seems calm in any season.

HIKES

I list two good hikes below. Orient yourself from the bottom of Boulevard Albert I (where it meets the beach). That tower on the hill is your destination for the first hike. The longer Cap d'Antibes hike begins on the next beach, just over that hill. The two hikes are easy to combine by bus, bike, or car.

▲▲Chapelle et Phare de la Garoupe Hike

The territorial views—best in the morning, skippable if it's hazy—from this viewpoint more than merit the 20-minute uphill climb from Plage de la Salis (a few blocks after Maupassant Apartments, where the road curves left, follow signs and the rough, cobbled Chemin du Calvaire up to lighthouse tower). An orientation table explains that you can see from Nice to Cannes and up to the Alps.

Getting There: Take bus #2 or bus #14 to the Plage de la Salis stop and find the trail a block ahead. By car or bike, follow signs for *Cap d'Antibes,* then look for *Chapelle et Phare de la Garoupe* signs.

▲▲Cap d'Antibes Hike
(Sentier Touristique de Tirepoil)

Cap d'Antibes itself is filled with exclusive villas and mansions protected by high walls. Roads are just lanes, bounded on both sides by the high and greedy walls in this home of some of the most

expensive real estate in France (and where "public" seems like a necessary evil). But all the money in the world can't buy you the beach in France, so a thin strip of rocky coastline forms a two-mile long, parklike zone with an extremely scenic, mostly paved but often rocky trail (Sentier Touristique de Tirepoil).

As you walk, you'll have fancy fences with security cameras on one side and dramatic sea views on the other. The public space is rarely more than 50 yards wide and often extremely rocky—impassible if not for the paved trail carved out of it for the delight of hikers.

At a fast clip you can walk the entire circle in just over an hour. Don't do the hike without the tourist map (available at hotels or the TI). While you can do it in either direction (or in partial segments), I'd do the entire loop counterclockwise like this:

From the La Fontaine bus stop (see "Getting There," below), walk five minutes down Avenue Mrs. L. D. Beaumont to the gate of the Villa Eilenroc. From here leave the road and enter a trail, skirting the villa on your left, and walk five more minutes to the rocky coastal trail. Now turn left and follow the trail for nearly an hour around Cap Gros. There's no way to get lost without jumping into the sea or scaling villa security walls. You return to civilization at a tiny resort (Plage de la Garoupe), with an expensive restaurant, a fine beach (both public and private), and a fun and inexpensive beachside bar/restaurant. From here it's a 10-minute walk uphill to your starting point and the bus stop. With a car (or bike), you could start and end at Plage de la Garoupe. For a shorter version, walk from Plage de la Garoupe to Cap Gros and back.

Getting There: Ride bus #2 from Antibes for about 15 minutes to the La Fontaine stop at Rond-Point A. Meiland (next to the recommended Hôtel Beau-Site). By car or bike, follow signs to *Cap d'Antibes,* then to *Plage de la Garoupe,* and park there. The trail begins at the far-right end of Plage de la Garoupe.

NEAR ANTIBES
Juan-les-Pins Town

The low-rise town of Juan-les-Pins, sprawling across the Cap d'Antibes isthmus from Antibes, is where the action is...after hours. It's a modern waterfront resort with good beaches, plenty of lively bars and restaurants, and a popular jazz festival in July. The town is also known for its clothing boutiques that stay open until midnight (people are too busy getting tanned to shop at normal hours). As locals say, "Party, sleep in, shop late, party more."

Getting There: Buses, trains, and even a tourist train (see "Getting Around Antibes" on page 389) make the 10-minute trip to and from Antibes constantly.

Renoir Museum (Musée Renoir)

Halfway between Antibes and Nice, above Cagnes-sur-Mer, Pierre-Auguste Renoir found his Giverny. Here, the artist spent the last 12 years of his life (1907-1919) tending his gardens, painting, and even dabbling in sculpture (despite suffering from rheu-

matoid arthritis). His home
was later converted into a small
museum. Visitors get a personal look into Renoir's later
years but very little art. You'll
see his studio, wheelchair, and
bedroom; take a stroll in his
gardens; and enjoy several of
his and other artists' paintings
of people and places around

Cagnes-sur-Mer. It's a pleasant place and an enjoyable pilgrimage
for his fans.

Cost and Hours: €4, Wed-Mon 10:00-12:00 & 14:00-18:00,
Oct-April until 17:00, closed Tue year-round, Chemin des Col-
lettes, tel. 04 93 20 61 07.

Getting There: It's complicated by public transport (and not
worth the trouble for most), but manageable by car: Go to Cagnes-
sur-Mer, then follow brown *Musée Renoir* signs.

Biot Village

The artsy pottery and glassblowing village of Biot is popular with
aesthetic types and home to the Fernand Léger Museum.

Getting There: Biot is easy to reach on bus #10 from Antibes'
city bus station (2/hour). The best parking is just above the town,
allowing direct access to its pretty pedestrian street.

Sleeping in Antibes

Several sleepable options are available in the town center, but my
favorite Antibes hotels are farther out and most convenient for
drivers.

OUTSIDE THE TOWN CENTER

$$$ Hôtel Pension le Mas Djoliba* is a traditional manor house
with chirping birds and a flower-filled moat. While convenient
for drivers, it's workable for walkers (10-minute walk to Plage de
la Salis, 15 minutes to old Antibes). Bigger rooms are worth the
additional cost, and several rooms come with small decks (several
good family rooms, no elevator but just three floors, *boules* court
and loaner balls; 29 Avenue de Provence—from Boulevard Albert
I, look for gray signs two blocks before the sea, turn right onto
Boulevard Général Maizière, and follow signs; tel. 04 93 34 02 48,
www.hotel-djoliba.com, contact@hotel-djoliba.com, Delphine).

$$ Hôtel la Jabotte is a cozy little hotel hidden along an
ignored alley a block from the famous beaches and a 20-minute
walk from the old town. Run with panache by Nathalie, the hotel's

rich colors and decor show a personal touch. The immaculate rooms have tight bathrooms and individual terraces facing a small, central garden where you'll get to know your neighbor (no TVs, free breakfast for Rick Steves readers, 13 Avenue Max Maurey, take the third right after passing Hôtel Josse, tel. 04 93 61 45 89, www.jabotte.com, info@jabotte.com). The hotel can shuttle clients to the train station, hiking trails, restaurants, etc. in their small tuk-tuk vehicle for a small fee.

$$ Hôtel Beau-Site,*** my only listing on Cap d'Antibes, is a 10-minute drive from town. It's a terrific value if you want to get away...but not *too* far away. (Without a car, you'll feel isolated.) Helpful Nathalie and Francine welcome you with a pool, a comfy patio garden, and free, secure parking. Rooms are spacious and comfortable, and several have balconies (electric bikes available, 141 Boulevard Kennedy, tel. 04 93 61 53 43, www.hotelbeausite.net, contact@hotelbeausite.net). The hotel is a 10-minute walk from Plage de la Garoupe on the Cap d'Antibes loop hike (described earlier).

$ Bastide de la Brague is an easygoing bed-and-breakfast hacienda up a dirt road a 10-minute drive east of Antibes. The fun-loving family (wife Isabelle, who speaks English, and hubby Franck) rent seven comfy rooms; several are ideal for families, and breakfast is included (55 Avenue No. 6, tel. 04 93 65 73 78, www.labastidedelabrague.com, bastidebb06@gmail.com). From Antibes, follow *Nice par Bord de la Mer* signs, turn left and then right at the roundabout (toward Groules), then follow the green signs. Antibes bus #10 drops you five minutes away, and if arranged in advance, they can pick you up at the Biot or Antibes train station.

IN THE TOWN CENTER

$$$ Hôtel la Place*** is central, pricey, and cozy. It overlooks the ugly bus station with tastefully designed rooms and a comfy lounge (no elevator, 1 Avenue 24 Août, tel. 04 97 21 03 11, www.la-place-hotel.com, contact@la-place-hotel.com).

$ Hôtel Relais du Postillon,** is a mellow, central place above a peaceful café with 16 impeccable rooms at very fair rates. The furnishings are beautiful, and several rooms have small balconies or terraces (tiny elevator, pay parking, 8 Rue Championnet, tel. 04 93 34 20 77, www.relaisdupostillon.com, relais@relaisdupostillon.com).

$ Modern Hôtel,** in the pedestrian zone behind the city bus station, is suitable for budget-conscious travelers. The 17 standard-size rooms are simple and spick-and-span (no elevator, 1 Rue Fourmillière, tel. 04 92 90 59 05, www.modernhotel06.com, modern-hotel@wanadoo.fr).

Eating in Antibes

Antibes is a fun and relaxed place to dine out. But there are preciously few really good options in Antibes, and those get booked up on weekends in particular (when you're smart to book a day ahead). All but one of my recommendations are within a few blocks of each other, so it's easy to comparison shop.

Antibes' **Market Hall** (Marché Provençal) has great ambience and is popular with budget-minded diners each evening after the market stalls close. It's not *haute cuisine*, but prices are usually reasonable, and slurping mussels under a classic 19th-century canopy can make for a great memory. To start your soirée, consider a glass of wine from one of several wine bars that call the market hall home.

$$ Try **Chez Lulu** for an ultimate family-style dining adventure that seems utterly out of place on the Riviera. Diners fork over €26 and settle in, while charismatic owner Frank (who speaks flawless English), his wife Alice, and—when they're busy—their granddaughter dish out charcuterie, salads, soups, a main course, and desserts to be shared. Tables seat 6-10, and the setting is warm and convivial. Don't come for a romantic meal. You'll be on a first-name basis with your neighbors, cut your own bread, and serve your own soup (fun!). Book a day ahead or arrive early (from 19:00, closed Sun-Mon, tel. 04 89 89 08 92, 5 Rue Frédéric Isnard).

$$$$ **Larazur** is the love child of a young couple who both worked as chefs at Michelin-starred restaurants and wanted a quieter life in the south. Lucas does the cooking while Jeanne runs the restaurant. The setting is relaxed yet elegant, and the attention to quality is obvious (book ahead, closed Mon-Tue, 8 Rue des Palmiers, tel. 04 93 34 75 60).

$$ **L'Aubergine** is an intimate and très Provençal place where hustling Madame Jenny delivers traditional cuisine at fair prices. The menu offers a good variety and includes bouillabaisse and tasty desserts (from 18:30, closed Wed, 7 Rue Sade, tel. 04 93 34 55 93).

$$$$ **Le Vauban** is a dressy place with red-velvet chairs and serious service. It's popular with locals for special events and its seafood (closed for lunch Mon and Wed, closed all day Tue, opposite 4 Rue Thuret, tel. 04 93 34 33 05, www.levauban.fr).

$$$ **Le Comptoir de la Tourraque** is a cool wine-bistro sort of place, favored by locals for its reliable cuisine and convivial atmosphere (closed Wed, 1 Rue de la Tourraque, tel. 04 93 5 24 86).

$$ **Le Brulot,** an institution in Antibes, is known for its Provençal cuisine and meat dishes (most cooked over an open fire). It's a small, rustic place with tables crammed every which way (big, splittable portions, come early or book ahead, closed Sun, 2 Rue Frédéric Isnard, tel. 04 93 34 17 76).

$ La Casa di Luciano serves hearty pizza and big portions of pasta. It works for families, but it's no place for a foodie. This raucous and welcoming place has indoors-only seating in an atmospheric, air-conditioned cellar under stone arches (open daily for dinner only, 3 Rue Frédéric Isnard, tel. 04 93 34 19 19).

$$$ La Taille de Guêpe is family-run by Olivier in the kitchen and Katy in the relaxing garden-like dining room. The chef has worked for several years with flowers; the colorful varieties you find on your plate are all edible and add a twist to the fresh, fine, and light food. The *moëlleux au chocolat* is a perfect way to end your meal. *Menus*, enjoyed with cheap and good local wine, are a good deal (reservations recommended, closed Sun-Mon, 24 Rue de Fersen, tel. 04 93 74 03 58).

Picnic on the Beach or Ramparts: Romantics on a shoestring can drop by the handy **L'Épicerie du Marché** (a little grocery store open daily until 23:00, up the hill from the market hall at 3 Cours Masséna) and assemble their own picnic dinner to enjoy on the beach or ramparts. There's also a **Monoprix** on Place Général de Gaulle (Mon-Sat until 20:30, Sun until 12:30).

Antibes Connections

For a comparison of train and bus connections, see the "Public Transportation in the French Riviera" sidebar on page 278.

From Antibes by Train: TGV and local trains serve Antibes' little station. Trains go to **Cannes** (2/hour, 15 minutes), **Nice** (2/hour, 20 minutes), **Grasse** (1/hour, 40 minutes), **Villefranche-sur-Mer** (2/hour, 40 minutes), **Monaco** (2/hour, 50 minutes), and **Marseille** (16/day, 2.5 hours).

By Bus: All the buses listed below serve the Pôle d'Echange regional bus station (behind the train station); they do not enter the center of Antibes. Handy **bus #200** ties everything together from Cannes to Nice, but runs at a snail's pace when traffic is bad. It goes west to **Cannes** (35 minutes) and east to near **Biot** village (15 minutes—bus #10 is better, see page 401), **Cagnes-sur-Mer** (25 minutes), and **Nice** (1.5 hours). For bus details, including info on tickets, routes, frequencies, and travel times, see page 276. **Bus #250** runs to **Nice Airport** (2/hour, 40 minutes).

Cannes

Cannes (pronounced "can"), famous for its May film festival, is the sister city of Beverly Hills. That says it all. When I asked at the TI for a list of museums and sights, they just smiled. Cannes—with big, exclusive hotels lining mostly private stretches of perfect, sandy beach—is for strolling, shopping, dreaming of meeting a movie star, and lounging on the seafront. Cannes has little that's unique to offer the traveler...except a mostly off-limits film festival and quick access to two undeveloped islands. You can buy an ice-cream cone at the train station and see everything before you've had your last lick. Money is what Cannes has always been about—wealthy people come here to make the scene, and there's always enough *scandale* to go around. The king of Saudi Arabia purchased a serious slice of waterfront just east of town and built his compound with no regard to local zoning regulations. Money talks on the Riviera...and always has.

GETTING TO CANNES

Don't sleep or drive in Cannes. Day-trip here by train or bus. It's a breeze, as frequent trains and buses link to Cannes from seafront cities like Antibes (15 minutes by train) and Nice (30 minutes; longer by bus). For details, see the transportation chart on page 278. From Grasse, you can take a direct bus to Cannes. Buses stop next to the train station. A car is a headache best avoided in Cannes, though there's a darn scenic drive just west of Cannes (from Fréjus on D-6098).

Orientation to Cannes

Buses stop in front of the train station, where you'll find a TI (to the left as you exit the train station), baggage storage (to the right as you exit), and a handy train-information desk with maps of the city. If you must drive, store your car at the parking garage next to the train station.

Tourist Information: Cannes' main TI is located in the Film Festival Hall at 1 Boulevard de la Croisette (daily July-Aug 9:00-20:00, Sept-June 10:00-19:00). Another TI is next to the train station (same hours, 4 Place de la Gare).

Handy Cannes and St-Tropez Phrases

Where is a movie star?	*Où est une vedette?*
I am a movie star.	*Je suis une vedette.*
I am rich and single.	*Je suis riche et célibataire.*
Are you rich and single?	*Etes-vous riche et célibataire?*
Are those real?	*Ils sont des vrais?*
How long is your yacht?	*Quelle est la longeur de votre yacht?*
How much did that cost?	*Combien coûtait-il?*
You can always dream...	*On peut toujours rêver...*

Cannes Walk

This self-guided cancan will take you to Cannes' sights in a level, one-hour walk at a movie-star pace.

• *Walk straight out of the train station, crossing the bus station/street in front and turn left. Make a quick right on Rue des Serbes, and stroll for five unglamorous minutes to the beachfront. Cross the busy Boulevard de la Croisette, turn left on the promenade, and walk a few blocks down until you're about opposite the Marriot Casino. Now get familiar with...*

The Lay of the Land: Cannes feels different from its neighbors to the east. You won't find the pastel oranges and pinks of Old Nice and Villefranche-sur-Mer. Cannes was never part of Italy—and its architecture and cuisine reminds me more of Paris than Nice.

Face the water. The land jutting into the sea on your left is actually two islands, St-Honorat and Ste-Marguerite. St-Honorat has been the property of monks for over 500 years; today its abbey, vineyards, trails, and gardens can be visited by peace-seeking travelers. Ste-Marguerite, which you also can visit, is famous for the stone prison that housed the 17th-century Man in the Iron Mask (whose true  identity remains unknown). For more on visiting these islands, see page 409.

Now look far to your right. Those striking mountains sweeping down to the sea are the Massif de l'Esterel. Their red-rock outcrops oversee spectacular car and train routes (see page 410). Closer in, the hill with the medieval tower caps Cannes' old town (Le Suquet). This hilltop offers grand views and pretty lanes—and the only place in Cannes where you feel its medieval past. Below the old town, the port welcomes yachts of all sizes...provided they're really big.

ANTIBES & NEARBY

Face inland. Closer, on the left, find the unexceptional, cream-colored building with the tinted windows overlooking the sea. That convention-center-like structure is home of the famous film festival (we'll visit there soon). Back the other way, gaze up the boulevard. That classy building with twin black-domed roofs is Hôtel Carlton, our eventual target and as far as we'll go together in that direction.

• *Continue with the sea on your right and stroll the...*

Promenade (La Croisette): You're walking along Boulevard de la Croisette—Cannes' famed two-mile-long promenade. First

popular with kings who wintered here after Napoleon fell, the elite parade was later joined by British aristocracy. Today, Boulevard de la Croisette is fronted by some of the most expensive apartments and hotels in Europe. If it's lunchtime, you might try one of the beach cafés.

• *Stop when you get to...*

Hôtel Carlton: This is the most famous address on Boulevard de la Croisette (small Db-€1,500, more spacious Db-€7,000). Face the beach. The iconic Cannes experience is to slip into a robe (ideally, monogrammed with your initials), out of your luxury hotel (preferably this one), and onto the beach or pier. While you may not be doing the "fancy hotel and monogrammed robe" ritual on this Cannes excursion, you can—for about €25—rent a

chair and umbrella and pretend you're tanning for a red-carpet premiere. Cannes has a few token public beaches, but most beaches are private and run by hotels like the Carlton. You could save money by sunning among the common folk, but the real Cannes way to flee the rabble and paparazzi is to rent a spot on a private beach.

Cross over and wander into the hotel—you're welcome to browse (harder during the festival). Ask for a hotel brochure, verify room rates, check for availability. How do people afford this? Groupon? Imagine the scene here during the film festival. An affordable café (considering the cost of a room) lies just beyond the champagne lounge.

• *You can continue your stroll down La Croisette, but I'm doubling back to the cream-colored building that is Cannes'...*

Film Festival Hall: Cannes' film festival (Festival de Cannes), staged since 1946, completes the "Big Three" of Riviera events (with Monaco's Grand Prix and Nice's Carnival). The hall where the festival takes place—a busy-but-nondescript convention center that also hosts the town TI—sits plump on the beach. You'll recognize the formal grand entryway (most likely without the famed red carpet). Find the famous (Hollywood-style) handprints in the sidewalk nearby (also by the entry to the TI). To get inside during the fes-

tival, you have to be a star (or a photographer—some 3,000 paparazzi attend the gala event, and most bring their own ladders to get above the crowds).

The festival originated in part as an anti-fascist response to Mussolini's Venice Film Festival. Cannes' first festival was due to open in 1939, on the very day Hitler invaded Poland. Because of World War II, the opening was delayed until 1946. Cannes' film festival is also famous as the first festival to give one vote per country on the jury (giving films from smaller countries a better chance).

Though generally off-limits to curious tourists, the festival is everything around here—and is worth a day trip to Cannes if you happen to be in the region when it's on. The town buzzes with megastar energy, press passes, and revealing dresses. Locals claim that it's the world's third-biggest media event, after the Olympics and the World Cup (soccer). The festival prize is the Palme d'Or (like the Oscar for Best Picture). The French press can't cover the event enough, and the average Jean in France follows it as Joe would the World Series in the States. In 2016, Woody Allen's film *Café Society* opened the festival, but the Palme d'Or was awarded to the British film *I, Daniel Blake*. The festival celebrated its 70th anniversary in 2017. American actors Jessica Chastain and Will Smith served on the main jury, and the Palme d'Or went to a Swedish film, *The Square*.

• *Around the other side of the festival hall is the port (Gare Maritime).*

The Port and Old Town (Le Suquet): The megayachts line up closest to the Film Festival Hall. After seeing these amazing boats, everything else looks like a dinghy. Boat service to St-Tropez and the nearby islands of St-Honorat and Ste-Marguerite depart from the far side of the port (at Quai Laubeuf; for boat info, see "Activities in Cannes," later).

Cannes' oldest neighborhood, Le Suquet, crowns the hill past the port. Locals refer to it as their Montmartre. Artsy and charming, it's a steep 15-minute walk above the port, with little of interest except the panoramic views from its ancient church, Notre-Dame-de-l'Espérance (Our Lady of Hope).

• *To find the views in Le Suquet, aim for its clock tower and pass the bus station at the northwest corner of the port, then make your way up*

Yachters' Itinerary

If you're visiting Cannes on your private yacht, here's a suggested itinerary:
1. Take in the Festival de Cannes and the accompanying social scene. Organize an evening party on your boat.
2. Motor over to Monte Carlo for the Grand Prix, scheduled—conveniently for yachters—just after the film festival.
3. On your way back west to St-Tropez, deconstruct events from the film festival and Grand Prix with Brigitte Bardot.
4. Drop down to Porto Chervo on Sardinia, one of the few places in the world where your yacht is "just average."
5. Head west to Ibiza and Marbella in Spain, where your friends are moored for the big party scene.

---

cobbled Rue Saint-Antoine (next to the Café St. Antoine). Turn left on Place du Suquet, and then follow signs to Traverse de la Tour *for the final leg.*

Cue music. Roll end credits. Our film is over. For further exploration, look for Cannes' "underbelly" between Le Suquet and the train station—narrow lanes with inexpensive cafés and shops that regular folks can afford.

Activities in Cannes

Shopping

Cannes is made for window shopping (the best streets are between the station and the waterfront). For the trendiest boutiques, stroll down handsome Rue d'Antibes (parallel to the sea about three blocks inland). Rue Meynadier anchors a pedestrian zone with more affordable shops closer to the port. To bring home a real surprise, why not consider cosmetic surgery? Cannes is well known as *the* place on the Riviera to have your face (or other parts) realigned.

Boat Excursions to St-Honorat and Ste-Marguerite Islands

Two boat companies ferry tourists 15 minutes from the Quai Laubeuf dock in Cannes' port to twin islands just offshore: St-Honorat and Ste-Marguerite. Both outfits charge the same (€15 round-trip) and run every half hour (daily 9:00-18:00). There's no ferry between the two islands. For the Ste-Marguerite schedule, go to TransCoteAzur.com; for St-Honorat hours, it's CannesIlesDelerins.com.

The islands offer a refreshing change from the town scene, with almost no development, good swimming, and peaceful walking paths. On Ste-Marguerite you can hike, visit the castle (part of which is now a youth hostel) and the cell where the mysterious Man in the Iron Mask was imprisoned (with a good little museum with decent English explanations featuring cargo from a sunken Roman vessel), and tour the Musée de la Mer's ancient collection and underwater exhibits. On St-Honorat you can hike seafront trails and visit the abbey where monks have lived and prayed for 16 centuries. Today they make fine wines in their free time. St-Honorat also has a few shops and a restaurant.

Cannes Connections

From Cannes by Train to: Antibes (2/hour, 15 minutes), **Nice** (2/hour, 30 minutes), **Monaco** (2/hour, 70 minutes), **Grasse** (rail service may be suspended for station construction; if running, trains generally hourly, 30 minutes).

By Bus: Bus **#200** heads east from Cannes along the Riviera, stopping at **Antibes** (35 minutes) and **Nice** (2 hours; trip duration depends on traffic; for bus details, see page 278). **Bus #210** runs from the train station express on the freeway to **Nice Airport** (1-2/hour, 50 minutes, €20). Both buses stop at the Cannes train station.

By Boat: Trans Côte d'Azur runs boat excursions from Cannes to **St-Tropez** (€50 round-trip, 1 hour each way; July-Aug daily 1/day; June and Sept 1/day Tue, Thu, and Sat-Sun only; no service Oct-May; tel. 04 92 98 71 30, www.trans-cote-azur.com). This boat trip is popular—book a few days ahead from June to September.

By Cruise Ship: Ships tender passengers to the west side of Cannes' port. From here, it's an easy walk into town: Head inland, with the port on your right-hand side. Note that the tender dock is near the end of my Cannes Walk; if planning to follow it, you can either start the walk here and do it in reverse or stroll about 10 minutes around the port to the walk's starting point (see page 406). If heading to points beyond Cannes, it takes about 15 minutes to walk from the tender dock to the train station, where you can catch a train for Antibes, Nice, or Villefranche-sur-Mer.

St-Tropez

St-Tropez is a busy, charming, and traffic-free port town smoth-

ered with fashion boutiques, elegant restaurants, and luxury boats. If you came here for history or quaintness, you caught the wrong yacht. But if you have more money than you know what to do with, you're home. There are 5,700 year-round residents...and more than 100,000 visitors daily in the summer. If St-Tropez is on your must-visit list, hit it on your way to or

from Provence—and skip it altogether in summer and on weekend afternoons.

As with lots of now-famous villages in southern France, St-Tropez was "found" by artists. Paul Signac brought several of his friends to St-Tropez in the late 1800s, giving the village its first whiff of popularity (get rid of the yachts filling the harbor, and the town would resemble what it looked like then). But it wasn't until Brigitte Bardot made the scene here in the 1956 film...*And God Created Woman* that St-Tropez became synonymous with Riviera glamour. Since then, it's the first place that comes to mind when people think of the jet set luxuriating on Mediterranean beaches. For many, the French Riviera begins here and runs east to Menton, on the Italian border.

The village is the attraction here; the nearest big beach is miles away. Window shopping, people-watching, tan maintenance, and savoring slow meals fill people's days, weeks, and, in some cases, lives. Here, people dress up, size up one another's yachts or cars, and troll for a partner. While the only models you'll see are in the shop windows, Brigitte Bardot still hangs out on a bench in front of the TI signing autographs (Thu 15:00-17:30, and if you believe that...).

Wander the harborfront, where fancy yachts moor stern-in, their carefully coiffed captains and first mates enjoying *pu-pus* for happy hour—they're seeing and being seen. Take time to stroll the back streets (the small lanes below La Citadelle are St-Tropez's most appealing) while nibbling a chocolate-and-Grand Marnier crêpe. Find the big Place des Lices (good cafés and local hangout), and look for some serious games of *pétanque (boules)*.

St-Tropez lies between its famous port and the hilltop Cita-delle (with great views). The network of lanes between the port and Citadelle are strollable in a Carmel-by-the-Sea sort of way. The main **TI** is on the starboard side of the port (to the right as you face

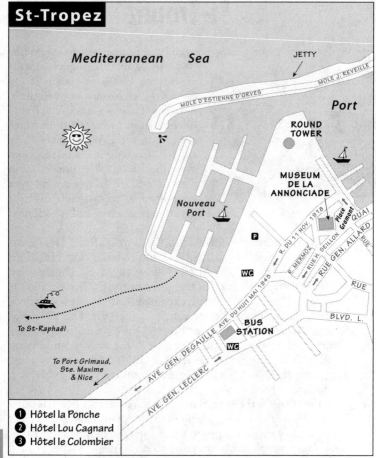

St-Tropez

Mediterranean   Sea

JETTY

MOLE J. REVEILLE

MOLE D'ESTIENNE D'ORVES

Port

ROUND
TOWER

MUSEUM
DE LA
ANNONCIADE

Nouveau
Port

R. DU 11 NOV. 1918

Place
Grémont

QUAI

R. MERMOZ

RUE H. SEILLON

RUE GEN. ALLARD

RUE

To St-Raphaël

WC

AVE. DU HUIT MAI 1945

BLVD. L.

BUS
STATION

WC

To Port Grimaud,
Ste. Maxime
& Nice

AVE. GEN. DEGAULLE

AVE. GEN. LECLERC

❶ Hôtel la Ponche
❷ Hôtel Lou Cagnard
❸ Hôtel le Colombier

the sea), where Quai Suffren and Quai Jean Jaurès meet (tel. 08 92 68 48 28, www.sainttropeztourisme.com). Pick up their helpful walking tour brochure, ask about events in town, and get maps and bus information if you plan to hike along the coast.

Getting There: With no trains to St-Tropez, buses and boats are your only options without a car. Varlib **buses** connect to St-Tropez from nearby train stations. From the east, catch bus #7601 from behind St-Raphaël's train station (goes via Ste-Maxime); from the west, take bus #7801 or #7802 from Toulon's train station (if arriving at either station by train, check bus schedules to St-Tropez in advance to ensure you make the connection; www.varlib. fr). Buses arriving in St-Tropez leave you a few minutes' walk to the port, near the parking lot—Parking du Vieux Port—on Avenue Général de Gaulle.

Boats connect to St-Tropez from St-Raphaël twice daily (tel.

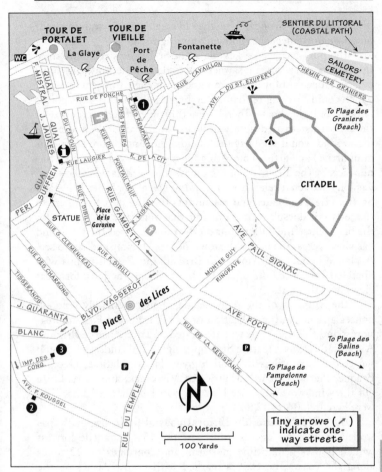

04 94 95 17 46, www.bateauxsaintraphael.com) and from Ste-Maxime about hourly (tel. 04 94 49 29 39, www.bateauxverts. com). For boats connecting St-Tropez with Nice, see page 335; with Cannes, page 410.

If arriving by **car,** prepare for traffic in any season—worse on weekends (forget driving on Sunday afternoons), always ugly during summer, and downright impossible between St-Tropez and Ste-Maxime on weekends. You can avoid this bottleneck by taking the autoroute to Le Luc and following the windy D-558 to St-Tropez from here (via La Garde-Freinet and Port Grimaud). The last few miles to St-Tropez are along a too-long, two-lane road with one way in, one way out, and too many people going exactly where you're going. There are two main parking lots: Parking des Lices (near recommended hotels) and Parking du Port (best for day-trippers).

Visiting St-Tropez: Use the TI's self-guided walking tour brochure to connect the following highlights.

The **port** has been a key player in St-Tropez's economy since the 18th century, when it saw a brisk trade in wine, cork, and lumber. St-Tropez's shipyards were famous for their three-mast ships, which could carry more than 1,000 barrels of wine. Today's port is famous for its big boats. There's something bizarre about the size of those boats, stern-tied tightly in such a small harbor. While strolling around, you'll see busy deckhands (hustling before their captains arrive) and artists competing for room. The red-tabled **Le Sénéquier,** by the TI, is one of the town's most venerated cafés—and has long attracted celebrities, including the philosopher Jean-Paul Sartre. High-end cafés and restaurants line the port from here to the jetty—it doesn't seem to matter that you can't see the sea for the big yachts. The bulky **Tour du Portalet** tower at the port's end has views across the bay to the town of Ste-Maxime and out to sea. A plaque honors the American, British, and French troops who liberated Provence on August 15, 1944. Climb the jetty for great views over the port.

The Museum of the Annonciade, though generally ignored, houses an enchanting collection of works from the Post-Impressionist and Fauvist artists who decorated St-Tropez before Brigitte. Almost all canvases feature St-Tropez sights and landscapes. You'll see colorful paintings by Paul Signac, Henri Matisse, Georges Braque, Pierre Bonnard, Maurice de Vlaminck, and more. Gaze out the windows and notice how the port has changed since they were here (tel. 04 94 17 84 10).

The scenic **Sentier du Littoral coastal path,** originally patrolled by customs agents, runs past the 1558 Citadelle fortress (which houses a maritime museum) and continues for 12 miles along the coast. The trail is marked with yellow dashes on the pavement, walls, and trees. Leave St-Tropez along the road below the Citadelle, pass the Sailors' Cemetery, and you'll join the path before long.

Several companies offer mildly interesting **boat tours** of the surrounding coastline. You'll learn a smidgen about St-Tropez's history and a lot about the villas of the rich and famous (details at TI).

The vast *pétanque (boules)* **court** on Place des Lices is worth your attention. Have a drink at Le Café and take in the action.

Nearby: Although more modern than St-Tropez, **Port Grimaud** (located a few miles toward Ste-Maxime) is no less attractive or upscale. This "Venice of Provence" was reclaimed from a murky lagoon about 40 years ago and is now lined with four miles of canals, lovely homes, and moorage for thousands of yachts. It's a fascinating look at what clever minds can produce from a swamp.

Park at the lot across from the town entry (TI next to the parking lot, www.grimaud-provence.com), and cross the barrier and bridge into a beautiful world of privilege. Climb the church bell tower for a good panorama view.

Sleeping in St-Tropez: If you're spending the night here, remember that high season in St-Tropez runs from June through September, and weekends are busy year-round. Hotels worth considering include: **$$$$ Hôtel la Ponche****** (central and luxurious, 3 Rue des Remparts, tel. 04 94 97 02 53, www.laponche.com); **$$$ Hôtel le Colombier**** (small, adorable, and on a quiet street—Impasse des Conquêtes, tel. 04 94 97 05 31, lecolombierhotel.free.fr); and **$$ Hôtel Lou Cagnard**** (pretty courtyard garden, 18 Avenue Paul Roussel, tel. 04 94 97 04 24, www.hotel-lou-cagnard.com).

ANTIBES & NEARBY

INLAND RIVIERA

St-Paul-de-Vence • Vence •
Grasse • Grand Canyon du Verdon

For a verdant, rocky, fresh escape from the beaches, head inland and upward. Some of France's most perfectly perched hill towns and splendid scenery hang overlooked in this region that's more famous for beaches and bikinis. A short car or bus ride away from the Mediterranean reaps big rewards: lush forests, deep canyons, and swirling hilltop villages. A longer drive brings you to Europe's greatest canyon, the Grand Canyon du Verdon.

PLANNING YOUR TIME

With one full day, consider renting a car and doing my self-guided Inland Riviera driving tour (below). Start in Nice or Antibes and arrive in St-Paul-de-Vence as early as you can to minimize crowds. Visit the village and Fondation Maeght, then head to nearby Vence for lunch. End your day with a visit to the perfume city of Grasse. (This same trip can be done by bus if you depart early in the morning and forgo Grasse.)

    With two days (and a car), conclude your driving tour with an overnight in Vence, then spend your second day visiting the Grand Canyon du Verdon (ideally ending in the Luberon, Cassis, or Aix-en-Provence).

GETTING AROUND THE INLAND RIVIERA

By Car: Driving is the best way to tour this area, though summer and weekend traffic and parking challenges will test your patience. Consider renting a car for a day (for rental places, see pages 389 and 288). I describe the best route later.

    By Bus: Buses get you to many of the places in this chapter. Vence, St-Paul-de-Vence, and Grasse are well-served by bus from Nice (about 2/hour). (Grasse also has train service from Nice, Antibes, and Cannes, but trains may not run for part of 2018.) Within

Inland Riviera

the area, bus #510/511 runs from Vence to Grasse via Tourrettes-sur-Loup and Le Bar-sur-Loup (6/day, 15 minutes to Tourrettes-sur-Loup, 35 minutes to Le Bar-sur-Loup, 50 minutes to Grasse). Bus connections for the Gorges du Loup, the village of Gourdon, or the Gorges du Verdon are either too complicated or nonexistent.

With a Local Guide: The owners of the recommended Frogs' House in St-Jeannet, **Benôit and Corinne,** are happy to organize cooking classes, wine tastings, hiking trips, and other excursions around their native area (see page 426).

See page 280 for guides with cars who can get you to places you would not find yourself.

Inland Riviera Driving Tour

This splendid self-guided loop drive connects St-Paul-de-Vence, Vence, Tourrettes-sur-Loup, and Grasse. Some of the villages can be linked by bus, but a car is essential to do the loop as described. Each stop is only minutes away from the next, but allow 45 minutes to drive from Nice or Antibes to the first stop, St-Paul-de-Vence. Be aware of bicyclists sharing the road, particularly on weekends.

Start early to see St-Paul-de-Vence without the mobs (have breakfast there, at the recommended **Café de la Place**). If you won't be visiting the Gorges du Verdon (or if you care more about nature than art), take the beautiful long way around from Vence to Gourdon (described later, under "Alternate Route") and skip Tourrettes-sur-Loup and the Gorges du Loup (you won't miss them, trust *moi*). Be prepared for twisty mountain roads and tailgating French drivers; they come with the territory. Note that most of the towns and sights on this drive are explained in detail later in this chapter.

For background on the region's hill towns, see "The Life of a Hill Town in Provence" sidebar on page 172.

FROM NICE TO GRASSE

Drivers go through Cagnes-sur-Mer (passing the Renoir Museum—see page 400), then follow *Vence* and *St-Paul-de-Vence* signs into the village. In **St-Paul-de-Vence,** park as close to the center as you can. Or, you can continue to the **Fondation Maeght** and park for free, then walk 20 minutes into town. Parking is also free along the road to Fondation Maeght (look for *Parking Conseillé* signs).

After exploring St-Paul-de-Vence, continue to artsy **Vence,** a few miles away with many good lunch options. From Vence, visit Matisse's famous **Chapel of the Rosary** (limited opening hours and sparse parking). The best views of Vence are a mile beyond the chapel, where there's a turnaround.

Next, head for slippery-sloped **Tourrettes-sur-Loup** (from Vence, follow D-2210)—or skip it and follow the "Alternate Route" described later. From Tourrettes-sur-Loup, continue along D-2210 (great views of Tourrettes-sur-Loup a quarter-mile after leaving— look for the bus stop labeled *Chemin de la Gare*). Before long, you'll see views of Le Bar-sur-Loup, clinging to its hillside in the distance. (Sugar addicts can detour quickly down to Pont-du-Loup and visit the small candied-fruit factory of **Confiseries Florian**).

Follow *Gourdon* and *Gorges du Loup* signs to the right along D-6 and climb into the teeth of a rocky canyon, the **Gorges du Loup.** It's a mostly second-gear road that winds between severe rock faces above a surging stream. (Buses cannot enter the Gorges du Loup, so nondrivers must continue directly to Grasse.) Several miles into the gorge, you can visit the Cascades du Saut du Loup **waterfall,** which may have you thinking you've made a wrong turn onto Hawaii (€1, easy walk down).

The drive passes all too quickly to where the road hooks back, crossing Pont du Bramafen and up toward Gourdon on D-3. Climb above the canyon you just drove through and watch the world below miniaturize. At the top, the village of **Gourdon**—known as the "Eagle's Nest" (2,400 feet)—waits for tourists with shops, good lunch options, and grand panoramas.

From Gourdon, slide downhill—passing stone quarries—toward **Grasse.** Enjoy sensational views down to (literally) overlooked Le Bar-sur-Loup. Follow signs to

Grasse, then *Centre-Ville,* then *Office de Tourisme.* Park under the TI at Parking Notre Dame des Fleurs.

After mastering your scent in Grasse—the capital of perfume—return to your Riviera home base (allow 45 minutes to Nice or 30 minutes to Antibes via Cannes and the autoroute), or continue to the Gorges du Verdon.

ALTERNATE ROUTE

If you won't be visiting the Gorges du Verdon, consider this dilly of a detour (ideal if staying in Vence): Follow the route described above until **Vence,** then find D-2 just before the bridge that leads to St-Jeannet, and follow signs for *Col de Vence* (the Vence pass) and *Coursegoules.* The road rises beyond the tree line into a barren landscape to the pass in about 15 minutes. (For a 45-minute uphill hike to views over Vence and the Riviera, pass Château St-Martin, drive another half-mile, then look for the faded brown trailhead sign to *Baou des Blancs;* park in small dirt lot 50 yards before.) From the pass (3,000 feet), continue on D-2, trading rocky slabs for lush forests, pastures, and vast canyons.

You'll soon pass the postcard-perfect village of **Coursegoules** (worth a photo but not a detour), then follow signs to *Gréolières.* At a roundabout just before Gréolières, find D-3, which leads to Nice, Gorges du Loup, and Gourdon. But first, continue a few minutes past **Gréolières** to the pullout barely above the village, with stirring views of its ruined castle. Consider a coffee break in Gréolières before backtracking to the roundabout, following signs to *Gourdon.* After visiting **Gourdon,** you can continue to Grasse, or return to Nice or Antibes.

St-Paul-de-Vence

This most famous of Riviera hill towns is also the most-visited village in France. I believe it. This incredibly situated village—with

views to the sea and the Alps—is understandably popular. Every cobble and flower seems just so, and the setting is postcard-perfect, but it can also feel like an overrun and over-restored artist shopping mall. Avoid visiting between 11:00 and 18:00, particularly on weekends. Beat the crowds by skipping breakfast at your hotel and eating here, or come for dinner and experience the village at its tranquil best.

Orientation to St-Paul-de-Vence

Tourist Information: The helpful TI, just through the gate into the old town on Rue Grande, has maps with minimal explanations of key buildings, and loaner *boules* for *pétanque* on the square (daily 10:00-18:00, June-Sept until 19:00, closed for lunch on weekends, tel. 04 93 32 86 95, www.saint-pauldevence.com, serviceguide@saint-pauldevence.com).

Arrival in St-Paul-de-Vence: Arrive early to park for free or in a pay lot near the village (cars are not allowed inside St-Paul; see page 418 for suggestions). Bus #400 (connects with Nice and Vence) stops on the main road, just above the village. If the traffic-free lane leading into the old town is jammed, walk along the road that veers up and left just after Café de la Place, and enter the town through its side door.

Sights in St-Paul-de-Vence

The Old Town

St-Paul's old town has no essential sights, though its lovely cobbled lanes and peekaboo views delight most who come. You'll pass two vintage eateries before piercing the walls of the old town. The recommended **La Colombe d'Or** is a historic hotel and a good spot for a meal. Back when the town was teeming with artists, this restaurant served as their clubhouse. Its walls are covered with paintings by Picasso, Miró, Braque, Chagall, and others who received free meals in exchange for their art. **Café de la Place** is a classic spot to have a coffee and croissant and watch waves of tourists crash into town (daily from 7:00, tel. 04 93 32 80 03). On the square, serious *boules* competitions take place.

After entering the walls of St. Paul, meander deep to find its quieter streets and panoramic views. How many art galleries can this village support? Imagine the time it took to create the intricate stone patterns in the street you're walking along. Visit **Marc Chagall's grave** in the cemetery at the opposite end of town, a 10-minute walk keeping straight along the main drag (from the cemetery entrance, turn right, then left to find Chagall's grave). Walk up the stairs to the **view platform** above the cemetery and try to locate the hill town of Vence at the foot of an impressive mountain. Is the sea out there—somewhere?

▲Fondation Maeght

This inviting, pricey, and far-out private museum is situated a steep walk or short drive above St-Paul-de-Vence. Fondation Maeght (fohn-dah-shown mahg) offers an excellent introduction to modern Mediterranean art by gathering many of the Riviera's most famous artists under one roof. Sadly, there are no English explanations.

Cost and Hours: €15, €5 to take photos, daily 10:00-18:00, July-Sept until 19:00, tel. 04 93 32 81 63, www.fondation-maeght. com.

Getting There: The museum is a steep uphill-but-doable 20-minute walk from St-Paul-de-Vence and the bus stop. Parking is usually available (and free) in the lower lot, signed *Parking Conseille*. From the lower lot, a shortcut on a steep, dirt path through the trees leads directly to the green gate in front of the ticket booth.

Visiting the Museum: The founder, Aimé Maeght, long envisioned the perfect exhibition space for the artists he supported and

befriended as an art dealer. He purchased this arid hilltop, planted 35,000 plants, and hired an architect (José Luis Sert) with the same vision.

A sweeping lawn laced with amusing sculptures and bending pine trees greets visitors. On the right, a chapel designed by Georges Braque—in memory of the Maeghts' young son, who died of leukemia—features a moving purple stained-glass work over the altar. The unusual museum building is purposely low profile to let its world-class modern art collection take center stage. Works by Fernand Léger, Joan Miró, Alexander Calder, Georges Braque, and Marc Chagall are thoughtfully arranged in well-lit rooms. The backyard of the museum has views, a Gaudí-esque sculpture labyrinth by Miró, and a courtyard filled with the wispy works of Alberto Giacometti. The sculptures are the only permanent collection in the museum, though there's a good selection of paintings by the famous artists here year-round. For a review of modern art, see "The Riviera's Art Scene" on page 281. The museum also has a great gift shop and cafeteria.

Eating in St-Paul-de-Vence

$$ Le Tilleul is a good place to dine well in St-Paul, either at inviting tables on the broad terrace or in its pleasant interior (daily, near the TI on Place du Tilleul, tel. 04 93 32 80 36, www.restaurant-letilleul.com).

Book well ahead for **$$$$ La Colombe d'Or,** a veritable institution in St. Paul where the menu hasn't changed in 50 years (see description earlier). Dine on good-enough cuisine inside by the fire to best feel its pulse (closed Nov-Dec, tel. 04 93 32 80 02, www. la-colombe-dor.com; for reservations, email contact@la-colombe-dor.com).

Vence

Vence is a well-discovered yet appealing town set high above the Riviera. While growth has sprawled beyond Vence's old walls, and cars jam its roundabouts, the mountains are front and center and the breeze is fresh. Vence bubbles with workaday life—and ample tourist activity in the day—but is quiet at night, with fewer visitors and cooler temperatures than along the coast. You'll also find good choices for affordable hotels and restaurants. Vence makes a handy base for travelers wanting the best of both worlds; it's a hill-town refuge near the sea. Some enjoy the Gorges du Verdon as a long day trip from Vence (see the route described on page 431).

Orientation to Vence

Tourist Information: Vence's fully loaded TI faces the main square at 8 Place du Grand Jardin, across from the merry-go-round. It offers free Wi-Fi, bus schedules, and a city map with a well-devised self-guided walking tour that incorporates informative wall plaques. Pick up the list of art galleries with helpful descriptions of the collections. Ask about their *pétanque* instructions with *boules* to rent, and about guided walking tours in English (Mon-Sat 9:00-19:00, Sun 10:00-18:00; Nov-March 10:00-17:00 and closed Sun; tel. 04 93 58 06 38, www.ville-vence.fr).

Arrival in Vence: Bus #94 (from Nice) or #400 (from Nice, Cagnes-sur-Mer, and St-Paul-de-Vence) drops you at the bus stop labeled *Halte Routière de l'Ara* on a roundabout at Place Maréchal Juin, a 10-minute walk to the town center (along Avenue Henri Isnard or Avenue de la Résistance). If arriving by **car,** follow signs to *cité historique* and park in the underground Parking Grand Jardin, across from the TI.

Helpful Hints: Market day in the *cité historique* (old town) is on Friday mornings on Place Clemenceau. A big all-day antiques market is on Place du Grand Jardin every Wednesday. If you miss market day, a Monoprix **supermarket** is on Avenue de la Résistance, across from the entrance to the Marie Antoinette parking lot (grocery store upstairs, Mon-Sat 8:30-20:00, Sun 9:00-13:00). For a **taxi,** call 04 93 58 11 14.

Sights in Vence

Explore the narrow lanes of the old town using the TI's worthwhile self-guided tour map. Connect the picturesque streets, enjoy a drink on a quiet square, inspect an art gallery, and find the small 11th-century cathedral with its colorful Chagall mosaic of Moses (for background, see the Chagall Museum description on page 307. And, of course, visit Matisse's Chapel. If you're in Vence later in the day, enjoy the *boules* action across from the TI (or rent a set from the TI and join in).

Château de Villeneuve

This 17th-century mansion, adjoining an imposing 12th-century watchtower, bills itself as "one of the Riviera's high temples of modern art," with a rotating collection. Check with the TI to see what's showing in the temple. The museum offers a loaner guide with English explanations of the collection.

Cost and Hours: €6, Tue-Sun 11:00-18:00, closed Mon, tel. 04 93 58 15 78.

▲Chapel of the Rosary (Chapelle du Rosaire)

The chapel—a short drive or 20-minute walk from town—was designed by an elderly and ailing Henri Matisse as thanks to the Dominican sister who had taken care of him (he was 81 when the chapel was completed—see the timeline of Matisse's life on page 316). While the chapel is the ultimate pilgrimage for his fans, the experience may underwhelm others. (Picasso thought it looked like a bathroom.)

Cost and Hours: €7; Mon, Wed, and Sat 14:00-17:30 plus Tue and Thu 10:00-12:00 & 14:00-18:00, Nov-March until 17:00; Sun only open for Mass at 10:00 followed by tour of chapel; closed Fri year-round; last entry 30 minutes before closing, 466 Avenue Henri Matisse, tel. 04 93 58 03 26.

Getting There: On foot, it's a 20-minute walk from the TI. Turn right out of the TI and take your first right. Then take a quick left onto Avenue Henri Isnard and continue all the way to the traffic circle. Turn right across the one-lane bridge on Avenue Henri Matisse, following signs to *St-Jeannet.* **By car,** follow signs toward *St-Jeannet,* cross the bridge, and start looking for parking—the chapel is about 400 yards after the bridge toward St-Jeannet.

Visiting the Chapel: The modest chapel holds a simple series of charcoal black-on-white tile sketches and uses three symbolic colors as accents: yellow (sunlight and the light of God), green (nature), and blue (the Mediterranean

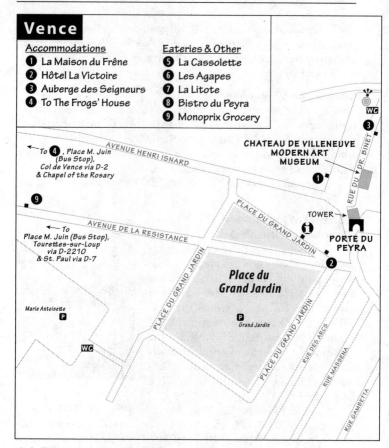

Vence

Accommodations
1. La Maison du Frêne
2. Hôtel La Victoire
3. Auberge des Seigneurs
4. To The Frogs' House

Eateries & Other
5. La Cassolette
6. Les Agapes
7. La Litote
8. Bistro du Peyra
9. Monoprix Grocery

CHATEAU DE VILLENEUVE
MODERN ART
MUSEUM

TOWER →

PORTE DU
PEYRA

To ④ , Place M. Juin
(Bus Stop),
Col de Vence via D-2
& Chapel of the Rosary

AVENUE HENRI ISNARD

PLACE DU GRAND JARDIN

To
Place M. Juin (Bus Stop),
Tourettes-sur-Loup
via D-2210
& St. Paul via D-7

AVENUE DE LA RESISTANCE

*Place du
Grand Jardin*

Grand Jardin

PLACE DU GRAND JARDIN

Marie Antoinette

WC

RUE DES ARCS

RUE MASSENA

RUE GAMBETTA

INLAND RIVIERA

sky). Bright sunlight filters through the stained-glass windows and does a cheery dance across the sketches.

Your entry ticket includes a 20-minute tour from one of the kind nuns who speak English. Downstairs, you'll find displays of the vestments Matisse designed for the priests, his models of the chapel, and sketches.

Matisse was the master of leaving things out. Decide for yourself whether Matisse met the goal he set for himself: "Creating a religious space in an enclosed area of reduced proportions and to give it, solely by the play of colors and lines, the dimensions of infinity."

Sleeping in Vence

These places tend to close their reception desks between 12:00 and 16:00. Make arrangements in advance if you plan to arrive during this time.

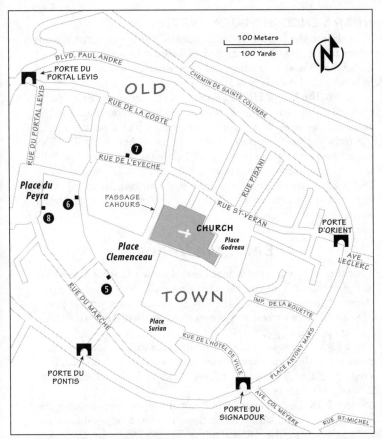

$$$ La Maison du Frêne, centrally located behind the TI, is a modern, art-packed B&B with four sumptuous suites. Energetic and art-crazy Thierry and Guy make fine hosts (RS%, includes good breakfast, kids under 12 free; next to the Château de Villeneuve at 1 Place du Frêne; tel. 04 93 24 37 83, www.lamaisondufrene.com, contact@lamaisondufrene.com).

$ Hôtel La Victoire is a solid value right on the main square next to the TI. Rooms are comparatively small but have all the comforts, and it's warmly run and well-maintained by Pierre (1 Place du Grand Jardin, tel. 04 93 24 15 54, www.hotel-victoire. com).

$ Auberge des Seigneurs feels medieval. Located in a 17th-century building, it has six simple but spacious rooms over a well-respected restaurant (Wi-Fi in lobby, no air-con, no elevator, no TV, 1 Rue du Docteur Binet, tel. 04 93 58 04 24, www.auberge-seigneurs.com, sandrine.rodi@wanadoo.fr).

INLAND RIVIERA

NEAR VENCE IN ST-JEANNET

To melt into the Inland Riviera's quiet side, drive 15 minutes from Vence to the remarkably situated, no-tourist-in-sight hill town of St-Jeannet. Views are endless and everywhere. It's so quiet, it's hard to believe the beach is only 10 miles away.

At **$ The Frogs' House,** Benôit and Corinne welcome travelers with a full menu of good rooms, cooking lessons, hikes in the area, and day trips. If you don't have wheels, they'll pick you up at the train station or airport. Rooms are small but sharp (includes hearty breakfast, some rooms with balconies, family rooms, full-house rentals available in winter, tel. 04 93 58 98 05, mobile 06 28 06 80 28, www.thefrogshouse.fr, info@thefrogshouse.com). Park in the lot at the bottom of St-Jeannet, a few blocks from this small hotel.

Eating in Vence

Tempting outdoor eateries litter the old town. Lights embedded in the cobbles illuminate the way after dark. Vence has a terrific choice of good restaurants. The first three I list have similar prices (about €30 for a three-course *menu*) and quality. All have outside dining options.

$$$ La Cassolette is an intimate place with reasonable prices and a romantic terrace across from the floodlit church (closed Tue-Wed, 10 Place Clemenceau, tel. 04 93 58 84 15, www.restaurant-lacassolette-vence.com).

At **$$$ Les Agapes,** Chef Jean-Philippe goes beyond the standard fare with lavish presentations, creative food combinations, and moderate (for the Riviera) prices. Try the *sphere chocolat* dessert to round out your meal (closed Mon year-round, closed Sun off-season, 4 Place Clemenceau, tel. 04 93 58 50 64, www.les-agapes.net).

$$$ La Litote is lauded by locals as a fine value, with outdoor tables on a quiet, hidden square and a cozy interior (closed Sun year-round, closed Mon off-season, 7 Rue de l'Evêché, tel. 04 93 24 27 82).

For less expensive, casual dining, head to Place du Peyra, where you'll find ample outdoor seating and early dinner service. At the basic **$$ Bistro du Peyra,** enjoy a relaxed dinner salad or pasta dish outdoors to the sound of the town's main fountain (closed Mon-Tue off-season, 13 Place du Peyra, tel. 04 93 58 67 63).

Between Vence and Grasse

The following sights are connected by the Inland Riviera driving tour (see page 417).

Tourrettes-sur-Loup

This unspoiled and picturesque town, hemmed in by forests, looks like it's ready to skid down its hill. Stroll the beautifully preserved, narrow medieval lanes, admire the wall-to-wall homes (built for defense, not the view), have an ice cream, and finish with a view drink (described below). Known as the *Cité des Violettes,* this small village produces more violets than anywhere else in France, most of which end up in perfume. In early March, Tourrettes-sur-Loop fills with almost 10,000 visitors (hard to imagine) for the annual Violet Festival.

Park in the lot at the village center near the **TI** (Mon-Sat 9:30-13:00 & 14:00-18:00, closed Sun, tel. 04 93 24 18 93, www.tourrettessurloup.com). Wednesday is **market day** (on Place de la Libération). If it's lunchtime, sit outside at the *pâtisserie* on Place de la Libération, which has delicious *pissaladière* (pizza-like dough topped with onions, olives, and anchovies) and the filling *tourte de Blettes* (Swiss chard tart).

With your back to the TI, walk to the right and under the clock tower, and onto Grande Rue. Stroll in a counterclockwise direction, ending up back at the parking lot. Along the way, you'll find a smattering of arts and crafts boutiques—though fewer than in the "Vence towns"—and a handful of places to eat or take a break.

Tom's Ice Cream may entice you with its violet-flavored scoops or tasty coffee and free Wi-Fi (daily from 13:30, 25 Grand Rue, tel. 04 93 24 12 12). Finish your walk with a coffee—or better, a glass of wine on the tiny back terrace at **La Cave de Tourrettes.** This small wine bar serves salads and quiches, with a daily by-the-glass selection and vast cellar. The sliver-sized balcony has panoramic views (closed Mon, near the St. Grégoire church and parking lot, 8 Rue de la Bourgade, tel. 04 93 24 10 12).

More views of Tourrettes-sur-Loup await a minute away on the drive to Pont-du-Loup.

Confiseries Florian

This candied-fruit factory hides between trees down in Pont-du-Loup (though their big, bright sign is hard to miss). Frequent 10-minute tours of the factory cover the candied-fruit process and explain the use of flower petals (like violets and jasmine) in their products. Everything they make is fruit-filled—even their choco-

INLAND RIVIERA

late (with oranges). The tour ends with a tasting of the *confiture* in the dazzling gift shop.

Cost and Hours: Tours are free, daily 9:00-12:00 & 14:00-18:30, gift shop stays open during lunch in summer, tel. 04 93 59 32 91, www.confiserieflorian.com.

Gorges du Loup

The Inland Riviera is crawling with spectacular canyons only miles from the sea. Slotted between Grasse and Vence, the Gorges du Loup is the easiest gorge to reach and works well with a day trip from the Nice area. You can drive about five miles right up into the canyon (on D-6)—passing waterfalls and sheer rock walls—then return on the gorge's rooftop (on D-3) to the "Eagle's Nest" village of Gourdon for magnificent vistas and a complete change of scenery.

Gourdon

This 2,400-foot-high, cliff-topping hamlet features grassy picnic areas, a short lineup of tourist shops, and a few good lunch options. The village's most famous building is its château, which is best enjoyed from the outside. Walk out to the broad terrace for the splendid view (TI in the far corner). A trail (Chemin du Paradis) leads down those cliffs from the far left side of the village to Le Bar-sur-Loup (1 hour)—now *that's* steep. This part of the village features fabulous vistas, a  tiny Romanesque church, and a nice option for lunch with a view.

Overlooking the grandeur is **$$ La Taverne Provençale**, which boasts a popular spread of outdoor tables and serves pizza, pasta, salads, and more (daily, tel. 04 93 09 68 22).

Grasse

The historic and contemporary capital of perfume, Grasse offers a contrast to the dolled-up hill towns above the Riviera. Though famous for its pricey product, Grasse's urban center is an unpolished but intriguing collection of walking lanes, peekaboo squares, and vertical staircases. The place feels in need of a graffiti-facelift and a jobs program for its large immigrant population. For me, Grasse is refreshingly real. Its historic alliance with Genoa explains the Italian-esque look of the old city. Still, the only good reasons to visit Grasse are if you care about perfume, or if you're heading to or from the Gorges du Verdon.

Orientation to Grasse

All sights in Grasse cluster near the Cours Honoré Cresp, also referred to as Place du Cours.

Tourist Information: The TI is a 10-minute walk from the center on Place de la Buanderie, where buses from Nice and Cannes stop (daily July-mid-Sept 9:00-19:00, shorter hours off-season, tel. 04 93 36 66 66, www.grasse.fr). Pick up an English map with a simple, self-guided tour of the old city. If heading to the Gorges du Verdon, get specifics here.

Arrival in Grasse: Buses from Cannes and Nice (#500) are better than trains, as they stop at the TI and cost only €1.50. To reach the town center from the TI, walk out to Avenue Thiers, turn left, and merge onto Boulevard du Jeu de Ballon. Nice and Cannes buses also stop, along with buses from other destinations, at the main bus stop at the *gare routière,* next to the train station.

When work is completed at the station sometime in 2018, fifteen **trains** a day will connect Grasse with Nice (1 hour), Antibes (40 minutes), and Cannes (30 minutes). Taxis usually wait at the station and are the best option to reach the town center. Bus #5 also runs from the train station to the town center (€1.50 round-trip, none on Sun, every 40 minutes, schedule at sillages.paysdegrasse. fr).

Those arriving by **car** are confounded by Grasse's size, hilly terrain, and inconsistent signage. Follow signs to *Centre-Ville,* then *Office de Tourism,* and park at Parking Notre Dame des Fleurs (under the TI, direct access to the old town) or at Parking Honoré Cresp (follow *Sortie Parfumerie* signs directly to the Fragonard Perfume Factory).

Sights in Grasse

▲International Museum of Perfume
(Musée International de la Parfumerie, MIP)

This city museum is a magnificent—if overwhelming—tribute to perfume, providing a thorough examination of its history and production from ancient Greece until today. The museum is well-designed, with excellent English explanations, a good audioguide, and impressive multimedia exhibits that could keep a perfume fan busy for days. Start in the Sensorial Room, where you'll spend nine minutes getting mellow while preparing your senses for the visit. The three floors below—organized chronologically—teach you everything there is to know about perfume. Your visit ends with a

Fragrant Grasse

Grasse has been at the center of the fragrance industry since the 1500s, when it was known for its scented leather gloves. The cultivation of aromatic plants around Grasse slowly evolved to produce ingredients for soaps and perfumes, and by the 1800s, Grasse was recognized as the center for perfume (thanks largely to its flower-friendly climate), making it a wealthy city.

It can take a ton of carefully picked petals (like jasmine)—that's about 10,000 flowers—to make about two pounds of essence. A damaged flower petal is bad news. Today, perfumes are made from as many as 500 different scents; most are imported to Grasse from countries around the world. The "blender" of these scents and the perfume mastermind is called the "nose" (who nose best). The five master "noses" who work here must study their profession longer than a doctor goes to med school (seven years). They must show that they have the gift before entering "nose school" (in Versailles), and they cannot drink alcohol, ever.

Skip the outlying perfumeries with French-only tours. Only three factories out of forty open their doors to visitors, and only one is worth visiting: Fragonard Perfume in Grasse.

cool display of perfume packages for every year since 1900 and a chance to sniff 32 key perfume ingredients. Allow at least one hour to see everything.

Cost and Hours: €4, keep ticket for 50 percent off at the gardens (see below); daily 10:00-19:00, Oct-April 10:30-17:30, audioguide-€1, two blocks above Fragonard Perfume at 2 Rue Jeu de Ballon, tel. 04 97 05 58 00, www.museesdegrasse.com.

Perfume Gardens (Les Jardins du MIP): You can also visit the museum's gardens about five miles from Grasse. These terraced gardens feature acres of important plants and flowers used in perfume production (€4, 50 percent off with perfume museum ticket, includes videoguide, same hours as museum, see website or ask at museum for location).

Fragonard Perfume Factory (Visite de l'Usine)

This functioning factory, located dead-center in Grasse, provides frequent, fragrant, informative 20-minute tours and an interesting "museum" to explore while you wait. Pick up the English brochure describing what's in the museum cases, then drop down to where the tour begins. On your tour, you'll learn that the difference between perfume, eau de toilette, and cologne is only a matter of perfume percentages. You'll also learn how the product is made today, as well as how they used to do it (by pressing flowers in animal fat). The tour ends with a whiff in the elegant gift shop.

Cost and Hours: Free guided tour, daily 9:00-18:00, closes for lunch Nov-Jan, just off Cours Honoré Cresp at 20 Boulevard Fragonard, tel. 04 93 36 44 65, www.fragonard.com.

Museum of Provençal Costume and Jewelry (Musée Provençal du Costume et du Bijou)

This small, dimly lit museum displays traditional dresses and jewelry from the 18th and 19th centuries. Upon leaving, you'll be given a card you can exchange for a free gift at a shop next door.

Cost and Hours: Free, daily 10:00-13:00 & 14:00-18:30, closed Sun in winter, a block above the *parfumerie* on the pedestrian street at 2 Rue Jean Ossola, tel. 04 93 36 44 65, www.fragonard. com.

Fragonard Museum (Musée Fragonard)

This free, air-conditioned museum houses paintings by three of Grasse's most famous artists: Jean-Honoré Fragonard, Marguerite Gérard, and Jean-Baptiste Mallet. Ask for the English explanations at the welcome desk.

Cost and Hours: Free, daily 10:00-18:00, just a few doors down from the costume museum, 14 Rue Jean Ossola, tel. 04 93 36 02 07, www.fragonard.com.

Old Grasse

Just above Fragonard Perfume, Rue Jean Ossola leads into the labyrinthine ancient streets that form an intriguing pedestrian area. To get a good taste of old Grasse, you can follow the TI's minimalist self-guided tour with your map (takes an hour at a brisk pace, read the posted information plaques as you go) or, better, wander at will and read the plaques when you see them.

Start by strolling up Rue Jean Ossola (just above Boulevard Fragonard), then turn right down Rue Gazan to find the Romanesque cathedral opposite an unusual WWI monument (it's worth peering into the cathedral to see its tree-trunk-like columns and austere decor). Find the view terrace behind the cathedral. Double back to Rue Jean Ossola, turn right, then make a left up bohemian Rue de l'Oratoire and pop out onto a terrific square, making a left just after #27 Place aux Aires (with more good eating options).

Grand Canyon du Verdon

Two hours north of Nice and three hours east of Avignon lies the Parc Naturel Régional du Verdon (a.k.a. Gorges du Verdon). This immense area of natural beauty is worth ▲▲▲...even to Arizonans.

For millions of years, this region was covered by the sea. Over time, sediments and the remains of marine animals were deposited

INLAND RIVIERA

here, becoming thick layers of limestone as they were buried. Later, plate tectonics uplifted the limestone and erosion exposed it, and the Verdon River—with help from Ice Age glaciers—carved out the gorges and its side canyons. At their deepest points, the gorges drop 2,200 feet to the river. At the bottom, the canyons narrow to as little as 26 feet across, while at the top, the canyon walls spread as far as 4,700 feet apart.

The Verdon River is named for its turquoise-green hue. The striking color comes from very fine particles of rock suspended in the water, pulverized by glaciers high at the river's source. It's a sight that has inspired visitors since Ligurian Celts ruled the region.

PLANNING YOUR TIME

The Grand Canyon du Verdon, Europe's greatest canyon, offers a magnificent detour between the Riviera and Provence (figure seven hours with modest canyon time between Nice and the Luberon or Aix-en-Provence; see my self-guided driving tour of the Inland Riviera on page 417). I prefer to stop and smell the canyon, overnighting en route (suggestions later in this chapter). You can reach the canyon on a very long round-trip drive from the Nice area if you leave early (easier if staying in Vence or Antibes). To do this, take the most direct route to or from the canyon and make it a one-way loop (from Nice take the route via Grasse, tour the canyon in the westbound direction, leave the route just before the Lac de Ste-Croix, and connect to the autoroute back to Nice near Draguignan; details below). The canyon can be overrun with cars in summer and on weekends, but is quiet most days in the off-season.

Here are some rough driving times: Riviera to Grasse—1 hour, Grasse to Balcon de la Mescla—1.5 hours, Balcon de la Mescla to Aiguines—1.5 hours with photo stops, Aiguines to Moustiers-Ste-Marie—20 minutes, Moustiers-Ste-Marie to Manosque (en route to Provence)—1.5 hours.

ORIENTATION TO GRAND CANYON DU VERDON

The Parc Naturel Régional du Verdon, far more than just its famous canyon, is a vast area mixing alpine scenery with misty villages, meandering streams, and seas of gentle meadows. The canyon is the heart of the park, where colossal slabs of white and salmon-colored limestone plunge impossible distances to the snaking Verdon River far below. You need a car, ample time, and a lack of vertigo to enjoy

this area. If traveling in summer or on holiday weekends, go really early or skip it. Fill your tank before leaving Grasse or Moustiers-Ste-Marie. Roads crawl along the length of the canyon on both sides (Rive Gauche and Rive Droite); the Rive Gauche works best for most, though both are spectacular.

The Grand Canyon du Verdon is located between the villages of Moustiers-Ste-Marie and Aiguines to the west and Castellane to the east. The most scenic driving segments are along the south side (Rive Gauche) between Aiguines and the Balcon de la Mescla, and the north side (Rive Droite) between Moustiers-Ste-Marie and the Point Sublime overlook. Thrill seekers head for the Castellane area, where the whitewater rafting, climbing, and serious hiking trails are best.

There are fewer pullouts and viewpoints than you'd expect, but picnickers will find some good choices for the perfect lunch stop.

GRAND CANYON DU VERDON DRIVING TOUR
From the Riviera to Provence
For drivers connecting the Riviera with Provence via the canyon, this self-guided drive along the Rive Gauche offers the most accessible and most scenic tour of the gorges. Coming from the Riviera, you'll drive the canyon from east to west. The basic route: Drive through Grasse and toward Castellane, then turn off to hit the canyon at the Balcon de la Mescla. After seeing the canyon's most scenic stretch, you can either split off (after Aiguines) to return to the Riviera, or continue through Moustiers-Ste-Marie and on to Provence. (For drivers coming *from* Provence, this tour works in reverse, west to east; see "Approaching from Provence," at the end of the tour.)

INLAND RIVIERA

Cannes to Balcon de la Mescla: The most direct route from the Riviera follows D-6185, which starts near Cannes (A-8 autoroute from Nice to Cannes saves time) and passes through Grasse, changing to D-6085 and continuing north toward Digne and Castellane. You'll turn left off D-6085 well before Castellane, following signs to the *Gorges du Verdon* and *Draguignan* (an impressive medieval bridge stands just north of the road, about 2 miles/3 kilometers before Comps-sur-Artuby, signed *La Souche*). Turn right onto D-71 at Comps-sur-Artuby, following signs to *Gorges du Verdon, Rive Gauche* (not *Rive Droite*). In a few minutes, you'll reach a pullout with a good view of the village of Trigance.

Driving along D-71, you'll arrive quickly at the canyon rim at the Balcon de la Mescla. Stop at **Le Relais de Balcon** café/gift shop, with a good selection of maps and books. The lookout on the lower side of the café/gift shop is best.

Along the Canyon, from Balcon de la Mescla to Aiguines: From here, follow the canyon lip for about 90 serpentine minutes (including ample stops). You'll drive at an escargot's pace, navigating hairpin turns along the Corniche Sublime while enjoying views of rocky masses and vanishing-point views up the canyon. Hikes into the canyon are too long and steep for most. You're better off walking along the main road for a bit, or detouring down some of the short paths scattered alongside the road. There are small pullouts along the route that come without warning. Don't expect US National Park conditions—you won't see a ranger, signage is minimal, and the road rarely has a shoulder.

A little beyond the Balcon de la Mescla, you can amble across Europe's second-highest bridge, the **Pont de l'Artuby,** and imagine working on its construction crew. There's a large parking lot at the far end of the bridge; get out and breathe here. About two miles (3 kilometers) past the bridge, you'll find a dirt pullout on the north side of the road. A 10-minute stroll along the path leads to sensational views of the canyon and acres of limestone to scramble over.

About halfway through the canyon is the recommended cliff-hanger **Hôtel-Restaurant Grand Canyon du Verdon.** This funky, concrete place looks slapped together, but the café terrace has tables with stupendous views (drinks, snacks, and meals available at fair prices). If your driver feels cheated about missing the views, make sure you stop here for a break.

Back along the main road, the **Col d'Illoire**—the last pass before leaving the canyon—provides sweeping views from the western portal. Park in the large pullout, where you'll find a few picnic tables scattered above and some good rock-scampering just below.

Aiguines: Just west of the canyon, the small village of Aiguines squats below waves of limestone and overlooks the long turquoise Lac de Ste-Croix. This unspoiled village has a hand-

ful of shops, recommended hotels, and cafés. It's an outdoorsy, popular-with-hikers place most canyon visitors cruise right through. Detour onto the grounds of the 15th-century château for the view over Aiguines (with picnic benches and a fun play area for kids; château interior closed to the public). Aiguines' **TI** is on the main drag (July-Aug daily 8:30-18:00; Sept-June Mon-Fri 9:00-12:00 & 14:00-17:00, closed Sat-Sun; Allée des Tilleuls, tel. 04 94 70 21 64, www.aiguines. com).

For more views over Aiguines and the lake, stroll up one of the many staircases along the main drag to the small **Chapelle St. Pierre.** From here, you can walk up the small road five minutes to the campground café, with nice tables on its broad view terrace (ideal for a predinner drink or morning coffee).

Returning to the Riviera: If you're day-tripping from the Riviera rather than continuing to Provence, follow signs for *Aups* (D-957) as you leave Aiguines, then *Draguignan,* then *Nice* via A-8.

Aiguines to Moustiers-Ste-Marie: If you're continuing to Provençal destinations, head for Moustiers-Ste-Marie and continue the tour below.

Barely 50 years old, the man-made **Lac de Ste-Croix** is about six miles long and is the last stop for water flowing out of the Gorges du Verdon. For a fun lake/river experience, rent a canoe or a pedal boat at either side of the low bridge halfway between Moustiers and Aiguines (no motor boats are allowed). You can paddle under the bridge, then follow the aquamarine inlet upstream as far as 2.5 miles, tracing the river's route up the gorge on its final journey to the lake.

Moustiers-Ste-Marie: Here's another pretty Provençal face lined with boutiques—though this one comes with an impressive setting, straddling a small stream at the base of the limestone cliffs of the Gorges du Verdon. The town is busy, with tourists clamoring for the locally famous china. Parking can be difficult, especially in high season. The **TI** is in the center, next to the church (daily 10:00-12:30 & 14:00-18:00, no midday break July-Aug, free Wi-Fi, Place de l'Eglise, tel. 04 92 74 67 84, www.moustiers.fr). There's a small supermarket at the bottom of

the town near the parking lots, and a smaller outlet is in the town center near the TI.

You can escape some of the crowds by climbing 20 minutes on a steep, ankle-twisting path (262 steps) to the **Chapelle Notre-Dame de Beauvoir**—a simple chapel that has attracted pilgrims for centuries. A notebook in the chapel allows travelers to pen a request for a miracle for a loved one. For most, the chapel does not warrant the effort, though you'll get great views over the village by walking a short way up the path.

Moustiers-Ste-Marie to Provence: From here it's another 1.5-2 hours to most Provençal destinations. From Moustiers-Ste-Marie, head for Riez, then Gréoux-les-Bains. From Gréoux-les-Bains, follow signs for *Manosque,* then *Apt* for Luberon and Avignon; or use A-51 south to reach Aix-en-Provence, Lourmarin in the Luberon, Cassis, Marseille, or Arles.

Approaching from Provence

Drivers coming from Provence can do the above tour from west to east (Moustiers-Ste-Marie to the Balcon de la Mescla).

All roads from Provence pass through Gréoux-les-Bains, an hour northeast of Aix-en-Provence. Those coming from Cassis, Aix-en-Provence, the southern Luberon, and Arles will find A-51 north the fastest path; those coming from the central Luberon and Avignon should take D-900 via Apt (turns into D-4100), then follow signs for *Manosque.* From Gréoux-les-Bains, follow signs to *Riez, Moustiers-Ste-Marie,* and *Aiguines* before entering the Grand Canyon du Verdon (Rive Gauche). Ignore the *Grand Canyon du Verdon* signs as you leave Moustiers-Ste-Marie—they lead to the Rive Droite. Follow the *Aiguines* signs instead to make sure you are going to the Rive Gauche.

Leave the canyon after the Balcon de la Mescla. To get to Nice, follow signs for *Comps-sur-Artuby* (and *Draguignan* for a short distance), then *Grasse* and *Nice.* The fastest way from Grasse to Nice is via Cannes and A-8.

SLEEPING AND EATING NEAR THE GRAND CANYON DU VERDON

These places are listed in the order you'll reach them on the self-guided driving tour from east to west. Most hotels in this area want you to take half-pension, but it is rarely required outside of high season. Budget-minded travelers will find lots of places to picnic, but bring groceries with you as stores are scarce (grocery stores and bakeries are in Gréoux and Moustiers if coming from the west, but there's not much if coming from the east—stock up before you head out).

Midway Through the Canyon

$$ Hôtel-Restaurant Grand Canyon du Verdon** is housed in a funky structure that must have been grandfathered-in to own such an unbelievable location—2,500 feet high on the Corniche Sublime. The hotel rents 15 basic, alpine-modern rooms—half on the canyon side (pricier), and many with decks (worth reserving ahead, easy parking, closed Nov-March, tel. 04 94 76 91 31, www.hotel-canyon-verdon.com, hotel.gd.canyon.verdon@wanadoo.fr).

In Aiguines

$ Hôtel du Vieux-Château,** which has been in business for 200 years, is Aiguines' most characteristic hotel. Its 10 snug rooms are red-tiled, spotless, and cool—literally, as there's little direct light. The hotel's cozy restaurant has simple, hearty fare and good soups (Place de la Fontaine, closed Nov-March, tel. 04 94 70 22 95, www.hotelvieuxchateau.fr, contact@hotelvieuxchateau.fr).

$ Hôtel Altitude 823,** just below, offers more predictable comfort with less character but better views (no air-con, closed Nov-Feb, tel. 04 98 10 22 17, www.hotel-altitude823-verdon.com, altitude823@laposte.net, helpful owners Patrice and Rosélyne).

In Moustiers-Ste-Marie

$ Le Mas du Loup is a good-value *chambre d'hôte,* a 10-minute walk outside of town. Charming Julie welcomes guests to her five-bedroom *bastide,* where all rooms come with private patios and comfortable beds (cash only, includes breakfast, free parking, tel. 04 92 74 65 61, mobile 06 71 71 81 36, www.le-mas-du-loup.fr, masduloup7@hotmail.fr).

¢ Restaurant/Chambres Clerissy has four spacious and spotless rooms. It's good for families and individuals (cash only, Place du Chevalier de Blacas, in the village center across from the left transept of the church, tel. 04 92 77 29 30, mobile 06 76 12 40 66).

Eating: There is no shortage of dining options in Moustiers-Ste-Marie. The simple **$ Restaurant Clerissy** (whose rooms are listed earlier) offers inexpensive and simple meals (crêpes and pizza) and appealing indoor and outdoor tables. **$$ Côté Jardin** is a quiet haven a few steps south of the old town, with a pleasing garden setting, great views, and good cuisine at fair prices (closed Mon evening and all day Tue, €25-38 *menus,* tel. 04 92 74 68 91).

INLAND RIVIERA

TRAVELING WITH CHILDREN

With relatively few must-see museums, plenty of outdoor activities, and cooperative weather, Provence and the French Riviera are practically made for kids. This part of France has beaches, fun canoeing on safe rivers, good biking, Roman ruins to scramble over, abundant sunshine, and swimming pools everywhere. Teenagers love the seaside resorts (Cassis and Antibes are best) and enjoy the hustle and bustle of cities like Avignon, Arles, Aix-en-Provence, and Nice. Younger kids tend to prefer the rural areas, which offer more swimming pools, open spaces, and parks.

Trip Tips

PLAN AHEAD
Involve your kids in trip planning. Have them read about the places that you may include in your itinerary (even the hotels you're considering), and let them help with your decisions.

Where to Stay
- Hotel selection is critical. In my recommendations, I've identified hotels that seem particularly kid-friendly (pools, table tennis, grassy areas, easygoing owners, etc.). Most hotels have some sort of crib you can use.
- Minimize hotel changes by planning three-day stays.
- Aim for hotels with restaurants, so older kids can go back to the room while you finish a pleasant dinner.
- If you're staying for a week or more in one place, a great option is to rent a *gîte* (see "Gîtes" on page 478).

What to Bring (or Not)
- Don't bother bringing a car seat—car-rental agencies usually rent them, though you must reserve one in advance.

Parenting French-Style

Famous for their topless tanning, French women are equally comfortable with public breastfeeding of their babies: No need for shawls or "hooter hiders" here. Changing tables are nonexistent, so bring a roll-up changing mat and get comfortable changing your baby on your knees, on a bench, or wherever you find enough space.

French grandmothers take their role as community elders seriously and won't hesitate to recommend that you put more sunscreen on your child in the summer, or add a layer of clothing if it's breezy.

Rather than saying *bonjour* to French children, say *coucou* (coo-coo) if they are young and *salut* (sal-oo) if they are pre-teens or older.

- Bring your own drawing supplies and English-language picture books, as these supplies are pricey in France.
- If your kids love peanut butter, bring it from home (hard to find in France).

EATING
Provence offers plenty of food options for children.

What to Eat (and Drink)
- Kid-friendly foods that are commonly available and easy to order include crêpes (available at many takeout stands), *croque monsieurs* (grilled ham and cheese sandwiches), and *tartines* (open-faced sandwiches). Plain pasta is available at many cafés and some bistros (ask for *pâtes nature*). Carry a baguette to snack on. In the south of France, pizza is omnipresent.
- For breakfast, try a *pain au chocolat* (chocolate-filled pastry) or dip your baguette in a *chocolat chaud* (hot chocolate). Fruit, cereals, and yogurt are usually available.
- Help your kids acquire a taste for Nutella, the tasty hazelnut-chocolate spread available everywhere. Look for organic *(bio)* stores in cities, where you can find numerous nut butters and *Chocolade*, a less-sugary version of Nutella.
- For older kids, be aware that the drinking age is 16 for beer and wine and 18 for the hard stuff: Your waiter will assume that your teen will have wine with you at dinner. Teens are also welcome in most bars and lounges (there's no 21-and-older section).

When and Where to Eat
- Eat dinner early (restaurants open for dinner at 19:00-19:30, cafés open earlier).

Books and Films for Kids

Get your kids into the traveling spirit with books and movies about France, Provence, and the French Riviera. For longer drives, audio books can be fun for the whole family (if carefully chosen)—I recommend Peter Mayle's *A Year in Provence.* (Also see "Books and Films," including some good choices for teenagers, on page 531.)

Anatole (Eve Titus, 1956). This Caldecott Honor Book introduces young readers to the great world of French food via a mouse who finds work in a cheese factory.

Anni's Diary of France, by Anni Axworthy. This fun, picture-filled book about a young girl's trip will inspire your little ones.

Camille and the Sunflowers (Laurence Anholt, 1994). In a tale based on a true story, the postman's son Camille befriends his town's new resident, Vincent van Gogh.

The Cat Who Walked Across France (Kate Banks, 2004). Beautiful illustrations accompany the marvelous journey of a cat through France—including a stop at Pont du Gard near Avignon.

Discovering Great Artists: Hands-On Art for Children in the Styles of the Great Masters (MaryAnn Kohl, 1997). Get to know your favorite artists, from the Renaissance to the present day, by learning their techniques through various art activities.

Getting to Know France and French (Nicola Wright, 1993). This illustrated guide is a fun crash course for younger travelers, featuring history, school life, food, festivals, and language.

- Skip romantic eateries. Try relaxed cafés (or fast-food restaurants) where kids can move around without bothering others.
- Picnics work well. *Boulangeries* are good places to grab off-hour snacks when restaurants aren't serving. (See page 484 for picnic tips.)

SIGHTSEEING

The key to a successful Provence family vacation is to slow down. Tackle one or two key sights each day, mix in a healthy dose of pure fun at a park or square, and take extended breaks when needed.

Planning Your Time

- Lower your sightseeing ambitions and let kids help choose daily activities. Plan longer stays at fewer stops—you won't regret it.
- To make your trip fun for everyone in the family, mix heavy-duty sights with kids' activities, such as playing *mini-golf* or *boules,* renting bikes or canoes, and riding the little tourist trains popular in many towns.
- Older kids and teens can help plan the details of a museum

Henri's Scissors (Jeanette Winter, 2013). This beautiful picture book illustrates how Matisse found new inspiration in paper cut-outs as he lay in bed near the end of his life.

How Would You Survive in the Middle Ages? (Fiona MacDonald, 1995). MacDonald makes history fun for kids and adults alike in this engaging guide to life in the Middle Ages.

The Lady and the Squire (Terry Jones, 2000). In this fun read by a former Monty Python member, the Duke of Lancaster's squire, Tom, makes a fantastical visit to 19th-century Avignon.

Madeline (Ludwig Bemelmans, 1939). Kids love the *Madeline* series, which follows the adventures of a Parisian girl and her boarding-school pals. A live-action 1998 film brings the stories to life.

Picasso and the Girl with a Ponytail (Laurence Anholt, 2002). This picture book relates the story of Sylvette, who models for Picasso and then eventually becomes a painter herself.

Ratatouille (2007). In this animated film named for the famous Provençal dish, a mouse becomes a chef at a fine French restaurant.

The Red Balloon (1956). A small boy chases his balloon through the streets of Paris in this classic of French cinema.

When Pigasso Met Mootisse (Nina Laden, 1998). A silly picture-book take on the tempestuous relationship between Picasso and Matisse, which ultimately ended in friendship.

visit, such as what to see, how to get there, and ticketing details.

Successful Sightseeing

- Museum audioguides are great for older children. For younger children, hit the gift shop first so they can buy postcards and have a scavenger hunt to find the pictured artwork. When boredom sets in, try "I spy" games or have them count how many babies or dogs they can spot in all the paintings in the room.
- Bring a sketchbook to a museum and encourage kids to select a painting or statue to draw. It's a great way for them to slow down and observe.
- If you're in France near Bastille Day, remember that fireworks stands pop up everywhere on the days leading up to July 14. Putting on their own fireworks show can be a highlight for teenagers.

CHILDREN

Making or Finding Quality Souvenirs

- One of my favorite suggestions is to buy your child a trip journal, where he or she can record observations, thoughts, and favorite sights and memories. This journal could end up being your child's favorite souvenir.

- For a group project, keep a family journal. Pack a small diary and a glue stick. While relaxing at a café over a *citron-pressé* (lemonade), take turns writing about the day's events and include mementos such as ticket stubs from museums, postcards, or stalks of lavender.

- Let kids pick out some toys and books. The best and cheapest toy selections are usually in department stores, like Monoprix and Galeries Lafayette. Note that Legos are sometimes different in Europe than in the US, and the French have wonderful doll clothes with a much wider selection than typically found in the US. Kids like the French adventure comics Astérix and Tintin (both available in English, sold in bigger bookstores with English sections).

MONEY, SAFETY, AND STAYING CONNECTED

Before your trip gets underway, talk to your kids about safety and money.

- Give your child a money belt and an expanded allowance; you are on vacation, after all. Let your kids budget their funds by comparing and contrasting the dollar and euro.

- If you allow older kids to explore a museum or neighborhood on their own, be sure to establish a clear meeting time and place.

- It's good to have a "what if" procedure in place in case something goes wrong. Give your kids your hotel's business card, your phone number (if you brought a mobile phone), and emergency taxi fare. Let them know to ask to use the phone at a hotel if they are lost. And if they have mobile phones, show them how to make calls in France (see page 500).

- If traveling with older kids, you can help them keep in touch with friends at home with cheap texting plans and by email. Hotel guest computers and Wi-Fi hotspots are a godsend. Readily available Wi-Fi (at hotels, some cafés, and all Starbucks and McDonald's) makes bringing a mobile device worthwhile. Most parents find it worth the peace of mind to buy a supplemental messaging plan for the whole family: Adults can stay connected to teenagers while allowing them maximum independence (see page 499).

Top Kids' Sights and Activities

ATTRACTIONS

These are listed in no particular order:

- Pont du Gard. An entire wing of the museum is dedicated to kids, who can also swim or take a canoe trip on the river nearby (see page 136).
- Cassis. Boat trip to the *calanques,* or the port and beaches for teenagers (see page 240).
- Monaco. Changing of the Guard in Monaco (see page 377) and Oceanography Museum (see page 379).
- Pedal boats on the Mediterranean (in Cassis; see page 244) and into the Grand Canyon du Verdon (from Lac de St-Croix; see page 435).
- Biking or in-line skating on the Promenade des Anglais in Nice (see page 288).
- Biking through vineyards to small villages, from Vaison-la-Romaine (see page 162).
- Les Baux's castle ruins, with medieval weaponry and great walls to climb (see page 76).
- Canoeing on the Ardèche River (see page 181) or the Sorgue River (see page 192).
- Boat trips from Nice (see page 291), Villefranche-sur-Mer (see page 347), or St-Tropez (see page 414).

Honorable mention goes to Arles' Ancient History Museum (see page 59), horseback riding and public beaches in the Camargue (see page 93), Roman arenas in Nîmes (see page 128) and Arles (see page 49), the beaches of Antibes (see page 399), and the narrow-gauge train ride from Nice (see page 321).

ACTIVITIES

Movies

It's fun to take kids to movies (even if not in English) just to see how theaters work elsewhere. Movies shown in their original language—usually with subtitles—are listed as *v.o.* at the box office. (One showing could be *v.o.* and the next could be dubbed in French, labeled *v.f.;* be aware that *v.o.* movies are hard to find outside major cities.) *Dessin animé* means "cartoon." While many live-action movies can be found in their original language with French subtitles, cartoons and kids' movies (intended for an audience that doesn't read so well yet) are almost always dubbed.

Swimming

I've listed swimming pools in many places—they're great for kids. But be warned: Public pools in France commonly require a small, Speedo-like bathing suit for boys and men (American-style swim

CHILDREN

trunks won't do)—though they usually have these little suits for sale. At hotel pools, any type of swimsuit will do.

Rides

You'll find old-style merry-go-rounds in many cities, perfect for younger travelers (my daughter's goal was to ride a merry-go-round in every town...she came close). There are also little tourist trains in nearly every city.

Farms

Visits to local goat-cheese makers in early spring yield good kid rewards (look for *fromage fermier de chèvre* signs along the country roads). Goats are social animals and goat-cheese makers will usually let your child hold or pet one. You can also pick up some superb fresh cheese for your picnic.

Boules

Consider buying a set of *boules* (a.k.a. *pétanque*, a form of outdoor bowling—for the rules, see sidebar on page 38). Play *boules* before dinner, side by side with real players on the village court. Get your *boules de pétanque* at sporting-goods stores or larger department stores. Since they're heavy, buy a set only if you'll be driving. The *boules* also make fun, if weighty, souvenirs, and are just as enjoyable to play back at home. TIs in some towns, such as Vence, have *boules* to rent.

SHOPPING

Provence and the Riviera offer France's best shopping outside of Paris, with a great range of reasonably priced items ideal for souvenirs and gifts. And, if approached thoughtfully, shopping in the south of France can be a culturally enlightening experience. There's no better way to mix serious shopping business with travel pleasure than at the weekly markets *(marchés)* in towns and villages throughout the region. These traditional market days offer far more than fresh produce and fish; in many cases, about half the market is devoted to durable goods (baskets, tablecloths, pottery, and fabrics)—*très* handy for gifts. If you miss market day, most Provençal towns have more than enough small shops that sell local products—and more than enough kitschy souvenirs. (They're often selling the same items you can find more cheaply at weekly markets.) If you crave French fashion, the destinations in this book have ample clothing boutiques.

In this chapter, you'll find information about shopping for souvenirs, navigating market days, and browsing boutiques. For information about VAT refunds and customs regulations, see page 468. For a comparison of French to US clothing sizes, see the appendix.

WHAT TO BUY

Here's a shopping list of locally made goods in Provence and the Riviera. You'll find most of these items in tourist-oriented boutiques, though many of them are cheaper on market days. If you buy more expensive, nonperishable goods, most stores will work with you to send them home.

- **Jams** *(confiture)* containing lush and often exotic fruits, such as *fruit de la passion* (passion fruit), *figues* (figs), and *pastèque* or *citre* (different types of watermelon).

- **Honey** *(miel)*, particularly lavender *(lavande)* or rosemary *(romarin)*. Stronger palates should try the chestnut *(châtaigne)* or even oak-flavored *(chêne)* honey.
- Tins of **tapenade** (olive paste) and all kinds of **olives**: black, green, and stuffed with garlic or anchovies.
- **Olive-wood products,** such as utensils and bowls. Olives are not just for nibbling; in Provence, the entire tree is used.
- Canned **pâtés,** including the buttery, rich foie gras (its "home" is Périgord, but you'll also find it in the markets of Provence). Canned goose, duck, and pork pâté can be imported to the US, but not beef.
- Packets of **herbs** (including the famous *herbes de Provence*), **salt** from the Camargue (look for *Fleur de Sel* for the best, and use sparingly), and bottles or tins of **olive oil** from local trees (Nyons is France's olive capital, though Les Baux is rightly proud of its olives as well). Most of these items can be found in attractive packaging that can be saved and enjoyed long after the product itself is gone.
- Sweets, including the famous *nougat de Montélimar* (a rich, chewy confection made with nuts and honey, sometimes flavored with lavender or other fragrances), *calissons* (orange-and-almond-flavored candy, shaped like the nut and originally from Aix-en-Provence), and **chocolates** from the Provençal producer Puyricard.
- **Soaps and lotions,** particularly those "perfumed" with local plants such as lavender *(lavande)*, rosemary *(romarin)*, or linden *(tilleul)*. You'll also find colorful **sachets** containing the same fragrances.
- Brightly colored **table linens.** Souleiado and Les Olivades are the most famous local manufacturers, but good-quality knockoffs can be found in most any market or store. Waterproof versions are great for outdoor use.
- **Cloth bags** with French designs for grocery shopping (can be packed easily and cost pennies).
- Local **pottery** *(poterie;* faïence is hand-painted *poterie)*. Terre Provence is a well-known (and pricey) brand, but many other producers offer excellent quality, usually for less. Serious potters can plan ahead to visit a pottery fair featuring the best of the regions' potters.
- *Santons,* the tiny, brightly adorned clay or wood Provençal figurines. Originally designed for traditional Christmas crèche scenes, today's *santons* ("little saints") represent all walks of life—from the local *boulanger* to the woman sewing bright Provençal cloth to the village doctor. The most famous *santon* makers are in Séguret and Aubagne. All *santon* makers be-

long to the *santon*-maker guild (think medieval stonecutters or woodworkers), and each *santon* is handmade and signed.

MARKET DAY

Market day *(jour de marché)* is a big deal throughout France, and in no other region is it more celebrated than in Provence and the Riviera. Markets have been a central feature of life in rural areas since the Middle Ages. No single event better symbolizes the French preoccupation with fresh products—and their strong ties to the soil—than the weekly market. Many locals mark their calendars with the arrival of fresh produce.

Market day is as important socially as it is commercially—it's a weekly chance for locals to resume friendships and get the current gossip. Here, neighbors can catch up on Henri's barn renovation, see photos of Jacqueline's new grandchild, and relax over *un café*. Dogs are tethered to café tables while friends exchange kisses. Tether yourself to a table and observe: three cheek-kisses for good friends (left-right-left), a fourth for friends you haven't seen in a while. (The appropriate number of kisses varies by region—Paris, Lyon, and Provence have different standards).

Provence is a Mediterranean melting pot where Italy, Spain, and North Africa intersect with France to do business. Notice the ethnic mix of the vendors (and the products they sell). Spices from Morocco and Tunisia, fresh pasta from Italy, saffron from Spain, and tapenade from Provence compete for your attention at Provence's *marchés*.

Types of Markets: There are two kinds of weekly open-air markets—*les marchés* and *les marchés brocantes*.

Les marchés are more general in scope, more common, and more colorful, featuring products from area farmers and artisans. These markets can offer a mind-boggling array of choices, from the perishable (produce, meats, cheeses, breads, and pastries) to the nonperishable (kitchen wares, inexpensive clothing, brightly colored linens, and pottery).

Les marchés brocantes specialize in quasi-antiques and flea market bric-a-brac (think rummage sale). *Brocantes* markets began in the Middle Ages, when middlemen would gather to set up small stalls and sell old, flea-infested clothes and the discarded possessions of the wealthy at bargain prices to eager peasants. Buyers were allowed to *rummage* through piles of aristocratic garbage.

Many *marchés* have good selections of produce and some *brocantes*. The best of all market worlds may rest in the town of Isle-sur-la-Sorgue, where on Sunday mornings, a brilliant food *marché* tangles with an active flea market and a good selection of antiques.

I've listed days and locations for both market types throughout this book. Notice the signs as you enter towns indicating the *jours de marché* (essential information to any civilized soul, and a reminder not to park on the streets the night before—be on the lookout for *stationnement interdit* signs that mark "no parking" areas). Most *marchés* take place once a week in the town's main square; larger *marchés* spill into nearby streets.

Usually, the bigger the market, the greater the overall selection, particularly of nonperishable goods. Bigger towns (such as Arles) may have two weekly markets, one a bit larger than the other, with more nonperishable goods; in other towns (including Isle-sur-la-Sorgue), the second weekly market may simply be a smaller version of the main market day. The biggest market days are usually on weekends so everyone can go. In the largest cities (such as Avignon and Nîmes), modern market halls have been established, with produce stands and meat counters selling fresh goods daily.

Market Day Tips: Markets begin at about 8:00, with setup commencing in the predawn hours (for some, a reason not to stay in a main-square hotel the night before market day). They usually end by 13:00.

At the root of a good market experience is a sturdy shopping basket or bag. (You'll need your own bag—small plastic ones are no longer legal in France.) Find the vendor selling baskets and other wicker items and go local (*osier* is the French name for wicker, *cade* is the Provençal name—from the basket-making Luberon village of Cadenet); you can also find plastic and nylon versions. Most baskets are inexpensive, make for fun and colorful souvenirs, and come in handy for holding odd-shaped or breakable carry-ons on the plane trip home. An alternative is a cloth shopping bag. With bag or basket in hand, shop for your heaviest items first. (You don't want to put a kilo of fresh apples on top of the bread you bought for your picnic.)

It's a joy to assemble picnics at an open-air market. Most perishable items are sold directly from the producers—no middlemen, no credit cards, just really fresh produce (*du pays* means "grown locally"). Sometimes you'll meet a widow selling a dozen eggs, two rabbits, and a wad of herbs tied with string. But most vendors follow a weekly circuit of markets they feel works best for them, showing up in the same spot every week, year in and year out. At a favorite market, my family has done business with the same olive vendor and "cookie man" for 22 years.

It's bad form to be in a hurry on market day. Allow the crowd

Key Shopping Phrases

English	French
Just looking.	*Je regarde.* (zhuh ruh-gard)
How much is it?	*Combien?* (koh<u>n</u>-bee-a<u>n</u>)
Too big/small/expensive	*Trop grand/petit/cher* (troh grah<u>n</u>/puh-tee/shehr)
May I try it on?	*Je peux l'essayer?* (zhuh puh lay-say-yay)
Can I see more?	*Je peux en voir d'autres?* (zhuh puh ah<u>n</u> vwahr doh-truh)
I'd like this.	*Je voudrais ça.* (zhuh voo-dray sah)
On sale	*Solde* (sohld)
Discounted price	*Prix réduit* (pree ray-dwee)
Big discounts	*Prix choc* (pree shohk)

to set your pace. Observe the interaction between vendor and client. Notice the joy they can find in chatting each other up. Wares are displayed with pride. Generally, the rule is "don't touch"—instead, point and let them serve you. If self-serve is allowed, the seller will hand you a biodegradable bag. Remember, they use metric weight. Ask for *un kilo* (about 2 pounds), *un demi-kilo* (about 1 pound—also called *une livre*), or *un quart de kilo* (pronounced "car-kilo," about half a pound). Many vendors speak enough English to assist you in your selection. Your total price will be hand-tallied on small scraps of paper and given to you. Vendors are normally honest. If you're struggling to find the correct change, just hold out your hand and they will take only what is needed. (Still, you're wise to double-check the amount you just paid for that olive tree.)

What to Look For: Markets change seasonally. In April and May, look for asparagus (green, purple, or the prized white—after being cooked, these are dipped in vinegar or homemade mayonnaise and eaten by hand). In late spring, shop for strawberries, including the best: *fraises des bois* (wild strawberries). Almost equally prized are the strawberries called *gariguettes* and *maras des bois*. Soon after, you'll see cherries and other stone fruits, plus the famously sweet Cavaillon melons (resembling tiny cantaloupes, often served cut in half with a spoonful or two of the sweet Rhône white wine Beaumes-de-Venise). Don't worry if these are split open—the abundance of sugar and sunshine are the cause (*fendus* melons are considered the sweetest). In late June and early September, watch for figs (*figues*). From July through September, essential vegetables for the Provençal dish ratatouille—including eggplant, tomatoes, zucchinis, and peppers—come straight from the open fields. In the fall, you'll see stands selling game birds, other beasts of the hunt, and a glorious array of wild mushrooms.

After November and throughout the winter, look for little (or big, depending on your wallet size) black truffles. Truffles preserved and sealed in jars can safely be brought back to the United States. The Luberon is one of Provence's largest truffle-producing areas. The town of Carpentras hosts a truffles-only market on Friday mornings in winter. Listen carefully and you might hear the Provençal language being spoken between some vendors and buyers. Richerenches—Northern Provence's truffle capital—holds its own winter truffle market; during its annual truffle-themed Mass, some parishioners give a truffle as a small offering instead of money. *Vive la France.*

For more immediate consumption in any season, look for local cheeses (cow, called *vache;* sheep or ewe, called *brebis;* or the Provençal favorite: goat cheese, or chèvre, named *picodons*). Cheeses range from very fresh (aged one day) to aged for weeks. The older the cheese, the more dried and shrunken. Some may even be speckled with edible mold. Cheeses come in many shapes (round, logs, pyramids) and various sizes (from single-bite mouthfuls to wheels that will feed you for several meals). Some are sprinkled with herbs or spices. Others are more adorned, such as those rolled in ash *(à la cendre)* or wrapped in leaves *(banon).* Watch for the locally produced *banon de banon,* a goat cheese soaked in *eau-de-vie* (the highly alcoholic "water of life"), then wrapped in chestnut leaves and tied with string—*oh là là*.

Next, move on to the usually huge selection of sausages (many also rolled in herbs or spices). Samples are usually free—try the *sanglier* (boar). Be on the lookout for locally produced wines and ciders (free tastings are standard). Find samples of foie gras (available in take-it-home tins), good with the sweet white wine of Beaumes-de-Venise. These items make perfect picnic fare when teamed with a crusty baguette.

You'll often pass vendors selling paella made *sur place* (on the spot) in huge traditional round pans. Paella varies by area and chef, but most recipes include the traditional ingredients of fresh shellfish, chicken, and sausages mixed into saffron-infused rice. And throughout France, you'll see vans selling sizzling, spit-roasted chicken (perfectly bagged for carrying out) or pizza (made to your liking on the spot). *Bon appétit!*

CLOTHING BOUTIQUES

Those who prefer fashion over food will be happy to learn they don't have to go to Paris to enjoy the latest trends. The stylish boutiques lining the shopping streets of Avignon, Nîmes, Aix-en-Provence, St-Rémy, Uzès, Nice, and the ultra-trendy Juan-les-Pins offer more than sufficient selection and style for the fashion-conscious. While many shopkeepers speak some English, an effort to speak even a minimum of French earns better service. These tips should get you off on the right track:

- In small stores, always say, *"Bonjour, Madame (*or *Mademoiselle* or *Monsieur)"* when entering. And remember to say, *"Au revoir, Madame/Mademoiselle/Monsieur"* when leaving.
- The customer is not always right; in fact, some clerks figure they're doing you a favor by waiting on you.
- Except in department stores, it's not normal for the customer to handle clothing. Ask first before you pick up an item: *"Je peux?"* (zhuh puh), meaning, "Can I?"
- By law, the price of items in a window display must be visible, often written on a slip of paper set on the floor or framed on the wall. This gives you an idea of how expensive or affordable the shop is.
- For clothing-size comparisons between the US and France, see the appendix.
- Forget returns (and don't count on exchanges).
- Observe French shoppers, then imitate them.
- Saturday afternoons are *très* busy and not for the faint of heart.
- Stores are closed on Sunday and usually on Monday mornings.
- Smaller shops may close for lunch
- Don't feel obliged to buy. If a shopkeeper offers assistance, just say, *"Je regarde, merci,"* meaning, "Just looking, thanks."
- For information on VAT refunds and customs regulations, see page 468.

FRANCE: PAST & PRESENT

FRENCH HISTORY IN AN ESCARGOT SHELL

About the time of Christ, Romans "Latinized" the land of the Gauls. With the fifth-century A.D. fall of Rome, the barbarian Franks and Burgundians invaded. Today's France evolved from this unique mix of Latin and Celtic cultures.

While France wallowed with the rest of Europe in medieval darkness, it got a head start in its development as a nation-state. In 507, Clovis, the king of the Franks, established Paris as the capital of his Christian Merovingian dynasty. Clovis and the Franks would eventually become Louis and the French. The Frankish military leader Charles Martel stopped the spread of Islam by beating the Spanish Moors at the Battle of Poitiers in 732. And Charlemagne, the most important of the "Dark Age" Frankish kings, was crowned Holy Roman Emperor by the pope in 800. Charles the Great presided over the "Carolingian Renaissance" and effectively ruled an empire that was vast for its time.

The Treaty of Verdun (843), which divided Charlemagne's empire among his grandsons, marks what could be considered the birth of Europe. For the first time, a treaty was signed in vernacular languages (French and German), rather than in Latin. This split established a Franco-Germanic divide and heralded an age of fragmentation. While petty princes took the reigns, the Frankish king ruled only Ile de France, a small region around Paris.

Vikings, or Norsemen, settled in what became Normandy. Later, in 1066, these "Normans" invaded England. The Norman king, William the Conqueror, consolidated his English domain, accelerating the formation of modern England. But his rule also muddied the political waters between England and France, kicking off a centuries-long struggle between the two nations.

In the 12th century, Eleanor of Aquitaine (a separate country

Typical Church Architecture

History comes to life when you visit a centuries-old church. Even if you wouldn't know your apse from a hole in the ground, learning a few simple terms will enrich your experience. Note that not every church has every feature, and a "cathedral" isn't a type of church architecture, but rather a designation for a church that's a governing center for a local bishop.

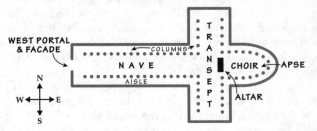

Aisles: The long, generally low-ceilinged arcades that flank the nave.

Altar: The raised area with a ceremonial table (often adorned with candles or a crucifix), where the priest prepares and serves the bread and wine for Communion.

Apse: The space beyond the altar, generally bordered with small chapels.

Barrel Vault: A continuous round-arched ceiling that resembles an extended upside-down U.

Choir: A cozy area, often screened off, located within the church nave and near the high altar where services are sung in a more intimate setting.

Cloister: Covered hallways bordering a (usually square-shaped) open-air courtyard, traditionally where monks and nuns got fresh air.

Facade: The exterior surface of the church's main (west) entrance, usually highly decorated.

Groin Vault: An arched ceiling formed where two equal barrel vaults meet at right angles. Less common usage: medieval jock strap.

Narthex: The area (portico or foyer) between the main entry and the nave.

Nave: The long, central section of the church (running west to east, from the entrance to the altar) where the congregation sits or stands through the service.

Transept: In a traditional cross-shaped floor plan, the transept is one of the two parts forming the "arms" of the cross. The transepts run north-south, perpendicularly crossing the east-west nave.

West Portal: The main entry to the church (on the west end, opposite the main altar).

in southwest France) married Louis VII, king of France, bringing Aquitaine under French rule. They divorced, and she married Henry of Normandy, soon to be Henry II of England. This marital union gave England control of a huge swath of land, from the English Channel to the Pyrenees. For 300 years, France and England would struggle for control of Aquitaine. Any enemy of the French king would find a natural ally in the English king.

In 1328, the French king Charles IV died without a son. The English king (Edward III), Charles IV's nephew, was interested in the throne, but the French resisted. This quandary pitted France, the biggest and richest country in Europe, against England, which had the largest army. They fought from 1337 to 1453 in what was modestly called the Hundred Years' War.

Regional powers from within France actually sided with England. Burgundy took Paris, captured the royal family, and recognized the English king as heir to the French throne. England controlled France from the Loire north, and things looked bleak for the French king.

Enter Joan of Arc, a 16-year-old peasant girl driven by religious voices. France's national heroine left home to support Charles VII, the dauphin (boy prince, heir to the throne but too young to rule). Joan rallied the French, ultimately inspiring them to throw out the English. In 1430, Joan was captured by the Burgundians, who sold her to the English, who then convicted her of heresy and burned her at the stake in Rouen. But the inspiration of Joan of Arc lived on, and by 1453 English holdings on the Continent had dwindled to the port of Calais.

By 1500 a strong, centralized France had emerged, with borders similar to those of today. Its kings (from the Renaissance François I through the Henrys and all those Louises) were model divine monarchs, setting the standard for absolute rule in Europe.

Outrage over the power plays and spending sprees of the kings—coupled with the modern thinking of the Enlightenment (whose leaders were the French *philosophes*)—led to the French Revolution in 1789. In France, it was the end of the *ancien régime*, as well as its notion that some are born to rule, while others are born to be ruled.

The excesses of the Revolution in turn led to the rise of Napoleon, who ruled the French empire as a dictator. Eventually, *his* excesses ushered him into a South Atlantic exile, and after another half-century of monarchy and empire, the French settled on a compromise role for their leader. The modern French "king" is ruled by a constitution. Rather than dress in leotards and powdered wigs, the president goes to work in a suit and carries a briefcase.

The 20th century spelled the end of France's reign as a military and political superpower. Devastating wars with Germany in 1870,

1914, and 1940—and the loss of her colonial holdings—left France with not quite enough land, people, or production to be a top player on a global scale. But the 21st century may see France rise again: Paris is a cultural capital of Europe, and France—under the EU banner—is a key player in unifying Europe as a single economic power. And when Europe becomes a superpower, Paris may yet be its capital.

CONTEMPORARY POLITICS IN FRANCE

Today, the political issues in France are—like everywhere—the economy, terrorism, and immigration.

French unemployment remains high (over 10 percent, even higher for youth) and growth has flatlined. France has not balanced its books since 1974, and public spending—at 56 percent of GDP—chews up a bigger chunk of output than any other eurozone country. The challenge for French leadership is to address its economic problems while maintaining the high level of social services that the French people expect from their government.

France also has its economic strengths: a well-educated workforce, an especially robust service sector and high-end manufacturing industry, and more firms big enough to rank in the global Fortune 500 than any other European country. Ironically, while France's economy may be one of the world's largest, the French remain skeptical about the virtues of capitalism and its requisite work ethic. Globalization conflicts in a fundamental way with French values—many fear losing what makes their society unique in the quest for a bland, globalized world. Business conversation is generally avoided, as it implies a fascination with money that the French find vulgar; it's considered gauche even to ask what someone does for a living. In France, CEOs are not glorified as celebrities—chefs are.

The French believe the economy should support social good, not vice versa. This has produced a cradle-to-grave social security system of which the French are proud. France's poverty rate is half of that in the US, proof to the French they are on the right track. On the other hand, if you're considering starting a business in France, think again—taxes are formidable (figure a total small-business tax rate of around 66 percent—and likely to increase). French voters are notorious for their belief in the free market's heartless cruelty, and they tend to see globalization as a threat rather than a potential benefit. France is routinely plagued with strikes, demonstrations, and slowdowns as workers try to preserve their hard-earned rights in the face of a competitive global economy.

Another ongoing issue French leaders are working to address is immigration, which is shifting the country's ethnic and cultural makeup in ways that challenge French society. Ten percent

Top French Notables in History

Madame and Monsieur Cro-Magnon: Prehistoric hunter-gatherers who moved to France (c. 30,000 B.C.), painted cave walls at Lascaux and Font-de-Gaume, and eventually settled down as farmers (c. 10,000 B.C.).

Vercingétorix (72-46 B.C.): This long-haired warrior rallied the Gauls against Julius Caesar's invading Roman legions (52 B.C.). Defeated by Caesar, France fell under Roman domination, resulting in 500 years of peace and prosperity. During that time, the Romans established cities, built roads, taught in Latin, and converted people to Christianity.

Charlemagne (742-814): For Christmas in 800, the pope gave King Charlemagne the title of Emperor, thus uniting much of Europe under the leadership of the Franks ("France"). Charlemagne stabilized France amid centuries of barbarian invasions. After his death, the empire was split, carving the outlines of modern France and Germany.

Eleanor of Aquitaine (c. 1122-1204): The beautiful, sophisticated ex-wife of the King of France married the King of England, creating an uneasy union between the two countries. During her lifetime, French culture was spread across Europe by roving troubadours, theological scholars, and skilled architects pioneering "the French style"—a.k.a. Gothic.

Joan of Arc (1412-1431): When France and England fought the Hundred Years' War (1337-1453), this teen—guided by voices in her head—rallied the French troops. Though Joan was captured and burned as a heretic, the French eventually drove England out for good, establishing the current borders. Over the centuries, the church upgraded Joan's status from heretic to saint (canonized in 1920).

François I (1494-1547): This Renaissance king ruled a united, modern nation, making it a cultural center that hosted the Italian Leonardo da Vinci. François set the tone for future absolute monarchs, punctuating his commands with the phrase, "For such is our pleasure."

Louis XIV (1638-1715): Charismatic and cunning, the "Sun King" ruled Europe's richest, most populous, most powerful nation-state. Every educated European spoke French, dressed in Louis-style leotards and powdered wigs, and built Versailles-like palaces. Though Louis ruled as an absolute monarch (distracting the nobility with courtly games), his reign also fostered the arts and philosophy, sowing the seeds of democracy and revolution.

Marie Antoinette (1755-1793): The Austrian-born wife of Louis XVI came to symbolize (probably unfairly) the decadence of France's ruling class. When the Revolution broke out (1789), she was arrested, imprisoned, and executed—one of thousands guillotined on Paris' Place de la Concorde as an enemy of the people.

Napoleon Bonaparte (1769-1821): This daring young military man became a hero during the Revolution, fighting Europe's royalty. He went on to conquer much of the Continent, become leader of France, and, eventually, rule as a dictator with the title of Emperor. In 1815, an allied Europe defeated and exiled Napoleon, reinstating the French monarchy—though future kings and emperors (including Napoleon's nephew, who ruled as Napoleon III) were somewhat subject to democratic constraints.

Claude Monet (1840-1926): His Impressionist paintings captured the soft-focus beauty of the belle époque—middle-class folk enjoying drinks in cafés, walks in gardens, and picnics along the Seine. At the turn of the 20th century, French culture reigned supreme while its economic and political clout was fading, and was soon shattered by World War I.

Charles de Gaulle (1890-1970): This career military man helped France survive occupation by Nazi Germany with his rousing radio broadcasts and unbending faith in his countrymen. He left politics after World War II, but following France's divisive wars in Vietnam and Algeria, he became president of the Fifth Republic in 1959. De Gaulle shocked allies by granting Algeria independence, blocking Britain's entry into the Common Market, and withdrawing from the military wing of NATO. Student riots in the late 1960s eventually led to his resignation in 1969.

Recent French Notables: Which French personalities of the last century will history remember? Marcel Marceau (1923-2007), world-famous mime? Brigitte Bardot (b. 1934), film actress, crusader for animal rights, and popularizer of the bikini? President François Mitterrand (1916-1996), the driving force behind Paris' La Grande Arche and Opéra Bastille? Chef Paul Bocuse (b. 1926), inventor of nouvelle cuisine? Yves Saint Laurent (1936-2008), the great fashion designer? Jean-Marie Le Pen (b. 1928), father of the far-right National Front party...and 2017 presidential runner-up Marine Le Pen? Bernard Kouchner (b. 1939), co-founder of Doctors Without Borders? Zinédine Zidane (b. 1972), star soccer player, whose Algerian roots helped raise the status of Arabs in France? Or will it be actress Catherine Deneuve (b. 1943), NBA star Tony Parker (b. 1982), or wrestler-turned-actor Andre the Giant (1946-1993)? (Giants all.)

of France's population is now of North African descent, mainly immigrants from former colonies. Many immigrants are Muslim, raising cultural questions in this heavily Catholic society with a history of official state secularism. The government has (quite controversially) made it illegal for women to wear a full, face-covering veil *(niqāb)* in public. Debates continue about whether banning the veil enforces democracy—or squelches diversity.

A series of terrorist attacks in France in recent years has battered the nation's self-confidence. Locals have had to adjust to life with armed soldiers patrolling rail stations and streets. Many of the attackers were French citizens as well as immigrants. The attacks have left the French questioning their process of assimilating immigrants into the body politic.

France is part of the 28-member European Union, the "United States of Europe" that has successfully dissolved borders and implemented a common currency, the euro. France's governments have been decidedly pro-EU and critical to the EU's success. But many French are Euro-skeptics, afraid that EU meddling threatens their job security and social benefits. The Brexit vote in 2016 focused attention on France. Is a Frexit possible? The EU can survive sans Britain but probably not sans France.

France is governed by a president elected by popular vote every five years. The president then selects the prime minister, who in turn chooses the cabinet ministers. Collectively, this executive branch is known as the *gouvernement*. The parliament consists of a Senate (348 seats) and Assemblée Nationale (577 seats).

In France, voters have an array of political parties to choose from, making compromise and coalition-building essential to keeping power. Even the biggest parties rarely get more than one-third of the seats in parliament. And, because the parliament can force the *gouvernement* to resign at any time, it's essential that the *gouvernement* work with them.

For a snapshot of the current political landscape, look no further than the 2012 and 2017 elections. (French elections last only several months, with one TV debate—yes, the French election season is that short). In 2012, socialist François Hollande defeated center-right incumbent Nicolas Sarkozy. But when Hollande's term became fraught by scandal, rocked by terrorist events, and weighed down by a flat economy, Hollande opted against running for re-election in 2017. That left the field wide open.

The 2017 election was a wild ride, with events never seen before in France. Eleven candidates competed in the French version of a primary, reducing the field to two for the final vote. For the first time since de Gaulle, neither of the two finalists were from the traditional right and left parties. (Imagine a US presidential election sans Republican or Democrat!) Emmanuel Macron, a

Trouble in Paradise: Population Growth in Southern France

Life is not as perfect as it may appear amid the breezy, sun-kissed beaches, cities, and villages of Provence and the French Riviera. The south of France has become a bouillabaisse of people in search of their Provençal paradise. While some say the influx into this region has invigorated the culture, many residents are feeling growing pains. Two major trends are fueling the population boom in the south: northern Europeans looking for their place in the sun, and North African immigrants looking for a better life. These trends meet head on in southern France.

Cheap flights and lightning-fast train service have enabled northern Europeans to experience the south of France as a weekend getaway...and a growing number are choosing to stay. Thanks to its sunny climate, relatively inexpensive homes (compared to northern Europe), and plentiful transportation options, this region is an understandably big draw. Unfortunately, as wealthy northerners pick off local homes and inflate prices, the average Jean is losing out.

France has long looked across the Mediterranean to its old colonies for cheap sources of manual labor. When these workers came, they brought their families, who stayed in France and had families of their own. Today, France has Europe's second-largest Muslim population—only Russia's is greater.

Five million North Africans legally reside in France—and many more illegally. Around 100,000 illegal immigrants arrive in France each year, about half of whom are North African. Most live in the south (more than a quarter of Marseille's population is North African). This concentration of immigrants among a very Catholic French population, combined with high unemployment, has led to the rise of racist politics.

This anti-immigrant movement has been spearheaded by the National Front party, which wants to keep "France for the French." National Front presidential candidate Marine Le Pen carried the anti-immigrant torch and added populist policies in the 2017 election. Although popular, she failed to overcome centrist Emmanuel Macron, proving—for now—that the National Front is still a minority.

centrist businessman, had no party affiliation and had never held elected office. Marine Le Pen, though a politician, represented the far-right National Front party, once a pariah party tarnished by accusations of anti-Semitism.

Le Pen rallied support by proposing to limit immigration and step back from the EU. Macron proposed a moderate stay-the-course plan that attracted both liberals and moderate conservatives. The tone of the debates was uncharacteristically nasty—something totally unheard of in genteel France. The French were presented with a stark choice: moderate vs. extreme. In the end, they overwhelmingly chose the moderate path.

Macron won with a whopping 66 percent of the vote. Still, Le Pen's result was the best yet for a National Front candidate. At 39, Macron is France's youngest leader since Napoleon Bonaparte (and looks even younger). His success was completely unpredicted. He won as an outsider, representing a change from traditional party politics. (Sound familiar?)

On the other hand, Macron carries on a tradition shared by many recent French leaders: unorthodox sexual relations that would raise eyebrows in America. Past leaders such as Jacques Chirac and François Mitterand were noted for their mistresses. Sarkozy divorced his wife to marry a young supermodel who previously dated Mick Jagger. Hollande was once photographed arriving by motorcycle for a rendezvous with a mistress. And Macron, though happily married, met his bride when he was 16 and she was his high school teacher.

For more about French history, consider Europe 101: History and Art for the Traveler *by Rick Steves and Gene Openshaw, available at www.ricksteves.com.*

PRACTICALITIES

Tourist Information 461
Travel Tips 462
Money 463
Sightseeing. 469
Sleeping. 471
Eating. 482
Staying Connected 498
Transportation 503
Resources from Rick Steves 526

This chapter covers the practical skills of European travel: how to get tourist information, pay for things, sightsee efficiently, find good-value accommodations, eat affordably but well, use technology wisely, and get between destinations smoothly. To round out your knowledge, check out "Resources from Rick Steves." For more information on these topics, see www.ricksteves.com/travel-tips.

Tourist Information

The French national tourist office is a wealth of information. **Before your trip,** scan their website—http://us.france.fr. It has particularly good resources for special-interest travel and plenty of free-to-download brochures.

In France, a good first stop is generally the tourist information office (abbreviated **TI** in this book). You can get plenty of information online—but I still make a point to swing by the local TI to confirm sightseeing plans, pick up a city map, and get information on public transit (including bus and train schedules), walking tours, special events, and nightlife. Prepare a list of questions and a proposed plan to double-check. Some TIs have information on the entire country or at least the region, so try to pick up maps and printed information for destinations you'll be visiting later in your trip. Towns with a lot of tourism generally have English-speaking guides available for private hire through the TI (about €100-150 for a two-hour guided town walk).

The French call TIs by different names: *Office de Tourisme* and *Bureau de Tourisme* are used in cities; *Syndicat d'Initiative* and *Information Touristique* are used in small towns. Also look for *Accueil* signs in airports and at popular sights. These information booths are staffed with seasonal helpers who provide tourists with limited, though generally sufficient, information. Smaller TIs are often closed from 12:00 to 14:00 and on Sundays.

Travel Tips

Emergency and Medical Help: In France, dial 112 for any emergency (their 911). For English-speaking police, call 17. To summon an ambulance (SAMU in French), call 15. If you get sick, do as the locals do and go to a pharmacist for advice. Or ask at your hotel for help—they'll know the nearest medical and emergency services.

Theft or Loss: To replace a passport, you'll need to go in person to an embassy or consulate (see page 529). If your credit and debit cards disappear, cancel and replace them (see "Damage Control for Lost Cards" on page 467). File a police report, either on the spot or within a day or two; you'll need it to submit an insurance claim for lost or stolen rail passes or travel gear, and it can help with replacing your passport or credit and debit cards. For more information, see www.ricksteves.com/help.

Time Zones: France, like most of continental Europe, is generally six/nine hours ahead of the East/West Coasts of the US. The exceptions are the beginning and end of Daylight Saving Time: Europe "springs forward" the last Sunday in March (two weeks after most of North America), and "falls back" the last Sunday in October (one week before North America). For a handy online time converter, see www.timeanddate.com/worldclock.

Business Hours: You'll find much of rural France closed weekdays from 12:00 to 14:00 (lunch is sacred). On Sunday, most businesses are closed (family is sacred), though some small shops such as *boulangeries* (bakeries) are open until noon, special events and weekly markets pop up, and museums are open all day (but public transportation options are scant). On Mondays, some businesses are closed until 14:00 and possibly all day. Smaller towns are often quiet and downright boring on Sundays and Mondays, unless it's market day. Saturdays are virtually weekdays, with earlier closing hours at some shops. Banks are generally open on Saturday

PRACTICALITIES

and closed on Sunday and possibly Monday. Friday and Saturday evenings are lively; Sunday evenings are quiet.

Watt's Up? Europe's electrical system is 220 volts, instead of North America's 110 volts. Most newer electronics (such as laptops, battery chargers, and hair dryers) convert automatically, so you won't need a converter, but you will need an adapter plug with two round prongs, sold inexpensively at travel stores in the US. Avoid bringing older appliances that don't automatically convert voltage; instead, buy a cheap one in Europe. You can buy low-cost hair dryers and other small appliances at Darty and Monoprix stores, which you'll find in major cities (ask your hotelier for the closest branch).

Discounts: Discounts for sights are generally not listed in this book. However, many sights offer discounts for youths (usually up to age 18), students (with proper identification cards, www.isic.org), families, and groups of 10 or more. Always ask, and have your passport available at sights for proof. Seniors (age 60 and over) may get the odd discount, though these are often limited to citizens of the European Union (EU). To inquire about a senior discount, ask, *"Réduction troisième âge?"* (ray-dewk-see-ohn trwah-zee-ehm ahzh).

Online Translation Tips: Google's Chrome browser instantly translates websites. You can also paste text or the URL of a foreign website into the translation window at Translate.google.com. The Google Translate app converts spoken English into most European languages (and vice versa) and can also translate text it "reads" with your smartphone's camera. It's not perfect...some results can be way off—and funny.

Money

Here's my basic strategy for using money in Europe:
- Upon arrival, head for a cash machine (ATM) at the airport and load up on local currency, using a debit card with low international transaction fees.
- Withdraw large amounts at each transaction (to limit fees) and keep your cash safe in a money belt.
- Pay for most items with cash.
- Pay for larger purchases with a credit card with low (or no) international fees.

PLASTIC VERSUS CASH

Although credit cards are widely accepted in Europe, day-to-day spending is generally more cash-based than in the US. I find cash is the easiest—and sometimes only—way to pay for cheap food, bus fare, taxis, tips, and local guides. Some businesses (especially

PRACTICALITIES

> ## Exchange Rate
>
> ### 1 euro (€) = about $1.10
>
> To convert prices in euros to dollars, add about 10 percent: €20=about $22, €50=about $55. (Check www.oanda.com for the latest exchange rates.) Just like the dollar, one euro (€) is broken down into 100 cents. Coins range from €0.01 to €2, and bills from €5 to €200 (bills over €50 are rarely used; €500 bills are being phased out).

smaller ones, such as B&Bs and mom-and-pop cafés and shops) may charge you extra for using a credit card—or might not accept credit cards at all. Having cash on hand helps you out of a jam if your card randomly doesn't work.

I use my credit card to book and pay for hotel reservations, to buy advance tickets for events or sights, and to cover major expenses (such as car rentals or plane tickets). It can also be smart to use plastic near the end of your trip, to avoid another visit to the ATM.

WHAT TO BRING

I pack the following and keep all of it safe in my money belt.

Debit Card: Use this at ATMs to withdraw local cash.

Credit Card: Use this to pay for larger items (at hotels, larger shops and restaurants, travel agencies, car-rental agencies, and so on).

Backup Card: Some travelers carry a third card (debit or credit; ideally from a different bank), in case one gets lost, demagnetized, eaten by a temperamental machine, or simply doesn't work.

Euros: For an emergency reserve, consider bringing €200 in hard cash in €20-50 bills (bring euros, as dollars can be hard to change in France).

BEFORE YOU GO

Use this pre-trip checklist.

Know your cards. Debit cards from any major US bank will work in any standard European bank's ATM (ideally, use a debit card with a Visa or MasterCard logo). As for credit cards, Visa and MasterCard are universal, American Express is less common, and Discover is unknown in Europe.

Newer credit and debit cards have chips that authenticate and secure transactions. In Europe, the cardholder inserts the chip card into the payment machine slot, then enters a PIN. (In the US, you provide a signature to verify your identity.)

Any American card, whether with a chip or an old-fashioned magnetic stripe, will work at Europe's hotels, restaurants, and shops. I've been inconvenienced a few times by self-service payment machines in Europe that wouldn't accept my card, but it's never caused me serious trouble.

If you're concerned, ask if your bank offers a true chip-and-PIN card. Cards with low fees and chip-and-PIN technology include those from Andrews Federal Credit Union (www.andrewsfcu.org) and the State Department Federal Credit Union (www.sdfcu.org).

Report your travel dates. Let your bank know that you'll be using your debit and credit cards in Europe, and when and where you're headed.

Know your PIN. Make sure you know the numeric, four-digit PIN for each of your cards, both debit and credit. Request it if you don't have one and allow time to receive the information by mail.

Adjust your ATM withdrawal limit. Find out how much you can take out daily and ask for a higher daily withdrawal limit if you want to get more cash at once. Note that European ATMs will withdraw funds only from checking accounts; you're unlikely to have access to your savings account.

Ask about fees. For any purchase or withdrawal made with a card, you may be charged a currency conversion fee (1-3 percent), a Visa or MasterCard international transaction fee (1 percent), and—for debit cards—a $2-5 transaction fee each time you use a foreign ATM (some US banks partner with European banks, allowing you to use those ATMs with no fees—for example, Bank of America customers pay no transaction fee when using French Paribas-BNP ATMs).

If you're getting a bad deal, consider getting a new debit or credit card. Reputable no-fee cards include those from Capital One, as well as Charles Schwab debit cards. Most credit unions and some airline loyalty cards have low-to-no international transaction fees

IN EUROPE
Using Cash Machines

European cash machines have English-language instructions and work just like they do at home—except they spit out local currency instead of dollars, calculated at the day's standard bank-to-bank rate.

In most places, ATMs are easy to locate—in France ask for a *distributeur* (dee-stree-bew-tur). When possible, withdraw cash from a bank-run ATM located just outside that bank. Ideally use it during the bank's opening hours; if your card is munched by the machine, you can go inside for help.

If your debit card doesn't work, try a lower amount—your request may have exceeded your withdrawal limit or the ATM's limit. If you still have a problem, try a different ATM or come back later—your bank's network may be temporarily down.

PRACTICALITIES

Avoid "independent" ATMs, such as Travelex, Euronet, Moneybox, Cardpoint, and Cashzone. These have high fees, can be less secure than a bank ATM, and may try to trick users with "dynamic currency conversion" (see below).

Exchanging Cash

Avoid exchanging money in Europe; it's a big rip-off. In a pinch you can always find exchange desks at major train stations or airports—convenient but with crummy rates. Banks in France may not exchange money unless you have an account with them.

Using Credit Cards

European cards use chip-and-PIN technology, while most cards issued in the US use a chip-and-signature system. But most European card readers can automatically generate a receipt for you to sign, just as you would at home. If a cashier is present, you should have no problems. Some card readers will instead prompt you to enter your PIN (so it's important to know the code for each of your cards).

In France, self-service payment machines (transit-ticket kiosks, parking, etc.) are a headache, as US chip-and-signature cards aren't configured for unattended transactions. If your card won't work, look for a cashier who can process your card manually—or pay in cash.

Drivers Beware: Be aware of potential problems using a US credit card to fill up at an unattended gas station, enter a parking garage, or exit a toll road. Carry cash and be prepared to move on to the next gas station if necessary. When approaching a toll plaza, use the "cash" lane. For more tips, see the "Driving" section, later.

Dynamic Currency Conversion

Some European merchants and hoteliers cheerfully charge you for converting your purchase price into dollars. If it's offered, refuse this "service" (called dynamic currency conversion, or DCC). You'll pay extra for the expensive convenience of seeing your charge in dollars. Some ATM machines also offer DCC, often in confusing or misleading terms. If an ATM offers to "lock in" or "guarantee" your conversion rate, choose "proceed without conversion." Other prompts might state, "You can be charged in dollars: Press YES for dollars, NO for euros." Always choose the local currency.

Security Tips

Pickpockets target tourists. To safeguard your cash, wear a money belt—a pouch with a strap that you buckle around your waist like a belt and tuck under your clothes. Keep your cash, credit cards, and passport secure in your money belt, and carry only a day's spending money in your front pocket or wallet.

Before inserting your card into an ATM, inspect the front. If anything looks crooked, loose, or damaged, it could be a sign of a card-skimming device. When entering your PIN, carefully block other people's view of the keypad.

Don't use a debit card for purchases. Because a debit card pulls funds directly from your bank account, potential charges incurred by a thief will stay on your account while the fraudulent use is investigated by your bank.

While traveling, to access your accounts online, be sure to use a secure connection (see page 502).

Damage Control for Lost Cards

If you lose your credit or debit card, report the loss immediately to the respective global customer-assistance centers. Call these 24-hour US numbers collect: Visa (tel. 303/967-1096), MasterCard (tel. 636/722-7111), and American Express (tel. 336/393-1111). In France, to make a collect call to the US, dial 08 00 90 06 24, then say "operator" for an English-speaking operator. European toll-free numbers (listed by country) can be found at the websites for Visa and MasterCard.

For another option (with the same results), you can call these toll-free numbers in France: Visa (tel. 08 00 90 11 79) and MasterCard (tel. 08 00 90 13 87). American Express has a Paris office, but the call isn't free (tel. 01 47 77 70 00, greeting is in French, dial 1 to speak with someone in English).

You'll need to provide the primary cardholder's identification-verification details (such as birth date, mother's maiden name, or Social Security number). You can generally receive a temporary card within two or three business days in Europe (see www.ricksteves.com/help for more).

If you report your loss within two days, you typically won't be responsible for unauthorized transactions on your account, although many banks charge a liability fee of $50.

TIPPING

Tipping *(donner un pourboire)* in France isn't as automatic and generous as it is in the US. For special service, tips are appreciated, but not expected. As in the US, the proper amount depends on your resources, tipping philosophy, and the circumstances, but some general guidelines apply.

Restaurants: At cafés and restaurants, a service charge is included in the price of what you order, and it's unnecessary to tip extra, though you can for superb service. For details on tipping in restaurants, see page 487.

Taxis: For a typical ride, round up your fare a bit (for instance, if the fare is €13, pay €14). If the cabbie hauls your bags and zips you to the airport to help you catch your flight, you might want to toss in a little more. But if you feel like you're being driven in circles or otherwise ripped off, skip the tip.

Services: In general, if someone in the tourism or service industry does a super job for you, a small tip of a euro or two is appropriate...but not required. If you're not sure whether (or how much) to tip, ask a local for advice.

GETTING A VAT REFUND

Wrapped into the purchase price of your French souvenirs is a Value-Added Tax (VAT) of about 20 percent. You're entitled to get most of that tax back if you purchase more than €175 (about $195) worth of goods at a store that participates in the VAT-refund scheme. Typically, you must ring up the minimum at a single retailer—you can't add up your purchases from various shops to reach the required amount. (If the store ships the goods to your US home, VAT is not assessed on your purchase.)

Getting your refund is straightforward...and worthwhile if you spend a significant amount on souvenirs.

Get the paperwork. Have the merchant completely fill out the necessary refund document, called a *bordereau de détaxe*. You'll have to present your passport. Get the paperwork done before you leave the store to ensure you'll have everything you need (including your original sales receipt).

Get your stamp at the border or airport. Process your VAT document at your last stop in the European Union (such as at the airport) with the customs agent who deals with VAT refunds. Arrive an additional hour before you need to check in to allow time to find the customs office—and to stand in line. Some customs desks are positioned before airport security; confirm the location before going through security.

It's best to keep your purchases in your carry-on. If they're too large or dangerous to carry on (such as knives), pack them in your checked bags and alert the check-in agent. You'll be sent (with your tagged bag) to a customs desk outside security; someone will examine your bag, stamp your paperwork, and put your bag on the belt. You're not supposed to use your purchased goods before you leave. If you show up at customs wearing your chic new shoes, officials might look the other way—or deny you a refund.

Collect your refund. Many merchants work with services, such as Global Blue or Premier Tax Free, that have offices at major airports, ports, or border crossings (either before or after security, probably strategically located near a duty-free shop). At Paris' Charles de Gaulle, you'll find them at the check-in area (or ask for help at an orange ADP info desk). These services, which extract a 4 percent fee, can refund your money immediately in cash or credit your card (within two billing cycles). Other refund services may require you to mail the documents from home, or more quickly, from your point of departure (using an envelope you've prepared in advance or one that's been provided by the merchant). You'll then have to wait—it can take months.

CUSTOMS FOR AMERICAN SHOPPERS

You can take home $800 worth of items per person duty-free, once every 31 days. Many processed and packaged foods are allowed, including vacuum-packed cheeses, dried herbs, jams, baked goods, candy, chocolate, oil, vinegar, mustard, and honey. Fresh fruits and vegetables and most meats are not allowed, with exceptions for some canned items. As for alcohol, you can bring in one liter duty-free (it can be packed securely in your checked luggage, along with any other liquid-containing items).

To bring alcohol (or liquid-packed foods) in your carry-on bag on your flight home, buy it at a duty-free shop at the airport. You'll increase your odds of getting it onto a connecting flight if it's packaged in a "STEB"—a secure, tamper-evident bag. But stay away from liquids in opaque, ceramic, or metallic containers, which usually cannot be successfully screened (STEB or no STEB).

For details on allowable goods, customs rules, and duty rates, visit http://help.cbp.gov.

Sightseeing

Sightseeing can be hard work. Use these tips to make your visits to Provence and the French Riviera's finest sights meaningful, fun, efficient, and painless.

MAPS AND NAVIGATION TOOLS

A good map is essential for efficient navigation while sightseeing. The maps in this book are concise and simple, designed to help you locate recommended destinations, sights, and local TIs, where you can pick up more in-depth maps. More detailed maps are sold at newsstands and bookstores.

You can also use a mapping app on your mobile device. Be aware that pulling up maps on the fly or looking up turn-by-turn walking directions usually requires an Internet connection—to use this feature, it's smart to get an international data plan (see page 498). With Google Maps or City Maps 2Go, it's possible to download a map while online, then go offline and navigate without incurring data-roaming charges—though you can't search for an address or get real-time walking directions. A handful of other apps, including Apple Maps, OffMaps, and Navfree, also allow you to use maps offline.

PLAN AHEAD

Set up an itinerary that allows you to fit in all your must-see sights. For a one-stop look at opening hours in the bigger cities, see the "At a Glance" sidebars for Arles, Avignon, Marseille, Nice, and Monaco. Most sights keep stable hours, but you can easily confirm the latest by checking with the TI or visiting museum websites.

Don't put off visiting a must-see sight—you never know when a place will close unexpectedly for a holiday, strike, or restoration. Many museums are closed or have reduced hours at least a few days a year, especially on holidays such as Christmas, New Year's, and Labor Day (May 1). A list of holidays is on page 530; check online for possible museum closures during your trip. In summer, some sights may stay open late; in the off-season, hours may be shorter.

Going at the right time helps avoid crowds. This book offers tips on the best times to see specific sights. Try visiting these busy villages and sights on weekdays, and arrive early (usually best) or very late in the day: Les Baux, Pont du Gard, Séguret, Roussillon, Fontaine de Vaucluse, Nice's Chagall and Antibes' Picasso museums, St-Paul-de-Vence, Eze-le-Village, and St-Tropez. Evening visits (when possible) are usually peaceful, with fewer crowds. Keep in mind that French monuments and cities (and some villages) are beautifully lit at night, making evening walks a joy.

If you plan to hire a local guide, reserve ahead by email. Popular guides can get booked up.

Study up. To get the most out of the self-guided tours and sight descriptions in this book, read them before you visit.

AT SIGHTS

Here's what you can typically expect:

Entering: Several cities offer sightseeing passes that can be worthwhile values. You may not be allowed to enter if you arrive less than 30 to 60 minutes before closing time. And guards start ushering people out well before the actual closing time, so don't save the best for last.

Many sights have a security check, where you must open your bag or send it through a metal detector. Allow extra time for these lines in your planning. Some sights require you to check daypacks and coats. (If you'd rather not check your daypack, try carrying it tucked under your arm like a purse as you enter.)

At churches—which often offer interesting art (usually free) and a cool, welcome seat—a modest dress code (no bare shoulders or shorts) is encouraged though rarely enforced.

Photography: If the museum's photo policy isn't clearly posted, ask a guard. Generally, taking photos without a flash or tripod is allowed. Some sights ban selfie sticks; others ban photos altogether.

Temporary Exhibits: Museums may show special exhibits in addition to their permanent collection, which can elevate the entry price.

Expect Changes: Artwork can be on tour, on loan, out sick, or shifted at the whim of the curator. Pick up a floor plan as you enter, and ask museum staff if you can't find a particular item. Say the title or artist's name, or point to the photograph in this book and ask for its location by saying, *"Où est?"* (oo ay).

Audioguides and Apps: Many sights rent audioguides, which generally offer worthwhile recorded descriptions in English. If you bring your own earbuds, you can enjoy better sound. To save money, bring a Y-jack and share one audioguide with your travel partner. Increasingly, museums and sights offer apps—often free—that you can download to your mobile device (check their websites).

Services: Important sights may have a reasonably priced on-site café or cafeteria (handy places to rejuvenate during a long visit). The WCs at sights are free and generally clean.

Before Leaving: At the gift shop, scan the postcard rack or thumb through a guidebook to be sure that you haven't overlooked something that you'd like to see.

Every sight or museum offers more than what is covered in this book. Use the information in this book as an introduction—not the final word.

Sleeping

Accommodations in Provence and the Riviera are a good value and generally easy to find. Choose from one- to five-star hotels

(two and three stars are my mainstays), bed-and-breakfasts (*chambres d'hôtes,* usually cheaper than hotels), hostels, campgrounds, and even homes (*gîtes,* rented by the week).

I favor hotels and restaurants that are handy to your sightseeing activities. Rather than list hotels scattered throughout a city, I choose hotels in my favorite neighborhoods. My recommendations run the gamut, from dorm beds to fancy rooms with all of the comforts.

Extensive and opinionated listings of good-value rooms are a major feature of this book's Sleeping sections. I like places

Sleep Code

Hotels are classified based on the average price of a standard double room without breakfast in high season.

$$$$	**Splurge:** Most rooms over €250
$$$	**Pricier:** €190-250
$$	**Moderate:** €130-190
$	**Budget:** €70-130
¢	**Backpacker:** Under €70
RS%	**Rick Steves discount**
*	**French hotel rating system** (0-5 stars)

Unless otherwise noted, credit cards are accepted, hotel staff speak basic English, and free Wi-Fi is available. Comparison-shop by checking prices at several hotels (on each hotel's own website, on a booking site, or by email). For the best deal, book directly with the hotel. Ask for a discount if paying in cash; if the listing includes **RS%,** request a Rick Steves discount.

that are clean, central, relatively quiet at night, reasonably priced, friendly, small enough to have a hands-on owner or manager and stable staff, and run with a respect for French traditions. I'm more impressed by a convenient location and a fun-loving philosophy than flat-screen TVs and a fancy gym. Most places I recommend fall short of perfection. But if I can find a place with most of these features, it's a keeper.

Book your accommodations as soon as your itinerary is set, especially if you want to stay at one of my top listings or if you'll be traveling during busy times. Wherever you're staying, be ready for crowds during these holiday periods: Easter weekend, Labor Day, Ascension weekend, Pentecost weekend, Bastille Day and the week during which it falls, and the winter holidays (mid-Dec-early Jan).

See page 530 for a list of major holidays and festivals in France; for tips on making reservations, see page 478.

RATES AND DEALS

I've categorized my recommended accommodations based on price, indicated with a dollar-sign rating (see sidebar). The price ranges suggest an estimated cost for a one-night stay in a standard double room with a private toilet and shower in high season, don't include breakfast, and assume you're booking directly with the hotel (not through a booking site, which extracts a commission). Room prices can fluctuate significantly with demand and amenities (size, views, room class, and so on), but relative price categories remain constant.

Room rates are especially volatile at larger hotels that use "dynamic pricing" to set rates. Prices can skyrocket during festivals and conventions, while business hotels can have deep discounts on weekends when demand plummets. Of the many hotels I recommend, it's difficult to say which will be the best value on a given day—until you do your homework.

Once your dates are set, check the specific price for your preferred stay at several hotels. You can do this either by comparing prices online on the hotels' own websites, or by emailing several hotels directly and asking for their best rate. Even if you start your search on a booking site such as TripAdvisor or Booking.com, you'll usually find the best deal through a hotel's own website. (While many hotels are contractually obligated not to undercut booking site prices, when you go direct, the hotel avoids the 15-20 percent commission, giving them wiggle room to treat you better—offering perhaps a nicer room or free breakfast.) Some hotels offer a discount to those who stay longer than three nights. To cut costs further, try asking for a cheaper room (for example, with a shared bathroom or no window).

Additionally, some accommodations offer a special discount for Rick Steves readers, indicated in this guidebook by the abbreviation "RS%." Discounts vary: Ask for details when you reserve. Generally, to qualify you must book directly (that is, not through a booking site), mention this book when you reserve, show this book upon arrival, and sometimes stay a certain number of nights. In some cases, you may need to enter a discount code (which I've provided in the listing) in the booking form on the hotel's website. Rick Steves discounts apply to readers with ebooks as well as printed books. Understandably, discounts do not apply to promotional rates.

Hotels in France must charge a daily tax *(taxe de séjour)* of about €1-3 per person per day. Some hotels include it in their prices, but most add it to your bill.

TYPES OF ACCOMMODATIONS
Hotels

In this book, the price for a double room will normally range from €70 (very simple; toilet and shower down the hall) to €400-plus (grand lobbies, maximum plumbing, and the works), with most clustering around €130 (with private bathrooms).

The French have a simple hotel rating system based on amenities and rated by stars (indicated in this book by asterisks, from * through *****). One star is modest, two has most of the comforts, and three is generally a two-star with a fancier lobby and more elaborately designed rooms. Four-star places give a bit more comfort than those with three. Five stars probably offer more luxury than

PRACTICALITIES

PRACTICALITIES

French Hotel-Room Lingo

Study the price list on the hotel's website or posted at the desk, so you know your options. Receptionists often don't mention the cheaper rooms—they assume you want a private bathroom or a bigger room. Here are the types of rooms and beds:

French	English
une chambre avec douche et WC (ewn shahm-bruh ah-vehk doosh ay vay-say)	room with private shower and toilet
une chambre avec bain et WC (ewn shahm-bruh ah-vehk ban ay vay-say)	room with private bathtub and toilet
une chambre avec cabinet de toilette (ewn shahm-bruh ah-vehk kah-bee-nay duh twah-leht)	room with a toilet (shower down the hall)
une chambre sans douche ni WC (ewn shahm-bruh sahn doosh nee vay-say)	room without a private shower or toilet
chambres communiquantes (shahm-bruh koh-mew-nee-kahnt)	connecting rooms (ideal for families)
une chambre simple, une single (ewn shahm-bruh san-pluh, ewn san-guhl)	a true single room
un grand lit (uhn grahn lee)	double bed (55 in. wide)
deux petits lits (duh puh-tee lee)	twin beds (30-36 in. wide)
un lit queen-size (uhn lee "queen size")	queen-size bed (63 in. wide)
un king size (uhn "king size")	king-size bed (usually two twins pushed together)
un lit pliant (uhn lee plee-ahn)	folding bed
un berceau (uhn behr-soh)	baby crib
un lit d'enfant (uhn lee dahn-fahn)	child's bed

you'll have time to appreciate. Two-star and above hotels are required to have an English-speaking staff, though nearly all hotels I recommend have someone who speaks English.

The number of stars does not always reflect room size or guarantee quality. One- and two-star hotels are less expensive, but some three-star (and even a few four-star hotels) offer good value, justifying the extra cost. Unclassified hotels (no stars) can be bargains...or depressing dumps.

Within each hotel, prices vary depending on the size of room,

---

Keep Cool

If you're visiting in the summer, booking an air-conditioned room is the way to go. Most French air conditioners are operated with a control stick (like a TV remote). You'll likely see these symbols and features: fan icon (click to toggle through wind power, from light to gale); louver icon (steady airflow or waves); snowflake and sunshine icons (cold air or heat); clock ("O" setting: run X hours before turning off; "I" setting (wait X hours to start); and the temperature control (20 degrees Celsius is comfortable; also see the thermometer diagram on page 535). When you leave your room for the day, turning off the air-conditioning is good form.

---

whether it has a tub or shower, and the bed type (tubs and twins cost more than showers and double beds). If you have a preference, ask for it. Hotels often have more rooms with tubs (which the French prefer) and are inclined to give you one by default. You can save lots by finding the rare room without a private shower or toilet.

Most French hotels now have queen-size beds—to confirm, ask, *"Avez-vous des lits queen-size?"* (ah-vay-voo day lee queen-size). Some hotels push two twins together under king-size sheets and blankets to make *le king-size*. If you'll take either twins or a double, ask for a generic *une chambre pour deux* (room for two) to avoid being needlessly turned away. Many hotels have a few family-friendly rooms that open up to each other *(chambres communiquantes)*.

Arrival and Check-In: Hotel elevators are becoming more common, though some older buildings still lack them. You may have to climb a flight of stairs to reach the elevator (if so, you can ask the front desk for help carrying your bags up). Elevators are typically very small—pack light, or you may need to send your bags up without you.

When you check in, the receptionist will normally ask for your passport and keep it for anywhere from a couple of minutes to a couple of hours. The EU requires that hotels collect your name, nationality, and ID number. Relax. Americans are notorious for making this chore more difficult than it needs to be.

If you're arriving in the morning, your room probably won't be ready. Check your bag safely at the hotel and dive right into sightseeing.

Hotel lobbies, halls, and breakfast rooms are off-limits to smokers, though they can light up in their rooms. Still, I seldom smell any smoke in my rooms. Some hotels have nonsmoking rooms or floors—ask.

In Your Room: Extra pillows and blankets are often in the closet or available on request. To get a pillow, ask for *"Un oreiller, s'il* *vous plaît"* (uhn oh-ray-yay, see voo play). Towels and linens aren't always replaced every day. Hang your towel up to dry.

Most hotel rooms have a TV, telephone, and free Wi-Fi (although in old buildings with thick walls, the Wi-Fi signal doesn't always make it to the rooms; sometimes it's only available in the lobby). There's often a guest computer with Internet access in the lobby. Simpler places rarely have a room phone, but usually have free Wi-Fi.

Breakfast and Meals: Most hotels offer some kind of breakfast (see page 484), but it's rarely included in the room rates—pay attention when comparing rates between hotels. The price of breakfast correlates with the price of the room: The more expensive the room, the more expensive the breakfast. This per-person charge rises with the number of stars the hotel has and can add up, particularly for families. While hotels hope you'll buy their breakfast, it's optional unless otherwise noted; to save money, head to a bakery or café instead.

Some hoteliers, especially in resort towns, strongly encourage their peak-season guests to take *demi-pension* (half-pension)—that is, breakfast and either lunch or dinner. By law, they can't require you to take half-pension unless you are staying three or more nights, but, in practice, some do during summer. And though the food is usually good, it limits your ability to shop around. I've indicated where I think *demi-pension* is a good value.

Hoteliers uniformly detest it when people bring food into bedrooms. Dinner picnics are particularly frowned upon: Hoteliers worry about cleanliness, smells, and attracting insects. Be tidy and considerate.

Checking Out: While it's customary to pay for your room upon departure, it can be a good idea to settle your bill the day before, when you're not in a hurry and while the manager's in. Some hoteliers will ask you to sign their *Livre d'Or* (literally "Golden Book," for client comments). They take this seriously and enjoy reading your remarks.

Hotelier Help: Hoteliers can be a good source of advice. Most know their city well, and can assist you with everything from public transit and airport connections to calling an English-speaking doctor, or finding a good restaurant, Wi-Fi hotspot (*point Wi-Fi,* pwan wee-fee), a late-night pharmacy, or a self-service launderette (*laverie automatique,* lah-vay-ree oh-to-mah-teek). English works in all but the cheapest places.

Hotel Hassles: Even at the best places, mechanical breakdowns occur: sinks leak, hot water turns cold, toilets may gurgle or smell, the Wi-Fi goes out, or the air-conditioning dies when you need it most. Report your concerns clearly and calmly at the front desk. For more complicated problems, don't expect instant results.

Above all, keep a positive attitude. Remember, you're on vacation. If your hotel is a disappointment, spend more time out enjoying the place you came to see.

If you find that night noise is a problem (if, for instance, your room is over a nightclub), ask for a quieter room in the back or on an upper floor. To guard against theft in your room, keep valuables out of sight. Some rooms come with a safe, and other hotels have safes at the front desk. I've never bothered using one and in a lifetime of travel, I've never had anything stolen from my room.

Modern Hotel Chains: France is littered with ultramodern hotels, providing drivers with low-stress accommodations and often located on cheap land just outside town. You'll find some in city centers as well. The clean and inexpensive Ibis Budget chain (about €55/room for up to three people), the more attractive and spacious standard Ibis hotels (€80-110 for a double), and the cushier Mercure and Novotel hotels (€130-250 for a double) are all run by the same company, Accor (www.accorhotels.com). Though hardly quaint, these can be a good value (look for deals on their websites), particularly when they're centrally located; I list several in this book. Other chains to consider are Kyriad, with moderate prices and good quality (www.kyriad.com) and the familiar-to-Americans Best Western (www.bestwestern.com). Château and Hotels Collection has more cushy digs (www.chateauxhotels.com).

Bed & Breakfasts

B&Bs (*chambres d'hôte*, abbreviated "CH") generally are found in smaller towns and rural areas. They're usually family-run and a great deal, offering double the cultural intimacy for less than most hotel rooms. While you may lose some hotel conveniences—such as lounges, TVs, daily bed-sheet changes, and credit-card payments—I happily make the trade-off for the personal touch and lower rates. It's always OK to ask to see the room before you commit. And though some CHs post small *Chambres* or *Chambres d'hôte* signs in their front windows, many are found only through the local tourist office.

I recommend reliable CHs that offer a good value and/or unique experience (such as CHs in renovated mills, châteaux, and wine *domaines*). While *chambres d'hôte* have their own star-rating system, it doesn't correspond to the hotels' rating system. To avoid confusion, I haven't listed these stars for CHs. But virtually all of my recommended CHs have private in-room bathrooms and Wi-Fi, and some have common rooms with refrigerators. Doubles generally cost €60-80; fancier places are about €100-120. Breakfast is usually included, but not always—ask. *Tables d'hôte* are CHs that offer an optional, reasonably priced, home-cooked dinner (usually a fine value, must be requested in advance). And though your hosts

Making Hotel Reservations

Reserve your rooms as soon as you've pinned down your travel dates. For busy national holidays, it's wise to reserve far in advance (see page 530).

Requesting a Reservation: It's easiest—and generally cheaper—to book your room through the hotel's official website (not a booking agency's site.) If there's no reservation form, or for complicated requests, send an email. Most recommended hotels take reservations in English.

Here's what the hotelier wants to know:
- type(s) of rooms you need and size of your party
- number of nights you'll stay
- your arrival and departure dates, written European-style as day/month/year (for example, 18/06/19 or 18 June 2019)
- special requests (such as en suite bathroom vs. down the hall, cheapest room, twin beds vs. double bed, quiet room)
- applicable discounts (such as a Rick Steves reader discount, cash discount, or promotional rate)

Confirming a Reservation: Most places will request a credit-card number to hold your room. If they don't have a secure online reservation form—look for the https—you can email it (I do), but it's safer to share that confidential info via a phone call or fax.

Canceling a Reservation: If you must cancel, it's courteous—and smart—to do so with as much notice as possible, especially for smaller family-run places (which describes most of the hotels

may not speak English, they will almost always be enthusiastic and pleasant.

Gîtes

Throughout France you can find reasonably priced rental homes, and nowhere are there more options than in Provence and the Riviera. Because this region is so small, you could rent one home in Provence and one in the Riviera, and day-trip to most of the sights described in this book.

Countryside *gîtes* (pronounced "zheet") are usually urbanites' second homes, rentable by the week, from Saturday to Saturday. The objective of the *gîte* program was to save characteristic rural homes from abandonment and to make it easy and affordable for families to enjoy the French countryside. The government offers subsidies to renovate such homes, and then coordinates rentals to make it financially feasible for the owner. Today, France has more than 9,000 *gîtes*. One of your co-authors restored a farmhouse in

PRACTICALITIES

From:	rick@ricksteves.com
Sent:	Today
To:	info@hotelcentral.com
Subject:	Reservation request for 19-22 July

Dear Hotel Central,

I would like to stay at your hotel. Please let me know if you have a room available and the price for:
• 2 people
• Double bed and en suite bathroom in a quiet room
• Arriving 19 July, departing 22 July (3 nights)

Thank you!
Rick Steves

I list). Cancellation policies can be strict; read the fine print or ask about these before you book. Many discount deals require pre-payment, with no refunds for cancellations.

Reconfirming a Reservation: Always call or email to recon-firm your room reservation a few days in advance. For chambres d'hôtes or very small hotels, I call again on my day of arrival to tell my host what time to expect me (especially important if arriving late—after 17:00).

Phoning: For tips on calling hotels overseas, see page 500.

Burgundy, and although he and his wife are American, they re-ceived the same assistance that French owners get.

Gîtes are best for drivers (they're usually rural, with little pub-lic-transport access) and ideal for families and small groups (since they can sleep many for the same price). Homes range in comfort from simple cottages and farmhouses to restored châteaux. Most have at least two bedrooms, a kitchen, a living room, and a bath-room or two (BYO soap, shampoo, etc.). Sheets or linens may be included or provided for a bit extra. Like hotels, all *gîtes* are rated for comfort from one to four *épis* (ears of corn). Two or three *épis* generally indicate sufficient quality, but I'd lean toward three for more comfort. Prices generally range from €500 to €1,500 per week, depending on house size and amenities such as pools. Some owners may not speak English, so be prepared for doing business in French. For more information on *gîtes*, visit www.gites-de-france.com (with the most rentals), www.gite.com, or www.provence-guide.com.

The Good and Bad of Online Reviews

User-generated review sites and apps such as Yelp, Booking.com, and TripAdvisor can give you a consensus of opinions about everything from hotels and restaurants to sights and nightlife. If you scan reviews of a hotel and see several complaints about noise or a rotten location, it tells you something important that you'd never learn from the hotel's own website.

But as a guidebook writer, my sense is that there is a big difference between the uncurated information on a review site and a guidebook. A user-generated review is based on the experience of one person, who likely stayed at one hotel in a given city and ate at a few restaurants there (and who doesn't have much of a basis for comparison). A guidebook is the work of a trained researcher who, year after year, visits many alternatives to assess their relative value. I recently checked out some top-rated user-reviewed hotel and restaurant listings in various towns; when stacked up against their competitors, some were gems, while just as many were duds.

Both types of information have their place, and in many ways, they're complementary: If something is well-reviewed in a guidebook, and also gets good ratings on one of these sites, it's likely a winner.

Short-Term Rentals

A short-term rental—whether an apartment, house, or room in a local's home—is an increasingly popular alternative, especially if you plan to settle in one location for several nights. For stays longer than a few days, you can usually find a rental that's comparable to—and cheaper than—a hotel room with similar amenities.

Many places require a minimum night stay, and compared to hotels, rentals usually have less-flexible cancellation policies. And you're generally on your own: There's no hotel reception desk, breakfast, or daily cleaning service. Apartments are available in larger towns such as Avignon, Aix-en-Provence, and Nice. It's usually more expensive to stay in an apartment than in a *gîte*.

Finding Accommodations: Aggregator websites such as Airbnb, FlipKey, Roomorama, Booking.com, and the Home-Away family of sites (HomeAway, VRBO, and VacationRentals) let you browse properties and correspond directly with European property owners or managers. If you prefer to work from a curated list of accommodations, consider using a rental agency such as InterhomeUSA.com or RentaVilla.com. Agency-represented apartments typically cost more, but this method often offers more help and safeguards than booking direct. To find a place, try the resources listed above, or one of these: **France Homestyle,** run by Claudette, a service-oriented French woman from Seattle who handpicks every home and apartment she lists (US tel. 206/325-0132, www.francehomestyle.com, info@francehomestyle.com), or **Ville et Village,** which has a bigger selection of higher-end places (US tel. 510/559-8080, www.villeetvillage.com).

Before you commit, be clear on the details, location, and amenities. I like to virtually "explore" the neighborhood using the Street View feature on Google Maps. Also consider the proximity to public transportation, and how well-connected the property is with the rest of the city. Ask about amenities (elevator, air-conditioning, laundry, Wi-Fi, parking, etc.). Reviews from previous guests can help identify trouble spots.

Be clear about the kind of experience you want: Just a key and an affordable bed...or a chance to get to know a local? There are typically two kinds of hosts: those who want minimal interaction with their guests, and hosts who are friendly and may want to interact with you. Read the promotional text and online reviews to help shape your decision.

Apartments and Rental Houses: If you're staying somewhere for four nights or longer, it's worth considering an apartment or house (shorter stays aren't worth the hassle of arranging key pickup, buying groceries, etc.). Apartment and house rentals can be especially cost-effective for groups and families. European apartments, like hotel rooms, tend to be small by US standards. But they often come with laundry machines and small, equipped kitchens, making it easier and cheaper to dine in. If you make good use of the kitchen (and Europe's great produce markets), you'll save on your meal budget.

Private and Shared Rooms: Renting a room in someone's home is a good option for those traveling alone, as you're more likely to find true single rooms—with just one single bed, and a price to match. Beds range from air-mattress-in-living-room basic to plush-B&B-suite posh. Some places allow you to book for a single night; if staying for several nights, you can buy groceries just as you would in a rental house. While you can't expect your host to also be your tour guide—or even to provide you with much info—some may be interested in getting to know the travelers who come through their home.

Other Options: Swapping homes with a local works for people with an appealing place to offer, and who can live with the idea of having strangers in their home (don't assume where you live is not interesting to Europeans). A good place to start is HomeExchange. To sleep for free, Couchsurfing.com is a vagabond's alternative to Airbnb. It lists millions of outgoing members, who host fellow "surfers" in their homes.

Confirming and Paying: Many places require you to pay the entire balance before your trip. It's easiest and safest to pay through

PRACTICALITIES

the site where you found the listing. Be wary of owners who want to take your transaction offline to avoid fees; this gives you no recourse if things go awry. Never agree to wire money (a key indicator of a fraudulent transaction).

Hostels

A hostel *(auberge de jeunesse)* provides cheap beds in dorms where you sleep alongside strangers for about €23-35 per night. Travelers of any age are welcome if they don't mind dorm-style accommodations and meeting other travelers. Most hostels offer kitchen facilities, guest computers, Wi-Fi, and a self-service laundry. Hostels almost always provide bedding, but not towels (although you can usually rent one for a small fee). Family and private rooms are often available.

Independent hostels tend to be easygoing, colorful, and informal (no membership required; www.hostelworld.com). You may pay slightly less by booking directly with the hostel. **Official hostels** are part of Hostelling International (HI) and share an online booking site (www.hihostels.com). HI hostels typically require that you either have a membership card or pay extra per night.

Camping

In Europe, camping is more of a social than an environmental experience. It's a great way for American travelers to make European friends. Camping sites average about €25 per night, and almost every destination recommended in this book has a campground within a reasonable walk or bus ride from the town center and train station. A tent, pillow, and sleeping bag are all you need. Many campgrounds have small grocery stores and washing machines, and some even come with cafés and miniature golf. Local TIs have camping information. You'll find more detailed information in the annually updated *Michelin Camping France,* available in the United States and at most French bookstores.

Eating

The French eat long and well—nowhere more so than in the south. Relaxed and tree-shaded lunches with a chilled rosé, three-hour dinners, and endless hours of sitting in outdoor cafés are the norm. Here, celebrated restaurateurs are as famous as great athletes, and mamas hope their babies will grow up to be great chefs. Cafés, cuisine, and wines should become a highlight of any French adventure: It's sightseeing for your palate. Even if the rest of you is sleeping in a cheap hotel, let your taste buds travel first-class in France. (They can go coach in Britain.)

You can eat well without going broke—but choose carefully:

Restaurant Price Code

I've assigned each eatery a price category, based on the average cost of a typical main course. Drinks, desserts, and splurge items (steak and seafood) can raise the price considerably.

$$$$	**Splurge:** Most main courses over €25
$$$	**Pricier:** €20-25
$$	**Moderate:** €15-20
$	**Budget:** Under €15

In France, a crêpe stand or other takeout spot is **$**; a sit-down brasserie, café, or bistro with affordable plats du jour is **$$**; a casual but more upscale restaurant is **$$$**; and a swanky splurge is **$$$$**.

You're just as likely to blow a small fortune on a mediocre meal as you are to dine wonderfully for €20. Read the information that follows, consider my restaurant suggestions in this book, and you'll do fine. I look for restaurants that are convenient to your hotel and sightseeing. When restaurant-hunting, choose a spot filled with locals, not the place with the big neon signs boasting, "We Speak English and Accept Credit Cards." Venturing even a block or two off the main drag can lead to higher-quality food for less than half the price of the tourist-oriented places.

RESTAURANT PRICING

I've categorized my recommended eateries based on price, indicated with a dollar-sign rating (see sidebar). The price ranges suggest the average price of a typical main course—but not necessarily a complete meal. Obviously, expensive items (steak, seafood, truffles), fine wine, appetizers, and dessert can significantly increase your final bill.

The categories also indicate a place's personality: **Budget** eateries include street food, takeaway, order-at-the-counter shops, basic cafeterias, bakeries selling sandwiches, and so on. **Moderate** eateries are nice (but not fancy) sit-down restaurants, ideal for a straightforward, fill-the-tank meal. Most of my listings fall in this category—great for a good taste of local cuisine on a budget.

Pricier eateries are a notch up, with more attention paid to the setting, presentation, and cuisine. These are ideal for a memorable meal that doesn't break the bank. This category often includes affordable "destination" or "foodie" restaurants. And **splurge** eateries are dress-up-for-a-special-occasion-swanky—typically with an elegant setting, polished service, pricey and intricate cuisine, and an expansive (and expensive) wine list.

I haven't categorized places where you might assemble a picnic, snack, or graze: supermarkets, delis, ice-cream stands, cafés or bars specializing in drinks, chocolate shops, and so on.

BREAKFAST

Most hotels offer an optional breakfast, which is usually pleasant and convenient (generally €10-20). They almost all offer a buffet breakfast (cereal, yogurt, fruit, cheese, ham, croissants, juice, and hard-boiled eggs). Some add scrambled eggs and sausage. Before committing to breakfast, scan the offerings to be sure it's to your liking. Once committed, it's self-service and as much as you want. Coffee is often self-serve from a machine or a thermos. If there's no coffee machine and you want to make your own *café au lait,* find the hot milk and mix it with your coffee. If your hotelier serves your coffee, ask for *café avec du lait.*

If all you want is coffee or tea and a croissant, the corner café offers more atmosphere and is less expensive (though you get more coffee at your hotel). Go local at the café and ask for *une tartine* (ewn tart-een), a baguette slathered with butter or jam. If you crave eggs for breakfast, drop into a café and order *une omelette* or *œufs sur le plat* (fried eggs). Some cafés and bakeries offer worthwhile breakfast deals with juice, croissant, and coffee or tea for about €7 (for more on coffee and tea drinks, see page 496).

To keep it cheap, pick up some fruit at a grocery store and pastries at your favorite *boulangerie* and have a picnic breakfast, then savor your coffee at a café bar *(comptoir)* while standing, like the French do.

PICNIC DINING AND FOOD TO GO

Whether going all out on a perfect French picnic or simply grabbing a sandwich to eat on an atmospheric square, dining with the town as your backdrop can be one of your most memorable meals.

Picnics

Great for lunch or dinner, French picnics can be first-class affairs and adventures in high cuisine. Be daring. Try the smelly cheeses, ugly pâtés, sissy quiches, and minuscule yogurts. Shopkeepers are accustomed to selling small quantities of produce. Get a succulent salad-to-go, and ask for a plastic fork. If you need a knife or corkscrew, borrow one from your hotelier (but don't picnic in your room, as French hoteliers uniformly detest this). Though drinking wine in public places is taboo in the US, it's *pas de problème* in France. Plastic bags are not available at markets in France; you'll need your own bag (cheap at stores) or daypack for carrying items.

Assembling a Picnic: Visit several small stores to put together a complete meal. Shop early, as many shops close from 12:00 or 13:00 to 15:00 for their lunch break. Say *"Bonjour madame/mon-*

Picnic Vocabulary

English	French
please	*s'il vous plaît* (see voo play)
a plastic fork	*une fourchette en plastique* (ewn foor-sheht ahn plah-steek)
a plastic cup	*un goblet en plastique* (uhn goh-blay ahn plah-steek)
a paper plate	*une assiette en papier* (ewn ah-see-eht ahn pahp-yay)
napkins	*les serviettes* (lay sehr-vee-eht)
a small box	*une barquette* (ewn bar-keht)
a knife	*un couteau* (uhn koo-toh)
a corkscrew	*un tire-bouchon* (uhn teer-boo-shohn)
sliced	*tranché* (trahn-shay)
a slice	*une tranche* (ewn trahnsh)
a small slice	*une petite tranche* (ewn puh-teet trahnsh)
more	*plus* (plew)
less	*moins* (mwan)
It's just right.	*C'est bon.* (say bohn)
That'll be all.	*C'est tout.* (say too)
Thank you.	*Merci.* (mehr-see)

sieur" as you enter, then point to what you want and say, *"S'il vous plaît."* For other terminology you might need while shopping, see the sidebar above.

At the ***boulangerie*** (bakery), buy some bread. A baguette usually does the trick, or choose from the many loaves of bread on display: *pain aux céréales* (whole grain with seeds), *pain de campagne* (country bread, made with unbleached bread flour), *pain complet* (wheat bread), or *pain de seigle* (rye bread). To ask for it sliced, say *"Tranché, s'il vous plaît."*

At the ***pâtisserie*** (pastry shop, which is often the same place you bought the bread), choose a dessert that's easy to eat with your hands. My favorites are *éclairs* (*chocolat* or *café* flavored), individual fruit *tartes* (*framboise* is raspberry, *fraise* is strawberry, *citron* is lemon), and *macarons* (made of flavored cream sandwiched between two meringues, not coconut cookies like in the US).

At the ***crémerie*** or ***fromagerie*** (cheese shop), choose a sampling of cheeses *(un assortiment).* I usually get one hard cheese (like Comté, Cantal, or Beaufort), one soft cow's milk cheese (like Brie or Camembert), one goat's milk cheese (anything that says chèvre), and one blue cheese (Roquefort or Bleu d'Auvergne). Goat cheese usually comes in individual portions. For all other large cheeses, point to the cheese you want and ask for *une petite tranche* (a small slice). The shopkeeper will show you the size of the slice about to be cut, then look at you for approval. If you'd like more, say, *"Plus."* If you'd like less, say *"Moins."* If it's just right, say *"C'est bon!"*

At the **charcuterie** or **traiteur** (for deli items, prepared salads, meats, and pâtés), I like a slice of *pâté de campagne* (country

pâté made of pork) and *saucissons secs* (dried sausages, some with pepper crust or garlic—you can ask to have it sliced thin like salami). I get a fresh salad, too. Typical options are *carottes râpées* (shredded carrots in a tangy vinaigrette), *salade de betteraves* (beets in vinaigrette), and *céleri rémoulade* (celery root with a mayonnaise sauce). The food comes in takeout boxes, and they may supply a plastic fork.

At a **cave à vin** you can buy chilled wines that the merchant is usually happy to open and re-cork for you.

At a **supermarché, épicerie,** or **magasin d'alimentation** (small grocery store or minimart), you'll find plastic cutlery and glasses, paper plates, napkins, drinks, chips, and a display of produce. Local *supermarchés* are less colorful than smaller stores, but cheaper, more efficient, and offer adequate quality. Department stores often have supermarkets in the basement. On the outskirts of cities, you'll find the monster *hypermarchés*. Drop in for a glimpse of hyper-France in action.

Another option is to visit open-air markets *(marchés),* which are fun and photogenic, but shut down around 13:00 (many are listed in this book; local TIs have complete lists). There's more information about these wonderful Provençal experiences in the Shopping chapter (see "Market Day" on page 447).

To-Go Food

You'll find plenty of to-go options at *crêperies,* bakeries, and small stands. Baguette sandwiches, quiches, and pizza-like items are tasty, filling, and budget-friendly (about €5).

Sandwiches: Anything served *à la provençale* has marinated peppers, tomatoes, and eggplant. A sandwich *à l'italienne* is a grilled *panini* (usually referred to as *pannini*). Here are some common sandwiches:

Fromage (froh-mahzh): Cheese (white on beige)

Jambon beurre (zhahn-bohn bur): Ham and butter (boring for most but a French classic)

Jambon crudités (zhahn-bohn krew-dee-tay): Ham with tomatoes, lettuce, cucumbers, and mayonnaise

Fougasse (foo-gahs): Bread rolled up with salty bits of bacon, cheese, or olives

Poulet crudités (poo-lay krew-dee-tay): Chicken with tomatoes, lettuce, maybe cucumbers, and always mayonnaise

Saucisson beurre (saw-see-sohn bur): Thinly sliced sausage and butter

Thon crudités (tohn krew-dee-tay): Tuna with tomatoes, lettuce, and maybe cucumbers, but definitely mayonnaise

Quiche: Typical quiches you'll see at shops and bakeries are *lorraine* (ham and cheese), *fromage* (cheese only), *aux oignons* (with onions), *aux poireaux* (with leeks—my favorite), *aux champignons* (with mushrooms), *au saumon* (salmon), or *au thon* (tuna).

Crêpes: The quintessentially French thin pancake called a crêpe (rhymes with "step," not "grape") is filling, usually inexpensive, and generally quick. Place your order at the *crêperie* window or kiosk, and watch the chef in action. But don't be surprised if they don't make the crêpe for you from scratch; at some *crêperies*, they might premake a stack of crêpes and reheat them when they fill your order.

Crêpes generally are *sucrée* (sweet) or *salée* (savory). Technically, a savory crêpe should be made with a heartier buckwheat batter, and is called a *galette*. However, many cheap and lazy *crêperies* use the same sweet batter *(de froment)* for both their sweet-topped and savory-topped crêpes. A *socca* is a chickpea crêpe.

Standard crêpe toppings include cheese *(fromage;* usually Swiss-style Gruyère or Emmental), ham *(jambon)*, egg *(œuf)*, mushrooms *(champignons)*, chocolate, Nutella, jam *(confiture)*, whipped cream *(chantilly)*, apple jam *(compote de pommes)*, chestnut cream *(crème de marrons)*, and Grand Marnier.

RESTAURANT AND CAFE DINING

To get the most out of dining out in France, slow down. Allow enough time, engage the waiter, show you care about food, and enjoy the experience as much as the food itself.

French waiters probably won't overwhelm you with friendliness. As their tip is already included in the bill (see "Tipping," below), there's less schmoozing than we're used to at home. Notice how hard they work. They almost never stop. Cozying up to clients (French or foreign) is probably the last thing on their minds. They're often stuck with client overload, too, because the French rarely hire part-time employees, even to help with peak times. To get a waiter's attention, try to make meaningful eye contact, which is a signal that you need something. If this doesn't work, raise your hand and simply say, *"S'il vous plaît"* (see voo play)—"please."

This phrase also works when you want to ask for the check. In French eateries, a waiter will rarely bring you the check unless you request it. Having the bill dropped off before asking for it is *très gauche* (even rude!) to the French. But busy travelers are often ready for the check sooner rather than later. If you're in a hurry, ask for the bill when your server comes to clear your plates or checks in to see if you want dessert or coffee. To request your bill, say, *"L'addition, s'il vous plaît."* If you don't ask now, the wait staff may become scarce as they leave you to digest in peace. (For a list of other restaurant survival phrases, see page 540.)

Note that all café and restaurant interiors are smoke-free. Today the only smokers you'll find are at outside tables, which—unfortunately—may be exactly where you want to sit.

For a list of common French dishes that you'll see on menus, see page 492. For specific suggestions on what to sample here in the south, see my cuisine suggestions in the introductions to Provence (page 30) and the Riviera (page 282). For details on ordering drinks, see page 496.

Tipping: At cafés and restaurants, a 12-15 percent service charge is always included in the price of what you order (*service compris* or *prix net*), but you won't see it listed on your bill. Unlike in the US, France pays servers a decent wage. Because of this, most locals only tip a little, or not at all. When dining, expect reasonable service. If you don't get it, skip the tip and move on. If you feel the service was good, tip a little—up to 5 percent. To tell the waiter to keep the change when you pay, say *"C'est bon"* (say bohn), meaning "It's good." If you are using a credit card, leave your tip in cash—credit-card receipts don't even have space to add a tip. Never feel guilty if you don't leave a tip.

Cafés and Brasseries

French cafés and brasseries provide user-friendly meals and a relief from sightseeing overload. They're not necessarily cheaper than many restaurants and bistros, and famous cafés on popular squares can be pricey affairs. Their key advantage is flexibility: They offer long serving hours, and you're welcome to order just a salad, a sandwich, or a bowl of soup, even for dinner. It's also OK to share starters and desserts, though not main courses.

Cafés and brasseries usually open by 7:00, but closing hours vary. Unlike restaurants, which open only for dinner and sometimes for lunch, some cafés and all brasseries serve food throughout the day (usually with a limited

Vegetarians, Allergies, and Other Dietary Restrictions

Many French people think "vegetarian" means "no red meat" or "not much meat." If you're a strict vegetarian, be specific: Tell your server what you don't eat—and it can be helpful to clarify what you do eat. Write it out on a card and keep it handy.

But be reasonable. Think of your meal (as the French do) as if it's a finely crafted creation by a trained artist. The chef knows what goes well together, and substitutions are considered an insult to his training. Picky eaters should try their best to just take it or leave it.

However, French restaurants are willing to accommodate genuine dietary restrictions and other special concerns, or at least point you to an appropriate choice on the menu. These phrases might help:

French	English
Je suis végétarien/végétarienne. (zhuh swee vay-zhay-tah-ree-an/vay-zhay-tah-ree-ehn)	I am vegetarian.
Je ne peux pas manger de _____. (zhuh nuh puh pah mahn-zhay duh _____)	I cannot eat _____.
Je suis allergique à _____. (zhuh sweez ah-lehr-zheek ah _____)	I am allergic to _____.
Pas de _____. (pah duh _____).	No _____.

menu during off hours), making them the best option for a late lunch or an early dinner. *Service Continu* or *Service Non-Stop* signs indicate continued service throughout the day. Cafés in smaller towns often close their kitchens from about 14:00 until 18:00.

Check the price list first, which by law must be posted prominently (if you don't see one, go elsewhere). There are two sets of prices: You'll pay more for the same drink if you're seated at a table *(salle)* than if you're seated or standing at the bar or counter *(comptoir)*. (For tips on ordering coffee and tea, see page 496.)

At a café or a brasserie, if the table is not set, it's fine to seat yourself and just have a drink. However, if it's set with a placemat and cutlery, you should ask to be seated and plan to order a meal. If you're unsure, ask the server before sitting down.

Ordering: A salad, crêpe, quiche, or omelet is a fairly cheap way to fill up. Each can be made with various extras such as ham, cheese, mushrooms, and so on. Omelets come lonely on a plate with a basket of bread.

Sandwiches, generally served day and night, are inexpensive, but most are very plain (*boulangeries* serve better ones). To get more than a piece of ham *(jambon)* on a baguette, order a *sandwich jambon crudités* (garnished with veggies). Popular sandwiches are the *croque monsieur* (grilled ham-and-cheese) and *croque madame (monsieur* with a fried egg on top).

Salads are typically large and often can be ordered with warm ingredients mixed in, such as melted goat cheese, fried gizzards, or roasted potatoes. One salad is perfect for lunch or a light dinner. See page 493 for a list of classic salads.

The daily special—*plat du jour* (plah dew zhoor), or just *plat*—is your fast, hearty, and garnished hot plate for about €12-20. At most cafés, feel free to order only *entrées* (which in French means the starter course); many people find these lighter and more interesting than a main course. A vegetarian can enjoy a tasty, filling meal by ordering two *entrées*.

Regardless of what you order, bread is free but almost never comes with butter; to get more bread, just hold up your basket and ask, *"Encore, s'il vous plaît?"*

Restaurants

Choose restaurants filled with locals. Consider my suggestions and your hotelier's opinion, but trust your instincts. If a restaurant doesn't post its prices outside, move along. Refer to my restaurant recommendations to get a sense of what a reasonable meal should cost.

Restaurants in the south open for dinner at 19:00 (cafés open earlier), and are most crowded about 20:30 (the early bird gets the table). Last seating is usually about 21:00 (22:00 in cities and on the French Riviera).

Tune into the quiet, relaxed pace of French dining. The French don't do dinner and a movie on date nights; they just do dinner. The table is yours for the night. Notice how quietly French diners speak in restaurants and how few mobile phones you see during a meal, and how this improves your overall experience. Go local.

Ordering: In French restaurants, you can choose something off the menu (called the *carte*), or you can order a multicourse, fixed-price meal (confusingly, called a *menu*). Or, if offered, you can get one of the special dishes of the day *(plat du jour).* If you ask for *un menu* (instead of *la carte*), you'll get a fixed-price meal.

Ordering **à la carte** gives you the best selection. I enjoy going à la carte especially when traveling with others and eating family style (waiters are usually happy to accommodate this approach and will bring small extra plates). It's traditional to order an *entrée* (a starter—not a main dish) and a *plat principal* (main course), though it's becoming common to order only a *plat principal*. *Plats* are generally more meat-based, while *entrées* usually include veggies. Multiple-course meals, while time-consuming (a positive thing in France), create the appropriate balance of veggies to meat. Elaborate meals may also have *entremets*—tiny dishes served between courses. Wherever you dine, consider the waiter's recommendations and anything *de la maison* (of the house), as long as it's not an organ meat (tripe, *rognons*, or andouillette).

Two people can split an *entrée* or a big salad (small-size dinner salads are usually not offered á la carte) and then each get a *plat principal*. At restaurants, it's inappropriate for two diners to share one main course. If all you want is a salad or soup, go to a café or brasserie.

Fixed-price **menus**—which usually include two, three, or four courses—are generally a better deal than eating à la carte, and help you pace your meal like the locals. At most restaurants offering fixed-price *menus*, the price for a two- or three-course *menu* is only slightly higher than a single main course from the à la carte list. With a three-course *menu* you'll choose a starter of soup, appetizer, or salad; select from three or four main courses with vegetables; and finish up with a cheese course and/or a choice of desserts. It sounds like a lot of food, but portions are smaller in France, and what we cram onto one large plate they spread out over several courses. If you're dining with a friend, one person can get the full *menu* while the other can order just a *plat* (and share the *menu* courses). Also, many restaurants offer less expensive and less filling two-course *menus*, sometimes called *formules*, featuring an *entrée et plat*, or *plat et dessert*. Many restaurants have a reasonable *menu-enfant* (kid's meal).

Wine and other drinks are extra, and certain premium items add a few euros to the price, clearly noted on the menu (*supplément* or *sup.*).

Lunch: If a restaurant serves lunch, it generally begins at 12:00 and goes until around 14:00, with last orders taken at about 13:30. If you're hungry when restaurants are closed (late afternoon), go to a *boulangerie*, brasserie, or café (see previous section). Even fancy places usually have affordable lunch *menus* (often called *formules* or *plat de midi*), allowing you to sample the same gourmet cooking for generally about half the cost of dinner.

In the south, I usually order *une entrée* and *un plat* from *la carte* (often as a two-course *menu* or *formule*), then find an ice-cream or crêpe stand and take a dessert stroll. If that sounds like too much, just order *un plat* (but don't skip the dessert stroll!).

PRACTICALITIES

FRENCH CUISINE

General styles of French cooking include *cuisine gastronomique* (classic, elaborately prepared, multicourse meals); *cuisine semi-gastronomique* or *bistronomie* (the finest-quality home cooking); *cuisine des provinces* (traditional dishes of specific regions); and *nouvelle cuisine* (a focus on smaller portions and closer attention to the texture and color of the ingredients). Sauces are a huge part of French cooking. In the early 20th century, the legendary French chef Auguste Escoffier identified five French "mother sauces" from which all others are derived: *béchamel* (milk-based white sauce), *espagnole* (veal-based brown sauce), *velouté* (stock-based white sauce), *hollandaise* (egg yolk-based white sauce), and *tomate* (tomato-based red sauce).

The following list of items should help you navigate a typical French menu. Galloping gourmets should bring a menu translator. The most complete (and priciest) menu reader around is *A to Z of French Food* by G. de Temmerman. The *Marling Menu-Master* is also good. The *Rick Steves French Phrase Book & Dictionary*, with a menu decoder, works well for most travelers. For specifics on specialties in Provence and the Riviera, see pages 30 and 282.

First Course *(Entrée)*

Crudités: A mix of raw and lightly cooked fresh vegetables, usually including grated carrots, celery root, tomatoes, and beets, often with a hefty dose of vinaigrette dressing. If you want the dressing on the side, say, *"La sauce à côté, s'il vous plaît"* (lah sohs ah koh-tay, see voo play).

Escargots: Snails cooked in parsley-garlic butter. You don't even have to like the snail itself. Just dipping your bread in garlic butter is more than satisfying. Prepared a variety of ways, the classic is *à la bourguignonne* (served in their shells).

Foie gras: Rich and buttery in consistency—and hefty in price—this pâté is made from the swollen livers of force-fed geese (or ducks, in *foie gras de canard*). Put small chunks on bread—don't spread it, and never add mustard. For a real French experience, try this dish with a sweet white wine (such as a Muscat).

Huîtres: Oysters, served raw any month, are particularly popular at Christmas and on New Year's Eve, when every café seems to have overflowing baskets in their window.

Œuf mayo: A simple hard-boiled egg topped with a dollop of flavorful mayonnaise.

Pâtés and **terrines:** Slowly cooked ground meat (usually pork, though game, poultry liver, and rabbit are also common) that is highly seasoned and served in slices with mustard and *cornichons* (little pickles). Pâtés are smoother than the similarly prepared but chunkier *terrines*.

Soupe à l'oignon: Hot, salty, filling French onion soup is a beef broth served with a baked cheese-and-bread crust over the top.

Salads *(Salades)*
With the exception of a *salade mixte* (simple green salad, often difficult to find), the French get creative with their *salades*. Here are some classics:

Salade de chèvre chaud: This mixed-green salad is topped with warm goat cheese on small pieces of toast.

Salade de gésiers: Though it may not sound appetizing, this salad with chicken gizzards (and often slices of duck) is worth a try.

Salade composée: "Composed" of any number of ingredients, this salad might have *lardons* (bacon), Comté (a Swiss-style cheese), Roquefort (blue cheese), *œuf* (egg), *noix* (walnuts), and *jambon* (ham, generally thinly sliced).

Salade gourmande: The "gourmet" salad varies by region and restaurant but usually features cured and poached meats served on salad greens with a mustard vinaigrette.

Salade niçoise: A specialty from Nice, this tasty salad usually includes greens topped with ripe tomatoes, raw vegetables (such as radishes, green peppers, celery, and perhaps artichoke or fava beans), tuna (usually canned), anchovy, hard-boiled egg, and olives.

Salade paysanne: You'll usually find potatoes *(pommes de terre)*, walnuts *(noix)*, tomatoes, ham, and egg in this salad.

Main Course *(Plat Principal)*
Duck, lamb, and rabbit are popular in France, and each is prepared in a variety of ways. You'll also encounter various stew-like dishes that vary by region. The most common regional specialties are described here.

Bœuf bourguignon: A Burgundian specialty, this classy beef stew is cooked slowly in red wine, then served with onions, potatoes, and mushrooms.

Confit de canard: A favorite from the southwest Dordogne region is duck that has been preserved in its own fat, then cooked in its fat, and often served with potatoes (cooked in the same fat). Not for dieters. (Note that *magret de canard* is sliced duck breast and very different in taste.)

Coq au vin: This Burgundian dish is rooster marinated ever so slowly in red wine, then cooked until it melts in your mouth. It's served (often family-style) with vegetables.

Daube: Generally made with beef, but sometimes lamb, this is a long and slowly simmered dish, typically paired with noodles or other pasta.

Escalope normande: This specialty of Normandy features turkey or veal in a cream sauce.

Gigot d'agneau: A specialty of Provence, this is a leg of lamb often grilled and served with white beans. The best lamb is *pré salé,* which means the lamb has been raised in salt-marsh lands (like at Mont St-Michel).

Le hamburger: This American import is all the rage in France. Cafés and restaurants serve it using local sauces, breads, and cheeses. It's fun to see their interpretation of our classic dish.

Poulet rôti: Roasted chicken on the bone—French comfort food.

Saumon and **truite:** You'll see salmon and trout *(truite)* dishes served in various styles. The salmon usually comes from the North Sea and is always served with sauce, most commonly a sorrel *(oseille)* sauce.

Steak: Referred to as *pavé* (thick hunk of prime steak), *bavette* (skirt steak), *faux filet* (sirloin), or *entrecôte* (rib steak), French steak is usually thinner and tougher than American steak and is always served with sauces (*au poivre* is a pepper sauce, *une sauce roquefort* is a blue-cheese sauce). Because steak is usually better in North America, I generally avoid it in France (unless the sauce sounds good). You will also see *steak haché,* which is a lean, gourmet hamburger patty served *sans* bun. When it's served as *steak haché à cheval,* it comes with a fried egg on top.

By American standards, the French undercook meats: Their version of rare, *saignant* (seh-nyahn), means "bloody" and is close to raw. What they consider medium, *à point* (ah pwan), is what an American would call rare. Their term for well-done, or *bien cuit* (bee-yehn kwee), would translate as medium for Americans.

Steak tartare: This wonderfully French dish is for adventurous types only. It's very lean, raw hamburger served with savory seasonings (usually Tabasco, capers, raw onions, salt, and pepper on the side) and topped with a raw egg yolk. This is not hamburger as we know it, but freshly ground beef.

Cheese Course (Le Fromage)

The cheese course is served just before (or instead of) dessert. It not only helps with digestion, it gives you a great opportunity to sample the tasty regional cheeses—and time to finish up your wine. Between cow, goat, and sheep cheeses, there are more than 350 different ones to try in France. Some restaurants will offer a cheese platter, from which you select a few different kinds. A good platter has at least four cheeses: a hard cheese (such as Cantal), a flowery cheese (such as Brie or Camembert), a blue or Roquefort cheese, and a goat cheese.

To sample several types of cheese from the cheese plate, say, *"Un assortiment, s'il vous plaît"* (uhn ah-sor-tee-mahn, see voo play). You'll either be served a selection of several cheeses or choose from a large selection offered on a cheese tray. If you serve yourself from the cheese tray, observe French etiquette and keep the shape of the cheese: Shave off a slice from the side or cut small wedges.

A glass of good red wine is a heavenly complement to your cheese course. With three-course *menus*, the last course is usually a choice between "*fromage*" or "*dessert*."

Dessert *(Le Dessert)*

If you order espresso, it will always come after dessert. To have coffee with dessert, ask for *"café avec le dessert"* (kah-fay ah-vehk luh day-sayr). See the list of coffee terms on page 497. Here are the types of treats you'll see:

Baba au rhum: Pound cake drenched in rum, served with whipped cream.

Café gourmand: An assortment of small desserts selected by the restaurant, served with an espresso—a great way to sample several desserts.

Crème brûlée: A rich, creamy, dense, caramelized custard.

Crème caramel: Flan in a caramel sauce.

Fondant au chocolat: A molten chocolate cake with a runny (not totally cooked) center. Also known as *moelleux* (meh-leh) *au chocolat*.

Fromage blanc: A light dessert similar to plain yogurt (yet different), served with sugar or herbs.

Glace: Ice cream—typically vanilla, chocolate, or strawberry.

Ile flottante: A light dessert consisting of islands of meringue floating on a pond of custard sauce.

Mousse au chocolat: Chocolate mousse.

Profiteroles: Cream puffs filled with vanilla ice cream, smothered in warm chocolate sauce.

Riz au lait: Rice pudding.

Sorbets: Light, flavorful, and fruity ices, sometimes laced with brandy.

Tartes: Open-face pie, often filled with fruit.

Tarte tatin: Apple pie like grandma never made, with caramelized apples, cooked upside down, but served upright.

BEVERAGES

In stores, unrefrigerated soft drinks, bottled water, and beer are one-third the price of cold drinks. Bottled water and boxed fruit juice are the cheapest drinks. Avoid buying drinks to-go at street-side stands; you'll pay far less in a shop.

In bars and at eateries, be clear when ordering drinks—you can easily pay €10 for an oversized Coke and €15 for a supersized beer at some cafés. When you order a drink, state the size in centiliters (don't say "small," "medium," or "large," because the waiter might bring a bigger drink than you want). For something small, ask for 25 *centilitres* (vant-sank sahn-tee-lee-truh; about 8 ounces); for a medium drink, order 33 cl (trahnte-twah; about 12 ounces—a normal can of soda); a large is 50 cl (san-kahnt; about 16 ounces); and a super-size is one liter (lee-truh; about a quart—which is more than I would ever order in France). The ice cubes melted after the last Yankee tour group left.

Water, Juice, and Soft Drinks

The French are willing to pay for bottled water with their meal (*eau minérale;* oh mee-nay-rahl) because they prefer the taste over tap water. Badoit is my favorite carbonated water (*l'eau gazeuse;* loh gah-zuhz) and is commonly available. To get a free pitcher of tap water, ask for *une carafe d'eau* (ewn kah-rahf doh). Otherwise, you may unwittingly buy bottled water.

In France *limonade* (lee-moh-nahd) is Sprite or 7-Up. For a fun, bright, nonalcoholic drink of 7-Up with mint syrup, order *un diabolo menthe* (uhn dee-ah-boh-loh mahnt). For 7-Up with fruit syrup, order *un diabolo grenadine* (think Shirley Temple). Kids love the local orange drink, Orangina, a carbonated orange juice with pulp (though it can be pricey). They also like *sirop à l'eau* (see-roh ah loh), flavored syrup mixed with bottled water.

For keeping hydrated on the go, hang on to the half-liter mineral-water bottles (sold everywhere for about €1-2) and refill. Buy juice in cheap liter boxes, then drink some and store the extra in your water bottle. Of course, water quenches your thirst better and cheaper than anything you'll find in a store or café. I drink tap water throughout France, filling up my bottle in hotel rooms.

Coffee and Tea

The French define various types of espresso drinks by how much milk is added. To the French, milk is a delicate form of nutrition: You need it in the morning, but as the day goes on, too much can upset your digestion. Therefore, the amount of milk that's added to coffee decreases as the day goes on. The average French person thinks a *café au lait* is exclusively for breakfast, and a *café crème* is only appropriate through midday. You're welcome to order a milkier coffee drink later in the day, but don't be surprised if you get a funny look.

Provence is known for its herbal and fruit teas. Look for *til-leul* (linden), *verveine* (verbena), or interesting blends such as *poire-vanille* (pear-vanilla).

By law, a waiter must give you a glass of tap water with your coffee or tea if you request it; ask for *"un verre d'eau, s'il vous plaît"* (uhn vayr doh, see voo play).

Here are some common coffee and tea drinks:

Café (kah-fay): Shot of espresso

Café allongé, a.k.a. *café long* (kah-fay ah-lohn-zhay; kah-fay lohn): Espresso topped up with hot water—like an Americano

Noisette (nwah-zeht): Espresso with a dollop of milk (best value for adding milk to your coffee)

Café au lait (kah-fay oh lay): Espresso mixed with lots of warm milk (used mostly for coffee made at home; in a café, order *café crème*)

Café crème (kah-fay krehm): Espresso with a sizable pour of steamed milk (closest thing you'll get to an American-style latte)

Grand crème (grahn krehm): Double shot of espresso with a bit more steamed milk (and often twice the price)

Décaféiné (day-kah-fee-nay): Decaf—available for any of the above

Thé nature (tay nah-tour): Plain tea

Thé au lait (tay oh lay): Tea with milk

Thé citron (tay see-trohn): Tea with lemon

Infusion (an-few-see-yohn): Herbal tea

Alcoholic Beverages

The legal drinking age is 16 for beer and wine and 18 for the hard stuff—at restaurants it's normal for wine to be served with dinner to teens.

Wine: Wines are often listed in a separate *carte des vins*. House wine at the bar is generally cheap and good (about €3-6/glass). At a restaurant, a bottle or carafe of house wine costs €10-20. To order inexpensive wine at a restaurant, ask for table wine in a pitcher (only available when seated and when ordering food), rather than a bottle. Finer restaurants usually offer only bottles of wine. For specifics on Provençal wines, see page 32.

Here are some important wine terms:

Vin de pays (van duh pay): Table wine

Verre de vin rouge (vehr duh van roozh): Glass of red wine

Verre de vin blanc (vehr duh van blahn): Glass of white wine

Pichet (pee-shay): Pitcher

Demi-pichet (duh-mee pee-shay): Half-carafe

Quart (kar): Quarter-carafe (ideal for one)
Bouteille (boo-teh-ee): Bottle
Demi-bouteille (duh-mee boo-teh-ee): Half-bottle

Beer: Local *bière* (bee-ehr) costs about €5 at a restaurant and is cheaper on tap (*une pression;* ewn pres-yohn) than in the bottle. France's best-known beers are Alsatian; try Kronenbourg or the heavier Pelfort (one of your author's favorites). *Un panaché* (uhn pah-nah-shay) is a tasty French shandy (beer and lemon soda). *Un Monaco* is a red drink made with beer, grenadine, and lemonade.

Aperitifs: Champagne is a popular way to start your evening in France. For a refreshing before-dinner drink, order a *kir* (pronounced "keer")—a thumb's level of *crème de cassis* (black currant liqueur) topped with white wine (upgrade to a *kir royal* if you'd like it made with champagne). Also consider a glass of Lillet, a sweet, flowery fortified wine from Bordeaux. In Provence, try sweet wines *(vins doux naturel)* such as Muscat de Beaumes-de-Venise or Rasteau. Both should be served chilled (from the fridge, never with ice cubes) and are enjoyable before dinner or with certain desserts; they're terrific with foie gras, melons, peaches, or Roquefort cheese. Look also for sparkling wines, usually inexpensive versions of the pricey champagne.

After Dinner: If you like brandy, try a *marc* (regional brandy—e.g., *marc de Bourgogne*) or an Armagnac, cognac's cheaper twin brother. *Pastis,* the standard southern France aperitif, is a sweet anise (licorice) drink that comes on the rocks with a glass of water. Cut it to taste with lots of water.

Staying Connected

One of the most common questions I hear from travelers is, "How can I stay connected in Europe?" The short answer is: more easily and cheaply than you might think.

The simplest solution is to bring your own device—mobile phone, tablet, or laptop—and use it just as you would at home (following the tips below, such as connecting to free Wi-Fi whenever possible). Another option is to buy a European SIM card for your mobile phone—either your US phone or one you buy in Europe. Or you can use European landlines and computers to connect. Each of these options is described below, and more details are at www.ricksteves.com/phoning. For a very practical one-hour talk covering tech issues for travelers, see www.ricksteves.com/mobile-travel-skills.

USING A MOBILE PHONE IN EUROPE

Here are some budget tips and options.

Sign up for an international plan. Using your cellular network in Europe on a pay-as-you-go basis can add up (about $1.70/minute for voice calls, 50 cents to send text messages, 5 cents to receive them, and $10 to download one megabyte of data). To stay connected at a lower cost, sign up for an international service plan through your carrier. Most providers offer a simple bundle that includes calling, messaging, and data. Your normal plan may already include international coverage (T-Mobile's does).

Before your trip, call your provider or check online to confirm that your phone will work in Europe, and research your provider's international rates. Activate the plan a day or two before you leave, then remember to cancel it when your trip's over.

Use free Wi-Fi whenever possible. Unless you have an unlimited-data plan, you're best off saving most of your online tasks for Wi-Fi (pronounced *wee-fee* in French). You can access the Internet, send texts, and even make voice calls over Wi-Fi.

Most accommodations in Europe offer free Wi-Fi, but some—especially expensive hotels—charge a fee. Many cafés (including Starbucks and McDonald's) have free hotspots for customers; look for signs offering it and ask for the Wi-Fi password when you buy something. You'll also often find Wi-Fi at TIs, city squares, major museums, public-transit hubs, important train stations, airports, aboard trains and buses, and at some autoroute (highway) rest stops.

Minimize the use of your cellular network. Even with an international data plan, wait until you're on Wi-Fi to Skype, download apps, stream videos, or do other megabyte-greedy tasks. Using a navigation app such as Google Maps over a cellular network can take lots of data, so do this sparingly or use it offline.

Limit automatic updates. By default, your device constantly checks for a data connection and updates apps. It's smart to disable these features so your apps will only update when you're on Wi-Fi, and to change your device's email settings from "auto-retrieve" to "manual" (or from "push" to "fetch").

When you need to get online but can't find Wi-Fi, simply turn on your cellular network just long enough for the task at hand. When you're done, avoid further charges by manually turning off data roaming or cellular data (either works) in your device's Settings menu. Another way to make sure you're not accidentally using data roaming is to put your device in "airplane" mode (which also disables phone calls and texts), and then turn your Wi-Fi back on as needed.

It's also a good idea to keep track of your data usage. On your device's menu, look for "cellular data usage" or "mobile data" and reset the counter at the start of your trip.

Use Wi-Fi calling and messaging apps. Skype, Viber, FaceTime, and Google+ Hangouts are great for making free or low-cost

PRACTICALITIES

How to Dial

International Calls

Whether phoning from a US landline or mobile phone, or from a number in another European country, here's how to make an international call. I've used one of my recommended Paris hotels as an example (tel. 01 47 05 25 45).

Initial Zero: Drop the initial zero from international phone numbers—except when calling Italy.

Mobile Tip: If using a mobile phone, the "+" sign can replace the international access code (for a "+" sign, press and hold "0").

US/Canada to Europe

Dial 011 (US/Canada international access code), country code (33 for France), and phone number.

▸ To call the Paris hotel from home, dial 011 33 1 47 05 25 45.

Country to Country Within Europe

Dial 00 (Europe international access code), country code, and phone number.

▸ To call the Paris hotel from Spain, dial 00 33 1 47 05 25 45.

Europe to the US/Canada

Dial 00, country code (1 for US/Canada), and phone number.

▸ To call from Europe to my office in Edmonds, Washington, dial 00-1-425-771-8303.

Domestic Calls

To call within France (from one French landline or mobile phone to another), simply dial the phone number, including the initial 0 if there is one.

▸ To call the Paris hotel from Nice, dial 01 47 05 25 45.

More Dialing Tips

French Phone Prefixes: France doesn't use area codes. French phone prefixes vary by region or type of call. For instance, all Paris landline numbers start with 01, and all landlines in Provence and the Riviera begin with 04.

voice and video calls over Wi-Fi. With an app installed on your phone, tablet, or laptop, you can log on to a Wi-Fi network and contact friends or family members who use the same service. If you buy credit in advance, with some of these services you can call any mobile phone or landline worldwide for just pennies per minute.

Many of these apps also allow you to send messages over Wi-Fi to any other person using that app. Be aware that some apps, such as Apple's iMessage, will use the cellular network if Wi-Fi

Any number beginning with 06 or 07 is a mobile phone, and costs more to dial.

Toll and Toll-Free Calls: France's toll-free numbers start with 0800-0805 and are called *numéro vert* (green number); they work only from French phones. Any 08 number followed by 10-99 is a toll call (generally €0.10-0.50/minute; cost announced in French; you can hang up before being billed). International rates apply to US toll-free numbers dialed from France—they're not free.

More Phoning Help: See www.howtocallabroad.com.

European Country Codes		Ireland & N. Ireland	353 / 44
Austria	43	Italy	39
Belgium	32	Latvia	371
Bosnia-Herzegovina	387	Montenegro	382
Croatia	385	Morocco	212
Czech Republic	420	Netherlands	31
Denmark	45	Norway	47
Estonia	372	Poland	48
Finland	358	Portugal	351
France	33	Russia	7
Germany	49	Slovakia	421
Gibraltar	350	Slovenia	386
Great Britain	44	Spain	34
Greece	30	Sweden	46
Hungary	36	Switzerland	41
Iceland	354	Turkey	90

isn't available: To avoid this possibility, turn off the "Send as SMS" feature.

USING A EUROPEAN SIM CARD

With a European SIM card, you get a European mobile number and access to cheaper rates than you'll get through your US carrier. This option works well for those who want to make a lot of voice calls or needing faster connection speeds than their US carrier provides. Fit the SIM card into a cheap phone you buy in Europe

Tips on Internet Security

Make sure that your device is running the latest versions of its operating system, security software, and apps. Next, ensure that your device and key programs (like email) are password- or passcode-protected. On the road, use only secure, pass-word-protected Wi-Fi hotspots. Ask the hotel or café staff for the specific name of their Wi-Fi network, and make sure you log on to that exact one.

If you must access your financial info online, use a bank-ing app rather than accessing your account via a browser. A cellular connection is more secure than Wi-Fi. Avoid logging onto personal finance sites on a public computer.

Never share your credit-card number (or any other sensi-tive information) online unless you know that the site is secure. A secure site displays a little padlock icon, and the URL begins with https (instead of the usual http).

(about $40 from phone shops anywhere), or swap out the SIM card in an "unlocked" US phone (check with your carrier about unlock-ing it).

SIM cards are sold at mobile-phone shops, department-store electronics counters, some newsstands, and vending machines. Costing about $5-10, they usually include prepaid calling/messag-ing credit, with no contract and no commitment. Expect to pay $20-40 more for a SIM card with a gigabyte of data. If you travel with this card to other countries in Europe, there may be extra roaming fees.

I like to buy SIM cards at a phone shop where there's a clerk to help explain the options. Certain brands—including Lebara and Lycamobile, both of which operate in multiple European coun-tries—are reliable and economical. Ask the clerk to help you insert your SIM card, set it up, and show you how to use it. In some coun-tries, you'll be required to register the SIM card with your passport as an antiterrorism measure (which may mean you can't use the phone for the first hour or two).

Find out how to check your credit balance. When you run out of credit, you can top it up at newsstands, tobacco shops, mobile-phone stores, or many other businesses (look for your SIM card's logo in the window), or online.

PUBLIC PHONES AND COMPUTERS

It's possible to travel in Europe without a mobile device. You can make calls from your hotel (or the increasingly rare public phone), and check email or browse websites using public computers.

Most hotels charge a fee for placing calls—ask for rates before you dial. Prepaid international phone cards (cartes international) are not widely used in France, but can be found at some post offices, newsstands, street kiosks, tobacco shops, and train stations. Dial the toll-free access number, enter the card's PIN code, and then dial the number.

Public computers are not always easy to find. Some hotels have one in their lobby for guests to use; otherwise you may find one at an Internet café or public library (ask your hotelier or the TI for the nearest location). If typing on a European keyboard, use the "Alt Gr" key to the right of the space bar to insert the extra symbol that appears on some keys. To type an @ symbol on French keyboards, press the "Alt Gr" and "à/0" key. If you can't locate a special character, simply copy it from a Web page and paste it into your email message.

MAIL

You can mail one package per day to yourself worth up to $200 duty-free from Europe to the US (mark it "personal purchases"). If you're sending a gift to someone, mark it "unsolicited gift." For details, visit www.cbp.gov, select "Travel," and search for "Know Before You Go." The French postal service works fine, but for quick transatlantic delivery (in either direction), consider services such as DHL (www.dhl.com). French post offices are referred to as *La Poste* or sometimes the old-fashioned PTT, for "Post, Telegraph, and Telephone." Hours vary, though most are open weekdays 8:00-19:00 and Saturday morning 8:00-12:00. Stamps are also sold at *tabacs*. It costs about €1 to mail a postcard to the US. One convenient, if expensive, way to send packages home is to use the post office's Colissimo XL postage-paid mailing box. It costs €50-90 to ship boxes weighing 5-7 kilos (about 11-15 pounds).

Transportation

If you're debating between using public transportation, renting a car, or flying between destinations in Europe, consider these factors: Cars are best for three or more traveling together (especially families with small kids), those packing heavy, and those delving into the countryside. Trains and buses are best for solo travelers, blitz tourists, city-to-city travelers, and those who don't want to drive. Intra-European flights are an increasingly inexpensive option. While a car gives you more freedom, trains and buses zip you effortlessly and scenically from city to city, usually dropping you in the center, often near a TI. For more detailed information on transportation throughout Europe, including trains, flying, renting a car, and driving, see www.ricksteves.com/transportation.

If you plan to focus on Arles, Avignon, Aix-en-Provence, and seaside destinations along the Riviera, go by train. Stations are centrally located in each city, which makes hotel-hunting and sight-seeing easy. Buses and taxis pick up where trains leave off. While bus service can be sparse, taxis are generally available and reasonable. If relying on public transportation, visit fewer destinations, or hire one of the excellent minivan tour guides I recommend (see "Tours in Provence" on page 24).

I've included two sample itineraries—by car and by public transportation—to help you explore Provence and the French Riviera smoothly; you'll find these in the Introduction.

TRAINS

France's SNCF rail system (short for Société Nationale Chemins de Fer) sets the pace in Europe. Its high-speed trains (TGV, tay zhay vay; Train à Grande Vitesse—also called "InOui") system has inspired bullet trains throughout the world. The TGV, which requires a reservation, runs at 170-220 mph. Its rails are fused into one long, continuous track for a faster and smoother ride. The TGV has changed commuting patterns throughout France by putting most of the country within day-trip distance of Paris.

TGV trains serve these cities in Provence and the Riviera: Avignon, Arles (very few trains), Nîmes, Marseille, Orange, Aix-en-Provence, Antibes, Cannes, and Nice. Avignon and Aix-en-Provence have separate TGV stations on their outskirts (with bus connections into the town center)—note carefully which station your train serves (either "Centre-Ville" or "TGV"; if it's not specified, it's the central station).

Any staffed train station has schedule information, can make reservations, and can sell tickets for any destination. For more on train travel, see www.ricksteves.com/rail.

Schedules

Schedules change by season, weekday, and weekend. Verify train times shown in this book—online, check www.bahn.com (Germany's excellent all-Europe schedule site), or check locally at train stations. The French rail website is www.sncf.com; for online sales, go to http://en.voyages-sncf.com. If you'll be traveling on one or two long-distance trains without a rail pass, it's worth looking online, as advance-purchase discounts can be a great deal.

Bigger stations may have helpful information agents roaming the station (usually in bright red or blue vests) and at *Accueil* offices or booths. Make use of their help; don't stand in a ticket line if all you need is a train schedule.

Rail Passes

The single-country Eurail France Pass can be a good value for long-distance train travelers. Each day of use of your France Pass allows

French Train Terms and Abbreviations

SNCF (Société Nationale des Chemins de Fer): This is the Amtrak of France, operating all national train lines that link cities and towns.

TGV (Train à Grande Vitesse): SNCF's network of high-speed trains (twice as fast as regular trains) that connect major cities in France (also called "InOui"). These trains always require a reservation.

Intercité: These trains are the next best to the TGV in terms of speed and comfort.

TER (Transport Express Régional): These trains serve smaller stops within a region. For example, you'll find trains called TER Provence (Provence-only trains) and TER de Bourgogne (trains operating only in Burgundy).

PRACTICALITIES

you to take as many trips as you want on one calendar day (you could go from Paris to Beaune in Burgundy, enjoy wine tasting, then continue to Avignon, stay a few hours, and end in Nice—though I wouldn't recommend it).

But be aware that France's fast TGV and international trains require paid seat reservations (up to €35). Places for rail-pass holders can be limited—which means trains may "sell out" for pass holders well before they've sold out for ticket buyers. Reserving these fast trains at least several weeks in advance is recommended (for strategies, see "Reservations," later).

The France Pass plus regular seat reservation fee also covers you beyond national borders on direct Eurostar, Thalys, or TGV fast trains to London, Amsterdam, Brussels, Cologne, Barcelona, Madrid (from Marseille), and Basel. All Eurail passes allow up to two kids (ages 4-11) to travel free with an adult.

You'll save money with the second-class version of the France Pass, but first class gives you more options when reserving popular TGV routes. A first-class pass also grants you access to lounges in railway stations in Paris (Est, Nord, Montparnasse, and Gare de Lyon), Strasbourg, Bordeaux, Marseille, Nantes, Rennes, Lille Flandres, Lille Europe, and Lyon Part-Dieu. These first-class lounges are more basic than airport lounges and can be crowded in big cities—but they do offer free coffee and water, good chairs, Wi-Fi, and a place to charge your phone.

For very short trips in France, buy second-class point-to-point tickets (it's worth looking into advance-purchase discounts).

If your trip extends beyond France, consider the Eurail **Select Pass** for two to four adjacent countries directly connected by rail or ferry. Two-country Select Passes allow you to pair France with the Benelux region, Germany, Switzerland, Italy, or Spain. For more

PRACTICALITIES

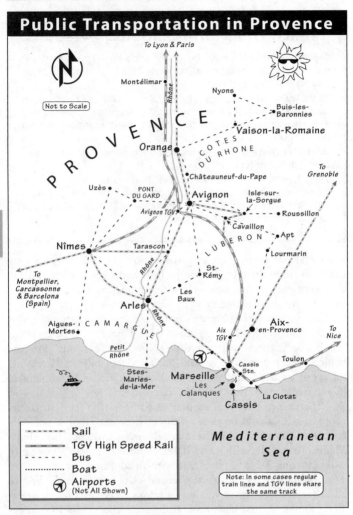

Public Transportation in Provence

To Lyon & Paris

N

Not to Scale

Montélimar

Rhône

Nyons

Buis-les-Baronnies

Vaison-la-Romaine

P R O V E N C E

Orange

CÔTES DU RHONE

To Grenoble

Uzès

PONT DU GARD

Châteauneuf-du-Pape

Avignon

Isle-sur-la-Sorgue

Avignon TGV

Roussillon

Cavaillon

Apt

Nîmes

Tarascon

L U B E R O N

Lourmarin

To Montpellier, Carcassonne & Barcelona (Spain)

Rhône

St-Rémy

Les Baux

Arles

C A M A R G U E

Aigues-Mortes

Aix TGV

Aix-en-Provence

To Nice

Petit Rhône

Toulon

Cassis Stn.

Stes-Maries-de-la-Mer

Marseille

Les Calanques

La Ciotat

Cassis

M e d i t e r r a n e a n S e a

— · — · — Rail
══════ TGV High Speed Rail
- - - - - Bus
········· Boat
✈ Airports (Not All Shown)

Note: In some cases regular train lines and TGV lines share the same track

detailed advice on figuring out the smartest rail-pass options for your train trip, visit www.ricksteves.com/rail.

Buying Tickets

Online: While there's no deadline to buy any train ticket, the fast, reserved TGV trains get booked up. Buy well ahead for any TGV you cannot afford to miss. Tickets go on sale 90 to 120 days in advance, with a wide range of prices on any one route. The cheapest tickets sell out early and reservations for rail-pass holders also go particularly fast.

To buy the cheapest advance-discount tickets (up to 60 percent less than full fare), visit http://en.voyages-sncf.com, three to four

Public Transportation on the French Riviera

Not to Scale

ITALY

FRANCE

To Grenoble

Veynes-Dévoluy

Ventimiglia

To Genoa & Cinque Terre

Digne-les-Bains

Eze-le-Village

La Turbie

Menton

Eze-Bord-de-Mer

Monaco

Manosque-Gréoux

Cap d'Ail

To Aix-en-Provence

Tourrettes

Vence

Nice

Beaulieu

Le Bar

St-Paul

Cap Ferrat

Villefranche-sur-Mer

Biot

Vallauris

Antibes

Grasse

Juan-les-Pins

RIVIERA

Cannes

Cap d'Antibes

To Toulon, Marseille, Avignon & Paris

St-Raphaël

To Toulon

St-Tropez

Note: In some cases regular train lines and TGV lines share the same track

Mediterranean Sea

Rail

TGV High Speed Rail

Bus

Boat

Airports (Not All Shown)

PRACTICALITIES

months ahead of your travel date. (A pop-up window may ask you to choose between being sent to the Rail Europe website or staying on the SNCF page—click "Stay.") Next, choose "Train," then "TGV." Under "Book your train tickets," pick your travel dates, and choose "France" as your ticket collection country. The cheapest (nonrefundable) tickets are called "Prems"; be sure it also says "TGV" (avoid iDTGV trains—they're very cheap, but this SNCF subsidiary doesn't accept PayPal). Choose the eticket delivery option (which allows you to print at home), and pay with your PayPal account to avoid credit-card approval issues. These low-rate tickets may not be available from Rail Europe or other US agents.

After the "Prems" rates are sold out, you can buy other fare types on the French site with a US credit card if it has been set up for the "Verified by Visa," "MasterCard SecureCode," or "American Express SafeKey" program. For a credit-card purchase, choose "USA" as your ticket collection country.

Otherwise, US customers can order through a US agency, such as at www.ricksteves.com/rail, which offers both etickets and home delivery, but may not have access to all the cheapest rates; or

Rail Passes and Train Travel in France

A Eurail France Pass lets you travel by train in France for three to eight days (consecutively or not) within a one-month period.

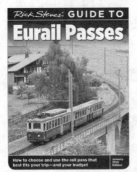

Discounted rates are offered for two or more people traveling together.

France can also be included in a Eurail Select Pass, which allows travel in two to four neighboring countries over two months, and it's covered (along with most of Europe) by the classic Eurail Global Pass.

Rail passes are sold only outside Europe (through travel agents or Rick Steves' Europe). For more on the ins and outs of rail passes, including prices, download my free guide to Eurail Passes (www.ricksteves.com/rail-guide) or go to www.ricksteves.com/rail.

If you're taking just a couple of train rides, look into buying individual point-to-point tickets, which may save you money over a pass. Use this map to add up approximate pay-as-you-go fares for your itinerary, and compare that to the price of a rail pass. Keep in mind that significant discounts on point-to-point tickets may be available with advance purchase.

Map shows approximate costs, in US$, for one-way, second-class tickets on faster trains.

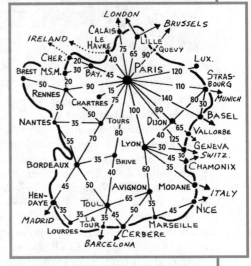

PRACTICALITIES

Coping with Strikes

Going on strike (en grève) is a popular pastime in this revolution-happy country. Because bargaining between management and employees is not standard procedure, workers strike to get attention. Trucks and tractors block main roads and autoroutes (they call it Opération Escargot—"Operation Snail's Pace"), baggage handlers bring airports to their knees, and museum workers make artwork off-limits to tourists. Métro and train personnel seem to strike every year—probably during your trip. What does the traveler do? You could jeter l'éponge (throw in the sponge) and go somewhere less strike-prone (Switzerland's nice), or learn to accept certain events as out of your control. Strikes in France generally last no longer than a day or two, and if you're aware of them, you can usually plan around them. Your hotelier will know the latest (or can find out). Make a habit of asking your hotel receptionist about strikes and checking with the TI. This website gives up to date information on train disruptions: www.sncf.com/en/news/timetables-traffic-updates.

Capitaine Train (www.captaintrain.com), which sells the "Prems" fare and iDTGV tickets.

Travelers with smartphones have the option of saving tickets and reservations directly to their phones (choose "m-ticket"). For more details, see http://en.voyages-sncf.com/en/mobile.

In France: You can buy train tickets in person at SNCF Boutiques or at any train station, either from a staffed ticket window or from a machine. You can buy tickets on the train for a €4-10 surcharge depending on the length of your trip, but you must find the conductor immediately upon boarding; otherwise it's a €35 minimum charge.

The ticket machines available at most stations are great time savers when other lines are long. But the machines probably won't accept your American credit card even if it has a chip, so be prepared with euro coins and bills. Some machines have English instructions, but for those that don't, here are the prompts. (Turn the dial or move the cursor to your choice, and press *"Validez"* to agree to each step.)

1. *Quelle est votre destination?* (What's your destination?)
2. *Billet Plein Tarif* (Full-fare ticket—yes for most.)
3. *1ère ou 2ème* (First or second class; normally second is fine.)
4. *Aller simple ou aller-retour?* (One-way or round-trip?)
5. *Prix en Euro* (The price should be shown if you get this far.)

Reservations

Reservations are required for any TGV train, *couchettes* (sleeping berths) on night trains, and some other trains where indicated in timetables. You can reserve any train at any station anytime before your departure or through SNCF Boutiques. If you're buying a point-to-point ticket for a TGV train, you'll reserve your seat when you purchase your ticket.

Popular TGV routes usually fill up quickly, making it a challenge to get reservations (particularly for rail-pass holders, who are allocated a very limited number of seats). It's wise to book well ahead for any TGV, especially on the busy Paris-Avignon-Nice line. If the TGV trains you want are fully booked, ask about TER trains serving the same destination, as these don't require reservations.

If you're using a rail pass, reservations cost €10-20 for domestic travel, depending on the kind of train they're for and where you buy them. Seat reservations on Thalys, Eurostar, and international TGV trains range from €10 to €38, with the price depending on route and class of service (and can cost up to €50 in first class on TGV trains to Swiss destinations).

Rail-pass holders can book TGV reservations directly at French stations up to departure, if still available, or book etickets at www.raileurope.com. Given the possible difficulty of getting TGV reservations with a rail pass, I recommend making those reservations online before you leave home.

If you're taking one of the rare overnight trains in France and need a *couchette*, it can be booked in advance through a US agent (such as www.raileurope.com).

Reservations are generally unnecessary for non-TGV trains (verify ahead, as some Intercité trains require reservations, like the Nice-Bordeaux train), but they are advisable during busy times (for example, Friday and Sunday afternoons, Saturday mornings, weekday rush hours, and holiday weekends; see "Holidays and Festivals" on page 530).

Baggage Check

Baggage check (*Consigne* or *Espaces Bagages*) is available only at a handful of the biggest train stations (about €5-10/bag per day depending on size), and is noted where available (which can depend on current security concerns, so be prepared to keep your bag). Some hotels and shops near stations will store your bag—I note these as well (if you don't see a bag-check service listed for your desired destination, ask at the station or the TI). For security reasons, all luggage should carry a tag with the traveler's first and last name and current address (though it's not enforced). This applies to hand luggage as well as bigger bags that are stowed. Free tags are available at train stations.

Train Tips
At the Station

- Arrive at the station with plenty of time before your departure to find your platform (platform numbers are posted about 15 minutes prior to departure), confirm connections, and so on. Large stations have separate information *(accueil)* windows; at small stations the ticket office gives information. Remember that Avignon and Aix-en-Provence have separate TGV stations that are outside the town center.

- Small stations are minimally staffed; if there is no agent at the station, go directly to the tracks and look for the overhead sign that confirms your train stops at that track.

- Larger stations have platforms with monitors showing TGV layouts (numbered forward or backward) so you can figure out where your car *(voiture)* will stop on the long platform and where to board each car.

Validating Tickets, Reservations, and Rail Passes

- You're required to activate *(composter,* kohm-poh-stay) all train tickets and reservations (when printed on official ticket stock) before boarding any SNCF train. Look for a yellow machine near the platform or waiting area to stamp your ticket or reservation. Reserved tickets that are printed at home on plain paper don't need validation (and won't fit in the machine). You also don't need to activate etickets on your phone.

- If you have a rail pass, get it activated at a ticket window before using it the first time (don't stamp it in the machine). If you're traveling with a pass and have a reservation for a certain trip, you must activate the reservation by stamping it.

- If you have a rail flexipass, write the date on your pass each day you travel (before or immediately after boarding your first train).

- Note that a Eurail pass must be kept in its cover, and you must fill in trip details on the cover as you go.

On the Train

- Before getting on a train, confirm that it's going where you think it is. For example, if you want to go to Antibes, ask the conductor or any local passenger, *"À Antibes?"* (ah ahn-teeb)

- Some longer trains split off cars en route. Make sure your train car is continuing to your destination by asking, for example, *"Cette voiture va à Avignon?"* (seht vwah-toor vah ah ah-veen-yohn; "This car goes to Avignon?").

- If a non-TGV train seat is reserved, it'll likely be labeled *réservé,* with the cities to and from which it is reserved.

- If you don't understand an announcement, ask your neighbor

Train-Ticket French

Hello, madam/sir, do you speak English?
Bonjour, madame/monsieur, parlez-vous anglais?
(bohn-zhoor, mah-dahm/muhs-yur, par-lay-voo ahn-glay)

I would like a departure for Avignon, on 10 May, about 9:00, the most direct way possible.
Je voudrais un train pour Avignon, pour le 10 Mai, vers 9:00, le plus direct possible.
(zhuh voo-dray uhn tran poor ah-veen-yohn, poor luh dees may, vehr nuhf, luh plew dee-rehk poh-see-bluh)

---

to explain: *"Pardon madame/monsieur, qu'est-ce qui se passe?"* (kehs kee suh pahs; "Excuse me, what's going on?").

- Verify with the conductor all of the transfers you must make: *"Correspondance à?"* ("Transfer to where?").

- To guard against theft, keep your bags in sight (directly overhead is ideal but not always possible—the early boarder gets the best storage space). If you must store them in the lower racks by the doors (available in most cars), pay attention at stops. Your bags are most vulnerable to theft before the train takes off and whenever it stops.

- Note your arrival time, so you'll be ready to get off.

- Use the train's free WCs before you get off (but not while the train is stopped in a station).

Low-Cost TGV Trains to Elsewhere in France

A TGV train called OuiGo (pronounced "we go") offers a direct connection from Disneyland Paris to select cities in southern and western France at rock-bottom fares with no-frills service. The catch: These trains leave from the Marne-la-Vallée TGV station, an hour from Paris on the suburban Train-A. So you can hang at Disneyland Paris before (or after) your trip south and connect with a direct TGV. You must print your own ticket ahead of time, arrive 30 minutes before departure, and activate your ticket. You can't use a rail pass, and you can only bring one carry-on-size bag plus one handbag for free (children's tickets allow you to bring a stroller). Larger or extra luggage is €5/bag if you pay when you buy your ticket. If you just show up without paying in advance, it's €20/bag on the train—yikes. There's no food service on the train (BYO), but children under age 12 pay only €5 for a seat. The website explains it all in easy-to-understand English (www.ouigo.com).

BUSES

Regional buses work well for many destinations not served by trains. Buses are almost always comfortable and air-conditioned.

A few bus lines are run by the SNCF rail system and are covered by your rail pass (show rail pass at station to get free bus ticket), but most bus lines are not covered. Bus stations *(gare routière)* are usually located next to train stations. Train stations usually have bus information where train-to-bus connections are important—and vice versa for bus companies. For dirt-cheap bus fares between cities in France, check out www.flixbus.fr and www.ouibus.com.

Bus Tips for Day Trips

- Read the train tips described earlier, and use those that apply (check schedules in advance, arrive at the station early, confirm the destination before you board, find out if you need to transfer, etc.).
- The bus company websites I've listed in this book are usually in French only. Here are some key phrases you'll see: *horaires* (schedules), *en semaine* (Monday through Saturday), *dimanche* (Sunday), *jours fériés* (holidays), *année* (bus runs all year on the days listed), *vac* (runs only during summer vacations), *scol/scolaire* (runs only when school is in session), *ligne* (route or bus line), and *réseau* (network—usually all routes).
- Use TIs to help plan your trip and verify times (TIs have regional bus schedules).
- Be aware that service is sparse or nonexistent on Sunday. Wednesday bus schedules often are different during the school year, because school is out this day (and regional buses generally operate school service).
- Confirm a bus stop's location in advance (rural stops are often not signed) and be at bus stops at least five minutes early.

TAXIS AND UBER

Most European taxis are reliable and cheap. In many cities, couples can travel short distances by cab for little more than two bus or subway tickets. Taxis can be your best option for getting to the airport for an early morning flight or to connect two far-flung destinations. If you like ride-booking services like Uber, these apps usually work in Europe just like they do in the US: You request a car on your mobile device (connected to Wi-Fi or a data plan), and the fare is automatically charged to your credit card. In France, Uber services generally work in only the largest cities.

RENTING A CAR

Rental companies require you to be at least 21 years old and to have held your license for one year. Drivers under the age of 25 may incur a young-driver surcharge, and some rental companies do not rent to anyone 75 or older. If you're considered too young or old, look into leasing (covered later), which has less-stringent age restrictions.

Research car rentals before you go. It's cheaper to arrange car rentals from the US. Consider several companies to compare rates. Most of the major US rental agencies (including Avis, Budget, Enterprise, Hertz, and Thrifty) have offices throughout Europe. Also consider the two major Europe-based agencies, Europcar and Sixt, and the French agency, ADA (www.ada.fr). It can be cheaper to use a consolidator, such as Auto Europe/Kemwel (www.autoeurope.com—or the often cheaper www.autoeurope.eu) or Europe by Car (www.europebycar.com), which compares rates at several companies to get you the best deal—but because you're working with a middleman, it's especially important to ask in advance about add-on fees and restrictions.

Always read the fine print or query the agent carefully for add-on charges—such as one-way drop-off fees, airport surcharges, or mandatory insurance policies—that aren't included in the "total price."

For the best deal, rent by the week with unlimited mileage. I normally rent the smallest, least-expensive model with a stick shift (cheaper than an automatic). This size works well for two people; I'd go up a size for more than two (e.g. equivalent to a Renault Mégane in size). Almost all rentals are manual by default, so if you need an automatic, request one in advance and be warned that these cars are usually larger models. Roads and parking spaces are narrow in France, so you'll do yourself a favor by renting the smallest car that meets your needs.

Figure on paying roughly $250 for a one-week rental. Allow extra for supplemental insurance, fuel, tolls, and parking. For trips of three weeks or more, leasing can save you money on insurance and taxes.

Picking Up Your Car: Compare pick-up costs (downtown can be less expensive than the airport or train station) and explore drop-off options. Always check the hours of the location you choose: Many rental offices close on Sunday and at lunch (about 12:00-13:30). At major locations like rail stations, you can usually drop off a car after-hours (put keys in lockbox).

When selecting a location, don't trust the agency's description of "downtown" or "city center." In some cases, a "downtown" branch can be on the outskirts of the city—a long, costly taxi ride from the center. Before choosing, plug the addresses into a mapping website. You may find that the "train station" location is handier. Returning a car at a big-city train station or downtown agency can be tricky; get precise details on the car drop-off location and hours, and allow ample time to find it.

If you want a car for only a day or two (e.g., for the Côtes du Rhône wine route or Luberon villages), you'll likely find it easy to rent on the spot just about anywhere in France. In many cases, this is a worthwhile splurge. All you need is your American driver's license and a major credit card (figure €60-90/day; some include unlimited mileage, others give you 100 kilometers—about 60 miles—for free).

When you pick up the rental car, check it thoroughly and make sure any damage is noted on your rental agreement. Rental agencies in Europe tend to charge for even minor damage, so be sure to mark everything. Before driving off, find out how your car's gearshift, lights, turn signals, wipers, radio, and fuel cap function, and know what kind of fuel the car takes (diesel vs. unleaded). When you return the car, make sure the agent verifies its condition with you. Some drivers take pictures of the returned vehicle as proof of its condition.

Car Insurance Options

When you rent a car, you are liable for a very high deductible, sometimes equal to the entire value of the car. Limit your financial risk with one of these options: Buy Collision Damage Waiver (CDW) coverage with a low or zero deductible from the car-rental company, get coverage through your credit card (free, if your card automatically includes zero-deductible coverage), or get collision insurance as part of a larger travel-insurance policy.

Basic **CDW** includes a very high deductible (typically $1,000-1,500), costs $15-30 a day (figure roughly 30-40 percent extra), and reduces your liability, but does not eliminate it. When you reserve or pick up the car, you'll be offered the chance to "buy down" the basic deductible to zero (for an additional $10-30/day; this is sometimes called "super CDW" or "zero-deductible coverage").

If you opt for **credit-card coverage,** you'll technically have to decline all coverage offered by the car-rental company, which means they can place a hold on your card (which can be up to the full value of the car). In case of damage, it can be time-consuming to resolve the charges with your credit-card company. Before you decide on this option, quiz your credit-card company about how it works.

If you're already purchasing a **travel-insurance policy** for your trip, adding collision coverage can be an economical option. For example, Travel Guard (www.travelguard.com) sells affordable renter's collision insurance as an add-on to its other policies; it's valid everywhere in Europe except the Republic of Ireland, and some Italian car-rental companies refuse to honor it, as it doesn't cover you in case of theft.

For more on car-rental insurance, see www.ricksteves.com/cdw.

Leasing

For trips of three weeks or more, consider leasing (which automatically includes zero-deductible collision and theft insurance). By technically buying and then selling back the car, you save lots of money on tax and insurance. Leasing provides you a brand-new car with unlimited mileage and a 24-hour emergency assistance program. Pick-up and drop-off locations are limited to a few major cities (listed on websites). You can lease for as little as 21 days to as long as five and a half months; Idea Merge offers two-week leases. Car leases must be arranged from the US; some companies allow drop off in different countries.

These reliable companies offer 21-day lease packages:

Auto France (Peugeot cars only, US tel. 800-572-9655, www.autofrance.net)

Europe by Car (Citroën cars only, US tel. 800-223-1516, www.ebctravel.com)

Idea Merge (ask about two-week leases; Citroën only, US tel. 503-715-5810, www.ideamerge.com)

Kemwel (Peugeot only, US tel. 877-820-0668, www.kemwel.com)

RV and Campervan Rental

Even given the extra fuel costs, renting your own rolling hotel can be a great way to save money, especially if you're sticking mainly to rural areas. Keep in mind that RVs in France are much smaller than those you see at home. Companies to consider:

Van It (rents pop-top VW Eurovan campers that are easy to maneuver on small roads, mobile 06 70 43 11 86, www.van-it.com)

Idea Merge (best resource for small RV rental, see listing above)

Origin (current-model Volkswagen vans fully equipped for 2-3 people, rates less than RVs, mobile 06 80 01 72 77, www.origin-campervans.com)

Navigation Options

If you'll be navigating using your phone or a GPS unit from home, remember to bring a car charger and device mount.

Your Mobile Device: The mapping app on your mobile phone works fine for navigation in Europe, but for real-time turn-by-turn directions and traffic updates, you'll generally need Internet access. And driving all day while online can be very expensive. Helpful exceptions are Google Maps, Here WeGo, and Navmii, which provide turn-by-turn voice directions and recalibrate even when they're offline.

Download your map before you head out—it's smart to select a large region. Then turn off your cellular connection so you're not charged for data roaming. Call up the map, enter your destination, and you're on your way. View maps in standard view (not satellite view) to limit data demands.

GPS Devices: If you prefer the convenience of a dedicated GPS unit, consider renting one with your car ($10-30/day). These units offer real-time, turn-by-turn directions and traffic without the data requirements of an app. Note that the unit may only come loaded with maps for its home country; if you need additional maps, ask. Also make sure your device's language is set to English before you drive off.

A less expensive option is to bring a GPS device from home. Be aware that you'll need to buy and download European maps before your trip.

Maps and Atlases: Even when navigating primarily with a mobile app or GPS, I always make it a point to have a paper map. It's invaluable for getting the big picture, understanding alternate routes, and filling in when my phone runs out of juice. The free maps you get from your car-rental company usually don't have enough detail. It's smart to buy a better map before you go, or pick one up at a European gas station, bookshop, newsstand, or tourist shop.

Michelin maps are available throughout France at bookstores, newsstands, and gas stations (about €6 each, cheaper than in the US). The orange Michelin map #527 (1:275,000 scale) covers this book's destinations with good detail for drivers. Michelin map #332 is good for the Luberon and the Côtes du Rhône, and map #340 is best for the Bouches-du-Rhône (the southern area around Arles). Drivers going beyond Provence and the Riviera should consider the soft-cover Michelin France atlas (the entire country at 1:200,000, well-organized in a €20 book with an index and maps of major cities). Spend a few minutes learning the Michelin key to get the most sightseeing value out of these maps.

DRIVING

It's a pleasure to explore France by car, but you need to know the rules.

Road Rules: Seat belts are mandatory for all, and children under age 10 must be in the back seat with a special seat. In city and town centers, traffic merging from the right (even from tiny side streets) may have the right-of-way *(priorité à droite)*. So even when you're driving on a major road, pay attention to cars merg-

PRACTICALITIES

ing from the right. In contrast, cars entering the many suburban roundabouts must yield *(cédez le passage)*. You can't turn right on a red light, U-turns are illegal, and on expressways it's illegal to pass drivers on the right.

When navigating France's narrow streets, you'll likely encounter short sections where cars must pass single file, one direction at a time. At those spots you'll see a sign with thick and thin arrows pointing up and down. A thick (white) arrow pointing up in the direction you're traveling means you have priority to pass through the section; a red arrow indicates you must yield to cars coming the other way.

Be aware of typical European road rules; for example, many countries require headlights to be turned on at all times (in France, they must be used in any case of poor visibility), and nearly all forbid talking on a mobile phone without a hands-free headset. Ask your car-rental company about these rules, or check the US State Department website (www.travel.state.gov, search for your country in the "Learn about your destination" box, then click "Travel and Transportation").

Speed Limits: Because speed limits are by road type, they typically aren't posted, so it's best to memorize them:
- Two-lane D and N routes outside cities and towns: 90 km/hour
- Two-lane roads in villages: 50 km/hour (unless posted at 30 km/hour)
- Divided highways outside cities and towns: 110 km/hour
- Autoroutes (toll roads): 130 km/hour (unless otherwise posted)

If it's raining, subtract 10 km/hour on D and N routes and 20 km/hour on divided highways and autoroutes. Speed-limit signs are a red circle around a number; when you see that same number again in gray with a broken line diagonally across it, this means that limit no longer applies. Speed limits drop to 30-50 km/hour in villages (always posted) and must be respected.

AND LEARN THESE ROAD SIGNS

STOP

Speed Limit (km/hr)
Yield
No Passing
End of No Passing Zone

One Way
Intersection
Main Road
Expressway

Roundabout Ahead
Danger
No Entry
All Vehicles Prohibited

No Through Road
Restrictions No Longer Apply
Yield to Oncoming Traffic
No Stopping

Parking
No Parking
Customs or Toll Road
Peace

French Tollbooths

For American drivers, getting through the toll payment stations on France's autoroutes is mostly about knowing which lanes to avoid—and having cash on hand. Skip lanes marked with a lowercase "t"—they're reserved for cars using the automatic Télépéage payment system. A pictograph of a credit card (usually a blue sign) means credit or debit cards only (your US card very likely won't work, so avoid this line). Look instead for green arrows above tollbooths and/or icons showing bills or coins, which indicate which lanes accept cash. Slow down as you approach tollbooths to study your options, and pull off to the side if you aren't positive of the tollbooth to choose.

Exits are entirely automated (if you have a problem at the tollbooth, press the red button for help). Have smaller bills ready (payment machines won't accept €50 bills). Shorter autoroute sections have periodic tollbooths, where you can pay by dropping coins into a basket (change is given for bills, but keep a good supply of coins handy to avoid waiting for an attendant).

To estimate how much cash to have on hand for tolls, use the planning tool at ViaMichelin.com.

Road speeds are monitored regularly with cameras—a mere two kilometers over the limit yields a pricey ticket (a minimum of about €70). The good news is that signs warn drivers a few hundred yards before the camera and show the proper speed (see image above). Look for a sign with a radar graphic that says *Pour votre sécurité, contrôles automatiques.* The French use these cameras not to make money but to slow down traffic—and it works.

Tire Pressure: In Europe, tire pressure is measured in *bars* of pressure. To convert to PSI (pounds per square inch) the formula is: $bar \times 14.5$ = PSI (so 2 *bars* would be 2×14.5, or 29 PSI). To convert to *bar* pressures from PSI, the formula is: PSI $\times 0.07$ = *bar* (so 30 PSI $\times 0.07$ would be 2.1 *bar*). Your car's recommended tire pressure is usually found on a sticker mounted on the driver-side doorframe.

Pulling to the Side of the Road: All rental cars are equipped with a yellow safety vest and triangle. You must wear the vest and display the triangle whenever you pull over on the side of the road (say, to fix a flat tire). If you don't, you could be fined.

Fuel: Gas *(essence)* is expensive—about $5.50 per gallon. Diesel *(gazole)* costs less—about $5 per gallon. Know what type of fuel your car takes before you fill up. Many Americans get marooned by filling with unleaded in a diesel car. Most rentals are diesel; if yours is one of them, use the yellow pump. Fuel is most expensive on autoroutes and cheapest at big supermarkets. Your US credit

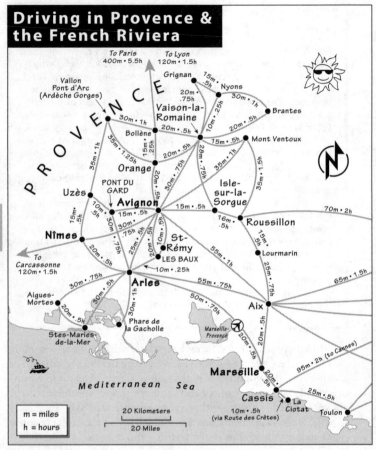

Driving in Provence & the French Riviera

To Paris 400m · 5.5h
To Lyon 120m · 1.5h

PROVENCE

Vallon Pont d'Arc (Ardèche Gorges)

Grignan
15m · .5h
Nyons
20m · .75h
30m · 1h
Brantes
Vaison-la-Romaine
20m · .5h
10m · .25h
20m · .5h
Mont Ventoux
15m · .5h
20m · .5h
Bollène
35m · 1h
15m · .25h
35m · 1.25h
20m · .5h
30m · 1h
35m · 1.5h
Orange
20m · .75h
20m · .5h
30m · .5h
Isle-sur-la-Sorgue
Uzès
PONT DU GARD
15m · .5h
10m · .5h
30m · .5h
Avignon
15m · .5h
70m · 2h
Nîmes
15m · .5h
30m · .75h
30m · .5h
16m · .5h
Roussillon
10m · .5h
25m · .5h
St-Rémy
15m · .5h
LES BAUX
55m · .5h
Lourmarin
20m · .5h
20m · .5h
10m · .25h
25m · .75h
To Carcassonne 120m · 1.5h
65m · 1.5h
30m · .75h
Arles
55m · .75h
Aigues-Mortes
30m · .5h
50m · .75h
20m · .5h
Aix
Phare de la Gacholle
30m · 1h
Marseille-Provence
20m · .5h
Stes-Maries-de-la-Mer
95m · 2h (to Cannes)
20m · .5h
Mediterranean Sea
Marseille
25m · .5h
Cassis
La Ciotat
Toulon
10m · .5h (via Route des Crètes)

m = miles
h = hours

20 Kilometers
20 Miles

and debit cards without a chip won't work at self-serve pumps—so you'll need to find gas stations with attendants (all autoroute stations have them), or get a chip-and-PIN card before your trip and hope that it works (see page 466). Most drivers will spend about $150 per week on gas to prowl the roads in Provence and the French Riviera.

Plan ahead for Sundays, as most gas stations in town are closed. I fill my tank every Saturday. If stuck on a Sunday, use an autoroute, where the gas stations are always staffed.

Autoroutes and Tolls: Autoroute tolls are pricey, but the alternative to these super-"feeways" usually means being marooned in countryside traffic—especially near the Riviera. Autoroutes save enough time, gas, and nausea to justify the cost. Mix high-speed "autorouting" with scenic country-road rambling.

You'll usually take a ticket when entering an autoroute and pay when you leave. Figure roughly €1 in tolls for every 15 kilometers

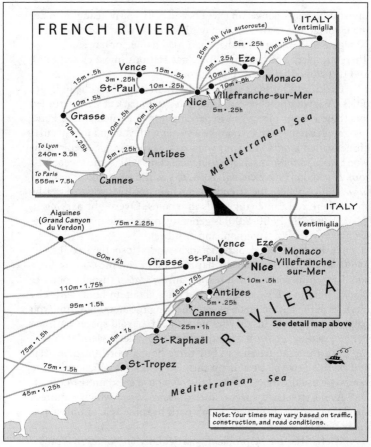

driven on the autoroute (or about €15 for two hours). Cash (coins or bills under €50) is your best payment option as most US credit cards won't work (for more on paying at tollbooths, see the sidebar on page 519). Estimate your distance and toll costs, then make sure that you have enough cash before entering the autoroute.

Autoroute gas stations are open on Sundays and usually come with well-stocked minimarts, clean restrooms, sandwiches, maps, local products, cheap vending-machine coffee, and Wi-Fi. Many have small cafés or more elaborate cafeterias with reasonable prices. For more information, see www.autoroutes.fr.

Highways: Roads are classified into departmental (D), national (N), and autoroutes (A). D routes (usually yellow lines on maps) are often slower but the most scenic. N routes and important D routes (red lines) are the fastest after autoroutes (orange lines on maps). Green road signs are for national routes; blue are for autoroutes. Some roads in France have had route-number changes (mostly N roads converting to D roads). If you're using an older map, the actual route name may differ from what's on your map. Navigate by destination rather than road name...or buy a new map. There are plenty of good facilities, gas stations (most closed Sun), and rest stops along most French roads.

Parking: Finding a parking place can be a headache in larger cities. Ask your hotelier for ideas, and pay to park at well-patrolled lots (blue *P* signs direct you to parking lots in French cities). Parking garages require that you take a ticket with you and pay at a machine (called a *caisse*) on your way back to the car. US credit cards won't work in these machines, but euro coins will (some accept bills too). If you don't have enough coins to pay the fee, find the garage's *accueil* office, where the attendant can help or direct you to a nearby shop where you can change bills into coins. Overnight parking in garages (usually 19:00-8:00) is generally reasonable (priciest in cities like Paris, Nice, Avignon, and Antibes).

Curbside metered parking also works (usually free 12:00-14:00 & 19:00-9:00, and all day and night in Aug). Look for a small machine selling time (called an *horodateur,* usually one per block), plug in a few coins (€1.50-2 buys about an hour, varies by city), push the button, get a receipt showing the amount of time you have, and display it inside your windshield. (Avoid spaces outlined in blue, as they require a special permit.) For cheap overnight parking until the next afternoon, buy three hours' worth of time after 19:00. This gets you until noon the next day, after which two more hours are usually free (12:00-14:00), so you're good until 14:00.

Avoid streetside spaces labeled *"zone bleue,"* which require a special tag to be displayed. Don't park in these spaces unless you enjoy tickets.

Theft: Theft is a problem, particularly in southern France. Thieves easily recognize rental cars and assume they are filled with a tourist's gear. Try to make your car look locally owned by hiding the "tourist-owned" rental-company decals and putting a French newspaper in your back window. Be sure all of your valuables are out of sight and locked in the trunk—or, even better, with you or in your room. And don't assume that just because you're parked on a main street that you'll be fine. Thieves work fast.

Driving Tips

- France is riddled with roundabouts—navigating them is an art. The key is to know your direction and be ready for your turnoff. If you miss it, take another lap (or two). See the diagram on page 524.
- At intersections and roundabouts, French road signs use the name of an upcoming destination for directions—the highway number is usually missing. That upcoming destination could

French Road Signs

Signs You Must Obey

Allumez vos feux	Turn on your lights
Cédez le Passage	Yield
Déviation	Detour
Dépassement Interdit	No passing
Parking Interdit/Stationnement Interdit	No parking
Priorité à Droite	Right-of-way is for cars coming from the right
Rappel	Remember to obey the sign
Vous n'avez pas la priorité	You don't have the right of way (when merging)

Signs for Your Information

Autres Directions	Other directions (follow when leaving a city)
Centre Commercial	Shopping center (not city center)
Centre-Ville	City center
Feux	Traffic signal
Horodateur	Ticket-vending machine for parking
Parc de Stationnement/Parking	Parking lot
Route Barrée	Road blocked
Rue Piétonne	Pedestrian-only street
Sauf Riverains	Local access only
Sortie des Camions	Work truck exit
Suivre... (e.g., Pont du Gard, suivre Nîmes)	Follow... (e.g., for Pont du Gard, follow signs for Nîmes)
Toutes Directions	All directions (follow when leaving a city)

Signs Unique to Autoroutes

Aire	Rest stop with WCs, telephones, and sometimes gas stations
Bouchon	Traffic jam ahead
Fluide	No traffic ahead
Péage	Toll
Par Temps de Pluie	When raining (modifies speed limit signs)
Télépéage	Automated tollbooths

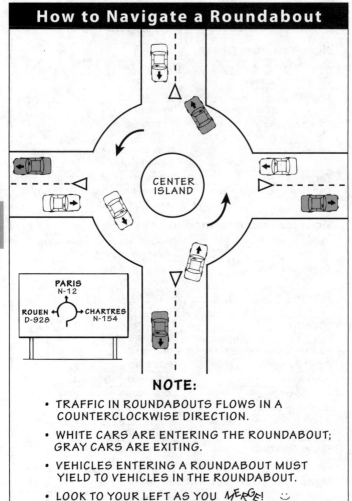

How to Navigate a Roundabout

CENTER ISLAND

PARIS
N-12

ROUEN ←
D-928

→ CHARTRES
N-154

NOTE:

- TRAFFIC IN ROUNDABOUTS FLOWS IN A COUNTERCLOCKWISE DIRECTION.

- WHITE CARS ARE ENTERING THE ROUNDABOUT; GRAY CARS ARE EXITING.

- VEHICLES ENTERING A ROUNDABOUT MUST YIELD TO VEHICLES IN THE ROUNDABOUT.

- LOOK TO YOUR LEFT AS YOU MERGE! ☺

be a major city, or it could be the next minor town up the road. Check your map ahead of time and get familiar with the names of towns and cities along your route—and even major cities on the same road beyond your destination.

- When navigating into cities, approach intersections cautiously, stow the map, and follow the signs to *Centre-Ville* (city center). From there, head to the TI *(Office de Tourisme)* or your hotel.

- When leaving or just passing through cities, follow the signs for *Toutes Directions* or *Autres Directions* (meaning "anywhere else") until you see a sign for your specific destination. Look also for *Suivre* signs telling you to follow *(suivre)* signs for the (usually more important) destination listed.

- Driving on any roads but autoroutes will take longer than you think, so allow plenty of time for slower traffic (tractors, trucks, and hard-to-decipher signs all deserve blame). First-timers should estimate how long they think a drive will take... then double it. I pretend that kilometers are miles (for distances) and base my time estimates accordingly.
- While locals are eating lunch (12:00-14:00), many sights (and gas stations) are closed, so you can make great time driving—but keep it slow when passing through villages.
- Be very careful when driving on smaller roads—many are narrow and flanked by little ditches that lure inattentive drivers. I've met several readers who "ditched" their cars (and had to be pulled out by local farmers).
- On autoroutes, keep to the right lanes to let fast drivers by, and be careful when merging into a left lane, as cars can be coming at high speeds.
- Motorcycles will scream between cars in traffic. Be ready—they expect you to make space so that they can pass.
- Keep a stash of coins handy for parking and small autoroute tolls.

BIKING

You'll find areas in France where public transportation is limited and bicycle touring might be a good idea. For many, biking is a romantic notion, and the novelty wears off after the first hill or headwind. Realistically evaluate your physical condition, be clear on the limitations bikes present, and consider an electric bike. Start with an easy pedal, then decide how ambitious you feel. Most find that one hour on a narrow, hard seat is enough. I've listed bike-rental shops where appropriate (TIs can also guide you), and I've suggested a few of my favorite rides. For a good touring bike, figure about €14 for a half-day and €20 for a full day. You'll pay more for better equipment; generally the best is available through bike shops, not at train stations or other outlets. French cyclists often do not wear helmets, though most rental outfits have them (for a small fee).

FLIGHTS

The best comparison search engine for both international and intra-European flights is Kayak.com. An alternative is Google Flights, which has an easy-to-use system to track prices. For inexpensive flights within Europe, try Skyscanner.com.

Flying to Europe: Start looking for international flights about four to six months before your trip, especially for peak-season travel. Off-season tickets can usually be purchased a month or so in advance. Depending on your itinerary, it can be efficient to fly into one city and out of another. If your flight requires a connection in Europe, see our hints on navigating Europe's top hub airports at www.ricksteves.com/hub-airports.

Flying Within Europe: If you're visiting one or more French cities on a longer European trip—or linking up far-flung French cities (such as Paris and Nice)—a flight can save both time and money. When comparing your options, factor in the time it takes to get to the airport and how early you'll need to arrive to check in.

Well-known cheapo airlines include Easyjet and Ryanair. Also check Air France for specials. But be aware of the potential drawbacks of flying with a discount airline: nonrefundable and nonchangeable tickets, minimal or nonexistent customer service, pricey and time-consuming treks to secondary airports, and stingy baggage allowances with steep overage fees. If you're traveling with lots of luggage, a cheap flight can quickly become a bad deal. To avoid unpleasant surprises, read the small print before you book. These days you can also fly within Europe on major airlines affordably—and without all the aggressive restrictions—for around $100 a flight.

Flying to the US and Canada: Because security is extra tight for flights to the US, be sure to give yourself plenty of time at the airport. It's also important to charge your electronic devices before you board because security checks may require you to turn them on (see www.tsa.gov for the latest rules).

Resources from Rick Steves

Begin your trip at www.ricksteves.com: My mobile-friendly **website** is *the* place to explore Europe. You'll find thousands of fun articles, videos, photos, and radio interviews organized by country; a wealth of money-saving tips for planning your dream trip; monthly travel news dispatches; a video library of my travel talks; my travel blog; and my latest guidebook updates (www.ricksteves.com/update).

Our **Travel Forum** is an immense yet well-groomed collection of message boards, where our travel-savvy community answers questions and shares their personal travel experiences—and our well-traveled staff chimes in when they can be helpful (www.ricksteves.com/forums).

Our **online Travel Store** offers travel bags and accessories that I've designed specifically to help you travel smarter and lighter. These include my popular bags (rolling carry-on and backpack versions, which I helped design...and live out of four months a year), money belts, totes, toiletries kits, adapters, other accessories, and a wide selection of guidebooks and planning maps.

Choosing the right **rail pass** for your trip—amid hundreds of options—can drive you nutty. Our website will help you find the perfect fit for your itinerary and your budget: We offer easy, one-stop shopping for rail passes, seat reservations, and point-to-point tickets (www.ricksteves.com/rail).

Small Group Tours: Want to travel with greater efficiency and less stress? We offer more than 40 itineraries and have over 900 departures annually reaching the best destinations in this book... and beyond. We offer an 11-day Paris and the Heart of France tour (focusing on the best of the north), a 13-day Loire to the South of France tour, a 14-day Best of Eastern France tour, a 7-day in-depth Paris city tour, and a 13-day My Way France tour. You'll enjoy great guides, a fun bunch of travel partners (with small groups of around 24 to 28 travelers), and plenty of room to spread out in a big, comfy bus when touring between towns. You'll find European adventures to fit every vacation length. For all the details, and to get our Tour Catalog, visit www.ricksteves.com or call us at 425/608-4217.

PRACTICALITIES

Books: *Rick Steves Provence & the French Riviera* is one of many books in my series on European travel, which includes country guidebooks (including France); city guidebooks (Paris, Rome, Florence, London, etc.); Snapshot guidebooks (excerpted chapters from my country guides); Pocket guidebooks (full-color little books on big cities); "Best Of" guidebooks (condensed country guidebooks in a full-color, easy-to-scan format); and my budget-travel skills handbook, *Rick Steves Europe Through the Back Door.* Most of my titles are available as ebooks.

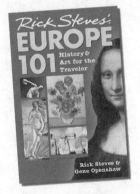

My phrase books—for French, Italian, German, Spanish, and Portuguese—are practical and budget-oriented. My other books include *Europe 101* (a crash course on art and history designed for travelers); *Mediterranean Cruise Ports* and *Northern European Cruise Ports* (how to make the most of your time in port); and *Travel as a Political Act* (a travelogue sprinkled with tips for bringing home a global perspective). A more complete list of my titles appears near the end of this book.

TV Shows: My public television series, *Rick Steves' Europe*, covers Europe from top to bottom with more than 100 half-hour episodes, and we're working on new shows every year. We have 13 episodes on France—that's over 6 hours of vivid video coverage of one of my favorite countries. To watch full episodes online for free, see www.ricksteves.com/tv.

Travel Talks on Video: You can raise your travel I.Q. with video versions of our popular classes (including my talks on travel skills, packing smart, cruising, tech for travelers, European art for travelers, travel as a political act, and individual talks covering most European countries—including France). See www.ricksteves.com/travel-talks.

Radio: My weekly public radio show, *Travel with Rick Steves*, features interviews with travel experts from around the world. It airs on 400 public radio stations across the US, and you can also

listen to it as a podcast on iTunes, iHeartRadio, Stitcher, Tune In, and other platforms. A complete archive of programs (more than 400 in all) is available at www.soundcloud.com/rick-steves. Most of this audio content is available for free through my **Rick Steves Audio Europe** app.

APPENDIX

Useful Contacts 529
Holidays and Festivals 530
Books and Films 531
Conversions and Climate. 533
Packing Checklist 536
Pronunciation Guide
for Place Names. 537
French Survival Phrases. 539

Useful Contacts

Emergency Needs

Police, Fire, and Ambulance: 112 (Europe-wide in English)
Police: Tel. 17
Emergency Medical Assistance (called "SAMU"): Tel. 15
Collect Calls to the US: Dial 08 00 90 06 24, then say "operator" for an English-speaking operator.
Riviera Medical Services: Tel. 04 93 26 12 70, www.rivieramedical. com (has list of English-speaking physicians in the Riviera region and can help make an appointment or call an ambulance)

Embassies and Consulates

US Consulate in Marseille: Tel. 04 91 54 92 00 (12 Boulevard Paul Peytral, 13006 Marseille, www.consulats-marseille.org/ Etats-Unis)
US Consulate and Embassy in Paris: Tel. 01 43 12 22 22 (4 Avenue Gabriel, to the left as you face Hôtel Crillon, Mo: Concorde, http://france.usembassy.gov)

Canadian Consulate and Embassy in Paris: Tel. 01 44 43 29 02 (35 Avenue Montaigne, Mo: Franklin D. Roosevelt, www.amb-canada.fr). For 24/7 emergency assistance, call collect to Canadian tel. 613/996-8885.

Australian Consulate in Paris: Tel. 01 40 59 33 00 (4 Rue Jean Rey, Mo: Bir-Hakeim, www.france.embassy.gov.au)

Holidays and Festivals

This list includes selected festivals in the Provence and French Riviera region, plus national holidays observed throughout France. Many sights and banks close on national holidays—keep this in mind when planning your itinerary. Before planning a trip around a festival, verify its dates by checking the festival's website, France's tourist office (www.franceguide.com), or my "Upcoming Holidays and Festivals in France" web page (www.ricksteves.com/europe/france/festivals). Hotels get booked up on Easter weekend, Labor Day, Ascension Day, Pentecost, Bastille Day, and the winter holidays.

Jan 1	New Year's Day
Jan 6	Epiphany
Feb	Carnival-Mardi Gras, parades and fireworks, Nice (www.nicecarnaval.com)
April	Easter weekend (Good Friday-Easter Monday): March 30-April 2, 2018; April 19-22, 2019
April	Feria de Pâques, bullfights, coincides with Easter weekend, Arles
May 1	Labor Day
May 8	V-E (Victory in Europe) Day
May	Cannes Film Festival: May 6-14, 2018; (www.festival-cannes.com)
May	Ascension: May 10, 2018; May 30, 2019
Late May	Monaco Grand Prix, auto race: May 24-27, 2018 (www.acm.mc)
May/June	Pentecost: May 20, 2018; June 9, 2019
June 21	Fête de la Musique, free concerts and dancing in the streets throughout France
Mid-June-early Aug	Chorégies d'Orange, music and opera performed in a Roman theater (www.choregies.fr)
July	Aix Festival, classical music and opera (www.festival-aix.com)
July	Avignon Festival, theater, dance, and music (www.festival-avignon.com)

July	Tour de France, national bicycle race culminating in Paris (www.letour.fr)
July	Jazz à Juan, international jazz festival, Antibes/Juan-les-Pins (www.jazzajuan.com)
July 14	Bastille Day, fireworks, dancing, and revelry
Mid-July	Nice Jazz Festival (www.nicejazzfestival.fr)
July-Aug	Cannes Festival of Pyrotechnic Art, fireworks (www.festival-pyrotechnique-cannes.com)
Aug 15	Assumption of Mary
Mid-Sept	Féria du Riz, bullfights, Arles
Nov 1	All Saints' Day
Nov 11	Armistice Day
Dec 25	Christmas Day
Dec 31	New Year's Eve

Books and Films

To learn more about France past and present, and specifically Provence and the French Riviera, check out a few of these books and films. To learn what's making news in France, you'll find *France 24 News* online at www.France24.com/en. See the Traveling with Children chapter for recommendations for kids.

Nonfiction

A to Z of French Food, a French to English Dictionary of Culinary Terms (G. de Temmerman, 1995). This is the most complete (and priciest) menu reader around—and it's beloved by foodies.

At Home in France (Ann Barry, 1996). An American author describes her visits to her country house.

The Course of French History (Pierre Goubert, 1988). Goubert provides a basic summary of French history.

A Distant Mirror (Barbara Tuchman, 1987). Respected historian Barbara Tuchman paints a portrait of 14th-century France.

French or Foe? (Polly Platt, 1994). This best seller, along with its follow-up, *Savoir-Flair!*, is an essential aid for interacting with the French and navigating the intricacies of their culture.

A Goose in Toulouse and other Culinary Adventures in France (Mort Rosenblum, 2000). This series of essays provides keen insights on rural France through its focus on cuisine.

La Seduction: How the French Play the Game of Life (Elaine Sciolino, 2011). Sciolino, former Paris bureau chief of the *New York Times*, gives travelers a fun, insightful, and tantalizing peek into how seduction is used in all aspects of French life—from small villages to the halls of national government.

Portraits of France (Robert Daley, 1991). Part memoir, part travelogue, this is a charming reminiscence of the writer's lifelong relationship with France, including marrying a French girl on his first trip there.

Postcards from France (Megan McNeill Libby, 1997). This perceptive account tells the adventures of an American exchange student adjusting to life in France.

The Road from the Past: Traveling Through History in France (Ina Caro, 1994). Caro's enjoyable travel essays take you on a chronological journey through France's historical sights.

Sixty Million Frenchmen Can't Be Wrong (Jean-Benoit Nadeau and Julie Barlow, 2003). This is a must-read for anyone serious about understanding French culture, contemporary politics, and what makes the French tick.

Travelers Tales: Paris and *Travelers' Tales: France* (edited by James O'Reilly, Larry Habegger, and Sean O'Reilly, 2002). Notable writers explore Parisian and French culture.

Two Towns in Provence (M. F. K. Fisher, 1964). Aix-en-Provence and Marseille are the subjects of these two stories by the celebrated American food writer. She also writes about her life in France in *Long Ago in France: The Years in Dijon* (1929).

A Year in Provence and *Toujours Provence* (Peter Mayle, 1989/1991). Mayle's memoirs include humorous anecdotes about restoring and living in a 200-year-old farmhouse in a remote area of the Lubéron.

The Yellow House: Van Gogh, Gauguin, and Nine Turbulent Weeks in Arles (Martin Gayford, 2006). This historical account vividly chronicles Van Gogh and Gauguin's tumultuous stay in Arles.

Fiction

The Fly-Truffler (Gustaf Sobin, 1999). After the death of his young wife, a Provençal man stays in touch with her spirit through intimate dream visions.

Hotel Pastis (Peter Mayle, 1993). Mayle, whose nonfiction books are recommended earlier, also writes fiction set in Provence, including this book and *A Good Year*.

Joy of Man's Desiring (Jean Giono, 1935). Giano captures the charm of rural France. (The author also wrote the Johnny Appleseed eco-fable set in Provence, *The Man Who Planted Trees*.)

Film and TV

The Chorus (2004). Filled with angelic choir music, this touching film tells the story of a schoolteacher and the boys he brings together.

Cyrano de Bergerac (1990). A homely, romantic poet woos his love
with the help of another, better-looking man (look for scenes
filmed at the Abbaye de Fontenay).

Dirty Rotten Scoundrels (1988). Steve Martin and Michael Caine
star in this hilarious flick, filmed in and around Villefranche-
sur-Mer.

French Kiss (1995). This romantic comedy includes scenes in the
French countryside and Cannes, as well as Paris.

The Horseman on the Roof (1995). The beautiful Juliette Binoche
seeks her missing husband in this romance-drama set in 1830s
southern France.

Jean de Florette (1986). This marvelous tale of greed and intolerance
follows a hunchback as he fights for the property he inherited
in rural France. Its sequel, *Manon of the Spring* (1986), continues with his daughter's story.

My Father's Glory and *My Mother's Castle* (1991). These companion
films, based on the memoirs of writer/filmmaker Marcel Pag-
nol, show his early life in Provence.

The Return of Martin Guerre (1982). A man returns to his village in
southwestern France from the Hundred Years' War—but is he
really who he claims to be?

Ronin (1998). Robert De Niro stars in this crime caper, which includes a car chase through Paris and scenes filmed in Nice,
Villefranche-sur-Mer, and Arles.

To Catch a Thief (1955). Alfred Hitchcock's thriller showcases both
the French Riviera and crackling performances by Grace Kelly
and Cary Grant.

APPENDIX

Conversions and Climate

NUMBERS AND STUMBLERS

- Europeans write a few of their numbers differently than we do.
  1 = 1, 4 = 4, 7 = 7.
- In Europe, dates appear as day/month/year, so Christmas
  2019 is 25/12/19.
- Commas are decimal points and decimals are commas. A dollar and a half is $1,50, one thousand is 1.000, and there are
  5.280 feet in a mile.
- When counting with fingers, start with your thumb. If you
  hold up your first finger to request one item, you'll probably get
  two.
- What Americans call the second floor of a building is the first
  floor in Europe.
- On escalators and moving sidewalks, Europeans keep the left
  "lane" open for passing. Keep to the right.

METRIC CONVERSIONS

A **kilogram** equals 1,000 grams (about 2.2 pounds). One hundred **grams** (a common unit at markets) is about a quarter-pound. One **liter** is about a quart, or almost four to a gallon.

A **kilometer** is six-tenths of a mile. To convert kilometers to miles, cut the kilometers in half and add back 10 percent of the original (120 km: 60 + 12 = 72 miles). One **meter** is 39 inches—just over a yard.

1 foot = 0.3 meter	1 square yard = 0.8 square meter
1 yard = 0.9 meter	1 square mile = 2.6 square kilometers
1 mile = 1.6 kilometers	1 hectare = 2.47 acres
1 centimeter = 0.4 inch	1 ounce = 28 grams
1 meter = 39.4 inches	1 quart = 0.95 liter
1 kilometer = 0.62 mile	1 kilogram = 2.2 pounds
32°F = 0°C	

CLOTHING SIZES

When shopping for clothing, use these US-to-European comparisons as general guidelines (but note that no conversion is perfect).

Women: For pants and dresses, add 32 in France (US 10 = French 42). For blouses and sweaters, add 8 for most of Europe (US 32 = European 40). For shoes, add 30-31 (US 7 = European 37/38).

Men: For shirts, multiply by 2 and add about 8 (US 15 = European 38). For jackets and suits, add 10. For shoes, add 32-34.

Children: Clothing is sized by height—in centimeters (2.5 inches = 1 cm), so a US size 8 roughly equates to 132-140. For shoes up to size 13, add 16-18, and for sizes 1 and up, add 30-32.

NICE'S CLIMATE

First line, average daily high; second line, average daily low; third line, average days without rain. For more detailed weather statistics for destinations in this book (as well as the rest of the world), check www.wunderground.com.

J	F	M	A	M	J	J	A	S	O	N	D
50°	53°	59°	64°	71°	79°	84°	83°	77°	68°	58°	52°
35°	36°	41°	46°	52°	58°	63°	63°	58°	51°	43°	37°
23	22	24	23	23	26	29	26	24	23	21	21

Fahrenheit and Celsius Conversion

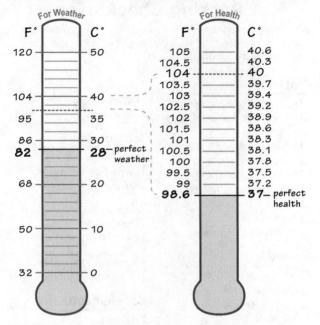

Europe takes its temperature using the Celsius scale, while we opt for Fahrenheit. For a rough conversion from Celsius to Fahrenheit, double the number and add 30. For weather, remember that 28°C is 82°F—perfect. For health, 37°C is just right. At a launderette, 30°C is cold, 40°C is warm (usually the default setting), 60°C is hot, and 95°C is boiling. Your air-conditioner should be set at about 20°C.

Packing Checklist

Whether you're traveling for five days or five weeks, you won't need more than this. Pack light to enjoy the sweet freedom of true mobility.

Clothing

- ❑ 5 shirts: long- & short-sleeve
- ❑ 2 pairs pants (or skirts/capris)
- ❑ 1 pair shorts
- ❑ 5 pairs underwear & socks
- ❑ 1 pair walking shoes
- ❑ Sweater or warm layer
- ❑ Rainproof jacket with hood
- ❑ Tie, scarf, belt, and/or hat
- ❑ Swimsuit
- ❑ Sleepwear/loungewear

Money

- ❑ Debit card(s)
- ❑ Credit card(s)
- ❑ Hard cash ($100-200 in US dollars)
- ❑ Money belt

Documents

- ❑ Passport
- ❑ Tickets & confirmations: flights, hotels, trains, rail pass, car rental, sight entries
- ❑ Driver's license
- ❑ Student ID, hostel card, etc.
- ❑ Photocopies of important documents
- ❑ Insurance details
- ❑ Guidebooks & maps
- ❑ Notepad & pen
- ❑ Journal

Toiletries Kit

- ❑ Basics: soap, shampoo, toothbrush, toothpaste, floss, deodorant, sunscreen, brush/comb, etc.
- ❑ Medicines & vitamins
- ❑ First-aid kit
- ❑ Glasses/contacts/sunglasses
- ❑ Sewing kit
- ❑ Packet of tissues (for WC)
- ❑ Earplugs

Electronics

- ❑ Mobile phone
- ❑ Camera & related gear
- ❑ Tablet/ebook reader/media player
- ❑ Laptop & flash drive
- ❑ Headphones
- ❑ Chargers & batteries
- ❑ Smartphone car charger & mount (or GPS device)
- ❑ Plug adapters

Miscellaneous

- ❑ Daypack
- ❑ Sealable plastic baggies
- ❑ Laundry supplies: soap, laundry bag, clothesline, spot remover
- ❑ Small umbrella
- ❑ Travel alarm/watch

Optional Extras

- ❑ Second pair of shoes (flip-flops, sandals, tennis shoes, boots)
- ❑ Travel hairdryer
- ❑ Picnic supplies
- ❑ Water bottle
- ❑ Fold-up tote bag
- ❑ Small flashlight
- ❑ Mini binoculars
- ❑ Small towel or washcloth
- ❑ Inflatable pillow/neck rest
- ❑ Tiny lock
- ❑ Address list (to mail postcards)
- ❑ Extra passport photos

Pronunciation Guide for Place Names

When using the phonetics: Try to nasalize the n sound (let the sound come through your nose). Note that the "ahn" combination uses the "ah" sound in "father," but the "an" combination uses the "a" sound in "sack." Pronounce the "ī" as the long "i" in "light." If your best attempt at pronunciation meets with a puzzled look, just point to the place name on the list.

Aigues-Mortes	ayg-mort
Aiguines	ayg-ween
Aix-en-Provence	ehks ahn proh-vahns
Antibes	ahn-teeb
Ardèche Gorges	ar-dehsh gorzh
Arles	arl
Avignon	ah-veen-yohn
Balazuc	bah-lah-zewk
Bedoin	buh-dwan
Biot	bee-oht
Bonnieux	bohn-yuh
Brantes	brahnt
Buis-les-Barronnies	bwee-lay-bah-roh-nee
Buoux	byoo
Cairanne	kay-rahn
Camargue	kah-marg
Cannes	kan
Cap Ferrat	kahp feh-rah
Cassis	kah-see
Cavaillon	kah-vī-yohn
Châteauneuf-du-Pape	shah-toh-nuhf-dew-pahp
Côte du Rhône	koht dew rohn
Crestet	kruh-stay
Eze-Bord-de-Mer	ehz-bor-duh-mehr
Eze-le-Village	ehz-luh-vee-lahzh
Gigondas	zhee-gohn-dahs
Gordes	gord
Gourdon	goor-dohn
Grasse	grahs
Grignan	green-yahn
Isle-sur-la-Sorgue	eel-sewr-lah-sorg
Joucas	zhoo-kahs
Juan-les-Pins	zhwahn-lay-pan
Le Trophée des Alpes	luh troh-fay dayz ahlp
La Turbie	lah tewr-bee

Pronunciation Guide for Place Names
(continued)

Lacoste	lah-kohst
Le Bar-sur-Loup	luh bar-sewr-loo
Les Baux	lay boh
Lourmarin	loor-mah-ran
Luberon	lew-buh-rohn
Marseille	mar-say
Ménerbes	may-nehrb
Menton	mahn-tohn
Monaco	moh-nah-koh
Monte Carlo	mohn-tay kar-loh
Mont Ventoux	mohn vahn-too
Moustier-Ste-Marie	moost-yay-sahnt-mah-ree
Nice	nees
Nîmes	neem
Nyons	nee-yohns
Oppède-le-Vieux	oh-pehd-luh-vee-uh
Orange	oh-rahnzh
Pont du Gard	pohn dew gar
Port Grimaud	por gree-moh
Provence	proh-vahns
Roussillon	roo-see-yohn
Saignon	sayn-yohn
Séguret	say-gew-ray
Ste-Jalles	san-zhahl
St-Jean	san-zhahn
St-Paul-de-Vence	san-pohl-duh-vahns
St-Rémy-de-Provence	san-ray-mee-duh-pro-vahns
St-Saturnin-lès-Apt	san-sah-tewr-nan-lehz-ahpt
St-Tropez	san-troh-pay
Stes-Maries-de-la-Mer	sahnt-mah-ree-duh-lah-mehr
Suzette	sew-zeht
Tourrettes-sur-Loup	too-reht-sewr-loo
Uzès	ew-zehs
Vaison-la-Romaine	vay-zohn lah roh-mehn
Vallauris	vah-loh-rees
Vence	vahns
Viens	vee-ahn
Villa Kérylos	vee-lah kay-ree-lohs
Villefranche-sur-Mer	veel-frahnsh-sewr-mehr

French Survival Phrases

When using the phonetics, try to nasalize the n̠ sound.

English	French	Pronunciation
Good day.	Bonjour.	bohn̠-zhoor
Mrs. / Mr.	Madame / Monsieur	mah-dahm / muhs-yuh
Do you speak English?	Parlez-vous anglais?	par-lay-voo ahn̠-glay
Yes. / No.	Oui. / Non.	wee / nohn̠
I understand.	Je comprends.	zhuh kohn̠-prahn̠
I don't understand.	Je ne comprends pas.	zhuh nuh kohn̠-prahn̠ pah
Please.	S'il vous plaît.	see voo play
Thank you.	Merci.	mehr-see
I'm sorry.	Désolé.	day-zoh-lay
Excuse me.	Pardon.	par-dohn̠
(No) problem.	(Pas de) problème.	(pah duh) proh-blehm
It's good.	C'est bon.	say bohn̠
Goodbye.	Au revoir.	oh ruh-vwahr
one / two	un / deux	uhn̠ / duh
three / four	trois / quatre	trwah / kah-truh
five / six	cinq / six	sank / sees
seven / eight	sept / huit	seht / weet
nine / ten	neuf / dix	nuhf / dees
How much is it?	Combien?	kohn̠-bee-an̠
Write it?	Ecrivez?	ay-kree-vay
Is it free?	C'est gratuit?	say grah-twee
Included?	Inclus?	an̠-klew
Where can I buy / find...?	Où puis-je acheter / trouver...?	oo pwee-zhuh ah-shuh-tay / troo-vay
I'd like / We'd like...	Je voudrais / Nous voudrions...	zhuh voo-dray / noo voo-dree-ohn̠
...a room.	...une chambre.	ewn shahn̠-bruh
...a ticket to ___.	...un billet pour ___.	uhn̠ bee-yay poor ___
Is it possible?	C'est possible?	say poh-see-bluh
Where is...?	Où est...?	oo ay
...the train station	...la gare	lah gar
...the bus station	...la gare routière	lah gar root-yehr
...tourist information	...l'office du tourisme	loh-fees dew too-reez-muh
Where are the toilets?	Où sont les toilettes?	oo sohn̠ lay twah-leht
men	hommes	ohm
women	dames	dahm
left / right	à gauche / à droite	ah gohsh / ah drwaht
straight	tout droit	too drwah
When does this open / close?	Ça ouvre / ferme à quelle heure?	sah oo-vruh / fehrm ah kehl ur
At what time?	À quelle heure?	ah kehl ur
Just a moment.	Un moment.	uhn̠ moh-mahn̠
now / soon / later	maintenant / bientôt / plus tard	man̠-tuh-nahn̠ / bee-an̠-toh / plew tar
today / tomorrow	aujourd'hui / demain	oh-zhoor-dwee / duh-man̠

In a French Restaurant

English	French	Pronunciation
I'd like / We'd like...	Je voudrais / Nous voudrions...	zhuh voo-dray / noo voo-dree-ohn
...to reserve...	...réserver...	ray-zehr-vay
...a table for one / two.	...une table pour un / deux.	ewn tah-bluh poor uhn / duh
Is this seat free?	C'est libre?	say lee-bruh
The menu (in English), please.	La carte (en anglais), s'il vous plaît.	lah kart (ahn ahn-glay) see voo play
service (not) included	service (non) compris	sehr-vees (nohn) kohn-pree
to go	à emporter	ah ahn-por-tay
with / without	avec / sans	ah-vehk / sahn
and / or	et / ou	ay / oo
special of the day	plat du jour	plah dew zhoor
specialty of the house	spécialité de la maison	spay-see-ah-lee-tay duh lah may-zohn
appetizers	hors d'oeuvre	or duh-vruh
first course (soup, salad)	entrée	ahn-tray
main course (meat, fish)	plat principal	plah pran-see-pahl
bread	pain	pan
cheese	fromage	froh-mahzh
sandwich	sandwich	sahnd-weech
soup	soupe	soop
salad	salade	sah-lahd
meat	viande	vee-ahnd
chicken	poulet	poo-lay
fish	poisson	pwah-sohn
seafood	fruits de mer	frwee duh mehr
fruit	fruit	frwee
vegetables	légumes	lay-gewm
dessert	dessert	day-sehr
mineral water	eau minérale	oh mee-nay-rahl
tap water	l'eau du robinet	loh dew roh-bee-nay
milk	lait	lay
(orange) juice	jus (d'orange)	zhew (doh-rahnzh)
coffee / tea	café / thé	kah-fay / tay
wine	vin	van
red / white	rouge / blanc	roozh / blahn
glass / bottle	verre / bouteille	vehr / boo-tay
beer	bière	bee-ehr
Cheers!	Santé!	sahn-tay
More. / Another.	Plus. / Un autre.	plew / uhn oh-truh
The same.	La même chose.	lah mehm shohz
The bill, please.	L'addition, s'il vous plaît.	lah-dee-see-ohn see voo play
Do you accept credit cards?	Vous prenez les cartes?	voo pruh-nay lay kart
tip	pourboire	poor-bwahr
Delicious!	Délicieux!	day-lees-yuh

For more user-friendly French phrases, check out *Rick Steves' French Phrase Book and Dictionary* or *Rick Steves' French, Italian & German Phrase Book.*

INDEX

A

Abbeys: about, 206–207; Montmajour, 51, 81; Notre-Dame de Sénanque, 204–205; St. Hilaire, 210
Absinthe: 393–394
Accommodations: *See* Sleeping; *and specific destinations*
Aigues-Mortes: 94
Aiguines: 434–435; sleeping, 437
Air-conditioning, in hotels: 475
Airfares (airlines): 8, 14, 525–526
Airports: Marseille, 225; Nice, 336–337
Aix-en-Provence: 252–269; eating, 266–268; helpful hints, 256–257; history of, 258; as home base, 22; maps, 254–255; sights/activities, 259–265; sleeping, 265–266; tourist information, 253; tours, 257; transportation, 253, 256, 268–269; walking tour, 259–265
Aix-en-Provence City Hall: 263
Albert I, Prince of Monaco: 377–379
Albert II, Prince of Monaco: 371, 377–378
Albert I Park (Nice): 297
Allen, Paul: 291, 343
Almanac: 4–5
Alpilles Mountains: 50–51, 73, 74
Amphithéâtre: *See* Arena
Ancient History Museum (Arles): 43, 59–62
Ancient Romans: *See* Romans, ancient
Angladon Museum (Avignon): 110–111
Antibes: 386–404; eating, 403–404; helpful hints, 389, 392; as home base, 273–274; maps, 387, 390–391; sights/activities, 392–401; sleeping, 401–402; tourist information, 388; transportation, 388–389, 404; walking tour, 392–394
Antibes Harbor: 386, 393
Antibes History and Archaeology Museum: 394, 398
Antique Toy and Doll Museum (Isle-sur-la-Sorgue): 191
Apartment rentals: 481; Riviera, 275

Apple Store (Aix): 256, 259
Apps: 16, 499; maps and navigation tools, 469–470, 516–517; messaging, 499–501; sightseeing, 471
Apt: 214
Aquarium, in Monaco: 379
Aqueducts: 29, 81; Pont du Gard, 136, 139–141
"Arc de Triomphe" (Orange): 152
Archaeological museums: 128, 318–319, 398
Archaeological sites: Chauvet Pont-d'Arc, 181–182. *See also* Romans, ancient
Ardèche Gorges: 181–182
Arena (amphithéâtre): Arles, 43, 49–50; Nîmes, 128–129
Arlaten Folk Museum (Arles): 57
Arles: 40–72; at a glance, 43; arrival in, 41–42; eating, 68–71; excursion areas, 73–94; helpful hints, 42–43, 46; as home base, 21; maps, 44–45, 66–67, 74; planning tips, 40–41; sights/activities, 46–64; sleeping, 64–68; special events, 64, 530, 531; tourist information, 41; transportation, 41–42, 46, 71–72; walking tour, 46–58
Arles Ancient History Museum: 43, 59–62
Arles City Hall: 52–53
Arles Classical Theater: 51–52
Arles Cryptoporticos: 53
Arles Forum Square: 43, 57–58; eating, 69
Art: of the Riviera, 281–282. *See also* Art museums; *and specific artists*
Art museums: Château de Villeneuve (Vence), 423; Collection Lambert (Avignon), 111; Fondation Maeght (St-Paul-de-Vence), 418, 420–421; Fondation Van Gogh (Arles), 43, 56; Fondation Villa Dartis (Isle-sur-la-Sorgue), 191; La Charité Museum (Marseille), 227, 233; Musée Angladon (Avignon), 110–111; Musée Calvet (Avignon), 111; Musée d'Art Moderne et d'Art Contemporain (Nice), 291, 318;

Musée des Beaux-Arts (Nice), 318; Musée du Petit Palais (Avignon), 104; Musée Granet (Aix), 261; Musée Léger (Museum) (Biot), 401; Musée Masséna (Nice), 319; Musée Matisse (Nice), 291, 314–318; Musée National Marc Chagall (Nice), 291, 307–314; Musée Picasso (Antibes), 395, 398; Musée Réattu (Arles), 43, 63; Musée Renoir (Cagnes-sur-Mer), 400–401; Musée Yves Brayer (Les Baux), 79

Atelier de Cézanne (Aix): 264
ATMs: 16, 463–467
Attitude, French: 7
Audio Europe, Rick Steves: 16, 528
Avenue Jean Médecin (Nice): 300
Avignon: 95–121; at a glance, 102; eating, 116–120; excursion areas, 122–143; helpful hints, 97, 100; as home base, 21; maps, 98–99, 114–115, 123; sights/activities, 102–112; sleeping, 112–116; special events, 101, 530; tourist information, 96; tours, 101, 122–124; transportation, 96, 120–121; walking tour, 102–110
Avignon City Hall: 103
Avignon Festival: 101, 530
Avignon Passion Pass: 96
Avignon ramparts: 105
Avignon Synagogue: 109
Avignon Wine Tour: 25

B
Baie des Anges: 295–296, 367
Balazuc: 182
Balcon de la Mescla: 434
Ballooning: 200
Bando: wines, 39, 283
Banks: alerting before travel, 16. *See also* Money
Barbegal Roman Aqueduct: 81
Bardot, Brigitte: 5, 411, 457
Basse Corniche: 351–352
Bastille Day: 441, 531
Baths of Constantine (Arles): 62–63
Baux: *See* Les Baux
Bay of Angels: 295–296, 367
Beaches: Antibes, 387, 392, 399; the Camargue, 90–91; Cannes, 405; Cap d'Ail, 368; Cap Ferrat, 356–357, 359; Cassis, 244, 245;

Juan-les-Pins, 400; Menton, 384; Nice, 289, 296–298, 306, 331; Pont du Gard, 138–139; St-Tropez, 411, 414
Beaulieu-sur-Mer: 360, 368; hiking, 356, 358–359
Beaumes-de-Venise: 37, 176
Bed & breakfasts (B&Bs): overview, 477–478. *See also specific destinations*
Beer: 439, 498
Beverages: 496–498. *See also* Wine and vineyards
Biking (bike rentals): 525; Antibes, 389; Arles, 42; Avignon, 100; Cassis, 248; Côtes du Rhône, 166; Gigondas, 176; Isle-sur-la-Sorgue, 188, 193; Luberon, 186; Mont Ventoux, 179; Nice, 288, 293; Provence, 24; St-Rémy, 83; Stes-Maries, 93; Vaison-la-Romaine, 159, 162; Villefranche, 342
Biot: 401
Bird-watching: 90, 91, 92
Boat travel (boating): maps, 506, 507; Antibes, 389; Avignon, 100; Cannes, 409–410; Cassis, 237; Lac de Ste-Croix, 435; Marseille, 236–237; Nice, 291–292, 335–336; Riviera, 280, 291–292, 335–336; St-Tropez, 412–413, 414; Villefranche, 347. *See also Calanques; Canoeing and kayaking; Cruise ships*
Bonbon Museum (Uzès): 142
Bonnieux: 209; eating, 202, 209; market, 186, 209
Books, recommended: 531–532; for children, 440–442
Bookstores: 97, 197, 256–257, 389
Bouillabaisse: 282–283, 349, 403, 459
Boules: 43, 342, 411, 414, 444; about, 38
Boulevard La Canebière (Marseille): 222, 230–231
Brantes: 181
Braque, Georges: 261, 396, 414, 420, 421
Brayer, Yves: 79; Museum (Les Baux), 79
Breakfast: overview, 484
Brunet Chocolatier (Aix): 262
Budgeting: 6, 8–10
Buis-les-Barronnies: 181; market, 145, 180, 181

Bullfights (bullgames): 93, 129, 530, 531; Arles, 63–64
Buoux: 215–216
Buses: 513; best two-week trip, 14–15; Luberon, 185; maps, 506, 507; Nice, 285, 335; Provence, 23; Riviera, 275–277, 278–279, 366–369, 417–418. *See also specific destinations*
Business hours: 462–463

C

Cabs: 513; tipping, 468. *See also specific destinations*
Café at Night (Van Gogh): 57–58
Café la Nuit (Van Gogh): 58, 69
Cafés (brasseries): overview, 487–490. *See also specific destinations*
Cagnes-sur-Mer: 400–401
Cairanne: 178–179
Calanque d'En-Vau: 247
Calanque Port-Miou: 247
Calanques: 237, 246–248
Calder, Alexander: 421
Calissons d'Aix: 256, 446
Calvet Museum (Avignon): 111
Camargue, the: 90–94; transportation, 91–92; wildlife, 91
Camargue Museum (Stes-Maries): 91–92
Campervan rentals: 516
Camping (campgrounds): 482
Camus, Albert: 217
Candy museum, in Uzès: 142
Cannes: 405–410
Cannes Film Festival: 275, 322, 405, 407–408, 530
Canoeing and kayaking: Ardèche Gorges, 181; the Calanques, 247–248; Lac de Ste-Croix, 435; Pont du Gard, 138; Sorgue River, 191
Cap Canaille (Cassis): 245, 248
Cap d'Ail: 368
Cap d'Antibes: 394; hiking, 399–400; sleeping, 402
Cap Ferrat: 353–360, 367–368; cruises, 291–292, 347; map, 354; planning tips, 353, 355; sights/activities, 355–359; sleeping, 359–360; tourist information, 353
Cap Gros: 400
Cardin, Pierre: 209
Car insurance: 515–516

Car leasing: 516
Carpentras: market, 146, 450
Carré d'Art (Nîmes): 132
Car rentals: 8–9, 513–515. *See also specific destinations*
Carrières de Lumières (Les Baux): 80
Car travel (driving): 516–525; best two-week trip, 12–13; distances and time, 520–521; general tips, 522, 524–525; road signs, 518; the Camargue, 91–92; inland Riviera, 417–419; Luberon, 184–185; Nice, 285, 288; Provence, 23–24; Riviera, 277, 280, 417; Three Corniches, 351–352. *See also specific destinations*
Casinos: Monte Carlo, 379–382; Nice, 297
Cassis: 39, 240–252, 443; eating, 250–251; helpful hints, 244–245; maps, 221, 242–243; sights/activities, 245–248; sleeping, 248–250; tourist information, 240–241; transportation, 241, 244, 252; wines, 39, 244–245, 248
Castellum (Nîmes): 134
Castle Hill (Nice): 291, 298, 320–321
Cathédrale de la Nouvelle Major (Marseille): 233–234
Cathédrale de Monaco: 378
Cathédrale Russe (Nice): 291, 319–320
Cathedral of the Holy Savior (Aix): 264–265
Cathedrals: *See* Churches and cathedrals
Caumont Centre d'Art (Aix): 260–261
Cavaillon: market, 186
Cavaillon melons: 31, 449
Caveau de Gigondas: 177
Cave de Cairanne: 178–179
Cave du Verger des Papes (Châteauneuf): 154
Cave la Romaine (Vaison-la-Romaine): 161
Cell phones: *See* Smartphones
Centre de la Vieille Charité (Marseille): 227, 233
Cézanne, Paul: 20, 110, 253, 261, 264; Atelier de Cézanne (Aix), 264
Chagall, Marc: 420, 421, 422–423; biographical sketch, 312–313; Museum (Nice), 291, 307–314; painting style, 310

Changing of the Guard (Monaco): 377–378
Chapelle Cocteau (Villefranche): 343, 346
Chapelle du Rosaire (Vence): 418, 423–424
Chapelle et Phare de la Garoupe: 399
Chapelle Notre-Dame de Beauvoir (Moustiers-Ste-Marie): 436
Chapelle St. Pierre (Aiguines): 435
Chapel of Penitents (Les Baux): 79
Chapel of St. Pierre (Villefranche): 343, 346
Chapel of the Rosary (Vence): 418, 423–424
Charité Museum (Marseille): 227, 233
Charlemagne: 452, 456
Château de Cassis: 250
Château de la Canorgue Winery: 208
Château de Lourmarin: 217–218
Château des Baux: 76, 78
Château de Villeneuve (Vence): 423
Château d'If (Marseille): 236–237
Château Eza: 362–363
Château Grimaldi (Antibes): 394
Châteauneuf-du-Pape: 36, 153–156
Château Redortier: 174
Chauvet Pont-d'Arc: 181–182
Cheeses: 31, 109, 117–118, 494–495
Chemins de Fer de Provence: 321
Children, traveling with: 438–444; books and films, 440–441; parenting French-style, 439; planning tips, 439–442; top sights and activities, 443–444
Chocolates: 55, 88, 130, 262, 427–428, 446
Churches and cathedrals: architecture, 453; Cathédrale de la Nouvelle Major (Marseille), 233–234; Church of the Immaculate Conception (Antibes), 394; Monaco Cathedral, 378; Nîmes Cathedral, 131; Notre-Dame d'Alidon Church (Oppède-le-Vieux), 211–212; Notre-Dame de la Garde (Marseille), 227, 235–236; Notre-Dame des Anges (Isle-sur-la-Sorgue), 189–190; Russian Cathedral (Nice), 291, 319–320; St-Jacques Church (Nice), 304; St. Michael's Church (Menton), 385; St. Michael's Church (Villefranche), 343, 346; St. Pierre Church (Avignon), 108; St. Réparate Cathedral (Nice), 305; Saint-Sauveur Cathedral (Aix), 264–265; St. Trophime Church (Arles), 43, 69–70; St. Vincent Church (Les Baux), 79
Church of the Immaculate Conception (Antibes): 394
Cicadas (cigales): 174
Citadel (Villefranche): 346–347
Climate: 4, 10–11, 534
Clothing: See Fashion
Clothing sizes: 534
Cocteau (Jean) Chapel (Villefranche): 343, 346
Coffee: 496–497
Col de la Chaîne Mountain Pass: 171–173
Col de Vence: 419
Col d'Illoire: 434
Collection Lambert (Avignon): 111
Collias: 138
Colline du Château (Nice): 291, 298, 320–321
Colorado Provençal: 213–214
Confiseries Florian (Pont-du-Loup): 418, 427–428
Connery, Sean: 291, 367
Conservatoire des Ocres et de la Couleur (Roussillon): 199
Constantine, Baths of (Arles): 62–63
Consulates: 529–530
Cooking classes: Châteauneuf-du-Pape, 155; Nice, 281, 292; Riviera, 281, 417; Vaison-la-Romaine, 159
Corkscrew Museum (Ménerbes): 210
Costs of trip: 6, 8–10
Côteaux d'Aix-en-Provence: 38–39
Côte d'Azur: See Riviera
Côtes de Provence: 37–38
Côtes du Rhône: 156–182; driving tours, 167–182; maps, 146–147, 168; markets, 145–146; planning tips, 144, 166; transportation, 145; wine and vineyards, 36–37, 153–155, 161, 166, 167–179; guided tours, 24–26. See also Orange
Côtes du Rhône Wine Road: 167–177
Count of Monte Cristo (Dumas): 236
Coursegoules: 419
Courses Camarguaises (Arles): 63–64
Cours Jean Jaurès (Avignon): 95

Cours Mirabeau (Aix): 253, 259–261; eating, 267–268
Cours St. Louis (Marseille): 231
Cours Saleya (Nice): 288, 298, 302–303, 330
Cousteau Aquarium (Monaco): 379
Coustellet: 207; market, 186
Crèche Municipale (Arles): 56
Credit cards: 16, 463–467
Crestet: 162, 170–171
Cruise ships: 23, 275; Cannes, 410; Marseilles, 239–240; Monaco, 383–384; Nice, 337–338; Ville-franche, 351. *See also* Boat travel
Cryptoporticos (Arles): 53
Cuisine: 492–495; of Provence, 30–32; of the Riviera, 282–283. *See also* Eating
Currency and exchange: 463–464
Customs regulations: 469
Cycling: *See* Biking

D

Daladier Bridge (Avignon): 97, 100
Debit cards: 16, 463–467
Denim: 124, 131
Dentelles de Montmirail: 171–173
Dietary restrictions: 489
Discounts: 463. *See also* Money-saving tips
Domaine de Cabasse: 169–170
Domaine de Cassan Winery: 175
Domaine de Coyeux Winery: 176
Domaine de la Citadelle Winery: 210
Domaine de Mourchon Winery: 170
Domaine de Tara: 200
Drinks: 496–498
Driving: *See* Car travel
Drôme Provençale Loop Drive: 180–181
Ducal Palace (Nice): 303
Dumas, Alexandre: 236
Dynamic currency conversion: 466

E

Easter Fair (Arles): 64, 530
Eating: 482–495; budgeting, 9; with children, 439–440; dietary restrictions, 489; restaurant phrases, 540; restaurant pricing, 483–484; tipping, 467, 488. *See also* Cuisine; Markets; *and specific destinations*
Eleanor of Aquitaine: 81, 452, 454, 456

Electricity: 463
Embassies: 529–530
Emergencies: 274, 462, 529
Entrevaux: 321
Espace Van Gogh (Arles): 55–56
Euro currency: 463–464
Euroméditerranée (Marseille): 234
Exchange rate: 464
Eze-Bord-de-Mer: 361, 362, 364, 368
Eze Church: 363
Eze-le-Village: 361–364

F

Fall Fair (Arles): 64, 531
Farm visits: 444
Fashion: boutiques, 288, 357, 400, 409, 435, 445, 450–451; clothing sizes, 534
Fenocchio (Nice): 305, 331–332
Feria de Pâques (Arles): 64, 530
Féria du Riz (Arles): 64, 531
Festival d'Avignon: 101, 530
Festivals: 530–531. *See also specific festivals*
Flamingos: 90, 91, 92, 94
Fondation Maeght (St-Paul-de-Vence): 418, 420–421
Fondation Van Gogh (Arles): 43, 56
Fondation Villa Dartis (Isle-sur-la-Sorgue): 191
Fontaine-de-Vaucluse: 192, 193
Fontvieille: sleeping, 68
Fontvieille (Monaco): 370, 378
Food: *See* Bouillabaisse; Cheeses; Chocolates; Cooking classes; Cuisine; Eating; *Macarons;* Markets; Olive oils; Tapenade; Truffles
Food tours: 26; Avignon, 101; Nice, 292; Riviera, 281
Fort Carré (Antibes): 398–399
Fort de Buoux: 215–216
Forum des Cardeurs (Aix): 266–267
Forum Square (Arles): *See* Place du Forum
Fountain Garden (Nîmes): 132–133
Fragonard Museum (Grasse): 431
Fragonard Perfume Factory (Eze-le-Village): 363
Fragonard Perfume Factory (Grasse): 430–431
François I: 236, 454, 456
Frank Gehry Tower (Arles): 43, 46
French language: *See* Language
French Riviera: *See* Riviera

French Riviera Pass: 274–275
Frioul Islands: 236–237

G
Gallimard (Eze-le-Village): 363
Gambling: *See* Casinos
Gauguin, Paul: 57–58
Gehry (Frank) Tower (Arles): 43, 46
Gignac: 214
Gigondas: 37, 176–177
Gites: 478–479
Glanum (St. Rémy): 83, 86–87
Gordes: 204–207; biking, 186;
  market, 186
Gorges de l'Ardèche: 181–182
Gorges du Loup: 419, 428
Gorges du Verdon: 431–437; driving
  tour, 433–436; map, 433
Goult: 200; eating, 200, 202
Gourdon: 419, 428
Grand Canyon du Verdon: 431–437;
  driving tour, 433–436; map, 433
Grande Corniche: 351–352, 364–365
Grand Prix of Monaco: 275, 322, 370,
  373, 377, 381, 530
Grasse: 419–420, 428–431
Great Maritime Port of Marseille: 234
Gréolières: 419
Gréoux-les-Bains: 436
Guidebooks, Rick Steves: 527
Gummi Bears: 142
Gypsies (Roma) of Stes-Maries-de-
  la-Mer: 93

H
Haribo: 142
Herbes de Provence: 446
High Corniche: 351–352, 364–365
Hiking: Antibes, 399–400; Ardèche
  Gorges, 181; Buoux, 215–216; the
  Calanques, 246–247; the Camar-
  gue, 91; Cap d'Antibes, 399–400;
  Cap Ferrat, 355, 356, 358–359;
  Colorado Provençal, 213–214;
  Eze-Bord-de-Mer, 364; Eze-le-
  Village, 364, 365; Gigondas, 176;
  Grand Canyon du Verdon, 434,
  435; Isle-sur-la-Sorgue, 189, 191;
  La Turbie, 365; Les Baux, 80;
  Mont Ventoux, 179; Nice, 306;
  Oppède-le-Vieux, 211; Pont du
  Gard, 138, 140–141; Roussillon,
  199; St-Rémy, 84; St-Tropez, 414;
  Vaison-la-Romaine, 162; Viens,
  203; Villefranche, 347–348, 355
Hill towns: overview, 172–173. *See
  also* Luberon hill towns
History: 452–455
Holidays: 530–531
Horseback riding, in the Camargue:
  93
Hostels: overview, 482. *See also specific
  destinations*
Hot-air ballooning: 200
Hôtel Carlton (Cannes): 407
Hôtel La Mirande (Avignon): 108,
  113
Hôtel Negresco (Nice): 293–294,
  322, 325
Hotels: glossary of terms, 474;
  overview, 473–477; rates and
  deals, 472–473; reservations, 15,
  478–479. *See also* Sleeping; *and
  specific destinations*

I
Iles du Frioul: 236–237
Imagine Tours: 23, 26, 97
Immigration (immigrants): 223, 234,
  455, 458, 549
Inland Riviera: 416–437; map, 417
International Museum of Perfume
  (Grasse): 429–430
Internet access: 502–503; with
  children, 442. *See also specific
  destinations*
Internet security: 502
Isle-sur-la-Sorgue: 186–194; eating,
  194; helpful hints, 187–189; map,
  188–189; market, 186, 191; sights/
  activities, 189–193; sleeping,
  193–194; tourist information, 187;
  transportation, 187; walking tour,
  189–191

J
Jardin de la Fontaine (Nîmes):
  132–133
Jardin d'Eté (Arles): 51
Jardin d'Eze: 363
Jardin du Rocher des Doms (Avi-
  gnon): 95, 102, 104–105
Jardin Exotique (Monaco): 379
Jeudi de Nîmes: 125, 128
Joan of Arc: 454, 456
John, Elton: 291, 367
Joucas: 202–203; sleeping, 201
Juan-les-Pins: 400

K

Kayaking: *See* Canoeing and kayaking
Kids, traveling with: 438–444; books
　and films, 440–441; parenting
　French-style, 439; planning tips,
　439–442; top sights and activities,
　443–444

L

La Canebière (Marseille): 222,
　230–231
La Capelière: 92
Lac de Ste-Croix: 435
La Charité Museum (Marseille):
　227, 233
La Ciotat: 248
La Citadelle (St-Tropez): 411, 414
La Colombe d'Or (St-Paul-de-
　Vence): 420, 421
La Commune Libre du Safranier
　(Antibes): 394
La Condamine (Monaco): 371
Lacoste: 209–210; eating, 202,
　209–210; market, 186
La Côte d'Azur: *See* Riviera
La Croisette (Cannes): 407
La Digue de la Mer: 92
La Fare: 175–176
Lagnes: 193
La Main Qui Pense (Arles): 56
Language: 4, 17; hotel phrases, 474;
　online translation tips, 463; picnic
　terms, 485; pronunciation guide,
　537–538; restaurant phrases,
　540; road signs, 523; shopping
　phrases, 449; survival phrases, 539;
　train terms, 512; wine terms, 35,
　497–498
Language barrier: 7
La Provence Profonde: 212–216
La Rotonde (Aix): 259
La Route des Crêtes: 248
La Seyne-sur-Mer: 23, 240
L'Atelier (Arles): 70–71
La Trophée des Alpes: 364–366
La Turbie: 364–366
Lavender: 11, 179–180, 205; about,
　178; festival, 10
Le Barroux: 172, 173
Le Bar-sur-Loup: 418, 428
Le Bassin (Isle-sur-la-Sorgue):
　190–191
Le Col de la Chaîne Mountain Pass:
　171–173

Le Colorado Provençal: 213–214
Léger, Fernand: 421; Museum (Biot),
　401
Le Jardin du Rocher des Doms (Avi-
　gnon): 95, 102, 104–105
Le Mistral: 167
Le Monastère St. Paul de Mausole
　(St-Rémy): 84–86
Le Musée Lapidaire (Avignon): 111
Le Panier (Marseille): 222, 227, 232
Le Petit Trains: *See* Tourist trains
Les Arcs-sur-Argens: 37–38
Les Baux: 74–82; eating, 82; map, 77;
　sights/activities, 76–81; sleeping,
　81–82; tourist information, 76;
　transportation, 75
Les Baux Castle Ruins: 76, 78
Les Deux Garçons (Aix): 261, 267
Le Sentier des Ocres (Roussillon):
　199
Les fêtes votives: 84
Les Halles (Avignon): 109, 120
Les Halles (Nîmes): 131
Le Suquet (Cannes): 406, 408–409
L'Occitane en Provence (Arles): 55
Louis XIV: 62, 190, 231, 232, 261,
　263, 363, 365, 456
Lourmarin: 184, 217–219; market,
　186, 218
Low Corniche: 351–352
Lower Town (Vaison-la-Romaine):
　157, 160, 163, 164–165
Luberon hill towns: 183–219; map,
　184–185; markets, 186; plan-
　ning tips, 183–184, 195; top
　restaurants, 202; transportation,
　184–186
LUMA Foundation (Arles): 43, 46

M

Macarons: 262, 485
Maeght Foundation (St-Paul-de-
　Vence): 418, 420–421
Mail: *See* Post offices
Maison Béchard (Aix): 260
Maison Camille Cayran (Cairanne):
　178–179
Maison Carrée (Nîmes): 131–132,
　135
Maison des Vins Côtes de Provence
　(Les Arcs-sur-Argens): 37–38
Maison Soulier Bakery (Arles): 55, 68
Malaucène: 170, 171, 180; market,
　145; sleeping, 174

Manville Mansion City Hall (Les Baux): 78–79
Maps: navigation tools, 469–470, 516–517. *See also* Map Index
Marchés: See Markets
Marie Antoinette: 456–457
Markets: 447–450; general tips, 448–449; key shopping phrases, 449; Aix-en-Provence, 256, 262; Antibes, 389, 393, 403; Arles, 42, 63; Avignon, 109, 120; Bonnieux, 186, 209; Buis-les-Barronnies, 145, 180, 181; Carpentras, 146, 450; Cassis, 244; Châteauneuf, 146, 153; Côtes du Rhône, 145–146; Coustellet, 186; Isle-sur-la-Sorgue, 186, 191; Lourmarin, 186, 218; Luberon, 186; Malaucène, 145; Marseille, 230–231, 238; Nice, 288, 298, 302–303; Nîmes, 131; Nyons, 145, 180; Orange, 145, 148; Roussillon, 186; St-Rémy, 83, 84, 88; St-Saturnin-lès-Apt, 186, 212; Sault, 179, 186; Tourrettes-sur-Loup, 427; Uzès, 141; Vacqueyras, 145, 176; Vaison-la-Romaine, 145, 157–158, 161; Vence, 422; Villefranche, 342
Marseille: 220–240; at a glance, 227; arrival in, 222–225; eating, 238–239; helpful hints, 225–226; maps, 221, 224, 228–229; planning tips, 222; sights/activities, 227–237; sleeping, 237–238; tourist information, 222; tours, 226–227; transportation, 222–225, 239–240; walking tour, 227–236
Marseille Chamber of Commerce: 231
Marseille City Hall: 232
Marseille History Museum: 231
Marseille Marine Museum: 231
Marseille Provence Cruise Terminal: 239–240
Mas de Lionne: 155
Masséna Museum (Nice): 319
Massif de l'Esterel: 406
Massif des Calanques: 246–248
Massif du Puget: 240
Matisse, Henri: 303, 414; biographical sketch, 316–317; Chapel of the Rosary (Vence), 418, 423–424; Museum (Nice), 291, 314–318
Maussane: 82; sleeping, 82

Mayle, Peter: 20, 167, 183, 195, 210, 217, 532
Mazarin Quarter (Aix): 253, 260–261; eating, 268; sleeping, 265–266
Medical help: 274, 462, 529
Medieval Garden (Uzès): 142
Ménerbes: 210–211
Menton: 384–385
Metric conversions: 533–534
Métro (Marseille): 224–225
Middle Corniche: 351–352
Mistral: 167
Mistral, Frédéric: 57
Mobile phones: *See* Smartphones
Modern and Contemporary Art Museum (Nice): 291, 318
Monaco: 368, 370–384; arrival in, 372–373; eating, 382; helpful hints, 373; layout of, 371–372; map, 374–375; nightlife, 373; sights/activities, 376–382; sleeping, 382; tourist information, 372; transportation, 372–373, 376, 383–384; walking tours, 376–379
Monaco Cathedral: 378
Monaco Grand Prix: 275, 322, 370, 373, 377, 381, 530
Monaco Post Office: 373, 379
Monasteries: about, 206–207; St. Paul Monastery and Hospital (St-Rémy), 58, 84–86
Monet, Claude: 457
Money: 16, 463–469; budgeting, 6, 8–10; with children, 442
Money belts: 442, 463, 464, 466–467
Money-saving tips: 463; Arles, 42; Avignon, 96; Riviera, 274–275; sleeping, 472–473
Mont-Alban Fort (Villefranche): 347–348
Monte Carlo: 371–372, 384
Monte Carlo Ballet: 373
Monte Carlo Casino: 379–382
Montmajour Abbey: 51, 81
Mont Rouge: 196
Mont Serein: 180
Mont Ventoux: 179–180
Moulin Saint Augustin: 207
Moustiers-Ste-Marie: 435–436; eating, 437; sleeping, 437
Movies, recommended: 532–533; for children, 440–442
Movie theaters: 443

Moyenne Corniche: 351–352

Murs: 203

Musée Angladon (Avignon): 110–111

Musée Archéologique (Nice):
318–319

Musée Calvet (Avignon): 111

Musée d'Art et d'Histoire (Orange):
152

Musée d'Art Moderne et d'Art Contemporain (Nice): 291, 318

Musée de la Camargue (Stes-Maries):
91–92

Musée de la Romanité (Nîmes): 128

Musée Départemental Arles Antique:
43, 59–62

Musée des Beaux-Arts (Nice): 318

Musée des Civilisations de l'Europe
et de la Méditerranée (Marseille):
234

Musée d'Histoire et d'Archéologie
(Antibes): 394, 398

Musée du Bonbon (Uzès): 142

Musée du Jouet et de la Poupée Ancienne (Isle-sur-la-Sorgue): 191

Musée du Petit Palais (Avignon): 104

Musée du Vin (Châteauneuf): 154

Musée Fragonard (Grasse): 431

Musée Granet (Aix): 261

Musée International de la Parfumerie
(Grasse): 429–430

Musée Léger (Museum) (Biot): 401

Musée Masséna (Nice): 319

Musée Matisse (Nice): 291, 314–318

Musée National Marc Chagall (Nice):
291, 307–314; map, 308; self-
guided tour, 308–314

Musée Océanographique (Monaco):
379

Musée Picasso (Antibes): 395, 398

Musée Provençal du Costume et du
Bijou (Grasse): 431

Musée Réattu (Arles): 43, 63

Musée Regards de Provence (Marseille): 234

Musée Renoir (Cagnes-sur-Mer):
400–401

Musée Yves Brayer (Les Baux): 79

Museum of Old Nîmes: 131

Museum of Santons (Les Baux): 80

N

Napoleon Bonaparte: 129, 260, 299,
319, 352, 457

Navette Fluviale (Avignon): 100

Nice: 284–338, 367; at a glance, 291;
arrival in, 285, 288; with children,
443; eating, 327–334; excursion
areas, 339–369; helpful hints,
288–289; as home base, 273; layout
of, 284; maps, 286–287, 294–295,
300–301, 324, 328–329, 333;
nightlife, 321–322; sights/activi-
ties, 292–321; sleeping, 322–327;
tourist information, 285; tours,
290–292; transportation, 285, 288,
289–290, 334–338; walking tours,
292–305. *See also* Vieux Nice

Nice Airport: 336–337

Nice Archaeological Museum:
318–319

Nice Carnival: 275, 322, 530

Nice Fine Arts Museum: 318

Nice Modern and Contemporary Art
Museum: 291, 318

Nice Narrow-Gauge Train: 321

Nice Opera House: 302

Nice Russian Cathedral: 291,
319–320

Nîmes: 124–136; eating, 135–136;
helpful hints, 125, 128; map,
126–127; sleeping, 134; tourist
information, 125; transportation,
125, 136; walking tour, 128–134

Nîmes Arena: 128–129

Nîmes Cathedral: 131

Nîmes Fountain Garden: 132–133

Nîmes Old City: 129–131

North African immigrants (immigration): 223, 234, 455, 458, 549

North African Market (Marseille):
227, 230–231, 238

Notre-Dame d'Alidon Church
(Oppède-le-Vieux): 211–212

Notre-Dame de la Garde (Marseille):
227, 235–236

Notre-Dame de l'Annonciation
(Nice): 304

Notre-Dame des Anges (Isle-sur-la-
Sorgue): 189–190

Notre-Dame de Sénanque Abbey:
204–205

Nyons: 180; market, 145, 180

O

Oceanography Museum (Monaco):
379

Ochre Cliffs (Roussillon): 199

Ochre Conservatory (Roussillon): 199

Old Grasse: 431
Old Nice: *See* Vieux Nice
Old Nîmes: 130–131
Old Port (Marseille): *See* Vieux Port
Olive oils: 88, 180, 207, 302, 331, 446
Oppède-le-Vieux: 211–212
Oppède-le-Vieux Castle: 211
Orange: 146–153; eating, 152; map, 149; sights, 148–152; sleeping, 152; tourist information, 148; transportation, 148, 153
Orange Roman Theater: 148–152
Orange Vélodrome (Marseille): 226
Ouvèze River: 157, 181

P

Packing tips (checklist): 16, 536
Palace of Justice (Aix): 262
Palace of the Popes (Avignon): 102, 106–107
Palais de la Bourse (Marseille): 231
Palais de la Méditerranée (Nice): 297
Palais des Papes (Avignon): 102, 106–107
Palais Lascaris (Nice): 304–305
Palais Maerterlinck: 367
Palais Princier (Monaco): 377–378
Panier District (Marseille): 222, 227, 232
Parc du Rocher des Doms (Avignon): 95, 102, 104–105
Parc Naturel Régional du Verdon: *See* Grand Canyon du Verdon
Passports: 14, 16, 373, 462
Perfume: about, 430; Fragonard Perfume Factory (Eze-le-Village), 363; Fragonard Perfume Factory (Grasse), 430–431; International Museum of Perfume (Grasse), 429–430
Pétanque: See Boules
Petit Palais Museum (Avignon): 104
Petit Trains: *See* Tourist trains
Phare de la Gacholle: 91
Philharmonic Orchestra (Monaco): 371, 373
Philip the Fair Tower (Villeneuve): 102, 111–112
Phoenicians, wine-growing almanac: 175
Phones: *See* Telephones
Picasso, Pablo: 57, 63, 110, 261, 420; biographical sketch, 396–397; Museum (Antibes), 395, 398

Picnics: 484–487; glossary of terms, 485. *See also* Markets
Place Albert I (Antibes): 387
Place Amélie Pollonnais (Villefranche): 350
Place Audiberti (Antibes): 389
Place aux Herbes (Nîmes): 130–131, 135
Place aux Herbes (Uzès): 142
Place aux Huiles (Marseille): 235, 239
Place Crillon (Avignon): 102, 118
Place d'Albertas (Aix): 262
Place de la Mirande (Avignon): 107–108
Place de la Poste (Roussillon): 201–202
Place de la République (Arles): 52–53
Place de la Tourette (Marseille): 235
Place de l'Horloge (Avignon): 102–103, 113
Place de l'Hôtel de Ville (Aix): 263
Place de République (St-Rémy): 84, 90
Place des Châtaignes (Avignon): 108, 119
Place des Corps-Saints (Avignon): 119
Place des Deux Garçons (Villefranche): 346
Place des Lices (St-Tropez): 411, 414
Place des Martyrs de la Résistance (Antibes): 387
Place des Quatre Dauphins (Aix): 261
Place des Trois Ormeaux (Aix): 267
Place du Centenaire (Eze-le-Village): 362
Place du Forum (Arles): 43, 57–58; eating, 69
Place du Marché (Marseille): 230
Place du Marché (Nîmes): 130, 135
Place du Palais (Avignon): 103–104
Place du Palais (Monaco): 376–377
Place Lamartine (Arles): 47, 63
Place Masséna (Nice): 284, 299–301, 321; eating, 332
Place Montfort (Vaison-la-Romaine): 157, 160, 165
Place Nationale (Antibes): 387, 389
Place Paul Doumier (Arles): 62, 70
Place Pie (Avignon): 119–120
Place Richelme (Aix): 262–263
Place Rossetti (Nice): 305
Plage d'Arles: 90–91

Plage de la Garoupe: 400
Plage de la Gravette (Antibes): 392, 399
Plage de la Paloma (Cap Ferrat): 357, 359
Plage de Passable (Cap Ferrat): 356–357, 359
Plage de Piemanço: 90–91
Plage du Bestouan (Cassis): 250
Plane trees: 260
Pointe Rouge: 237
Police: 529
Politics: 455, 458–460
Pont Daladier (Avignon): 97, 100
Pont d'Arc: 181
Pont d'Avignon: 102, 105–106
Pont de l'Artuby: 434
Pont du Gard: 136–141; the aqueduct, 136, 139–141; with children, 443; map, 137; orientation, 138; transportation, 136–137
Pont du Gard Museum: 139
Pont-du-Loup: 418, 427–428
Pont St. Bénezet (Avignon): 102, 105–106
Pont St. Julien: 208
Popes Palace (Avignon): 102, 106–107
Port Grimaud: 414–415
Post offices: 503; Monaco, 373, 379
Pottery: 56, 181, 401, 446
Prince's Palace (Monaco): 377–378
Promenade des Anglais (Nice): 3–6, 292–293, 296–298; eating, 334; guided walks, 292; map, 294; sleeping, 325–326; walking tour, 292–298
Promenade du Paillon (Nice): 301, 321
Promenades en Mer (Villefranche): 347
Pronunciation guide: 537–538
Provence: 20–269; at a glance, 8–9; best two-week trips, 12–15; cuisine, 30–32; helpful hints, 23; home base in, 21–22; map, 21; planning tips, 22; Roman history, 27–29; top 10 Provençal towns and villages, 25; tours, 23, 24–27; transportation, 23–24. *See also specific destinations*
Puymin: 160
Puyricard Chocolate (Arles): 55

Q
Quai des Etats-Unis (Nice): 297–298
Quai des Milliardaires (Antibes): 393
Quarries of Light (Les Baux): 80

R
Rabanel, Jean-Luc: 70–71
Rail passes: 14–15, 504–506, 508, 511, 527
Rasteau: 37
Réattu Museum (Arles): 43, 63
Remoulins: 136, 138
Renoir (Pierre-Auguste) Museum (Cagnes-sur-Mer): 400–401
Rental properties: 480–482; Riviera, 275
Resources from Rick Steves: 526–528
Restaurants: *See* Eating; *and specific destinations*
Rhône River: 40, 47–48, 90, 100, 105–106; cruises, 100
Rick Steves resources: 526–528
Riviera: 272–437; at a glance, 9; art scene, 281–282; best two-week trips, 12–15; cuisine, 282–283; helpful hints, 274–275; home base in, 273–274; inland, 416–437; maps, 273, 277, 341, 417; planning tips, 274, 339, 386, 417; top art sights, 281; tours, 280–281; transportation, 275–280, 416–417; wines, 283. *See also specific destinations*
Romans, ancient (Roman sites): 27–29, 60–61, 452; Aix-en-Provence, 258; Arles, 43, 48–53, 57, 59–63; Avignon, 102; Barbegal Aqueduct, 81; La Trophée des Alpes, 364–366; Nîmes, 128–134; Orange, 146–147, 148–152; Pont du Gard, 136, 139–141; Pont St. Julien, 208; Provence, 27–29; top 10 sight,s, 28; St-Rémy, 83, 86–87; Vaison-la-Romaine, 159–161
Roman World Museum (Nîmes): 128
Roma (Gypsies) of Stes-Maries-de-la-Mer: 93
Room and board: *See* Eating; Sleeping
Roquette (Arles): 58, 59, 62
Rosary Chapel (Vence): 418, 423–424
Roussillon: 22, 195–202; eating, 201–202; map, 197; market, 186; sights/activities, 196–200; sleeping,

200–201; tourist information, 196; walking tour, 196–199

Roussillon church: 197–198

Route des Crêtes: 248

Rue Biscarra (Nice): 332

Rue d'Antibes (Cannes): 409

Rue de la Calade (Arles): 52

Rue de la Calade (Les Baux): 79

Rue de la Cavalerie (Arles): 48–49

Rue de la Poissonnerie (Nice): 303–304

Rue de la République (Arles): 55

Rue de la République (Avignon): 95, 103

Rue de Porte de Laure (Arles): 51

Rue des Ciseaux d'Or (Avignon): 108

Rue des Fourbisseurs (Avignon): 108

Rue des Teinturiers (Avignon): 109–110, 118–119

Rue Droite (Nice): 304–305

Rue du Docteur Fanton (Arles): 56, 69–70; eating, 69–70

Rue du Vieux Sextier (Avignon): 108

Rue Emile de Loth (Monaco): 376

Rue Obscure (Nice): 346

Rue Président Wilson (Arles): 55

Rue Rossetti (Nice): 304, 305

Rue St. François de Paule (Nice): 301–302

Rue Saint-Saëns (Marseille): 239

Russian Cathedral (Nice): 291, 319–320

Rustrel: 214

RV rentals: 516

S

Sablet: 37, 177

Sade, Marquis de, Donatien Alphonse François: 209

Saignon: 214–215

St. Bénezet Bridge (Avignon): 102, 105–106

Sainte-Cécile-les-Vignes, market: 146

Ste-Jalles: 181

Ste-Marguerite Island: 406, 409–410

Stes-Maries-de-la-Mer: 92, 93

St. Hilaire Abbey: 210

St-Honorat Island: 406, 409–410

St-Jacques Church (Nice): 304

St. Jean-Cap-Ferrat: 357–358; sleeping, 359–360

St-Jeannet: 419, 423, 426

St. Julien Bridge: 208

St. Laurent Church (Marseille): 235

St. Marcellin-lès-Vaison: 162

St. Michael's Church (Menton): 385

St. Michael's Church (Villefranche): 343, 346

St. Pantaléon: 206

St-Paul-de-Vence: 418, 419–421

St. Paul Monastery and Hospital (St-Rémy): 58, 84–86

St. Pierre Chapel (Villefranche): 343, 346

St. Pierre Church (Avignon): 108

St-Rémy-de-Provence: 22, 83–90; eating, 88–90; maps, 85, 89; sights, 84–87; sleeping, 87–88; tourist information, 84; transportation, 83

St. Réparate Cathedral (Nice): 305

St-Saturnin-lès-Apt: 212–213; market, 186, 212; sleeping, 201, 213

Saint-Sauveur Cathedral (Aix): 264–265

St-Tropez: 411–415; map, 412–413

St. Trophime Church (Arles): 43, 69–70

St. Trophime Cloisters (Arles): 54–55

St. Vincent Church (Les Baux): 79

Salin de Giraud: 90, 91

Santons: 302, 446–447; Museum (Les Baux), 80

Sarah, Saint: 93

Sault: 179–170; market, 179, 186

Savannah College of Art and Design: 209

Seasons: 10–11

Séguret: 169–170

Sentier du Littoral: 414

Sentier Touristique Piétonnier de Tirepoil: 399–400

Shopping: 445–451; budgeting, 10; Cannes, 409; with children, 442; hours, 462–463; key phrases, 449; VAT refunds, 468–469; what to buy, 445–447. *See also* Fashion; Markets

Sightseeing: best two-week trips, 12–15; budgeting, 9–10; with children, 440–441; general tips, 469–471; priorities, 10; top kid-friendly sights, 443–444. *See also specific sights and destinations*

Signac, Paul: 411, 414

SIM cards: 501–502

Sleep code: 472

Sleeping: 471–482; budgeting, 9; with children, 438; glossary of terms,

474; online reviews, 480; rates and deals, 472–473; reservations, 15, 478–479; types of accommodations, 473–482. *See also specific destinations*

Smartphones: 16, 498–502; with children, 442. *See also* Apps

Soccer: 226, 342

Sorgue River: 109–110, 186, 190–191, 192; canoeing, 192

Special events: 530–531. *See also specific events*

Sports: *See Boules;* Bullfights; Soccer

Spring of Nemo (Nîmes): 132–133

Stamps, in Monaco: 371, 373, 376, 379

Starry Night (Van Gogh): 48

Strauss, Levi: 124

Suzette: 173–174

Swimming: 443–444. *See also* Beaches

Synagogue (Avignon): 109

T

Tapenade: 30, 88, 191, 446

Tavel: 37, 116

Taxes: VAT refunds, 468–469

Taxis: 513; tipping, 468. *See also specific destinations*

Tea: 496–497

Telephone numbers, useful: 529–530

Telephones: 498–503; with children, 442

Temperatures, average monthly: 534

Temple of Diana (Nîmes): 133

TGV: *See* Train travel

Theater (théâtre antique): Arles, 51–52; Orange, 148–152

Theft alerts: 16, 225–226, 288, 462, 466–467, 522

Thermes de Constantin (Arles): 62–63

Three Corniches: 351–352, 364–365

Time zones: 462

Tipping: 467–468, 488

Tollbooths: 519

Toulon: 23, 239–240

Tour guides: *See specific destinations*

Tourist information: 461–462. *See also specific destinations*

Tourist trains: Aix-en-Provence, 257; Antibes, 392; Avignon, 101; Cassis, 244; Marseille, 226–227; Monaco, 376; Nice, 290–291, 321; Vaison-la-Romaine, 159; Villefranche, 342

Tour Philippe-le-Bel (Villeneuve): 102, 111–112

Tourrettes-sur-Loup: 418, 427

Tours: of Provence, 24–27; Rick Steves, 527; of the Riviera, 280–281. *See also specific destinations*

Tower of Philip the Fair (Villeneuve): 102, 111–112

Toy and Doll Museum (Isle-sur-la-Sorgue): 191

Train travel: 504–512; baggage check, 510; best two-week trip, 14–15; coping with strikes, 509; general tips, 511–512; glossary of terms, 512; Luberon, 185; maps, 506, 507; Nice, 285, 334–335; Provence, 23; reservations, 509–510, 511; Riviera, 277, 278–279, 334–335, 336; terms and abbreviations, 505; tickets, 506–507, 509, 511. *See also* Tourist trains; *specific destinations*

Transportation: 503–526; budgeting, 8–9; maps, 506, 507. *See also specific destinations*

Travel insurance: 15–16

Travel smarts: 16–17

Travel tips: 462–463

Trinquetaille Bridge (Arles): 62

Trip costs: 6, 8–10

Trophée des Alpes: 364–366

Truffles: 210, 450

TV shows, recommended: 532–533

U

Uber: 290, 513

Upper Town (Vaison-la-Romaine): 161, 163, 164

Uzès: 141–143

Uzès Medieval Garden: 142

V

Vacqueyras: 176; market, 145, 176

Vaison-la-Romaine: 22, 157–165; eating, 164–165; helpful hints, 157–159; map, 158; sights/activities, 159–162; sleeping, 162–164; tourist information, 157; transportation, 157, 165

Vallauris: 398

Vallon-Pont-d'Arc: 181–182

Valréas: 178

Van Gogh, Vincent: 81, 110, 261; in Arles, 46–48, 55–56, 57–58; Fondation Van Gogh, 43, 56; in St-Rémy, 83, 84–86

VAT refunds: 468–469
Vegetarians: 489
Velleron: 193
Vence: 418, 422–426; eating, 426; map, 424–425; sights/activities, 422–424; sleeping, 424–426
Vercingétorix: 456
Verdon Gorge: *See* Grand Canyon du Verdon
Viens: 214; eating, 202, 214
Vieux Nice: 284, 291, 299–305; eating, 327, 330–332; maps, 300–301, 328–329; nightlife, 321–322; sleeping, 322, 326–327; walking tour, 299–305
Vieux Port (Marseille): 222, 227, 230, 231–232, 236; eating, 238–239; map, 228–229; sleeping, 237–238
Villa Dartis (Isle-sur-la-Sorgue): 191
Villa Ephrussi de Rothschild (Cap Ferrat): 353, 355–356, 367
Village des Bories: 205–206
Villa Kérylos: 360–361
Villa Masséna (Nice): 294–295
Villa Méditerranée (Marseille): 234
Villedieu: 162, 164; eating, 165
Villefranche-sur-Mer: 340–351, 367; eating, 349–350; helpful hints, 342; as home base, 274; maps, 341, 344–345; sights/activities, 342–348; sleeping, 348; tourist information, 340–341; transportation, 341, 342, 350–351; walking tour, 342–347
Villefranche-sur-Mer Citadel: 346–347
Villefranche-sur-Mer Harbor: 343
Villeneuve-lès-Avignon: 100–101, 111–112
Vineyards: *See* Wine and vineyards
Vinsobres: 178

Visitor information: 461–462. *See also specific destinations*
Visit Provence: 27, 122

W
Walking tours, self-guided: Aix-en-Provence, 259–265; Antibes, 392–394; Arles, 46–58; Avignon, 102–110; Isle-sur-la-Sorgue, 189–191; Marseille, 227–236; Monaco, 376–379; Nice, 292–305; Nîmes, 128–134; Villefranche, 342–347
Waterwheels: 110, 190
Weather: 10–11, 534
Wi-Fi: 16, 442, 498, 499–500, 502. *See also specific destinations*
Wine and vineyards: 34–35, 497–498; Aix-en-Provence, 253; Cassis, 39, 244–245, 248; Châteauneuf-du-Pape, 153–155; Côtes du Rhône, 36–37, 153–155, 161, 166, 167–179; guided tours, 24–26; key terms, 35, 497–498; Phoenicians, wine-growing almanac, 175; Provence, 32–39; guided tours, 24–26; Riviera, 283; tasting tips, 34; Uzès, 142
Wine Museum (Châteauneuf): 154
Wine Uncovered: 25–26
World War I: 104, 197–198, 431
World War II: 47, 104, 235, 245, 347

Y
"Yellow House" (Arles): 47
Yves Brayer Museum (Les Baux): 79

Z
Zidane, Zinédine: 226, 457

MAP INDEX

Color Maps
Provence: iv
French Riviera: v

Introduction
Provence & the French Riviera: 2–3
Top Destinations in Provence &
   the French Riviera: 11
Best Two-Week Trip by Car: 13

Provence
Provence: 21

Arles
Arles: 44–45
Arles Hotels & Restaurants: 66–67

Near Arles
Near Arles: 74
Les Baux: 77
St-Rémy Area: 85
Restaurants in St-Rémy's Old Town:
   89

Avignon
Avignon: 98–99
Avignon Hotels & Restaurants:
   114–115

Near Avignon
Near Avignon: 123
Nîmes: 126–127
Pont du Gard: 137

Orange & the Côtes du Rhône
The Côtes du Rhône Area: 146–147
Orange: 149
Vaison-la-Romaine: 158
Côtes du Rhône Driving Tour: 168

Hill Towns of the Luberon
Luberon: 184–185
Isle-sur-la-Sorgue: 188-189
Roussillon: 197

Marseille & Nearby
Marseille & Nearby: 221
Greater Marseille: 224

Marseille: 228–229
Cassis: 242–243
Aix-en-Provence: 254–255

French Riviera
The French Riviera: 273
Public Transportation Between
   Nice & Monaco: 277

Nice
Nice: 286–287
Promenade des Anglais Walk:
   294–295
Vieux Nice Walk: 300–301
Chagall Museum: 308
Nice Hotels: 324
Vieux Nice Hotels &
   Restaurants: 328–329
Nice Restaurants: 333

East of Nice
Between Nice & Monaco: 341
Villefranche-sur-Mer: 344–345
Cap Ferrat: 354

Monaco
Monaco: 374–375

Antibes & Nearby
Antibes Area: 387
Antibes: 390–391
St-Tropez: 412–413

Inland Riviera
Inland Riviera: 417
Vence: 424–425
Grand Canyon du Verdon: 433

Practicalities
Public Transportation in Provence:
   506
Public Transportation on the French
   Riviera: 507
Driving in Provence & the French
   Riviera: 520–521

Explore Europe

At ricksteves.com you can browse through thousands of articles, videos, photos and radio interviews, plus find a wealth of money-saving travel tips for planning your dream trip. And with our mobile-friendly website, you can easily access all this great travel information anywhere you go.

TV Shows

Preview the places you'll visit by watching entire half-hour episodes of Rick Steves' Europe (choose from all 100 shows) on-demand, for free.

ricksteves.com

your travel dreams into affordable reality

Radio Interviews

Enjoy ready access to Rick's vast library of radio interviews covering travel

tips and cultural insights that relate specifically to your Europe travel plans.

Travel Forums

Learn, ask, share! Our online community of savvy travelers is a great resource for first-time travelers to Europe, as well as seasoned pros. You'll find forums on each country, plus travel tips and restaurant/hotel reviews. You can even ask one of our well-traveled staff to chime in with an opinion.

Travel News

Subscribe to our free Travel News e-newsletter, and get monthly updates from Rick on what's happening in Europe.

Audio Europe™

Rick's Free Travel App

Get your FREE **Rick Steves Audio Europe**™ app to enjoy...

- Dozens of self-guided tours of Europe's top museums, sights and historic walks

- Hundreds of tracks filled with cultural insights and sightseeing tips from Rick's radio interviews

- All organized into handy geographic playlists

- For Apple and Android

With Rick whispering in your ear, Europe gets even better.

Find out more at ricksteves.com

Pack Light and Right

Gear up for your next adventure at ricksteves.com

Light Luggage

Pack light and right with Rick Steves' affordable, custom-designed rolling carry-on bags, backpacks, day packs and shoulder bags.

Accessories

From packing cubes to moneybelts and beyond, Rick has personally selected the travel goodies that will help your trip go smoother.

Rick Steves has

Experience maximum Europe

Save time and energy

This guidebook is your independent-travel toolkit. But for all it delivers, it's still up to you to devote the time and energy it takes to manage the preparation and logistics that are essential for a happy trip. If that's a hassle, there's a solution.

Rick Steves Tours

A Rick Steves tour takes you to Europe's most interesting places with great

guides and small groups of 28 or less. We follow Rick's favorite itineraries, ride in comfy buses, stay in family-run hotels, and bring you intimately

close to the Europe you've traveled so far to see. Most importantly, we take away the logistical headaches so you can focus on the fun.

Join the fun

This year we'll take thousands of free-spirited travelers—nearly half of them repeat customers—along with us on four dozen different itineraries, from Ireland to Italy to Athens. Is a Rick Steves tour the right fit for your travel dreams? Find out at ricksteves.com, where you can also request Rick's latest tour catalog. Europe is best experienced with happy travel partners. We hope you can join us.

BEST OF GUIDES

Full color easy-to-scan format, focusing on Europe's most popular destinations and sights.

Best of France
Best of Germany
Best of England
Best of Europe
Best of Ireland
Best of Italy
Best of Spain

COMPREHENSIVE GUIDES

City, country, and regional guides with detailed coverage for a multi-week trip exploring the most iconic sights and venturing off the beaten track.

Amsterdam & the Netherlands
Barcelona
Belgium: Bruges, Brussels,
  Antwerp & Ghent
Berlin
Budapest
Croatia & Slovenia
Eastern Europe
England
Florence & Tuscany
France
Germany
Great Britain
Greece: Athens & the Peloponnese
Iceland
Ireland
Istanbul
Italy
London
Paris
Portugal
Prague & the Czech Republic
Provence & the French Riviera
Rome
Scandinavia
Scotland
Spain
Switzerland
Venice
Vienna, Salzburg & Tirol

HE BEST OF ROME

e, Italy's capital, is studded with
an remnants and floodlit-fountain
es. From the Vatican to the Colos-
with crazy traffic in between, Rome
derful, huge, and exhausting. The
s, the heat, and the weighty history

of the Eternal City where Caesars walked
can make tourists wilt. Recharge by taking siestas, gelato breaks, and after-dark
walks, strolling from one atmospheric
square to another in the refreshing evening air.

Pantheon—which
t dome until the
r 2,000 years old
r over 1,500).

Athens in the Vat-
ies the humanistic
.

adiators fought
other, entertaining

Rome ristorante.
at St. Peter's
riously.

Rick Steves guidebooks are published by Avalon Travel,
an imprint of Perseus Books, a Hachette Book Group company.